SOCIETY ON THE EDGE

The social sciences underwent rapid development in postwar America. Problems once framed in social terms gradually became redefined as individual with regards to scope and remedy, with economics and psychology winning influence over the other social sciences. By the 1970s, both economics and psychology had spread their intellectual remits wide: psychology's concepts suffused everyday language, while economists entered a myriad of policy debates. Psychology and economics contributed to, and benefited from, a conception of society that was increasingly skeptical of social explanations and interventions. Sociology, in particular, lost intellectual and policy ground to its peers, even regarding "social problems" that the discipline long considered its settled domain. The book's ten chapters explore this shift, each refracted through a single "problem": the family, crime, urban concerns, education, discrimination, poverty, addiction, war, and mental health, examining the effects an increasingly individualized lens has had on the way we see these problems.

PHILIPPE FONTAINE is Professor of Economics at the École normale supérieure Paris–Saclay.

JEFFERSON D. POOLEY is Professor of Media and Communication at Muhlenberg College.

Society on the Edge

Social Science and Public Policy in the Postwar United States

Edited by

PHILIPPE FONTAINE
École normale supérieure Paris–Saclay

JEFFERSON D. POOLEY
Muhlenberg College, Pennsylvania

CAMBRIDGE
UNIVERSITY PRESS

CAMBRIDGE
UNIVERSITY PRESS

University Printing House, Cambridge CB2 8BS, United Kingdom

One Liberty Plaza, 20th Floor, New York, NY 10006, USA

477 Williamstown Road, Port Melbourne, VIC 3207, Australia

314–321, 3rd Floor, Plot 3, Splendor Forum, Jasola District Centre, New Delhi – 110025, India

79 Anson Road, #06-04/06, Singapore 079906

Cambridge University Press is part of the University of Cambridge.

It furthers the University's mission by disseminating knowledge in the pursuit of education, learning, and research at the highest international levels of excellence.

www.cambridge.org
Information on this title: www.cambridge.org/9781108487139
DOI: 10.1017/9781108765961

© Cambridge University Press 2021

First published 2021

A catalogue record for this publication is available from the British Library.

Library of Congress Cataloging-in-Publication Data

NAMES: Fontaine, Philippe, 1960- editor. | Pooley, Jefferson, editor.
TITLE: Society on the edge : social science and public policy in the postwar United States / edited by Philippe Fontaine, École normale supérieure Paris-Saclay, Jefferson D. Pooley, Muhlenberg College, Pennsylvania.
DESCRIPTION: Cambridge, United Kingdom ; New York, NY : Cambridge University Press, 2021. | Includes bibliographical references and index. w
IDENTIFIERS: LCCN 2020032756 | ISBN 9781108487139 (hardback) | ISBN 9781108732192 (paperback) | ISBN 9781108765961 (ebook)
SUBJECTS: LCSH: Social problems--United States--History--20th century. | Social sciences--United States--History--20th century. | United States--Social policy.
Classification: LCC HN57 .S6247 2021 | DDC 306.0973--dc23
LC record available at https://lccn.loc.gov/2020032756

ISBN 978-1-108-48713-9 Hardback
ISBN 978-1-108-73219-2 Paperback

Contents

Contributors

Savina Balasubramanian is Assistant Professor of Sociology and Affiliate Faculty in Women's Studies and Gender Studies at Loyola University Chicago. She is a historical sociologist of gender and science in global and transnational perspective. Her current book project examines the relationship between American demography and the politics of family planning in Cold War era India. Balasubramanian received her PhD from Northwestern University in 2018.

Charles Camic is the Lorraine H. Morton Professor of Sociology at Northwestern University. His areas of interest are sociological theory, history of the social sciences, and science studies. He is the author of *Veblen: The Making of an Economist Who Unmade Economics* (Harvard University Press, 2020).

Nancy D. Campbell is Professor and Department Head of Science and Technology Studies at Rensselaer Polytechnic Institute in Troy, New York, where she has taught for over two decades. Her most recent book is *OD: Naloxone and the Politics of Overdose Prevention* (Massachusetts Institute of Technology Press, 2020). She was a FRIAS Senior Fellow and Marie Curie Fellow of the European Union at the Freiburg Institute for Advanced Studies (FRIAS) in 2017–2018. She is one of three editors of the *Journal of the Social History of Alcohol and Drugs*. Her books include *Discovering Addiction: The Science and Politics of Substance Abuse Research* (University of Michigan Press, 2007), *Gendering Addiction: The Politics of Drug Treatment in a Neurochemical World* (coauthored with Elizabeth Ettorre; Palgrave, 2011), *The Narcotic Farm: The Rise and Fall of America's First Prison for Drug Addicts* (coauthored with J. P. Olsen and Luke Walden; Abrams, 2008), and *Using Women: Gender, Drug Policy, and Social Justice* (Routledge, 2000).

vi

Jean-Baptiste Fleury is Associate Professor of Economics at CY Cergy Paris University. His research focuses on the history of post–World War II economics, with particular emphasis on the expansion of its boundaries and its relationship with public policy. His articles have appeared in the *Journal of Economic Literature, Public Choice*, and *History of Political Economy*. He is currently working on a history of the emergence and development of the economics of crime after Gary Becker's seminal contribution in the late 1960s.

Philippe Fontaine is Professor of Economics at the École normale supérieure Paris–Saclay, research associate with the Center for Philosophy of Natural and Social Science at the London School of Economics, and an honorary member of the Institut universitaire de France. His main area of interest is the history of the social sciences after World War II, with special emphasis on the relations between economics and other social sciences. His latest book, coedited with Roger Backhouse, *A Historiography of the Modern Social Sciences*, was published with Cambridge University Press in 2014.

George C. Galster earned his PhD in Economics from Massachusetts Institute of Technology and is the Hilberry Professor of Urban Affairs Emeritus at Wayne State University. He has published 165 peer-reviewed articles, 9 books, and 43 book chapters on a wide range of urban topics. He has been a consultant to the US Departments of Housing and Urban Development and Justice, and served on the Consumer Advisory Council of the Federal Reserve's Board of Governors. The Urban Affairs Association placed him on their Service Honor Roll in 2014 and awarded him the prestigious Contributions to the Field of Urban Affairs prize in 2016.

Leah N. Gordon is Harry S. Levitan Director of Education and Associate Professor of Education at Brandeis University. She holds a joint PhD in History and Education from the University of Pennsylvania. She has particular interests in intellectual history; the history of education; the relationship between social science and social policy; and ideas about race, class, and inequality in modern America. Her first book, *From Power to Prejudice: The Rise of Racial Individualism in Midcentury America* (University of Chicago Press, 2015), received the 2016 Linda Eisenmann Prize from the History of Education Society. She is currently working on *Imagining Opportunity: Education and Equality in Modern America* (under contract with the University of Chicago Press), a history of the idea that schooling can equalize the social and economic structure. She has received awards and fellowships from the Spencer Foundation, the National Academy of Education, the American Council of Learned Societies, the Woodrow Wilson Foundation, Stanford University's Center for Comparative Studies in Race and Ethnicity, and the Teagle Foundation.

Andrew Jewett teaches modern US history and science studies. He has published *Science, Democracy, and the American University: From the Civil War to the Cold War* (Cambridge University Press, 2012) and *Science under Fire: Challenges to Scientific Authority in Modern America* (Harvard University Press, 2020). His current research explores how structures of scientific authority have intersected with racial discourses in the United States.

Alice O'Connor is Professor of History and Director of the Blum Center on Poverty, Inequality, and Democracy at the University of California, Santa Barbara. She teaches and writes about poverty and wealth, social and urban policy, the politics of knowledge, and the history of organized philanthropy in the United States. Among her publications are *Poverty Knowledge: Social Science, Social Policy, and the Poor in Twentieth-Century US History* (Princeton University Press, 2001); *Social Science for What? Philanthropy and the Social Question in a World Turned Rightside Up* (Russell Sage Foundation, 2007); and, with Gary Gerstle and Nelson Lichtenstein, the coedited volume *Beyond the New Deal Order: U.S. Politics from the Great Depression to the Great Recession* (University of Pennsylvania Press, 2019).

Jefferson D. Pooley is Professor of Media and Communication at Muhlenberg College in Allentown, Pennsylvania. His research interests center on the history of media research within the context of the social sciences, with a special focus on the early Cold War behavioral sciences. He also writes frequently on scholarly communication topics. He is the author of *James W. Carey and Communication Research: Reputation at the University's Margins* (Peter Lang, 2016), and coeditor of *The History of Media and Communication Research* (Peter Lang, 2008) and *Media and Social Justice* (Palgrave, 2011).

Joy Rohde is Associate Professor of Public Policy and History at the University of Michigan–Ann Arbor. Her book, *Armed with Expertise: The Militarization of American Social Research in the Cold War* (Cornell University Press, 2013), examines the Cold War origins and contemporary consequences of military support for social research. She is currently writing a book that investigates the relationship between computing, social science, and policy practice since World War II.

Andrew Scull is Distinguished Research Professor of Sociology and Science Studies at the University of California, San Diego, where he has taught for more than three decades. He previously held faculty positions at the University of Pennsylvania and Princeton University. He has written extensively on the history of Anglo-American psychiatry from the eighteenth through the twentieth centuries, and is past president of the Society for the Social History of Medicine and a former Guggenheim fellow. His many books include: *Museums of Madness* (Penguin, 1979), *Social Order/Mental Disorder* (University of California Press, 1989), *The Most Solitary of Afflictions* (Yale University Press, 1993), *Masters of Bedlam* (Princeton University Press, 1996), *Undertaker of the Mind* (University of California Press, 2001), *Madhouse* (Yale University Press, 2005), *Hysteria* (Oxford University Press, 2009), *Madness in Civilization: The Cultural History of Insanity from the Bible to Freud, and from the Madhouse to Modern Medicine* (Thames and Hudson and Princeton University Press, 2016, translated into a dozen languages), and *Psychiatry and Its Discontents* (University of California Press, 2019).

Preface

When we conceived this volume – a comparative history of the study of social problems in postwar America – we invited authors to draft accounts of scholarship on troubles that social scientists and the public had long recognized as persistent yet tractable. The authors' remit was to chart the changing division of labor, jurisdictional disputes, and moments of cooperation between the mainline social science disciplines in the decades after World War II. The problems of society tableau was, by intent, a means to an historiographical end. Here was a set of linked topics that, in its thematic breadth, demanded a multidisciplinary approach.

Contributors were invited to a pair of workshops at the École normale supérieure Paris–Saclay to present on their designated social problem, in papers that evolved into the book's nine chapters. As we held our second workshop in December 2018, "yellow vest" protestors were venting their wrath in the streets of Paris, ten kilometers away. Before the workshop, our North American visitors, alarmed by the accounts in the press and the disturbing images of demonstrators shouting their frustrations, had wondered whether Paris was worth a second visit. As the workshop got underway, it was clear that participants were struggling to understand the meaning behind the protests. Aware that social unrest is not necessarily correlated with hardship, they found it a challenge, nonetheless, to imagine such smoke without fire.

There was something paradoxical about holding a workshop on the problems of society in the postwar United States at a time when problems in French society seemed to demand attention. The professed problems of the yellow vest movements were, in space and time, far removed from the workshop's collection of US troubles. Yet they have something in common: They are both marked by the divergence between the social scientist's and the public's outlook, a gap widened by the disciplines' twentieth-century professionalization. France or the United States, the postwar era or the present: There is a constitutive tension in the construction of knowledge about society, a tension exacerbated when knowledge centers on society's problems. The cases collected in this volume, and the yellow vest movements too, reveal that public recognition need not correspond with the scholar's documentation of a problem's scope. There is, in other words, no necessary link between the apparent significance of a problem and whatever public clamor surrounds it. Pierre Bourdieu has quoted Jean-Paul Sartre's *Being and Nothingness* in this spirit (quoted in Bourdieu, *The Logic of Practice* (Stanford: Stanford University Press, 1990), 42):

It is necessary to reverse the common opinion and acknowledge that it is not the harshness of a situation or the sufferings it imposes that lead people to conceive of another state of affairs in which things would be better for everybody. It is on the day that we are able to conceive of another state of affairs, that a new light is cast on our trouble and our suffering and we *decide* that they are unbearable.

One lesson of the volume's chapters is that the salience of problems of society in the postwar United States has hinged on public recognition – that problem status is a definitional act, a social baptism that, moreover, needs regular renewal to maintain political standing. That conclusion offers lessons that go beyond the US situation.

The volume is meant to be useful not only to historians of social science but also to practicing social scientists interested in the complex interactions between public policy and their disciplines. A related aim is to improve our understanding of the way that problems of society emerge, prosper, and disappear. As such the volume is intended as a modest contribution to our collective ability to transform the social world.

Acknowledgments

We wish to thank the CNRS GDRI "History of the social sciences since 1945" for its generous support. We are also indebted to Craig Calhoun, Charles Camic, Jean-Baptiste Fleury, Leah Gordon, and Stephen Turner for their comments on our introduction. The quality of the final chapters was assured by both the authors and a number of referees who must remain nameless: We are grateful to them all.

Introduction

Whose Social Problems?

Philippe Fontaine and Jefferson D. Pooley

> Since ... people variously located in the social structure differ in their appraisal of a particular situation as a social problem, we should be prepared to find ... that the "solutions" proposed for coping with these problems also differ.
>
> Robert Merton and Robert Nisbet, *Contemporary Social Problems*, ix–x

1.1 A Sociologist's World?

At first glance, the 1961 collection *Contemporary Social Problems* is indistinguishable from dozens of similarly named textbooks. The volume, edited by Robert Merton and Robert Nisbet, was the latest installment in a long-running genre of works aiming to orient American sociology undergraduates to a range of "social problems." Like its predecessors, the Merton and Nisbet collection featured a chapter-by-chapter march through a succession of named problems such as crime, drug addiction, and family disorganization. So the 1961 textbook was, in its form, unremarkable.

But this was no ordinary social problems textbook. The first clue was authorship: Columbia's Robert Merton and the Berkeley-trained UC Riverside Dean Robert Nisbet were both theorists, known for grappling with European intellectual traditions. Merton was no stranger to empirical work, but his famous alliance with Paul Lazarsfeld at Columbia's Bureau of Applied Social Research epitomized – even symbolized – a postwar shift away from sociology's commitment to social problems in a reformist key. For his part, Nisbet's only other book, *The Quest for Community*, was a dense and idiosyncratic work of intellectual history. In short, Merton and Nisbet were among the least likely American sociologists to take up the genre.

A second clue, linked to the first, was the editors' first-paragraph claim that a comprehensive theory of social problems was still lacking. What unified their book's chapters was merely a "theoretical *orientation*." That common framework was a loose-fitting version of Merton's functionalism: The volume's contributors, and the editors themselves, stressed consequences over causes, pointed to latent social problems, and placed "systemic interdependence" at the center of analysis.[1]

The book's table of contents was the third clue. Many of the usual problems were represented, with chapters on juvenile delinquency, mental disorders, and race and ethnic relations. But there were a number of unusual inclusions – chapters that had rarely, if ever, appeared in social problems textbooks. One was devoted to traffic and transportation, and another, dropped in the third edition (1971), to the "military establishment."[2] Most surprisingly, Merton and Nisbet commissioned a "disaster" chapter, focused on calamities such as tornadoes, floods, and earthquakes, which seem only glancingly social.

The 1961 collection was, in short, a surprising intervention. The phrase itself, "social problems," was a token for an approach to sociology from which Merton and Nisbet had distanced themselves. The "social problems" course, the "social problems" textbook: These were the hallmarks of an older, "amateur" phase of the discipline's history, the kind of sociology that Merton and his Harvard teacher Talcott Parsons had, after World War II, helped expel to the margins. The whiff of reform and Midwestern starch hung about the phrase. The discipline's new elite, forged in shared wartime service, favored systematic theory, sophisticated quantitative methods, and value-free scientific rigor – very much like its counterpart in economics.

It was around this time, indeed, that some of these new-style economists – notably Gary Becker – were claiming rights over those social problems Merton and Nisbet meant to make their own. So the appearance of *Contemporary Social Problems* in 1961 – on the edge of the decade's social unrest – was a revival of a peculiar kind. Merton and Nisbet, having won the battle for the discipline, were now claiming the vanquished tradition's core domain. They were likely aware of the economists' nascent and still-marginal enterprise. But their aim was redemptive, not defensive: to introduce sociological theory into a social problems literature that was,

---

[1] Merton and Nisbet, *Contemporary Social Problems*, vii, viii, x.
[2] Merton and Nisbet, *Contemporary Social Problems*, 3rd ed.

in their view, theoretically impoverished and hopelessly fragmented.[3] Economists interested in "noneconomic" problems would have endorsed the critique, but their remedy was of a different, and more auspicious, character.

Though these economists were not cited, references to psychologists abound throughout the book. The relative prominence of psychology can be explained by its more constructive relationship with sociology, as exemplified by the expansion of interdisciplinary social psychology after the war.[4] But arguably more important still was what Ellen Herman has described as a shift "toward a larger jurisdiction for psychology."[5] With deep roots in the cross-disciplinary projects of the war, that shift marked psychology's increased involvement with a wide range of social problems during the early postwar decades. The discipline's protean character encouraged its broad application, and helped to spread its language to the other social sciences.[6] By 1961, psychology's expanded remit had registered with sociologists studying social problems, as an individualistic complement to their approach.[7] The result was that psychologists' efforts to expand their jurisdiction over social problems found a more receptive audience, at least initially, than did economists.

The appearance of psychologists and, more tentatively, economists on the social problems terrain was, in its way, a reminder that their study has always had a double character. The vocabulary of "social problems"

[3] Merton and Nisbet's charge was itself, arguably, unfair: The prewar social problems textbooks, and other works by their authors, were steeped in theory – albeit of a distinctive mode ("history of social thought"), with its own touchstones, referents, and Spencerian residues. See Turner and Turner, *Impossible Science*, 121–28; and Hinkle, *Developments in American Sociological Theory*, 7–12, 186–90. Still, Erwin Smigel, in the preface to his 1971 *Handbook on the Study of Social Problems*, admitted that "[w]e have not been able to find a unifying theory for the study of social problems." Smigel, "Preface," vii.
[4] Sewell, "Some Reflections on the Golden Age"; and House, "Social Psychology, Social Science, and Economics," 233–35.
[5] Herman, *Romance of American Psychology*, chap. 11. Herman's title, as she notes herself, is inspired from Abraham Maslow's title of part 1 in *Toward a Psychology of Being*.
[6] On the protean nature of psychology and its implications for the discipline's relevance to a wide range of issues, see Capshew, *Psychologists on the March*, 54.
[7] See Merton's comments on the "bridge-building game" between the two disciplines, delivered at a 1955 conference on juvenile delinquency: "The tactic that could be most helpful, it seems to me, would be for us to join together and fuse our respective sensitivities from time to time but, in the main, to continue to develop the conceptions most pertinent to each field." Merton, "Concluding Comments and an Example," 79.

developed primarily within sociology, but the study of the problems themselves was always and already a transdisciplinary endeavor. Sociologists have claimed the social problems label, but scholarship on the problems of society – the alternative phrase we adopt to signal this ecumenism – has featured the other social sciences too. In the decades after Merton and Nisbet's volume, sociology's always-partial claims for jurisdiction, if anything, weakened further.

The social problems literature in sociology had been ushered in fifty years earlier, in *Sociology and Modern Social Problems*, a 1910 "elementary text" authored by Missouri's Charles Ellwood and designed for sociology courses centered on "current social problems."[8] The volume treated the family as the main locus of social challenge, though a handful of late chapters addressed a series of related domains: population growth, immigration, the "negro problem," the "problem of the city," crime, and "poverty and pauperism." The text's basic orientation – even its reformist politics – would remain a staple of the social problems textbook for decades. The volume's chapter-per-problem format as well as its catalog of named problems were embraced by the many competing texts published in the 1920s and 1930s to service sociology's undergraduate curriculum.[9] Ellwood himself became the chief interwar proponent of "social problems" as the discipline's anchoring orientation.[10]

American sociology was, in organizational terms at least, built on the idea of "social problems." The phrase supplied a practical scheme to organize the would-be discipline. Even its subfields and journals began to mimic the problem-by-problem "sociology of" schematic pattern. The "social problems" construct, in short, helped sociology establish its distinctive identity – and its institutional foothold in the US academy. By the 1930s, however, advocates for a more rigorous, and resolutely quantitative, science of sociology took aim at the social problems paradigm. They lumped its textbooks and leading figures, Ellwood included, together with social work, public edification, settlement houses, and moralizing do-goodism.[11] This Depression-era assault on the social problems approach was, in its way, new.

---

[8] Ellwood, *Sociology and Modern Social Problems*, 3.
[9] Reinhardt, "Trends in the Teaching of 'Social Problems.'"
[10] Turner, "Life in the First Half-Century of Sociology" and LoConto, "Charles A. Ellwood and the End of Sociology."
[11] Turner and Turner, *The Impossible Science*, chaps. 2–3; Turner, *American Sociology*, chap. 2; and Bannister, *Sociology and Scientism*, chap. 13.

But the rhetoric of science – the boundary work with reform – had been a staple of the proto-discipline from its late nineteenth-century origins.[12]

What made the 1930s different was that sociologists turned on themselves. The rhetorical demarcation had, in preceding decades, existed in uneasy admixture with ongoing reform commitments.[13] Now advocates of a scientific sociology drew the border to exclude not just "outsiders" such as Christian temperance activists and social workers, but also those fellow sociologists insufficiently weaned from the discipline's reformist past. The sometimes-belligerent campaign was waged by evangelists for statistical methods.[14] Ellwood and his reform-minded allies answered in kind.[15] There was an organizational flashpoint – the mid-1930s fight over the American Sociological Society (ASS) and the Chicago-based *American Journal of Sociology* (*AJS*). At the time, some of the discipline's oldest and best-established outposts were scattered across the country's non-elite universities and colleges, with particular strength in Catholic institutions. Many of these programs retained an ameliorist orientation, with close ties to social reform movements – Christian and nominally secular – long

---

[12] Sociology, together with its barely differentiated siblings in the American Social Science Association, was baptized in applied social reform during the last decades of the nineteenth century. There is an extensive literature on the proto-discipline's engagements with, and resistance to, "reform" in all its typical (and often feminized) meanings. On the late nineteenth-century context, see, for example, Furner, *Advocacy and Objectivity* and Haskell, *Emergence of Professional Social Science*, esp. chaps. 9–10. On the settlement house movement, see, for example, Deegan, *Jane Addams and the Men of the Chicago School* and Lengermann and Niebrugge-Brantley, "Back to the Future." On the social survey movement, see, for example, O'Connor, *Poverty Knowledge*, 26–44 and Gordon, "Social Survey Movement and Sociology." On social work in particular, see Lengermann and Niebrugge, "Thrice Told."

[13] Calhoun, "Sociology in America," 10–19. Early figures in the discipline, such as Lester Ward, Albion Small, and Franklin Giddings, had made claims for sociology's scientific character, even as they remained variously entwined with reform groups and initiatives. Second-generation sociologists like W. I. Thomas and Robert Park – indeed, Ellwood himself – adopted a similar rhetoric of scientific distance, likewise belied in practice by their on-the-ground alliances with philanthropists and Social Gospel reformers. The main strategy to square the science/reform circle – a tack also adopted by the social problems textbook authors of the 1920s – was to insist on a division of labor: The sociologist supplies the analytical guidance, while the reformers and politicians are on the hook for implementation. Turner, "Origins of 'Mainstream Sociology' and Other Issues," 56–58.

[14] The backdrop to the struggle was mounting frustration with sociology's apparent public ineffectuality as symbolized by its virtual exclusion from the New Deal bureaucracies that employed so many economists and political scientists. See Camic, "On Edge."

[15] See, for example, Ellwood, *Methods in Sociology*.

after Chicago's department had rejected its reformist roots. In 1936, they won control of the ASS and launched a rival, ASS-sponsored flagship, the *American Sociological Review* (*ASR*). It was, however, a Pyrrhic victory: Soon enough the *ASR* itself became a platform for the very brand of rigorous, quantitative empiricism that Ellwood and his allies had earlier resisted.[16]

The Depression-era struggle over the discipline's future was not, however, resolved by the manifestos for quantification penned by advocates of a more scientific sociology. The key factors, instead, were generational turnover and World War II.[17] By the end of the war, when the academic job market picked up in earnest, many of the quantitative insurgents were nearing retirement. The result was a vacuum in disciplinary leadership that a younger cohort – figures such as Samuel Stouffer and Robert Merton – soon filled. The wartime mobilization was decisive for a number of mutually reinforcing reasons: Shared service in Washington and overseas, with all its agency-spawning cross-pollination, helped to connect young sociologists with each other and with like-minded social scientists from other disciplines. The team-based work itself, some of it employing new survey methods, was widely perceived as a down payment on a postwar social science of on-the-cusp promise.

There were other factors. Some members of the new elite, including Parsons (an erstwhile economist) and Lazarsfeld (an applied psychologist), were disciplinary outsiders with few commitments to prewar American sociology. There was, too, explicit postwar Congressional concern (buoyed by natural scientists) about the social sciences' alleged reformism, even before the "social"/"socialism" conflation became an early Cold War staple.[18] The post–World War II upstarts were, moreover, over-represented at Ivy League schools, maintained close ties to the New York foundation

---

[16] Lengermann, "Founding of the *American Sociological Review*"; Turner and Turner, *The Impossible Science*, 60–62, 81 n23; Abbott, *Department and Discipline*, 106–17; and Bannister, *Sociology and Scientism*, chaps. 14–15. As Lengermann's meticulous anatomy makes clear, the conflict was multi-dimensional, though it centered on a populist revolt against a perceived elite. The targets of the populists' ire included the Chicago department – in all its methodological diversity – as well as the discipline's leading evangelists for "scientific" quantification.

[17] Abbott and Sparrow, "Hot War, Cold War"; Steinmetz, "American Sociology before and after World War II"; Converse, *Survey Research in the United States*, chaps. 5–7; Turner and Turner, *The Impossible Science*, chap. 3; and Platt, *History of Sociological Research Methods in America*, 228–30.

[18] Solovey, "Riding Natural Scientists' Coattails."

world, and served as key brokers in the government/foundation patronage network of the 1950s.[19]

The relevant point is that sociology's "east coast fraternity," hitched to a cross-disciplinary movement to accent the science in social science, had displaced sociology's already-battered, teaching-oriented majority.[20] Clearly, the "postwar settlement," in its paradigmatic mix of survey methods and functional theory, was never accepted by the full discipline.[21] But the social problems tradition, in particular, was widely discredited.[22] Indeed, it served as a symbolic and field-defining rejected past. The movement to remake sociology as a science was won, in other words, through a series of repudiations, articulated in a litany of pejoratives: speculative, edifying, reformist, Christian, and impressionistic. Methodological rigor and theoretical sophistication were the proposed substitutes. For the theory, the Ivy departments turned to European sociology as an alternative genealogy, with such remarkable success that the field's classical pantheon was – after

---

[19] On the early Cold War brokerage and patronage networks, see Crowther-Heyck, "Patrons of the Revolution" and Solovey, *Shaky Foundations*, chaps. 2–3.

[20] Abbott and Sparrow, "Hot War, Cold War," 296. The standard story of mid-century American sociology treats the changes outlined here as (using the department shorthands) a displacement of Chicago by Harvard and Columbia. Chicago, in these accounts, is treated as a bastion of textured and qualitative empiricism then smothered by an alliance of quantitative technicians and high functionalists at Harvard and Columbia. This account is caricatural. Columbia's department, for instance, was already prominent decades before the fateful 1941 meeting of Merton and Lazarsfeld. For its part, the interwar Chicago department was both more plural, and less dominant, than the typical interwar account allows. (As Andrew Abbott has shown, the idea of the "Chicago School" was a retroactive creation of the early 1950s, when the department briefly embodied the traits it projected onto its past. Abbott, *Department and Discipline*, chap. 2.) But the main problem with the Chicago-Harvard-Columbia emplotment is that most of the country's interwar departments and programs, and many of its sociologists, are left out.

[21] Steinmetz, "American Sociology before and after World War II," 339.

[22] In a soon-famous 1943 *AJS* study, a young C. Wright Mills surveyed interwar social problems textbooks to sketch out what he called American sociology's "common style of thought." He treated the books (over thirty of them) as a proxy for the discipline's "professional ideology" – as a more-or-less faithful register of its commitments. The texts, he added, are "empirically confused," fragmentary, and indifferent to structural patterns – and thereby leave out the "larger problems of social structure." The typical sociologist, in Mills' wartime portrait, was provincial, small-minded, and Babbitt-like. Mills, "Professional Ideology of Social Pathologists," 165–66. A similarly caustic account, published two years later, came from criminologist Edwin Sutherland: "The textbooks display a minimum of abstraction and a maximum of the commonplace." Sutherland, "Social Pathology," 430. See also Emil Bend and Martin Vogelfanger's quarter-century textbook survey, "New Look at Mills' Critique."

the war – almost completely repopulated by European figures like Max Weber and Emile Durkheim.[23]

The discipline's new, Eastern seaboard mainstream did not, crucially, rule out problem-oriented work. Indeed, many of its core commitments – around methodological rigor and theory-building, for example – were forged in the wartime mobilization. The lessons of the war, in turn, helped guide the self-identified "behavioral sciences" movement among sociologists and other social scientists during the early Cold War: Problem-oriented work, funded by foundation or government patrons, was especially well suited to the large-scale, team-based empirical projects that general theory-building required.[24] So work on *problems*, even those within the traditional social problems array, was perfectly compatible with the postwar formation – even if, in practice, the early Cold War mix of projects was heavy on overseas propaganda and morale topics. The point is that applied work was welcomed into the house of the ascendant behavioral sciences while the meliorist social problems tradition was not.[25]

The Society for the Study of Social Problems (SSSP) was founded in 1951 as a protest against the postwar marginality of that meliorist tradition.[26] The new group openly defined itself against the behavioral sciences vanguard. Its aim was to shelter a reformist alternative to the apolitical mainstream by then ensconced in the ASS leadership. The SSSP's founders, and its early membership, were largely drawn from the same Midwestern departments

[23] See, for example, Connell, "Why is Classical Theory Classical?" and Scaff, "Max Weber and the Social Sciences."

[24] The best overview of the "behavioral sciences" movement – the self-understood clustering of sociologists, social psychologists, and political scientists (the latter with their own, complementary "behavioralism" moniker) in the early Cold War, with participation from some anthropologists and a handful of economists – remains Crowther-Heyck, *Herbert A. Simon*, chap. 5. For a history of the label including the crucial role of the modern Ford Foundation, see Pooley, "'Not Particularly Felicitous' Phrase."

[25] This distinction helps explain our interpretive difference with Arnold Rose. In his posthumous 1971 history of social problems research, Rose discerned a drop-off of sociological interest in the interwar period, with a postwar revival linked to the war's boost to applied research. Rose, "History and Sociology of the Study of Social Problems," 7–9. Our own review of the primary and secondary literature, however, suggests that the interwar period represented the heyday of self-conscious sociological engagement with "social problems" – and that, by the early postwar years, that tradition was marginalized. Rose's postwar narrative conflates a broader problem orientation, or openness to applied work, with the reformist social problems tradition.

[26] On the SSSP, see Skura, "Constraints on a Reform Movement" and Abbott, *Department and Discipline*, 78–79.

that had long incubated the discipline's undergraduate substrate.[27] Especially in its first decade, the SSSP was the organizational redoubt for the discipline's half-vanquished social problems tradition. The SSSP was a backlash organization. The group took aim at the rising generation of Eastern seaboard sociologists who had refined and tested new quantitative methods, as well as affirmed the primacy of disciplinary issues – taken as "scientific" problems – over the older, reform-tainted social problems formulation. But the SSSP was not, by its own self-definition, bounded by a putative "social problems" subfield. The group, instead, represented an alternative – and besieged – orientation toward sociology as a whole. It was fitting, then, that Alvin Gouldner, Merton's former student, delivered the group's presidential address at its annual meeting in 1961.[28] The speech was an unbridled attack on the postwar sociological establishment. Gouldner assailed sociologists' claims to value freedom, in a line of critique that would – by the end of the decade – find wide appeal among student protesters.[29] The mantle of objectivity, to Gouldner, was a license to neglect real human problems in the service of professional self-interest. "In return for a measure of autonomy and social support," he wrote, "many social scientists have surrendered their critical impulses." The "dominant drift" of American sociology, he concluded, was a self-chosen segregation, a moral abnegation.[30] The antiseptic detachment of Merton and Nisbet's *Contemporary Social Problems*, published the same year, was a case in point.

By the early 1960s, then, the discipline's erstwhile social problems tradition had weakened, and alternative bids for the domain were gathering momentum. The SSSP claimed the interwar legacy, though with a leftward, minoritarian pitch. That claim was not, however, honored by the postwar mainstream. Over the subsequent, turbulent decade, American sociology settled into a

---

[27] The founders enlisted the University of Chicago's department as a symbolic ally, with cooperation from notable Chicago figures Ernest W. Burgess (the SSSP's first president) and Herbert Blumer (its third). Skura, "Constraints on a Reform Movement," 71. Alfred McClung Lee was, however, the organization's real leader, and he assumed, from the beginning, a defiant posture toward the discipline's elites. Lee, based at Brooklyn College, positioned his pugilistic 1954 presidential address as a David-and-Goliath rejoinder to Harvard's Samuel Stouffer's speech as ASS president the year before. Lee, "Sociologists in an Integrating Society."

[28] Gouldner, "Anti-Minotaur."

[29] If the social problems tradition had supplied, for the early postwar elites, a useful symbolic contrast, the idea of an establishment-cozy "mainstream" furnished something similar for post-1968 sociologist-dissidents. See Calhoun and VanAntwerpen, "Orthodoxy, Heterodoxy, and Hierarchy."

[30] Gouldner, "Anti-Minotaur," 206, 207.

pattern of joint custody of the social problems terrain. The social movement activism of the early 1960s, at places such as Greensboro and Port Huron, had mushroomed into nationwide protest and unrest – including conservative backlash – by the decade's end. Many of the demonstrations and disturbances centered on the "classic" social problems: race relations, urban life, crime, the family, poverty, education, and war. The political system registered the public clamor around these issues, by way of campaigns, commissions, policy proposals, programs, and legislation. The qualified interventionism of Lyndon Johnson's Great Society platform was only the most visible stimulus.

One result was an efflorescence of sociological work on the conventional social problems, some of it sponsored by government agencies and the big foundations themselves. On the heels of the vast postwar expansion of the US university system, and sociology in particular, the discipline produced a massive wave of scholarship – much of it consciously policy-relevant. The 1960s unrest helped to yoke the behavioral sciences – the sociological elite included – to domestic problems. The RAND Corporation's turn from war-gaming to urban poverty was, in that decade, a highly visible instance.[31] Radical interventions, allied with the New Left student movement and growing black militancy, cohabitated with the cross-tabulated sobriety of the discipline's mainstream. This was, taken as a whole, a lively postscript to Merton and Nisbet's improbable claim on the discipline's social problems tradition.

But the main result of the 1960s for sociology was, if anything, the unraveling of the discipline's claim to sovereignty over the "social problems" domain. By the end of the decade, sociology's hold on social problems had weakened. The fall-off looked steeper still by the close of the twentieth century, at least as registered in political and policy impact.[32] By contrast, psychologists and economists won a larger jurisdiction for their disciplines in the wake of the 1960s. Psychologists benefited from the growing belief that problems of society could be approached with the techniques of individual diagnosis, while economists capitalized on the pervasiveness of the market metaphor. More generally, their work seemed congruent with the intellectual assumptions of the last third of the twentieth century. In Daniel Rodgers' words, the disciplines contributed to and built upon "conceptions of human nature that stressed choice, agency, performance, and desire."[33]

---

[31] Light, *From Warfare to Welfare.*
[32] For a merciless account of sociology's general loss of policy influence in the two decades after 2000, see Turner, "More American Sociology Seeks to Become a Politically-Relevant Discipline."
[33] Rodgers, *Age of Fracture,* 3.

The book's nine chapters explore this apparent shift in the postwar division of labor in social science, each refracted through a single "problem": the family, crime, the black ghetto, education, discrimination, poverty, addiction, war, and mental health. The authors' accounts address three major themes. The first is *problem status* itself: How and when did the issue (poverty, for example, or crime) come to be viewed as a problem of public significance, and to whom? For most chapters, this question implicates the interwar period and the wartime context itself. Each chapter traces its designated problem's career – the waxing and waning of social-scientific interest, public concern, and political intervention in that particular area. Documenting shifts in the *disciplinary division of labor* since World War II is the collection's second aim. The relative contributions of the various social sciences – in cooperation or rivalry, as these patterns shifted over time – are taken up by each chapter in accounts that, juxtaposed to one another, record the disciplines' contrasting fortunes. The book's chapters all take up, finally, the signal question of social problems' *explanation*. Did the leading approaches of one or another social scientist or discipline point to individuals as the source of the problem? Or did they stress social conditions that supersede and overlay the experience of the individual? To what extent, if at all, were structural or systemic accounts accorded priority in one period or another? The answers to these questions have obvious implications for policy. The contributors investigate, in the context of their problem-subject, the vexed and bidirectional relationship between social science and the political system over the postwar decades.

The balance of this introduction follows a similar format. We take up, first, the question of social problem status, move on to assess the redrawn boundaries of postwar social science, and conclude with a meditation on the paired questions of policy and explanatory resonance. Our aim is to make sense of a tension exposed by the chapters, taken as a whole. The authors document a divergence between developments *internal* to the social sciences, on the one hand, and the fate of competing disciplinary frameworks at the level of *policy and politics*, on the other. Crudely speaking – that is, with the variation across the problem domains bracketed – the core social sciences, sociology included, remain active contributors to the problem-specific literatures through the period under study. On the question of reigning explanatory mode, there is, again, no simple shift from, say, structural or systemic explanations to those that favor individual factors. And yet the chapters, taken together, register clear disciplinary "winners" at the level of policy and politics: namely, economics and psychology. The volume's contributions, likewise, trace a postwar attenuation of social-structural ways of seeing problems like racial prejudice and poverty – though again, only at the intersection of politics and social science.

We conclude by grappling with this discrepancy. Disciplinary frameworks such as *homo economicus* and psychological individualism, we argue, both contributed to, and benefited from, a conception of society that, by the 1970s, was increasingly skeptical of social explanations and interventions. Likewise, academic discourse and public debate were embedded in, and helped to reinforce, a social imaginary that was already tuned to personal frames of understanding. Psychology and economics thrived because they resonated with the era's growing individualism, while also helping to underwrite it. The story is one of an elective affinity between these disciplines and a public imagination that was decreasingly social-structural and decidedly not sociological.

1.2 Problem Status

Sociologists, as the term "social problems" took hold in the early interwar years, raised the obvious definitional question: What counts as a social problem? The field's textbooks and coursework supplied an ad hoc answer, in their problem-a-week inventories: A social problem, according to their implicit argument, is one of the pathologies listed in the table of contents. A more deliberate literature of reflection, making the number of people affected a defining characteristic of a social problem, began to appear in the early 1920s, and then reappeared in regular installments – across commentaries, presidential addresses, and theoretical treatises – for the balance of the century.

The key issues, if not the problem-designates themselves, have remained consistent over the decades. Are social problems merely "what people think they are" – in the blunt words of an influential 1941 intervention?[34] Or are there objective criteria – actual social conditions, for instance – that scholars might use to qualify an issue as problematic? If indeed "objective" conditions are a legitimate yardstick, what is the measure of social *health* that specifies the pathology? The main (if often implicit answer) in the interwar years was *order* – stability in the face of rapid, centrifugal social change. "Social disorganization" was the ur-problem, in other words – the

---

[34] Fuller and Myers, "Some Aspects of a Theory of Social Problems," 25. For all their subjectivist bravado, Fuller and Myers remained committed to a definition that includes an "objective phase" – a "verifiable condition, situation, or event."

byproduct of modernity expressed through crime, poverty, and the other specific problems. An alternative approach, one that looked to prevailing *norms*, gained some traction in the 1930s: A social problem is defined by the gap between consensus values and conditions on the ground. If social scientists can identify the norms and their violation, they can name the pathology. A late-appearing rival to the *order* and *norm* theories, which won significant uptake only in the 1970s, dispensed with objective conditions altogether. A social problem, on the strong subjectivist view, is what people call a social problem.

The point is that a discourse on problem status – a running debate on the definition of a "social problem" itself – developed alongside the teaching and empirical study of specific pathologies. The disputes and definitional struggles took place, for the most part, among sociologists, but they are, nevertheless, relevant to the analysis of problems of society in general.[35] The act of naming problems, in patterned repetition, has helped to call those very problems into existence – and to attract the attention of a growing number of observers to their significance. There is a creative, illocutionary character to the designation of social pathology. So too with the running deliberation – the meta-discourse, as it were – over what elevates a topic to problem status. Our own approach, moreover, to the problems of society and their study – the object of this volume – is indebted to the discourse, in particular the subjectivist turn of the 1970s. So it is worth recounting here.

As we have seen, Ellwood's (1910) textbook initiated the ad hoc tradition of social problem designation: Social problems, in effect, are what sociologists think they are. That there are identifiable "social evils" was, for Ellwood, a given, and so his stepwise elaboration required no warrant. The pathologies were announced by the chapter titles: "The Problem of the Modern Family," "The Immigration Problem," "The Problem of the City," and on down the list.[36] Ellwood's textbook was reissued in 1919 in an enlarged edition, and by the middle of the next decade four competitors had emerged to serve the

---

[35] There is no robust history of the "social problems" discourse in American sociology. The best overview is Senn and Senn, "What is a Social Problem?" See also Martindale, "Social Disorganization" and Spector and Kitsuse, *Constructing Social Problems*, chaps. 2–3, though the narrative is set up against the authors' theory. Two other brief histories appeared in the 1971 *Handbook on the Study of Social Problems*: Rose, "History and Sociology of the Study of Social Problems"; and Chall, "Notes Toward a History."

[36] Ellwood, *Sociology and Modern Social Problems*, 5–6, 13.

proliferating core course in the discipline.[37] These five texts, placed side by side, demonstrate the arbitrary (or at least eclectic) character of the problem selection process. Only the family is named as a problem across all five books, while just poverty and labor conditions appear in three. There is a long tail of singletons (like "The 'revolt of the young'" in one, or "The drug habit" in the other), and just a handful of topics that appear twice: race, immigration, crime, health, education, and war. Perhaps it is fitting that a sociologist, writing in 1929, managed to identify 396 "major" social problems.[38]

A survey of American sociology departments, published that year, found that over half offered a generic "Social Problems" course, with many programs also reporting specialized courses such as "Drug Addiction and Alcoholism." The departments, taken together, listed forty-four distinct problems covered in their core "Social Problems" courses, though a handful of topics stood out: poverty, crime, the family, race problems, population, immigration, and divorce were each reported by about two-thirds of respondents.[39] So some stability – perhaps achieved through self-generated momentum, cross-pollination, and the textbook/course interplay – was evident by the end of the decade.

We conducted our own analysis of textbooks published in the early postwar years, tallying the chapter-problems of the six leading volumes.[40] Some of the same topics were prominent: crime and the family appeared in all six books, with race and poverty included in all but one volume. A few of the leading problems in 1929 were less salient by the early 1950s: Only three books devoted a chapter to immigration, with still fewer devoted to population (two) or divorce (one). Newly prominent on the textbook agenda were mental health (five chapters) and education (four) – neither of which had made the top ten in 1929. Perhaps reflecting the temper of the time,

---

[37] Ellwood, *Sociology and Modern Social Problems*, rev. and enlarged ed. The others were Binder, *Major Social Problems* (1920); Parsons, *Introduction to Modern Social Problems* (1924); Beach, *Introduction to Sociology and Social Problems* (1925); and Queen and Mann, *Social Pathology* (1925). Two other major texts appeared in 1927: Odum's *Man's Quest for Social Guidance* and Bossard's *Problems of Social Well-Being*. A 1929 survey of departments found that Queen and Mann, Odum, and Bossard were the most frequently used. Reinhardt, "Trends in the Teaching of 'Social Problems,'" 383.
[38] Bowden, "Our 396 Major Social Problems." Wrote Bowden: "We have many social problems." 397.
[39] Reinhardt, "Trends in the Teaching of 'Social Problems,'" 382.
[40] The six were selected on the basis of a total count of book reviews from 1930 to 1960 in JSTOR's "Sociology" journal collection, with the earliest edition appearing in the 1950s chosen for analysis. The books are Horton and Leslie, *Sociology of Social Problems* (1955); Landis, *Social Problems in Nation and World* (1959); Merrill, *Social Problems* (1950); Neumeyer, *Social Problems and the Changing Society* (1953); Raab and Selznick, *Major Social Problems* (1959); and Weaver, *Social Problems* (1951).

chapters on civil liberties, natural resources, and mass communication each made an appearance.

The topical drift over the decades is one index of what long prevailed as the main method for identifying problems: the fiat of sociologist-authors.[41] This untheorized, taken-for-granted adhocracy – together with an unexamined substrate of gauzy reformism – was already provoking critique in the interwar years.[42] The charge of reformism was, to a point, fair. The interwar social problems orientation was predicated on faith in guided progress. The common view was that – with the help of social science, moral uplift, and modest government intervention – modernity's rough edges could be smoothed out. This bundle of assumptions was shared with other Progressive reformers, and consistent, too, with most of the American discipline's late nineteenth-century pioneers. The basic idea was that the onrush of social change had outpaced society's ability to hold itself together – but that "social control" could be re-established. The agitations of urban-industrial civilization, in other words, had so jostled the social order that social problems – byproducts of disorder – had shaken loose. These problems, crucially, were fixable: Social institutions and norms, with the aid of social science, just needed to catch up with social reality. Social problems, whatever their magnitude, were amenable to social intervention.

Summarized in the language of the time, social problems resulted from the "social disorganization" generated by "cultural lag," thereby requiring the remedy of "social control."[43] This worldview furnished, for

[41] The unarticulated selection process remains a fixture of the textbook market, as Joel Best observed in 2006: "publishers continue to churn out old-style, theoretically incoherent textbooks for traditional problem-of-the-week courses." Best, "Whatever Happened to Social Pathology?" 536.

[42] This avoidance of theory was a point of pride to Ellwood back in 1910: The book, he wrote, "is not intended to be a contribution to sociological theory, and no attempt is made to give a systematic presentation of theory. Rather, the student's attention is called to certain obvious and elementary forces in the social life, and he is left to work out his own system of social theory." Ellwood, *Sociology and Modern Social Problems*, 3.

[43] "Social control" was already in wide circulation by the 1890s. "Social disorganization" was popularized by W. I. Thomas and Florian Znaniecki's *The Polish Peasant in Europe and America* (1918), while "cultural lag" was not coined by Chicago sociologist William Ogburn until 1922. Ogburn, *Social Change*, Part IV. Even so, the ideas behind cultural lag and behind social disorganization were prevalent from the beginning of the social problems tradition. Take the case of Ellwood's initial 1910 text: "old habits are usually not replaced by new habits without an intervening period of confusion and uncertainty. In other words, in the transition from old habit to the new habit there is much opportunity for disorganization and disintegration." Ellwood, *Sociology and Modern Social Problems*, 131.

interwar American sociologists, an implicit theory of social pathology. Social problems were problems of modernity, brought on by the kinetic novelty of the factory floor and tenement congestion. Social order was the background against which problems were identified. What then counts as a social problem? Disorder, the unraveling of norms, the attenuation of social bonds, as expressed in the broken family or the juvenile delinquent. The task of the sociologist, in the view of interwar social pathologists, was to diagnose the breakdown of order – the deviations from the solidarity that society's progress required. Theirs was, in other words, an under-articulated functionalism, with cohesion as the normative benchmark. The problems, moreover, were linked to solutions: The social scientist not only named the pathology, but also lent a hand in devising the treatment. For most interwar authors, the point was not explicit activism – which, after all, smacked of social work and moralistic reformism.[44] Instead, the sociologist, and perhaps social science as a whole, furnished expert guidance to the actual agents of social control.

So the mainline stance toward social problems was objectivist: Pathologies are real and discernible. Already by the mid-1920s, however, a dissenting view crept in, one that insisted on public *recognition* for an issue to count as a problem. Writing in 1924, the sociologist Clarence Case tethered problem status to the "attention of a considerable number of competent observers within a society," who clamor for a social remedy. Case's was the first articulation of a subjectivist alternative, one that (in his words) sees a social problem as "partly a state of the social mind and hence not purely a matter of unfavorable objective conditions." Here public consternation was a necessary, if not yet sufficient, criterion for problem status: The "public mind ... *recognizes the existence* of the problem; and perceives also the fact that it must be collectively solved." This alternative to the prevailing certitude – that there were problems out there that sociologists can identify – was, in a way, subjectivist twice over. The social scientist deferred to the public's judgment that a state of affairs is problematic, which also entailed deference to a set of social norms – the ones that were violated. There was even a third dimension of relevant public belief: the shared view that a given problem is in fact addressable. For all the weight he granted to collective

---

[44] From Ellwood on, the social problems literature took exquisite pains to distinguish sociology and/or social science, with its scientific character, from the work of reformers, social workers, and legislators.

belief, Case preserved a role for objective inquiry: A social scientist must still ratify that "adverse social conditions" obtain.[45]

Case's qualified subjectivism was subsequently endorsed by a number of other interwar sociologists who emphasized the importance of value *conflict* in the definitional process.[46] Indeed, Richard Fuller's quarrel with the mainstream "social disorganization approach" concerned its neglect of clashing norms. Warring interest groups cannot even agree on what counts as a problem, let alone a solution, since they bring incompatible values to the battlefield. Consider the "problem" of unemployment, which many economists and employers take to be an inevitable byproduct of a market economy. Treating labor-market conditions, in this example, "as if they were objective states of social disorganization gets us nowhere." The "clash of social interests" is the core of any social problem, and so the task of the social scientist is to analyze that definitional struggle.[47] Thus, according to Fuller and a co-author, social problems are "what people think they are." Conditions on the ground matter, but they do not "assume a prominent place in a social problem until a given people define them as hostile to their welfare."[48]

The objectivist view – that social problems exist regardless of whether people recognize them – persisted into the postwar decades. Merton and Nisbet, for example, assigned sociologists the task of identifying those *latent* problems that the public failed to acknowledge.[49] But proponents

---

[45] Case, "What is a Social Problem?" 268, 269, 271 (italics in the original). Case staked out his claim against Hornell Hart's 1923 definition, which hinges on (objectively) measured impact: "*A social problem is a problem which actually or potentially affects large numbers of people in a common way so that it may best be solved by some measure or measures applied to the problem as a whole rather than by dealing with each individual as an isolated case, or which requires concerted or organized human action.*" Hart, "What is a Social Problem?" 349 (italics in the original). Hart, Case notes, defines a social problem "in terms of objective data." For Case, "these are not social problems in the full sense, but simply the adverse conditions of life which form one side of social problems, the other being the more or less prevalent social attitude toward those conditions." Case, "What is a Social Problem?" 272.
[46] Waller, "Social Problems and the Mores"; Fuller, "Sociological Theory and Social Problems"; Fuller, "Problem of Teaching Social Problems"; Fuller, "Social Problems"; and Fuller and Myers, "Some Aspects of a Theory of Social Problems."
[47] Fuller, "Problem of Teaching Social Problems," 421, 422.
[48] Fuller and Myers, "Some Aspects of a Theory of Social Problems," 25. Every social problem, therefore, has "both an objective and a subjective aspect."
[49] Writes Merton, in the volume's conclusion: "For the sociologist to confine himself only to the conditions in society which a majority of people regard as undesirable would be to exclude study of all manner of other conditions that are in fact at odds with the declared values and purposes of those who accept or endorse these conditions. Such a limitation would require the sociologist to subscribe to an extreme subjectivism, under the self-deceiving guise of retaining the objectivity of the scientific observer." Merton, "Social Problems and Sociological Theory," 708.

of a more subjectivist cast were increasingly vocal, notably within the new SSSP. The emergence of labeling theory was especially important. As outlined in Edwin Lemert's *Social Pathology* (1951) and popularized by Howard Becker's *Outsiders* (1963), labeling theory proposed that normative majorities assign deviant status to the nonconformist minorities in their midst.[50] So deviance – and by extension other kinds of social pathology – has nothing to do with "bad" behavior itself. "The deviant is one to whom that label has been successfully applied," wrote Becker in 1963. "Deviant behavior is behavior that people so label."[51] Becker and other self-styled sociologists of deviance, in effect, turned the study of social problems on its head. The foundational moral calculus, that problems are *problematic*, was discarded in favor of an underdog morality – one that, at least implicitly, celebrated the outsider.[52] This shift reflected a more general drift away from the small-town meliorism that C. Wright Mills had mocked. The postwar "social problems" discourse, at the SSSP and within its *Social Problems* journal, was more insistently qualitative, sympathetic to the stigmatized, and sensitive to the social process of definition. The new orientation registered the moral energies of the Civil Rights Movement, the student New Left, and the counterculture, as well as the wider postwar culture of expressive individualism that, in myriad ways, celebrated nonconformity. The congealing, in the late 1960s and 1970s, of "symbolic interactionism" as a self-conscious alternative to mainstream sociology – erected around Herbert Blumer's influential reading of George Herbert Mead – was a crucial development too. Much of the subsequent sociology of deviance was conducted under its banner, and even the early postwar exemplars of the labeling approach were retroactively classified as interactionist.

The result was that much of the 1960s and 1970s "social problems" scholarship – if not the typical textbook – filtered its work through a subjectivist lens. Becker himself, in the introduction to his 1966 *Social*

---

[50] Lemert, *Social Pathology* and Becker, *Outsiders*. In an insightful 1962 paper, Kai Erikson argued that deviance – far from being a problem – is in fact crucial for the renewal and sustenance of social order. "Thus deviance cannot be dismissed as behavior which disrupts stability in society," he wrote, "but is itself, in controlled quantities, an important condition for *preserving* stability." Erikson, "Notes on the Sociology of Deviance," 310.

[51] Becker, *Outsiders*, 9.

[52] In a remarkably scabrous 1968 takedown of his SSSP colleague Becker, Alvin Gouldner assailed the sociology of deviance for its romantic embrace of the stigmatized, characterized by a "collector's aesthetic." Among other things, the Becker approach lets the "overdogs" – the truly powerful – off the hook. His is the "sociology of young men with friends in Washington." Gouldner, "The Sociologist as Partisan," 106–11. Gouldner's critique from the left is echoed in Liazos, "Poverty of the Sociology of Deviance."

Problems: A Modern Approach, embraced Fuller's "what people think they are" definition.[53] But Becker also registered a wider turn to the *process* of problem formation – to the messy, power-laden definitional struggle over a problem's "career."[54] To a significant degree, that is, sociologists shifted their gaze from the underlying social issues to the people and institutions that go about *naming* problems. This was, for Becker and others, contested terrain, pockmarked by definitional conflict among citizens, professional experts, politicians, and, of course, social scientists. The problematic people, so called, were in the mix too, shaped by but also reacting to their ascribed deviancy – an especially salient point within a racialized public and policy discourse that frequently blamed victims for their own plight and would increasingly do so in the years to come.[55] Becker, in 1966, called on sociologists to "take the point of view of those who are defined as causing the problem instead of those who so define it."[56] His proposal was to assume the perspective of the "other" – to study, in W. E. B. Du Bois's haunting phrase, how it feels to be a problem.[57] On this view there are no social problems as such, just ways of seeing people as problems – as nuts, sluts, and perverts, in Liazos' critical shorthand.[58]

Problems, according to this new, more interactionist approach, have a natural history of sorts – a trajectory that the social scientist might trace.[59] Inchoate concern and organized advocacy, often transmitted through mass media, generate the widespread recognition that problem status requires. What follows, typically, is an institutionalization of the problem: the emergence of organizations and professionals who claim, in effect, custody. These are, to borrow a pair of prominent concepts in the literature, "control institutions" staffed by the "troubled persons professions" – such as social work or policy analysis – which subsist on the putatively troubled.[60] Once

---

[53] Becker, "Introduction," 2–5.
[54] "The chapters of this book," Becker wrote, "do not so much treat 'social problems' as they do areas in which various people – citizens, politicians, professional experts, cultural critics, social scientists, and other interested parties – define many kinds of social problems as arising." Becker, "Introduction," 7.
[55] On the politics of social scientific problem definition, around poverty, deficiency, and race in particular, see O'Connor, *Poverty Knowledge*, 10–16.
[56] Becker, "Introduction," 27.
[57] Du Bois, *Souls of Black Folk*, 1–3.
[58] Liazos, "Poverty of the Sociology of Deviance," 103. Leah Gordon suggested this point in conversation.
[59] The idea that social problems have a career, with identifiable stages, appears in a number of reflective accounts from the period.
[60] "Control institutions" are described in Erikson, "Notes on the Sociology of Deviance," 310. Joseph Gusfield discusses the "troubled persons professions" in "Constructing the Ownership of Social Problems," 432–33.

these are established and institutionalized, the contest over "ownership" – the authority to name the problem, suggest solutions, and marshal a response – continues along lines of stratified power.[61]

It was inevitable, perhaps, that the century's drift toward a more definitional approach to the study of social problems would arrive at a pure and uncompromising subjectivism. In a pair of 1973 papers, sociologists John Kitsuse and Malcolm Spector staked out a strong constructionist position, one that proudly neglects "real" social conditions.[62] They even faulted apparent allies, like Becker and Fuller, for not going far enough – for clinging, needlessly, to the view that objective conditions help establish problem status.[63] The word "putative" is the decisive departure in their definition of social problems: *"the activities of groups making assertions of grievances and claims with respect to some putative conditions."*[64] The task of the social scientist is to document and explain the claim-making, and nothing more than that. Spector and Kitsuse concede that actors often marshal evidence about social conditions, but those assertions are merely gist for the analytical mill: "Here *their* causal analysis, not the sociologist's, is the crucial input." The process of claiming and naming – of calling out an issue as a problem – is what matters in the study of social problems. The intrinsic gravity of a problem is almost irrelevant; social problem status is a symbolic achievement, resulting from a complex and contested social baptism.

In a 1971 paper, Herbert Blumer – the Chicago veteran and godfather of symbolic interactionism – more or less anticipated the position that Kitsuse and Spector would so forcefully propound. Social problems are not born, Blumer claimed; they are made – legitimated, in other words, through a process of collective definition. There is, he wrote, a "selective process in which, so to speak, many budding social problems are choked off, others are

---

[61] Gusfield develops the idea of problem "ownership" in his important 1981 book, *The Culture of Public Problems*, 10–13, in the context of drunk driving.

[62] Kitsuse and Spector, "Toward a Sociology of Social Problems" and Spector and Kitsuse, "Social Problems." Spector and Kitsuse codified their approach in a 1987 book, *Constructing Social Problems*.

[63] Kitsuse and Spector, "Toward a Sociology of Social Problems," 412–13. Kitsuse and Spector were right that Case, Waller, Fuller, and even postwar labeling theorists such as Becker all carved out a role for the social scientist to, in effect, verify the public's problem recognition by holding it up against actual social conditions. Becker: "Objective conditions are an important part of our conception of a social problem, then, because the definition of a social problem by participants in the society is likely to refer to a situation in society which can, as Fuller and Myers say, 'be checked as to existence and magnitude (proportions) by impartial and trained observers.'" Becker, "Introduction," 6.

[64] Kitsuse and Spector, "Toward a Sociology of Social Problems," 414, 415 (italics in original).

ignored, others are avoided, others have to fight their way to a respectable status, and others are rushed along to legitimacy by a strong and influential backing."[65] Blumer, like others before him, highlighted the *career* of the typical social problem – the series of stages through which a problem passes, from legitimation to (in some cases) government intervention.

So Blumer, in a sense, furnished a digest of the literature of reflection on social problems, or at least its terminus in subjectivism. What distinguished his 1971 contribution, however, was its claim that social scientists rarely have anything to do with that process of collective definition. Blumer chided his fellow social scientists for their policy pretensions and inflated sense of public efficacy. Social-scientific knowledge, to the extent it enters the definitional stream at all, is often "ignored, distorted, or smothered by other considerations."[66] Powerful interest groups, politicians, media coverage, public opinion polls, outside shocks, and legislative horse-trading, among other factors, are normally far more decisive than social science over the course of a problem's career.[67]

We take issue with Blumer's last point, even as we endorse the subjectivist program that his paper encapsulates. The chapters of this volume, like the classic sociology textbook, are devoted to specific problems of society, one after another. It is true, too, that our selection process for the chapter topics honors the view that social problems are what people say they are. But for us, and for this project, the social scientist is decisive. The chapters' attention, in other words, lingers on those problems that economists, psychologists, and the rest – even sociologists – took to be most trenchant over the postwar decades. Major research projects, commissions and reports, works of public resonance, expert testimony – moments in which social scientists and their work joined the definitional fray – are at the heart of the volume's topical chapters. These interventions often withered on the vine of official indifference, as Blumer observed – or else registered their impact at the more subterranean level of language. But social scientists, in each of the postwar cases, were among the significant definers. They helped to designate the problems and – in complex interplay with other social and political currents – to give shape to the policy responses.

The point, contra Blumer, is that social scientists were in the mix, as postwar America grappled with its increasingly visible challenges. The

---

[65] Blumer, "Social Problems as Collective Behavior," 303.
[66] Blumer, "Social Problems as Collective Behavior," 304.
[67] Friedrich Hayek, in a well-known 1949 essay, already pointed out the growing influence of these "professional secondhand dealers in ideas." Hayek, "Intellectuals and Socialism," 417.

chapters, with that baseline, attend to the *relative* contributions of the social science disciplines – their shifting prominence and claims to topical "ownership" vis-à-vis their counterparts. Here the case of sociology is instructive: For all its preoccupation with the "social problems" domain, the discipline has watched its rivals – notably psychology and economics – lay increasingly credible claims to the problems themselves.

1.3 Disciplinary Division of Labor

By the time Richard Swedberg considered the history of interaction between economics and sociology, in 1991, economics imperialism, with Gary Becker as its flag bearer, had made a name for itself. The uncoordinated attempts that had characterized its beginnings in the late 1950s had now coalesced, creating new momentum for the discipline's inroads into the realm of other social sciences. Becker's "economic approach to human behavior" was now complemented by a similar effort in sociology with the publication of James Coleman's monumental treatise in rational choice sociology – *Foundations of Social Theory* – in 1990. Disciplinary boundaries had inexorably shifted and jurisdictional changes were not temporary or accidental.[68]

As Swedberg described the nature of these changes, he offered a four-fold periodization of the relationship between economics and social analysis: the time of political economy (late eighteenth to late nineteenth-century); the *Methodenstreit* (1880s–1910s); mutual ignorance and distortion in the social sciences (1920s–1960s); and economic imperialism and the challenge of redrawing the boundaries in the social sciences (1970s–).[69] As a broad characterization of changing boundaries, Swedberg's periodization fares well, but its third and fourth periods suffer from imprecisions. It is surprising indeed that the opening years of the "mutual ignorance" period coincide with the creation of the Social Science Research Council (SSRC) and that its end dovetails with what can be considered as the closing of the most prolific period for interdisciplinary work in the US social sciences. Likewise, placing the start of economics imperialism in the 1970s illustrates the frequent emphasis on the movement's heyday at the expense of its first significant inroads in the late 1950s and early 1960s. To some extent, the shortcomings of Swedberg's last two periods reflect his own biases as an economic sociologist: the minimization of the role of political science in the redefinition of the division of labor in the US social sciences in the early

---

[68] Swedberg, *Economics and Sociology* and Coleman, *Foundations of Social Theory*.
[69] Swedberg, *Economics and Sociology*, 14–15.

1920s, and the temptation to cast sociology as the main rival to economics in the 1970s.

The changing division of labor among the US social sciences since 1918 cannot be understood without bearing in mind that their practitioners viewed disciplinary boundaries through the prism of solving important problems of society. Clearly by the first decade of the twentieth century, the departmental structure of the American university as we know it was in place – with the caveat that many departments remained bi-disciplinary.[70] It was, even into the 1930s, common for sociologists to coexist with either economists or political scientists in the same department. Likewise, most social sciences had their own professional societies, which strengthened a nascent sense of identity among disciplinary brethren, but did not stand in the way of organizing common annual meetings, which remained the norm until the 1940s.[71]

By the early 1920s, increasing specialization was already raising fears. The tendency to disciplinary isolation accentuated those fears, with the benefits of specialization often contrasted with the costs of excessive departmentalization and compartmentalization. Specialization itself was not regarded as evil, but its acceleration in a time of rapid social change could, according to this view, prove counterproductive. The concern was that social scientists, confined to their disciplines, were badly positioned to grasp and address problems of a complex, interrelated, and fast-changing society. Specialization encouraged intellectual particularisms that made synthesis – the integration of research findings from different social sciences – more problematic. Increased specialization accompanied the professionalization of social science disciplines, but it would be an exaggeration to suggest that their practitioners saw problems of society as falling under the exclusive jurisdiction of any particular discipline.

To varying degrees, each of the core social sciences – economics, sociology, and political science – addressed problems such as crime, addiction, the family, prejudice, poverty, and education. And in the 1920s, at least, they stood on similar footing, as measured by prestige, legitimacy, and co-equal membership in the SSRC. By providing flexible institutional structures supporting multidisciplinary research work, the SSRC, created in 1923, helped address concerns raised by increased specialization. Its primary purpose was to advance the research methods of political science and related social sciences by encouraging greater cooperation between existing disciplinary associations, including the American Statistical Association. By the mid-1920s,

---

[70] Abbott, *Chaos of Disciplines*, 122–31.
[71] Young, "Emergence of Sociology from Political Economy."

the American Psychological Association, the American Anthropological Association, and the American Historical Association had all joined the SSRC. As political scientist and SSRC co-founder Charles Merriam pointed out, the organization was established to support "cases where problems overlap the boundaries of one or more of the special fields concerned."[72]

By the late 1920s, the sociologist William Ogburn and the anthropologist Alexander Goldenweiser drew a portrait of the US social sciences in which their interrelations, more than their general nature, stood out: "The problems of living society," they wrote, "do not range themselves so as to fit the artificial isolation forced upon the social sciences by differences of specific subject and method. These problems are what they are. If they are to be solved, whatever knowledge we possess about society must be called into service, wherever needed."[73]

Ogburn and Goldenweiser offered a handful of examples that, with the exception of taxation – described as the concern of economics and political science – would have slotted into most social problems textbooks of the time. Thus, poverty was described as falling in the domains of psychology, economics, sociology, political science, ethics, and education. With a few variations, the same argument was repeated for immigration, race problems, and crime. Ogburn and Goldenweiser's book stood as a good illustration of the position of leading social scientists on disciplinary specialization in the wake of the SSRC's creation. Increased specialization allowed for greater professionalization and more "scientific" approaches, but social problems themselves did not fall under the exclusive preserve of any single discipline.

In the eyes of Ogburn and Goldenweiser and many others, synthesizing the research findings of various social sciences appeared much more important than sanctifying their modes of expertise. Synthesis was supposed to open new horizons for future developments in the US social sciences, but with the unprecedented economic crisis of the 1930s, the sense of urgency thrust certain disciplines to the forefront. In the process, it became even more obvious that the pressing problems of American society not only did not "fit the artificial isolation forced upon the social sciences by differences of specific subject and method," but actually played a role in redrawing the boundaries attached to these differences.[74] Until the late 1920s, social scientists had tended to emphasize interdisciplinary

[72] See Worcester, *Social Science Research Council*, 14 and Merriam, "Annual Report of the Social Science," 185.
[73] Ogburn and Goldenweiser, *Social Sciences and Their Interrelations*, 7–8.
[74] Ogburn and Goldenweiser, *Social Sciences and Their Interrelations*, 7.

cooperation as a prerequisite for solving social problems. With the crisis of the 1930s, however, uneven participation in policymaking marked the disciplines' diverging fortunes.

With the Great Depression and the New Deal, the pace of social change continued to occupy the minds of social scientists, if only because there was so much uncertainty as to the kind of social order that would emerge from those troubled years. Yet, the threat that large-scale economic disorganization posed to capitalism itself quickly took precedence. As Charles Camic has shown, the 1930s were not a happy time for sociologists, whose nascent public stature suffered at the expense of other social scientists, economists in particular. Among the significant changes in the substance and organization of American culture, Camic listed "a fundamental reordering of the prestige hierarchy of academic disciplines as a result of trends that predated the Depression."[75]

Even before economic hardship struck the whole US society, indeed, there was a gradual shift in emphasis toward economic problems following the depression of 1920–1921. Though social problems still concerned the community of social scientists as a whole, the centrality of economic problems in American society, together with Secretary of Commerce Herbert Hoover's marked trust in economic expertise, granted economists a comparative advantage over other social scientists. As early as August 1927, plans were discussed for a study of recent economic changes, which would improve the understanding of the American economy as a whole with the aim to draw down unemployment. Following the recruitment of collaborators, work and discussions were undertaken under the directorship of economic historian Edwin Gay and empirical economist Wesley Mitchell from the National Bureau of Economic Research (NBER). Both Gay and Mitchell were known for promoting the collection of data as a major resource in the search for the solutions to society's problems.[76]

That two institutional economists found themselves at the center of a national survey commissioned by the federal government need not be taken as evidence that policymakers favored one stream of thought over another, or that economics alone carried professional expertise. The growing faith in professional expertise was tethered to statistical methods more than disciplinary background, so differences in recognition depended on social scientists' familiarity with these methods as much as their activism in the

[75] Camic, "On Edge," 226.
[76] It is worth remembering that Gay and Mitchell played an important role in the creation of the NBER in 1920 and the SSRC in 1923.

service of society, with Mitchell illustrating the former trait and Gay the latter. When it came to advising policymakers, however, differences in theoretical orientations within economics could prove influential, because different conceptions of disciplinary boundaries implied differential attention to noneconomic factors in devising solutions to economic problems. Institutional economists such as Mitchell and Gay showed greater sensitivity to the relationships between economic and social organization than their neoclassical counterparts, a tendency that helped give quantitative economic research greater public relevance than it would have had otherwise.

The Committee on Recent Economic Changes' final report was completed in February 1929. As Gay noted in the introduction, the report emphasizes the causes of American prosperity and suggests that its current features resembled those of "former major periods of prosperity." As he referred to maladjustments of economic growth, Gay likewise found similarities with the past, but also noted that "the rapidity and vigor of growth of some elements is so great as seriously to unbalance the whole organism." In an argument reminiscent of the cultural lag hypothesis, Gay observed a shift in the "psychological attitude" toward change in material conditions, with "quick adaptation and rapid mutation" increasingly regarded with "more social concern." The economic historian hinted that "something distinctly different from our former experience is taking place" and that "there seem now to be differences of degree which approach differences in kind."[77] Gay's remarks should not be taken as prophesizing the coming economic crisis; instead, they reflected acute perception that change in the adaptive culture failed to synchronize with change in the material culture, making the perspective of a new type of social organization altogether likely. It is ironic that such concern, which emerged in a time of accelerated changes accompanying economic prosperity, became even more paramount when policymakers began to ponder the best way to adjust social organization to the economic dislocations of the late 1920s and early 1930s.

From that perspective, the decision of now-President Hoover to create the multidisciplinary Research Committee on Social Trends in the autumn of 1929 is less perplexing. The Committee, the culmination of the growing stature of the social sciences throughout the 1920s, seemed especially suited to dealing with the undesirable social consequences of economic prosperity. Yet by the time its report was published in 1933, after four years of economic hardship, its motivation was hardly in phase with current preoccupations.

[77] Gay, "Introduction," 10–12.

In keeping with the spirit of the 1920s, the report viewed the "outstanding problem" of American society "as that of bringing about a realization of the interdependence of the factors of our complicated social structure, and of interrelating the advancing sections of our forward movement so that agriculture, labor, industry, government, education, religion and science may develop a higher degree of coordination in the next phase of national growth." In a time of severe recession, that concern seemed incongruous to say the least. More importantly, in keeping with the emphasis on the social consequences of economic prosperity, the report presented itself as a study of social change, pointing to the interrelations between various social trends at a time when economic changes were on everyone's mind. Of course, the contributors to the volume saw economic changes, like many other changes, as parts of a broader pattern of overall social change, but the "central view of the American problem as revealed by social trends" cut against the inclination to concentrate on economic concerns in the midst of a depression.[78]

Whatever interest sociologists and other social scientists might have had in economic matters, it is understandable that economics, which was still methodologically pluralistic at the time and certainly more open to the other social sciences than it became after World War II, acquired the status of a reference discipline in the eyes of policymakers. Though the merits of economists and the impact of their ideas on economic policymaking were already recognized in the pre–New Deal era, the kind of stature the discipline achieved during the New Deal was of a different nature. Its practitioners' strong commitment to objectivity and quantification combined with a sense of economic urgency to create unprecedented expectations.[79]

In economics, the great figure of the 1930s was John Maynard Keynes, but the message of *The General Theory of Employment, Interest, and Money* reached the United States much later. If one wants to form a clear idea of the influence of economists on the public stage in the United States, a good place to start is with US economics itself. By the mid-1930s, the discipline encompassed a variety of perspectives – a pluralism inadequately captured

[78] President's Research Committee on Social Trends, *Recent Social Trends*, xii, xiii. Comparing its work to Hoover's Committee on Recent Economic Changes, Mark C. Smith presents the Committee on Social Trends project as a "similar but more ambitious study of American society." Smith, *Social Science in the Crucible*, 71.
[79] Barber, *From New Era to New Deal*. Likewise, Michael A. Bernstein's *A Perilous Progress* offers a detailed story of the years prior to 1939, pointing to the gradual strengthening of the economics profession, its sensitivity to objectivity, and its participation in the realization of a public purpose.

by the sharp distinction between neoclassicism and institutionalism.[80] Economics allowed for a variety of theoretical approaches at the same time that its policy recommendations, being less systematized, suffered from inadequate disciplinary demarcation. As a result, the distinction between abstract and empirical work lacked the clarity it later achieved. The absence of a common theoretical framework encompassing pure and applied economics meant that the shared identity of economists in the 1930s resulted more from efforts at "shaping an authoritative community," to use Michael A. Bernstein's phrase, than from attempts at defining an orthodoxy around a certain conception of scholarly research. The identity of economists built upon a professionalizing, not a disciplinarizing, vision.

While economists, together with political scientists and legal scholars, filled top New Deal policy posts, sociologists continued to publish "social problem" treatises to a curiously indifferent public. Though plainly relevant to the decade's struggles, sociology's litany of social problems fell outside the main New Deal frame.[81] Sociologists were not long in registering the weakening of their position in academia and among policymakers. Throughout the 1930s, they missed no opportunity to voice their concern about the discipline's lowly place in society. They variously lamented the "almost complete disregard of the depression in the programs of important sociological meetings," argued for increasing attention to the sociology of economic relations, attributed the lesser influence of sociologists in the current national crisis to an "inferiority complex," and pointed to the relatively greater role of economists in contemporary life and the weak presence of sociologists in the bureaus, divisions, offices, and sections of the Roosevelt administration.[82]

These concerns, voiced in a 1934 special issue of *Social Forces*, illustrated sociologists' perceived need to deal with wider social and economic problems, which, as sociologist Luther L. Bernard put it, "are not treated specifically under the heading of conventional economics." Bernard, the ASS's president in 1932,

[80] Roger Backhouse notes: "In the 1920s and 1930s, US economics was pluralistic.... Classical economists (Frank Taussig at Harvard) and institutionalists (John Commons at Wisconsin and Wesley Mitchell and John Maurice Clark at Columbia) flourished alongside neoclassical economists (Irving Fisher at Yale) and Marshallians (Edward Chamberlin at Harvard). Some individuals defied classification (Frank Knight at Iowa and then at Chicago). By 1960, all this had changed, and neoclassical economics, or at least the neoclassical synthesis of Paul Samuelson's textbook, was unquestionably dominant." Backhouse, "Transformation of US Economics," 85.
[81] Camic, "On Edge."
[82] All these points are made in a 1934 *Social Forces* symposium devoted to examining questions concerning the role of sociology in the New Deal.

added: "In fact such problems as those of poverty and relief, social welfare, the standard of living, profits and social service, the function of capitalism in civilization, collective ownership and control, wages and welfare, child labor and child welfare, conditions of work, and social reform can be treated adequately only from a sociological standpoint." The reference to conventional economics implied that sociology could join with alternative streams of thought, institutional economics in particular, which were closer to the other social sciences and took these problems seriously. At the same time, Bernard's chauvinist claim that a "sociological standpoint" was required suggested that sociologists should hold the upper hand in this potential collaboration.[83]

In the late 1930s, the growing significance of ideologies of economic planning notwithstanding, social scientists outside economics had not relinquished the hope for a brighter future.[84] Moreover, the role of institutional economists in the New Deal left the door open for consideration of solutions that took the contributions of other social sciences into account. As we have seen, sociologists showed growing awareness of the need to make a special effort to demonstrate the public significance of their field. In 1937, a number of "monographs appeared in print, under SSRC's imprint, with the titles standardized in the form of *Research Memorandum on [X Topic] in the Depression*. The thirteen topics covered were family, religion, education, rural life, internal migration, minority peoples, crime, health, recreation, reading, consumption, social work, and relief policies." With a few exceptions, the topics addressed resembled those appearing in the social problems literature of the time, even though the contributing authors were not all associated with that tradition.[85] This initiative did not produce durable results and eventually failed in its attempt to strengthen a sociological vision of the Depression on the public stage. The divisions in sociology did not help, but economics was not especially unified either. Its greater public recognition by the end of the 1930s derived from a special combination of disinterested scholarship, unmistakable resonance with current problems, and a sense of identity based on professional expertise.

---

[83] Bernard, Contribution to "Questions for Sociology," 167–68. Camic places the arguments of sociologists within two broader, distinct strategies: one that made economic and political changes associated with the Depression and the New Deal expressions of long-term cultural trends, and the other that emphasized mores, customs, values, ideals, and attitudes and the particular institutions that supported them. Camic, "On Edge," 277–80.

[84] Balisciano, "Hope for America."

[85] Camic, "On Edge," 268.

By the time the war started, the division of labor in the core social sciences was mostly unchanged. In political science, from the early 1920s, various efforts to bring a scientific viewpoint to the study of politics and to define the discipline as a policy science won its practitioners more recognition on the public stage. Different disciplines were nominated as suitable complements to political science in its analysis of political questions: psychology and statistics for Charles Merriam, physics for Bennett Munro, and classical economics for George E. G. Catlin.[86] As the role of political scientists in the New Deal amply demonstrated, however, the discipline enjoyed enough professional credit for its own expertise over political systems to be recognized.[87]

In sociology, too, avowed appeals to science and quantitative methods gained traction from the 1920s and, as in political science, that aspiration coexisted with a professed belief in the necessary involvement with public issues. Up to the late 1920s and early 1930s, sociology to a large extent centered on the study of social problems, which more or less coincided with the problems of US society. The New Deal marked a turning point, as we have seen, with economic problems acquiring increased political salience. Sociologists suffered from their relative neglect of economic issues, but eventually reacted by arguing that their discipline offered a broader treatment of the problems affecting US society. Reorganizing the insights of economics and political science within a broader sociological framework could help restore sociologists' public stature.

While it is undeniable that the 1930s marked an important stage in the quantification of economics, the consolidation of its professional authority, and the affirmation of its relevance for the treatment of public problems, it would be an exaggeration to suggest that its estrangement from other social sciences had already begun. Part of its success derived from its concentration on economic problems at a time when those called for special attention. Yet, in the late 1930s and early 1940s, economics was still methodologically pluralistic and its internal diversity comparable to those of political science and sociology. Within the division of labor in the social sciences, the place of economics had not changed much from the 1920s, even though its position in their hierarchy had certainly improved.

---

[86] Somit and Tanenhaus, *Development of Political Science*, 110–17.
[87] Writing on the nature of the social sciences in the mid-1930s, Charles A. Beard noted that political science "is that division of social study which is concerned with government.... It is usually a plane-surface description of those aspects of human nature and human activity which pertain to government." Beard, *Nature of the Social Sciences*, 73.

The war itself created an even more challenging combination of circumstances for the social sciences, with new problems coming to the fore. Professional societies reacted to this sea change with variable success, which eventually impacted the relative prestige of social science disciplines on the public stage. The impact of the war on social science is well known. The government's need for rapid solutions together with its lack of patience for departmental boundaries took prewar efforts to mobilize social science to a new scale and encouraged a move in the direction of problem-oriented, cross-disciplinary team work. That does not mean that the government had a definitive idea of its actual needs, or that social scientists knew precisely the nature and scope of their possible contribution. But overall, the two parties found their bearings and established a form of collaboration that survived the war for two decades before a new turn toward specialization, helped by a new patronage system, began around the mid-1960s.[88]

Rather than changing the division of labor entirely, the war confronted its practitioners with new questions and new forms of research organization that made that division less constraining. In the process, wartime service favored greater awareness of applied work and more opportunity for disciplinary interaction. The prewar social sciences did not lack applied and interdisciplinary ambitions, but war problems, of a different nature from those of adjusting to modernity, provided even more incentive for social scientists to cross disciplinary boundaries. Leaving their departments to join governmental agencies, social scientists were encouraged to curb their natural inclination to consider problems – economic, political, and sociological – primarily associated with their own discipline. The enthusiasm for interdisciplinary work came together with a conception of what it meant to be scientific based on methods of investigation rather than objects of study.

Many social scientists, notably economists, sociologists, and political scientists, were recruited to the war effort, working in various capacities and locations.[89] Economists worked as general, technical problem-solvers, collaborating with natural scientists and engineers as well as with other social scientists. They were especially active in the Office of Strategic Services (OSS), the Enemy Objectives Unit, and the Statistical Research Group, where they dealt with problems related to military strategy and tactics as well as more traditional economic topics.[90] It was during the war

[88] Crowther-Heyck, "Patrons of the Revolution."
[89] Backhouse and Fontaine, *History of the Social Sciences*, 186–88.
[90] Guglielmo, "Contribution of Economists to Military Intelligence."

that economists began to develop a sense of separation from the other social sciences – a self-segregation of the privileged that sharpened in the postwar decades.[91]

Sociologists' experience in the war "comprised two types of service – in war-related research and in the military." Like economists, sociologists worked in a number of agencies, including the OSS Research & Analysis Branch, the Army's Research Branch, the Department of Agriculture (where they represented a significant contingent), and the Labor Department.[92] To some extent, war service helped sociology regain academic standing vis-à-vis its neighbors, in part through ambitious cross-disciplinary projects with social psychologists, anthropologists, and political scientists working in the federal government's sprawling propaganda bureaucracy.

Political scientists, with their ties to law and public administration, likewise participated in military activities and civilian work in connection with national defense.[93] As of 1941, they were especially active in two federal agencies: the Office of Price Administration, where, together with economists, they helped keep prices under control and organize the rationing of consumer goods; and the Office of the Coordinator of Information, an intelligence organization later divided into the OSS and the Office of War Information, where they interacted with sociologists in particular.

By 1945, political scientist Pendleton Herring, who held several positions in Washington during the war, was already drawing conclusions from the mobilization of his peers: "As professors of a distinctive discipline, we have taught our courses and expected of our colleagues in other departments that respect for jurisdictional boundaries which serves as the greatest safeguard to our scholarly mysteries and the readiest protection of academic amenities. Changes are already upon us that promise to alter greatly these familiar and pleasant arrangements." Like many of his colleagues who had worked in wartime service, Herring was aware of the growing interest of other social scientists in understanding governmental activities and, as a result, concluded that "the study of governmental problems cannot be the concern of one discipline to the same extent as in the past." At the same time, he noted that problems formerly associated with the subject matter of

---

[91] Pooley and Solovey, "Marginal to the Revolution." The self-segregation, though real and traceable, was by no means absolute. A number of economists made serious efforts to work with other social scientists throughout the early postwar decades.
[92] Abbott and Sparrow, "Hot War, Cold War," 26.
[93] Ogg, "News and Notes."

other social sciences had piqued the interest of political scientists. Overall, Herring viewed the process of cooperation among the social sciences as a way of inventing new tools of analysis and of creating new sources for data.[94]

Herring's conclusions for political science could be easily extended to the other social sciences, whose practitioners had similarly experienced the increased permeability of disciplinary boundaries during the war and its beneficial effects on knowledge creation and policy relevance. Social scientists had objective reasons to think of themselves as active participants in the war effort, but their recognition in the early postwar years did not match their actual contribution and hardly equaled that of physical scientists. With the exception of economists, whose recognition in high circles was made obvious with the creation of the Council of Economic Advisers in 1946, social scientists took a painful measure of the gap between their sense of accomplishment and their invisibility to policymakers. As the war came to an end in Europe, George A. Lundberg, a former president of the ASS, betrayed these mixed feelings when he complained "that social research was [seen as] a kind of luxury to which surplus funds might be devoted as a sort of advertising stunt reflecting the benevolence of donors, or in any event as a side issue not vitally concerned with the serious business of managing society. If social research is really to flourish," the quantitative sociologist concluded, "this view must change. Sooner or later it will change."[95] How long it took, exactly, is difficult to say, but it is clear that the decade following World War II was not an easy ride for the US social sciences.

Economics' gradual shift toward hypothetico-deductive modeling marked its entry into a new era, with greater methodological agreement and lessened contacts with other social sciences as the new trends. For social sciences other than economics, the late 1940s reinforced the view that they were lacking in comparison with the natural sciences. According to Michigan psychologist and academic entrepreneur Donald Marquis, the social sciences (economics included) followed imperfectly the sequence of six steps supposed to characterize the scientific process.[96] The idea that the social sciences lagged behind the natural sciences became the rhetoric of social scientists willing to push the agenda of the so-called "behavioral

---

[94] Herring, "Political Science in the Next Decade," 758, 759. A decade later, political scientist David Easton continued to deplore overspecialization and the disintegration of social knowledge "into a multitude of intellectual feudalities," but remarked: "Today this condition has stimulated a movement towards a re-integration of our compartmentalized knowledge." Easton, *Political System*, 101.

[95] Lundberg, "Social Sciences in the Postwar Era," 138.

[96] Marquis, "Scientific Methodology in Human Relations."

sciences." Self-identified behavioral scientists endorsed a cross-disciplinary, problem-oriented approach – compatible, in their view, with theoretical and methodological sophistication akin to the natural sciences. Disciplinary divides were routinely, and as a matter of principle, breached, but the shared domains of study were not, for the most part, oriented to the litany of social problems that had preoccupied their interwar predecessors.

From the late 1940s onward, the political context, notably the "antifoundation sentiment in American politics," was not especially favorable to the social sciences, as "they became deeply entangled with the domestic and international dimensions of the Cold War."[97] As earlier criticisms about their confusion between social advocacy and scientific objectivity resurfaced and took on a new political sharpness, the wartime accomplishments of the social sciences were gradually sidelined. From the late 1940s to the mid-1950s, McCarthyism impacted the social sciences and natural sciences alike, but the hierarchy of the sciences, reinforced by the growing prestige of physics after the war, protected the latter more than the former. The various attacks against the social sciences tarnished their reputation, but they did not stall – and may have even spurred – the effort to establish legitimacy through natural-science mimicry. As a result, as suggested by Roger Geiger, the social sciences were "far more vigorous by 1956, and much less in need of reformation, than had been the case at the end of the 1940s."[98]

The porousness of disciplinary boundaries in war work and the effort to turn the experience of interdisciplinary interaction into a model for future research did not, in themselves, shift any jurisdictional claims nor reorder the prewar hierarchy of prestige. The war helped create new methods, new subfields, and new collaborations, to be sure, but, overall, these changes were compatible with the existing disciplinary structure. As it turned out, cross-disciplinary research ventures represented an alternative form of production and dissemination of social-scientific knowledge more than an effort to loosen the disciplinary yoke.[99]

From that perspective, it is not surprising that the first serious challenges to the prevailing disciplinary division of labor came from social scientists who, with unblushing ambition, plied their tools in the traditional domains of their disciplinary rivals. The opposite tack – to assert that a discipline

---

[97] Solovey, "Cold War Social Science," 4. See also Solovey, *Shaky Foundations*, 119–27.
[98] Geiger, *Research and Relevant Knowledge*, 104. On the postwar campaign for scientific legitimacy in social science, see Haney, *Americanization of Social Science*, chap. 2.
[99] Fontaine, "Introduction."

Like sociology, in the early 1960s political science was marked by "a mood of sympathy toward 'scientific' modes of investigation and analysis." Published at a time when a number of political scientists were trying to promote a "scientific outlook" through the analysis of individuals, Downs' reliance on rational man provided a nice illustration of the explanatory power attached to simple behavioral assumptions for the study of political behavior. Yet, as Dahl noted, behavioral political scientists had a greater ambition, namely, "understanding the psychological characteristics of *homo politicus*: attitudes, belief, predispositions, personality factors." And here he mentioned examples from sociology, psychology, and political science – not economics.[110]

Throughout the 1960s, the continuing incursions of economists into the domains of sociology and political science marked a shift in the disciplinary division of labor in the three core social sciences. Before Becker's and Downs' work, sociologists and political scientists' belief in the benefits of interacting with economics rested on the experience of war service and multidisciplinary team work. Within certain limits, that attitude continued to reflect the spirit of the SSRC enterprise: Political scientists and sociologists alike held that learning from other social sciences was a necessary step in the vexing effort to solve society's problems.

With economists' first attempts to investigate "noneconomic" topics, differentiating the various social-scientific approaches – the economic, the political, and the sociological – to problems of society took precedence over their integration. To some extent, Becker's and Downs' effort in the late 1950s, and those of others in the early 1960s, marked the beginning of a declining concern for a general understanding of society. That decline coincided with the waning of a cross-disciplinary age in social science, with the individual disciplines set in new, competitive relief. It is no exaggeration to suggest that economists, who had been used to cultivating their difference with other social sciences, benefited from that reorientation, which later encouraged the affirmation and propagation of economic reasoning within society at large.[111] In policy circles, too, economists revealed ambitions that would have appeared excessive only a few years earlier. By 1963, as suggested by Bernstein, "federal economists were now very much part of an effort to stimulate social and political change in modern American society."[112]

---

[110] Dahl, "Behavioral Approach in Political Science," 766, 769.
[111] Craig Calhoun regards economics as the main competitor to sociology in the project of a general understanding of social life. It should be made clear, however, that Calhoun talks about claims not achievements, for neither sociology nor economics offers an integrative approach. Calhoun, "Sociology, Other Disciplines," 180,
[112] Bernstein, *Perilous Progress*, 139.

As Hamilton Cravens rightly put it, "the social sciences were more the creature of politics than the other way around."[113] This explains why the launch of the Great Society programs exacerbated tensions within social science. The wave of programs and initiatives testified to the recognition that persisting social and political ills deserved special attention at a time when, by their own admission, sociologists largely neglected social disruption and political scientists paid inadequate attention to political crises. For their part and despite notable achievements, economists were reminded that policy shifts could diminish their comparative advantage over the other social sciences – making it crucial to reaffirm their jurisdictional claim over a variety of social problems.

By the late 1960s, the core social sciences found themselves in contrasting situations. Just as political scientist David Easton deemed behavioralism in need of revamping, and hoped to see more intellectual resources devoted to studying the problems of the day, so Alvin Gouldner pointed to the crisis of Western sociology and hoped to find a better reflection of social conflict in social theory. At about the same time, economist Mancur Olson, then Deputy Assistant Secretary for Social Indicators, felt the need to remind the readers of *The Public Interest* that "if poverty is not an economic problem, then nothing is." And in case this was not clear enough, he insisted: "it is futile to attempt to determine the division of labor between social science disciplines in terms of the objects they are supposed to consider. Reality cannot be divided into departments the way universities are, and no logically defensible division of subject matters is possible. The various disciplines are, however, distinguished by their prejudices and their methods."[114]

Social scientists outside economics had good reason for their frustration. The effort to make their disciplines more publicly appealing in the past decade had produced mixed results, as if the shift away from social advocacy had eventually diverted them from problems themselves. While the scientific accomplishments of economics translated into increased prestige, with the Council of Economic Advisers standing as the epitome of economic expertise in policy circles, those of other social scientists found lesser resonance among policymakers – and sometimes occasioned skepticism, as illustrated by the repeated failures of Senator Walter Mondale's bills to create a Council of Social Advisers in the late 1960s and

---

[113] Cravens, "Have the Social Sciences Mattered in Washington?" 129.
[114] Easton, "New Revolution in Political Science"; Gouldner, *Coming Crisis of Western Sociology*; and Olson, "Economics, Sociology," 97.

early 1970s.[115] If the prosperity of US capitalism in the 1950s and 1960s was often credited to economists, the social and political crises of the 1960s seemed to underscore the lack of relevance and meaningfulness of other social sciences for understanding contemporary problems of society.

From the late 1960s through the 1970s, changes in the economic and political context, together with cultural shifts, fueled the ongoing redefinition of the boundaries between the social sciences. Becker's *Economic Approach to Human Behavior*, published in 1976, included subjects such as discrimination, democracy, crime, fertility, marriage, and, more generally, social interactions. Potentially, such a range of issues could bring economics closer to sociology, especially as the latter had experienced notable transformations in the late 1960s and early 1970s. With the invention of a "mainstream" in sociology came repeated critiques of its orientations and calls for reform. The revolt against the mainstream implied a greater role for issues such as race, class, and gender, which partly paralleled Becker's own effort in economics.[116] Yet, the heart of the "economic approach" – the "combined assumptions of maximizing behavior, market equilibrium, and stable preferences, used relentlessly and unflinchingly" – suggested less collaborative prospects.[117] Moreover, Becker's approach was in tune with more general trends in the realm of ideas in a way that sociology, with the emergence of neo-Marxian perspectives, was not. Those trends historian Daniel Rodgers has aptly described as the result of a process whereby "conceptions of human nature that in the post–World War II era had been thick with context, social circumstance, institutions, and history gave way to conceptions of human nature that stressed choice, agency, performance, and desire."[118]

1.4 From Social Problems to Individual Problems?

How do social problems come to exist and persist? The question has threaded through the reflective literature on social problems that sociologists have produced since the interwar years. Writing in 1941, for example, Richard Fuller proposed a "natural history approach," with the aim to trace the "common order of development through which all social problems pass."[119] Some thirty years later, Malcolm Spector and John Kitsuse rephrased the

---

[115] Solovey, "To Measure, Monitor, and Manage."
[116] Calhoun and VanAntwerpen, "Orthodoxy, Heterodoxy, and Hierarchy," 376–85.
[117] Becker, *Economic Approach to Human Behavior*, 5.
[118] Rodgers, *Age of Fracture*, 3.
[119] Fuller and Myers, "Natural History of a Social Problem," 320, 321.

point with antiseptic precision: The "central problem for a theory of social problems," they wrote, "is to account for the emergence, maintenance, and history of claim-making and responding activities."[120] The idea that social problems have careers is, in short, a recurring theme.

Most of the major mid-century social problems remain, as it were, recognized. Crime, poverty, addiction, and the others were, into the new millennium, still considered problems of society. What had changed, for many problem domains at least, was their public etiology – the prevailing frame by which they were explained. Trends in US politics and policy since the mid-1960s, registered by the social sciences too, had challenged their "social" dimension.

C. Wright Mills, back in 1959, furnished a useful vocabulary to address this shift. In *The Sociological Imagination*, he lamented the claustrophobic consciousness of everyday life in America. For most people, problems are experienced as private – as a "series of traps." Problems that are, to Mills, manifestly social come across, to the average American, as personal. Caught up in "private orbits" and the "close-up scenes" of family and work life, the public has the nagging sense that something is off.[121] But they have lost the power, Mills thought, to link their private struggles to structural forces – the kind of linkage that the Great Depression, for example, had made conspicuous.

Mills' project was to encourage a new consciousness, a "sociological imagination," that restores the relationship between "the personal troubles of milieu" and "the public issues of social structure." Employment, war, marriage, the city: The key to the sociological imagination, he claimed, is the awareness that these perceived problems are "caused by structural changes" – and therefore resistant to personal solutions. Mills' complaint was that private troubles are no longer translated into public issues: "Much private uneasiness goes unformulated," he wrote in 1959, "much public malaise and many decisions of enormous structural relevance never become public issues."[122] The sociological imagination is Mills' solution to a meta-problem: The process by which society's problems come to be recognized has, he claimed, broken down.

The distinction between public issues and private troubles, trenchant as it is, implies that the former – recognized social problems – present a structural explanation by default. For Mills, a problem's private enclosure

[120] Spector and Kitsuse, "Social Problems," 146.
[121] Mills, *The Sociological Imagination*, 1.
[122] Mills, *The Sociological Imagination*, 8, 10, 12.

just means that it is understood as personal. Once a concern wins public
recognition, its systemic nature is (or so Mills suggests) revealed too. But
the lesson of the post-1960s era is that public resonance and personal frames
of explanation can co-exist. Social problems can, in effect, be stripped of
their social character. As a whole, the social dimension of the problems has
thinned out over these decades. The prevailing explanatory schemes, and
especially those policy interventions with meaningful purchase, have been
cast in increasingly individual terms. And the declining significance of the
social has a correlate in the disciplinary division of labor: psychology and
economics lay claim to political territory once occupied by sociology.

The waning of the social, as a cross-problem pattern, demands an
explanation. One clue, we think, resides in the broader US political
economy. Scholars of the postwar social-problems array have remarked
on the decisive importance of the welfare state – even in its limited, US
form. Joseph Gusfield, in his 1989 SSSP presidential address, argued
that the very concept "social problem" is "embedded in the development
of the welfare state." The idea that societies have fixable problems – and
that they have a responsibility to go about fixing them – is, he noted, a
recent development. Private troubles can only become public issues once
the modern, democratized state has emerged. Its moral substrate is the
"optimism of a sense of progress" according to which "most of life's
difficulties are inherently remediable."[123] For Gusfield, this entailed, among
other things, the rise of the "troubled persons professions," who service –
and profit from – the public's will to intervene. For our purposes, the crucial
point is that the very conceivability of social problems as such – as social
and resolvable – presupposes an interventionist state.[124]

Since the mid-1970s, of course, the US version of the postwar Keynesian
welfare state has come under unremitting attack. Sharp cuts to safety
net programs, selective deregulation, free-falling marginal tax rates, and
enfeebled union protections were secured, at different registers, in both

[123] Gusfield, "Constructing the Ownership of Social Problems," 432.
[124] The linkage of the welfare state, sociology, and social problems is a major theme of
Alvin Gouldner's (1970) *The Coming Crisis of Western Sociology*. Writes Gouldner:
"The needs of the new Welfare State, then, constitute both the growth opportunities
and the limiting conditions that shape modern Academic Sociology as an institution;
Academic Sociology flourishes in a period when Keynesian economics permit effective
intervention with respect to the more traditional economic factors. Sociology is thus
the N + I science of the Welfare State, providing it with an expert, university-based
staff which addresses itself to the 'other,' the noneconomic social problems: racial
conflict, deviant behavior, delinquency, crime, the social consequence of poverty."
Gouldner, *Coming Crisis of Western Sociology*, 161.

Republican and Democratic administrations through the 1990s. This bundle of changes, paired with steep upticks in income inequality and labor precarity, is often called "neoliberalism" – a term that, given its political freight and competing definitions, we use sparingly.[125] For now, the welfare state's partial rollback suggests a tantalizing question: If social problems, as such, presume an interventionist state, what is their fate when intervention takes on an entirely new meaning? Might, in other words, a relationship obtain between the prevailing US political economy and the country's designated problems? If so – and this is our crucial question – how are the social sciences implicated, if at all?

We can only gesture at some tentative answers, supported by the volume's chapters. There is, to be sure, nothing neatly causal to report: The social sciences, in their changing configuration, did not convert, as it were, public issues into private troubles in the quarter-century since the Carter Administration. But the social sciences, economics and psychology in particular, are in the explanatory mix. To even approach the issue is to back into a sociology-of-knowledge thicket since there are so many layers of mutual entanglement: popular beliefs, the political system, the policy-making process, the influence industries, and the social sciences themselves. There are, moreover, elective affinities – resonances – among the layers as they have co-evolved in the postwar era, so that claims of directional influence are cripplingly hard to sustain.

The chapters nevertheless document an overall drift since the 1960s: an attenuation of social ways of seeing society's problems, and their replacement, to some extent, by economic and psychological framings. Writ large, problems once cast as social were refracted, by the 1980s, through individualistic prisms, especially at the level of policy and public debate. The social sciences contributed to this shift, but were also – in their patterns of public prominence – remapped by the changes they helped bring about. The process was complicated by the suffusion of social-scientific concepts to the general populace and throughout the political system, alongside the spread of certain tools – such as cost–benefit analysis – into the policy-making arena.

For our purposes, three dimensions of the social sciences of social problems are worth isolating: *explanation, prescription,* and the *frame of analysis.* Along each dimension, a social scientist's program might have, at the very least, implications for the way that problems are understood

---

[125] See Rodgers, "Uses and Abuses of 'Neoliberalism,'" and the linked forum: Ott et al., "Debating the Uses and Abuses of 'Neoliberalism.'"

and addressed. For example, we can distinguish between explanations for a problem such as crime that are structural – rooted in, say, the history of institutionalized racism or the economy's lopsided distribution of wealth – and more individualistic frameworks that assign blame to personal failures or even crude self-interest. Interventions – proposed or implied – might hinge on that diagnosis, with a remedial strategy such as redistributive spending arising from a structural explanation. Or, on the individualistic account, a "family values" public information campaign or stiff mandatory prison sentences might follow. All of this (the explanation and even the remedy) could be guided by the mode of analysis – the methods chosen, paired with key disciplinary assumptions.

Words such as "structural" and "individualistic" are, of course, blunt designators. We have already referred to explanation – the realm of causes – as well as remedies (implied or prescribed). The question of method we have invoked too. At all three levels we are keen to maintain a distinction – a soft one – between the *structural* and the *individualistic*, but without imposing our definition on the volume's authors – who have their own reasons to frame the stakes differently. Nor do we mean to invoke the contrast in the ontological sense – that is, in terms of what the real stuff of society is (e.g., individuals, systems, or social relations) – even if those commitments might ground explanatory accounts or methodological decisions.[126]

If the question is how problems arise and why they persist, one set of answers looks to the aggregated beliefs and actions of individuals. Mental illness, from one angle, is quintessentially private, possibly biological – if also affected by immediate social experience like early family history. A more structural account might, by contrast, stress the social conditions and institutions (notably including the "psy-disciplines") that help produce the diagnoses and treatment regimens that organize individual lives. Thus for explanations to qualify as structural in the loose sense we invoke here, they must point to the hard cake of law, institutions, or political economy. Attitudes and actions take primacy in the more individualistic accounts.

[126] See the interesting discussion in Tilly, *Durable Inequality*, 17–24. Of course, a commitment to viewing social life through the prism of the individual makes it harder to even conceive of supra-individual factors such as institutions or political-economic dynamics. Likewise, an ontology that privileges systems or groups is ipso facto averse to explanations at the level of individual minds or behavior. Only those ontological schemes that foreground social relations, social process, or the dynamic, mutual constitution of subjectivity and structure are, as it were, truly agnostic on the explanatory questions we are interested in.

Attempts to address social problems might, accordingly, target structural impediments or, instead, dispositions and behavior. It's true that there is, strictly speaking, no necessary overlap between a given causal story about a problem and its proposed solutions. Individualistic accounts, after all, often seek to explain socially patterned outcomes. Those conditions – a racial wage gap, for example – could accommodate a range of would-be remedies, including policies, such as social welfare spending, that do not target the underlying "cause." Nevertheless, interventions may be suggested, or discouraged, by the kind of explanation that elicits the greatest public resonance.

In other words, our two explanation types – individualistic and social-structural – in effect nominate their causal agents as targets for intervention. So if the public tends to see crime through an individualist prism, social-scientific explanations supporting individual agency will generate more appeal among policymakers. Making the crimes cost more (through harsher sentences or stepped-up enforcement), for instance, can appear as the most sensible policy response. If, instead, social forces find greater public resonance, social-scientific explanations of crime centered on social structures can attract policymakers much more effectively. Boosting the economic fortunes of potential perpetrators, for instance, will appear as a more fitting response. Explanations and policy interventions have affinities, in other words, along the structural/individualistic lines we have drawn. In the context of politics, moreover, policies must be promoted and justified on the basis – at least in part – of causal accounts. Explanations furnish distinctive kinds of rhetorical resources: Most individualistic explanations invoke, at least implicitly, intention, while many structural explanations point to unintended consequences. A remedy such as school-funding redistribution, for example, is hard to defend if the education problem is really about bad teachers and indifferent parents.

There is, finally, the frame of analysis – by which we mean methodology in the broad sense, inclusive of underlying assumptions. Here again a crude distinction may be drawn between approaches that position individual agency as the unit of analysis and those scholarly strategies that attempt to account for structural forces first and foremost. These methodological choices are, at the same time, dueling ways of seeing society. A commitment to methodological individualism, in other words, entails a social aperture whose exposure is narrowed. Survey methods that treat populations as individuals-in-aggregate, for example, might boost a more individualist problem diagnosis – as might a framework that, in the microeconomic mode, assumes rational maximizers. A political-economic analysis will, with its focus sharpened to pick out large-scale systems, be prone to see the pivotal role of institutions. There is nothing determinate about these methodological nudges, but because they come with specific questions, they privilege certain understandings of a problem.

The point of drawing this contrast, between the structural and the individualistic, is to better specify patterns of change in the postwar social science engagement with social problems. As sketched across these three dimensions (explanation, prescription, and frame of analysis), the claim that "social" problems have lost some of their social character can be more precisely articulated. The draining out of the social is really about the declining fortunes of structural approaches to US society's problems – and the ascendancy of more individualistic alternatives.

Consider economics. The discipline has maintained, at least since the 1930s, outsized policy prominence relative to its social science peers. But that fact obscures an array of relevant changes that, taken together, mark the period since the late 1950s and mid-1960s as distinctive. The economists who staffed the New Deal were, after all, much more pluralistic by the standards of the postwar discipline, with intellectual coordinates, in many cases, that were hard to distinguish from their sociologist or political science peers. The story of economists' war-won prestige in the early postwar decades is well known, but the discipline's mathematized orthodoxy was only secured at the end of the 1950s.[127] Well into the 1960s, moreover, the field's mainstream paired its microeconomic neoclassicism with a Keynesian macroeconomics. Already by the late 1950s, however, Chicago figures like Gary Becker were taking microeconomics on the road – applying a utility maximization framework to domains well beyond the discipline's inherited jurisdiction. By the early 1970s, the Keynesian consensus in the macroeconomic realm was, in the face of stagflation, unsettled. It is easy to exaggerate, but the trend, since then, has been the ascent of the "economic approach" within the discipline itself.

Meanwhile, the political climate for economists had improved, reflecting a trend toward "economization" – a way of framing political issues in economic terms.[128] The concept of "the economy," in the relevant sense as the sum total of economic activity, did not gain public or political

[127] Backhouse, "Transformation of US Economics."
[128] Berman, *Creating the Market University*, 174–77 (rendered as "economic rationalization"); and Berman, "Not Just Neoliberalism." Berman's use of "economization" is distinct from, for example, Murphy, *Economization of Life* or Callon, "Embeddedness of Economic Markets in Economics."

purchase until the early postwar decades.[129] By the late 1970s, as Elizabeth Popp Berman demonstrates in a variety of US policy contexts, thinking about government as mainly in the business of improving the economy had become pervasive. From regulatory rule-making all the way through to campaign discourse, policymakers and politicians increasingly framed their talk and their decisions around economic impact. Government's role is to prime and pump the economy – an assumption, by the late twentieth century, embraced across the political spectrum and reflected, too, in everyday talk. The belief, almost unquestioned, was that a strong economy is the public goal that matters most. To Berman, this form of economization is much more ubiquitous – and ultimately significant – than the market fundamentalism espoused by the political right with special vigor since the 1980s. Economization is, indeed, an enabling condition, a seedbed from which the far narrower "neoliberal" worldview could grow.[130]

There was no single engine driving the post-1960s process of economization, but US economists undoubtedly contributed, if only because they were also active in policy institutions like the Council of Economic Advisers and in public debates.[131] They were, at the same time, its main academic beneficiaries. Over this period they won unequaled levels of policy influence, even by the standards of the discipline's existing prominence.[132] While some of that sway took the form of promoting market liberalization and market creation – the "neoliberal" facet – the policy leverage was secured on other, more mainstream grounds too. Economists' elevated influence, moreover, was felt indirectly: through political and popular language, for example, and through the spread of policy instruments. These dynamics, in practice, generated feedback loops: The discipline's authoritative stature helped economists obtain positions – often prominent ones – in policy institutions, which then boosted the field's prestige.

---

[129] Berman, "Not Just Neoliberalism," 408; see also Mitchell, "Fixing the Economy"; Suttles, *Front Page Economics*, chap. 9; and Smith, *The Right Talk*, chap. 3.

[130] Writes Berman: "While neoliberalism is still an influential worldview, economization is in many ways a more powerful, and potentially more durable, trend." Berman, "Not Just Neoliberalism," 419.

[131] Berman, *Creating the Market University*, 46, 50 and Berman, "Not Just Neoliberalism," 408–9.

[132] There is a large literature that chronicles the post-1960s influence of economists on US politics and policy, only some of it related to the rise of so-called "neoliberalism." See, for example, Bernstein, *A Perilous Progress*, chap. 6; Hirschman and Berman, "Do Economists Make Policies?"; and Appelbaum, *Economists' Hour*.

That legitimacy, and those institutional footholds, helped in turn to promote and spread an economic way of thinking – a "cognitive infrastructure" that, once in circulation, did not depend on actual economists or their scholarship.[133] At varying levels of depth and sophistication, politicians, public intellectuals, and policy elites ventriloquize economists. Even barstool banter is sprinkled with economic concepts. So the idea, for example, that we are all calculating individuals – strategic managers of our own best interests – has seeped deeper into the social imaginary with the aid, at least, of economic thinking.[134] Put differently, the country's individualistic spine was arguably straightened in the homo economicus mold. And if economists helped to underwrite the culture's entrepreneurial ethos, they also reaped its legitimizing rewards – as an everyday warrant for the discipline's distinctive style of reasoning.[135] That way of thinking, suffused with disciplinary argot such as "externalities" and "marginal cost,"

---

[133] This analysis draws heavily from Hirschman and Berman, "Do Economists Make Policies?" Angus Burgin's and Daniel Stedman Jones' analyses of neoliberalism – *The Great Persuasion* and *Masters of the Universe*, respectively – show that economic ideas, and not just economic theory, change society, and that they do it from within. So what matters is the seeming convergence between those ideas and the political climate. See Fontaine, "Other Histories of Recent Economics," 400–401.

[134] We are using the notion of "social imaginary" in Charles Taylor's sense: "By social imaginary, I mean something much broader and deeper than the intellectual schemes people may entertain when they think about social reality in a disengaged mode. I am thinking, rather, of the ways people imagine their social existence, how they fit together with others, how things go on between them and their fellows, the expectations that are normally met, and the deeper normative notions and images that underlie these expectations." Taylor, *Modern Social Imaginaries*, 23. Taylor, focused on the broad sweep of modernity, claims that a major economic dimension was stitched into the Western social imaginary centuries before Becker's *Economic Approach to Human Behavior*. See Taylor, *Modern Social Imaginaries*, chap. 5.

[135] Hirschman and Berman borrow the "style of reasoning" concept from Ian Hacking, "Statistical Language, Statistical Truth, and Statistical Reason." The economic style of reasoning, according to Hirschman and Berman, "includes basic concepts such as incentives, growth, efficiency and externalities. It includes economic ways of approaching problems: by using models, systematically weighing costs and benefits, analysing quantitative empirical data, considering incentives, and thinking marginally. It suggests causal policy stories … linked to economic theories: that investing in education will increase human capital and thus raise wage levels, or that increased government spending will stimulate the economy. And it makes certain methodological assumptions: about the importance of quantification and the possibility of using monetary value as a means of commensuration, for example." Hirschman and Berman, "Do Economists Make Policies?" 794. See also Berman, *Thinking Like an Economist*, chaps. 1–2.

has taken special hold among policy analysts, most of whom are not card-carrying economists.[136]

A related development, stressed by Berman and Daniel Hirschman, was the rapid uptake of "policy devices" such as cost–benefit analysis or Congressional Budget Office bill-scoring.[137] Some of these devices, created or co-authored by economists, settled into the policymaking sediment in this period. Once lodged in rule-making practices, or even established by statute, the instruments – at least the successful ones – enjoy an effortless and durable legitimacy. As authorless doxa, their status as containers of particular values, often economic ones, goes mostly unseen. But the devices bear those values in consequential ways, Frankenstein-like. Their assumptions ricochet across the policy landscape – the antitrust fixation on price, for example, or the auctioning off of the public spectrum to the highest bidder.

The point is that economics – with its surging fortunes since the mid-1960s – has helped to undermine the idea that problems of society are social. To do so, economists did not have to deny the social character of these problems. Instead they drew attention to their microeconomic dimension

---

[136] Hirschman and Berman, "Do Economists Make Policies?" 795. Policy analysis is an especially amorphous, cross-disciplinary academic field whose history has yet to be written. With roots in public administration and Daniel Lerner and Harold Lasswell's mid-century "policy sciences" program, policy analysis as a self-understood label took hold in the late 1960s and early 1970s, with especially heavy contributions from political scientists housed in public policy schools, newly established or re-branded from public administration in this period. See Torgerson, "Policy Analysis and Public Life," 235–43; DeLeon, *Advice and Consent*, chap. 2; and Fleishman, "New Framework for Integration," 734–38. By the mid-1970s, the think tank sector, often tied to funded political agendas, was growing dramatically, employing policy analysts and the emerging policy evaluation toolkit. See Medvetz, *Think Tanks in America*, chaps. 2–3 and Smith, *The Right Talk*, chaps. 4–5. Economic modes of analysis have been fundamental to the academic field's approach and curricula, and to the practices of policy analysts in government and the think tank sector, ever since. See Fleishman, "New Framework for Integration," 739–41; Haveman, "Policy Analysis and Evaluation Research," 193, 197–202; House, "Social Psychology, Social Science, and Economics," 237–39; and Berman, *Thinking Like an Economist*, chap. 1.

[137] Hirschman and Berman, "Do Economists Make Policies?" 796–800. They concede that economists were co-authors, as it were, with other disciplines in the creation of many widely deployed policy instruments. They adapt the "policy device" concept from the "market device" idea outlined in Fabian Muniesa, Yuval Millo, and Michel Callon's "An Introduction to Market Devices." Hirschman and Berman develop an interesting distinction between "devices for seeing" and "devices for choosing." The "seeing" kind is about understanding, usually through a quantitative prism. "Choosing" devices, by contrast, grease the wheels of decision-making. Hirschman and Berman, "Do Economists Make Policies?" 797.

at a time when governments, confronted with the limits of the welfare state, found increasing merit in rational pricing. The social problems tradition within sociology had embraced the view that poverty, crime, and the other issues are fixable dislocations of modernity. That worldview had indeed helped underwrite the wider belief that government has an obligation to intervene – as expressed, to some extent, in US social policy through the Great Society. The claim that a problem like racism has social roots, with attendant social remedies, has since become less legible. As we have suggested, the discipline of economics was both a contributor to, and beneficiary of, a way of seeing society's problems through a cost–benefit prism. That worldview did not rule out the possibility of government intervention, but did contribute to reorienting governmental action toward creating favorable conditions for market pricing. Economists lay claim to "ownership," in Gusfield's sense, of no single problem in particular, but instead the whole array. Those jurisdictional bids were contested, of course, and strands of post-1960s quantitative sociology have – in some problem domains – remained a significant presence. It is also true that work on the full spread of society's "problems" has continued apace within sociology. The scholarship, however, failed to gain much policy purchase through the 1990s. If anything, sociologists positioned their interventions as a rearguard defense against policy rollbacks. Likewise, it was the rare work of sociology that resonated in the political sphere or with the wider public. By the late 1970s, in short, it had become harder to think like a sociologist and get noticed.

The case of psychology is harder to pin down, though the discipline's swelling influence in certain problem domains – like addiction and mental illness – is well documented by the volume's chapters.[138] The more crucial influence, however, was indirect, at the level of everyday discourse. The American vernacular, by the second half of the twentieth century, was littered with psychological concepts – the ideas, to some extent, and even the diagnostic language. Psychology supplied, as it were, a vocabulary of popular knowledge – and a way of seeing problems. Viewed through the prism of popular psychology, problems are personal. They are, in C. Wright Mills' phrase, "private troubles." Structural explanations fall outside the frame, and remedies, too, have a narrow, therapeutic character.

---

[138] The historiographical debate over whether psychological social psychology has shed much of its "social" character over the twentieth century operates at a different academic register than the popularization dynamics that we gloss here. See Greenwood, *Disappearance of the Social in American Social Psychology*.

It is true that the line from popular psychology to the postwar politics and policy of society's problems is hard to draw. Still, the therapeutic ethos – its baseline individualism – has helped seed the ground conditions for political intervention. Indeed, we refer to *psychologization* to capture this dynamic – with the parallel to, and example of, economics very much in mind. If the ends of public life have come to be recognized – by politicians, policymakers, journalists, and voters – as economic, something analogous can be said about private life: The injunction, issued with new urgency since the 1960s, has been to seek personal fulfillment. What counts as pathology, in a culture of self-actualization, is the individual's state of mind – her mental life as shaped by upbringing and immediate social experience. To the extent that psychological categories define the boundaries of the problematic, they limit the range of imagined explanations – and interventions – to the personal sphere.[139]

Neither the popularization nor the self-fulfillment culture was entirely new. The language of Freudian psychoanalysis, for example, had entered into popular circulation in the 1920s.[140] And cultural historians have documented expressions of yearning for "authentic" experience among late nineteenth-century American elites, which – by the 1920s – had spread in contradictory coevolution with mass consumerism.[141] But developments in the postwar decades were of a different character: Psychotherapy, as a practice and as an idea, took off, as psychologists broke psychiatry's monopoly on professional therapy in the late 1940s.[142] Federal legislation – the National Mental Health Act of 1946 and the Community Mental Health

---

[139] There is no treatment of "psychologization" comparable to Berman's elaboration of "economization." Jan De Vos has employed the term in a roughly analogous, though heavily theorized, way to the sense we invoke here: "Psychologization is the overflow of the knowledge of psychology into society altering the way in which 'man' is present with himself, others and the world. Psychologization is the process in which psychological signifiers and discursive schemes result in the typical dualism within modern humankind which reflects upon itself having adopted the academic, psychologizing gaze." De Vos, "From Milgram to Zimbardo," 158. See also De Vos, *Psychologization and the Subject of Late Modernity*. The term also appears, in passing, in other academics' works, to refer to the popular incorporation of psychological concepts. Rutherford, *Beyond the Box*, 12. Nikolas Rose, in his Foucaldian genealogies of the psy-disciplines, occasionally invokes the term, and with a similar meaning. Rose, *Governing the Soul*, 38, 248.

[140] See, for example, Burnham, *After Freud Left*, part 1.

[141] Lears, *No Place of Grace*; Lears, "From Salvation to Self-Realization"; Susman, "'Personality' and the Making of Twentieth-Century Culture"; and Leach, *Land of Desire*.

[142] Herman, *Romance of American Psychology*, chap. 9 and Cushman, *Constructing the Self, Constructing America*, chap. 8.

Centers Act of 1963 – helped finance an army of trained psychotherapists. Clinical psychology, a specialty that scarcely existed before the war, came to dwarf the discipline's academic ranks.[143] Therapy for the "normal" American – the merely neurotic – quickly lost its stigma, producing an explosive growth in demand.

By the 1960s psychology had, in Ellen Herman's words, become "public culture," infused into social movement politics and mass media.[144] The postwar growth of humanistic psychology – epitomized by figures like Carl Rogers and Abraham Maslow – directly fed a popular fixation on self-fulfillment.[145] The 1970s efflorescence of encounter groups, New Age spirituality, and the human potential movement was itself just one tributary in a broad-stream therapeutic culture expressed – with inescapable ubiquity – in mass-circulation magazine advice, confessional talk show television, and the self-help book trade. So there was, in the decades after World War II, a lava-like flow of psychological concepts into the postwar American lexicon – transforming the meaning of the social world to its actors themselves. Of course, the postwar American social imaginary was already tuned to personal frames of understanding, long before the publication of the *Diagnostic and Statistical Manual of Mental Disorders – III* in 1980.

If anything, disciplinary frameworks such as psychological individualism and homo economicus took hold, at the level of everyday life, because they resonated with preexisting currents of American atomism. But the disciplines were not simple beneficiaries of the country's Lockean and bootstrapist legacies. They also helped to rechannel the social imaginary in distinct, if overlapping, ways: through the spread of an entrepreneurial ethos, for example, or the thorough-going embrace of psychological talk. As a shared substrate of common sense – of a "worldview" in the everyday sense – the social imaginary helps to set the parameters of political possibility. It is easier, in other words, to treat government as the problem, or to accept that there's no such thing as society, when the social is imagined as a collection of self-determining individuals. It is here, at the indirect and hard-to-measure level of popular sentiment, that psychology and economics may have their greatest import. Even if psychology's direct policy influence was more intermittent and domain-specific than that of economics, the two disciplines helped, in tandem, to peg the boundaries of the politically thinkable to the postulate of self-reliance. By the 1980s it was harder to see

---

[143] Capshew, *Psychologists on the March*, chaps. 6 and 8.
[144] Herman, *Romance of American Psychology*, 310. See also chaps. 9–11.
[145] Grogan, *Encountering America*.

private troubles as expressions of social problems, or to target those troubles with collective intervention.[146]

The new prominence of economics and psychology coincided with the hardening of disciplinary boundaries among the social sciences. By the 1970s, partly due to a shift in the patronage system, specialization gained ground, with disciplinary concepts and techniques gradually supplanting the use of broad, integrative concepts and theories. Economists overtook other social scientists in studying society's problems and advising policymakers, while psychologists registered their social-problems influence at the level of everyday language and the spread of a popular therapeutic ethos.

The volume's chapters, taken together, reveal a paradox – or at least a discrepancy. In the realm of policy and politics, the postwar story has an arc: Social problems became economic problems, personal problems, or both. Economists, and to a lesser extent psychologists, displaced sociologists at the public center of the social science of society's problems. That is the more-or-less consistent takeaway from the chapters' problem-by-problem accounts – but mainly, as it turns out, for the high-stakes domain of policy, politics, and public discourse. The chapters tell a different story about the social sciences themselves. Debates that in the early postwar period were plural and polyphonic remained so – at least in many cases – by the late 1980s.

Social scientists, as Savina Balasubramanian and Charles Camic show in their chapter, were already fretting about the family early in the twentieth century. The institution, according to sociologists through the late interwar period, was especially vulnerable to the disorganization wrought by modern social change. Concern for the family's fate took on a new, international cast in the early Cold War period, in conjunction with the rise of demography as a cross-disciplinary field. In the contest with the Soviets, the drive to modernize the "new states" had, as its demographic dimension, a concern for large family size. The claim that economic development and insulation from socialism hinged on fertility control was advanced by demographers, many but not all housed in sociology. By the mid-1960s, a domestic-facing research landscape was gathering momentum, supported by government and foundation interest in the family's role as transmitter of inequality. The domain of family demography, a resource-intensive specialty clustered in

---

[146] Indeed, the two disciplines' implicit models of selfhood had, by the last quarter of the century, formed a curious cocktail – of strategic self-objectification mixed with authentic self-fulfillment. The injunction, fully realized on the new millennium's social media platforms, was to treat yourself as a product promoted through the calculated appearance of authenticity. Pooley, "The Consuming Self."

cross-disciplinary centers, spread throughout the remainder of the century – dwarfing other claimants, including Gary Becker's microeconomics of the family.

In his chapter on education, Andrew Jewett traces the peculiar – and sometimes hands-off – relationship of the mainline social sciences to education research over the course of the twentieth century. The existence of low-status education schools, operating as standalone units on the professional margins of the US university, colored the shape and volume of social-scientific inquiry in shifting ways. Into the 1950s, Jewett observes, education was typically positioned as a solution for other problems of society, rather than its own focal concern. With the Cold War and the federal government's new mandate to steward economic growth as backdrop, "fixing" the nation's schools took on special urgency, as exemplified in the early 1980s by a policy and political climate increasingly oriented to national competitiveness. In Jewett's account, social scientists from the main disciplines move in and out of the education domain, sometimes yielding jurisdiction to "ed school" faculty whose radicalism has tended to marginalize their contributions since the 1960s. From the 1970s on, meanwhile, the policy prominence of economics has increased. The human capital framework, in particular, supplied an individualistic and vocational lens to assess the school system, one that sidelined the stratification and inequality concerns of other social scientists and educational researchers. Jewett's account, in other words, documents the post-1960s split-screen dynamic outlined above: social-scientific pluralism juxtaposed with the overarching policy influence of economics and, to a lesser extent, psychology.

Alice O'Connor's chapter on poverty describes the broad arc of twentieth-century poverty knowledge in terms of "disembedding." Progressive era social research had cast poverty as a structural problem, one that would require structural solutions. When journalists and politicians thrust poverty back onto the social-scientific agenda in the 1960s, the issue was framed – by economists and other social scientists – in narrow and absolute terms, to the explicit exclusion of inequality. Economists in the postwar policy firmament were decisive and notably aloof, but the behavioral science–orientation of their noneconomist colleagues contributed to the War on Poverty's circumscribed ambitions too. By the time the political currents shifted in the 1970s, the stage was set for a further disembedding – a re-pauperization of the poverty problem that culminated in Bill Clinton's mid-1990s welfare rollback. O'Connor's account foregrounds the often-determinate role played by politics and – in the case of the neoconservative think tank – mezzo-level policy discourse. But social scientists were not impotent bystanders in the disembedding process. They had, in the War on Poverty years, laid the groundwork for the dodging of inequality questions – and, ironically, for the personal-responsibility moralism that, in the Clinton era, marked a full retreat from liberal social provision.

Leah N. Gordon, in her chapter, recounts how social scientists, during and after the war, tended to treat discrimination as a system – one with interlocking legal, political, and economic dimensions. By the 1950s systemic frameworks had receded in favor of more individualistic explanations for the "race problem." The study of discrimination remained strikingly cross-disciplinary, but the lens of prejudice – individual attitudes in the aggregate – was newly prominent, supported by philanthropy and Cold War discretion. Gary Becker brought microeconomics to discrimination in this period, too, in an approach that, like the psychology of prejudice, stressed the causal priority of dispositions. The announcement of formal equality in the civil rights legislation of the mid-1960s complicated the study of race for the balance of the century. Systemic accounts were partially revived, and evidence for persisting racial inequality was widely documented. But causal factors proved harder to identify, Gordon concludes. In the wake of de jure segregation, even radical critics of "institutional racism" and "internal colonialism" conceded that discrimination's effects were easier to describe than its causal dynamics. Quantitative sociologists and economists deployed a cascade of measures that demonstrated disparate outcomes, though again without clear explanatory accounts rooted in discrimination. By the 1980s the conservative rhetoric of "colorblindness" had, as it were, turned the discrimination question on its head.

George C. Galster's chapter addresses the "black ghetto" – the persistent concentration of African-American poverty in the country's inner cities. The interwar Chicago School's race-agnostic paradigm was, Galster shows, challenged by a handful of high-profile sociologists and economists in the mid-1940s, in works that, though they documented a discriminatory thicket, failed to win public or policy traction. Only with the televised urban riots of the mid- to late 1960s, in the midst of Johnson's Great Society, did the black ghetto attain full-fledged problem status. Social scientists registered the new stakes in a wave of studies that, in effect, established the battle lines for decades. Works that stressed the spatially concentrated legacy of racial discrimination were pitted – in a highly charged political climate – against culture-of-poverty accounts. The research lines, in turn, informed competing remedies, notably geographic dispersal, community development, and – in a reflection of the country's rightward drift – outright disengagement. The broad, if uneven patterns in the post-1960s scholarship, according to Galster, are a de-emphasis of race on the one hand, and the strengthening of individualistic frames on the other. There is, moreover, a rough disciplinary divide: Sociologists, he shows, have tended to highlight spatial and social factors, with economists and political scientists favoring, for the most part, more individualist and class-based accounts.

The story of crime, as related in Jean-Baptiste Fleury's chapter, has a familiar arc. Interwar criminology was dominated by sociologists, who cited modern social conditions as the main source of crime. Together with social psychologists and legal scholars, sociologists had swapped out environmental explanations for the biological accounts prevalent in the late nineteenth-century. In the early postwar decades, the study of crime came to center on juvenile delinquency, with a rough division of labor established between sociologists and psychologists. The overall explanatory frame remained environmental, though low-income and subcultural factors had, by the 1950s, largely supplanted immigration and urbanization. New philanthropic attention to delinquency helped guide the federal government's adoption of community action programs under the Democratic administrations of the 1960s, with heavy involvement from social scientists. Johnson's twinned Wars on Poverty and Crime were, at least initially, predicated on the postwar consensus that the root causes of crime were social. As Fleury recounts, an uptick in crime and the urban riots of the mid- to late 1960s put Johnson and the Great Society's social policies on the defensive – as Republicans refined a racialized backlash politics of "law and order." By the late 1960s a handful of social scientists had launched high-profile attacks on the prevailing criminological mainstream, coinciding with a federally sanctioned turn toward "crime control" and standalone programs in "criminal justice." Though still prominent, sociologists shared jurisdiction with other social scientists, including a growing and influential contingent of economists. By the 1980s, crime had been sheared off from other social issues, with the field now centered on crime's efficient management.

Nancy D. Campbell's chapter takes up the case of drug addiction. The social science of the "opium problem" (an early label) was, from its 1910s beginning, entangled with the federal government. Federal institutions generally promoted research that located addiction in personal psychology or the properties of drugs and their effects on the brain. There was, from the 1930s onward, a marginal but persistent alternative – exemplified by sociologists Alfred Lindesmith and Howard S. Becker – focused on the social process of definition, one that involved "addicts" themselves interacting with their social environment. An avalanche of new interest in the 1960s and 1970s – a response to a perceived drugs crisis and follow-on funding and policy mandates that brought into being the National Institute on Drug Abuse (NIDA) – brought epidemiologists, economists, and anthropologists into the research mix. In Campbell's account, the social sciences of addiction is a century-long jurisdictional melee, with the notable inclusion of fields bordering on, or fully within, the natural sciences. And so her conclusion – that the least "social" among them, neuroscience, came to dominate by the 1990s – provides support, with a natural-science asterisk, for the volume's social-attenuation thesis.

In his chapter on mental health, Andrew Scull traces the social sciences' relatively light pre–World War II engagement with mental health issues, with the partial exception of sociology. The postwar expansion of federal research funding, paired with explosive treatment demand for returning veterans, transformed psychology, swelling its ranks (as we have seen) with clinicians. Federal largesse, especially from the new National Institute of Mental Health (NIMH), underwrote a surprisingly diverse range of projects, with psychologists, psychiatrists, and, to a lesser degree, sociologists as the main beneficiaries. As psychology swelled under its postwar "scientist-practitioner" settlement, sociology remained comparatively small and, by the 1960s, increasingly critical of psychiatry and the country's mental health institutions. Meanwhile, as Scull describes, psychiatry had rapidly shed its psychoanalytic character by the 1980s, a response to dried-up funding and the psychopharmacological revolution. The chapter addresses the relative neglect of mental health by economists up through the 1990s – even as the discipline (as documented by the volume's other chapters) marched its toolkit through many other social problem domains. Scull's explanation for the anomaly is that mental health, in all its stigmatized irrationality, was a step too far for a discipline committed to the everyday fact, and scholarly application, of reason. With its tight discipline and established policy sway, economists had "no need to chase after scraps from the table served up by NIMH" (p. 352).

The social science of war, as Joy Rohde demonstrates in her concluding chapter, is a curious case. If education *gained* problem status in the early postwar period, war followed the opposite arc, shedding its social problem framing. From the interwar years through to the late 1940s, war was a public-facing problem whose solution – the eradication of armed conflict – seemed within reach for many social scientists and their internationalist allies. Quincy Wright's magisterial and multidisciplinary 1942 *A Study of War* exemplified the social-scientific ambition to foster peace through an expert-guided world order. The Cold War, however, abruptly stalled war's brief career as a social problem. The Soviet threat, and the national security state erected in response, helped to reframe the social science of war in management terms. For the next two decades most social scientists of war – though split on methodology and approach – hitched their study to the Cold War struggle. By the late 1960s the Vietnam debacle had implicated Defense-sponsored work on counter-insurgency and psychological warfare, leading to a public backlash against military entanglements. Many social scientists, Rohde shows, abandoned the study of war in Vietnam's wake, ceding the domain to political science in general and international relations in particular. The result was a social science of war that remained centered on statecraft and security into the 1980s.

So the volume's problem-specific accounts describe, from a bird's-eye view, an intriguing gap between developments internal to the social-scientific discourse on the one hand, and public prominence on the other. The picture is one of academic pluralism juxtaposed with a lopsided resonance at the level of politics and policy. In the second domain, the more public constellation, economics and psychology won an outsized influence that, however, was not always reflected in the problem-specific academic literatures traced by the book's authors.

What are we to make of this discrepancy? One answer, which we reject, is a variation on the theme that Herbert Blumer, in his 1971 paper, put forward: Social scientists and their work are side-shows in the political process. What matters, in the end, are the prevailing political winds; politicians and policymakers will, perhaps, raid the academic storehouse, but for their own justificatory ends. The policy shelf is well stocked with academic literature fit for any particular political platform to, in effect, check out. All the agency on this view lies with the politicians and their house intellectuals and functionaries. If governments are constrained by organized interests and more diffuse publics, then something gauzier – like the prevailing social imaginary – furnishes those limits. On this account, social science is an inert and ineffectual bystander – a supplier of raw materials, at best.

The problem with this position, for all its obvious truth, is that the constitutive contributions of social scientists to the underlying conditions of reception are written off. We have, by invoking the pair of ungainly process nouns "economization" and "psychologization," tried to gesture at the dynamism – the mutual shaping – that enmeshes social scientists in the politics of American social problems. The very seedbed of legibility is fertilized, in part, by the circulation of social-scientific knowledge. If the individualisms of economics and psychology have resonated in the century's last twenty-five years, the explanation is not merely their good fortune. If their normative, explanatory, and methodological frameworks are a good match for the prevailing politics, one reason is that psychology and economics have helped to sculpt the very popular and political space in which they flourish. The disciplines have, crucially, helped set the conditions for their own success.

Bibliography

Abbott, Andrew. *Department and Discipline: Chicago Sociology at One Hundred.* Chicago: University of Chicago Press, 1999.
Abbott, Andrew. *Chaos of Disciplines.* Chicago: University of Chicago Press, 2001.
Abbott, Andrew, and James T. Sparrow. "Hot War, Cold War: The Structure of Sociological Action, 1940–1955." In *Sociology in America: A History*, edited by Craig Calhoun, 281–313. Chicago: University of Chicago Press, 2007.
Appelbaum, Binyamin. *The Economists' Hour: False Prophets, Free Markets, and the Fracture of Society.* New York: Little, Brown, 2019.
Backhouse, Roger E. "The Transformation of US Economics, 1920–1960, Viewed through a Survey of Journal Articles." In *From Interwar Pluralism to Postwar Neoclassicism*, edited by Mary S. Morgan and Malcolm Rutherford, 85–107. Durham: Duke University Press, 1998.
Backhouse, Roger E., and Philippe Fontaine, eds. *The History of the Social Sciences since 1945.* Cambridge: Cambridge University Press, 2010.
Backhouse, Roger E., and Philippe Fontaine, "Economics and Other Social Sciences: A Historical Perspective." *Annals of the Fondazione Luigi Einaudi* 52, no. 2 (2018): 7–44.
Balisciano, Márcia L. "Hope for America: American Notions of Economic Planning between Pluralism and Neoclassicism, 1930–1950." In *From Interwar Pluralism to Postwar Neoclassicism*, edited by Mary S. Morgan and Malcolm Rutherford, 153–78. Durham: Duke University Press, 1998.
Banfield, Edward C. "Review of *An Economic Theory of Democracy*, by Anthony Downs." *Midwest Journal of Political Science* 2, no. 3 (1958): 324–25.
Bannister, Robert C. *Sociology and Scientism: The American Quest for Objectivity, 1880–1940.* Chapel Hill: University of North Carolina Press, 1987.
Barber, William J. *From New Era to New Deal: Herbert Hoover, the Economists, and American Economic Policy, 1921–1933.* Cambridge: Cambridge University Press, 1985.
Beach, Walter G. *An Introduction to Sociology and Social Problems.* New York: Houghton Mifflin, 1925.
Beard, Charles A. *The Nature of the Social Sciences in Relation to Objectives of Instruction.* New York: Charles Scribner's Sons, 1934.
Becker, Gary S. *The Economic Approach to Human Behavior.* Chicago: University of Chicago Press, 1976.
Becker, Howard S. *Outsiders: Studies in the Sociology of Deviance.* New York: Free Press, 1963.
Becker, Howard S. "Introduction." In *Social Problems: A Modern Approach*, edited by Howard S. Becker, 1–31. New York: John Wiley 1966.
Bend, Emil, and Martin Vogelfanger. "A New Look at Mills' Critique." In *Mass Society in Crisis*, edited by Bernard Rosenberg, 271–81. New York: Macmillan, 1964.

Bergson, Abram. "Review of *An Economic Theory of Democracy*, by Anthony Downs." *American Economic Review* 48, no. 3 (1958): 437–40.

Berman, Elizabeth Popp. *Creating the Market University: How Academic Science Became an Economic Engine*. Princeton: Princeton University Press, 2012.

Berman, Elizabeth Popp. "Not Just Neoliberalism: Economization in US Science and Technology Policy." *Science, Technology, & Human Values* 39, no. 3 (2013): 397–431.

Berman, Elizabeth Popp. *Thinking Like an Economist: How Economics Became the Language of US Public Policy*. Princeton: Princeton University Press, forthcoming.

Bernard, Luther L. "Contribution to 'Questions for Sociology: An Informal Round Table Symposium'." *Social Forces* 13, no. 2 (1934): 165–70.

"Questions for Sociology: An Informal Round Table Symposium." *Social Forces* 13, no. 2 (1934): 165–223.

Bernstein, Michael A. *A Perilous Progress: Economists and Public Purpose in Twentieth-Century America*. Princeton: Princeton University Press, 2001.

Best, Joel. "Whatever Happened to Social Pathology? Conceptual Fashions and the Sociology of Deviance." *Sociological Spectrum* 26, no. 6 (2006): 533–46.

Binder, Rudolph M. *Major Social Problems*. New York: Prentice-Hall, 1920.

Blumer, Herbert. "Social Problems as Collective Behavior." *Social Problems* 18, no. 3 (1971): 298–306.

Bossard, James H. S. *Problems of Social Well-Being*. New York: Harper & Bros, 1927.

Bowden, A. O. "Our 396 Major Social Problems and Issues and the Schools." *Journal of Educational Sociology* 2, no. 7 (1929): 397–411.

Burgin, Angus. *The Great Persuasion: Reinventing Free Markets since the Depression*. Cambridge: Harvard University Press, 2012.

Burnham, John, ed. *After Freud Left: A Century or Psychoanalysis in America*. Chicago: University of Chicago Press, 2012.

Calhoun, Craig. "Sociology, Other Disciplines, and the Project of a General Understanding of Social Life." In *Sociology and its Publics: The Forms and Fates of Disciplinary Organization*, edited by Terence C. Halliday and Morris Janowitz, 137–95. Chicago: University of Chicago Press, 1992.

Calhoun, Craig. "Sociology in America: An Introduction." In *Sociology in America: A History*, edited by Craig Calhoun, 1–38. Chicago: University of Chicago Press, 2007.

Calhoun, Craig, and Jonathan VanAntwepren. "Orthodoxy, Heterodoxy, and Hierarchy: 'Mainstream' Sociology and Its Challengers." In *Sociology in America: A History*, edited by Craig Calhoun, 367–410. Chicago: University of Chicago Press, 2007.

Callon, Michel. "The Embeddedness of Economic Markets in Economics." In *The Laws of the Markets*, edited by Michel Callon, 1–57. Oxford: Blackwell.

Camic, Charles. "On Edge: Sociology during the Great Depression and the New Deal." In *Sociology in America: A History*, edited by Craig Calhoun, 225–80. Chicago: University of Chicago Press, 2007.

Capshew, James H. *Psychologists on the March: Science, Practice, and Professional Identity in America, 1929–1969*. Cambridge: Cambridge University Press, 1999.

Case, Clarence M. "What Is a Social Problem?" *Journal of Applied Sociology* 8 (1924): 268–73.

Chall, Leo P. "Notes Toward a History of the Literature of Social Problems." In *Handbook on the Study of Social Problems*, edited by Erwin O. Smigel, 399–407. Chicago: Rand McNally, 1971.

Cole, Arthur H. "Economic History in the United States: Formative Years of a Discipline." *Journal of Economic History* 28, no. 4 (1968): 556–89.

Coleman, James S. *Foundations of Social Theory.* Cambridge: Belknap Press of Harvard University Press, 1990.

Committee on Recent Economic Changes of the President's Conference on Unemployment, ed. *Recent Economic Changes in the United States.* New York: NBER, 1929.

Connell, R. W. "Why is Classical Theory Classical?" *American Journal of Sociology* 102, no. 6 (1997): 1511–57.

Converse, Jean M. *Survey Research in the United States: Roots and Emergence, 1890–1960.* Berkeley: University of California Press, 1987.

Cravens, Hamilton. "Have the Social Sciences Mattered in Washington?" In *The Social Sciences Go to Washington: The Politics of Knowledge in the Postmodern Age,* edited by Hamilton Cravens, 129–33. New Brunswick: Rutgers University Press, 2004.

Crowther-Heyck, Hunter. *Herbert A. Simon: The Bounds of Reason in Modern America.* Baltimore: Johns Hopkins University Press, 2004.

Crowther-Heyck, Hunter. "Patrons of the Revolution: Ideals and Institutions in Postwar Behavioral Science." *Isis* 97, no. 3 (2006): 420–46.

Cushman, Philip. *Constructing the Self, Constructing America: A Cultural History of Psychotherapy.* New York: Da Capo Press, 1995.

Dahl, Robert A. "The Behavioral Approach in Political Science: Epitaph for a Monument to a Successful Protest." *American Political Science Review* 55, no. 4 (1961): 763–72.

Dahl, Robert A. *Who Governs? Democracy and Power in an American City.* New Haven: Yale University Press, 1961.

Deegan, Mary Jo. *Jane Addams and the Men of the Chicago School: 1892–1918.* Chicago: University of Chicago Press, 1988.

DeLeon, Peter. *Advice and Consent: The Development of the Policy Sciences.* New York: Russell Sage Foundation, 1989.

De Vos, Jan. "From Milgram to Zimbardo: The Double Birth of Postwar Psychology/ Psychologization." *History of the Human Sciences* 23, no. 5 (2010): 156–75.

De Vos, Jan. *Psychologization and the Subject of Late Modernity.* New York: Palgrave MacMillan, 2013.

Diamond, Martin. "Review of *An Economic Theory of Democracy,* by Anthony Downs." *Journal of Political Economy* 67, no. 2 (1959): 208–11.

Du Bois, W. E. B. *The Souls of Black Folk: Essays and Sketches.* Chicago: A. C. McClurg & Co., 1903.

Easton, David. *The Political System: An Inquiry into the State of Political Science.* New York: Alfred A. Knopf, 1953.

Easton, David. "The New Revolution in Political Science." *American Political Science Review* 63, no. 4 (1969): 1051–61.

Ellwood, Charles A. *Sociology and Modern Social Problems.* New York: American Book Company, 1910.

Ellwood, Charles A. *Sociology and Modern Social Problems.* Revised and enlarged ed. New York: American Book Company, 1919.

Ellwood, Charles A. *Methods in Sociology: A Critical Study.* Durham: Duke University Press, 1933.

Erikson, Kai T. "Notes on the Sociology of Deviance." *Social Problems* 9, no. 4 (1962): 307–14.

Farr, James. "Political Science." In *The Cambridge History of Science (The Modern Social Sciences)*, edited by Theodore M. Porter and Dorothy Ross, vol. 7, 306–28. Cambridge: Cambridge University Press, 2003.

Fleishman, Joel L. "A New Framework for Integration: Policy Analysis and Public Management." *American Behavioral Scientist* 33, no. 6 (1990): 733–54.

Fleury, Jean-Baptiste. "Wandering through the Borderlands of the Social Sciences: Gary Becker's *Economics of Discrimination*." *History of Political Economy* 44, no. 1 (2012): 1–40.

Fontaine, Philippe. "Introduction: The Social Science in a Cross-Disciplinary Age." *Journal of the History of the Behavioral Sciences* 51, no. 1 (2015): 1–9.

Fontaine, Philippe. "Other Histories of Recent Economics: A Survey." *History of Political Economy* 48, no. 3 (2016): 373–421.

Frank, Lawrence K. "Social Problems." *American Journal of Sociology* 30, no. 4 (1925): 462–73.

Fuller, Richard C. "Sociological Theory and Social Problems." *Social Forces* 15, no. 4 (1937): 496–502.

Fuller, Richard C. "The Problem of Teaching Social Problems." *American Journal of Sociology* 44, no. 3 (1938): 415–35.

Fuller, Richard C. "Social Problems." In *An Outline of the Principles of Sociology*, edited by Robert E. Park, 3–59. New York: Barnes & Noble, 1939.

Fuller, Richard C., and Richard R. Myers. "The Natural History of a Social Problem." *American Sociological Review* 6, no. 3 (1941): 320–29.

Fuller, Richard C., and Richard R. Myers. "Some Aspects of a Theory of Social Problems." *American Sociological Review* 6, no. 1 (1941): 24–32.

Furner, Mary O. *Advocacy and Objectivity: A Crisis in the Professionalization of American Political Science, 1865–1905*. Lexington: University Press of Kentucky, 1975.

Gay, Edwin. "Introduction." In *Recent Economic Changes in the United States*, vol. 1, edited by Committee on Recent Economic Changes of the President's Conference on Unemployment, 1–12. New York: NBER, 1929.

Geiger, Roger L. *Research and Relevant Knowledge: American Research Universities since World War II*. New York: Oxford University Press, 1993.

Gordon, Michael. "The Social Survey Movement and Sociology in the United States." *Social Problems* 21, no. 2 (1973): 284–98.

Gouldner, Alvin W. "Anti-Minotaur: The Myth of a Value-Free Sociology." *Social Problems* 9, no. 3 (1962): 199–213.

Gouldner, Alvin W. "The Sociologist as Partisan: Sociology and the Welfare State." *American Sociologist* 3, no. 2 (1968): 103–16.

Gouldner, Alvin W. *The Coming Crisis of Western Sociology*. New York: Basic Books, 1970.

Greenwood, John. *The Disappearance of the Social in American Social Psychology*. Cambridge: Cambridge University Press, 2004.

Grogan, Jessica. *Encountering America: Humanistic Psychology, Sixties Culture, and the Shaping of the Modern Self*. New York: Harper Perennial, 2013.

Guglielmo, Mark. "The Contribution of Economists to Military Intelligence During World War II." *Journal of Economic History* 68, no. 1 (2008): 109–50.

Gusfield, Joseph R. *The Culture of Public Problems: Drinking-Driving and the Symbolic Order*. Chicago: University of Chicago Press, 1981.

Gusfield, Joseph R. "Constructing the Ownership of Social Problems: Fun and Profit in the Welfare State." *Social Problems* 36, no. 5 (1989): 431–41.

Hacking, Ian. "Statistical Language, Statistical Truth, and Statistical Reason: The Self-Authentication of a Style of Scientific Reasoning." In *The Social Dimensions of Science*, edited by Ernan McMullin, 130–57. Notre Dame: University of Notre Dame Press, 1992.

Haney, David P. *The Americanization of Social Science: Intellectuals and Public Responsibility in the Postwar United States*. Philadelphia: Temple University Press, 2008.

Hart, Hornell. "What is a Social Problem?" *American Journal of Sociology* 29, no. 3 (1923): 345–52.

Haskell, Thomas L. *The Emergence of Professional Social Science: The American Social Science Association and the Nineteenth-Century Crisis of Authority*. Champaign: University of Illinois Press, 1977.

Haveman, Robert H. "Policy Analysis and Evaluation Research after Twenty Years." *Policy Studies Journal* 16, no. 2 (1987): 191–218.

Hayek, Friedrich A. "The Intellectuals and Socialism." *University of Chicago Law Review* 16, no. 3 (1949): 417–33.

Herman, Abbott P. "The Disproportionate Emphasis on Description in Social Problem Texts." *Social Problems* 1, no. 3 (1954): 105–9.

Herman, Ellen. *The Romance of American Psychology: Political Culture in the Age of Experts, 1940–1970*. Berkeley: University of California Press, 1995.

Herring, Pendleton. "Political Science in the Next Decade." *American Political Science Review* 39, no. 4 (1945): 757–66.

Hinkle, Roscoe C. *Developments in American Sociological Theory, 1915–1950*. Albany: State University of New York Press, 1994.

Hirschman, Daniel, and Elizabeth Popp Berman. "Do Economists Make Policies? On the Political Effects of Economics." *Socio-Economic Review* 12, no. 4 (2014): 779–811.

Horton, Paul B., and Gerald R. Leslie. *The Sociology of Social Problems*. New York: Appleton-Century-Crofts, 1955.

House, James S. "Social Psychology, Social Science, and Economics: Twentieth Century Progress and Problems, Twenty-first Century Prospects." *Social Psychology Quarterly* 71, no. 3 (2008): 232–56.

Kitsuse, John I., and Malcolm Spector. "Toward a Sociology of Social Problems: Social Conditions, Value-Judgments, and Social Problems." *Social Problems* 20, no. 4 (1973): 407–19.

Landis, Paul H. *Social Problems in Nation and World*. New York: Lippincott, 1959.

Leach, William R. *Land of Desire: Merchants, Power, and the Rise of a New American Culture*. New York: Vintage, 1993.

Lears, Jackson. *No Place of Grace: Antimodernism and the Transformation of American Culture, 1880–1920*. Chicago: University of Chicago Press, 1981.

Lears, Jackson. "From Salvation to Self-Realization: Advertising and the Therapeutic Roots of the Consumer Culture, 1880–1930." In *The Culture of Consumption: Critical Essays in American History, 1880–1980*, edited by Richard Wightman Fox and Jackson Lears, 1–38. New York: Pantheon Books, 1983.

Lee, Alfred McClung. "Sociologists in an Integrating Society: Significance and Satisfaction in Sociological Work." *Social Problems* 2, no. 2 (1954): 57–66.

Lemert, Edwin M. *Social Pathology: A Systematic Approach to the Theory of Sociopathic Behavior*. New York: McGraw Hill, 1951.

Lengermann, Patricia. "The Founding of the *American Sociological Review*: The Anatomy of a Rebellion." *American Sociological Review* 44, no. 2 (1979): 185–98.

Lengermann, Patricia, and Gillian Niebrugge. "Thrice Told: Narratives of Sociology's Relation to Social Work." In *Sociology in America: A History*, edited by Craig Calhoun, 63–114. Chicago: University of Chicago Press, 2007.

Lengermann, Patricia, and Jill Niebrugge-Brantley. "Back to the Future: Settlement Sociology, 1885–1930." *American Sociologist* 33, no. 3 (2002): 5–20.

Liazos, Alexander. "The Poverty of the Sociology of Deviance: Nuts, Sluts, and Perverts." *Social Problems* 20, no. 1 (1972): 103–20.

Light, Jennifer S. *From Warfare to Welfare: Defense Intellectuals and Urban Problems in Cold War America.* Baltimore: Johns Hopkins University Press, 2003.

Lindblom, Charles E. "In Praise of Political Science." *World Politics* 9, no. 2 (1957): 240–53.

Lipset, Seymour M., and Neil Smelser. "Change and Controversy in Recent American Sociology." *British Journal of Sociology* 12, no. 1 (1961): 41–51.

LoConto. "Charles A. Ellwood and the End of Sociology." *American Sociologist* 42, no. 1 (2011): 112–28.

Lundberg, George A. "The Social Sciences in the Postwar Era." *Sociometry* 8, no. 2 (1945): 137–49.

Marquis, Donald G. "Scientific Methodology in Human Relations." *Proceedings of the American Philosophical Society* 92, no. 6 (1948): 411–16.

Martindale, Don. "Social Disorganization: The Conflict of Normative and Empirical Approaches." In *Social Problems: A Modern Approach*, edited by Howard S. Becker, 340–67. New York: John Wiley & Sons, 1966.

Maslow, Abraham H. *Toward a Psychology of Being*, 2nd ed. New York: D. Van Nostrand Company, 1968.

Medvetz, Thomas. *Think Tanks in America.* Chicago: University of Chicago Press, 2012.

Merriam, Charles E. "Annual Report of the Social Science Research Council." *American Political Science Review* 20, no. 1 (1926): 185–89.

Merrill, Francis E. *Social Problems.* New York: Knopf, 1950.

Merton, Robert K. "Concluding Comments and an Example of Research." In *New Perspectives for Research on Juvenile Delinquency*, edited by Ellen Witmer and Ruth Kotinsky, 75–92. Washington, DC: US Department of Health, Education, and Welfare, 1956.

Merton, Robert K. "Social Problems and Sociological Theory." In *Contemporary Social Problems: An Introduction to the Sociology of Deviant Behavior and Social Disorganization*, edited by Robert K. Merton and Robert A. Nisbet, 697–737. New York: Harcourt, Brace & World, 1961.

Merton, Robert K., and Robert A. Nisbet, eds. *Contemporary Social Problems: An Introduction to the Sociology of Deviant Behavior and Social Disorganization.* New York: Harcourt, Brace & World, 1961.

Merton, Robert K., and Robert A. Nisbet, eds. *Contemporary Social Problems: An Introduction to the Sociology of Deviant Behavior and Social Disorganization.* 3rd ed. New York: Harcourt, Brace & World, 1971.

Mills, C. Wright. "The Professional Ideology of Social Pathologists." *American Journal of Sociology* 49, no. 2 (1943): 165–80.

Mills, C. Wright. *The Sociological Imagination.* Oxford: Oxford University Press, 1959.

Mitchell, Timothy. "Fixing the Economy." *Cultural Studies* 12, no. 1 (1998): 81–101.

Muniesa, Fabian, Yuval Millo, and Michel Callon. "An Introduction to Market Devices." *Sociological Review* 55, no. 2S (2007): 1–12.

Murphy, Michelle. *The Economization of Life*. Durham: Duke University Press, 2017.

Neumeyer, Martin H. *Social Problems and the Changing Society*. New York: Van Nostrand, 1953.

Nisbet, Robert A. *The Quest for Community: A Study in the Ethics of Order and Freedom*. Oxford: Oxford University Press, 1953.

O'Connor, Alice. *Poverty Knowledge: Social Science, Social Policy, and the Poor in Twentieth-Century US History*. Princeton: Princeton University Press, 2001.

Odum, Howard W. *Man's Quest for Social Guidance: The Study of Social Problems*. New York: H. Holt and Company, 1927.

Ogburn, William F. *Social Change with Respect to Culture and Original Nature*. New York: B. W. Huebsch, 1922.

Ogburn, William F., and Alexander Goldenweiser, eds. *The Social Sciences and Their Interrelations*. Boston: Houghton Mifflin, 1927.

Ogg, Frederic A. "News and Notes: Political Scientists in the War." *American Political Science Review* 36, no. 4 (1942): 728–33.

Olson, Mancur, Jr. "Economics, Sociology, and the Best of All Possible Worlds." *Public Interest* 12 (1968): 96–118.

Ott, Julia, Mike Konczal, N. D. B. Connolly, Timothy Shenk, and Daniel Rodgers. "Debating the Uses and Abuses of 'Neoliberalism': Forum." *Dissent*, January 22, 2018, www.dissentmagazine.org/online_articles/debating-uses-abuses-neo liberalism-forum

Park, Robert E. "Sociology and the Social Sciences." *American Journal of Sociology* 26, no. 4 (1921): 401–24.

Park, Robert E. "Sociology and the Social Sciences: The Social Organism and the Collective Mind." *American Journal of Sociology* 27, no. 1 (1921): 1–21.

Park, Robert E. "Sociology and the Social Sciences: The Group Concept and Social Research." *American Journal of Sociology* 27, no. 2 (1921): 169–83.

Parsons, Philip A. *An Introduction to Modern Social Problems*. New York: Alfred A. Knopf, 1924.

Platt, Jennifer. *A History of Sociological Research Methods in America: 1920–1960*. Cambridge: Cambridge University Press, 1996.

Pooley, Jefferson. "The Consuming Self: From Flappers to Facebook." In *Blowing Up the Brand*, edited by Melissa Aronczyk and Devon Powers, 71–89. New York: Peter Lang, 2010.

Pooley, Jefferson. "A 'Not Particularly Felicitous' Phrase: A History of the 'Behavioral Sciences' Label." *Serendipities* 1, no. 1 (2016): 38–81.

Pooley, Jefferson, and Mark Solovey. "Marginal to the Revolution: The Curious Relationship between Economics and the Behavioral Sciences Movement in Mid-Twentieth-Century America." In *The Unsocial Social Science? Economics and Neighboring Disciplines since 1945*, edited by Roger E. Backhouse and Philippe Fontaine, 199–233. Durham: Duke University Press, 2010.

Porter, Theodore M., and Dorothy Ross. "Introduction: Writing the History of Social Science." In *The Cambridge History of Science (The Modern Social Sciences)*, edited by Theodore M. Porter and Dorothy Ross, vol. 7, 1–10. Cambridge: Cambridge University Press, 2003.

President's Research Committee on Social Trends. *Recent Social Trends in the United States.* New York: McGraw-Hill, 1933.

Queen, Stuart A., and Delbert M. Mann. *Social Pathology.* New York: Thomas Y. Crowell Co., 1925.

Raab, Earl, and Gertrude J. Selznick. *Major Social Problems.* Evanston: Row, Peterson, 1959.

Reinhardt, J. M. "Trends in the Teaching of 'Social Problems' in Colleges and Universities in the United States." *Social Forces 7,* no. 3 (1929): 379–84.

Rodgers, Daniel T. *Age of Fracture.* Cambridge: Belknap Press of Harvard University Press, 2011.

Rodgers, Daniel T. "The Uses and Abuses of 'Neoliberalism'." *Dissent,* 65, no. 1 (2018): 78–87.

Rose, Arnold M. "History and Sociology of the Study of Social Problems." In *Handbook on the Study of Social Problems,* edited by Erwin O. Smigel, 3–18. Chicago: Rand McNally and Co., 1971.

Rose, Nikolas S. *Governing the Soul: The Shaping of the Private Self.* London: Routledge, 1999.

Rutherford, Alexandra. *Beyond the Box: B.F. Skinner's Technology of Behavior From Laboratory to Life, 1950s–1970s.* Toronto: University of Toronto Press, 2009.

Scaff, Lawrence A. "Max Weber and the Social Sciences in America." *European Journal of Political Theory 3,* no. 2 (2004): 121–32.

Senn, Mary S., and Peter R. Senn. "What is a Social Problem? A History of its Definition." In *Jahrbuch für Soziologiegeschichte 1993,* edited by Carsten Klingemann, Michael Neumann, Karl-Siegbert Rehberg, Ilja Srubar, and Erhard Stölting, 211–46. Wiesbaden: VS Verlag für Sozialwissenschaften, 1995.

Sewell, William H. "Some Reflections on the Golden Age of Interdisciplinary Social Psychology." *Annual Review of Sociology 15,* no 1. (1989): 1–17.

Skura, Barry. "Constraints on a Reform Movement: Relationships between SSSP and ASA, 1951–1970." *Social Problems 24,* no. 1 (1976): 15–36.

Smigel, Erwin O. "Preface." In *Handbook on the Study of Social Problems,* edited by Erwin O. Smigel, vii–viii. Chicago: Rand McNally and Co., 1971.

Smith, Mark A. *The Right Talk: How Conservatives Transformed the Great Society into the Economic Society.* Princeton: Princeton University Press, 2007.

Smith, Mark C. *Social Science in the Crucible: The American Debate over Objectivity and Purpose, 1918–1941.* Durham: Duke University Press, 1994.

Solovey, Mark. "Riding Natural Scientists' Coattails onto the Endless Frontier: The SSRC and the Quest for Scientific Legitimacy." *Journal of the History of the Behavioral Sciences 40,* no. 4 (2004): 393–422.

Solovey, Mark. "Cold War Social Science: Specter, Reality, or Useful Concept?" In *Cold War Social Science: Knowledge Production, Liberal Democracy, and Human Nature,* edited by Mark Solovey and Hamilton Cravens, 1–22. New York: Palgrave Macmillan, 2012.

Solovey, Mark. *Shaky Foundations: The Politics–Patronage–Social Science Nexus in Cold War America.* New Brunswick: Rutgers University Press, 2013.

Solovey, Mark. "To Measure, Monitor, and Manage the Nation's Social Progress." Working Paper, University of Toronto, 2019.

Somit, Albert, and Joseph Tanenhaus. *The Development of Political Science: From Burgess to Behavioralism.* Boston: Allyn and Bacon, 1967.

Spector, Malcolm, and John I. Kitsuse. "Social Problems: A Re-Formulation." *Social Problems* 21, no. 2 (1973): 145–59.

Spector, Malcolm, and John I. Kitsuse. *Constructing Social Problems*. New York: Aldine de Gruyter, 1987.

Stedman Jones, Daniel. *Masters of the Universe: Hayek, Friedman, and the Birth of Neoliberal Politics*. Princeton: Princeton University Press, 2012.

Steinmetz, George. "American Sociology before and after World War II: The (Temporary) Settling of a Disciplinary Field." In *Sociology in America: A History*, edited by Craig Calhoun, 314–66. Chicago: University of Chicago Press, 2007.

Susman, Warren L. "'Personality' and the Making of Twentieth-Century Culture." In *New Directions in American Intellectual History*, edited by John Higham and Paul K. Conkin, 212–26. Baltimore: Johns Hopkins University Press, 1979.

Sutherland, Edwin H. "Social Pathology." *American Journal of Sociology* 50, no. 6 (1945): 429–35.

Suttles, Gerald D. *Front Page Economics*. Chicago: University of Chicago Press, 2010.

Swedberg, Richard. *Economics and Sociology – Redefining Their Boundaries: Conversations with Economists and Sociologists*. Princeton: Princeton University Press, 1990.

Swedberg, Richard. "'The Battle of the Methods': Toward a Paradigm Shift?" In *Socioeconomics: Toward a New Synthesis*, edited by Amitai Etzioni and Paul R. Laurence, 13–33. Armonk: M.E. Sharpe, 1991.

Swedberg, Richard, and Mark Granovetter. "Introduction." In *The Sociology of Economic Life*, edited by Mark Granovetter and Richard Swedberg, 1–26. Boulder: Westview Press, 1992.

Taylor, Charles. *Modern Social Imaginaries*. Durham: Duke University Press, 2004.

Thomas, W. I., and Florian Znaniecki. *The Polish Peasant in Europe and America*. Boston: Gorham Press, 1918.

Tilly, Charles. *Durable Inequality*. Berkeley: University of California Press, 1998.

Torgerson, Douglas. "Policy Analysis and Public Life: The Restoration of Phronesis." In *Political Science in History: Research Programs and Political Traditions*, edited by James Farr, John S. Dryzek, and Stephen T. Leonard, 225–52. Cambridge: Cambridge University Press, 1995.

Turner, Jonathan H. "The More American Sociology Seeks to Become a Politically-Relevant Discipline, the More Irrelevant it Becomes to Solving Societal Problems." *American Sociologist* 50, no. 4 (2019): 456–87.

Turner, Stephen P. "The Origins of 'Mainstream Sociology' and Other Issues in the History of American Sociology." *Social Epistemology* 8, no. 1 (1994): 41–67.

Turner, Stephen P. "A Life in the First Half-Century of Sociology: Charles Ellwood and the Division of Sociology." In *Sociology in America: A History*, edited by Craig Calhoun, 115–54. Chicago: University of Chicago Press, 2007.

Turner, Stephen P. *American Sociology: From Pre-Disciplinary to Post-Normal*. New York: Palgrave Pilot, 2013.

Turner, Stephen P., and Jonathan H. Turner. *The Impossible Science: An Institutional Analysis of American Sociology*. Newbury Park: Sage Publications, 1990.

Walker, Harvey. "Political Scientists and the War." *American Political Science Review* 39, no. 3 (1945): 555–74.

Waller, Willard. "Social Problems and the Mores." *American Sociological Review* 1, no. 6 (1936): 922–33.

Weaver, William W. *Social Problems*. New York: Dryden Press, 1951.

Worcester, Kenton W. *Social Science Research Council, 1923–1998*. New York: SSRC, 2001.

Wright, Quincy. *A Study of War*. Chicago: University of Chicago Press, 1942.

Young, Cristobal. "The Emergence of Sociology from Political Economy in the United States: 1890 to 1940." *Journal of the History of the Behavioral Sciences* 45, no. 2 (2009): 91–116.

2

Family

Savina Balasubramanian and Charles Camic

Many "social problems" follow the trajectory of a life history. They seize the attention of intellectuals and the public at a historical moment, hold interest for a time, and then fade – whether "resolved" or not. Attention moves on. But the belief that the "family" presents social problems has been more durable, historically speaking. For as long as writers, whether religious or secular, have taken pen to paper, they have raised alarm about some aspect of family life: witness – to look no further – the jeremiads of religious leaders since antiquity, or the programs for a new social order advocated by conservative, liberal, and radical social thinkers ever since the Age of the Enlightenment. In America in our own day – again, to look no further – there is no religious sect, no political party, no rising generation of women and men that is wholly content with the contemporary family and regards it as an oasis cleansed of all social problems.

How historical actors have defined and interpreted those problems has varied greatly, even when one restricts the focus to a single location, a short span of time, and (for the purposes of this volume) a fairly small group of knowledge-makers: namely, American social scientists in the period after World War II, who considered the contemporary family as rife with social problems. Chapters 4–7 in this volume touch on aspects of the subject, inasmuch as the subject of family has spilled over onto the social scientific study of other problems, such as poverty, crime, urban life, and discrimination.

In this chapter, we trace how the family per se has been problematized differently at different moments in twentieth-century American intellectual history. For this purpose, we begin with a background section that sketches the prevailing approach to the family before 1945, an era when many social scientists, their eyes trained primarily on the United States, saw the modern family as an institution in the throes of *social disorganization and decline*. We then turn to developments in the half-century after World War II, dividing this era into two overlapping periods: the period from 1945 to the mid-1960s, when the global issue of *family size* gained priority as the major problem of the family; and the period from the mid-1960s to the 1990s, when those priorities shifted to the role of the family in the *transmission of social inequality* in American society.

The words we have just italicized encapsulate what constituted, in our assessment of the historical evidence, the overarching problem of concern among leading social scientists actively engaged, during these periods, in discussing the phenomenon of the contemporary family; and it is from this angle alone that we examine pre- and postwar writings on the family. We want to stress this qualifier to warn readers not to expect an exhaustive coverage of social scientific work on the family in any of these periods. At every point, scholarship on the family was extensive, diffuse, and marked by crosscurrents; conversely, occasionally social scientists showed little interest in picturing the family as a major problem at all. This literature defies the intellectual historian's impulse to characterize it as a totality, or to boil it all down to this or that theory or empirical claim – however significant that theory or claim becomes in retrospect (whereas, when viewed in context, it was often just another eddy in a vast intellectual sea). Following the example of other chapters in this book, we will concentrate on the ideas of sociologists and, to a lesser degree, on those of economists, with no more than a few side-glances into other academic disciplines. At the same time, our narrative will consider the research of an overlapping, multidisciplinary group of experts, namely, demographers, who played a pivotal part in conceptualizing the problems of the contemporary family in the postwar period.

Across these time periods, there was a tendency among the social scientists whose ideas we consider to regard the family as a conduit that channels certain broad (or macro-level) social forces to small kinship groups comprised of interacting individuals whose (micro-level) behaviors combine to reproduce (or change) those broader forces. Where does this circular process start or end? what weights attach to particular moments of it? and what drives it? On these questions social scientists have disagreed.[1] Likewise, they have disagreed over whether social conditions or problems external to the family "cause" its internal problems, or whether ameliorating the latter furnishes a "solution" for larger social maladies.[2] In either case,

[1] Adams, "Fifty Years of Family Research."
[2] For simplicity's sake, we use more contemporary wording (macro/micro, structure/agency, external/internal) in the last two sentences than did most social scientists in the first half of the twentieth century.

social scientists have generally held to the convention of using the word "family" (at least when affixed to Western societies in the twentieth century) to refer to a nuclear family consisting of a heterosexual couple and small number of children.[3] Indeed, for most of the authors mentioned in this chapter, the standard practice was to regard contemporary societies in which a large number of households *depart* from this norm as *prima facie* evidence that something had gone wrong: that the family *was* a social problem of one kind or another.

2.1 Historical Background: The Problem of Family Disorganization and Decline

Writing in 1926, Ernest Burgess, a leading figure at the venerable Department of Sociology at the University of Chicago and one of the nation's premier sociologists of the family, looked back on his speciality area as it stood at the time America entered World War I.[4]

Nine years ago I gave for the first time a course on the family. There was even then an enormous literature in this field. But among all the volumes upon the family, ethnological, historical, psychological, ethical, social, economic, [and] statistical ... there was to be found not a single work that even pretended to study the modern family as a behavior or as a social phenomenon.[5]

The comment shows the myopia of the young academic (Burgess was barely 30 in 1917): He conceded that, "yes," other writers – economists included – had dealt with the family, but complained that they had all failed at the job, coming up short with regard to the concepts suitable for understanding the contemporary family. The historical part of the claim was inaccurate. Since the start of the American university in the 1880s, social scientists had been analyzing the phenomenon of the family – and its attendant problems – with concepts akin to those Burgess would use. This was true, for example, of Albion Small and George Vincent in *An Introduction to the Study of Society* (1894) – the urtext of the Chicago School of sociology – as well as W. E. B. Du Bois in *The Philadelphia Negro* (1899), Charles Ellwood in *Sociology and Modern Social Problems* (1910), and James Dealey in *The Family in Its Sociological Aspects* (1912).

---

[3] Locke, "Mobility and Family Disorganization," 494.
[4] On the Chicago School of sociology, see Abbott, *Department and Discipline*; Bulmer, *Chicago School of Sociology*; and Fitzpatrick, *Endless Crusade*.
[5] Burgess, "Family as a Unity," 3.

Even so, Burgess saw older works like these as amateur efforts when compared with an alternative opened up by the encompassing theory of social change that he and his senior colleague Robert Park had set forth in their *Introduction to the Science of Sociology* (1921). This theory centered on social "institutions" – economic organizations, the state, the legal system, churches, and so forth – and on how they function when buffeted by major transformations of the time: viz., industrialization, internal migration, foreign immigration, and urbanization. To make sense of these changes, Park and Burgess proposed a three-stage model of organization–disorganization–reorganization. Citing observational studies and descriptive statistical data, they asserted that macro-level changes undermined the well-integrated institutions of the past, destabilizing them up to the point where they reorganized in order to function effectively under modern conditions.[6]

Extending this grand theory specifically to the family, the Chicagoans maintained that here too was a social institution in the midst of social change. As such, it was experiencing a concatenation of dislocations that went with the stage of social disorganization.[7] Topping the list of these dislocations was the nation's rising divorce rate, but other problems drew extensive notice by sociologists: declining marriage and fertility rates, rising numbers of out-of-wedlock births, marital discord and dissatisfaction, the breakdown of parental oversight of children's development, desertion of the household by husbands/fathers, and employment outside of the household by wives/mothers.[8] By the later 1920s, these problems were the subject not only of dozens of articles in sociological journals, but also of such classic books as *Social Problems of the Family* (1927) by Ernest Groves and *Family Disorganization* (1927) by Ernest Mowrer (a student of Burgess).[9]

To some sociologists, however, there was an important difference between the family and many of the other social institutions embraced within Park and Burgess's model. Whereas institutions such as the state and the economy moved over time from the stage of disorganization to the stage of reorganization, the family showed little movement toward reorganization, because the social role of the family was shrinking. That, at any rate, was

[6] Park and Burgess, *Introduction to the Science of Sociology*.
[7] Burgess, "Foreword," ix–x.
[8] We could extend this list. Looking back on the literature on the sociology of the family, Sprey commented on tendency to classify "every conceivable family problem under the heading of disorganization." Sprey, "Family Disorganization," 398.
[9] Hart, "Trends of Change in Textbooks"; Groves, *Social Problems of the Family*; and Mowrer, *Family Disorganization*.

the assessment of social scientists like Burgess's Chicago colleague William F. Ogburn, who proposed that "there had been a decline in the institutional functions of the family." He elaborated:

> In colonial times in America the family was a very important economic organization .... The home was ... a factory. Civilization was based on a domestic system of production of which the family was the center.... But changes set in as manufacturing technique evolved, as economic division of labor progressed and as trade developed.... This loss of economic functions has been a factor in many social questions, including the position of women in society, the stability of the family and the birth rate. [Furthermore,] the family has been losing other functions as well. The government is assuming a larger protective role with its policing forces, its enormously expanded schools, its courts and its social legislation. Religious observances within the home are said to be declining. [As well,] it has been said that some homes are merely 'parking places' for parents and children who spent their active hours elsewhere.[10]

Rather than question any of these what "has been said" statements, moreover, Ogburn plied on, attributing these problems – along with "increased divorce," "broken homes," and "defective personality development" – to "the weakening of the functions which served to hold the family together." In his view, although these maladies especially beset "poorer families," no income group was immune; rather, all could benefit from publicly supported "efforts to deal with family problems," through (for instance) social work services and family clinics.[11]

In these proposals to strengthen the family, we see the activist spirit of the New Deal, which was then taking form, drawing on the advice of academic economists, political scientists, sociologists, and legal experts.[12] To be sure, repairing the American family was not among the principal objectives of the New Deal. Nevertheless, the adverse effects of the Great Depression on families were plain to everyone, and government interventions into the family life – via unemployment insurance, housing assistance, aid for children in fatherless households, and job creation programs – were parts of the New Deal mix.[13] Behind these policies, furthermore, lay the research of experts from the Bureau of Agricultural Economics (a research branch of the US Department of Agriculture from the 1920s to the 1950s). These

[10] Ogburn and Tibbitts, "Family and Its Functions," 661–62 and President's Research Committee on Social Trends, "Review of Findings," xlv. In quoting, we have combined passages from these two sources, since Ogburn wrote the latter, as well as the former.
[11] Ogburn and Tibbitts, "Family and Its Functions," 702–8.
[12] Barber, *From New Era to New Deal* and Camic, "On Edge."
[13] Kennedy, *Freedom from Fear*, 164–66.

experts included rural sociologists and farm economists who studied the "family-farm institution," and researchers in the emerging speciality area of "home economics," who grappled with topics such as "the economics of household consumption" and the "economic choices" made by "family units."[14] The Bureau produced major monographs such as sociologist Conrad Taeuber and Rachel Rowe's *Five Hundred Families Rehabilitate Themselves* (1941).

None of this work called into dispute the Chicago School's "social disorganization" template, which was nothing if not adaptable. During the Depression and the New Deal, studies of the topic continued at a brisk pace, with "economic disintegration" included prominently among the sources of family disorganization – as, for example, in monographs like Robert Angell's *The Family Encounters the Depression* (1936), Ruth Shonle Cavan and Katherine Howland Ranck's *The Family and the Depression* (1938), and Winona Louise Morgan's *The Family Meets the Depression* (1939). The looming entry of the United States into World War II furnished another occasion to extend the concept, with family researchers, such as sociologist Willard Waller and his collaborators sending up alerts about the "disorganizing effect of the war," especially its "disintegrating influence" on the family, where it "leaves a heritage of damaged family solidarity, mounting divorce and increased delinquency."[15] This way of thinking pervaded the well-noticed publications of the National Council on Family Relations (NCFR), a multidisciplinary nonprofit organization, which Burgess cofounded in 1938 to promote academic research and social policies to remediate family disorganization.[16]

Nevertheless, perhaps the most influential application of "social disorganization" appeared in studies of the African-American family. Here, the seminal work was *The Negro Family in the United States* (1939), authored by another Burgess student, E. Franklin Frazier, who sought to make sense of the "tide of family disorganization [which] followed as a natural

[14] On "home economics," see Kyrk, *Theory of Consumption*, 402; Kyrk, *Economic Problems of the Family*; and Kyrk's student, Reid, *Economics of Household Production*. On the Bureau of Agricultural Economics, see Larson and Zimmerman, *Sociology in Government*.
[15] Waller, Goldstein, and Frank, "Family and National Defense," 1. In the aftermath of the war, these themes echoed through the classic work of Samuel Stouffer et al., *The American Soldier*.
[16] On the origins (and extremely multidisciplinary character) of the NCFR, see Sayre, "Work of the National Conference"; Folsom, "Report of Committee"; and Nye, "Fifty Years of Family Research," 306.

consequence of the impact of modern civilization upon ... Negro families," and which registered in problems such as "immorality, delinquency, desertions, and broken homes."[17] Drawing on the analysis Frazier provided, the Swedish economist Gunnar Myrdal, visiting the United States in the late 1930s, painted an identical picture of family problems in his 1,500-page best seller *An American Dilemma* (1944). Going forward, similar accounts of the African-American family appeared as well in works like *Black Metropolis* (1945) by St. Clair Drake and Horace Cayton – young scholars trained at the University of Chicago – who plumbed the "social disorganization in the Black Ghetto."[18]

While the Chicago School's practice of viewing family problems through the lens of "disorganization" remained strong into the late 1930s and throughout the war, two other perspectives were, by that time, also attracting growing attention among social scientists. Neither of these contradicted the approach of Park and Burgess and their students, and it was not unusual to find the different approaches comingling. All the same, these perspectives threw into relief phenomena that were less visible from the angle of "social disorganization."

One of these was social stratification: the hierarchical arrangement of the members of a society into different social strata. At certain points in modern intellectual history, social scientists have equated social strata with "classes" in a Marxist sense (of ownership of the means of production). But during the interwar and wartime period, most American sociologists – along with anthropologists and economists interested in social structures – treated social strata, or "classes," in a colloquial sense, as groups constituted on the basis of some combination of occupation, income, inherited wealth, social prestige, and education. Matters of definition aside, this period was the era of community network studies in an ethnographic vein mined by Robert and Helen Lynd in *Middletown* (1929) and *Middletown in Transition* (1937) and excavated further by W. Lloyd Warner, a Harvard social anthropologist turned University of Chicago sociologist. Intentionally centering his research on midsize American towns that were "better integrated" than the disorganized urban areas that inspired Park and Burgess, Warner and his collaborators produced a series of books that described the family lifestyle

---

[17] Frazier, *Negro Family in the United States*, 364; O'Connor, *Poverty Knowledge*; and Chapter 4: Poverty.

[18] Myrdal, *American Dilemma*, 927–55 and Drake and Cayton, *Black Metropolis*, 202. For a valuable discussion of these and other works in this family of studies, see Furstenberg, "Making of the Black Family."

differences of the upper classes, middle classes, and lower classes, and then analyzed the consequences of these differences. They also examined the incidence (by social class) of problems such as divorce, illegitimacy, and female labor force participation, and they brought into the foreground the problem of social mobility, which they conceptualized in terms of the differential chances that individuals had of moving up or down the socioeconomic status (SES) hierarchy – thereby gaining or losing economic, political, and social advantages.[19]

The second perspective that gained salience during this period bore the strong impress of World War II. A joint production of sociologists, cultural anthropologists, and social psychologists, this perspective repurposed research on the relationship of family structure, child-rearing methods, and personality formation in order to plumb the roots of democracy and authoritarianism – political systems that scholars regarded as underpinned by different learned sets of cultural values and patterns of conduct.[20] Galvanized most immediately by the Frankfurt School's *Studien über Authorität und Familie* (Horkheimer, 1936), but drawing intellectual support from the multidisciplinary field of "culture and personality," this literature on family political socialization (as we would now call it) grew rapidly. Issues of the *American Sociological Review* from the late 1930s, for instance, contained articles on the problems associated with the German family, the Chinese family, and the Soviet family (as contrasted with the democratically organized American family); and the wartime years unleashed a flood of "national character" studies, often funded by the federal government, in which researchers examined the family origins of the attitudes and behaviors of the modal – highly stereotyped – personalities of peoples of foreign nations. Continuing in this tradition, this era also launched the research project that eventuated in *The Authoritarian Personality* (1950), where émigré Theodor W. Adorno (and his multidisciplinary team of collaborators) elaborated and empirically tested the thesis that authoritarian personalities arose from families that used punitive child-rearing practices.

In different ways, these modes of thinking about the family – in terms of social organization, social mobility, and political personality

[19] Warner, "Social Anthropology and the Modern Community," 795. Of the many books in the series, especially important were Warner and Lunt, *Social Life of a Modern Community* and Warner and Lunt, *Status System of a Modern Community*. To describe social mobility as a "problem" is not to suggest that the writers named were critical of it; mostly they were not, in the belief that social mobility served positive functions. For discussion of these studies, see Furstenberg, "Making of the Black Family."
[20] Zimmerman, "Types of Families."

formation – drew increasingly on information contemporaries usually referred to as "demographic." In the early years of the Chicago School, this information generally amounted to little more than raw figures that untutored researchers in various subfields culled from local government records by counting and percentaging the number of people in this or that demographic category (age, employment status, and so on). During the Great Depression, however, experts in the subject began to appear on the American intellectual landscape in conjunction with the development of the field of demography. This speciality traced its origins as a profession to the founding in 1931 of the Population Association of America (PAA), which consisted initially of a tiny, loose-knit, and heterogeneous assortment of researchers from sociology, economics, biology, and statistics, as well as officials at insurance companies and other private organizations interested in the size, composition, and distribution of the nation's population and, by extension, in statistical projections of birth and death rates. Funded by the Milbank Memorial Fund (MMF), a foundation seeking to develop a national population policy, the membership of PAA was often split in its views about basic population trends, with some researchers worried, for example, about the rapid growth of the American population, others by its shrinking size.[21]

As important as demographers' debates over matters of substance was the emerging infrastructure of demographic research. Here again the MMF took the lead, establishing at Princeton University in 1935 the Office of Population Research (OPR), which launched and thereafter maintained a successful program of research on fertility and mortality rates and population movements, which by the 1940s turned "primarily toward international demography."[22] Office of Population Research's success occurred even though it was little more than a poorly attached institutional satellite, partly because neither at Princeton nor anywhere elsewhere was there a separate "Department of Demography" (an institutional constraint that remains true even now, in the 2020s). As a result, OPR subsisted mainly on funding from extramural sources, in particular private foundations. Also, as many of the lead researchers at OPR had faculty appointments in sociology departments (at Princeton or elsewhere), it was with sociology that demography tended to be affiliated organizationally. Even when these affiliations with sociology were the strongest, however, demography functioned more as an "interdiscipline" than as a freestanding discipline

---

[21] Weeks, "Early Years of the PAA" and President's Research Committee on Social Trends, "Review of Findings," xv–xx.
[22] Taeuber, "Population Studies," 256.

in its own right.[23] (Due to this organizational peculiarity, individual demographers have typically had one foot in their "home" department and another in its adjacent demography unit. To convey this fact, we will use hyphenated neologisms, such as "sociologist-demographer" or "economist-demographer," except in passages where "demographer" suffices.)

Significantly, the early years of OPR coincided also with a heavy stream of demographic research issuing from various agencies of the federal government in response, first, to the New Deal demand for data on the US population and, subsequently, to the wartime need for projections of population trends in allied and enemy nations. These agencies included the Census Bureau, as well as the Bureau of Agricultural Economics, the Works Progress Administration, the National Housing Agency, and the War Production Board.[24] Working with seemingly limitless resources, the staff members at these agencies – researchers trained mainly in sociology, though also in economics, public administration, and statistics – mounted national and regional surveys that grafted additional questions onto familiar Census-type questions, designed to improve projections of birth rates, population makeup, internal migration patterns, and so on: questions that elicited more and more information about the problems of the American family. The move toward seeking such data was a natural one; for, from demographers' concerns about the size and composition of populations, there soon arose a strong interest in the primary site for population reproduction, viz., the family – and, therefore, in reliable data on birth rates, marriage rates, the age distribution of women and men at marriage, divorce rates, rates of illegitimacy, and so forth. These data proved relatively easy to collect and analyze by increasingly sophisticated statistical methods. Out of the 1930 decennial Census, for example, came a large volume entitled *Families*. When Paul Glick (a new PhD in sociology from the University of Wisconsin) joined the Census Bureau in 1939 as a "family analyst," one of his first assignments was to augment the research in *Families* with "ten book-size reports from the 1940 census that dealt with family composition, age at marriage, fertility, employment of women, family income, and housing characteristics of families." Immediately afterward, wartime conditions stimulated a demand for an even broader range of "marriage and family statistics," as sociologist-demographer Philip Hauser (a freshly minted University of Chicago PhD, then working at the Census Bureau) described.[25]

---

[23] Stycos, "Introduction."
[24] Hauser, "Wartime Development in Census Statistics."
[25] Glick, "Fifty Years of Family Demography," 861–62. The *Families* volume is referenced in Glick, "Fifty Years of Family Demography," 861.

Around the same time, Hauser also predicted that "population problems will be among the major problems of postwar adjustment," and that "in the troubled days which lie ahead" demographers will play an increasingly central role.[26] Not surprisingly, Hauser's predictions were borne out. Owned exclusively by no single academic discipline, these data would become the lifeblood for social scientists concerned with the family as a social problem.

2.2 Postwar Period I, 1945–1965: The Problem of Family Size

During the two decades that followed World War II, all of these approaches continued forward, some changing in the number of adherents they attracted, some changing in their substantive character. For its part, the idea that family problems were part of a larger process of social disorganization slowly waned, as the model itself faded throughout sociology in tandem with the dwindling influence of the Chicago School. Yet many of the family maladies that earlier writers had included under the header of "disorganization" remained subjects of active investigation among researchers who identified with the speciality area of "the sociology of the family" – or "family studies," as scholars outside of sociology often called it. As represented in the area's flagship journal, the *Journal of Marriage and Family* (a publication of the NCFR), this list of topics continually expanded, with more articles on premarital sexuality, birth control, the mental and physical health of the family members, the family life cycle, and (perhaps above all) the strains between the "sex roles" of husbands and wives inside and outside the household.[27]

To social scientists within and outside the sociology of the family, this work sometimes felt lightweight and insignificant, leading to calls to rethink its agenda. This was the view of leading family sociologist Leonard Cottrell, who wrote of his subfield in 1948: "there is little or no concerted attack on a carefully selected series of problems which are agreed upon as fundamental; … for the most part, research is being conducted by scattered and isolated investigators who are frequently working on relatively trivial problems."[28] Even so, new conceptual winds blew through the area now and then, as in 1947 when family sociologist Reuben Hill interjected the factor of individual economic choice into a discussion of the social problems of the family, asserting that

---

[26] Hauser, "Population and Vital Phenomena," 322.
[27] Adams, "Fifty Years of Family Research" and Nye, "Fifty Years of Family Research." For a view from the times, see Komarovsky and Waller, "Studies of the Family."
[28] Cottrell, "Present Status and Future Orientation of Research," 123.

A man can get his meals cooked and his clothes mended more cheaply without a wife than with one. Most able-bodied women can provide themselves with better clothes through their own efforts than with the pay envelope of a husband. Economically, marriage has become a luxury and parenthood a positive expense. Most couples actually live more frugally together than they did separately; they economize to marry.[29]

Looking beyond the subfield of the sociology of the family per se, one finds, too, expanding bodies of research on most of the other problems we flagged in the previous section. We see this in the honor roll of classic ethnographic accounts, by anthropologists and sociologists, of underprivileged urban communities – with some of these studies emphasizing the role of cultural beliefs (the so-called culture of poverty), others the role of social-structural factors (racial and ethnic discrimination, residential segregation, and limited employment opportunities) in perpetuating the collateral problems of family life. These classics included Hylan Lewis's *Blackways of Kent* (1955), Elliot Liebow's *Tally's Corner* (1967), and Ulf Hannerz's *Soulside* (1969).[30] In different ways, these case studies descended from Frazier and Warner, whose influence also lay behind the advances made throughout this period in theories of social stratification and in the refinement of statistical techniques for analyzing intergenerational mobility.[31]

On top of all of this, there was an explosion of research on the relationship between family socialization and troublesome kinds of personality development. Some of this work took the form of wide-angled books, mixing sociology with anthropology, such as C. K. Yang's *The Chinese Family in the Communist Revolution* (1954), Ezra Vogel's *Japan's New Middle Class* (1963), and H. Kent Geiger's *The Family in Soviet Russia* (1968). More typical were smaller-scale studies, often by social psychologists, of the effects of different culture-based and/or class-based child-rearing styles on children's attitudes and behaviors, political and otherwise.[32]

---

[29] Hill, "American Family," 125, 130. There is an interesting historical twist perhaps worth noting here: At the time he made these points, Hill was teaching at a small agricultural college, Iowa State College, in the same department from which future pioneer of the "new home economics," Theodore W. Schultz, had resigned in 1943 to join the faculty at the University of Chicago. Schultz's time on the Iowa State faculty coincided with that of Margaret Reid, the progenitor of "home economics." In 1948, Reid herself became a professor of economics at the University of Chicago.

[30] See also Chapter 5: Discrimination.

[31] These advances were brought together in a widely read text, Bendix and Lipset, *Class, Status, and Power*.

[32] Zigler, "Social Class and the Socialization Process." O'Connor usefully situates the torrent of child-rearing studies within "the behavioral sciences 'revolution'" of the 1950s. O'Connor, *Poverty Knowledge*, 103–7. This revolution was part of what House calls the "golden age of social psychology." House, "Social Psychology, Social Science," 232.

Dwarfing all these problems, however, was the problem of family size, which had stayed for decades on the periphery of social scientific research, but now moved to the forefront. Here, the geopolitics of the Cold War era provided the backdrop. For no American social scientist of the postwar period was unaware that she or he was living in a world overshadowed by the military, economic, and ideological rivalry between the Soviet and American powers, as each bloc fought to control the "new nations" of the "Third World." Under this new order, American foreign policy interests centered on containing the threat of communism and spreading Western-style capitalism, Western-tinted democracy, and Western-flavored values to nonaligned and decolonizing countries. The American federal government – particularly the Department of State and the Department of Defense – often looked to the nation's social scientific experts to illuminate how to achieve these new developmental objectives, all of which the Truman, Eisenhower, and Kennedy administrations took deadly seriously. Vice versa, American social scientists eagerly latched onto these objectives as compelling rationales for their scholarship, holding fast to "economic growth" as the *sine qua non* of national development and to "democracy" as its *prima facie* mode. From these grand notions, scholars were led to assign priority to the problem of family size, endowing it with nothing short of world-historical significance.[33]

We see this, in the first instance, in writings coming from the theoretical side of the social sciences – writings intellectual historians have subsequently lumped together under the loose (and sometimes misleading) rubric of "modernization theory." Expressed in different forms in different disciplines, modernization theory's most vigorous spokespersons were sociologist Talcott Parsons and many of his leading students, along with economists Walt W. Rostow and Alexander Gerschenkron, communications scholar Daniel Lerner, political scientist Edward Banfield, and psychologist David McClelland, all of whom posited an evolutionary distinction between backward-facing societies (call them "underdeveloped," "peasant," "agrarian," "nonindustrial," or "traditional") and forward-facing societies ("advanced," "developed," "urbanized," "industrial," or "modern"), the latter resting on capitalist institutions, democratic practices, and a commitment to values such as individualism and personal achievement. Few hesitated to apply the distinction to the contemporary Cold War situation by locating the world's "new nations" in the traditional category and worrying that,

---

[33] Gilman, *Mandarins of the Future*; Engerman, *Price of Aid*; and Latham, *Modernization as Ideology*.

inasmuch as these nations failed to modernize, they would be highly susceptible to Soviet influence and capture.

Preventing this catastrophic possibility required removing barriers to modernization, not least the problem of high birth rates and large family size. "If western civilization is to survive at all," wrote Parsons, non-Western nations needed to adopt the form of "a modern urbanized industrial society," a change dependent in part on declining birth rates. Traditional familial societies, however, hampered the speed of this decline, posing "a profounder population crisis very closely connected with the major problems of [the] whole society."[34]

This modernization perspective dovetailed with the views of a number of contemporary American macroeconomists. In terms of the United States, economists of varying stripes and convictions, including Arthur F. Burns, Paul A. Samuelson, James Tobin, and Milton Friedman, voiced the idea that economic growth should be a primary aim of national policymaking and a principal standard to which political leaders' competence should be held.[35] Looking abroad, Rostow applied a similar outlook to the situation in low-income countries, stylizing the process of modernization into separate "stages," which together ensured the conditions for "traditional societies" to experience what he termed the "takeoff" to rapid economic growth and increased development.[36]

Initially, family size per se was a problem in the margins of these writings, though Parsons' postwar essays already assigned it a greater role in the modernization process. According to his work, and that of Rostow and Lerner, for example, nuclear families that saw the usefulness of fewer children and investing resources that would otherwise be set aside for basic survival into capital formation, consumption, and familial economic "achievement" were the functional bedrocks of modernity.[37] Although other modernization theorists rarely formulated the point so crisply, most implicitly linked increased production outside the family to controlled reproduction within the family. Among those sociologists who held this view, Marion Levy and Wilbert Moore (both students of Parsons) and William Goode (Moore's student) were some of the most insistent. In his oft-cited treatise *World Revolution and Family Patterns*, Goode argued that the "Western" conjugal

---

[34] Parsons, *Essays in Sociological Theory*, 259, 275–76, Japan.
[35] Yarrow, *Measuring America*; Collins, *More*; and Hirschman, "Inventing the Economy."
[36] Rostow, *Stages of Economic Growth*, chaps. 2–5.
[37] Lerner, *The Passing of Traditional Society*; Parsons and Bales, *Family, Socialization, and the Interaction Process*; and Rostow, *Stages of Economic Growth*.

model of male-headed, small nuclear family would eventually spread globally, accompanying "revolutionary" social and economic transformations toward industrialization and urbanization.[38] The effects would include shrinking population growth rates, transitions to democratic capitalism, and increases in national economic growth in non-Western and decolonizing countries. Insofar as modernization theorists conceptualized "tradition" and social "backwardness" as global social problems, they likewise characterized nonnuclear family and kinship structures, as well as families that exhibited high fertility, as related social problems.[39]

In advancing these arguments, social theorists of the period converged with researchers at the more heavily empirical end of the social sciences, demographers in particular.[40] Postwar demographers' focus on overpopulation further shifted social scientists' locus of concern away from the social disorganization of the American family to the "fecund family" in the "developing world" as a global social problem in need of speedy intervention.[41] Intertwined with these research developments was a far-reaching shift in the way demographers theorized demographic change itself – a theoretical shift that pushed the family into even greater prominence within their field.[42] During the prewar period, demographers' prevailing theoretical explanation for changes in population dynamics was "demographic transition theory." First elucidated in its classical form by sociologist-demographer Warren Thompson in 1929, this theory posited that historical declines in national fertility in Western European countries and the United States operated as *ex post facto* evidence of industrialization and urbanization. This classical view changed, however, in the immediate aftermath of World War II, shifting demography's geographic focus from Western countries to the developing world. The crucible for this shift was the OPR at Princeton. Whereas classical transition theory asserted that lowered fertility was a *response* to industrialization and urbanization, after the war OPR demographers began to assert that proactive fertility control was a *necessary antecedent* to the promise of modernization in these regions.

Much of this rethinking was the result of demographers' anxieties about the global fate of capitalist democracy after the "fall of China" in 1949, when

---

[38] Goode, *World Revolution and Family Patterns.*
[39] Gerschenkron, *Economic Backwardness in Historical Perspective.*
[40] Balasubramanian, "Communicating Contraception"; Connelly, *Fatal Misconception*; and McCann, *Figuring the Population Bomb.*
[41] Greenhalgh, "Social Construction of Population Science"; Murphy, *Economization of Life*; and Merchant, "Prediction and Control."
[42] Bashford, *Global Population.*

they began to wonder whether the pressures of high fertility rates in countries that had yet to experience high levels of industrialization and urbanization would breed conditions ripe for the establishment of communism.[43] Skeptical that industrialization and urbanization would proceed apace in these regions – and convinced that their high fertility rates and low mortality rates were likely impeding those processes to begin with – OPR sociologist-demographers Frank Notestein, Kingsley Davis, and Dudley Kirk, and economist-demographer Ansley Coale, became concerned that the "problem [was] too urgent to permit [them] to await the results of gradual processes of urbanization, such as took place in the Western world." If left unchecked, overpopulation would not only stymie economic development but would also set the stage for the rise of totalitarian governments and communist rebellion.[44] Davis, by then an associate professor of sociology at Columbia University, averred that global population growth was a "Frankenstein" that would set the stage for the rise of "completely planned economies."[45]

This specter led to an enormous expansion of the infrastructure for demographic research, which had previously consisted mainly of OPR and a handful of federal government agencies. Supporting this expansion was an infusion of resources by philanthropists and government agencies, such as Frederick Osborn of the Carnegie Corporation and John D. Rockefeller III of the Rockefeller Foundation, and federal officials in the Department of State and US Agency for International Development (USAID), who were collectively concerned about stitching global population control into the fabric of American foreign policy.[46] The Ford Foundation was responsible for the creation of sixteen new interdisciplinary university centers for demographic and population research between 1951 and 1967, and foundation and federal government monies supported many of these centers' activities.[47] Simultaneously, a number of prominent postwar demographers assumed positions of power in independent organizations that funded population research, most significantly the Population Council. From their new organizational perches, leading demographers promoted

[43] Balasubramanian, "Communicating Contraception" and Connelly, *Fatal Misconception.*
[44] Davis, *Population of India and Pakistan* and Notestein, "Summary of the Demographic Background of Problems," 253.
[45] Davis, *Population of India and Pakistan,* 220 and Hodgson, "Demography as Social Science."
[46] Sharpless, "World Population Growth" and Sharpless, "Population Science, Private Foundations."
[47] Greenhalgh, "Social Construction of Population Science," 42–43.

research agendas that foregrounded problems of family size, fertility decision-making, and reproductive and sexual behaviors.[48]

What was more, demographic researchers did not stop with "causes and consequences," as we have already mentioned. Instead, proponents of modernization theory and economic growthism, working in collaboration, fueled the expansion of international family planning research. One of the most influential of these collaborations was between Ansley Coale and the University of Pittsburgh economist Edgar M. Hoover.[49] Published in 1958, their study of population dynamics in newly independent India projected population growth rates in two hypothetical scenarios: one in which the Indian government promoted fertility control through programmatic policy over the next twenty-five years and another in which it made no such "special efforts."[50] Coale and Hoover modeled rates of increase in India's population on the country's GDP per capita, thereby explicitly articulating transition theory in macroeconomic terms. Arguing that the former scenario would alleviate population pressures on national economic growth if executed appropriately, they concluded that a direct program of fertility control would free up capital to be funneled into economic growth, rather than consumption for basic survival.

For demographers, this was an opportunity to legitimize the place of lowering family size in the US government's international development endeavors. Davis reiterated his new faith in government-led family planning programs and the distribution of effective contraceptive technologies among citizens. Notestein and Kirk elaborated this line of reasoning; they appealed to American agricultural (development) economists and to political leaders alike to take the promotion of smaller family size seriously as a determinant of economic growth and political stability.[51] Set in this light, the family appeared not only as a social problem, but also as a compelling *solution* to a complex of related social problems. Not only this, but the revision of demographic transition theory enabled sociologist-demographers and economists to promote medical and biomedical contraceptives as "direct" technological antidotes to postcolonial underdevelopment.[52] Worth noting,

---

[48] Balasubramanian, "Communicating Contraception."
[49] Coale and Hoover, *Population Growth and Economic Development*.
[50] Hodgson, "Demography as Social Science," 25–26 and McCann, *Figuring the Population Bomb*.
[51] Notestein, "Economic Problems of Population Change" and International Planned Parenthood Federation, *Sixth International Conference on Planned Parenthood*.
[52] Connelly, *Fatal Misconception*; McCann, *Figuring the Population Bomb*; Murphy, *Economization of Life*; Notestein, "Summary of the Demographic Background of Problems," 254; and Takeshita, *Global Biopolitics of the IUD*.

too, is that in the course of fielding local family planning programs, the study of family size also opened itself up to social-psychological approaches for understanding how to change people's attitudes and behaviors at the family level, approaches that grew out of the broader behavioral sciences "revolution" of the 1950s. These included survey research to ascertain "knowledge, attitudes, and practices" regarding birth control, as well as experiments on the effectiveness of various mass communications strategies at promoting contraception and favorable attitudes toward smaller families.[53]

Considering these intellectual and institutional developments together, what the period between 1945 and 1965 reveals, then, is that when it came to research on family size and international family planning, American social scientists across the major disciplines did not seek to wrest professional jurisdiction from each other. On the contrary, against the backdrop of an escalating Cold War and rapid decolonization, they collaborated to present measures for limiting family size and restraining global population growth as fruitful development aid initiatives in the service of urgent foreign policy objectives. Whereas during the prewar period, the sociological concept of "disorganization" dominated discussions of the family as a social problem, it could no longer do so after 1945. In this period, the intersecting politics of overpopulation, economic growth, and international development placed the problem of family size at the forefront of the social sciences, with demographers standing at the cutting edge.

2.3 Postwar Period II, Mid-1960s–1990s: Problem of Family Transmission of Social Inequality

The start of our first period is easy to date – this volume concerns the historical era that begins in 1945. However, there is no equivalent date – no exact calendar year – that marks the beginning of the second postwar period. Many social scientists who were active scholars in the first period remained so for decades afterward, carrying out research that was scarcely different from the work they had been doing previously – or, for that matter, from what their teachers had been doing *before* the war. In 1966, nearly a half-century after members of the Chicago School began framing

---

[53] Balasubramanian, "Communicating Contraception"; Murphy, *Economization of Life*; and Parry, *Broadcasting Birth Control*. See Greenhalgh, "Social Construction of Population Science," and Merchant, "Prediction and Control," for how dissidents within demography sought to critique these new disciplinary objectives but were systematically sidelined.

family problems as expressions of social disorganization and institutional decline, the *Journal of Marriage and Family* still ran as its lead an article on "Family Disorganization: Toward a Conceptual Clarification," while a 1989 issue of the *American Journal of Sociology* featured a "test of the social disorganization theory," which dealt with "family disruption" in terms Chicagoans of the 1920s would have immediately recognized.[54] Likewise, deep into this second period, studies of family political socialization and other research on the disruptive effects of certain child-rearing practices continued to appear, even as the "culture and personality" school closed shop in cultural anthropology and social psychology.[55] Most importantly, demographic research on pressing international issues of family size, population growth, and family planning remained a tall presence in the social sciences, securely anchored in journals such as *Studies in Family Planning, Demography,* and *Family Planning Perspectives,* founded in 1963, 1964, and 1969, respectively.

For all this, however, family size and family disorganization gradually ceased to command their previous centrality among scholars in the United States. As we have seen, interest in the family went together with broad theories of social change, in particular from modernization theory. However, the death of modernization theory during this period dissolved this linkage, allowing a great deal of family scholarship to drift loose as a differentiated speciality area, with few connections to the mainland. In the previous subsection (p. 78), we quoted Cottrell's (1948) remark that research on the family was "being conducted by scattered and isolated investigators who are frequently working on relatively trivial problems." By the 1980s, well-placed commentators were repeating this criticism, averring that the study of marriage and the family had become "an intellectual backwater in sociology."[56]

At this date, the list of specific family problems under active investigation was longer than ever, having grown to include newer problems associated with cohabitation, abortion, intergroup marriage, post-divorce adjustment, remarriage, job pressures on parents, and life-course changes. Notwithstanding this constantly expanding list, research on specific family problems no longer constituted a hotspot in sociology or neighboring disciplines – *except*

[54] Sprey, "Family Disorganization" and Sampson and Groves, "Community Structure and Crime."

[55] This was part of the decline of the field of social psychology more generally. See House, "Social Psychology, Social Science," 235–37.

[56] Hannan, "Families, Markets, and Social Structures," 65. As few years later Adams observed: "family social science continues to be relatively low in status." Adams, "Fifty Years of Family Research," 12.

inasmuch as these problems also fell within the bounds of family demography (see below). This was true despite the publication of well-respected books such as Christopher Lasch's *Haven in a Heartless World* (1977), Jessie Bernard's *The Future of Marriage* (1982), Lenore Weitzman's *The Divorce Revolution* (1985), and Arlie Russell Hochschild's *The Second Shift* (1989).

   To be sure, scholarly concern over certain aspects of the family exhibited itself in other subfields. In the intellectual space vacated by the demise of modernization theory, the second period saw the dramatic growth, spearheaded by sociologists and political scientists, of comparative-historical research. In large part, these new specialties focused on the historical study of the world's resource-poor nations, usually with an eye on their economic and political struggles, but in doing so researchers often considered topics like family property holdings and kinship networks.[57] Still further, comparative-historical scholarship on wealthier nations frequently called forth analyses of household organization and domestic relations, particularly as these intersected with changing practices of gender and sexuality – and with the development of state social policies to address family problems. Then too, this second period brought a sharp uptick of ethnographic research on socially and economically disadvantaged urban areas; this research concentrated especially on African-American communities and on the "problems" of family life in these communities (see Chapter 6: The Black Ghetto).[58]

   These diverse lines of research drew inspiration and sustenance from real-time developments outside the academy, most visibly the Civil Rights Movement, the Women's Liberation Movement, and the protest movement against the Vietnam War, which themselves bore the influence of neo-Marxist class analytics, radical feminist thought, and theories of racial oppression and colonialism.[59] Their combined effect was to reshape American thinking about one social problem after another by inviting knowledge-makers to reckon with some of the fault lines of their own society – in other words, the overarching problem of social inequality. In the process, many more specific family-associated problems were set in a fresh, panoptic light through the research of another multidisciplinary ensemble, one in which sociologists (in their capacity as demographers) played a leading role once again, though sharing the stage with other social scientists, economists among them.

---

[57] Articles in the journal *Social Politics* (founded in 1987) offer many illustrations.
[58] Furstenberg, "Making of the Black Family."
[59] Self discusses the different ways these movements politicized the family. Self, *All in the Family*.

In this new era, research funding, from both federal agencies and private foundations, was of decisive importance once more. In her chapter, Alice O'Connor describes the historical context, tracing the path from the Kennedy administration's investment in programs to overcome conditions of economic deprivation in resource-poor nations to the Johnson administration's commitment to ameliorating equivalent conditions in the United States itself (see Chapter 4: Poverty). This commitment was embodied in the passage of the Civil Rights Act of 1964 and the simultaneous launch of the War on Poverty. Designed and operated with guidance from social scientists, these initiatives signaled growing attention to the income gap between rich and poor Americans, to questions about causes of socioeconomic inequality, and to government measures for addressing poverty and inequality. Almost immediately, these concerns turned the national and academic spotlight onto the American family.

We see this turn as early as 1965, when political scientist Daniel Moynihan, Assistant Secretary in the US Department of Labor, issued his instantly controversial report, *The Negro Family: The Case for National Action*. In this, Moynihan wove together the old family disorganization theory with postwar arguments about the dangers of large family size to diagnose urban poverty as the result of the "highly unstable ... family structure of lower class Negroes." Moynihan saw this condition reflected in demographic trends like rising rates of illegitimacy and divorce in African-American communities, as well as in the growing prevalence of large households headed by single mothers.[60] This strong emphasis on the family reappeared the following year in a Department of Health, Education, and Welfare report, *Equality of Educational Opportunity*. Written by sociologist James S. Coleman on the basis of research carried out under a contract from the Department, the report purported to show that students' academic performance was more strongly influenced by their family backgrounds than by the resources of their schools. For most social scientists and policymakers, the immediate takeaway was that families created inequalities of educational opportunity that public spending on schooling could not of itself eradicate.[61]

Influential though they were, government reports like these relied on cross-sectional data, which did not allow researchers to nail down causal relationships between factors (e.g., family characteristics, community conditions, and family SES). Better data and data-analytic techniques were in the pipeline, however. In 1968, for example, Office of Economic

[60] Moynihan, *Negro Family*, 50. See also Chapter 4: Poverty.
[61] Coleman et al., *Equality of Educational Opportunity*. See also Chapter 3: Education.

Opportunity officials invited economist James N. Morgan (of the University of Michigan's Survey Research Center) to conduct a multiyear survey of 2,000 low-income households – an invitation Morgan accepted provided the study would also include, for the purposes of a broader study of social inequality, 3,000 nonpoor households. Eventually, this survey evolved into the multidisciplinary Panel Study of Income Dynamics (PSID), which has run continuously to the present day, generating troves of information on American families and their members, considered intra- and intergenerationally. This information has included data on race, fertility, family size, marriage and divorce, out-of-wedlock births, childcare arrangements, schooling, labor force participation, earnings, occupational mobility, wealth, health, and the use of government services. By the year 2000, these data yielded literally hundreds of articles, appearing in leading journals of economics, sociology, and demography, on the interface between socioeconomic inequalities and other family problems. The PSID data also resulted in a ten-volume series – *Five Thousand American Families* – where economists sympathetic to government assistance policies argued that poverty is not a permanent condition, but one that many families cycle through, pulled out with the aid of government safety net programs.[62]

Nearly simultaneous with the launch of the PSID was the publication in 1967 of a landmark study of social inequality, *The American Occupational Structure*, by sociological theorist Peter Blau and sociologist-demographer Otis Dudley Duncan, who followed the tradition of social mobility research that went back to Warner and Frazier. Using a 1962 survey of over 20,000 men, which was carried out by the Census Bureau and funded by grants from the National Science Foundation and the National Institutes of Health, Blau and Duncan examined the intergenerational transmission of social inequality through the prism of the jobs that survey respondents held in the nation's "stratified hierarchy of occupations." The authors' central thesis was the dual argument that, "for the large majority of men" the "primary determinant" of social class position was their occupational position *and* that occupational position was "affected," in turn, by the social background factors they brought with them when they entered the labor market. Blau and Duncan illustrated the latter contention by means of a "path diagram" – a mode of multivariable statistical analysis their book made famous. In its "basic" form, their model of occupational "attainment" took the shape depicted in Figure 2.1.

---

[62] Morgan, *Five Thousand American Families*. We base our account of the history of the PSID project on Duncan, Hofferth, and Stafford, "Evolution and Change in Family Income."

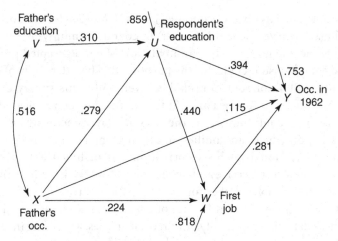

Figure 2.1 Path diagram from Peter Blau and Otis Dudley Duncan's *The American Occupational Structure* (1967), 170.

The upshot of this social mobility model was that a man's occupation in 1962 – the "dependent," or outcome, variable on the right side of the diagram – was determined by a set of "independent" variables (here, the respondent's father's education and occupation), as well as by mediating, or "intervening variables" (here, the respondent's education and first job).[63] Blau and Duncan then elaborated the model by incorporating other variables, including the respondent's race, level of educational attainment, and, significantly, "the structure of [his] family relations" (size of his parental family, marital status, number of children fathered, and so on). In this way, they made the phenomenon of "family" into a nexus of variables that served to transmit the inequalities existing in one generation into inequalities in the next generation.[64] In the spirit of the War on Poverty, Blau and Duncan saw this evidence as promoting the cause of equality of opportunity. For, what their data suggested was that "helping children from large families to obtain a better education would suffice to remove the occupational disadvantages they now tend to experience, [whereas] the compounded handicaps of Negroes ... would have to be attacked on many different levels."[65] (Blau and Duncan did not spell out what this multilevel attack would look like.)

---

[63] Blau and Duncan, *American Occupational Structure*, 5–6, 19, 170–71.
[64] We see the same development in the Coleman Report, as well as in the work of PSID researchers.
[65] Blau and Duncan, *American Occupational Structure*, 442.

The American Occupational Structure provided a flexible template for literally hundreds of subsequent studies of social inequality.[66] In some of these, researchers zeroed in on particular variables (say, family structure) in Blau and Duncan's model and on *their* determinants. In other cases, investigators focused on other outcome variables, substituting educational attainment or income (for example) for occupational position. And in still other instances, researchers examined the direct and indirect effects of additional variables: school characteristics, religious affiliations, measured intelligence, age, mental health and health conditions, subjective aspirations and attitudes, and numerous spousal attributes. Up until the mid-1970s, many of these studies stuck to path-analytic statistical approaches, although these methods were gradually replaced by log-linear regression and survival analysis, which were better suited to the testing of causal hypotheses and the treatment of longitudinal data.[67]

In Blau and Duncan's book and later studies, family-related factors, while ordinarily included at some stage in the statistical analysis, were typically only part of the story of the transmission of social inequalities from one generation to the next – and, in the years ahead, this usually remained their role. That said, many researchers assigned particular importance to family factors, agreeing with sociologist Richard Curtis's view that "households organized as families are essential units in theory on inequality."[68] However, like many other factors in the basic Blau-Duncan model, family-related factors continually gave rise to additional questions that called out for more detailed research to measure the strength and directionality of the relationship between different family attributes and dimensions of social inequality. This research formed a substantial piece of the core of what was then crystalizing as the speciality area of "family demography."[69]

From its outset, this speciality found its academic home base in the cluster of population or demography centers that had been established in our first period. This was so because research of the sort pioneered by Blau and Duncan was "big science"; it made heavy logistical demands that were beyond the capacity of solo family researchers. These demands included managing giant data sets purchased from the Census Bureau and other agencies; conducting large, PSID-like panel studies; maintaining

---

[66] Hout and Janus, "Educational Mobility in the United States," 167–68.
[67] Teachman, Paasch, and Carver, "Thirty Years of *Demography*."
[68] Curtis, "Household and Family in Theory," 168. Jencks et al. presented a more qualified view of the role of the family in their widely debated book, *Inequality*.
[69] Keyfitz, *Applied Mathematical Demography* and Sweet, "Demography and the Family."

state-of-the-art computational facilities; and preparing multi-million dollar grant applications to the federal government and private foundations to cover the expenses of all these things, as well as the salaries of support staff of professionals in nontenured academic positions.[70]

By and large, grants of this type were project grants, attracting the interest of external funders, though only so long as funders' attention held firm. While precarious, this funding situation had the upside of continually enlarging the bounds of family demography, bringing within its jurisdiction one social problem after another, most of which researchers conceptualized as fitting into the larger study of social inequality. Sociologist-demographer Samuel Preston has described the situation:

Research directions in demography are more sensitive to demand for demographic products and less dependent on internally generated pressures than those in other social sciences.... The sensitivity of demography to external priorities [causes the field to be] associated closely with a series of perceived national and international problems. The funding generated by the search for solutions to these problems has attracted many people to the field in 'soft-money' positions.... When funding priorities shift, their own priorities can change.[71]

This is not to say that monies to study certain older topics entirely dried up; throughout this second period, family researchers continued to find support for work on subjects that had interested academics and policymakers during previous periods, including marriage rates, divorce rates, fertility and family planning, family size, husbands' and wives' employment status, and so on. But now sharing the limelight were studies of the causes and effects of problems having to do, too, with new household forms (cohabiting couples, same-sex couples, female-headed households, households with aging relatives), patterns of residential and educational segregation, household financial and social resources (government benefits, child custody payments, savings, inheritances, and the availability of affordable childcare), *and* racial, ethnic, and generational disparities in these patterns.[72]

By the end of the twentieth century, family demographers broadened their reach still further, as illustrated by a major project titled the "Fragile Families & Child Wellbeing Study," which tracked (so far up to the age of 15) 5,000 children, most of them born to unmarried parents between

---

[70] Preston, "Contours of Demography."
[71] Ibid., 595.
[72] As we have already indicated, many of these topics were significant for nondemographers as well.

1998 and 2000. Under the direction of sociologist-demographer Sara McLanahan (from Princeton's OPR) and economist-demographer Irwin Garfinkel (of the Columbia Population Research Center), and supported with grants from the National Science Foundation, the Department of Health and Human Services, the Shriver National Institute of Child Health and Human Development, and over twenty private foundations, the study asked how children born into these "fragile" families fare as they grow up, and how they are affected by government policies. To address these questions, investigators interviewed mothers and fathers (from different socioeconomic backgrounds) to collect data on their demographic characteristics, their employment, educational, health, and incarceration histories, the characteristics of their neighborhoods, their participation in government programs, and their relationships, parenting behaviors, and subjective attitudes. In addition, researchers conducted in-home interviews in order to gather information on children's cognitive and emotional development, mental and physical health, and home environments.[73]

Entering the twenty-first century, family demographers' expansionism continued. Thus, to take one example, the Center for Demography at the University of Wisconsin at Madison, with funding from the Shriver Institute and the National Institute of Aging, designated "family and households" as its top research project, clarifying that label to mean "the study of family and intergenerational factors critical to understanding population health; sociodemographic variation in formation and dissolution of family relationships, social changes contributing to these patterns (e.g., growing socioeconomic inequality); and the role of families in shaping and mitigating social and health inequalities."[74] The chasm between, on the one hand, the multifunctional view of the family represented here, and on the other hand, the dominant prewar view of the family as an institution on the decline – a mere "parking place" – can hardly be overstated. To quote Preston's takeaway from recent work in family demography: "even in counties with the best-developed economies and state bureaucracies, the large majority of adults continue to live in intimate relations with a member of the opposite sex and to bear and raise children," constituting family-like units that still perform "an enormous array of socially vital functions, from socializing children to caring for the elderly to transferring income."[75]

[73] "Fragile Families & Child Wellbeing Study" (website), https://fragilefamilies.princeton.edu.
[74] Center for Demography and Ecology, "Research" (website), https://cde.wisc.edu/research. This website gives "Fertility, Families and Households" as the full title of this project, but then proceeds to omit "fertility" from its description.
[75] Preston, "Contours of Demography," 601.

To investigate the ever-expanding list of subjects that family demographers claimed during our second period, demography centers also expanded their faculty rolls to include scholars from more and more academic disciplines.[76] Within the ranks of its researchers in family demography, an American demography center by century's end contained sociologists, economists, psychologists, anthropologists, and statisticians, plus scholars from departments of human development, public administration and public policy, social work, educational policy, nursing and other health sciences, gerontology, and environmental studies.[77] This multidisciplinary confluence facilitated the transfer of substantive and methodological knowledge across fields. In the typical case, sociologist-demographers constituted a plurality, though rarely a majority, of a demography center's faculty, and in their research on the family they proved receptive to inputs from a variety of disciplines, including economics, from which they drew advanced econometric methods of data analysis.[78]

In this context, family demographers solidified their position as the leading voices in the study of the problems of the family, even in the face of criticisms of their work from scholars outside of demography.[79] Surveying social scientific research on the family in 1988, sociologist Bert Adams observed that "family demography represents the upper end of the status continuum for the family field" and that it was overshadowing – in quantity as well as in standing in the academy and beyond – other studies of the family.[80] By the 1980s, social problem-focused articles by family demographers appeared frequently in top general-interest journals like the *American Journal of Sociology* and the *American Sociological Review*. Likewise, in the period between 1987 and 1992, the leading demography journal, *Demography*, saw a 14 percent rise in articles in the area (the largest increase for any area), at the same time as articles on fertility

---

[76] House, "Social Psychology, Social Science," 246–48 and Preston, "Contours of Demography," 601–3.
[77] We base this statement on our examination of the websites of all the major demography centers in the United States as of December 2018.
[78] Demography centers were not the only place where social scientists from different disciplines encountered one another's views. Local and national funding panels were another.
[79] Critics faulted (though not always fairly) studies in family demography for being too individualistic and decontextualized, among other flaws. By the end of our second period, demographers were attempting to address these critiques. Preston, "Contours of Demography," 598–99.
[80] Adams, "Fifty Years of Family Research," 12.

and contraception dropped 12 percent.[81] When the multidisciplinary
International Encyclopedia of the Social and Behavior Sciences appeared in
2001, summarizing scholarship during the previous quarter century, ten
of its thirteen entries on the family – including those on "Family Theory"
and "Family as Institution" – were written by researchers in demography
concerned with aspects of the problem of social inequality.[82]

So entrenched was the approach of family demographers, in fact, that it
was barely affected by the appearance of what future intellectual historians
are likely to regard as the most intellectually innovative contribution to the
study of the family during this second period. This was the development
of what is now usually referred to as the "economics of the family," an
approach that emerged in the mid-1970s in the work of two future Nobelists
in economics from the University of Chicago, Theodore W. Schultz and Gary
S. Becker – the guiding lights of what proponents of the approach initially
called the "new home economics."[83] (The label later gave way to variants of
the "Chicago School of family economics.") As formulated particularly in
Becker's *A Treatise on the Family* (1981), the approach stretched the tenets
of mainstream economics beyond the marketplace by theorizing family
behaviors as "active choices by maximizing agents" – i.e., preference-bearing
individuals engaged in rational decision-making in the face of "incentives"
and given "constraints."[84] Becker mostly carried out this theorizing in
abstract terms (often using mathematical formulas); his primary focus was
not on empirical data, but on recasting neoclassical principles formally and
then systematically deriving from them corollaries that pertained to the
family – and that might, going forward, be tested empirically.

The antecedents of this approach went back to our first period, when
Schultz and Becker were both focused on questions of international
economic growth and family size. In a 1960 volume *Demographic and
Economic Change in Developed Countries*, for instance, Becker argued that
"student[s] of consumption economics need to pay more attention to the
determinants of family size than they have in the past." Following his own

[81] Teachman, Paasch, and Carver, "Thirty Years of *Demography*," 529.
[82] Smelser and Bates, *International Encyclopedia of the Social & Behavioral Sciences.*
[83] Schultz, *Economics of the Family.* On the shifting labels, see Willis, "What Have We
Learned from the Economics of the Family?" 70–72. The approach had no connection
to the earlier Chicago School of sociology. Proponents initially spoke of the *new* home
economics to distinguish their work from the "home economics" that appeared during
the prewar period.
[84] Becker, *Treatise on the Family.* Quoting Willis, "What Have We Learned from the
Economics of the Family?" 76.

advice, he then laid out an "economic analysis of fertility" that described the problem of "family size" in terms of cost-benefit decisions having to do with prospective parents' "demand for children" in relation to the cost of children as a "consumer durables."[85] In the course of the next decade, partly in connection with his book *Human Capital* (1964), Becker elaborated this theory until it included decisions not only about family size, but also about marriage, divorce, the household division of labor, women's participation in the labor force, and parents' "altruistic" investment of their resources in the human capital of their children.[86]

Embracing Becker's work as a successful exercise of "economic imperialism" – a triumphant move to capture "areas traditionally deemed to be outside the realm of economic theory" – many economists followed its example, publishing dozens of rational-choice studies of the family-associated topics like those Becker wrote about.[87] Amplifying this development was the fact that, in accord with the neoliberal policy orientation of the Reagan–Bush presidencies, economists took hold of more academic bases and became even more of a force than previously in shaping national economic policy. Still further, economists' policy attitudes at this point trended strongly in a free market direction and away from the state-interventionist programs of family researchers going back to beginnings of the social sciences in the United States.[88] Becker's views were part of this newer trend, as he made explicit: "A progressive system of government redistribution is usually said to narrow the inequality in disposable income" across families, but such a system "may well widen the inequality ... because parents are discouraged from investing in their children by lower after-tax rates of return." Indeed, for Becker and his disciples, many of the family issues on the nation's agenda were less "social problems" – as they

[85] Becker, "Economic Analysis of Fertility."
[86] Becker, *Treatise on the Family*; Becker, *Human Capital*; Becker, "Theory of Social Interactions"; and Becker, "Altruism in the Family." On the background and implications of Becker's notion of altruism, see Fontaine, "From Philanthropy to Altruism" and Fontaine, "Beyond Altruism?"
[87] We take "economic imperialism" from Edward Lazear, who writes: "modern economic imperialism's birth is due primarily to Gary Becker." Lazear, "Economic Imperialism," 104n7. In addition to Lazear, we draw on the following accounts of Becker's influence on economists' research on the family: Bergstrom, "Economics in a Family Way"; Pollack, "Gary Becker's Contributions to Family and Household Economics"; Sawhill, "Economic Perspectives on the Family"; and Willis, "What Have We Learned from the Economics of the Family?" On Schultz's influence, see Bowman, "On Theodore W. Schultz's Contributions to Economics."
[88] Bernstein, *Perilous Progress*; House, "Social Psychology, Social Science"; and O'Connor, *Poverty Knowledge*.

had been throughout the twentieth century – than results of individual choices. But we should be careful of overstatement here; for even at the height of Beckerism during this second period, there were still plenty of economists (and economist-demographers) who rejected, in part or all, this conservative policy stance and its accompanying conception of the family.[89] The same was true outside of economics, where reactions to Becker's theory of the family were even more mixed. (Imperialism tends to be unpopular among peoples threatened with subjugation.) To cite a single example: The 2014 *Wiley Blackwell Companion to the Sociology of Families*, a multi-authored 27-chapter, 560-page digest of family research from recent decades, contained only *two* citations to Becker.[90] Elsewhere, Becker's theories fared better, in the sense that they appeared, with modest frequency, in research on subjects such as divorce and women's labor force participation. These appearances were especially visible in studies by family demographers, who could scarcely neglect the microeconomics of the family as they worked side-by-side with economists at population centers. Of the approximately 700 articles published in *Demography* in the 20 years after the *Treatise* was published, 56 (roughly 8 percent) cited the book, decoratively in some cases, more substantively in others.[91] In many of the latter instances, authors used Becker's theory to derive specific hypotheses that they then juxtaposed with alternative hypotheses in order to conduct empirical tests of competing explanations for family-related phenomena, tests that sometimes confirmed Becker's views, but most times did not.[92] And it was in this manner, too, that social scientists, in and out of family demography, generally responded to all of Becker's work: welcoming it as a go-to source of testable hypotheses that were easier to specify than those drawn from the less formal scholarship of other social scientists, but greeting his economic imperialism otherwise with deep skepticism.[93]

Be this as it may, there is little evidence that the new microeconomics of the family prompted much social scientific rethinking, either during our

[89] Becker, *Treatise on the Family*, 213. On the policy views of other economists, see Haveman, "New Policy for the New Poverty."
[90] Treas, Scott, and Richards, *Wiley Blackwell Companion*.
[91] We base these numbers on our own JSTOR research, May 25, 2019.
[92] Illustrative of this practice is the work of leading family sociologist-demographer Sara McLanahan (and her collaborators); see McLanahan and Bumpass, "Intergenerational Consequences of Family Disruption"; McLanahan and Casper, "Growing Diversity and Inequality"; McLanahan and Percheski, "Family Structure and the Reproduction of Inequalities"; and McLanahan and Sandefur, *Growing Up with a Single Parent*.
[93] For one of many examples, see England and Budig, "Gary Becker and the Family," 102.

second period or since, of the conviction that the overarching problem of the family lay in perpetuating social inequalities. For his part, Becker, aware of Blau and Duncan's work, retorted with a short chapter in his *Treatise* on "Inequality and Intergenerational Mobility," which minimized the role of the family in the reproduction of inequality – consistent with his claim in *Human Capital* that "although earnings of parents and children are positively related, the relation is not strong."[94] Few scholars concerned with the family were satisfied with this view. Sociologist Michael Hannan described Becker's analysis of "the heritability of parental advantage … the least convincing of the theories in the treatise," while the eminent economist Arthur Goldberger deemed Becker's account as inferior to that of family demographers, who formed "the main line of sociological research on family background and socioeconomic achievement." In Goldberger's assessment, Becker's microeconomic approach risked seriously "understat[ing] the influence of family background on inequality."[95] With that overhanging problem, however, social scientists were not about to quit and move on, as they had at earlier points in the twentieth century. As our second period ended, there was yet on the horizon no family problem so pervasive, or so consuming of social scientific attention, as the family's role in transmitting social inequalities from generation to generation.

Bibliography

Abbott, Andrew. *Department and Discipline: Chicago Sociology at One Hundred.* Chicago: University of Chicago Press, 1999.

Adams, Bert N. "Fifty Years of Family Research: What Does It Mean?" *Journal of Marriage and Family* 50, no. 1 (1988): 5–17.

Adorno, Theodor W., Else Frenkel-Brunswik, Daniel J. Levinson, and R. Nevitt Sanford. *The Authoritarian Personality.* New York: Harper & Row, 1950.

Angell, Robert C. *The Family Encounters the Depression.* New York: Charles Scribner's Sons, 1936.

Balasubramanian, Savina. "Communicating Contraception: Social Science and the Politics of Population Control in Cold War India." PhD diss., Northwestern University, 2018.

Barber, William J. *From New Era to New Deal: Herbert Hoover, the Economists, and American Economic Policy, 1933–1945.* Cambridge: Cambridge University Press, 1985.

Bashford, Alison. *Global Population: History, Geopolitics, and Life on Earth.* New York: Columbia University Press, 2014.

[94] Becker, *Treatise on the Family*, 201–32 and Becker, *Human Capital*, 21.
[95] Hannan, "Families, Markets, and Social Structures," 68 and Goldberger, "Economic and Mechanical Models," 513.

Becker, Gary S. "An Economic Analysis of Fertility." In *Demographic and Economic Change in Developed Countries*, 209–40. New York: Columbia University Press, 1960. https://www.nber.org/chapters/c2378.pdf

Becker, Gary S. "A Theory of Social Interactions." *Journal of Political Economy* 82, no. 6 (1974): 1063–93.

Becker, Gary S. "Altruism in the Family and Selfishness in the Market Place." *Economica* 48, no. 189 (1981): 1–15.

Becker, Gary S. *A Treatise on the Family*. Enlarged ed. Chicago: University of Chicago Press, 1991. First published 1981.

Becker, Gary S. *Human Capital: A Theoretical and Empirical Analysis with Special Reference Education*. 3rd ed. Chicago: University of Chicago Press, 1993. First published 1964.

Bendix, Reinhard, and Seymour Martin Lipset, eds. *Class, Status, and Power: A Reader in Social Stratification*. New York: Free Press, 1957.

Bergstrom, Theodore C. "Economics in a Family Way." *Journal of Economic Literature* 34, no. 4 (1996): 1903–34.

Bernard, Jessie. *The Future of Marriage*. New Haven: Yale University Press, 1982.

Bernstein, Michael A. *A Perilous Progress: Economists and Public Purpose in Twentieth Century America*. Princeton: Princeton University Press, 2001.

Blau, Peter M., and Otis Dudley Duncan. *The American Occupational Structure*. New York: Free Press, 1967.

Bowman, Mary Jean. "On Theodore W. Schultz's Contributions to Economics." *Scandinavian Journal of Economics* 82, no. 1 (1980): 80–107.

Broderick, Carlfred B. "To Arrive Where We Started: The Field of Family Studies in the 1930s." *Journal of Marriage and Family* 50, no. 3 (1988): 569–84.

Bulmer, Martin. *The Chicago School of Sociology*. Chicago: University of Chicago Press, 1984.

Burgess, Ernest W. "The Family as a Unity of Interacting Personalities." *The Family* 7 (1926): 3–9.

Burgess, Ernest W. "Foreword." In *Family Disorganization*, edited by Ernest Mowrer, vii–xi. Chicago: University of Chicago Press, 1927.

Caldwell, J. C. "Demography and Social Science." *Population Studies* 50, no. 3 (1996): 305–33.

Camic, Charles. "On Edge: Sociology during the Great Depression and the New Deal." In *Sociology in America: A History*, edited by Craig Calhoun, 225–80. Chicago: University of Chicago Press, 2007.

Cavan, Ruth Shonle, and Katherine Howland Ranck. *The Family and the Depression*. Chicago: University of Chicago Press, 1938.

Center for Demography and Ecology. "Research." Accessed December 9, 2018. https://cde.wisc.edu/research

Coale, Ansley, and Edgar M. Hoover. *Population Growth and Economic Development in Low-Income Countries: A Case Study of India's Prospects*. Princeton: Princeton University Press, 1958.

Coleman, James, Ernest Q. Campbell, Carol J. Hobson, et al. *Equality of Educational Opportunity*. Washington, DC: Department of Health, Education, and Welfare, 1966.

Collins, Robert M. *More: The Politics of Economic Growth in Postwar America*. Oxford: Oxford University Press, 2000.

Connelly, Matthew. *Fatal Misconception: The Struggle to Control World Population.* Cambridge: The Belknap Press of Harvard University Press, 2008.

Cottrell, Leonard S., Jr. "The Present Status and Future Orientation of Research on the Family." *American Sociological Review* 13, no. 2 (1948): 123–36.

Crimmins, Eileen M. "Demography: The Past 30 Years, the Present, and the Future." *Demography* 30, no. 4 (1993): 579–91.

Curtis, Richard F. "Household and Family in Theory on Inequality." *American Sociological Review* 51, no. 2 (1986): 168–83.

Davis, Kingsley. "Demographic Fact and Policy in India." In *Demographic Studies of Selected Areas of Rapid Growth*, 35–57. New York: Milbank Memorial Fund, 1944.

Davis, Kingsley. "The World Demographic Transition." *Annals of the American Academy of Political and Social Science* 237, no. 1 (1945): 1–11.

Davis, Kingsley. *The Population of India and Pakistan.* Princeton: Princeton University Press, 1951.

Dealey, James Quayle. *The Family in Its Sociological Aspects.* New York: Houghton Mifflin, 1912.

Drake, St. Clair, and Horace Cayton. *Black Metropolis: A Study of Negro Life in a Northern City.* Chicago: University of Chicago Press, 1945.

Du Bois, W. E. B. *The Philadelphia Negro.* New York: Oxford University Press, 2007. First published 1899 by University of Pennsylvania Press (Philadelphia).

Duijker, Hubertus Carl Johannes, and Nico H. Frijda. *National Character and National Stereotypes.* Amsterdam: North-Holland, 1960.

Duncan, Greg J., Sandra L. Hofferth, and Frank P. Stafford. "Evolution and Change in Family Income, Wealth, and Health: The Panel Study of Income Dynamics, 1968–2000 and Beyond." In *A Telescope on Society: Survey Research & Social Science at the University of Michigan & Beyond*, edited by James S. House, F. Thomas Juster, Robert L. Kahn, Howard Schuman, and Eleanor Singer, 156–93. Ann Arbor: University of Michigan Press, 2004.

Ehrlich, Paul R. *The Population Bomb.* New York: Buccaneer Books, 1968.

Ellwood, Charles. *Sociology and Modern Social Problems.* New York: American Book Company, 1910.

Engerman, David C. *The Price of Aid: The Economic Cold War in India.* Cambridge: Harvard University Press, 2018.

England, Paula, and Michelle J. Budig. "Gary Becker and the Family." In *Required Reading: Sociology's Most Influential Books*, edited by Dan Clawson, 95–111. Amherst: University of Massachusetts Press, 1998.

Enke, Stephen. "The Economic Aspects of Slowing Population Growth." *Economic Journal* 76, no. 301 (1966): 44–56.

Enke, Stephen. "Birth Control for Economic Development." *Science* 164, no. 388 (1968): 798–802.

Fitzpatrick, Ellen. *Endless Crusade: Women Social Scientists and Progressive Reform.* New York: Oxford University Press, 1990.

Folsom, Joseph K. "Report of Committee on Marriage and Family Research." *Living* 2, no. 2 (1940): 53–54.

Fontaine, Philippe. "From Philanthropy to Altruism: Incorporating Unselfish Behavior into Economics, 1961–1974." *History of Political Economy* 39, no. 1 (2007): 1–46.

Fontaine, Philippe. "Beyond Altruism? Economics and the Minimization of Unselfish Behavior, 1975–1993." *History of Political Economy* 44, no. 2 (2012): 195–233.

"Fragile Families & Child Wellbeing Study." Accessed May 24, 2019. https://fragilefamilies.princeton.edu

Frank, Lawrence K. "Social Change and the Family." *Annals of the American Academy of Political and Social Science* 160 (March 1932): 94–102.

Frazier, E. Franklin. *The Negro Family in the United States.* Chicago: University of Chicago Press, 1939.

Furstenberg, Frank F. "The Making of the Black Family: Race and Class in Qualitative Studies in the Twentieth Century." *Annual Review of Sociology* 33 (2007): 429–48.

Geiger, H. Kent. *The Family in Soviet Russia.* Cambridge: Harvard University Press, 1968.

Gerschenkron, Alexander. *Economic Backwardness in Historical Perspective: A Book of Essays.* Cambridge: Belknap Press of Harvard University Press, 1962.

Gilman, Nils. *Mandarins of the Future: Modernization Theory in Cold War America.* Baltimore: Johns Hopkins University Press, 2004.

Glander, Timothy. *Origins of Mass Communications Research in the American Cold War: Educational Effects and Contemporary Implications.* Mahwah: Lawrence Erlbaum Associates, 2000.

Glick, Paul C. "Fifty Years of Family Demography." *Journal of Marriage and Family* 50, no. 4 (1988): 861–73.

Goldberger, Arthur S. "Economic and Mechanical Models of Intergenerational Transmission." *American Economic Review* 79, no. 3 (1989): 504–13.

Goode, William J. *World Revolution and Family Patterns.* Glencoe: Free Press, 1963.

Greenhalgh, Susan. "The Social Construction of Population Science: An Intellectual, Institutional, and Political History of Twentieth-Century Demography." *Comparative Studies in Society and History* 38, no. 1 (1996): 26–66.

Groves, Ernest R. *Social Problems of the Family.* Philadelphia: Lippincott, 1927.

Halfon, Saul. *The Cairo Consensus: Demographic Surveys, Women's Empowerment, and Regime Change in Population Policy.* Lanham: Rowman and Littlefield, 2006.

Hannan, Michael T. "Families, Markets, and Social Structures." *Journal of Economic Literature* 20, no. 1 (1982): 65–72.

Hannerz, Ulf. *Soulside: Inquiries into Ghetto Culture and Community.* New York: Columbia University Press, 1969.

Hart, Hornell. "Trends of Change in Textbooks on the Family." *American Journal of Sociology* 39, no. 2 (1933): 222–30.

Hauser, Philip M. "Population and Vital Phenomena." *American Journal of Sociology* 48 (1942): 309–22.

Hauser, Philip M. "Wartime Development in Census Statistics." *American Sociological Review* 10 (1945): 160–69.

Haveman, Robert H. "New Policy for the New Poverty." *Challenge* 31 (1988): 27–36.

Hill, Reuben. "The American Family: Problem or Solution?" *American Journal of Sociology* 53, no. 2 (1947): 125–30.

Hirschman, Daniel. "Inventing the Economy, Or: How We Learned to Stop Worrying and Love the GDP." PhD diss., University of Michigan, 2016.

Hochschild, Arlie Russell. *The Second Shift: Working Parents and the Revolution at Home.* New York: Viking, 1989.

Hodgson, Dennis. "Demography as Social Science and Policy Science." *Population and Development Review* 9, no. 1 (1983): 1–34.

Hodgson, Dennis. "Demography: Twentieth-Century History." In *International Encyclopedia of the Social and Behavioral Sciences*, edited by Neil J. Smelser and Paul Bates, vol. 5, 3493–98. Amsterdam: Elsevier, 2001.

Horkheimer, Max, ed. *Studien über Autorität und Familie*. Paris: Felix Alcan, 1936.

House, James S. "Social Psychology, Social Science, and Economics." *Social Psychology Quarterly* 71, no. 3 (2008): 232–56.

Hout, Michael, and Alexander Janus. "Educational Mobility in the United States since the 1930s." In *Whither Opportunity: Rising Inequality, Schools, and Children's Life Chances*, edited by Greg J. Duncan and Richard J. Murname, 165–86. New York: Russell Sage Foundation, 2011.

Immerwahr, Daniel. *Thinking Small: The United States and the Lure of Community Development*. Cambridge: Harvard University Press, 2015.

International Planned Parenthood Federation. *The Sixth International Conference on Planned Parenthood: Report of the Proceedings, 14–21 February 1959*. London: International Planned Parenthood Federation, 1959.

Jencks, Christopher, Marshall Smith, Henry Acland, et al. *Inequality: A Reassessment of the Effect of Family and Schooling in America*. New York, Basic Books, 1972.

Kahl, Joseph. *The Measurement of Modernism*. Austin: University of Texas Press, 1968.

Kennedy, David M. *Freedom from Fear: The American People in the Depression and War, 1929–1945*. New York: Oxford University Press, 1999.

Keyfitz, Nathan. *Applied Mathematical Demography*. New York: John Wiley & Sons, 1977.

Komarovsky, Mirra, and Willard Waller. "Studies of the Family." *American Journal of Sociology* 50, no. 6, (1945): 443–51.

Kyrk, Hazel. *A Theory of Consumption*. Boston: Houghton Mifflin, 1923.

Kyrk, Hazel. *Economic Problems of the Family*. New York: Harper, 1933.

Larson, Olaf F., and Julie N. Zimmerman. *Sociology in Government*. University Park: Pennsylvania State University Press, 2003.

Lasch, Christopher. *Haven in a Heartless World: The Family Besieged*. New York: Norton, 1977.

Latham, Michael E. *Modernization as Ideology: American Social Science and "Nation-Building" in the Kennedy Era*. Chapel Hill: University of North Carolina Press, 2003.

Latham, Michael E. *The Right Kind of Revolution: Modernization, Development, and U.S. Foreign Policy from the Cold War to the Present*. Ithaca: Cornell University Press, 2010.

Lazear, Edward. "Economic Imperialism." *Quarterly Journal of Economics* 115, no. 1 (2000): 99–146.

Lerner, Daniel. *The Passing of Traditional Society: Modernizing the Middle East*. Glencoe: Free Press, 1958.

Levy, Marion. *Modernization and the Structure of Societies*. Princeton: Princeton University Press, 1966.

Lewis, Hylan. *Blackways of Kent*. Chapel Hill: University of North Carolina Press, 1955.

Liebow, Elliot. *Tally's Corner*. Boston: Little, Brown, 1967.

Locke, Harvey J. "Mobility and Family Disorganization." *American Sociological Review* 5, no. 4 (1940): 489–94.

Lynd, Robert S., and Helen Merrill Lynd. *Middletown: A Study in American Culture.* New York: Harcourt, Brace, 1929.

Lynd, Robert S., and Helen Merrill Lynd. *Middletown in Transition: A Study in Cultural Conflicts.* New York: Harcourt, Brace, 1937.

MacRae, Duncan, Jr. "Review Essay: The Sociological Economics of Gary S. Becker." *American Journal of Sociology* 83, no. 5 (1978): 1244–58.

McCann, Carole R. *Figuring the Population Bomb: Gender and Demography in the Mid-Twentieth Century.* Seattle: University of Washington Press, 2016.

McLanahan, Sara, and Larry Bumpass. "Intergenerational Consequences of Family Disruption." *American Journal of Sociology* 94, no. 1 (1988): 130–52.

McLanahan, Sara, and Lynne M. Casper. "Growing Diversity and Inequality in the American Family." In *State of the Union: America in the 1990s,* edited by Reynolds Farley, vol. 2, 1–46. New York: Russell Sage Foundation, 1995.

McLanahan, Sara, and Christine Percheski. "Family Structure and the Reproduction of Inequalities." *Annual Review of Sociology* 34 (2008): 257–76.

McLanahan, Sara, and Gary Sandefur. *Growing Up with a Single Parent: What Hurts, What Helps.* Cambridge: Harvard University Press, 1994.

Merchant, Emily K. "Prediction and Control: Global Population, Population Science, and Population Politics in the Twentieth Century." PhD diss., University of Michigan, 2015.

Morgan, James. N. *Five Thousand American Families: Patterns of Economic Progress.* Vol. 1. Ann Arbor: Institute for Social Research, University of Michigan, 1974.

Morgan, Winona Louise. *The Family Meets the Depression.* Minneapolis: University of Minnesota Press, 1939.

Mowrer, Ernest R. *Family Disorganization: An Introduction to Sociological Analysis.* Chicago: University of Chicago Press, 1927.

Moynihan, Daniel P. *The Negro Family: The Case for National Action.* Washington, DC: US Department of Labor, 1965.

Murphy, Michelle. *The Economization of Life.* Durham: Duke University Press, 2017.

Myrdal, Gunnar. *An American Dilemma.* New York: Harper & Row, 1944.

Niemi, Richard, and Barbara I. Sobieszek. "Political Socialization." *Annual Review of Sociology* 3 (1977): 209–33.

Notestein, Frank. "Summary of the Demographic Background of Problems of Underdeveloped Areas." *Milbank Memorial Fund Quarterly* 26, no. 3 (1948): 249–55.

Notestein, Frank. "Economic Problems of Population Change." In *Proceedings of the Eighth International Conference of Agricultural Economists,* 3–31. New York: Oxford University Press, 1953.

Nye, F. Ivan. "Fifty Years of Family Research, 1937–1987." *Journal of Marriage and Family* 50, no. 2 (1988): 305–16.

O'Connor, Alice. *Poverty Knowledge: Social Science, Social Policy, and the Poor in Twentieth Century U.S. History.* Princeton: Princeton University Press, 2001.

Ogburn, William F., with the assistance of Clark Tibbitts. "The Family and Its Functions." In *Recent Social Trends in the United States,* vol. 1, 661–708. New York: McGraw-Hill, 1933.

Park, Robert E., and Ernest W. Burgess. *Introduction to the Science of Sociology.* Chicago: University of Chicago Press, 1921.

Parry, Manon. *Broadcasting Birth Control: Mass Media and Family Planning.* New Brunswick: Rutgers University Press, 2013.

Parsons, Talcott. *Essays in Sociological Theory.* New York: Free Press, 1949.
Parsons, Talcott and Robert F. Bales. *Family, Socialization and Interaction Process.* Glencoe: Free Press, 1955.
Pollack, Robert A. "Gary Becker's Contributions to Family and Household Economics." *Review of Economics of the Household* 1, no. 1–2 (2003): 111–41.
Pooley, Jefferson. "From Psychological Warfare to Social Justice: Shifts in Foundation Support for Communication Research." In *Media and Social Justice*, edited by Sue Curry Jansen, Jefferson Pooley, and Lora Taub-Pervizpour, 211–40. New York: Palgrave Macmillan, 2011.
President's Research Committee on Social Trends. "A Review of Findings by the President's Research Committee on Social Trends." In *Recent Social Trends in the United States*, vol. 1, xi–xxiii. New York: McGraw-Hill, 1933.
Preston, Samuel H. "The Contours of Demography: Estimates and Projections." *Demography* 30, no. 4 (1993): 593–606.
Reid, Margaret Galpin. *The Economics of Household Production.* New York: John Wiley, 1934.
Rosier, Martin, and Carla Willig. "The Strange Death of the Authoritarian Personality." *History of the Human Sciences* 15, no. 4 (2002): 71–96.
Rostow, W. W. *The Stages of Economic Growth: A Non-Communist Manifesto.* Cambridge: Cambridge University Press, 1964.
Ryder, Norman B. "Comment." In *Economics of the Family: Marriage, Children, and Human Capital*, edited by Theodore W. Schultz, 76–80. Chicago: University of Chicago Press, 1973.
Sabin, Paul. *The Bet: Paul Ehrlich, Julian Simon, Our Gamble Over Earth's Future.* New Haven: Yale University Press, 2014.
Sampson, Robert J., and W. Byron Groves. "Community Structure and Crime: Testing Social Disorganization Theory." *American Journal of Sociology* 94, no. 4 (1989): 774–802.
Sawhill, Isabel V. "Economic Perspectives on the Family." *Daedalus* 106, no. 2 (1977): 115–25.
Sayre, Paul. "The Work of the National Conference on Family Relations." *Living* 1, no. 2–3 (1939): 49–50.
Schultz, Theodore W., ed. *Economics of the Family: Marriage, Children, and Human Capital.* Chicago: University of Chicago Press, 1973.
Self, Robert O. *All in the Family: The Realignment of American Democracy Since the 1960s.* New York: Hill and Wang, 2012.
Sharpless, John. "World Population Growth, Family Planning, and American Foreign Policy." *Journal of Policy History* 7, no. 1 (1995): 72–102.
Sharpless, John. "Population Science, Private Foundations, and Development Aid: The Transformation of Demographic Knowledge in the United States, 1945–1965." In *International Development and the Social Sciences: Essays on the History and Politics of Knowledge*, edited by Frederick Cooper and Randall Packard, 176–202. Berkeley: University of California Press, 1997.
Small, Albion, and George Vincent. *An Introduction to the Study of Society.* New York: American Book Company, 1894.
Smelser, Neil J., and Paul Bates, eds. *International Encyclopedia of the Social & Behavioral Sciences.* Amsterdam: Elsevier, 2001.
Sprey, Jetse. "Family Disorganization: Toward a Conceptual Clarification." *Journal of Marriage and Family* 28, no. 4 (1966): 398–406.

Stouffer, Samuel A., Edward A. Suchman, Leland C. Devinney, et al. *The American Soldier*. 2 vols. Princeton: Princeton University Press, 1949.

Stycos, J. Mayone. "Introduction." In *Demography as an Interdiscipline*, edited by J. Mayone Stycos, vii–ix. New Brunswick: Transaction Publishers, 1989.

Stycos, J. Mayone, and Kurt W. Back. *The Family and Population Control: A Puerto Rican Experiment in Social Change*. Chapel Hill: University of North Carolina Press, 1959.

Sweet, James A. "Demography and the Family." *Annual Review of Sociology* 3 (1977): 363–405.

Taeuber, Conrad, and Rachel Rowe. *Five Hundred Families Rehabilitate Themselves*. Washington, DC: US Department of Agriculture, 1941.

Taeuber, Irene. "Population Studies in the United States." *Population Index* 12, no. 4 (1946): 254–69.

Takeshita, Chikako. *The Global Biopolitics of the IUD: How Science Constructs Contraceptive Users and Women's Bodies*. Cambridge: MIT Press, 2011.

Teachman, Jay D., Kathleen Paasch, and Karen Price Carver. "Thirty Years of Demography." *Demography* 30, no. 4 (1993): 523–32.

Thompson, Warren. "Population." *American Journal of Sociology* 34, no. 1 (1929): 959–75.

Treas, Judith, Jacqueline Scott, and Martin Richards, eds. *The Wiley Blackwell Companion to the Sociology of Families*. West Sussex: Wiley, 2014.

Vogel, Ezra F. *Japan's New Middle Class: The Salary Man and His Family in a Tokyo Suburb*. Berkeley: University of California Press, 1963.

Waller, Willard, Sidney E. Goldstein, and Lawrence K. Frank. "The Family and National Defense." *Marriage and Family Living* 3, no. 1 (1941): 1–3.

Warner, W. Lloyd. "Social Anthropology and the Modern Community." *American Journal of Sociology* 46, no. 6 (1941): 785–96.

Warner, W. Lloyd, and Paul S. Lunt. *The Social Life of a Modern Community*. New Haven: Yale University Press, 1941.

Warner, W. Lloyd, and Paul S. Lunt. *The Status System of a Modern Community*. New Haven: Yale University Press, 1942.

Weeks, John R. "The Early Years of the PAA." Population Association of America. www.populationassociation.org/about/history-of-paa. Accessed July 28, 2020.

Weitzman, Lenore J. *The Divorce Revolution*. New York: Collier Macmillan, 1985.

Willekens, Frans, and Evert van Imhoff. "Families and Households, Formal Demography of." In *International Encyclopedia of the Social and Behavioral Sciences*, edited by Neil J. Smelser and Paul Bates, vol. 7, 5271–75. Amsterdam: Elsevier, 2001.

Willis, Robert J. "What Have We Learned from the Economics of the Family?" *American Economic Review* 77, no. 2 (1987): 68–81.

Yang, C. K. *The Chinese Family in the Communist Revolution*. Cambridge: Massachusetts Institute of Technology Press, 1954.

Yarrow, Andrew L. *Measuring America: How Economic Growth Came to Define American Greatness in the Late Twentieth Century*. Amherst: University of Massachusetts Press, 2010.

Zigler, Edward. "Social Class and the Socialization Process." *Review of Educational Research* 40, no. 1 (1970): 87–110.

Zimmerman, Carle C. "Types of Families-Communist, Fascist, Democratic." *Living* 2, no. 1 (1940): 12–15.

3

Education

Andrew Jewett

Unlike crime, drug abuse, or war, education is not in itself a phenomenon that social scientists have aimed to eliminate, minimize, or contain. Like the family, rather, it is an institution that social scientists and other commentators have defined as problematic or unproblematic according to numerous (and often competing) criteria. Moreover, US social scientists, like Americans in general, have also viewed education as a crucial means of addressing other social problems. Most importantly, they have emphasized education's potential to create a common, democratic culture and to foster vocational success, thereby ensuring social mobility. Such lofty expectations have produced an enormous ideological investment in schooling, across virtually all levels of American society.

Education has also been distinctive in policy terms. As in other areas central to nineteenth-century social life, such as agriculture and Native American policy, the US state built up significant bureaucratic capacities long before the New Deal created a welfare state in the 1930s. Unusually, however, the federal government held almost none of that power. Although the prospect of federal aid for education drew widespread support through the twentieth century, conflicts over whether the Constitution allowed funding for Catholic schools blocked any movement on that front until the 1960s. Thus, while the United States had a strong capacity to educate students, funding, decision-making, and administration remained highly decentralized. Individual states set budgets and possessed other broad powers, but real discretion lay with school boards and superintendents in the many thousands of local districts scattered across the country. Thus, education was neither a domain that the growing federal state addressed for the first time in the 1930s nor a function that federal officials took over from localities and religious charities during that era.

Finally, social-scientific research on education has been unusual in structural, institutional terms as well. Like other applied areas that became coded feminine by the twentieth century – social work being a primary example – education was a low-status domain that many scholars avoided. By World War I, moreover, a discrete field of educational research, housed in professional schools of education, had emerged, creating a strong institutional boundary that has varied over time in its intellectual porosity. Educational researchers have always learned from mainstream social scientists and have often been trained by them. But their distinctive concerns have also led them to emphasize concepts and theories lying outside the main currents of social-scientific thought. Meanwhile, social scientists have dipped selectively into educational research, sometimes interacting closely with its practitioners, theories, and problems but often keeping the field at arm's length. Indeed, the existence of separate programs for the study of education has allowed mainstream social scientists to distance themselves from an institution that has long served as a lightning rod for ideological criticism in American public life.

When social-scientific research on education has nonetheless emerged, however, it has resembled work on other social problems in important ways. As elsewhere, research interests in the field have strongly tracked shifts in national politics and the policy environment. The post–World War II period brought a campaign to foster social adjustment through education, although that impulse also provoked fears of excessive conformity and a loss of individual autonomy. By the late 1950s, the black freedom movement and battles over *Brown* v. *Board of Education*'s injunction to desegregate public schools directed attention to racial inequalities in education (see Chapter 5: Discrimination). The "urban crisis" of the 1960s deepened a nascent pattern of convergence and collaboration between social scientists and educational researchers, who increasingly joined forces to explore how schooling perpetuated – and perhaps could mitigate – urban poverty (see Chapter 6: The Black Ghetto). But with the rightward shift in American politics during the 1970s and 1980s, mainstream social scientists distanced themselves once again from educational problems and educational researchers.

Throughout much of this period, and indeed up to our own day, widespread perceptions of a national educational crisis heightened the perceived stakes of social-scientific research on kindergarten to twelfth grade (ages five to eighteen) and higher education. Since the 1950s, conservatives and some groups of liberals have argued that the American educational system fails to give students basic competence, let alone excellence, in traditional academic fields. Many, especially since the 1960s, have also charged that the schools and colleges serve as breeding grounds for radicalism. Among left-leaning scholars, however, a very different crisis narrative has prevailed since the 1960s: that the schools systematically consign poor and minority children to socioeconomic disadvantage. These competing discourses of crisis have identified education as a social problem in its own right, though one that is inseparable from other social problems.

By the 1980s, the perception of a crisis centered on inadequate academic preparation had come to dominate the national policy conversation, even when questions of access and equity arose as well. To the extent that policy experts have drawn on social science since the 1980s, they have mainly looked to psychological theories about students' cognitive development and economists' portraits of education as a form of "human capital" in which investment could boost the country's economic standing. Such work is hardly confined to the mainstream disciplines; many educational researchers till these fields as well. Conversely, social scientists often join educational researchers in decrying urban poverty and beating the drum for social justice. Yet, a combination of historical legacies and elite academia's persistent discomfort with applied work and vocational training have given the education schools a reputation for shoddy, politically driven scholarship, at a time when national leaders stress the need for academic excellence in the context of global economic competition.[1] Many critics, in fact, see education schools as a key contributor to education's status as a social problem.

3.1 Interwar Precedents

In the United States, both the social sciences and the educational system took their familiar shapes in the late nineteenth and early twentieth centuries, in conjunction with the broad reform impulse known as Progressivism. In an important sense, the whole project of social science constituted a vast educative endeavor in those years. Increasingly rejecting economic and biological explanations, practitioners identified what anthropologists came to call "culture" as the source of human behavior. These social scientists aimed to change American culture so that citizens would support progressive social and political reforms in response to industrialization and corporate consolidation.[2]

---

[1] A recent example is Hess and Pickett, "Celebrating a Century of Advocacy Masquerading."
[2] This paragraph and the next draw on Jewett, *Science, Democracy, and the American University*.

To that end, Progressive social scientists worked not only to develop new theoretical understandings but also to teach citizens about the distinctive patterns of social causation and goals of social action in an industrial society. Focusing especially on childhood socialization, they called for an educational system grounded in scientific thinking, which would keep individuals oriented toward the common good amid rapid technological and economic changes. In this understanding, expert knowledge and techniques would anchor a modern curriculum, while also helping educational leaders align their institutions with both children's needs and social goals.

This reform project intersected at numerous points with the crystallization of the modern American school system during the same years. The program of universal public education had first taken shape before the Civil War, amid the explosion of evangelical reform efforts. During those years, Massachusetts' Horace Mann and other reformers taught a generalized form of Protestant Christianity alongside basic literacy, numeracy, and patriotic narratives. By 1900, however, a slapdash array of one-room schoolhouses had developed into an age-graded system stretching from kindergarten to twelfth grade (K-12). By 1930, the vast bulk of American children attended such schools regularly and made it at least partway through high school (typically ninth through twelfth grade). The system also took on a more secular cast, especially after the complaints of Catholic and Jewish parents led many urban districts to eliminate Bible lessons in the 1860s and 1870s.[3]

As the twentieth century dawned, parents and students typically emphasized schooling's vocational function: preparation for the workplace, including specialized skills as well as literacy and numeracy. Meanwhile, administrators, local politicians, and many theorists of education aimed to inculcate a common American culture, including everything from nationalist lore down to personal hygiene. Other models could be found: private academies or "Latin schools" for the college-bound, a handful of public equivalents, and by the 1920s, a network of "progressive schools" experimenting with project-based, experiential learning. For the most part, however, K-12 education aimed at workforce preparation and Americanization.[4]

Conversely, a host of Progressive social scientists, from Lester Frank Ward in the 1870s to John Dewey in the 1910s, identified education as a means of fundamental social change. Theoretically minded social psychologists

---

[3] Graham, *Schooling America* and Green, *The Bible, the School, and the Constitution.*
[4] On the vocational orientation, see especially Groeger, "Political Economy of Education and Social Inequality."

such as Dewey, G. Stanley Hall, and James Mark Baldwin worked to engage students – and thereby promote various programs of social reform – by aligning pedagogical techniques and curricular content with the developmental needs of children. Sociologists such as Albion Small and Edward A. Ross likewise emphasized the schools' potential contributions to social change in an increasingly industrial, urban, and demographically diverse country. These Progressive social scientists targeted what William F. Ogburn later dubbed "cultural lag": the temporal mismatch between accelerating changes in technology and economic organization, on the one hand, and a highly inertial political culture, on the other. They aimed to transform social institutions and values inherited from an age of family farming and small-scale, competitive enterprise to make them fit a modern mass-production economy, in part by applying social-scientific methods to the task of educational reform. Progressives in the social sciences identified formal and informal education as uniquely powerful means of changing minds and thereby minimizing cultural lag.[5]

After World War I, however, education – especially K-12 schooling – became far less central to the reform visions and research agendas of American social scientists. This development both reflected and accelerated a growing institutional divide between social science departments and schools of education. Education schools emerged in two ways. First, the "normal schools" created in the nineteenth century to train teachers eventually grew into nonselective regional colleges that offered education programs alongside many other courses of study. Second, many established universities converted departments of education into professional schools, seeking to facilitate research and graduate training in the field. In both contexts, an increasingly professionalized and self-contained cadre of educational researchers plied their trade alongside faculty engaged in training future teachers and administrators. The creation of the American Educational Research Association in 1916 and the *Journal of Educational Research* in 1920 reflected the maturation of the new field, defined by its object of study rather than a distinctive theory or method.[6]

---

[5] Reuben, "Education," 621, 626; Walters, "Betwixt and Between Discipline and Profession," 641–42; and Snedden, "Field of Educational Sociology." The classic formulation of the cultural lag idea is Ogburn, *Social Change with Respect*. On the influence of the Progressive context, see also Johanningmeier and Richardson, *Educational Research, the National Agenda, and Educational Reform*.

[6] Reuben, "Education," 629; Labaree, *Trouble with Ed Schools*; and Perry, "What History Reveals about the Education Doctorate." On the AERA's early history, see Mershon and Schlossman, "Education, Science, and the Politics of Knowledge."

In the 1920s and 1930s, the deepening institutional split between education schools and the social science disciplines became an intellectual boundary as well. Examining dissertations in sociology and economics during the period from 1920 to 1924, F. W. Hoffer found that only 4.9 percent of the former and 3.2 percent of the latter addressed education. The subject drew far less interest than topics such as the family, industrial labor, community organization, race, and even "personality, leadership, and creative effort." Sociologists were also more than twice as likely to have studied religion than education. Five years later, the psychologist Charles H. Judd complained that the influential Social Science Research Council (SSRC), like other broad-gauged scholarly organizations, had not targeted educational research in its funding: "Evidently, the view of these research councils is that their fields of inquiry are distinct from" that of education schools, Judd noted. In a list of more than 180 grantees from the SSRC's 1933 decennial report, only six – five of them psychologists – examined education. It was left to the American Council of Education to step in, with funding from the educationally oriented Julius Rosenwald Fund.[7]

Changing reform visions contributed to the divergence in research foci. The resounding defeat of Progressives in national elections after 1920 shattered the assumption of many social scientists that the middle-class public shared their beliefs and values. In response, some shifted their attention from K-12 schooling to higher education, adult education, and popular writing, seeking to change the minds of voters and leaders. Others abandoned the goal of thoroughgoing cultural change and instead sought to bypass what they now deemed a fundamentally irrational electorate by forging an alliance of social scientists and bureaucrats that would manage political affairs with minimal input from voters. Neither version of interwar Progressivism gave a central role to public K-12 schooling – or to the distinctive expertise of educational researchers. To be sure, educational researchers and many social scientists still agreed on the need for scientifically grounded social reform. That ambition informed an emerging focus on "character education" and the analysis (often quantitative) of what social psychologists came to call "attitudes." Studies of attitudes identified a key site of intervention by experts and institutional leaders and also promised a way to measure the reformers' success in changing individual minds and the broader culture. Yet, educational researchers and mainstream social scientists increasingly sought to reach different segments

---

[7] Hoffer, "Five Years of Ph.D. Research"; Judd, "National Program of Educational Research," 587; and Social Science Research Council, *Decennial Report*, 85–102.

of the population, even when their political goals, theoretical frameworks, and research methods overlapped.[8]

Moreover, a growing number of social scientists came to believe that they could improve the reliability of their findings only if they bracketed all practical concerns and focused on theoretical and methodological innovation. Although the mainstream social sciences have never been nearly as pure and abstract as either defenders or critics believed, the perceived boundary between theory and application hardened after World War I and claims of rigorous value-neutrality multiplied. Even the sociologist Ogburn, a fervent champion of strict objectivity, still believed that scientific inquiry's ultimate purpose was to inform social change. But in the new, objectivist model of social science, which took hold across the disciplines by the 1940s, those scholars who addressed practical questions in the absence of theoretical or methodological ambition – including researchers in educational schools – were not true scientists. Even many of the social scientists who concerned themselves with education upheld the new model, agreeing with the sociologist Robert C. Angell that the social scientist should no more be "concerned with meeting the practical problems of 'controlled education' than is the physicist in showing Henry Ford what are the best types of electrical units for his cars." With such a sensibility afoot, the stage was set for further intellectual isolation between the education schools and the social sciences.[9]

Still, despite the growing institutional divide and the accompanying theory/practice split, a number of important concepts and techniques flowed across the border. Mental testing represented the main point of contact between social science and educational research in the 1920s, as it would in subsequent decades. Squadrons of educational researchers followed the behaviorist psychologist Edward Thorndike in developing and honing psychological tests of intelligence. They believed that a single, innate, quantifiable trait – the intelligence quotient (IQ) – reliably predicted

[8] Jewett, *Science, Democracy, and the American University*; American Association of School Administrators, *Character Education*; Hartshorne, "Sociological Implications of the Character Education"; Shuttleworth, "Decade of Progress in Methods of Measuring Character"; Thurstone, "Attitudes Can Be Measured"; Hart, *Progress Report on a Test*; Murphy and Likert, *Public Opinion and the Individual*; and Fleming, "History of a Concept."
[9] Bannister, *Sociology and Scientism*; Reuben, *Making of the Modern University*; Walters, "Betwixt and Between Discipline and Profession," 643–44; Ogburn, "Folk-Ways of a Scientific Sociology"; Angell, "Science, Sociology, and Education," 408; and Reuben, "Education," 629.

academic outcomes and could be quickly and accurately measured through pencil-and-paper exams. Such tests enabled public school administrators to sort a rapidly expanding, polyglot student population into differentiated tracks pegged to specific vocational futures. Although Dewey, with his expansive vision of participatory democracy, is the era's best-remembered theorist of education, most educational researchers in the 1910s and 1920s actually embraced more centrist, technocratic modes of Progressivism. Seeking a rigorous, experimental, and ideally quantitative science of education that could reliably answer practical questions of application, they emphasized "social efficiency": the maximal adjustment of schools and children to the functional needs of the workplace and other social institutions.[10]

Other lines of connection to the mainstream social sciences emerged as well. One important body of work centered on organizational efficiency. As the school system mushroomed and high school attendance became typical among noncollege-bound students, educational researchers and mainstream political scientists such as Columbia's Frank J. Goodnow helped school districts around the country undertake administrative reforms to streamline and centralize their efforts. Another area of research centered on curriculum design and sought to align the content of schooling with the varied functional needs of adults. This work fed into a vaguely defined field of "educational sociology" that began to coalesce in the 1920s with a number of textbooks and a new professional journal.[11]

As the 1920s boom gave way to the Depression and New Deal, social scientists and educational researchers shared in the opprobrium heaped on advocates of "modern" thoughtways by both religious traditionalists and political conservatives. Yet, the education schools gained a special reputation for secularism and radicalism in the 1930s. Many critics blamed changes in schooling on the "educationists" who had embraced modern ideas and applied them in practice, rather than the social scientists who had spun such fantasies in the first place. (Meanwhile, the institutional divide enabled mainstream social scientists to insulate themselves from educational controversies if they wished.) As the Depression worsened, moreover, a prominent group of "social reconstructionists" in leading

---

[10] Reuben, "Education," 629; Lagemann, *An Elusive Science*; Smeyers and Depaepe, "Lure of Psychology for Education," 323; Kliebard, *Struggle for the American Curriculum*; and Labaree, "Public Goods, Private Goods."

[11] Reuben, "Education," 626; Walters, "Betwixt and Between Discipline and Profession," 649–54; and Roucek, "Changing Concepts and Recent Trends."

education schools sought to turn the K-12 system into the instrument of a peaceful, social-democratic revolt against capitalism. Such ambitions were not unknown among mainstream social scientists; the anthropologist Margaret Mead and the sociologist Robert Lynd, among others, also considered what the reconstructionists frankly called "indoctrination." But the reconstructionists' stark anticapitalism and casual dismissal of students' intellectual autonomy gave their work added notoriety. Social reconstructionism helped fuel a broad public perception that education schools such as Columbia's Teachers College – home to the leading reconstructionists as well as Dewey, a fierce critic of traditional religion – peddled ideology in the guise of scholarship and perhaps represented an entering wedge for "godless communism."[12]

3.2 Postwar Patterns

During and after World War II, both right-wing anticommunism and a new belief in democracy's potential led many scholars to position themselves as celebrants rather than critics of American institutions. Many social scientists now asserted that the nation featured a thoroughly liberal consensus that could be redirected into more progressive channels, if only citizens understood the contours and proper applications of their liberal tradition. This "consensus liberalism" held that Americans had always embraced a framework of liberal values that experts could demonstrate how to properly implement under modern conditions. Social scientists drawn to consensus liberalism typically argued that antiracism, welfare liberalism, and other left-leaning policies reflected foundational American values. When they applied this perspective to education, they focused largely on inculcating a set of "democratic ideals" defined in civil-libertarian terms, emphasizing intellectual freedom, cultural pluralism, and meritocracy. Anthropologists such as Mead, Ruth Benedict, Gene Weltfish, and Ashley Montagu, having long identified childhood socialization as a key point of intervention, led the way in fighting racism and religious bigotry during World War II. The liberal consensus, as portrayed by these figures, centered on shared commitments to tolerance, civil liberties, and individual autonomy.[13]

---

[12] Graham, *Schooling America*; Mead, *Growing Up in New Guinea*; Lynd, *Knowledge for What?*; and Gaston, *Imagining Judeo-Christian America*.

[13] Jewett, *Science, Democracy, and the American University*; Jewett, "Naturalizing Liberalism"; and Cohen-Cole, *Open Mind*.

Postwar consensus liberalism hardly mollified conservatives in Congress and elsewhere, who still held that social scientists wanted Soviet-style collectivism. Once again, however, educational researchers bore the brunt of the criticism – and sometimes from the left as well as the right. After World War II, educational theorists and school administrators raised the ire of many commentators by promoting a "life adjustment" curriculum that aimed to fit students seamlessly into adult society by preparing them for marriage, childrearing, and even leisure as well as citizenship and work. A growing body of specialized educational research supported this instrumental understanding of education's purposes. Sociologists of education, for example, identified schooling as a means of combatting social disorganization and the resulting crime and delinquency. The curriculum designer David Snedden had long advocated "scientific valuations" of various school subjects, assessing their capacity to be "functional now or later in the lives of persons of varying native endowments and environmental opportunities." Snedden and his allies sought "reliable schemes of objectives for controls of the learning processes fostered by, or permitted in, schools, churches, households, workshops, and even theaters and other places of pleasure." Although talk of planning and social control vanished from the life adjustment movement by the late 1940s, the goals of sorting students by their future prospects and preparing them to operate within established institutions remained.[14]

Even then, the life adjustment curriculum was not simply conservative. (Indeed, some 1950s critics said it brainwashed students into supporting New Deal liberalism.) Rather, life adjustment reflected the broader turn toward consensus liberalism. In the mainstream social sciences, the growing emphasis on consensus even appeared among sociologists of the Chicago School, who had long highlighted the tense, conflictual relations between immigrant groups in urban environments. By the 1940s, Chicago School sociologists had begun to incorporate cultural anthropology, with its increasingly holistic emphasis on shared cultural patterns. Many of them refigured the clashes of marginalized groups – both with one another and with mainstream society – as not just social but also cultural in character, while arguing that these cultural differences undermined social cooperation and negotiation by hindering the inculcation of shared national understandings.[15]

---

[14] Graham, *Schooling America* and Snedden, "Field of Educational Sociology," 13.
[15] Burgess et al., *Environment and Education* and Johnson, *Education and the Cultural Process.*

Although consensus liberalism, which permeated the social sciences by the 1950s, directed attention to childhood socialization as a site for the production of tolerant, democratic citizens, it rarely gave rise to detailed analyses of schooling itself. That tendency could already be seen in a pair of wartime publications that brought Chicago School sociologists together with cultural anthropologists to discuss educational issues. The theme of the *Environment and Education* volume was "broad enough for anything," noted a reviewer. Contributors adopted a "total-environment conception of education" and discussed the educative effects of urban settings and social status, along with the more general process of personality development. The second symposium, on "Education and the Cultural Process," defined education in equally broad, Deweyan terms as a society's "transmission of and diffusion of an existing cultural tradition." Although a few of the participants here focused on formal education, the symposium's overarching theme obscured the specificity of school and university settings.[16]

After the war, the pattern of discussing socialization in the round, while largely ignoring the specifics of formal education, persisted. For example, surprisingly little discussion of schooling appeared in canonical works on prejudice and "authoritarian personalities," or the array of psychological studies aimed at defining and measuring the "open-mindedness" that differentiated democracy from totalitarianism. The same held true for sociological studies by David Riesman and William H. Whyte, Jr., who criticized conformity and "massification" in the name of authentic individuality – and produced unexpected bestsellers in the process. Similarly, although Talcott Parsons' version of structural-functionalism alluded to education through its Durkheim-inspired invocation of a shared framework of social values, and also underwrote studies of the professions as key features of modern societies, little of the research it spawned focused on educational institutions as such. Moreover, Parsons' influential style of sociological reasoning prioritized general theories and foundational principles over specific applications.[17]

Overall, then, specialized studies of education rarely appeared in the mainstream social sciences during the 1940s and 1950s. The particular

---

[16] Davis, "Review of *Environment and Education*"; Hulett, "Review of *Environment and Education*"; and Johnson, "Introduction to Symposium," 630.

[17] Cohen-Cole, *Open Mind*; Riesman, *Lonely Crowd*; and Whyte, *Organization Man*. For exceptions, see the "Jacob report" controversy, discussed in Jewett, "Naturalizing Liberalism"; Parsons, "School Class as a Social System"; and David Riesman's numerous later writings on the subject, including *Constraint and Variety in American Education* and Jencks and Riesman, *The Academic Revolution*.

contours of educational agencies drew little attention outside the marginal subfield of educational sociology and the largely self-contained body of psychological research on intelligence testing. When the *Annals of the American Academy of Political and Social Science* published a special issue on education in 1949, neither of the coeditors and only two of the twenty-three contributors (the sociologist James H. S. Bossard and the organizational theorist Ordway Tead) came from the social sciences. In fact, even mainstream psychologists, with a few notable exceptions, largely turned away from educational questions and applications in the wake of World War II. Many social scientists at the time agreed with the sociologist Joseph Roucek that educational research, as a field, was fundamentally unscientific, offering only "a series of clichés gathered from other disciplines and unrelated to social forces or empirical facts." Roucek dismissed its practitioners as mere "educationists" whose work was riddled with "social philosophy," lacking conceptual precision and empirical rigor.[18]

3.3 Policy Shifts

During the same years, however, the roles of K-12 and higher education in American society changed dramatically, in ways that reshaped the policy environment and eventually led mainstream social scientists to rejoin the conversation in the early 1960s. For one thing, both World War II and the Cold War amplified the perceived importance of fostering specific values and traits in students, both in the longstanding sense of Americanization and the newer idiom of character education. At the same time, both assimilation and character training were increasingly subsumed under the project of creating a democratic culture comprising democratic personalities, each harboring a foundational commitment to democracy over and against its totalitarian competitors. The wartime experience also led federal officials to recognize the instrumental importance of the knowledge produced in universities, facilitating the postwar emergence of an extensive "military-industrial complex" based on federal contracts with university-based researchers (and, increasingly, dedicated research centers) whose work bore promise for national security purposes. The natural

[18] "Critical Issues and Trends in American Education"; Bossard, "Social Change in the United States"; Tead, "New Frontiers in Higher Education"; Berliner, "100-Year Journey of Educational Psychology"; Roucek, "Review of *The Conceptual Structure of Educational Research*," 101; and Roucek, "Changing Concepts and Recent Trends," 242. Moreover, Bossard's article discussed the changing social context, not schooling itself.

sciences and engineering obviously figured prominently, but area studies and other segments of the humanities and social sciences benefited greatly as well. Economic knowledge also held a special importance for the postwar American state, since it had committed itself to managing economic cycles and ensuring steady growth by applying economic expertise. Finally, the question of racial equality began to come to the fore in the late 1940s and increasingly dominated national debates over education by the 1950s (see Chapter 5: Discrimination).

Even before Pearl Harbor, university professors and administrators had begun to emphasize the capacity of their institutions to produce democratic citizens armed for the ideological struggle against totalitarianism. The preferred avenue was "general education": distinctive courses instilling a shared framework of cultural values. At Harvard, for example, President James B. Conant and the authors of the famed "Redbook" report identified the outline of Western civilization – a combination of technical knowhow and ethical principles – as the needed foundation for democratic education at both the high school and collegiate levels.[19]

College attendance boomed at the same time, particularly after the 1944 "GI Bill" brought a massive wave of returning veterans into higher education. At a time when conflicts over funding for parochial schools prevented federal aid to K-12 education, the GI Bill allowed veterans to attend religious institutions, public universities, or any other schools they chose. Within a few years, the growing flood of federal research grants – mainly from military agencies, but also the National Institutes of Health and, after 1950, the National Science Foundation – had combined with the GI Bill to place American colleges and universities on stable financial footing. Although veterans largely sought vocational skills and many researchers emphasized their instrumental contributions to national security, the universities continued to layer education for democratic citizenship onto those goals. Indeed, the land-grant schools added liberal arts departments such as philosophy and history to leaven their focus on agriculture and engineering.[20]

In the wake of the war, President Truman commissioned a report that synthesized all of these themes and added a new one: equal access, especially for racial minorities. *Higher Education for American Democracy*, published

[19] Jewett, *Science, Democracy, and the American University* and Cohen-Cole, *Open Mind*.
[20] Edmondson, "Without Comment or Controversy"; Geiger, *Research and Relevant Knowledge*; Lowen, *Creating the Cold War University*; and Loss, *Between Citizens and the State*.

in 1947, was notable for its very existence; it marked the first systematic attempt by a US president to analyze any form of education from a federal standpoint. Its conclusions resonated with the contemporary discussion as well. The President's Commission on Higher Education averred that decisions about higher education in the United States would determine the direction, and possibly the fate, of Western civilization. The Commission proposed a massive expansion of US higher education: nearly tripling the rate of college enrollments by 1960, with public universities taking on most of the new students. (Indeed, the committee recommended prohibiting federal aid to religious institutions, on First Amendment grounds.) The report also aimed to subordinate disciplinary knowledge to the problems of everyday life, including the problem of defending democracy against the Soviets. Finally, the Commission sought to maximize access to higher education among all social groups and specifically targeted racism and religious bigotry as well as class inequality. It proposed not only federal aid to higher education but also specific policies aimed at equalizing access, such as creating community colleges and providing financial aid for poor students.[21]

By the end of the 1950s, federal agencies had begun to leave their mark on K-12 education as well. The launch of the Sputnik satellite in 1957 fueled intense concern that the Soviet Union was producing far more scientific and technical experts than the United States. Government spending on defense-related work had dramatically altered research priorities, graduate education, and even undergraduate teaching in the top tier of universities. But where would those researchers come from in the first place? The National Defense Education Act of 1958 sought to strengthen science, engineering, mathematics, and modern language training in the schools as well as colleges and universities. At the same time, the National Science Foundation created a series of curricular study committees that produced new textbooks for high school science classes, with the goal of reorienting K-12 science training toward the production of future researchers rather than scientifically informed citizens. For the first time in decades, top researchers took a hand in textbook design.[22]

Indeed, leading scientists sometimes joined military leaders and other critics in attacking the life adjustment curriculum, arguing that schooling

[21] President's Commission on Higher Education, *Higher Education for American Democracy*. The report drew widespread criticism from advocates of both religious colleges and the traditional liberal arts curriculum. Schrum, "Establishing a Democratic Religion."
[22] Geiger, *Research and Relevant Knowledge*; Lowen, *Creating the Cold War University*; and Rudolph, *Scientists in the Classroom*.

should aim at academic excellence rather than skills for everyday life. The 1950s saw the emergence of a nationwide debate over the American educational system as a whole that has continued ever since. For the first time, influential critics argued that schools in the United States were fundamentally broken, requiring an entirely new approach. In this view, the entire country – not individual districts or states – faced a choice between wallowing in academic mediocrity or moving forward by consciously redesigning its educational institutions. Ironically, some of the most powerful calls for systematic change on a national scale came from political conservatives such as Bernard Iddings Bell. But a range of figures, including Mortimer Smith, Arthur Bestor, Rudolf Flesch, and Hyman Rickover, charged that the life adjustment model denied students competence in the traditional academic subjects that reformist educators had systematically marginalized since the early twentieth century.[23]

Although these developments altered the policy environment, they rarely inspired mainstream social scientists to undertake detailed, specialized studies of education. By the late 1950s, however, the growing ties between K-12 education and federal policy began to resuscitate interest in the field. Central here was the desegregation imperative of the Supreme Court's unanimous *Brown* decision in 1954. The majority opinion, written by Chief Justice Earl Warren, cited social-scientific research on prejudice, cultural environments, and individual self-perception, especially studies by the psychologists Kenneth Clark and Mamie Clark. The Clarks had found that racism and segregation adversely affected black children's self-esteem from a very young age. Their writings enabled Warren to argue that segregation denied black children an equal education by damaging their personalities and limiting their ability to learn – and thereby allowed him to avoid the even more contentious claim that segregation violated other Constitutional rights.[24]

Such work sidestepped the questions of curricular content that drove so much educational controversy in the 1950s and shifted the focus to access for racial minorities. In the late 1950s and early 1960s, the culturalist orientation of antiracist work increasingly intersected with experiments in urban education, including those at the Clarks' Harlem-based Northside Center for Child Development, and with a turn among psychologists against the view of academic aptitude as a fixed and easily quantifiable phenomenon. In this context, small groups of social scientists returned

[23] Graham, *Schooling America*, 111–13 and Hartman, *Education and the Cold War*.
[24] Reuben, "Education," 630–31 and Scott, *Contempt and Pity*.

to educational questions, exploring anew the interconnections between personality, culture, and society. Institutional developments shaped the growing rapprochement as well. Funders such as the Ford Foundation and the Department of Health, Education, and Welfare sponsored research on education by mainstream social scientists, who also began to find new avenues for employment in education schools.[25]

By the early 1960s, this cluster of intellectual and institutional innovations had fueled the argument that "cultural deprivation," not lack of aptitude, explained educational outcomes among underprivileged minorities – and perhaps even their poverty itself. The discovery of the "urban crisis" and the consequent determination of the expert-friendly Kennedy and Johnson administrations to root out poverty and injustice brought cultural deprivation theories to the forefront of policy discussions, as social-scientific research on education and inequality grew dramatically in both scope and salience (see Chapter 4: Poverty and Chapter 6: The Black Ghetto). Federal initiatives such as the Head Start program for young children and Title I of 1965's Elementary and Secondary Education Act, which directed federal aid to schools with low-income student populations, were designed to overcome the cultural deprivation of racial minorities and the poor.[26]

These policies both reflected and spurred a growing body of research on class, race, and education, as the search for policy relevance temporarily eclipsed the quest for theoretical and methodological sophistication among mainstream social scientists as well as educational researchers. The burst of research on education in the 1960s also expressed scholars' growing comfort with practical recommendations and even overt activism, at a time when social scientists found unusually receptive audiences in Washington and many of their own served at the highest levels of government. Not all of these studies, however, recommended federal action. Indeed, the cultural deprivation hypothesis could easily be used to rebut calls for policy interventions. Thus, the sociologist James S. Coleman's report *Equality of Educational Opportunity* famously argued that educational outcomes reflected students' experiences in their homes and neighborhoods, not district spending levels.[27]

Sociologists such as Coleman were central to the educational debates of the 1960s. (Not coincidentally, the discipline embraced the subfield of sociology of education in those years; the American Sociological Association assumed

[25] Reuben, "Education," 631–32.
[26] Reuben, "Education," 631–32.
[27] Reuben, "Education," 631 and Coleman, *Equality of Educational Opportunity*.

sponsorship of the newly renamed journal *Sociology of Education* in 1963.) Although an anthropologist, Oscar Lewis, had coined the term "culture of poverty" a few years earlier, by the mid-1960s sociologists were especially likely to argue that the urban poor constituted a distinctive subculture that sowed educational failure alongside other social pathologies. Their work found a receptive audience among like-minded administrators such as War on Poverty architect Daniel Patrick Moynihan, himself a trained social scientist. Unexpectedly leaked to the public, Moynihan's 1965 report *The Negro Family: The Case for National Action* caused an uproar by tracing poverty to cultural pathologies incubated in black families, especially those led by single mothers. Moynihan's work summarized and extended the burgeoning sociological literature on the intersections of culture, poverty, and education.[28]

The writings of economists were far less visible and controversial than the sociologists' cultural deprivation accounts, but they also shaped educational policy initiatives in the 1960s. Since the 1940s, Democratic leaders and some influential Republicans had committed themselves to steady economic growth through a Keynesian approach – using fiscal policy and countercyclical spending to smooth out the economic cycle and ensure steady investment and productivity gains. The Council of Economic Advisers (CEA), created in 1946 and headed by Leon Keyserling, quickly turned its attention from economic stability to growth, which supplanted high employment levels as a goal for the CEA and policymakers. The new federal commitment to expert oversight of the economy overlapped with the creation of aggregate national statistics to assess the country's economic health, not least in comparison with the expanding Soviet economy. As the American state took up economic management on a permanent basis, it met its new cognitive and political needs – knowing and promoting the efficacy of its interventions – through national indices that obscured subnational distinctions.[29]

In the early 1960s, the idea of "human capital" emerged at this point of convergence between governance demands, aggregate measures, and economic theorizing – and immediately became a leading framework for understanding K-12 education. With Cold War tensions easing, McCarthyite anticommunism waning, and the logjam on federal aid to education broken

---

[28] Lewis, *Five Families*; Reuben, "Education," 632; Moynihan, *Negro Family*; and Geary, *Beyond Civil Rights*.
[29] Collins, *Politics of Economic Growth* and Holden and Biddle, "Introduction of Human Capital Theory."

by the election of a Catholic president in 1960, policymakers no longer faced constant charges that the schools failed to instill patriotism or piety; they could now focus squarely on the vocational side of schooling. The human capital framework quickly became a central resource. Drawing a parallel between financial capital and vocationally relevant capacities, human capital theorists argued that education and other forms of training imbued individuals with technical skills and knowledge that dramatically improved their productivity, and thus the efficiency of the economy as a whole. Figures such as Theodore Schultz, Gary Becker, and Jacob Mincer identified immense social returns on such investments and called for federal spending on education at all levels. After 1960, the human capital idea, though still in its formative stage among economists, connected academic theorizing with federal imperatives – and, in the minds of policymakers, fused education with labor force preparation.[30]

The human capital literature brought a subset of professional economists squarely into debates over education policy. Over the years, individual economists had intermittently taken up educational questions. In 1948, the policy-oriented Keynesian Seymour E. Harris published a comprehensive study of school finance, but the major economics journals did not review it. A year earlier, the University of Virginia economist Tipton R. Snavely anticipated the human capital model by calling for massive public investments in "vocational, technical and scientific education" to pull the US South abreast of other regions economically. But it was not until the late 1950s and early 1960s that a coherent network of economists took up education as an area of dedicated concern.[31]

When it did emerge, the human capital approach powerfully shaped the educational initiatives of the Kennedy and Johnson administrations. After Eisenhower emphasized economic stability in his policies, Kennedy ran in 1960 on the promise of 5 percent growth per year. He then tapped Walter Heller, a vigorous champion of growth and a skilled translator of human capital theory and other economic concepts into policy terms, to head his Council of Economic Advisers. Via Heller, whose advice and rhetoric

[30] Holden and Biddle, "Introduction of Human Capital Theory." For more on the career of human capital theory in the economics of education field, see Teixeira, "Portrait of the Economics of Education"; Teixeira, "Human Capital Revolution"; and Teixeira, "Conquering or Mapping?" In 2018, the Trump administration proposed a single "Department of Education and the Workforce" that would merge the mandates of Education and Labor.
[31] Harris, *How Shall We Pay for Education?* and Snavely, "Place of Education in the Developing Economic Structure," 413.

124 *Andrew Jewett*

Kennedy followed closely, the human capital framework jumped to the top level of policy formation even as it was still under theoretical development by the likes of Schultz, Becker, and Mincer. The new approach, as interpreters have noted, helped convince policy elites that "the federal government has an important role to play in both funding and regulating public education, the central purpose of education is to increase students' future productivity and earnings capacity, and economists possess expert knowledge that gives them important insights into the educational process."[32]

On the intellectual side, one factor in human capital theory's meteoric rise was its fit with the contemporaneous idea that a "knowledge economy" was emerging in the United States and elsewhere. Theorists such as the sociologist Daniel Bell argued that technological innovation had fundamentally transformed the American economy, such that it now centered on expertise – instrumental knowledge – rather than the traditional inputs of capital and labor. Predictions differed on the long-term effects of the transition to a knowledge society, but one thing was clear: The bodies of knowledge that increasingly anchored economic activity were gained largely through formal education. Educational administrators themselves, such as the industrial relations theorist and University of California head Clark Kerr, assimilated the knowledge society idea to earlier visions of what Kerr called the "multipurpose university" and the historian Ethan Schrum dubs the "instrumental university": an institution that produced specialized knowledge and experts to meet whatever needs the surrounding society generated. The human capital framework did not always comport perfectly with portraits of the knowledge society or the instrumental university, but these schools of thought shared the assumption that technical knowledge and expertise anchored modern life.[33]

At the same time, the human capital orientation differed from these otherwise congruent approaches in one key regard. Like the prevailing forms of Keynesianism, human capital theory focused almost entirely on individuals and national aggregates and largely ignored subnational structures and social groups. As racial equality became a central federal goal, the human capital approach produced ambiguous effects. On the

[32] Holden and Biddle, "Introduction of Human Capital Theory," 541–42, 553–56, 570.
[33] Brick, *Transcending Capitalism* and Schrum, *Instrumental University*. Similar ideas about the importance of expertise circulated among the modernization theorists of the early 1960s, who imagined societies abroad converging on the American model and stressed the importance of three products of education: a highly trained technical elite, a widespread "achievement orientation," and a meritocratic distribution of vocational opportunities. Gilman, *Mandarins of the Future*.

one hand, it was fully meritocratic; it treated racialized minorities and women as abstract, formally equal individuals who were functionally interchangeable with members of dominant groups. One could thus argue that racism harmed the country by squandering the economic potential of its black citizens. But the emphasis on maximizing a national aggregate also meant that policymakers could ignore minority communities if investing in well-off individuals or institutions produced a greater return on investment. That version of the human capital approach, divested of a commitment to social justice, would become increasingly prominent as the political climate moved rightward in the 1970s and 1980s.

3.4 Critical Turns

For the radical critics of the mid- to late 1960s, human capital theory represented yet another example of the liberal establishment's centrist, procedural approach to questions of social justice. Indeed, it had emerged at a time when social scientists and educational theorists were eager not to be seen as advocating economic redistribution. Moreover, human capital theory ignored all of education's nonvocational elements, including not only the basic socialization function long ascribed to American schools but also the centuries-old discourse of liberal learning, with its emphasis on broadened perspectives, humane values, and other forms of personal development. The critical social scientists of the late 1960s and 1970s highlighted the dimensions of education that human capital theories obscured. Marxists described the school system as a tool for reproducing class divisions, not ensuring social mobility. Ethnographers, who were turning from "traditional" societies toward their own and examining cultural and social dynamics within US classrooms, likewise saw behind the human capital framework a technocratic vision that cast students as future cogs in an oppressive economic machine. The "critical pedagogy" of the Brazilian theorist Paulo Freire spread widely in radical circles, and some critics followed Ivan Illich in rejecting the very idea of schooling.[34]

Yet radical perspectives never fully dominated the subfields – sociology of education, anthropology of education, and so forth – that emerged at the intersections of educational research with the social sciences in the late 1960s and 1970s. Instead, those fields featured many competing

[34] Blaug, "Where Are We Now in the Economics of Education?"; Yon, "Highlights and Overview of the History of Educational Ethnography," 413; Freire, *Pedagogy of the Oppressed*; and Illich, *Deschooling Society*.

views, including progressive, multicultural, liberal, and neoconservative sensibilities. In the sociology of education, for example, calls for federal action on behalf of minority groups coexisted with high-profile works by James S. Coleman and Christopher Jencks, who argued that societies could not expect transformative changes from schooling alone – and perhaps not at all. Of course, it was these arguments, along with conventional liberal approaches, that drew the attention of policymakers. The pattern continued in the 1970s. Indeed, as the chastened economic climate gave rise to a full-throated defense of supply-side principles among Reaganite conservatives, prominent social scientists tended to pull back from educational discussions after 1970. Subfields such as sociology of education largely returned to marginal, low-status positions akin to that of educational research itself.[35]

Of those subfields, anthropology of education likely housed the highest percentage of social critics, if not always the most radical ones. Since World War II, ethnographers such as Mead had consistently advocated social equality. Mead and a number of other anthropologists also began working with or for education schools in the late 1940s and early 1950s, especially at Columbia and Harvard. George D. Spindler, jointly hired in anthropology and education at Stanford, formally launched the anthropology of education field with a major conference and the resulting 1955 volume *Education and Anthropology*. But it was only amid the ferment of the 1960s that the field took its present shape. Burgeoning interest in ethnographic approaches gave rise to a professional society, the Council on Anthropology in Education in 1968, and a journal, *Anthropology of Education*, in 1969.[36]

More overtly anticapitalist perspectives gained ground among economists of education as the 1960s gave way to the 1970s. Samuel Bowles and Herbert Gintis' 1976 classic *Schooling in Capitalist America* challenged the human capital theorists' assumption of an efficient, meritocratic system that tightly linked productivity, status, and pay to the technical knowledge acquired by individuals. In fact, not only Marxists such as Bowles and Gintis but also theorists of many other stripes began to argue that hiring decisions reflected far more than the maximization of employees' technical knowledge. They emphasized the affective outputs of education, the centrality of exchange

[35] Coleman, *Equality of Educational Opportunity*; Jencks, *Reassessment of the Effect of Family and Schooling*; Blaug, "Where Are We Now in the Economics of Education?" 17; and Reuben, "Education."
[36] Yon, "Highlights and Overview of the History," 413; Wooton, "Review of *Education and Anthropology*"; Mead, *School in American Culture*; Comitas and Dolgin, "On Anthropology and Education"; Spindler, *Education and Anthropology*; and Reuben, "Education."

value rather than use value in the "credentials market," and other features of the contemporary labor market. By the 1970s, a new generation of economists had rejected the idea that educational credentials represented the attainment of vocationally relevant forms of cognitive knowledge. The more radical among them argued that schooling reproduced class structures, rather than ensuring cross-class fluidity and the maximization of skills and knowledge across the economy.[37]

Ironically, critical perspectives did not make a significant mark in the politics of education. A number of political scientists began to systematically analyze education at the very end of the 1950s and the first years of the 1960s. Late in 1959, Thomas H. Eliot, a lawyer by training who had worked in government as well as legal practice before taking up an academic post in his mid-forties, published a groundbreaking article, "Toward an Understanding of Public School Politics," that the *Teachers College Record* enthusiastically reprinted. A few years later, Syracuse's Maxwell School of Citizenship and Public Affairs and the Center of Applied Research in Education in New York began publishing studies of both the economics and the politics of schooling, as did H. Thomas James at Stanford's School of Education. From its start, then, the politics of education field stood at the margins of the discipline, finding much of its support and appeal in professional schools.[38]

As in the other disciplines, interest in the politics of education blossomed after the mid-1960s. However, the subfield was slow to find professional expression. Although the American Educational Research Association created a specialty in the politics of education after its 1969 meeting, the Politics of Education Association emerged only in 1978. Nor did the field reflect much of the era's political radicalism. Indeed, its institutional marginality belied its practitioners' commitment to conventional, centrist formulations that echoed the postwar mainstream in political science. Through the upheavals of the 1960s and long beyond, students of the politics of education continued to follow the behavioral science approach of 1950s figures such as Gabriel Almond and David Easton, embracing the search for a comprehensive, theoretically grounded science of educational administration. The politics of education field retained the Parsonsian

---

[37] Bowles and Gintis, *Schooling in Capitalist America* and Blaug, "Where Are We Now in the Economics of Education?"
[38] Eliot, "Toward an Understanding of Public School Politics," 1959; Eliot, "Toward an Understanding of Public School Politics," 1960; and Scribner, Aleman, and Maxcy, "Emergence of the Politics of Education Field," 14.

assumptions of value consensus and social integration until the 1980s, when its "romance with behavioralism" finally ended and alternative, conflictual ("neoinstitutionalist") perspectives that had first emerged in the mid-1970s – rational choice perspectives, cultural analyses, and structuralist approaches – took hold. Even then, this work remained largely within the domain of educational administration rather than functioning as a subfield of political science.[39]

Psychology presented the opposite pattern; the field had always figured centrally in the study of education. Since the late 1800s, psychological research has often been closely tied to educational practices. Instrumentally, psychology has provided the testing tools and other quantitative measures used to assess aptitude and other elements of the educational experience. Ideologically, meanwhile, psychological conceptions of intelligence – if often rather outdated conceptions – have come to anchor popular understandings of the goals and structures of schooling. Still, most mainstream psychologists had shifted their attention away from education in the wake of World War II. One exception was the arch-behaviorist B. F. Skinner, whose emphasis on conditioned responses and sweeping ambition for social engineering led him to seek educational reforms. Among other innovations, Skinner created a "learning box" that mechanized the process of reinforcement. Another influential figure, though of a very different ilk, was Skinner's Harvard colleague Jerome Bruner. Picking up on the Swiss theorist Jean Piaget's work, Bruner helped to establish the postbehaviorist field of cognitive psychology and increasingly turned to developmental issues in the 1960s. At the same time, however, the deep theoretical disputes that accompanied the "cognitive revolution" of the 1960s left little room for the kinds of direct social criticism that emerged in many other fields. Most of the era's radical challenges came from maverick clinicians rather than academic theorists.[40]

The education schools offered a sharp contrast, as radical perspectives flourished among researchers there. The critics of the 1960s and 1970s often targeted experimental psychology's dominance over their field, fueling methodological diversification and borrowing from a host of other disciplines. Yet psychology itself remained important for educational researchers, if in newly varied forms. The psychological development of children became increasingly paramount as an overarching goal for

---

[39] Scribner, Aleman, and Maxcy, "Emergence of the Politics of Education Field."
[40] Cohen-Cole, *Open Mind* and Staub, *Madness Is Civilization.* An example of Skinner's work in the field is *The Technology of Teaching.*

education, replacing demands to fit students into broad moral or ideological molds. The humanistic, person-centered orientation of psychologists such as Carl Rogers appealed to many critical scholars. Elsewhere, developmental theories – starting with that of Piaget in the 1950s, and then Lev Vygotsky's constructivism in the 1970s – steadily replaced Thorndike's behaviorist model. The leading theories of education, as interpreters have noted, were still firmly rooted in psychological concepts, "even though the psychology of the educational reformers was not necessarily that of the psychologists."[41]

3.5 Toward the Present

Since the 1970s, critical orientations have persisted, and in certain regards deepened, among many sociologists of education, anthropologists of education, and educational researchers. A variety of post-Marxist perspectives emerged by the 1980s. Multiculturalism stressed the positive value of social and cultural diversity, while poststructuralism emphasized the contingent, constructed character of foundational categories of social thought. These perspectives found their greatest appeal in the humanities, but many social scientists developed them as well. Also highly influential was the work of the French sociologist Pierre Bourdieu, whose nuanced analyses of the interrelations between class position and the accumulation of various forms of "cultural capital" inspired numerous American social scientists and educational researchers. In a less radical vein, the psychologist Howard Gardner's "multiple intelligences" framework challenged the concept of intelligence as a singular, quantifiable trait.[42]

These innovations, however, coexisted with many other perspectives – rational choice models and the human capital approach among them – that fit much more neatly with prevailing national goals, especially as policy debates moved rightward. Intense though it was in the late 1960s, the political establishment's desire to promote social equality by reforming urban education has waxed and waned over time, and has typically been swamped in the public conversation by broader, more conservative critiques of the educational system as a whole. The ascendance of the Christian Right in the wake of *Roe* v. *Wade* added a new dimension, heightening

---

[41] Smeyers and Depaepe, "Lure of Psychology for Education," 325.
[42] Banks and McGee Banks, *Multicultural Education*; Peters and Burbules, *Poststructuralism and Educational Research*; Davies and Rizk, "Three Generations of Cultural Capital Research"; and Gardner and Hatch, "Multiple Intelligences Go to School."

longstanding fears of educational secularization. In a revealing incident from the early 1970s, Jerome Bruner and other members of the National Science Foundation's (NSF) social science curriculum committee tried to bring anthropological perspectives into high schools through their "Man: A Course of Study" (MACOS) curriculum. Religious conservatives fought back, taking their campaign against MACOS all the way to Congress and leading that body to crack down on the NSF's science education programs across the board.[43]

In the years since then, US educational policies have been mainly shaped by a convergence of human capital concerns and parents' intense preoccupation with economic positioning. By the 1970s, the Cold War conflict took a back seat to the new threats of Japanese and German competition. Public education, many now argued, should aim at economic growth and maximum productivity. In the 1980s, the push for economic competitiveness coalesced around the language of educational "excellence" and "standards." That discourse, captured in the influential 1983 report *A Nation at Risk*, suggested that the US school system was a dismal failure, not just for disadvantaged students but for all students and society at large. Its definition of excellence inaugurated the current era of educational reform, with its laser-like focus on high-stakes testing in traditional academic subjects such as reading and mathematics – and its inattention to most of the ideas prevailing in education schools. The new regime identifies federal investments in education as contributions to the production of a skilled workforce capable of sustaining the technological and economic dominance of the United States.[44]

Meanwhile, students and parents have become more and more preoccupied with getting a leg up in an increasingly credential-driven economy. As David Labaree has pointed out, the ideal of social mobility that drives so many families can be highly ambiguous in its impact on inequality. When poor and minority students work to move up the economic ladder, the social mobility ideal points toward equality and justice. But when the wealthy and advantaged seek to retain, or further improve, their positions, the conservative face of the social mobility approach shows itself. In either case, moreover, the goal is not to change economic and

---

[43] Cohen-Cole, *Open Mind*.
[44] Labaree, "Public Goods, Private Goods" and National Commission on Excellence in Education, *A Nation at Risk*. On the influence of such perspectives in education schools, see Wells and Roda, "Impact of Political Context on the Questions Asked and Answered."

social structures, but rather to maintain or improve one's position within them. Indeed, as Labaree notes, the social mobility ideal takes for granted a steep, hierarchical organization of both society at large and educational institutions, which sort individuals and thereby limit the candidate pools for the choicest opportunities at the top of the pyramid.[45]

In this climate, the approaches of critical theorists in the social sciences and education schools bear little relation to prevailing educational practices and norms, except where they overlap with the social mobility aims of the downtrodden. Institutionally, social-scientific studies of education flourish across a range of subfields and departments. Intellectually, however, many practitioners are farther from the political mainstream than they have been at any point since the 1930s. As in the past, their work tends to gain a purchase only insofar as it fits the needs of students, teachers, administrators, and policymakers, as well as cultural prescriptions regarding educational purposes and structures. If the intellectual and institutional convergence of the 1960s is to repeat itself, dramatic shifts across multiple domains of society will need to occur, in order to bring social-scientific knowledge and public policy into closer alignment on a national level once again.

Bibliography

American Association of School Administrators. *Character Education.* Washington, DC: The Department of Superintendence of the National Education Association of the United States, 1932.

Angell, Robert C. "Science, Sociology, and Education." *Journal of Educational Sociology* 1, no. 7 (1928): 406–13.

Banks, James A., and Cherry A. McGee Banks. *Multicultural Education: Issues and Perspective.* 9th ed. New York: Wiley, 2015.

Bannister, Robert C. *Sociology and Scientism: The American Quest for Objectivity, 1880–1940.* Chapel Hill: University of North Carolina Press, 1987.

Berliner, David C. "The 100-Year Journey of Educational Psychology: From Interest, to Disdain, to Respect for Practice." In *Exploring Applied Psychology: Origins and Critical Analyses,* edited by T. K. Fagan and G. R. VandenBos, 37–78. Washington, DC: American Psychological Association, 1993.

Blaug, Mark. "Where Are We Now in the Economics of Education?" *Economics of Education Review* 4, no. 1 (1985): 17–28.

Bossard, James H. S. "Social Change in the United States." *Annals of the American Academy of Political and Social Science* 265 (1949): 69–79.

---

[45] Labaree, "Public Goods, Private Goods." For a different take on the timing and causes of the research-policy divergence, see Nash, "Relationship between Academic Social Scientists and Educational Policymakers."

Bowles, Samuel, and Herbert Gintis. *Schooling in Capitalist America: Educational Reform and the Contradictions of Economic Life*. New York: Basic Books, 1976.

Brick, Howard. *Transcending Capitalism: Visions of a New Society in Modern American Thought*. Ithaca: Cornell University Press, 2006.

Burgess, Ernest W., W. Lloyd Warner, Franz Alexander, and Margaret Mead. *Environment and Education: A Symposium Held in Connection with the Fiftieth Anniversary Celebration of the University of Chicago*. Chicago: University of Chicago, 1942.

Cohen-Cole, Jamie. *The Open Mind: Cold War Politics and the Sciences of Human Nature*. Chicago: University of Chicago Press, 2014.

Coleman, James S. *Equality of Educational Opportunity*. Washington, DC: US Department of Health, Education, and Welfare, Office of Education, 1966.

Collins, Robert M. *More: The Politics of Economic Growth in Postwar America*. New York: Oxford University Press, 2000.

Comitas, Lambros, and Janet Dolgin. "On Anthropology and Education: Retrospect and Prospect." *Anthropology & Education Quarterly* 9, no. 3 (1978): 165–80.

"Critical Issues and Trends in American Education." *Annals of the American Academy of Political and Social Science* 265 (September 1949).

Davies, Scott, and Jessica Rizk. "The Three Generations of Cultural Capital Research: A Narrative Review." *Review of Educational Research* 88, no. 3 (2018): 331–65.

Davis, Kingsley. "Review of *Environment and Education*, by Ernest W. Burgess, W. Lloyd Warner, Franz Alexander, and Margaret Mead." *American Anthropologist* 44, no. 4 (1942): 712–13.

Edmondson, Elizabeth A. "Without Comment or Controversy: The G.I. Bill and Catholic Colleges." *Church History* 71, no. 4 (2002): 820–47.

Eliot, Thomas H. "Toward an Understanding of Public School Politics." *American Political Science Review* 53, no. 4 (1959): 1032–51.

Eliot, Thomas H. "Toward an Understanding of Public School Politics." *Teachers College Record* 62, no. 2 (1960): 118.

Fleming, Donald. "Attitude: The History of a Concept." *Perspectives in American History* 1 (1967): 287–365.

Freire, Paulo. *Pedagogy of the Oppressed*. New York: Seabury Press, 1970.

Gardner, Howard, and Thomas Hatch. "Multiple Intelligences Go to School: Educational Implications of the Theory of Multiple Intelligences." *Educational Researcher* 18, no. 8 (1989): 4–10.

Gaston, K. Healan. *Imagining Judeo-Christian America: Religion, Secularism, and the Redefinition of Democracy*. Chicago: University of Chicago Press, 2019.

Geary, Daniel. *Beyond Civil Rights: The Moynihan Report and Its Legacy*. Philadelphia: University of Pennsylvania Press, 2015.

Geiger, Roger L. *Research and Relevant Knowledge: American Research Universities since World War II*. New York: Oxford University Press, 1993.

Gilman, Nils. *Mandarins of the Future: Modernization Theory in Cold War America*. Baltimore: Johns Hopkins University Press, 2003.

Graham, Patricia Albjerg. *Schooling America: How the Public Schools Meet the Nation's Changing Needs*. New York: Oxford University Press, 2005.

Green, Steven K. *The Bible, the School, and the Constitution: The Clash That Shaped Modern Church-State Doctrine*. New York: Oxford University Press, 2012.

Groeger, Cristina. "The Political Economy of Education and Social Inequality in the United States, 1870–1940." PhD diss., Harvard University, 2017.

Harris, Seymour Edwin. *How Shall We Pay for Education? Approaches to the Economics of Education.* New York: Harper, 1948.

Hart, Hornell. *Progress Report on a Test of Social Attitudes and Interests.* Iowa City: University of Iowa, 1923.

Hartman, Andrew. *Education and the Cold War: The Battle for the American School.* New York: Palgrave Macmillan, 2008.

Hartshorne, Hugh. "Sociological Implications of the Character Education Inquiry." *American Journal of Sociology* 36, no. 2 (1930): 251–62.

Hess, Frederick M., and Francesca Pickett. "Celebrating a Century of Advocacy Masquerading as Education Research." *National Review* (blog), April 7, 2016. www.nationalreview.com/2016/04/education-research-radical-politics

Hoffer, F. W. "Five Years of Ph.D. Research in Economics and Sociology." *Social Forces* 4, no. 1 (1925): 74–77.

Holden, Laura, and Jeff Biddle. "The Introduction of Human Capital Theory into Education Policy in the United States." *History of Political Economy* 49, no. 4 (2017): 537–74.

Hulett, J. E. "Review of *Environment and Education*, by Ernest W. Burgess, W. Lloyd Warner, Franz Alexander, and Margaret Mead." *American Sociological Review* 7, no. 6 (1942): 881.

Illich, Ivan. *Deschooling Society.* New York: Harper & Row, 1971.

Jencks, Christopher, and David Riesman. *The Academic Revolution.* Chicago: University of Chicago Press, 1968.

Jencks, Christopher, et al. *Inequality: A Reassessment of the Effect of Family and Schooling in America.* New York: Basic Books, 1972.

Jewett, Andrew. *Science, Democracy, and the American University: From the Civil War to the Cold War.* New York: Cambridge University Press, 2012.

Jewett, Andrew. "Naturalizing Liberalism in the 1950s." In *Professors and Their Politics*, edited by Neil Gross and Solon Simmons, 191–216. Baltimore: Johns Hopkins University Press, 2014.

Johanningmeier, Erwin V., and Theresa Richardson. *Educational Research, the National Agenda, and Educational Reform: A History.* Charlotte: Information Age Publishing, 2008.

Johnson, Charles S. "Introduction to Symposium." *American Journal of Sociology* 48, no. 6 (1943): 629–32.

Johnson, Charles S. *Education and the Cultural Process: Papers Presented at Symposium Commemorating the Seventy-Fifth Anniversary of the Founding of Fisk University, April 29–May 4, 1941.* New York: Negro Universities Press, 1970.

Judd, Charles H. "A National Program of Educational Research." *Bulletin of the American Association of University Professors* 16, no. 8 (1930): 587–89.

Kliebard, Herbert M. *The Struggle for the American Curriculum, 1893–1958.* New York: Routledge & Kegan Paul, 1987.

Labaree, David F. "Public Goods, Private Goods: The American Struggle over Educational Goals." *American Educational Research Journal* 34, no. 1 (1997): 39–81.

Labaree, David F. *The Trouble With Ed Schools.* New Haven: Yale University Press, 2004.

Lagemann, Ellen Condliffe. *An Elusive Science: The Troubling History of Education Research.* Chicago: University of Chicago Press, 2000.

Lewis, Oscar. *Five Families: Mexican Case Studies in the Culture of Poverty.* New York: Basic Books, 1959.

Loss, Christopher P. *Between Citizens and the State: The Politics of American Higher Education in the 20th Century.* Princeton: Princeton University Press, 2012.

Lowen, Rebecca S. *Creating the Cold War University: The Transformation of Stanford.* Berkeley: University of California Press, 1997.

Lynd, Robert S. *Knowledge for What? The Place of Social Science in American Culture.* Princeton: Princeton University Press, 1939.

Mead, Margaret. *Growing Up in New Guinea: A Comparative Study of Primitive Education.* New York: W. Morrow & Company, 1930.

Mead, Margaret. *The School in American Culture.* Cambridge: Harvard University Press, 1951.

Mershon, Sherie, and Steven Schlossman. "Education, Science, and the Politics of Knowledge: The American Educational Research Association, 1915–1940." *American Journal of Education* 114, no. 3 (2008): 307–40.

Moynihan, Daniel Patrick. *The Negro Family: The Case for National Action.* Washington, DC: United States Department of Labor, Office of Policy Planning and Research, 1965.

Murphy, Gardner, and Rensis Likert. *Public Opinion and the Individual: A Psychological Study of Student Attitudes on Public Questions, with a Retest Five Years Later.* New York: Harper, 1938.

Nash, Margaret A. "The Relationship between Academic Social Scientists and Educational Policymakers: A Brief Historical Overview." In *New Foundations for Knowledge in Education Policy, Politics, and Administration: Science and Sensationalism,* edited by Douglas E. Mitchell, 3–28. Mahwah: Erlbaum, 2006.

National Commission on Excellence in Education. *A Nation at Risk: The Imperative for Educational Reform: A Report to the Nation and the Secretary of Education.* Washington, DC: United States Department of Education, 1983.

Ogburn, William Fielding. *Social Change with Respect to Culture and Original Nature.* New York: B. W. Huebsch, 1923.

Ogburn, William Fielding. "The Folk-Ways of a Scientific Sociology." *Scientific Monthly* 30, no. 4 (1930): 300–6.

Parsons, Talcott. "The School Class as a Social System: Some of Its Functions in American Society." *Harvard Educational Review* 29, no. 4 (1959): 297–318.

Perry, Jill Alexa. "What History Reveals about the Education Doctorate." In *Placing Practitioner Knowledge at the Center of Teacher Education: Rethinking the Policies and Practices of the Education Doctorate,* edited by Margaret Macintyre Latta and Susan Wunder, 51–72. Charlotte: Information Age Publishing, 2014.

Peters, Michael, and Nicholas C. Burbules. *Poststructuralism and Educational Research.* Lanham: Rowman & Littlefield, 2004.

President's Commission on Higher Education. *Higher Education for American Democracy.* Washington, DC: GPO, 1947.

Reuben, Julie A. *The Making of the Modern University: Intellectual Transformation and the Marginalization of Morality.* Chicago: University of Chicago Press, 1996.

Reuben, Julie A. "Education." In *The Cambridge History of Science (The Modern Social Sciences),* edited by Theodore M. Porter and Dorothy Ross, vol. 7, 621–34. New York: Cambridge University Press, 2003.

Riesman, David. *The Lonely Crowd: A Study of the Changing American Character.* New Haven: Yale University Press, 1950.

Riesman, David. *Constraint and Variety in American Education*. Lincoln: University of Nebraska Press, 1956.

Roucek, Joseph S. "Review of *The Conceptual Structure of Educational Research*, by T. R. McConnell, Douglas E. Scates, and Frank N. Freeman." *American Sociological Review* 8, no. 1 (1943): 101–2.

Roucek, Joseph S. "Changing Concepts and Recent Trends in American Educational Sociology." *International Review of Education* 4, no. 2 (1958): 240–44.

Rudolph, John L. *Scientists in the Classroom: The Cold War Reconstruction of American Science Education*. New York: Palgrave, 2002.

Schrum, Ethan. "Establishing a Democratic Religion: Metaphysics and Democracy in the Debates over the President's Commission on Higher Education." *History of Education Quarterly* 47, no. 3 (2007): 277–301.

Schrum, Ethan. *The Instrumental University: Education in the Service of the National Agenda after World War II*. Ithaca: Cornell University Press, 2019.

Scott, Daryl Michael. *Contempt and Pity: Social Policy and the Image of the Damaged Black Psyche, 1880–1996*. Chapel Hill: University of North Carolina Press, 1997.

Scribner, Jay D., Enrique Aleman, and Brendan Maxcy. "Emergence of the Politics of Education Field: Making Sense of the Messy Center." *Educational Administration Quarterly* 39, no. 1 (2003): 10–40.

Shuttleworth, Frank K. "A Decade of Progress in Methods of Measuring Character." *Journal of Educational Sociology* 4, no. 4 (1930): 233–41.

Skinner, B. F. *The Technology of Teaching*. New York: Appleton-Century-Crofts, 1968.

Smeyers, Paul, and Marc Depaepe. "The Lure of Psychology for Education and Educational Research." *Journal of Philosophy of Education* 46, no. 3 (2012): 315–31.

Snavely, Tipton R. "The Place of Education in the Developing Economic Structure of the South." *Southern Economic Journal* 13, no. 4 (1947): 404–15.

Snedden, David. "The Field of Educational Sociology." *Review of Educational Research* 7, no. 1 (1937): 5–14.

Social Science Research Council. *Decennial Report, 1923–1933*. New York: Social Science Research Council, 1934.

Spindler, George. *Education and Anthropology*. Stanford: Stanford University Press, 1955.

Staub, Michael E. *Madness Is Civilization: When the Diagnosis Was Social, 1948–1980*. Chicago: University of Chicago Press, 2011.

Tead, Ordway. "New Frontiers in Higher Education." *Annals of the American Academy of Political and Social Science* 265 (1949): 115–21.

Teixeira, Pedro Nuno. "A Portrait of the Economics of Education, 1960–1997." In *Toward a History of Applied Economics*, edited by Roger E. Backhouse and Jeff Biddle, 257–88. Durham: Duke University Press, 2000.

Teixeira, Pedro Nuno. "The 'Human Capital Revolution' in Economics." *History of Economic Ideas* 13, no. 2 (2005): 129–48.

Teixeira, Pedro Nuno. "Conquering or Mapping? Textbooks and the Dissemination of Human Capital Theory in Applied Economics." *European Journal of the History of Economic Thought* 25, no. 1 (2018): 106–33.

Thurstone, L. L. "Attitudes Can Be Measured." *American Journal of Sociology* 33, no. 4 (1928): 529–54.

Walters, Pamela Barnhouse. "Betwixt and Between Discipline and Profession: A History of Sociology of Education." In *Sociology in America: A History*, edited by Craig Calhoun, 639–65. Chicago: University of Chicago Press, 2007.

Wells, Amy Stuart, and Allison Roda. "The Impact of Political Context on the Questions Asked and Answered: The Evolution of Education Research on Racial Inequality." *Review of Research in Education* 40 (2016): 62–93.

Whyte, William H., Jr., *The Organization Man*. New York: Simon and Schuster, 1956.

Wooton, Flaud C. "Review of *Education and Anthropology*, by George D. Spindler and Lawrence K. Frank." *American Sociological Review* 20, no. 6 (1955): 770.

Yon, Daniel A. "Highlights and Overview of the History of Educational Ethnography." *Annual Review of Anthropology* 32 (2003): 411–29.

4

Poverty

Alice O'Connor

At an especially fraught moment in America's short-lived War on Poverty in the late 1960s, experts took to quoting a conversation between F. Scott Fitzgerald and Ernest Hemingway to explain the impasse that kept them, as social scientists, from arriving at a definitive consensus about the problem and how it could be resolved. It was a rare literary gesture to a conversation that (numerous citations to the contrary) never actually took place.[1] "The very rich are different from you and me," says Fitzgerald in the storied exchange, speaking as the keen if occasionally enamored observer of the psychology and folkways of the American aristocracy. "Yes, they have more money," Hemingway replies, in a social and literary put-down meant to bring the conceit – and the conversation – to an end.[2]

Apocryphal or not, for social scientists caught up in what was shaping up to be a surprisingly heated debate, the legendary Fitzgerald/Hemingway exchange captured two essential points. One was that on questions of poverty – its definition, measurement, and extent; its nature as a social problem; the appropriate policy response – social scientists felt hopelessly divided. The other was that in the escalating poverty wars, economists held themselves apart from everyone else. They, after all, were the first to put themselves squarely in Hemingway's camp, to advocate what economist Harold Watts approvingly called the "narrowly economic" approach to poverty. Poor people, that is, shared one clearly identifiable characteristic that distinguished them from everyone else in the affluent United States: They lacked sufficient income to meet basic subsistence needs. To suggest otherwise risked falling back on all-too-familiar tropes about the indolence of the "undeserving poor," or otherwise "blaming the victim," as writer

[1] Dow, "The Rich Are Different."
[2] Rainwater, "Lower-Class Culture and Poverty-War Strategy," 231.

137

William Ryan would later charge.[3] It also overlooked what economists thought to be the most obvious and efficient antipoverty solution: raise the incomes, through earnings and transfers, of the poor. This approach had the added advantage, to its advocates, of being based on an admittedly simplified but universally applicable and in their view nonjudgmental model of human behavior drawn from neoclassical economics, which treated firms and households as rational decision-makers whose economic and related life choices had to be understood within the context of the constraints – or lack thereof – their material circumstances imposed.

On the other side of the debate were those who, like the narrator of the short story that was the actual source of F. Scott Fitzgerald's quip, bore witness to what in this instance they claimed to be a distinctive "culture of poverty," replete with a far more elaborate – and decidedly less artfully rendered – inventory of socially dysfunctional attitudes, behaviors, habits, and psychological traits than any Fitzgerald attributed to the rich.[4] The poor were different, they argued, in ways that money alone would not fix, and that called into question whether even the most extensive remedial intervention would enable poor people to benefit from opportunities available to everyone else.[5] Nor could human behavior and motivation be reduced to the oversimplified schema of pecuniary incentives and calculated choices proposed in neoclassical economics. What economists insisted on treating as calculated choices, albeit within constraints, were in fact patterned behaviors conditioned by culturally specific values and

[3] Watts, "Economic Definition of Poverty" and Ryan, *Blaming the Victim*.
[4] The story is Fitzgerald's "The Rich Boy," published in 1926 as part of his collection *All the Sad Young Men*, and drawn extensively from his experience as a self-described "poor boy" at Princeton, a decidedly rich boy's school. The quote, in context, reads as follows: "Let me tell you about the very rich. They are different from you and me. They possess and enjoy early, and it does something to them, makes them soft where we are hard, and cynical where we are truthful, in a way that, unless you were born rich, it is very difficult to understand. They think, deep in their hearts, that they are better than we are because we had to discover the compensations and refuges of life for ourselves. Even when they enter deep into our world or sink below us, they still think that they are better than we are. They are different."
[5] The best known, starkest, and most controversial rendition of the "culture of poverty" was first articulated by Oscar Lewis in *Five Families*, and then in somewhat more popularized and novelistic form in *La Vida*. At the time, however, there were a number of variations on the theme, including a handful that argued that the alternative values and norms under observation were in fact adaptive to the conditions of deprivation, and – Lewis to the contrary – would quickly disappear under improved economic circumstances. For a fuller discussion of the genesis and variations on the theme, see O'Connor, *Poverty Knowledge*, chap. 8.

lifeways learned, rewarded, and perpetuated in families, communities, and peer groups.

How "the professors" arrived at this impasse had as much to do with the increasingly and, at least for some, unexpectedly divisive politics of fighting poverty as with their seemingly unbridgeable disciplinary and interpretive differences. Reflecting back on the experience of policy intellectuals a decade later, Brookings Institution economist Henry Aaron wrote that the 1960s had been hard on many of the liberal "faiths" animating the Great Society, not in the least the idea that social science could help to forge consensus around what – and not whether – the federal government could and should do to solve problems of poverty, racial discrimination, unemployment, and unequal opportunity.[6] By then, scholars had already been largely disabused of any notion they once might have harbored that their research would shape policy initiatives rather than the other way around. Indeed, as in other controversial areas of social policy, "poverty" emerged as a distinctive field of social-scientific expertise – with a distinctive empirical and analytical apparatus – only after the problem of "poverty in the midst of plenty" had been "rediscovered," formulated as a public issue, and elevated to the center of domestic social politics by journalists, public officials, political strategists, foundation officials, and only secondarily by social scientists operating as policy advisors.[7] Michael Harrington's *The Other America* (1962), written as a work of social journalism and a call to conscience, provided the basic framing that would inform the Kennedy/Johnson administration initiative, even after its basic premises had been undermined, of poverty as a "paradox" in the midst of prosperity – a problem of "other" people who, in the words later adopted by the President's Council of Economic Advisers (CEA), inhabited "a world apart, whose inhabitants are isolated from the mainstream of American life and alienated from its values."[8] Harrington was also the first to insert the terminology of the "culture of poverty," along with the proverbial Fitzgerald/Hemingway exchange, into the popular poverty discourse. (Harrington pronounced Fitzgerald's the

[6] Aaron, *Politics and the Professors*.
[7] Notably, the President's Council of Economic Advisers, in what for economists was a pathbreaking chapter on "Problem of Poverty" in its 1964 report, opened by acknowledging that they were following the President's lead, after LBJ had declared an "all-out war on poverty in America" in his State of the Union address. The aim of the chapter, accordingly, was to "provide some understanding of the enemy and to outline the elements of a strategy of attack." Council of Economic Advisers, *Annual Report of the Council of Economic Advisers*, 55.
[8] Council of Economic Advisers, *Annual Report of the Council of Economic Advisers*.

"better" of the views, adding that what was "true of the rich ... is ten times truer of the poor.")[9]

Poverty experts were also caught up in the decade's deeply conflicted racial politics, as they found themselves called to account for perpetuating racialized stereotypes of cultural deprivation and pathology as well as for the poverty program's failure to grapple with the structural and institutionalized racism documented – however partially and imperfectly – by the presidentially appointed National Advisory Commission on Civil Disorders (Kerner Commission) in its riveting 1968 report on the racial uprisings that had broken out in large and mid-sized American cities throughout the decade.[10]

The debacle of escalating war in Vietnam and the mood of division and distrust it engendered proved toxic as well, especially as it translated into presidential demands for domestic austerity that would drain resources for the War on Poverty. Both wars "attracted fierce resistance as well as strong partisans," Daniel Patrick Moynihan noted at the time, "and both came in a way to haunt their creators," in the face of an unbridgeable divide, with one side "demanding de-escalation and withdrawal, the other insisting on a total national effort for 'victory.'"[11] Moynihan himself was hardly a neutral bystander in these battles, having contributed mightily to the atmosphere of polarization with his 1965 report on *The Negro Family: The Case for National Action*, attributing the persistence and distinctive nature of black poverty to a so-called tangle of pathology that had forced "the Negro community" into a "matriarchal structure" that would perpetuate black disadvantage even after the pillars of Jim Crow segregation had crumbled.[12] Partly in reaction to the controversy over his report, Moynihan would go on to launch an all-out attack on the social theorists behind the concept of "maximum feasible participation" as what he alleged was an ill-defined and little understood – and politically subversive – strategy for ending poverty by empowering the poor.[13]

Caught up in the back and forth about just how "other" the proverbial "other Americans" were, few took notice of how narrowly construed and instrumental the social-scientific debate, and the still-emerging field of

[9] Harrington, *Other America*, 16.
[10] Kerner Commission, *Report of the National Advisory Commission*. On the report's problems, see McLaughlin, *Long Hot Summer*, among others.
[11] Moynihan, "Professors and the Poor," 17. This essay was also published in the August 1968 issue of *Commentary*.
[12] Moynihan, *Negro Family*.
[13] Moynihan, *Maximum Feasible Misunderstanding*.

poverty research, had already become. This was not for want of alternative perspectives, especially coming from the burgeoning ranks of antipoverty and social movement activism stimulated – in fact if not by design – by the War on Poverty's controversial Community Action Program. In drawing narrow boundaries around the problem, if in little else, poverty experts found common ground. Poverty research, as a social scientific and policy enterprise, would be about poor people and the identifiable demographic and behavioral attributes – age, race, skill or human capital deficiencies, family structure, values, and attitudes – that kept them from sharing in the unprecedented prosperity of the nation. It would be about the poor and otherwise "underdeveloped" places economic progress had left behind. For the economists and policy analysts heading the research division of the War on Poverty's newly established Office of Economic Opportunity (OEO), it would be about identifying the combination of policy and programmatic fixes that would "lift" low-income people above the only recently established federal poverty line, and effectively eliminate income poverty within a generation. It would not, as a narrowly circumscribed field, engage the structural inequities, systems of class, racial, and gender stratification, or the disparities of wealth, political, and economic power that kept upwards of one-quarter of American households in extreme economic need. Nor would it take up the challenge implicit in Harrington's *The Other America*, along with other prominent publications of the time, to the idea that the United States had emerged from the struggles of economic depression and war as a "classless" society with opportunities open to all.

This, too, reflected the politics of the moment, which in the context of Lyndon B. Johnson's declaration of "all-out war" on poverty called for defining the "enemy," as his CEA put it, in a way that could produce all-out victory. In what had become the prevailing cost/benefit calculation of the liberal administrative state, LBJ's political mandate also called for quantitative indicators, measurable "inputs" and outcomes, and concrete, realizable goals. Ending income deprivation was achievable in this calculus; ending inequality, let alone some other less tangible expression of social injustice, was not. The politics of the moment also called for maintaining an arm's distance between poverty and racial justice as social problems or policy issues, in what turned out to be a vain attempt to minimize racial backlash (see Chapter 5: Discrimination).

Still, if the politics of fighting the War on Poverty dictated a narrow definition of the problem, a set of more basic, first-order questions remained unresolved. The answers to these questions would prove especially consequential in shaping the relationship between social-scientific research and policy at the moment of poverty's "rediscovery," and in the decades to come. The first calls to mind the distinction between putatively objective or neutralized (but never entirely) research questions and the more explicitly normative "social question" that had animated reformist social investigators – from Charles J. Booth to the women of Hull House – to launch statistical surveys of poverty nearly a century before. To use historian Michael B. Katz's formulation: What *kind* of a problem was poverty?[14] Was it a problem of persons, who should get help based on some criteria of deservingness and need? Was it a problem of inadequate, dependency-inducing or otherwise misguided social provision? Was it a problem of absent or structurally blocked opportunity? Political power and representation? High unemployment, maldistribution, or some other expression of market failure? Such questions drew from social-scientific theory and research, but they originated from more fundamentally moral and ethical concerns that preoccupied the policy intellectuals of mid-century capitalist democracies, about the rights and obligations of social citizenship, and the scope of public responsibility for bringing them to fruition.

Another, related, first-order question spoke to what for all but the protagonists were the barely visible politics of mid–twentieth-century statecraft and liberal reform: What kind of knowledge was needed to fight a war on poverty? In an era that featured the "new" (Keynesian) economics of Kennedy's CEA in the headlines – and prompted British economic historian Michael Postan to write memorably of "A Plague of Economists" in contemporary public affairs – the answer had as much to do with the political organization as with the substantive boundaries of economic knowledge defined as disciplinary expertise.[15]

In what follows, I trace the shifting constellation of first- and second-order questions that influenced the identification of poverty as a problem and a priority for public intervention in the 1960s, at what by American standards was an extraordinarily expansive moment in political and social policy history. That the social-scientific experts defined "the poverty problem" narrowly, as a problem of persons lacking income or otherwise caught in a "cycle of poverty," had as much to do with the behavioral turn in postwar social science more widely as with the influence of economists and their new-found policy imperium alone. It also had to do with the imperatives – and boundaries – of Great Society liberal reform. But it can also be understood in terms of a series of more deeply rooted historical

[14] Katz, *The Undeserving Poor*, 268–70.
[15] Postan, "A Plague of Economists?"

transformations in social-scientific theory, knowledge practices, and in the political organization of expertise. I discuss how these developments played out in overlapping processes of disembedding: of social science from social reform; of economic from social and political knowledge; and of poverty from the study of structured patterns and experiences of stratification and inequality. The structurally disembedded, individualized concept of poverty that would emerge from these transformations presented Great Society liberal reformers with a legible problem that they could fix without recourse to major reforms. It would eventually be recast by neoliberal reformers to justify a more ideological form of disembedding that would shift the boundaries of responsibility for dealing with poverty from the social and the public to the individual and personal.

4.1 Embedded Poverty Knowledge

Looking back at his experience in the War on Poverty during an interview conducted in the 1980s, economist Robert Lampman made note of what a "shock" it was for economists of his generation to have "poverty" reemerge as a topic for economic research and policy intervention. Lampman himself was among a generation of economists whose careers had been shaped by the changes sweeping the profession in the immediate postwar decades. After completing his PhD in 1950 at the famously institutionalist University of Wisconsin Department of Economics – with its commitments to historical methods, labor movement politics, and laying the legislative and institutional groundwork for public regulation of corporate capitalism – Lampman joined a number of his peers in adopting the methods and preoccupations of the "neoclassical/Keynesian" synthesis that came to fruition in the Kennedy/Johnson CEA. Building on the methods developed by Simon Kuznets for measuring and tracking the distribution of national income, Lampman conducted a major study of historical trends in wealth distribution for the National Bureau of Economic Research.[16] That, and a study Lampman conducted for the Congressional Joint Economic Committee in 1959 tying the fate of the country's "low-income population" to trends in employment and economic growth, drew him squarely into the orbit of Keynesian economic management. "We never used the word 'poverty,'" he noted, referring to what he and his colleagues considered to be its moralistic and charity work overtones. "It had been consigned

---

[16] Lampman, *Oral History Interview*; O'Connor, *Poverty Knowledge*, 139–52; Bernstein, *A Perilous Progress*; and Huret, *Experts' War on Poverty*, 57–61.

to the dustbin," as professional economists sharpened the lines between theirs as an academic, theoretically grounded, and scientific discipline and the applied program- and practice-related knowledge generated by agency bureaucrats and social work professionals. Economists similarly eschewed references to "the poor," preferring terms such as "low-income" and "low-skilled," which were deemed more descriptively neutralized and salient to the questions of employment, human capital, and labor force participation dominating the field.[17] Nor did the terminology of "poverty" seem as relevant or applicable as it once might have to a postwar generation concerned with managing the nation's celebrated prosperity, conjuring images of Depression-era breadlines and mass immiseration as it did. At least one prominent effort at estimation seemed to bear that bias out: Poverty was at most an "afterthought," confined to "islands" of economic backwardness and individual "cases" of disabling needs, as John Kenneth Galbraith claimed in his best-selling 1958 book *The Affluent Society* – an assessment based on what he later acknowledged to be an artificially low household income yardstick of $1,000.[18]

Within a few years, such trepidation had all but disappeared. Poverty had been designated a major economic challenge – an indicator of ongoing economic hardship in an otherwise prosperous economy – by no less an authority than the CEA, which had devoted an entire chapter to the subject in its now famous 1964 *Annual Report*. Five years later, poverty appeared on the roster of leading social indicators as well, in the ultimately unsuccessful effort to establish a "'social report,' akin to the Economic Report of the President," as it was described by economist Mancur Olson, writing as the Department of Health Education and Welfare (HEW) staff member responsible for managing the project. Even there poverty was presented strictly in terms of income deprivation. "[I]f poverty is not an 'economic' problem, then nothing is," Olson wrote, in an essay reflecting on the often disputed, but in the end, necessarily blurred division of labor between economists and the other social scientists in matters of public policy.[19] Meantime, Lampman was gaining recognition as the country's leading poverty expert. After conducting the empirical research that informed the CEA *Report*, he went on to make studying the economics of poverty the centerpiece of his life's work, as a founder of the first federally funded

[17] Lampman, *Oral History Interview*, 16.
[18] O'Connor, *Poverty Knowledge*, 146–47 and Galbraith, *Affluent Society*.
[19] U.S. Department of Health, Education, and Welfare, *Toward a Social Report*; and Olson, "Economics, Sociology, and the Best of All Possible Worlds."

poverty research center, the University of Wisconsin's Institute for Research on Poverty, and standard-bearer for assessing policy proposals with the imprimatur to ask "what does it do for the poor?"[20]

Still, Lampman's recollection is salient for what it tells us about the dynamics shaping the trajectory of twentieth-century economics, and social science more generally, as the academic enterprise grew more disembedded from its roots in Progressive-era reform. In reality, though unacknowledged in Lampman's view, investigating poverty was one of the defining activities of the associations of academics, intellectuals, and social reformers who came together at the height of America's first Gilded Age to bring the statistical and otherwise methodologically innovative tools of empirical social investigation to bear on the vast disparities in wealth and welfare generated by unregulated industrial capitalism. The academically trained economists who organized the American Economic Association in 1885 recognized and encouraged the fluidity between their inquiries into political economy and the heterogeneous field of social economy – the rubric for the wide array of poverty, public health, housing, and related social welfare investigations launched by college-educated women and men associated with the settlement house movement and related efforts to make charitable and philanthropic work more scientific and systematic in its approach to social change.[21] This was especially the case for economics at the University of Wisconsin, which, thanks to Richard T. Ely, John R. Commons, and their students, had made the department the exemplar of the famed "Wisconsin tradition" of research in service to public policy they helped to establish. Commons and his student John Fitch were centrally involved in the renowned Pittsburgh Survey (1909–1914), which was the most ambitious and intellectually encompassing of the large-scale social surveys of its day, and the project that heralded the establishment of the Russell Sage Foundation as a new kind of philanthropy, devoted to promoting "social research for social betterment."[22] Inspired by Charles Booth's epic, seventeen volume *Life and Labour of the People in London* (1889–1903) and the widely circulated maps and investigations of earnings and ethnicity in the working-class immigrant neighborhood surrounding Chicago's Hull House settlement, the Pittsburgh Survey drew together an extraordinary collection of academically trained and "amateur" social investigators to study the homes, working, civic, and environmental

---

[20] Lampman, "What Does It Do for the Poor?"
[21] Furner, *Advocacy and Objectivity* and Rodgers, *Atlantic Crossings*.
[22] O'Connor, *Social Science for What?*

---

conditions of working-class Pittsburgh in the era of Carnegie Steel. It was also during that period that poverty research began to assume its modern form, laying critical groundwork for some of the measurements and protocols – including the notion of establishing what Booth referred to as the "line of poverty" – which would later be absorbed into the toolkit of a more fully professionalized social-scientific field.[23]

Linking social science to its roots in the progressive social survey reform tradition draws our attention to how earlier generations embedded the study of poverty in more broadly conceived investigations of the social-structural and political transformations of their times. This was especially evident in the case of the Pittsburgh Survey, which presented poverty as a problem of low wages, exploitative labor practices, and degraded social conditions in a series of volumes that together presented a documentary narrative of the consequences of unchecked, locally oligarchic industrial capitalism. They also laid out an agenda for labor reform. The Hull House surveys similarly framed poverty as a problem of exploited labor, while highlighting the significance of gender in studies that would help to instigate a virtual subgenre of feminized inquiry into sweatshop labor. Migration and urbanization also figured prominently as framing themes for this generation of poverty research, most prominently in W. E. B. Du Bois's pioneering study *The Philadelphia Negro*.[24] Notably diminished, though never entirely absent, was the obsession with routing out pauperism, public dependency, or indolence that had animated poverty investigations since the days of late eighteenth- and early nineteenth-century Anglo-American Poor Law Reform.[25] Studying poverty, in the newly scientific, structurally contextualized mode of social investigation, would facilitate a shift from charity, with its emphasis on blaming, punishing, or saving individuals, to public action and social-structural reform.

Progressive-era economic knowledge left another, darker legacy with its widespread, though by no means universal, embrace of eugenics and other variations on "race" science. Armed with popular but robustly refuted theories of white racial and cultural superiority – and often in the name of protecting "American" labor – Commons joined a number of his Progressive colleagues in supporting the racially restrictive immigration legislation that culminated in the Johnson–Reed Act of 1924. With a few notable exceptions, progressive economists were also traditionally masculinist

[23] Booth, *Life and Labour of the People* and O'Connor, *Poverty Knowledge*, chap. 1.
[24] Du Bois, *Philadelphia Negro*.
[25] Katz, *In the Shadow of the Poorhouse*.

in their approach to labor regulations and norms, making them resistant to treating women as permanent, equal rights–bearing members of the industrial workforce. While embedded in a structural critique of laissez-faire capitalism, Progressive views of poverty were also steeped in and, in important ways, reinforced the very ideas and ideologies that were used to justify, obscure, or otherwise explain away the structures of inequality that made women and nonwhite minorities disproportionately vulnerable to poverty.[26]

The Progressive-era practice of structurally and socially contextualized and embedded poverty research would continue during the interwar decades, even as changes in the production of social and economic knowledge tended to marginalize the reform sensibilities that animated earlier inquiries. These trends, toward the professionalization and disciplinary differentiation of social and economic knowledge, were actively encouraged by philanthropic funding agencies such as the Rockefeller Foundation and the Carnegie Corporation, which subsidized the expansion of research universities and corporatist policy think tanks while promoting an increasingly scientistic ideology that conflated objectivity with academic disengagement and political neutrality.

The impact of these changes could be seen in the highly influential body of urban research produced by the University of Chicago's Department of Sociology, which reached the height of its prestige under the direction of figures such as Robert E. Park and Ernest Burgess, and the publication of memorably titled studies such as Harvey Zorbaugh's classic survey of the social geography of inequality on Chicago's Near North Side, *Gold Coast and Slum*.[27] Although a number of Chicago-affiliated faculty and researchers were associated with local reform movements and drew on the survey and mapping techniques pioneered by the Hull House settlement, under Park's direction and throughout the interwar years, the department began to sharpen the lines between academic and applied or amateur investigation, to articulate more theoretical aspirations, and to embrace an ethos of academic detachment from the work of reform. Best known for its ecological theories of urban development and assimilationist models of ethnic succession, Chicago School sociology framed poverty as a symptom of the cultural dislocation and social "disorganization" experienced by the uprooted rural peasantries of Europe and the American South as they attempted to adjust to urban industrial life. As part of what Chicago

[26] Leonard, *Illiberal Reformers*, 109–85 and Recchiuti, *Civic Engagement*, 177–207.
[27] Zorbaugh, *Gold Coast and Slum*.

School theorists conceptualized as a naturalized process of resettlement and readjustment, poverty would be a temporary and largely internalized condition, as successive waves of migrants learned to assimilate and otherwise "reorganize" their own lives.

By pivoting its explanatory framework around naturalized assimilation processes rather than labor market institutions and inequities, Chicago School sociologists exhibited the growing tendency to link poverty and related problems to patterns and scientific models of human behavior, a tendency that would only accelerate in the post–World War II decades. As critics noted at the time and subsequently, Chicago sociologists also downplayed the depth and structural nature of racial barriers facing African-Americans and other nonwhite minorities, and obscured the degree to which the patterns of segregation and uneven mobility explained as natural in their ecological theories were rooted in actively discriminatory, officially sanctioned policies and social practices. To be sure, there were important exceptions to what Gunnar Myrdal criticized, caustically, as the "do-nothing (laissez-faire)" bias in Chicago School social ecology.[28] Chicago-trained sociologist Charles S. Johnson, then employed as research director for the Chicago Urban League, used the Chicago School's cyclical theory of racial conflict in his officially sponsored investigation of the devastating Chicago race riots of 1919, ultimately concluding that naturalized models of intergroup competition among migrants could not explain the extent, or the deliberately planned, officially sanctioned nature of the racial violence.[29] In the massive Depression-era (and WPA-funded) study of Chicago's African-American South Side *Black Metropolis*, sociologists St. Clair Drake and Horace Cayton similarly drew on Chicago sociology's assimilationist framework to show that African-Americans were not following the trajectory of progress it predicted, and that institutionalized color lines in employment, housing, and social relations were to blame.[30]

Still, the more lasting legacy of Chicago School urban ecology for later generations of poverty research and policy would stem from two of its more ecological and behavioral themes. One was E. Franklin Frazier's frequently reappropriated analysis of the breakdown and matriarchal reorganization of black family life under the pressures of slavery, post-Emancipation migration, and urbanization – in a series of "crises" that,

---

[28] Myrdal, *American Dilemma*, 1095.
[29] Chicago Commission on Race Relations, *Negro in Chicago*.
[30] Drake and Cayton, *Black Metropolis*.

in Frazier's ecological frame, left lower-class female-headed African-American families especially vulnerable to the "disorganizing" influences of urban life, while also pointing to a future in which black male industrial employment would facilitate a return to what he pictured as a more stable patriarchal family norm. In the decades to come, this analysis would be detached from its ecological frame and distilled into a repeatedly invoked imagery of black motherhood as a form of self-perpetuating pathology at the root of intergenerational poverty. The other was the Chicago School's indelible ecological map that located immigrant and black neighborhoods in "zones" of social disorganization – an analysis that, Robert Park to the contrary, would provide the rationale for a wide range of community action and development programs in future decades.[31]

4.2 Disembedding Poverty Knowledge

Standard narratives of postwar American history emphasize the degree to which poverty was rendered "invisible" by the combination of mass affluence, the broad if occasionally begrudging political acceptance of the moderately redistributionist New Deal welfare state, and the achievement of an unprecedented level of white working-class prosperity, especially among unionized industrial workers.[32] And in significant ways, poverty *did* lose public visibility as its incidence diminished in the immediate postwar decades, despite the still-widespread persistence of economic hardship. For many of the same reasons, it also lost purchase as a recognized social problem and political issue, as poverty became marginalized and disembedded from the primary institutional channels of economic research and policy.

Sustained economic growth was an important factor in this shift, assuring liberals in particular that the turmoil and displacement that had made poverty a first-order social question in the late nineteenth and early twentieth centuries had been resolved. Diminished extremes of income inequality between the very top and the broad middle segments of the earnings distribution, as reported by Simon Kuznets – a development economists would later, nostalgically, refer to as "the great compression" – contributed to the declining sense of urgency about poverty as well.[33] In

[31] Frazier, *Negro Family in the United States*; O'Connor, *Poverty Knowledge*, 77–84; and O'Connor, "Community Action, Urban Reform, and the War against Poverty."
[32] Patterson, *America's Struggle against Poverty*.
[33] Kuznets, *Shares of Upper Income Groups* and Goldin and Margo, "Great Compression."

Galbraith's well-known and apt observations, the "ancient preoccupations" with addressing inequality, insecurity, and privation had been replaced by "a preoccupation with productivity and production" in liberal economic thought and policy, in a prevailing approach that treated growth as an alternative to redistribution and poverty as a "residual" concern.[34] Poverty's marginalized position was only reinforced by the increasing professionalization and disciplinary organization of postwar economic knowledge around neoclassical principles and models, solidifying boundaries between economics as a theoretically grounded science and social work and welfare studies as applied fields. With the possible exception of welfare economics, a field that at the time was undergoing major challenges and transitions, the question of poverty did not lend itself to the kind of economic modeling encouraged by the growing influence of neoclassical theory in the field.

The stability – and stratified structure – of America's partial welfare state fostered a similar kind of complacency about poverty and inequality in liberal policy circles. Conservative animus notwithstanding, the social insurance, safety net, and labor protections of the New Deal welfare state – all bearing the imprint of the Wisconsin institutionalists – remained intact through the Eisenhower administration, along with, at least in the eyes of liberals, a basic commitment to the role of government in protecting citizens from the vicissitudes of life and labor in a capitalist economy. Vast areas of economic insecurity and need remained, especially for those barred from the benefits of social citizenship by the New Deal's racial and gender exclusions.[35] With rare exception, however, these issues were largely unacknowledged in legislative debates, and otherwise consigned to networks of expertise and advocacy – themselves segregated by race and gender – that emerged around means-tested social welfare programs.

The preoccupations of postwar affluence and a rising scientific positivism contributed to the marginalization of poverty in the noneconomic social sciences as well. With the extremes of economic inequality diminished or at least hidden from view, sociologists grew more interested in gauging and theorizing its impact, systemic functions, and noneconomic expressions than in tracing its structural roots. Some, inspired by Max Weber's stratificational theory (first introduced, in translation, by Talcott Parsons in the 1930s), focused on bringing a wider range of status and behavioral

[34] Galbraith, *Affluent Society*, 97–98, 239.
[35] Gordon, *Pitied but Not Entitled*; Quadagno, *Color of Welfare*; and Katznelson, *When Affirmative Action Was White*.

indicators – educational attainment, occupational and social prestige, access to social and political power, differences in "value orientation" – into the measurement of American class dynamics and social mobility.[36] Others took a lead from Robert Merton to recast Chicago School explanations of lower-class disorganization and deviance as expressions of structurally induced Durkheimian social anomie.[37] Joining the foundation- and government-subsidized quest for a comprehensive, theoretically robust science of human behavior, a number of studies incorporated psychological tests and concepts borrowed from interdisciplinary studies of "culture and personality" to map the outlines of distinctively lower-class behavior. Suffice it to say that the image of lower- (the almost uniformly preferred substitute for "working-") class life to emerge from these studies did not weather well; any lingering appreciation from Depression-era research had long since disappeared. Indeed, in lower-class culture, social scientists found the locus of values and culture "traits" quite the opposite of what prosperous, liberal America stood for: among them, political authoritarianism, harsh child-rearing practices, presentism, and a ubiquitously diagnosed inability to defer gratification. To be poor or "lower class" in affluent America was to be culturally and psychologically "other." To be black and poor was to be psychologically damaged, "scarred" – in the words of one of the many studies that anticipated the pathologizing themes of the Moynihan Report – by the racial oppression that was coming home to roost in the "crisis" of the black female-headed family.[38] While Moynihan drew on E. Franklin Frazier to depict a matriarchy descended from slavery and historically sustained by black male unemployment, he had a substantial trove of social science literature on the psychologically and culturally deviant "lower-class Negro" to back up his sensationalistic claims that the black family had hardened into a self-perpetuating "tangle of pathology" that threatened to send lower-class African-Americans into a permanent cycle of poverty and welfare dependency.

Even as postwar social scientists obsessed about the damage and dangers of lower-class culture, poverty as an economic and politically rooted problem was very much treated as the "residual" John Kenneth Galbraith had made it out to be. To the extent that they problematized it at all, poverty was reframed as a problem of culture and psychology, and of individuals

[36] Horowitz, "Max Weber and the Spirit of American Sociology" and Parsons, "Revised Analytical Approach."
[37] Merton, "Social Structure and Anomie."
[38] O'Connor, *Poverty Knowledge*, 102–13 and Scott, *Contempt and Pity*.

and groups, conceptually disembedded from structures of inequality. When income deprivation did reemerge as a public issue, formulated as a "paradox" in the midst of plenty, even the more structurally inclined analyses, including Galbraith's, dwelled on the internalized mechanisms through which poor people supposedly perpetuated their own oppression by allowing themselves to get caught in behavioral "cycles" that would be difficult to "break."

Exceptional cases of politically and structurally embedded poverty research did emerge in this period of postwar affluence. In two significant instances, they provide us with exceptions that prove the rule. One was the largely applied and program-related expertise developed by the growing cadres of professionally trained policy analysts, social work professionals, and midlevel civil servants who staffed or otherwise advised the public and private, federal, state, and local agencies of the postwar welfare state. Though academically trained with advanced degrees in one of the disciplines or in schools of policy or social work, the women who came up through these career paths were often cut off from academic opportunities – a limitation their similarly credentialed male counterparts, who moved between university and government posts with a greater degree of fluidity, did not encounter. As long-time if not career civil servants in postwar Washington, these men and women rose to high-level staff positions in the research and administrative bureaus of the Departments of Labor, Agriculture, Commerce, and the Social Security Administration. Through professional organizations such as the National Association of Social Workers, they also organized venues for lobbying and advocacy and, at critical moments, coalition-building to advance social-democratic labor and social welfare legislation.

In these and other ways, they continued the work of social economy pioneered by their Progressive-era forebears, with a special eye to gathering adequate and consistent data on the low-income populations who did not always register in the then-comparatively scant roster of federal-level income and labor surveys. They were also acutely aware of the inadequacies of the categorically targeted and otherwise stratified system of income maintenance created by the New Deal welfare state, especially for the growing numbers of single-mother households who were ineligible for the comparatively generous benefits of social insurance, and otherwise reliant on the federal/state program Aid to Dependent Children, colloquially known as "welfare." In research and advocacy work that would trigger McCarthyite suspicions and, for some in the network, investigation, they drew attention to these and other inadequacies and promoted measures that would strengthen and expand citizens' entitlement to adequate income. They also laid critical groundwork for later efforts to develop standardized measures of need and to shore up and integrate "rehabilitative" services into the nation's safety net programs – with decidedly mixed results.[39]

The other exception came in the form of the "discovery" and social-scientific construction of poverty as a globalized problem of "underdevelopment," in what would become a vast body of economic, sociological, and anthropological literature conducted in (or about) the decolonizing countries and regions of the postwar "third world."[40] Funded and initiated within the rapidly expanding internationalized infrastructure of Cold War era development, foreign aid, defense, and philanthropic agencies, this research was varied and internally contested, especially by scholars from once colonized regions (see Chapter 2: Family). In the United States during the early decades of the Cold War, the field was dominated by the theoretical framework encapsulated in economist Walt W. Rostow's *The Stages of Economic Growth*, published in 1960 – and provocatively but aptly subtitled "a non-communist manifesto" – as a blueprint for capitalist global economic development.[41] What Rostow and a number of others laid out was an abstracted, putatively universalistic model of economic and cultural modernization that positioned the postwar United States – with its high-consumption, growth-oriented, broadly affluent political economy – as the actual and normative apotheosis of historical advancement and development worldwide. Its sweeping, forward-moving vision of history presented capitalist economic development as a decidedly non-Marxist, multistaged progression from a traditional, agrarian, hierarchical, communal past to a modern, industrial, democratic, individuated future. Poverty in this scenario was a problem of structural underdevelopment, endemic to decolonizing third world countries without the economic and cultural resources necessary to get and stay on the modernizing path. It was also a condition the United States and other "advanced" industrialized democracies had presumably long since left behind.[42] Simon Kuznets presented a similarly stylized, if admittedly "conjectural" model of the relationship between national economic growth and income inequality in his 1954 presidential address to the American Economic

[39] Huret, *Experts' War on Poverty*; Mittelstadt, *From Welfare to Workfare*; Storrs, *Second Red Scare*; and Tani, *States of Dependency*.
[40] Escobar, *Encountering Development*, 21–54.
[41] Rostow, *Stages of Economic Growth*.
[42] Gilman, *Mandarins of the Future*; Cullather, *Hungry World*; and Ekbladh, *Great American Mission*.

Association, postulating that the famous inverted-U-shaped pattern (of initially rising, then falling levels of inequality) found in the United States and other developed industrial economies might someday apply to the underdeveloped countries of Latin America, Africa, and Asia – but only if they acquired the political and cultural capacity to create the conditions for capital accumulation, technological innovation, and protecting low-income populations from the ravages of change, as their first-world counterparts had. Understanding whether and how that might happen, Kuznets concluded, was critical to getting a firmer grip on the relationship between economic growth and inequality; it also called for "a shift from market economics to political and social economy."[43]

Whether at the behest of Kuznets or, more likely, one of the major international funding agencies (including, as scholars would later learn, the Central Intelligence Agency), overseas development generated wide-ranging opportunities for social-scientific research, leading to investments in new subfields such as development economics and interdisciplinary area studies while giving poverty – understood as a distinctively "third world" problem – a new relevance as a site for exploring the prospects for a decidedly Americanist vision of democratic capitalism. While continuing to invest in modernization theory and area studies as intellectual underpinnings for international development policy, major foundations turned to poverty alleviation as a universalizing thematic for a more varied set of research and community-based interventions they were sponsoring worldwide.[44]

It was in just this sort of "underdeveloped" world-spanning, universalizing project that anthropologist Oscar Lewis conducted the field research behind what would later become one of the most provocative and fought-over ideas in the American War on Poverty. Combining traditional ethnography with intimate, recorded oral histories and elaborate batteries of psychological tests, Lewis culled from research in sites targeted for economic development – in Mexico, India, and Puerto Rico – to track the emergence of what, in 1959, he labeled a "culture of poverty" that prevented certain subgroups of poor people from adapting to the structural transformations of their modernizing societies.[45] Lewis argued that this "culture," in the sense of a "design for living," was not a product of poverty per se, but had emerged among particular subgroups of poor people who had been uprooted from

[43] Kuznets, "Economic Growth and Income Inequality."
[44] Cullather, *Hungry World* and Immerwahr, *Thinking Small.*
[45] Lewis, *Five Families.*

more traditionally organized agrarian societies to find themselves at the very bottom of newly class-stratified capitalist societies.

In a number of wide-circulation books that would culminate with the publication of the sensationalistic *La Vida*, based on fieldwork in Puerto Rico and New York, in 1966, Lewis catalogued its features in vivid testimonials of lives threaded with economic precarity, overcrowded housing, sexual promiscuity, interpersonal cruelty, and domestic violence, coupled with an ever-expanding inventory of self-defeating behaviors, attitudes, values, and psychological disorders that, he argued, were sanctioned within the culture of poverty – and replicated across generational lines.[46] Lewis expressed sympathy for his subjects, and made it a point to note that some of their most grievous behavior was motivated by the very characteristics – individualistic acquisitiveness and greed – that made capitalism tick. But as the "culture of poverty" turned into an academic juggernaut, the concept quickly lost any viability as systemic critique – as Lewis lavished far more attention on documenting and diagnosing the deviant behavior than on developing a convincing structural analysis.[47] Although Michael Harrington borrowed the concept to shock affluent Americans into action in 1962, even in his critical voice the culture of poverty did more to underscore the otherness of poor people than to implicate the failures of democratic capitalism – an outcome Harrington more than counterbalanced in a lifetime of advocating programs of social-democratic reform.[48]

By the time *La Vida* was published in 1966, to considerable controversy, the social-scientific script on poverty had flipped. No longer considered an economic "afterthought," the problem of poverty warranted a separate chapter in the CEA *Annual Report* of 1964. Affecting upwards of thirty million people, and one-fifth of American families, it had been, and would continue to be, likened to having "a third world country in our midst." Economic growth at full employment was deemed the "number one weapon" by the Keynesian economists at the helm, coupled with education, job training, and other human capital–building interventions. Chastened by the firestorm provoked by the Moynihan Report, erstwhile theorists of lower-class culture were beginning to reexamine their own assumptions, methods, and cultural biases, lest their studies feed into ongoing attacks on "undeserving" welfare recipients. Conservative backlash politics had

[46] Lewis, *La Vida*.
[47] The most thorough excavations of Lewis's concept remain Rigdon, *Culture Façade* and O'Connor, *Poverty Knowledge*, 117–23.
[48] Isserman, *Other American*.

found a ready target in the cultural deviance of poor people – minority youth and single mothers in particular – but were more fully honed on the permissiveness of the liberal welfare state.

More important than the seeming divide, though, is to recognize the essential compatibility among the varied lines of postwar social-scientific thought about poverty and the poor. Ideas rooting poverty in cultural deprivation would continue to be deployed throughout the 1960s in support of remedial cycle-of-poverty-breaking interventions at home and in the developing world. Nor were they seen to be incompatible with the employment and labor market emphasis adopted by liberal economists. While keeping an arm's length from culture and psychology as meaningful frameworks for analysis, they too were convinced that explanations for the lingering problem of poverty could be located in the attributes of poor people and households – the absence of a male breadwinner, the lack of human capital and marketable skills – that prevented them from getting access to the opportunities and protections that a growing economy could and would provide. It was in this form, and as part of a discourse that focused narrowly on the character and characteristics of the poor, that the idea of a deviant, self-sabotaging but ultimately remediable subculture was absorbed into the canon of American poverty research, and would continue to exert a powerful influence well after it had been subject to criticism from the people it presumed to represent.

The effect, at the time and going forward, was to disembed poverty as a concept and as an issue from any meaningful grounding in class politics or analysis, let alone in the intersectional inequities of class, race, and gender. The poverty problem, so framed, would be made palatable to white liberal policymakers and politicians in affluent Cold War America, while offering reassurances that it could be eliminated without significant structural reform.

4.3 Poverty amidst Plenty

In *Progress and Poverty*, his extraordinarily popular and influential treatise first published in 1879, amateur economist and single-tax advocate Henry George made a direct link between the "increase of want" and the "increase of wealth," arguing that the economic immiseration of the laboring classes could be explained by the rampant speculation and rent-seeking of wealthy landowners.[49] *Progress and Poverty* inspired millions and sparked reform

---

[49] George, *Progress and Poverty*.

movements worldwide. It was also a political and cultural touchstone for John R. Commons and numerous other Progressive economists. Decades later, another generation of economists would signal how much things had changed, when the President's CEA explained the "paradox" of poverty amidst plenty by focusing on the "special handicaps" of the poor.[50]

By then, several groups variously situated within and otherwise aligned with the Kennedy and Johnson administrations had been promoting the idea of making poverty the target of some kind of remedial intervention, if not necessarily structural reform. After successfully courting West Virginia Democratic primary voters with promises of a domestic antipoverty platform, Kennedy launched his presidency by pledging leadership and support in the fight against global poverty. The Peace Corps and the Alliance for Progress (in Latin America) were created in 1961, signaling the administration's intent to join with the United Nations to make the 1960s the "decade of development," while stepping up the Cold War battle with the Soviets to win the allegiances of the third world.[51] The administration also embraced place, or "depressed-area," development as a thematic in a number of domestic legislative and administrative initiatives, starting with the successful passage of the Area Redevelopment Act in 1961 and a series of experimental urban reform initiatives funded by the National Institute of Mental Health (NIMH). Kennedy's Department of Labor made "manpower development" a signature issue, reflecting the burst of interest in human capital investments taking hold in the field.

The country's largest philanthropies took a similar loop back from their ongoing ventures in overseas development to an emerging interest in addressing what they continued to think of as isolated problems affecting poor people and places at home. Encouraged by the prospect of renewed government activism and their own connections in the Kennedy administration, program officers at the Ford Foundation initiated a series of urban and state-wide demonstration projects in education, social services, urban renewal, and juvenile delinquency prevention with the expectation that federal agencies would adopt and take them to scale. Two of these experiments would prove especially influential in the administration's domestic program, and in building the channels through which social-scientific ideas would be funneled into social policy. In its multicity "Gray Areas" demonstrations, the foundation adapted Chicago School models of urban migration in a grant program designed to "catalyze" comprehensive

[50] CEA, *Annual Report*, 72.
[51] Latham, *Modernization as Ideology* and Jahanbani, "Across the Ocean, Across the Tracks."

social service and educational interventions that would help the increasingly minority residents of central city neighborhoods to get on a pathway to employment and assimilation – all in the face of industrial job loss and white flight.

In Mobilization for Youth, an ambitious New York City–based initiative, the foundation joined the NIMH and the President's Committee on Juvenile Delinquency and Crime – the latter under the auspices of Attorney General Robert F. Kennedy's Department of Justice – to bring the most up-to-date thinking from social science and social work practice to bear on the prevention of juvenile delinquency. Tapping a body of research inspired by Robert Merton's theory of social anomie, Mobilization for Youth was becoming the best-known outlet for the "blocked opportunity" theory of delinquency, which called on youth-serving agencies, advocates, and activists to re-channel their reform energies toward local "systems" of education, social services, employment, and law enforcement rather than targeting problem youth (see Chapter 7: Crime). Along with the Ford Foundation's Gray Areas program, Mobilization for Youth would also be a source of ideas, models, and networks for Community Action in the War on Poverty.[52]

By 1963, White House advisors had come to think of poverty as a possible framework for bringing these otherwise uncoordinated domestic programs together, with an eye to identifying a distinctively "Kennedy" issue for the upcoming reelection campaign. Kennedy himself had become aware of Harrington's best-selling book, thanks to an extraordinary review published in *The New Yorker* earlier in the year.[53] Kennedy's CEA also had an as-yet unspecified antipoverty initiative in its sights, as part of the broader full-employment and economic stimulus package they had been urging the reluctant, fiscally cautious president to adopt. Given the go-ahead to develop what at that point was being framed as a comprehensive "attack," they too were aware of poverty's potential as a political strategy. As plans for the Civil Rights Movement's 1963 March on Washington for Jobs and Freedom became more widely known, task force members honed arguments that African-Americans would disproportionately benefit from an attack on poverty, even as the majority of beneficiaries would be white – making the initiative among the earliest examples of what liberals would come to refer to as "race-neutral" policies for addressing racial and economic inequality.[54]

[52] O'Connor, *Poverty Knowledge*, 124–32.
[53] Macdonald, "Our Invisible Poor."
[54] Brauer, "Kennedy, Johnson, and the War on Poverty."

But the real impetus for making poverty the focus of a major federal policy initiative came from Lyndon B. Johnson's official declaration of War on Poverty in 1964, in a characteristically dramatic escalation of JFK's "attack." This, more than any kind of social-scientific rediscovery or public awakening, gave ending poverty its singular priority on the Great Society's domestic policy agenda. LBJ's announcement also generated the logic and sense of political imperative that would shape poverty research as a major social-scientific enterprise, and as a specialized, multidisciplinary subfield detached from the broader social-scientific study of inequality. And it shaped the answers to the mission-defining questions that, as social scientists quickly learned, were far more contentious and consequential in practice than in theory: about the nature of the problem, the necessary scope of the response, the kind of knowledge required, and, ultimately, whether the burden of responding to poverty was really a public responsibility at all.

One thing seemed overdetermined from the start. To fulfill the president's mandate – "total victory" – the poverty problem would be narrowly delineated, in terms of deficits that could be remediated and measurable gaps that could be filled. Certainly, this was the view of the CEA economists; with Lampman as their designated representative to the administration's War on Poverty planning task force, they actively resisted efforts to turn the effort into an attack on inequality. "The Great Society is at war with poverty, not inequality," CEA member James Tobin would later write. That way, it would be possible to imagine raising all incomes above a basic level of subsistence, "while relative disparities in consumption are reduced little if at all."[55] Pressures from the Johnson administration pointed to a delimited effort as well. The president sent a powerful signal by dismissing proposals for direct government job creation, and by setting a ceiling on overall expenditures for the initiative. Under the rubric of "a hand-up, not a hand-out," the operation would be located in the newly created OEO, with a limited budget authorization and the mandate to leverage additional funds for fighting poverty through creative bureaucratic politics.[56] Community action would be included within this framework, at least in the administration's expectations, as a program emphasizing coordinated rehabilitative services rather than systemic change: "Breaking the cycle of poverty" was a well-known tagline among OEO programs designed to address cultural deprivation among the poor. These mandates, in turn, would privilege a certain kind of applied economic knowledge:

[55] Tobin, "It Can Be Done!" 14.
[56] Patterson, *America's Struggle against Poverty*, 138–49.

heavily quantitative, grounded in existing and newly generated statistical data, and defined around a fairly circumscribed set of questions about the characteristics of poor people and the measurable outcomes of antipoverty policies.

This narrow framing was reinforced by what on first glance may seem to have been a counterintuitive move: the decision to staff the OEO's research office with economists and systems analysts recruited from the RAND Corporation. Although admittedly inexpert in poverty, the analysts from RAND were legendary for having revolutionized policymaking in Robert McNamara's Department of Defense with the introduction of the Planning–Programming–Budgeting System (PPBS), a decision-making model that promised to turn federal dollars ("inputs") into more effective program outcomes. In response to a directive from administration budget officials, the PPBS system was soon adopted by all federal government departments, effectively institutionalizing the values and research priorities, as well as the decision-making and evaluation practices, of economic analysis within the leading social policy agencies. The PPBS mandate elevated efficiency, targeting, and measurability of outcomes as values in program design, as well as certain kinds of data – concrete, quantifiable, compatible with existing budget and planning systems – in knowledge-gathering. This approach stood in stark contrast to the participatory model of research and planning embraced by advocates and program staff in the OEO's Community Action Program, which among other things called for evidence of "maximum feasible participation" of poor people in local program design. Nor were community-based initiatives easy to translate into readily measurable inputs and outcomes favored by the PPBS system, especially as they began to target local institutions, power hierarchies, and systems of resource allocation for change. Olson, then staffing the HEW Office of the Assistant Secretary for Planning and Evaluation – one of the premier analytic policy "shops" – recognized the tension that the favored position of economic analysis was causing. Critics questioned whether "an economic approach is the most appropriate for dealing with the 'social' programs of government, or suited to an inevitably political environment," he acknowledged. But he also defended economic reasoning as a recognition that "social programs require scarce resources, and that is what economics is all about."[57]

These tensions would only become more concrete as the War on Poverty got underway, spilling over into key decisions such as the adoption of an

[57] Olson, "Economics, Sociology, and the Best of All Possible Worlds," 97 and O'Connor, *Poverty Knowledge*.

official and standardized poverty measurement. Here again the impetus was toward an approach that would define the poverty problem as limited and finite. On this point, the CEA economists had been and would continue to be adamant: The measure and official definition of poverty should be absolute, which is to say, tied to a measurable standard or "line" of subsistence below which no one could be expected to survive. To link the measure to some more relational gauge – a portion of median income was a commonly suggested option – would be to target a problem that would never go away, or, more pointedly, to fight a war the Great Society would never "win." They also insisted on basing the poverty measure on income alone, rather than attempting to incorporate softer indicators of social exclusion or disfranchisement, as the one variable that was readily measurable and basically universal as an indicator of need. The CEA had adopted this approach in assessing the size and characteristics of the population in poverty in its 1964 *Annual Report*, but skirted the issue of adopting an official measure in favor of using the broadly "reasonable" figure of $3,000 per family ($1,500 for individuals), which happened to fall in the middle of the poverty measures in use at the time. That left the ultimate decision in the hands of the economists in the OEO's new Office of Research, Planning, Programs, and Evaluation who, faced with numerous demands for a scientifically defensible yardstick for determining target groups, eligibility criteria, and, especially, tracking the progress of the high-profile agency's programs, were similarly inclined to adopt a measure based on minimum standards of subsistence: an absolute poverty line. This is what led them to a much-updated version of the measurement protocols rooted in the social survey tradition, and the research of a career government analyst named Mollie Orshansky.

The details of the adoption of the Orshansky poverty line are well known, and they underscore the multivalenced politics of coming up with an official measure of economic need. As a statistical analyst at the Children's Bureau and the Department of Agriculture (DOA), Orshansky had spent much of her early career assessing household expenditures and needs, basing the latter on what, since the earliest surveys of poverty, was considered the most "scientifically" calculable standard of subsistence: the cost of a calorically adequate, minimally nutritious diet. She subsequently joined the Social Security Administration's (SSA) research division, which by the late 1950s had begun to grapple with a significant (and later politically explosive) change in the composition of the welfare rolls, given the rapidly growing proportion of households headed by never-married, rather than widowed, single mothers. It was in work related to that project that Orshansky came up with the basic formula adopted by the OEO as the official measure of poverty, based on the cost of the DOA's minimalistic economy food plan, multiplied by three and adjusted for family size. Orshansky was among those who drew attention to the limitations of her measure – which she regarded as highly provisional and bare bones as an assessment of need. But in the face of immediate programmatic demands and a mounting counteroffensive from the Chamber of Commerce and the American Enterprise Institute (AEI), the measure had two significant virtues. One was that, though significantly more detailed and elaborate in approach, the Orshansky poverty line did not significantly alter the broad-gauged count provided in the CEA *Report*. The other was that, for much the same reason, Orshansky's measure was able to withstand the AEI's claim, offered up in an alternative statistical report by Rose Friedman, that the administration's estimates of poverty were grossly exaggerated and in fact should be cut in half.[58] This practice of manipulating measures to make poverty disappear would become standard among conservative think tanks in future decades, and remains so to this day.

This swift resolution aside, the Orshansky poverty line left many deeply dissatisfied. To European observers such as British social policy intellectuals Richard Titmuss and Peter Townsend, its basic approach was hopelessly outdated, and in many ways anachronistic for the dynamic, affluent society the United States had become. It was "too static, somehow locked up in the distant youth of the grandparental generation," Townsend wrote.[59] Many of their American counterparts agreed. Notable among the issues singled out for criticism were the very features that made the Orshansky poverty line attractive to the research and planning officers at the OEO. One problem was that it was wedded to an old-fashioned concept of basic subsistence, leaving no room to acknowledge changing standards of living or need. Another was its failure to recognize the importance of a whole host of nonmonetary resources – education, benefits, capital assets, access to legal representation, and social services – that were increasingly part of the basic requirements of social citizenship, and were just as unequally distributed as income. Most problematic was its reliance on a concept of absolute rather than relative deprivation, creating the illusion that poverty was confined to an identifiable and stable class of people rather than itself a hazard of market economies, and ignoring the fact that it was rooted in inequitable distributions of income, resources, and power.

[58] O'Connor, *Poverty Knowledge*, 182–85 and Huret, *Experts' War on Poverty*, 131–44.
[59] Townsend, "Introduction," x.

Beneath the surface of these mostly under-the-radar debates were deepening tensions that could not be mapped onto the frequently referenced Fitzgerald/Hemingway divide: between those who continued to treat poverty as a problem that could be fixed within the existing distributional system and those who insisted that the problem was the system of distribution itself. The latter approach would call not just for a more relational poverty measure but for a different kind of knowledge from what was being produced in the RAND-like research offices of the OEO and affiliated think tanks: focused on the institutions, practices, and norms of distribution rather than on the characteristics of households and individuals; prepared to investigate how the privileges of the affluent relied on the deprivation of the poor; and aimed at achieving a more equitable distribution of income and resources rather than the elimination of deprivation below an arbitrary poverty line.[60]

These tensions would only grow sharper and more overtly politicized – and less abstract – as the War on Poverty moved from the initial planning stages to the proverbial front lines. Social-scientific research came under a greater degree of public and political scrutiny than ever before, especially from within the rank and file of variously mobilized poor people's movements. Program evaluation was an increasingly volatile area of contention, as service providers questioned the validity of hastily constructed outcomes measures and resisted the idea of withholding services for the sake of the industry "gold standard" of controlled experimental design. The immense controversy surrounding the Moynihan Report was but the best known among a wider range of field-shaping debates, over the conceptual vagaries and methodological flaws of the culture of poverty in particular, that would invigorate theoretically critical and otherwise alternative lines of social research. Now-classic works of urban ethnography such as Elliot Liebow's *Tally's Corner* and Carol Stack's *All Our Kin* challenged the idea that a pathologically damaged, matriarchal subculture had taken hold of the black family and was permanently emasculating black men – in many ways anticipating critiques later levied by feminist theorists of poverty and the welfare state.[61] Others pointed to the limitations of Great Society political economy and economic analysis, noting the administration's failure to acknowledge the structural disadvantages faced by workers displaced by automation, by minorities and women shut out of better jobs, by women with childcare responsibilities, and in cities threatened by industrial

[60] Townsend, "Measures and Explanations of Poverty."
[61] Liebow, *Tally's Corner* and Stack, *All Our Kin.*

job loss.[62] In their highly influential book, *Regulating the Poor*, political scientist Frances Fox Piven and sociologist Richard Cloward shifted the focus of analysis entirely, to capitalism as a system of unequal political and social relations that revolved around employers' need for an impoverished, politically complacent working class.[63] Each of these varied interventions was influential in its own right, with wider reverberations in research, practice, and – in the case of Piven and Cloward in particular – social movement activism. The concept of cultural pathology – with its multiple variants – continued to cast a long shadow over public debate nevertheless, especially when deployed by conservative intellectuals and politicians in their concerted campaign to dismantle the welfare state.

Still, despite or perhaps because of these increasingly volatile debates, the economists' deliberately narrow and politically neutralized knowledge practices continued to prevail in official research and policy circles even after the technocratic exuberance surrounding Great Society reform had begun to fade. That analytic tilt would continue through much of the 1970s, even as the newly elected Republican President Richard M. Nixon began to court white working-class loyalties with promises of getting tough on crime and welfare – and a bold new approach to social provision known as the Family Assistance Plan (FAP) developed with advice from his specially appointed urban affairs advisor Daniel Patrick Moynihan. In the face of such overheated rhetoric, the economists staffing the OEO and HEW research offices sought to frame the debate around the goal of improving, expanding, and bringing economies of scale and efficiency to the hopelessly convoluted system. In collaboration with colleagues at the University of Wisconsin's Institute for Research on Poverty, they implemented what in retrospect may seem an outlandishly ambitious series of social experiments designed to test the feasibility of a universal basic income guarantee. In reality, the idea of some kind of simplified, universal minimum income had widespread support at the time – from the otherwise free-market right anchored by Milton Friedman (who favored a very low stipend that would replace all federal welfare, including Social Security) and the US Chamber of Commerce, to the women leading the National Welfare Rights movement, who sought a livable minimum of $5,600. The original idea for an experiment had been incubated in the Johnson administration OEO, as part of its ten-year PPBS plan to end income poverty by 1976, the nation's bicentennial year.

---

[62] Weir, *Politics and Jobs* and McKee, *Problem of Jobs*.
[63] Piven and Cloward, *Regulating the Poor*.

By the time the experiments were actually launched, beginning with sites in New Jersey, Pennsylvania, and rural North Carolina, talk of ending poverty, and the OEO itself were on the wane. The experiments themselves were presented as a test of a new and improved approach to "income maintenance," and funneled into debates about Nixon's FAP. By the end of the decade, it was clear that the politics of welfare reform were driving the reception of the income experiments, rather than the other way around. Citing preliminary (and later disputed) evidence from a later set of experiments linking income guarantees to increased marital break-up, recently elected Senator Moynihan (D-New York) withdrew his support for the idea. By then a very different approach to welfare reform was on the horizon and rapidly gaining steam. Sketched out in a "blueprint" circulated by California Governor Ronald Reagan, it promised to purge the rolls of those deemed undeserving or otherwise not entitled to public largesse, and a return to a bygone era of individual and family responsibility.[64]

4.4 Poverty, Social Science, and Neoliberal Reform

What some experienced as Moynihan's apostasy – after all, he had been among the chief architects and proponents of Nixon's FAP – actually points to an emerging dynamic in the politics of expertise that operated alongside and often apart from more overtly political agendas: as a tool for scrutinizing costs and benefits, assessing prospects and performance, and delivering predictable results, social science could be used to question, and ultimately undermine, the legitimacy of social reform. Thus, it was in a tone of tough-minded realism that *The Public Interest*, a journal founded in the mid-1960s to bring social-scientific rigor to policy debates, delivered a sobering verdict on the ten-year performance of the Great Society in a special issue published in 1974: praiseworthy for its public commitments, overblown in its promises, mixed in its performance, sometimes unintended in its consequences.[65]

A decade later *The Public Interest* was recognized as having become a platform for neoconservative social thought and policy analysis. In a series of essays on "the future of the welfare state," contributors drew on the logic of utility-maximizing actors – coupled with the virtues of the market and neo-Victorian self-reliance – to make a case for disembedding the

---

[64] O'Connor, "False Dawn of Poor Law Reform" and Kershaw and Fair, *New Jersey Income-Maintenance Experiment*.
[65] Ginzberg and Solow, "Some Lessons of the 1960's."

problem of poverty from the social responsibilities of the state. Two of the contributions stand out as indicative of how the case would play out. One was the essay by Charles Murray, arguing that progress against poverty had ended when the War on Poverty began. This essay would catch the attention of an up-and-coming conservative think tank that funded Murray to turn the essay into his massively influential antiwelfare missive *Losing Ground*.[66] The other was a reprint of Alexis De Tocqueville's "Memoir on Pauperism" (1835), a repudiation of the principle of public welfare.[67]

Although it tapped into age-old anxieties and resentments, this attack on the very foundations of social provision represented a development for which the basically liberal, but ideologically neutralized, "establishment" of poverty experts was unprepared: the mobilization of a conservative counterestablishment anchored in the explicitly ideological foundations, think tanks, advocacy organizations, legal institutes, and media outlets of the right. Reagan memorably provided the rhetorical frame for the new era of poverty research, which made ending dependency its central focus and put the existing poverty research establishment on the defensive. "My friends," he said in a quote that could well be offered as a distillation of *Losing Ground*, "some years ago the federal government declared war on poverty and poverty won."[68]

But it was the foot soldiers of the counterestablishment who marshaled the tools of policy analysis to mount an outright war on welfare and on the Keynesian underpinnings of postwar political economy, with lasting effects. Conservative movement think tanks such as the Heritage Foundation, the AEI, the Manhattan Institute, the Cato Institute, and the London-based Institute of Economic Affairs issued a steady barrage of books, reports, and well-placed policy briefs arguing that government intervention only made things worse – generally by coddling bad behavior, interfering in markets, and making it more profitable to rely on welfare than to work. These missives sent shudders through a poverty research establishment still reeling from the impact of the Reagan administration's budget cuts and efforts to "defund the left," and led to various efforts to challenge the right-wing think tanks on empirical and methodological grounds. Such challenges would only go so far, though, in debates that had never been driven or resolved with empirical evidence alone, and that would increasingly be framed around an artificially conceived ideological consensus that too much welfare and too little self-sufficiency was the problem, not the cure.

---

[66] Murray, *Losing Ground*.
[67] De Tocqueville, "Memoir on Pauperism" and Murray, "Two Wars against Poverty."
[68] Reagan, "Address Before a Joint Session of Congress."

But it was not until the mid-1990s, under the administration of President William Jefferson Clinton, that what Murray had proposed as a radical "thought experiment" – to end welfare – actually came to fruition. Clinton put a "New Democrat" gloss on Murray's frame, with a promise to "end welfare as we know it" honed in the centrist post–New Deal politics he cultivated as governor of Arkansas and as a presidential candidate. And although Clinton's proposed reform package was accompanied by promises of access to affordable healthcare coverage, tax subsidies for low-income workers, and related supports, the very title of the welfare-ending Personal Responsibility and Work Opportunity Reconciliation Act of 1996 indicates how dramatically disembedded from the tenets of liberal social provision the "poverty problem" had become. The Act itself made eligibility for welfare time limited and contingent on participation in the paid labor force. In provisions that smacked of a return to the old Poor Law tradition, cash assistance would be penurious and subject to the availability of funds. Even more striking in this regard were its so-called marriage promotion provisions, which required single mothers to establish paternity for purposes of child support and otherwise imposed sanctions on "illegitimacy." Indeed, well over half of the "findings" justifying the legislation had to do with the sanctity of the family and the "crisis" of family values that welfare "dependency" had wrought.[69]

Striking though this return to Poor Law principles may have seemed, in reality the impulse to pauperize the poverty problem had never entirely disappeared from either popular or social-scientific discourse. Despite being couched in the neutralized language of quantification, newly configured distinctions between short- and long-term welfare recipients reflected age-old concerns about undeservingness and, like the growing tendency to draw a line between welfare recipients and the "working poor," helped to naturalize the designation of welfare as a stigmatized, socially undesirable state. Meantime, the fallout from the end of welfare created ever more ways of categorizing the poor, as evaluations of the welfare-replacing Temporary Assistance for Needy Families (TANF) program distinguish among various groups of welfare "leavers," for example, and between presumably permanent leavers and "recidivists," in measuring the program's performance over time. More recently, the notion of "deep" or "extreme" poverty has emerged to highlight the growth in the proportion of poor people – largely as a result of the end of most welfare entitlements and the long-term erosion of the safety net – living at or below half the

[69] Kornbluh and Mink, *Ensuring Poverty*.

Alice O'Connor

poverty line, a concept one might also think of as a measure of the shift from poverty to pauperism in policy and research.[70] Despite its well-known and widely documented flaws, Moynihan's "tangle of pathology" would also be resurrected as a way of talking about ghettoized urban poverty and African-American families in the "underclass" debates of the late 1980s and early 1990s (see Chapter 6: The Black Ghetto).[71]

With the neoliberal turn in policy and politics heralding the "end of welfare as we know it," casual observers might be tempted to conclude that poverty research and policy had come full circle, to return to debates about whether poor people were "different" merely because they lacked income, or because of some deep, possibly irredeemable character flaw. That observation would not be mistaken. But it would be more apt to extend the circle back a century or more, to Progressive-era efforts to cast poverty as, at root, a social and structural rather than an individual and behavioral problem. The irony was that these debates were being resurrected at a moment when social scientists were "rediscovering" inequality as a serious social and economic problem, against the backdrop of visibly rising disparities of wealth and income, of economic hardship among a growing proportion of people with at least a tenuous foothold in the middle or working class, and structural and political transformations in capitalism that would put "life and labour" at the center of poverty knowledge once again. Only by then, after decades of disembedding poverty from the structures of inequality and the channels of reform, social science had lost the capacity to influence or meaningfully engage the first-order social questions upon which modern poverty research had been founded a century before.

Bibliography

Aaron, Henry J. *Politics and the Professors: The Great Society in Perspective.* Washington, DC: Brookings Institution, 1978.
Bernstein, Michael A. *A Perilous Progress: Economists and Public Purpose in Twentieth-Century America.* Princeton: Princeton University Press, 2001.
Booth, Charles. *Life and Labour of the People in London.* London: Macmillan, 1889.
Brauer, Carl. "Kennedy, Johnson, and the War on Poverty." *The Journal of American History*, 69, no. 1 (1982): 98–119.
Brick, Howard. *Transcending Capitalism: Visions of a New Society in Modern American Thought.* Ithaca: Cornell University Press, 2006.
Chicago Commission on Race Relations. *The Negro in Chicago: A Study of Race Relations and a Race Riot.* Chicago: University of Chicago Press, 1922.

[70] Edelman, *So Rich, So Poor.*
[71] Wilson, *Truly Disadvantaged* and Gans, *War against the Poor.*

Council of Economic Advisers. *The Annual Report of the Council of Economic Advisers.* Washington, DC: Council of Economic Advisers, 1964

Cullather, Nick. *The Hungry World: America's Cold War Battle against Poverty in Asia.* Cambridge: Harvard University Press, 2010.

De Tocqueville, Alexis. "Memoir on Pauperism." *The Public Interest* 70 (Winter 1983): 102–20.

Dow, Eddy. "The Rich Are Different." *The New York Times*, November 13, 1988. www.nytimes.com/1988/11/13/books/l-the-rich-are-different-907188.html?auth=login-smartlock

Drake, St. Clair, and Horace R. Cayton. *Black Metropolis: A Study of Negro Life in a Northern City.* New York: Harper & Row, 1962. First published 1945 by Harcourt Brace (New York).

Du Bois, W. E. B. *The Philadelphia Negro: A Social Study.* Philadelphia: University of Pennsylvania Press, 1996. First published 1899.

Edelman, Peter. *So Rich, So Poor: Why It's So Hard to End Poverty in America.* New York: The New Press, 2013.

Ekbladh, David. *The Great American Mission: Modernization and the Construction of an American World Order.* Princeton: Princeton University Press, 2010.

Escobar, Arturo. *Encountering Development: The Making and Unmaking of the Third World.* Princeton: Princeton University Press, 1996.

Fitzgerald, F. Scott. *All the Sad Young Men.* New York: Scribner's, 1926.

Frazier, E. Franklin. *The Negro Family in the United States.* Chicago: University of Chicago Press, 1939.

Furner, Mary O. *Advocacy and Objectivity: A Crisis in the Professionalization of American Social Science.* Lexington: University of Kentucky Press, 1975.

Galbraith, John Kenneth. *The Affluent Society.* New York: Houghton Mifflin, 1998. First published 1958.

Gans, Herbert J. *The War against the Poor: The Underclass and Antipoverty Policy.* New York: Basic Books, 1995.

George, Henry. *Progress and Poverty.* New York: Robert Schalkenbach Foundation, 1948. First published 1879 by D. Appleton and Co. (New York).

Gilman, Nils. *Mandarins of the Future: Modernization in Cold War America.* Baltimore: Johns Hopkins University Press, 2004.

Ginzberg, Eli, and Robert M. Solow. "Some Lessons of the 1960's." *The Public Interest* 34 (Winter 1974): 211–20.

Goldin, Claudia, and Robert A. Margo. "The Great Compression: The Wage Structure in the United States at Mid-Century." *The Quarterly Journal of Economics*, 107, no. 1 (1992): 1–34.

Goldstein, Alyosha. *Poverty in Common: The Politics of Community Action during the American Century.* Durham: Duke University Press, 2012.

Gordon, Linda. *Pitied But Not Entitled: Single Mothers and the History of Welfare.* Cambridge: Harvard University Press, 1994.

Harrington, Michael. *The Other America: Poverty in the United States.* New York: Macmillan, 1962.

Horowitz, Irving Louis. "Max Weber and the Spirit of American Sociology." *The Sociological Quarterly* 5, no. 4 (1964): 344–54.

Huret, Romain. *The Experts' War on Poverty: Social Research and the Welfare Agenda in Postwar America.* Ithaca: Cornell University Press, 2018.

Immerwahr, Daniel. *Thinking Small: The United States and the Lure of Community Development*. Cambridge: Harvard University Press, 2015.

Isserman, Maurice. *The Other American: The Life of Michael Harrington*. New York: Public Affairs Press, 2000.

Jahanbani, Sheyda. "'Across the Ocean, Across the Tracks': Imagining Global Poverty in Cold War America." *Journal of American Studies* 48, no. 4 (2014): 937–74.

Katz, Michael B. *In the Shadow of the Poorhouse: A Social History of Welfare in America*. New York: Basic Books, 1996.

Katz, Michael B. *The Undeserving Poor: America's Enduring Confrontation with Poverty*. New York: Oxford University Press, 2013.

Katznelson, Ira. *When Affirmative Action Was White: An Untold History of Racial Inequality in America*. New York: W. W. Norton, 2005.

Kerner Commission. *Report of the National Advisory Commission on Civil Disorders*. New York: Bantam Books, 1968.

Kershaw, David, and Jerilyn Fair. *New Jersey Income-Maintenance Experiment*. New York: Academic Press, 1976.

Kornbluh, Felicia, and Gwendolyn Mink. *Ensuring Poverty: Welfare Reform in Feminist Perspective*. Philadelphia: University of Pennsylvania Press, 2018.

Kuznets, Simon. *Shares of Upper Income Groups in Income and Savings*. New York: National Bureau of Economic Research, 1953.

Kuznets, Simon. "Economic Growth and Income Inequality." *The American Economic Review* 45, no. 1 (1955): 1–28.

Lampman, Robert J. "What Does It Do for the Poor? A New Test for National Policy." *The Public Interest* 34 (Winter 1974): 66–82.

Lampman, Robert J. *Oral History Interview with Laura Small. Poverty Institute Program*. Madison: University of Wisconsin, 1981.

Latham, Michael E. *Modernization as Ideology: American Social Science and "Nation-building" in the Kennedy Era*. Chapel Hill: University of North Carolina Press, 2000.

Leonard, Thomas C. *Illiberal Reformers: Race, Eugenics and American Economics in the Progressive Era*. Princeton: Princeton University Press, 2016.

Lewis, Oscar. *Five Families: Mexican Case Studies in the Culture of Poverty*. New York: Basic Books, 1959.

Lewis, Oscar. *La Vida: A Puerto Rican Family in the Culture of Poverty – San Juan and New York*. New York: Random House, 1966.

Liebow, Elliot. *Tally's Corner: A Study of Negro Streetcorner Men*. Boston: Little, Brown, 1967.

Macdonald, Dwight. "Our Invisible Poor." *The New Yorker*, 19 January 1963: 82–132.

McKee, Guian A. *The Problem of Jobs: Liberalism, Race, and Deindustrialization in Philadelphia*. Chicago: University of Chicago Press, 2008.

McLaughlin, Malcolm. *The Long Hot Summer*. New York: Palgrave Macmillan, 2014.

Merton, Robert K. "Social Structure and Anomie." *American Sociological Review* 3, no. 5 (1938): 672–82.

Mittelstadt, Jennifer. *From Welfare to Workfare: The Unintended Consequences of Liberal Reform: 1945–1965*. Chapel Hill: University of North Carolina Press, 2005.

Moynihan, Daniel Patrick. *The Negro Family: The Case for National Action [The Moynihan Report]. Office of Policy Planning and Research*. Washington, DC: US Department of Labor, 1965.

Moynihan, Daniel Patrick. "The Professors and the Poor." In *On Understanding Poverty: Perspectives from the Social Sciences*, edited by Daniel P. Moynihan. New York: Basic Books, 1968, 3–35.

Moynihan, Daniel Patrick. *Maximum Feasible Misunderstanding: Community Action in the War on Poverty*. New York: Free Press, 1969.

Murray, Charles A. "The Two Wars against Poverty: Economic Growth and the Great Society." *The Public Interest* 69 (Fall 1982): 3–16.

Murray, Charles A. *Losing Ground: American Social Policy, 1950–1980*. New York: Basic Books, 1984.

Myrdal, Gunnar. *An American Dilemma: The Negro Problem and Modern Democracy*. New York: Harper, 1944.

O'Connor, Alice. "Community Action, Urban Reform, and the War against Poverty: The Ford Foundation's Gray Areas Program." *Journal of Urban History* 22, no. 5 (1996): 586–625.

O'Connor, Alice. "The False Dawn of Poor Law Reform: Nixon, Carter, and the Quest for a Guaranteed Income." *Journal of Policy History* 10, no. 1 (1998): 99–129.

O'Connor, Alice. *Poverty Knowledge: Social Science, Social Policy, and the Poor in Twentieth-Century U.S. History*. Princeton: Princeton University Press, 2001.

O'Connor, Alice. *Social Science for What? Philanthropy and the Social Question in a World Turned Rightside Up*. New York: Russell Sage Foundation, 2007.

Olson, Mancur. "Economics, Sociology, and the Best of All Possible Worlds." *The Public Interest* 12 (Summer 1969): 96–118.

Parsons, Talcott. "A Revised Analytical Approach to the Theory of Social Stratification." In *Class, Status, and Power*, edited by Reinhard Bendix and Seymour Martin Lipset, 92–128. Glencoe: The Free Press, 1953.

Patterson, James T. *America's Struggle against Poverty*. Cambridge: Harvard University Press, 2004.

Piven, Frances Fox, and Richard Cloward. *Regulating the Poor: The Functions of Public Welfare*. New York: Pantheon Books, 1971.

Postan, Michael. "A Plague of Economists?" *Encounter*, January 1968: 42–47.

Quadagno, Jill. *The Color of Welfare: How Racism Undermined the War on Poverty*. New York: Oxford University Press, 1994.

Rainwater, Lee. "The Lower-Class Culture and Poverty-War Strategy." In *On Understanding Poverty: Perspectives from the Social Sciences*, edited by Daniel P. Moynihan, 229–59. New York: Basic Books, 1968.

Reagan, Ronald. "Address Before a Joint Session of Congress on the State of the Union." *The American Presidency Project*, January 25, 1988. www.presidency.ucsb.edu/ws/index.php?pid=36035

Recchiuti, John Louis. *Civic Engagement: Social Science and Progressive-Era Reform in New York City*. Philadelphia: University of Pennsylvania Press, 2007.

Rigdon, Susan M. *The Culture Façade: Art, Science, and Politics in the Work of Oscar Lewis*. Champaign: University of Illinois Press, 1988.

Rodgers, Daniel. *Atlantic Crossings: Social Politics in a Progressive Age*. Cambridge: Harvard University Press, 1998.

Rostow, W. W. *The Stages of Economic Growth: A Non-Communist Manifesto*. Cambridge: Cambridge University Press, 1960.

Ryan, William. *Blaming the Victim*. New York: Random House, 1971.

Scott, Daryl. *Contempt and Pity: Social Policy and the Image of the Damaged Black Psyche, 1880–1996.* Chapel Hill: University of North Carolina Press, 1997.

Stack, Carol. *All Our Kin: Strategies for Survival in a Black Community.* New York: Harper & Row, 1974.

Storrs, Landon. *The Second Red Scare and the Unmaking of the New Deal Left.* Princeton: Princeton University Press, 2013.

Tani, Karen M. *States of Dependency: Welfare, Rights, and American Governance, 1935–1972.* Cambridge: Cambridge University Press, 2015.

Tobin, James. "It Can Be Done! Conquering Poverty in the US by 1976." *The New Republic,* June 3, 1967: 14–18.

Townsend, Peter. "Introduction." In *The Concept of Poverty,* edited by Peter Townsend, ix–xi. New York: American Elsevier, 1970.

Townsend, Peter. "Measures and Explanations of Poverty in High Income and Low Income Countries." In *The Concept of Poverty,* edited by Peter Townsend, 1–45. New York: American Elsevier, 1970.

U.S. Department of Health, Education, and Welfare. *Toward a Social Report.* Ann Arbor: University of Michigan Press, 1970.

Watts, Harold. "An Economic Definition of Poverty." In *On Understanding Poverty: Perspectives from the Social Sciences,* edited by Daniel P. Moynihan, 316–29. New York: Basic Books, 1968.

Weir, Margaret. *Politics and Jobs: The Boundaries of Employment Policy in the United States.* Princeton: Princeton University Press, 1992.

Wilson, William Julius. *The Truly Disadvantaged.* Chicago: University of Chicago Press, 1987.

Zorbaugh, Harvey. *Gold Coast and Slum.* Chicago: University of Chicago Press, 1929.

5

Discrimination

Leah N. Gordon

In sociologist Robert MacIver's 1949 essay collection *Discrimination and the National Welfare*, two leading African-American social scientists depicted discrimination as a system. The problem of discrimination "touches all aspects of life in the South," sociologist Ira de Augustine Reid held – extending beyond prejudiced attitudes, discriminatory actions, or the law to involve "a complex of sentiments and practices embedded in the social structure that operates to cancel human sentiments and reasonable behavior."[1] To Reid, the Southern racial order was a system in which legal segregation and state policy reinforced interwoven social and cultural processes, creating a self-sustaining social order in which change might be difficult to engineer. Economist Robert Weaver, the second author, also cautioned against treating racial injustice in terms of individual morality, even though such an approach was "more palatable to the reading public," an approach he elaborated in his 1948 *The Negro Ghetto*. An individualized view of discrimination, he warned, obscured the interlocking public and private practices that generated housing segregation across Northern urban "black belts." By emphasizing the causal power of individual bigotry when explaining the race issue, social theorists also hid the often coordinated and mutually reinforcing processes by which the interests of real estate brokers, builders, lenders, and federal and state policymakers converged to relegate African-Americans to segregated, overpriced, and substandard housing.[2] In both the Southern context and across the urban North, Reid and Weaver made clear, discrimination functioned like a system that, while rooted in law and state policy, featured interlocking sociological, political-economic, and anthropological dimensions.

[1] Reid, "What Segregated Areas Mean," 7.
[2] Weaver, *Negro Ghetto*, vii, ix and Weaver, "Effect on Housing."

Throughout the second half of the twentieth century, Reid and Weaver's
views of discrimination as system competed with theories in which
discriminating individuals, acting in aggregate, constituted the root
cause (and in some cases the full extent) of the wider race problem. By
the late 1970s, when economists experimenting with "paired testing"
sought to measure discrimination in labor or housing markets, they
did not look to interconnected political, economic, social, and cultural
systems and associated profit motives. Instead, these thinkers measured
levels of discrimination by painstakingly counting the beliefs and actions
of individual discriminators one by one.[3] Proponents of paired testing
celebrated this methodological tool for its ability to expose "systemic
patterns of differential treatment" and "subtle forms of discrimination,"
while providing evidence that could be used in court. The approach
eventually expanded to encompass research on discrimination in
employment, mortgage and insurance applications, and even purchasing
cars, accessing health clubs, or hailing taxis.[4]

This chapter examines how social scientists conceptualized racial
discrimination from the 1940s to the 1990s, as one component of what
W. E. B. Du Bois famously termed "the problem of the twentieth century."[5]
It examines debates over whether racial discrimination was a problem of
individuals or systems; how it related to the more broadly defined problems
of racial injustice and inequality; how disciplinary divisions of labor shifted
over time; and how theories of and policies to address racial discrimination
intersected. The "race problem," an amorphous phrase popularized in
the early 1940s, linked distinct but interrelated issues – racial prejudice,
discrimination, conflict, inequality, segregation, and racialized poverty –
that American social scientists had long treated as among the most
pressing social problems. Without question, ideological, political, and
methodological factors affected how social scientists theorized the social
problem of racial discrimination. Their theories of the nature and causes

[3] Wienk et al., *Measuring Racial Discrimination in American Housing Markets*, ii, 3; Fix,
   Galster, and Struyk, *Clear and Convincing Evidence*, 1; and Oh and Yinger, "What Have
   We Learned from Paired Testing in Housing Markets?" 21.
[4] Fix, Galster, and Struyk, *Clear and Convincing Evidence*, 11, 12.
[5] Du Bois, *Souls of Black Folk*, 29. To keep the scope manageable, this chapter echoes
   one strand of mid–twentieth-century US social science on race, which prioritized
   discrimination against African-Americans, even though much other scholarship
   reached beyond this focus. Pettigrew, *Racial Discrimination in the United States*, xiv,
   xxix; McKee, *Sociology and the Race Problem*, 22–51, 273–81; Yu, *Thinking Orientals*;
   and Masuoka and Valien, *Race Relations*.

of the race issue, in turn, shaped imagined reformist solutions, even as questions of political feasibility circumscribed policy proposals. Indeed, as social scientists examined the race issue in the long postwar era, some questioned whether racial inequality in the absence of discrimination was a social problem at all.

Charles Tilly's distinction between *dispositional, systemic,* and *relational* social theories provides a useful framework for delineating the range of social scientific theories of racial discrimination. Motivated by concern with individual beliefs and behaviors, psychologists of prejudice, economists concerned with rational actors, and some scholars of race relations in other fields developed a collection of individualistic, dispositional paradigms that they applied to both prejudice and discrimination. Work of this type typically made individuals the unit of analysis, focused on motivations, and expressed special interest in a discriminating individual's intentions immediately before they acted in a discriminatory manner.[6] Rival, nonindividualistic explanations – including those Tilly termed "systemic" and "relational" theories – also circulated throughout the second half of the twentieth century. Often articulated by sociologists, anthropologists, economists, political scientists, and historians of race relations, systemic theories put (at times intersecting) social, cultural, political, economic, or legal systems at the center of analysis. They often presented societies or economies as "coherent, self-sustaining entities," and situated processes of change over time within this broader system. Relational theories focused less on the coherence of a social system than the relations among groups, centering power, intergroup conflict, and patterned interaction among distinct (rather than systemically linked) social groups as drivers of social structure and change.[7]

As I have argued elsewhere, particular scholars or studies often combined approaches or blurred Tilly's lines, especially lines between systemic and relational theories.[8] Still, when examining the social science of racial discrimination, the overall distinction between dispositional theories, on the one hand, and systemic and relational theories, on the other, helps to clarify both change over time and competition between frameworks in

---

[6] Tilly, *Identities, Boundaries, and Social Ties,* 14–16 and Rose, *Studies in the Reduction of Prejudice.*

[7] Tilly, *Identities, Boundaries, and Social Ties,* 14–16; Tilly, *Durable Inequality,* 6–7, 24; and Gordon, *From Power to Prejudice,* 8–10, 28–34. On interwar social ecology and social anthropology, see Bulmer, *Chicago School of Sociology;* McKee, *Sociology and the Race Problem,* 103–80; and O'Connor, *Poverty Knowledge,* 74–88.

[8] Gordon, *From Power to Prejudice;* Johnson, *Negro in American Civilization;* Thompson, "Introduction," *Race Relations and the Race Problem;* and Myrdal, *American Dilemma.*

any given period. Indeed, how one conceptualized the object of scientific investigation itself – as prejudice, discrimination, racial conflict, racial oppression, or racial inequality – rested on an implicit explanatory scheme with distinct policy implications. Dispositional approaches tended to suggest that individual discriminators should be reformed or their actions prevented or punished. Systemic and relational theories, in contrast, implied the need for more far-reaching changes to economic, legal, and political systems, even to liberal capitalism itself.[9]

Focused primarily on the half-century following World War II, this chapter chronicles change over time in which analytic and disciplinary frameworks set the terms of social scientific discussion on racial discrimination, only one subset of the broader race issue. It describes an evolution from (1) an interwar theoretical multiplicity to (2) a cross-disciplinary emphasis on discrimination viewed as a system in the wartime and immediate postwar years to (3) an emphasis on psychological and economic individualism in the early Cold War era to, finally, (4) a return to systemic theories of both discrimination and racial inequality, alongside their fracturing and frequent disembedding from the political and economic context in the three decades following the passage of the Civil Rights Act.

The ascent of psychological and economic individualism was most clearly evident in the early Cold War era, though social scientists paid careful attention to prejudice and individual acts of discrimination for the remainder of the century. Prejudiced personalities occupied thinkers across the behavioral sciences, while economists focused on "rational actors" slowly came to see discrimination as a problem within their purview.[10] Methodological and theoretical developments within the social sciences partly account for rising attention to individuals in research on racial discrimination. But this turn is little surprise given social scientists' need to navigate a rightward-moving American liberalism and its heightened anticommunist pressures.[11] Psychologists of prejudice, as well as economists focused on discriminating

[9] Gordon, *From Power to Prejudice*, 8–12.
[10] Adorno et al., *Authoritarian Personality*; Allport, *Nature of Prejudice*; Becker, *Economics of Discrimination*; and Jackson, *Gunnar Myrdal and America's Conscience*, 280–85. Daniel Rodgers sees the shift from midcentury visions of the social world as "thick with context" to a more individualized "disaggregation" after 1975, but notes that "[e]ven in a society that boasted of its individualism, race making made every self social." Rodgers, *Age of Fracture*, 3, 5, 112.
[11] Alpers, *Dictators, Democracy, and American Public Culture*; Ciepley, *Liberalism in the Shadow of Totalitarianism*; Dudziak, *Cold War Civil Rights*; and Isaac, "Human Sciences in Cold War America."

rational actors, would persist in the post–Civil Rights Act era and, by the mid-1970s, paired testing experiments provided new tools for asking old questions about racist individuals. By century's end, conservative colorblindness would rearticulate individualism on racial questions, despite its attention to the legal system, by treating any racial categorization (regardless of social, political, or economic context) as a racial harm.[12]

In the post–Civil Rights Act era, though many social scientists remained convinced that racial discrimination was not reducible to individuals, presenting discrimination as a system became less straightforward. The arrival of formal equality; the association of notions of institutional racism, internal colonialism, and power relations with political radicalism; and the growing authority of statistical methods in research on racial inequality complicated systemic and relational theorizing on the race issue. Alternatives to individualism circulated widely from 1964 through the 1990s, but many systemic and relational theories proved quiet or ambiguous on causality. Across diverse scholarly communities – from theorists of "institutional racism" sympathetic to Black Power movements; to sociologists or economists who treated racism as an unmeasurable residual when examining racial disparity in labor and housing markets; to proponents of deficiency paradigms who linked past discrimination and present inequality with fuzzy notions of pathology; to legal scholars focused on "disparate impact" – the consequences and contours of racial inequality were easier to delineate, and to measure scientifically, than its causes.[13]

The transformations of social scientific thought on racial discrimination in the four decades following World War II illuminate key themes of this volume. These include the growing influence, especially in the early Cold War era, of individualized psychological and economic frameworks at the expense of systemic and relational paradigms, even if attention to law, power, and system never fully disappeared. This history also addresses how research methods shaped research questions, with methods (as in the case of the postwar ascent of attitude testing) at times motivating and in other contexts (such as when regression analyses could not pinpoint distinct causes

---

[12] Fix, Galster, and Struyk, *Clear and Convincing Evidence*, 11; Crenshaw, "Color Blindness, History, and the Law"; and Bonilla-Silva, *Racism without Racists*.

[13] On institutional racism, see Ture and Hamilton, *Black Power* and Pettigrew, *Racial Discrimination in the United States*, x. On racism as a residual, see Darity and Mason, "Evidence on Discrimination in Employment" and Arrow, "What Has Economics to Say about Racial Discrimination?" On damage imagery, see O'Connor, *Poverty Knowledge*; Scott, *Contempt and Pity*; Katz, *Undeserving Poor*; and Geary, *Beyond Civil Rights*. On disparate impact, see Dobbin, *Inventing Equal Opportunity*, 129, 112, 110.

of racial inequality) constraining research agendas. In charting how social scientists imagined the role of racial discrimination in larger patterns of racial injustice, the chapter highlights the abilities of social science to not only measure but also define social problems, typically, in the process, prioritizing some reform approaches over others. There was, however, no smooth ascent of psychological and economic individualism over the long postwar era. A range of systemic theories persisted in the era of formal equality, but what it meant to view discrimination, and the race issue itself, as a system was less clear than when Reid and Weaver described their world in the late 1940s.

5.1 Prejudice and Race Relations in Social Science, 1920–1939

In the interwar years, psychological, sociological, anthropological, political-economic, and historical approaches to questions of racial equity and intergroup conflict flourished, which involved much cross-disciplinary borrowing. By the mid-1920s, as if belatedly responding to Du Bois' question "How does it feel to be a problem?" social scientists in many disciplines followed sociologist Robert Park and anthropologist Franz Boas in shifting attention away from "the Negro problem," a label that implicitly located the sources of racial disparity in minority communities themselves.[14] New terms like "race relations," "the race problem," or "the race issue" implied that patterns extending beyond minority communities were worthy of analysis, and that white attitudes, behaviors, institutions, and systems were to blame.[15] While the term discrimination was part of the language of civil rights protest in these years – emerging in campaigns for fair employment and open housing – it did not play as central a role in social science as it would following World War II.[16]

Instead, discussions of the race problem, dominated by psychologists, sociologists, and anthropologists, focused on prejudice, on the one hand, and race relations, on the other. Psychologists of prejudice used experimental or survey research techniques to measure racial beliefs or attitudes and their relationship to bigoted behaviors. Social ecologists associated with the Chicago School developed theoretical models like Park's analysis of the transnational and transhistorical race relations cycle, which – prompted by technological change and migration – moved in a predictable fashion

[14] Du Bois, *Souls of Black Folk*, 1.
[15] McKee, *Sociology and the Race Problem*, chap. 2.
[16] For a comprehensive overview of Northern civil rights struggles in the 1930s and 1940s, see Sugrue, *Sweet Land of Liberty*, part 1.

from conflict to cooperation to accommodation to assimilation. Critics worried that such frameworks implied a sense of teleology and inevitability, suggesting that policymakers wait for change to emerge on its own accord.[17] Social anthropologists, especially those associated with Lloyd Warner, John Dollard, Hortense Powdermaker, and the Caste and Class School, in contrast, often used case study or community study methods, and viewed race relations as a cohesive, and often impenetrable, cultural system featuring interlocking ideological, economic, social, political, and cultural processes that made change difficult to engineer.[18] Finally, political scientists, economists, and historians, many concerned with slavery and plantation economies, and a few with socialist or communist sympathies, explored the economic bases of the South's racial labor systems, and the legal and political structures, including the role of racial violence, that sustained it.[19]

Interdisciplinary exchange marked interwar scholarship on race. Lines between psychology, sociology, and anthropology, as well as between sociological and political-economic analyses, frequently blurred. Many of the key questions occupying scholars of the race issue were cross-disciplinary. Sociologists, psychologists, and anthropologists read each other's work, published in one another's journals, and often worked in multidisciplinary teams. Even as sociologists staked a claim to being "the social scientists who were most concerned with race relations," scholars with training and appointments in other disciplines, especially anthropologists and psychologists, published widely on the topic, at times in sociology journals.[20] Psychologists of prejudice paid considerable attention to sociological and anthropological considerations, especially how racial attitudes drew on and were situated in social and cultural contexts.[21] A key point of debate among anthropologists and sociologists, over whether the American racial situation was best analyzed as a problem of caste, class,

[17] Park, "Our Racial Frontier on the Pacific," 150; Bulmer, *Chicago School of Sociology*; Matthews, *Quest for an American Sociology*; McKee, *Sociology and the Race Problem*, 133–40; and O'Connor, *Poverty Knowledge*, 76–77. For a more critical view of social ecology, see Steinberg, *Race Relations*, 57–71.
[18] On Caste and Class, see McKee, *Sociology and the Race Problem*, chap. 4; Baker, *From Savage to Negro*; and Brick, *Transcending Capitalism*, 112–14.
[19] Myrdal, *American Dilemma*, 205–572 and Holloway, *Confronting the Veil*.
[20] McKee, *Sociology and the Race Problem*, 145.
[21] Selig, *Americans All*, 32–35, 20; Horowitz, "'Race' Attitudes," 159–65, 181–82; Horowitz and Horowitz, "Development of Social Attitudes in Children"; Jackson, *Social Scientists for Social Justice*, chaps. 2–3; Clark, *Prejudice and Your Child*, chap. 2; and Rose, *Studies in the Reduction of Prejudice*.

or some combination of the two, reached across disciplinary divides.[22] Historians, political scientists, and labor economists' analyses of the central role of labor exploitation in slavery-based and colonial economies also provided the starting point for sociological and anthropological discussions of race relations in the present and more recent past.[23]

Methods also crossed disciplinary boundaries. The Chicago School of social ecology, in particular, was methodologically capacious, using survey research techniques, case study methods associated with anthropology, and documentary sources.[24] The interwar study of the race issue was also interracial, though far from egalitarian, given the racial segregation of the academic institutions where interwar social scientists worked, significant disparities in research funding, and the pervasive assumption that historically black colleges and universities (HBCUs) were settings for leadership development but not cutting edge scientific research.[25] Organized around the psychology of prejudiced individuals and the sociological, anthropological, and political-economic systems in which those individuals interacted, interwar social science on race did not center the causal importance of discriminating individuals in the ways that much postwar research on race would. In fact, the centrality of social and political-economic systems to this interwar literature, in combination with the pervasiveness of state-sanctioned legal segregation, likely explains why the study of discrimination, when it emerged in earnest during World War II, was so often grounded in notions of system.

5.2 The American Creed and the System of Discrimination, 1939–1950

Concern with discrimination moved to the center of social scientific discourse on the race issue during World War II, and, though this literature continued to exhibit the theoretical and disciplinary breadth of the interwar years, it featured a new sense of urgency. This wartime and immediate postwar

[22] McKee, Sociology and the Race Problem, chaps. 3–4 and O'Connor, Poverty Knowledge, chap. 3.
[23] Holloway, Confronting the Veil; Myrdal, American Dilemma, 205–409; Cox, Caste, Class, and Race; Thompson, "Introduction"; Johnson, "Race Relations and Social Change"; Mayor's Commission on Conditions in Harlem, Complete Report of Mayor LaGuardia's Commission; and Chicago Commission on Race Relations, Negro in Chicago.
[24] Bogardus, "Measuring Social Distance"; Converse, Survey Research in the United States, 63, 60; and Bulmer, Chicago School of Sociology, 77, 92–93.
[25] Stanfield, Philanthropy and Jim Crow, 70, 79–90; Holloway and Keppel, Black Scholars on the Line; and Holloway, Confronting the Veil.

literature drew on interwar paradigms, especially notions of system at the heart of social ecology, caste and class, and political-economic theories of slavery and plantation societies. Between 1944 and 1950, however, a central strand of social scientific thought on the race issue viewed discrimination as a system, one rooted in law and state policy, but intersecting with social, cultural, and political-economic systems. It included ideologically disparate texts from leading African-American and white scholars, such as Gunnar Myrdal's *An American Dilemma* (1944), Robert Weaver's *The Negro Ghetto* (1948), St. Clair Drake and Horace Cayton's *Black Metropolis* (1945), Oliver Cromwell Cox's *Caste, Class, and Race* (1948), and Robert MacIver's *Discrimination and the National Welfare* (1949) and *The More Perfect Union* (1948).[26] The sociologists and economists (though Myrdal and Weaver worked outside the mainstream American economics profession) who led these discussions were concerned with how state-sanctioned patterns of discrimination violated "the American creed" by contradicting American ideals of democracy, civic inclusion, and equality of opportunity. While Southern de jure segregation was the clearest example of the systemic character of discrimination, scholars also depicted discrimination across the urban North and West as an interconnected set of formalized networks, policies, and processes. The system of discrimination they depicted was both public and private, knitted social, legal, political, and institutional arenas, and worked together as a coherent whole.

That social science on the race issue emphasized national unity and civic ideas was hardly surprising during, and in the wake of, World War II. As the nation fought a war against Nazi racism and in defense of democratic ideals – battles that occurred amid mounting civil rights activism, repeated incidents of violence against racial minorities, and accelerating movements for racial understanding and intergroup goodwill – support for civil rights became central to the political identity of American liberals.[27] Social scientific interest in the ways American racial discrimination violated national ideals also built on decades of African-American activism against disenfranchisement and de jure segregation across the South, and on

[26] Myrdal *American Dilemma*; Weaver, *Negro Ghetto*; Drake and Cayton, *Black Metropolis*; Cox, *Caste, Class, and Race*; MacIver, *Discrimination and the National Welfare*; and MacIver, *More Perfect Union*.

[27] Polenberg, *War and Society*, 97–98, cited in Jackson, *Gunnar Myrdal and America's Conscience*, 237; Sugrue, *Sweet Land of Liberty*, 44–58, 75–77; Jackson, *Gunnar Myrdal and America's Conscience*, 234–37, 273–79; Klarman, *From Jim Crow to Civil Rights*, chap. 4; Gordon, *From Power to Prejudice*, chap. 3; McKee, *Sociology and the Race Problem*, 257–58; and Jackson, *Gunnar Myrdal and America's Conscience*, 279–84.

accelerating legal efforts against housing and employment discrimination across the urban North and West.[28]

Discrimination – both its moral consequences for the white conscience and its political, economic, and legal consequences for African-Americans – was at the heart of Myrdal's enormous, Carnegie Corporation–commissioned *An American Dilemma* (1944), though this volume synthesized research that employed dispositional, systemic, and relational frameworks.[29] Carnegie had turned its attention to "the Negro problem" as part of a wider interest in "social problems," motivated in part by Depression-era economic dislocations, racial unrest in Harlem in 1935, and the sense that a "statesmanlike" figure was needed to survey the American racial situation in the tradition of European surveys of colonial contexts. The foundation chose Myrdal, a Swedish economist and social democrat, on a pair of related assumptions: that the leading American scholars of the race issue could not investigate the topic with sufficient objectivity, and that a social scientist from a nation lacking a colonial tradition was preferable.[30]

Myrdal's volume would come to be known for its individualism, in part because it made the case for racial liberalism – the political framework, rooted in opportunity-based egalitarianism, which prioritized nondiscrimination legislation, desegregation, and efforts to reduce prejudice – by centering an image of white America beset by a moral dilemma.[31] *"The American Negro problem is a problem in the heart of the American,"* Myrdal wrote in perhaps the most widely quoted statement from the enormous study. *"It is there that the interracial tension has its focus. It is there that the decisive struggle goes on...."*[32] Supporters and critics alike saw Myrdal's work as the first in a series of postwar studies that shifted attention from political economy toward individual prejudice and discrimination.[33] And yet Myrdal, an institutional economist and architect of the Swedish social welfare state, was an unlikely scholar to focus on individual beliefs. He came to the moral dilemma thesis,

[28] Hall, "Long Civil Rights Movement." On fair employment and open housing movements across the urban North and West in the 1930s and 1940s, see Sugrue, *Sweet Land of Liberty*, part 2; Pritchett, *Robert Clifton Weaver and the American City*, chap. 6; Gilmore, *Defying Dixie*; and Kelley, *Hammer and Hoe*.
[29] Myrdal, *American Dilemma*.
[30] Jackson, *Gunnar Myrdal and America's Conscience*, 28–29, 32.
[31] Jackson, *Gunnar Myrdal and America's Conscience*, chap. 7 and Gordon, *From Power to Prejudice*, 2–3.
[32] Myrdal, *American Dilemma*, xlvii (italics in original).
[33] Jackson, *Gunnar Myrdal and America's Conscience*, 241–62. For a few examples of critics from the left, see Cox, "American Dilemma" and Aptheker, "Negro People in America," 185–86.

historian Walter Jackson emphasizes, late in the project, having returned home to a war-torn Europe beset by evidence of irrationality and, some have speculated, out of a desire to make the volume more palatable to philanthropic sponsors.[34]

Myrdal's full analysis of discrimination was, however, hardly individualistic or atomized. His discussion of Southern politics elaborated the legal and political mechanisms, and the state-sanctioned violence, sustaining African-American disenfranchisement and denial of fair legal proceedings. Even though some aspects of African-American economic dislocation did not result from discrimination per se, state-sanctioned and widespread systems of economic discrimination were the most consequential violation of the American creed in a volume that viewed African-American economic circumstances as "pathological."[35] Far from a simple question of individual conscience, the discrimination at the heart of Myrdalian racial liberalism was systematic, institutionalized in public and private policies, complexly entangled with American political economy, and supported by law. And yet, reflecting what he considered to be the American liberal mainstream, Myrdal emphasized that racial inequality challenged the American creed only "in so far as Negro poverty is caused by discrimination."[36]

The concept of discrimination as a system garnered growing social scientific attention in the half decade after World War II. This was especially evident in classic works by leading African-American scholars: economist Robert Weaver's *The Negro Ghetto* (1948), sociologist/anthropologist St. Clair Drake and sociologist Horace Cayton's *Black Metropolis* (1945), and sociologist Oliver Cromwell Cox's *Caste, Class, and Race* (1948).[37] These authors diverged ideologically. Cox was known as a Marxist, though he rejected the label, while many criticized Weaver for excessive attention to the needs of the African-American middle class. All these authors contributed, however, to a view that situated race relations in large-scale, interlocking social, cultural, political, economic, and legal systems, while also making clear that legal segregation and discrimination were systems in and of themselves. In doing so, these works prefigured the attention to

[34] Jackson, *Gunnar Myrdal and America's Conscience*, chap. 4, especially 134, 185 and Winant, "Dark Side of the Force," 560.
[35] Myrdal, *American Dilemma*, li, 205–206.
[36] Myrdal, *American Dilemma*, 210, 214.
[37] Cox, *Caste, Class, and Race*; Weaver, *Negro Ghetto*; and Drake and Cayton, *Black Metropolis*.

social and political-economic systems in more radical theories of internal colonialism appearing in the second half of the 1960s.[38]

Cox was a prominent figure in a group of African-American intellectuals who viewed the American racial situation as part of a much larger anticolonial and anticapitalist struggle. He argued that ideological, institutional, and legal systems of discrimination had to be analyzed in conjunction with the capitalist interests that motivated them.[39] Discrimination adapted to and emerged from conflicts of interest, he suggested, within systems that were both political and economic in character. Arguing that "racial antagonism is part and parcel of this class struggle, because it developed within the capitalist system as one of its fundamental traits," Cox emphasized that "the interest behind racial antagonism is an exploitative interest – the peculiar type of economic exploitation characteristic of capitalist society…"[40] The systems doing the most important causal work in Cox's analysis, then, were political-economic systems, though social and cultural systems were closely intertwined with political economy.

Closer to the center of the mid-century antiracist liberal political spectrum, Weaver's *The Negro Ghetto* and Drake and Cayton's *Black Metropolis* also treated discrimination as a system intertwined with the economic interests that generated it. When examining the sources of housing segregation (and with it, overcrowding and dilapidation) across the Northern "Black Belts," Weaver cautioned against individualized moral frameworks that "divert attention from the economic motivations and institutions that must be recognized and understood," if the social problem of racial discrimination was to be fought through effective social planning.[41] Northern residential segregation emerged, he argued, from the collusive actions of "well-organized real estate dealers, home builders and home finance institutions" – groups that, aided by restrictive covenants and the policies of public home loan and public housing authorities, created an interconnecting public and private discriminatory system.[42] Drake

---

[38] McAuley, *Mind of Oliver C. Cox* and Pritchett, *Robert Clifton Weaver and the American City*, chap. 6.

[39] Cox, *Caste, Class, and Race*; McAuley, *Mind of Oliver C. Cox*; and Allport, *Nature of Prejudice*, 209.

[40] Cox, "American Dilemma," 143; McKee, *Sociology and the Race Problem*, 175; and Cox, *Caste, Class, and Race*, xxxi.

[41] Weaver, *The Negro Ghetto*, vii and Pritchett, *Robert Clifton Weaver and the American City*, chap. 6.

[42] Weaver, *Negro Ghetto*, vii, ix. On Weaver's work on employment discrimination, see Weaver, *Negro Labor*.

and Cayton acknowledged the same interlocking system – one rooted in economic interest but sustained by intersecting private and public policies and organizational practices.[43] Their Chicago School–inspired analysis of segregated Chicago emphasized that the nation's urban African-American neighborhoods were becoming more "concentrated" and their residents more racially isolated.

In the five years following World War II, some of the nation's best-known white sociologists also contributed to studies of discrimination as a social and legal system. Sponsored by the Jewish Theological Seminary's Institute for Religious and Social Studies, with some Rockefeller funding, Columbia sociologist Robert MacIver's *The More Perfect Union: A Program for the Control of Inter-group Discrimination in the United States* (1948) and his edited collection, *Discrimination and the National Welfare* (1949), brought together insights from sociology, psychology, anthropology, and economics (though represented by Weaver alone).[44] Explaining discrimination in many institutional contexts – housing, education, labor, trade unions, religious institutions, international affairs, business, and intergroup relations – MacIver's volumes broadly addressed "the relation of group to group in the United States," and aimed to translate scholarship into terms that activists might use. In contrast to the emphasis on the economic dimensions of discrimination in Cox and Weaver's work, MacIver (in all likelihood due to Rockefeller sponsorship) focused on racial and ethnic, rather than "economic or 'class,'" struggle, except when class antagonisms were "accentuated and made more divisive" by racial or ethnic antagonism.[45] Still, both texts presented discrimination as consequential due to its systemic dimensions, emphasized how legal segregation legitimized discrimination in other settings, and explored how legal, social, and cultural systems intersected.[46]

Conceptualizing discrimination as a system involved attention to the ways that discriminatory laws – especially state-sponsored segregation – rationalized discriminatory behaviors in realms outside the law and reinforced social and cultural systems. Legal scholar Milton Konvitz emphasized that, when the law discriminated, it encouraged citizens to

---

[43] Drake and Cayton, *Black Metropolis*, 17.
[44] MacIver, *More Perfect Union* and MacIver, *Discrimination and the National Welfare*. The latter included a widely cited essay by Robert Merton, as well as essays by Weaver, anthropologist Ira de A. Reid, educational philosopher Theodore Brameld, legal scholar Milton Konvitz, and others.
[45] MacIver, *More Perfect Union*, 11, 14 and Merton, "Discrimination and the American Creed," 100.
[46] MacIver, *Discrimination and the National Welfare*, 1.

discriminate.[47] While "the law says some forms of discrimination are legal and others are not," Konvitz argued, "the average citizen has no time or capacity for subtle distinctions."[48] Ira de A. Reid saw Southern segregationist laws as of especially great consequence, since they existed at the intersection – as a kind of linchpin – of the interlocking social, political, economic, and cultural systems – what Reid described as the "region's traditional system of racial exploitation." Prefiguring post-1964 theories of internal colonialism, Reid compared the South to colonial and apartheid contexts, and argued that "segregated areas in the United States represented the world's most systematic exploitation of citizens, deemed by their national constitution as equals." In arguing that "it is the area of 'Jim Crow' laws, statutes which regulate, tighten, freeze – even instigate – the practices and customs of race discrimination in general," Reid made clear the common view of *Discrimination and National Welfare* that "segregation is discriminatory."[49] Weaver's contribution to the volume built on *The Negro Ghetto* as well as his work on discriminatory labor markets to argue that, while labor market discrimination ensured that minorities often had less income with which to secure life's necessities, the intertwined public and private, legal and extra-legal systems generating housing segregation made a bad economic situation worse.[50]

Another set of alternatives to individually oriented research on racial discrimination in the immediate postwar years referred to "institutional racism," but with a different meaning than radical theorists would deploy in the Black Power era. This late-1940s work focused on small-scale institutions (business firms, government offices, or labor unions, for example) and their social norms and policies. Both MacIver and fellow sociologist Robert Merton explored whether there was a clear correlation between discriminatory beliefs and behaviors – and how institutional context might shape this relationship.[51] Merton's analysis built on a notion of institutional discrimination that was taking form in the work of three scholars with brief ties to the University of Chicago. In dissertations and articles, William C. Bradbury (whom Merton advised at Columbia), Joseph Lohman (a student of Robert Park's and a criminologist), and Dietrich Reitzes (a Chicago graduate student focused on discrimination in the medical field) asked whether and how the established

---

[47] Konvitz, "Discrimination and the Law," 51.
[48] Konvitz, "Discrimination and the Law," 52, 63.
[49] Reid, "What Segregated Areas Mean," 8, 11, 12.
[50] Weaver, "Effect on Housing," 25.
[51] Merton, "Discrimination and the American Creed," 47.

norms and social codes of labor unions, government offices, or business firms conditioned individuals' actions irrespective of their racial attitudes. Whether or not an individual acted on their attitudes, Lohman and Reitzes found, "will depend very greatly on the organizational context in which people behave."[52] The claim that institutional factors help determine when some prejudiced individuals discriminated, and others did not, had major implications for social planning, as MacIver, Merton, and colleagues recognized. In fact, Merton distinguished between four ways that prejudice and discrimination might be linked, and held that the failure to acknowledge the institutional and social dimensions of discrimination perpetuated the status quo.[53]

In the five years following the publication of Myrdal's *An American Dilemma*, then, a number of theories of discrimination circulated. All of them described discrimination as a system – rooted in law, state policy, and, increasingly, discrete social institutions – that was difficult to disentangle from social, cultural, political, and economic systems. Though racial inequalities could result from many atomized individuals acting without clear coordination, it was the planning and coordination by both public and private institutions that proved so consequential. While most of this literature separated "the race issue" from questions of socioeconomic inequality, thinkers at the far-left presented systems generating racial and socioeconomic hierarchy as one and the same. As we will see, attention to the social-structural, political-economic, and institutional sources of racial injustice – different systems that social scientists would posit as the root cause of racial injustice – would move back to the center of interdisciplinary research on the race issue in the post–Civil Rights Act era. Still, given the centrality of law and state policy to notions of discrimination as system in the immediate postwar years, the key social scientific question going forward would be: Once a system of discrimination was no longer enshrined in law, how could it be measured, evaluated, and effectively fought?

5.3 Prejudiced Personalities and Rational Actors, 1950–1957

The tide would turn in the late 1940s and 1950s, when two individualistically oriented, dispositional frameworks for conceptualizing racial discrimination – theories of prejudiced personalities and economic analyses of the "taste for

---

[52] Lohman and Reitzes, "Notes on Race Relations in Mass Society," 242; Reitzes, "Collective Factors in Race Relations"; and Bradbury, "Racial Discrimination in Federal Employment."

[53] MacIver, *More Perfect Union*, 14, 105.

discrimination," respectively – gained influence. Intellectual and political pressures, many with origins in earlier decades, intensified during World War II and converged in the Cold War era to favor "scientific" approaches that centered individuals as objects of analysis and causal agents. These included philanthropic support for the behavioral sciences; activist-inspired projects to explain Nazi racism and wartime domestic racial unrest; the rising appeal of methodological individualism, including new quantitative research methods; domestic McCarthyist pressures; and Cold War era struggles for the "hearts and minds" of postcolonial nations.[54]

Despite their individualistic frameworks, scholars concerned with prejudiced personalities and scholars endorsing rational actor approaches had fairly different institutional and political orientations. Many psychologists, social psychologists, and some sociologists and anthropologists who turned attention to prejudice had close ties to activist communities committed to civil rights and antiprejudice work. They also developed ideas amid expanded philanthropic enthusiasm for their approaches and shared assumptions across disciplinary lines.[55] In contrast, when economist Gary Becker turned attention to discrimination in the mid-1950s, his work remained outside his discipline's mainstream, while also being relatively cut off from activist efforts and from interdisciplinary research teams.[56]

Scientific, activist, and philanthropic priorities converged to promote the psychology of prejudice by the early 1950s, though the research area had earlier roots. It had been established as a field in the 1920s and 1930s, with sources in both personality theory and social-psychological concerns with the ways individuals were shaped by social and cultural environment.[57] After World War II, other social scientists took up the prejudice question too. The arrival of psychoanalytically oriented émigré scholars; the refining of quantitative attitude testing techniques, including new, easily replicated scales of authoritarianism and "politico-economic conservatism"; and the elaboration of interdisciplinary experiments, such as Samuel Stouffer's *The American Soldier* (1949) and Harvard's Department of Social Relations (founded in 1946), drew the attention of not only psychologists but also

---

[54] Gordon, *From Power to Prejudice*, 5–6; Herman, *Romance of American Psychology*, chaps. 5–6; Dudziak, *Cold War Civil Rights*; and Von Eschen, *Race Against Empire*.
[55] Rose, *Studies in Reduction of Prejudice* and Herman, *Romance of American Psychology*, especially 125–26 and 153–54.
[56] Murphy, "How Gary Becker Saw the Scourge of Discrimination."
[57] Nicholson, *Inventing Personality* and Greenwood, *Disappearance of the Social in American Social Psychology*.

sociologists and anthropologists.[58] Social scientific interest in prejudice, and action-oriented approaches to studying it, also drew from wartime and postwar activist concerns.

This was, after all, a period in which civil rights activism became increasingly visible nationwide, while the number of (often white-led) organizations focused on fighting prejudice and intergroup tensions exploded. The American Jewish Committee's "Studies in Prejudice" series; action research on minority self-esteem by social psychologist Kurt Lewin; and foundation-supported surveys of research on prejudice directed toward activist groups, such as Arnold Rose's *Studies in Reduction of Prejudice* (1947) and sociologist Robin M. Williams, Jr.'s, SSRC-sponsored *The Reduction of Intergroup Tensions* (1947), all exemplified this sort of action-oriented social science.[59] Interest in prejudice, its sources, and how to fight it was especially strong among religiously oriented groups like the American Jewish Congress, American Jewish Committee, and the Federal Council of Churches; the lines between research and activism, in short, were often fluid.[60] Sociologists like Louis Wirth and Charles S. Johnson were actively committed to using social science in the study of "social action," while the American Jewish Congress' Commission on Community Interrelations trained social psychologists who later served as expert witnesses in the NAACP's *Brown* v. *Board* litigation.[61]

At the same time, expanded foundation support for the behavioral sciences, a shift from sociology toward psychology as the discipline with the most authority on racial questions, McCarthyist ideological pressures, and the tendency for academic agenda-setters to treat racial issues as dangerously radical converged to promote the postwar flowering of dispositional, individualistic research on prejudice. The Ford Foundation launched its behavioral sciences initiative in 1951 and the Rockefeller Foundation began a similar project to support interdisciplinary research in human relations in the early 1950s.[62] In these same years, centers of disciplinary strength

[58] McKee, *Sociology and the Race Problem*, 257–58 and Jackson, *Gunnar Myrdal and America's Conscience*, 280–81.
[59] McKee, *Sociology and the Race Problem*, 258–59 and Jackson, *Gunnar Myrdal and America's Conscience*, 280–85.
[60] Jackson, *Gunnar Myrdal and America's Conscience*, 280–85 and McKee, *Sociology and the Race Problem*, 256–73.
[61] Gordon, *From Power to Prejudice*, chaps. 3–4 and Jackson, *Social Scientists for Social Justice*, 63–78, 109–24.
[62] Herman, *Romance of American Psychology*, 133, 184; Solovey, *Shaky Foundations*, chap. 3; Pooley and Solovey, "Marginal to the Revolution"; and Gordon, *Power to Prejudice*, chap. 2.

on racial issues shifted. While psychology did not displace sociological approaches to race, the discipline became, as historian of sociology James McKee argues, "more significant in the sociological study of race relations than at any previous time."[63] Two books, in particular – Theodor Adorno et al.'s *The Authoritarian Personality* (1950) and Gordon Allport's *The Nature of Prejudice* (1954) – were decisive for this new influence.

That the growth areas in research on race in the late 1940s and 1950s centered individual behavior and interpersonal and intergroup interaction, but failed to raise questions about class inequality or political-economic structures, was hardly coincidental. As Howard Brick and Joel Isaac have argued of social relations and the behavioral sciences more generally, while direct causal relationships between McCarthyist pressures and these paradigms are difficult to discern, their avoidance of questions of political economy made them more palatable in an anticommunist climate.[64] Foundations also tread with particular caution when addressing questions of race relations, which – as the NAACP's ongoing fights to distance itself from communist accusations made clear – was always tinged with radicalism.[65]

Although the psychology of prejudice had long been promoted by social psychologists who explored how individuals were shaped by social and cultural contexts, by the 1950s, some of the best-known works in the field isolated prejudice from social, cultural, and, especially, political-economic settings. The broad, cross-disciplinary influence of *The Authoritarian Personality* and *The Nature of Prejudice* exemplified this pattern, as well as the tendency to highlight prejudice when addressing the race issue. These texts explained prejudice by focusing on personality structures and cognitive and emotional predispositions, that – while linked to social, economic, political, and cultural context – could also function independently.[66]

While *The Authoritarian Personality* did not completely dismiss the social, political, and economic context, notions of what was politically possible converged with methodological considerations to explain the volume's individualism.[67] The most psychoanalytically oriented – and best-known – of the "Studies in Prejudice" series, the book viewed prejudice, in some cases,

---

[63] McKee, *Sociology and the Race Problem*, 295.
[64] Isaac, "Human Sciences in Cold War America," 736–40; Jewett, *Science, Democracy, and the American University*, 342–43; and Brick, *Transcending Capitalism*.
[65] Lagemann, *Politics of Knowledge*, 153–54, 166–70, 172, 146; O'Connor, *Social Science for What?*, 70; and Gilmore, *Defying Dixie*.
[66] Adorno et al., *Authoritarian Personality* and Allport, *Nature of Prejudice*, xviii.
[67] Pettigrew, *Racial Discrimination in the United States*, 13.

as separable from social or political-economic systems and, in the most extreme cases, as aspects of a distorted personality, akin to a psychological malady.[68] The availability of new methods may have explained some of this causal emphasis on the individual psyche. Adorno and colleagues' well-publicized "F scale" presented political ideas in largely psychological terms while investigating social developments with tools designed for individual psychological diagnosis.[69] But it was also the political context – especially given the "social problem" focus of the series and the editors' sense that educational solutions would be uncontroversial and easy to implement – that explained the book's emphasis on the psychological dimensions of prejudice. Even the more sociologically oriented studies in the series, such as *Dynamics of Prejudice* (1950), were constrained by the political climate: Bruno Bettelheim and Morris Janowitz, in that book, concluded that educational reforms were more feasible than progressive welfare or employment policies.[70]

Gordon Allport, who helped established Harvard's Department of Social Relations, also acknowledged the necessity of multidisciplinary approaches to research on the race issue, though his disciplinary orientation – including assumptions about methodological rigor – led him to emphasize the causal importance of individuals and their dispositions. Allport's *The Nature of Prejudice* (1954) included historical, sociological, economic, anthropological, and psychological perspectives. The volume, nonetheless, made "ethnic prejudice," defined as "an antipathy based upon a faulty and inflexible generalization," its central concept.[71] The notion of the prejudiced personality, one of the volume's central concepts, built on *The Authoritarian Personality* to suggest a personality type whose "habits of thinking" and "cognitive processes" could be distinguished from those of more tolerant individuals. The focus on prejudice was, partly, a consequence of Allport's epistemological assumptions, rooted in psychology, that social and cultural mores were only visible in, and effective through, individual actors – since, as Allport put it, "it is only *individuals* who can feel antagonism and practice discrimination."[72]

And yet *The Nature of Prejudice* was complex, calling emphatically for legal and institutional change while also drawing social scientific attention to individual belief and behavior. The book suggested that prejudice was of

---

[68] Cohen-Cole, "Thinking in Cold War America," 97–98.
[69] Herman, *Romance of American Psychology*, 58–60.
[70] Adorno et al., *Authoritarian Personality*, viii; Herman, *Romance of American Psychology*, 182–83, 185–86; and Bettelheim and Janowitz, *Dynamics of Prejudice.*
[71] Allport, *Nature of Prejudice*, xviii, 209, 9.
[72] Allport, *Nature of Prejudice*, 175, xviii.

social and political consequence, that discrimination had both individual and institutional dimensions, and that planned intergroup contacts were a key tool for reducing prejudice. Regardless of the potential needs and proclivities of prejudiced personalities, Allport argued that it was discriminatory laws and institutions that mattered most for policy, and he devoted a chapter to the argument that legal desegregation must precede changed racial attitudes.[73]

The expansion of methodological individualism across the interdisciplinary behavioral sciences was so pronounced that some sociologists expressed worries about the rise of "atomistic" paradigms. Writing in 1952, Robin M. Williams, Jr., expressed concern that students of race – especially sociologists – were focusing too much attention on prejudice, discrimination, and individual personalities. Too much work treated "prejudice as an unanalyzed aggregate of individual attitudes" that was, Williams argued, "divorced from the functioning of real personalities" as well as "from enduring social relations and the structural properties of groups and communities." Between 1948 and 1953, he lamented, the largest research area in the whole field of intergroup relations involved personality-based approaches to prejudice.[74]

Later research confirmed Williams' worries. A study of 255 journal articles published on intergroup relations in major social scientific journals between 1900 and 1958 found that "half of the papers concentrate on the individual level" rather than on "social systems," despite the fact that the group of journals examined were "largely sociological."[75] Suggesting, quite explicitly, that methodological considerations were to blame for this individualistic turn, Williams emphasized "how frequently one finds that the fulfillment of crucial research needs depends upon advances in research methods." He called for renewed attention to the systemic dimensions of "racial and cultural relations," and, in his own subsequent work, *Strangers Next Door* (1964), conducted a series of community studies, seeking to develop this methodological approach in a manner that was uncommonly quantitative.[76]

The other discipline that promoted individual causal frameworks and units of analysis in the study of discrimination in the Cold War era was economics, a field that paired policy relevance with an abstract, increasingly mathematical

[73] Allport, *Nature of Prejudice*, 174–75, 9, 461–78.
[74] Williams, "Review and Assessment of Research."
[75] Pettigrew, *Racial Discrimination in the United States*, 16.
[76] Williams, "Review and Assessment of Research," 68–69; Gordon, *Power to Prejudice*, chap. 3; and Williams, *Strangers Next Door*.

orientation after World War II. When economists "rediscovered" the race issue in the late 1950s and 1960s, the focus was on individuals viewed as rational actors. In the 1930s and 1940s, the scattered economists studying the race issue had adopted a framework that was deeply historical, institutionally rooted, and contextually attuned. Some were explicitly policy-oriented, making the case for centralized economic planning alongside federal efforts to combat discrimination, while others embraced Marxist assumptions.[77] Post–World War II economics saw growing institutional ties to policymaking and government bureaucracies. At the same time, as the neoclassical framework moved to the field's center by the late 1950s and into the 1960s, and methodological pluralism declined, the field became increasing theoretically focused, mathematical, statistical, and model-driven.[78] Economics journals, curricula, and departments actively marginalized institutionalists (as well as Marxists), who had been among the most active economic voices on racial issues in the interwar and wartime years, as technically incompetent and overly ideological. It was, as historian of economics Michael A. Bernstein contends, "in the elaboration of a science of rational choice that American economists had secured both rank and privilege."[79]

Mainstream economists would remain largely uninterested in racial questions until the mid-1960s. Gary Becker's *The Economics of Discrimination*, while originally published in 1957, would not become a classic until its second printing in 1971.[80] Still, Becker's interest in discrimination exposes the analytic fit between the psychology of prejudice and rational actor economic models. And in both cases, methodological considerations drove turns to the individual in research on racial discrimination. Like psychologists of prejudice, Becker pointed to the primary importance of discriminating individuals' dispositions. He viewed discrimination through a microeconomic lens – as something one could have a "taste" for. Since the "taste for discrimination," in Becker's terms, typically required that discriminating employers pay more for the labor they hired, discriminatory preferences were likely to raise costs and make discriminating employers less competitive against their more egalitarian

[77] Holloway, *Confronting the Veil*. On institutionalism, see Backhouse, "Economics," 40; Bernstein, *Perilous Progress*, 45–47, 88, chaps. 4–5; and Jackson, *Gunnar Myrdal and America's Conscience*, 204–7.
[78] Backhouse, "Economics," 40–41; Bernstein, *Perilous Progress*, 89, 93, 101, 106, 123; and Backhouse, "Transformation of U.S. Economics," 85–107, 105.
[79] Backhouse, "Economics," 40–41; Bernstein, *Perilous Progress*, 89, 93; and Backhouse, "Transformation of U.S. Economics," 101, 105–6, 123.
[80] Murphy, "How Gary Becker Saw the Scourge of Discrimination."

peers.[81] To Becker, the greater prominence of wage differentials between African-Americans and whites in the "socio-psychological" literature was a reflection of economists' methods, which had made it difficult to distinguish between an employer's failure to hire a minority worker on the basis of "objective facts" (usually involving the worker's training or capacities) and "an expression of taste or values" (discrimination against some ascribed characteristic).[82] As economist Kenneth Arrow argued in the 1970s, evidence of employers' "taste for discrimination" did "not contradict rational choice theory" entirely. In raising the issue, however, Becker complicated rational choice frameworks, since competition should have pressured discriminators to give up their "taste," if only because employers who did not discriminate were likely to "drive out the others."[83]

Becker also questioned a core tenet of much sociological, anthropological, and especially left-leaning political-economic literature of the 1930s and 1940s that had viewed discrimination as an interlocking political, economic, and social system. He was especially critical of frameworks like Cox's that assumed "political discrimination, class warfare, monopolies, and market imperfections" raised levels of discrimination within labor markets. Since individuals acting in aggregate could explain wage differentials, "political discrimination" was of secondary causal importance.[84] While interwar and wartime political economy had imagined capitalism as a system that intersected with other systems, for Becker the social and political-economic landscape in which racial discrimination took place was made up of isolated individuals – rational actors interacting in unfettered markets to secure their own interests. Though it would take years for Becker's economics of discrimination to be accepted by the discipline's mainstream, by the last quarter of the century, as we will see, *The Economics of Discrimination* had a far-reaching impact, shaping research on race (and later gender) and wage differentials, antidiscrimination legislation, and "premarket factors" (including education's impact on wages).[85]

The approach pioneered by Becker shared with the psychology of prejudice a view of discrimination as a problem perpetuated by individuals, with social, political, economic, or cultural systems as of marginal or secondary causal

---

[81] Becker, *Economics of Discrimination*, 14, 30.
[82] Murphy, "How Gary Becker Saw the Scourge of Discrimination" and Becker, *Economics of Discrimination*, 13–14.
[83] Arrow, "What Has Economics to Say about Racial Discrimination?" 94–96.
[84] Becker, *Economics of Discrimination*, 30.
[85] Becker, *Economics of Discrimination*, 7 and Posner, "Gary Becker's Contributions to Law and Economics."

importance.[86] In contrast to the multidisciplinary borrowing, and emphasis on system, of the interwar and wartime years, the Cold War era saw the ascent, albeit contested and complicated, of the psychology of prejudice and the "economic approach" to discrimination. Both dispositional, individualistic paradigms for understanding racial discrimination put individual prejudices and the discriminatory actions that resulted center stage. With important exceptions, these paradigms emphasized the causal significance of individual attitudes to racial conflict and inequality. They also treated discrimination as the behavioral consequence of biased beliefs, and tended to use individuals as units of analysis. While the specter of wartime racist irrationality and the appeal of individualistic methods certainly accounted for some of the appeal of these frameworks, the importance of the Cold War political context, while more difficult to prove, cannot be dismissed.

5.4 Discrimination and Inequality in the Era of Formal Equality, 1964–1975

Alternatives to individualistic psychological and economic paradigms returned to prominence in the decade after the passage of the Civil Rights Act. By then, systemic and relational theories had assumed a new character, and their proponents responded to new pressures. After the 1964 arrival of formal equality, social scientists across the disciplines expressed concern with delineating those causes of racial inequality that could not be explained by individual belief and behavior. They also raised questions about whether discrimination was itself the crux of the social problem being considered, or if racial inequality in the absence of discrimination constituted a racial harm. Systemic and relational theories tended to fall into new categories that borrowed from, but moved beyond, their interwar and wartime predecessors. One set involved radically inspired theories of power, internal colonialism, and institutional racism. In the other group were a range of quantitative sociological and economic studies on the sources of racial inequality. For both categories of scholarship, the systemic dimensions of discrimination in the era of formal equality were harder to identify than in earlier eras, when slavery or de jure segregation could be more readily conceptualized as a coordinated system. Thus, alternatives to individualism reclaimed a central place in the social science of racial discrimination after 1964, but these paid more attention to consequences than to causes. In the wake of legalized discrimination and segregation, and

---

[86] Murphy, "How Gary Becker Saw the Scourge of Discrimination," 7.

in a social scientific landscape where quantification increasingly signaled scientific authority, scholars approached efforts to delineate the systemic nature of discrimination, and to measure its mechanisms and causes, with less empirical precision, and in some instances less authority, than their counterparts in previous periods.

The literature on the race issue responded to the changed political landscape of the mid-1960s, one marked by a sense of both progress and crisis. The decade saw the arrival of formal equality with the Civil Rights Act, Voting Rights Act, and desegregation legislation, alongside recurring incidents of urban racial unrest, leading the Kerner Commission to famously proclaim: "Our nation is moving toward two societies, one black, one white – separate and unequal."[87] These years featured the War on Poverty's promise of "equality as a fact and as a result," alongside Lyndon Johnson's tendency, critics contended, to fight poverty "on the cheap," in part by prioritizing education, job training, and welfare for only the deserving poor. The "discovery" of not just poverty in a land of plenty, but also an urban crisis with tangled roots in structural transformations of the economy and systemic racial discrimination, also marked the Great Society era. Variants of African-American militancy – which drew on much longer radical and internationalist traditions and emphasized the economic dimensions of racial injustice – were increasingly visible alongside the marches and legislative gains of the civil rights struggle.[88]

Post-1964 literature on racial discrimination, inequality, and the relationship between the two also responded to an evolving intellectual climate. The era's scholarship reflected legacies of the movement of the sociological "center of gravity" from the conflict-oriented Chicago School of the 1930s to Harvard and Columbia in the 1950s, where structural-functionalists downplayed foundational social conflicts and envisioned in their place a teleological evolution toward social integration and cohesion.[89] This climate was also distinguished by new advances in quantitative

---

[87] US National Advisory Commission on Civil Disorders, *Report of the National Advisory Commission*, 1.

[88] On the War on Poverty and its limits, see Katz, *Undeserving Poor*, chap. 3; O'Connor, *Poverty Knowledge*, chaps. 6–8; and Sugrue, *Sweet Land of Liberty*, chap. 11, 366. On the blurred lines between militancy and pacifism, as well as economic and civic emphases in the Civil Rights and Black Power movements, see Sugrue, *Sweet Land of Liberty*, xxi–xxvii; Jackson, *From Civil Rights to Human Rights*; and Van DeBurg, *New Day in Babylon*.

[89] Winant, "Dark Side of the Force," 561–62; Pettigrew, *Sociology of Race Relations*, 183, 238–39; McKee, *Sociology and the Race Problem*, chap. 9; and Brick, *Transcending Capitalism*, 210.

methods in economics and sociology – especially computer-generated regression techniques and increasingly mathematical turns in economic modeling and quantitative sociology.[90] A series of multidisciplinary edited volumes – Talcott Parsons and Kenneth Clark's *The Negro American* (1966); Irwin Katz and Patricia Gurin's *Race and the Social Sciences* (1969); and Thomas Pettigrew's *Racial Discrimination in the United States* (1975) – echoed their wartime predecessors in expressing the view that social science should inform social planning. The volumes also highlighted a new landscape, in which questions about the relationship between discrimination and inequality were of increasing importance.[91] A number of themes marked this literature: (1) disagreement over ideological and policy commitments, even within the same volume; (2) concern with the persistence of racial disparity in the absence of formal, legal systems of racial discrimination; and (3) renewed attention to deficiency paradigms, which suggested that African-American beliefs and values reproduced the social and economic harms discrimination and economic dislocation had originally generated.[92] These volumes brought together scholars from fields deemed relevant to the race question. After 1964, these included sociology (especially its quantitative branch), economics (focused on labor, occupational mobility, and economic inequality), demography (with an emphasis on indices of racial disparity and family "disorganization"), psychology (with reduced, though still present, attention to white prejudice and considerable growth in concern with identity and pathology among racism's victims), and political science (which returned to prominence in race-related debates in this period).[93]

Ideological and theoretical divides were especially visible between thinkers who advocated consensus-oriented or more conflict-based frameworks,

[90] Backhouse, "Economics," 48. While econometrics is often treated as originating in the 1920s and 1930s, regression analysis "began to become established as a tool for empirical research in the 1950s," though "the use of tables of statistics or graphs in the *American Economic Review* (AER) was more common, rising from 50% in the 1920s to over 60% in 1955–1960." Backhouse, "Transformation of U.S. Economics," 95 and Pettigrew, *Sociology of Race Relations*, 316.

[91] Parsons and Clark, *Negro American* and Katz and Gurin, *Race and the Social Sciences*, vii–viii.

[92] Moynihan, *Negro Family*; O'Connor, *Poverty Knowledge*, chap. 8; Katz, *Undeserving Poor*, chap. 3; Patterson, *Freedom Is Not Enough*; Scott, *Contempt and Pity*; Geary, *Beyond Civil Rights*; and Geary, "Racial Liberalism, the Moynihan Report."

[93] While psychologists of prejudice continued to develop dispositional research, only two of thirty chapters in *The Negro American* focused on psychological approaches to prejudice: B. Sheatsley, "White Attitudes Toward the Negro" and Pettigrew, "Complexity and Change in American Racial Patterns."

Leah N. Gordon

even though both challenged individualistic paradigms. Parsons and Clark's *The Negro American* exemplified these fissures. The book's authors (and two editors) disagreed over whether racial progress could be achieved without racial conflict, over the necessity of racial integration, and over the political implications of the language of "power." On the one hand, consensus theorists – rooted in structural-functionalist sociology in which notions of social structure played a central role – presented discrimination as an aberration and American society as progressing inevitably toward cohesion. With demographer Philip Hauser, Parsons assumed that African-Americans would follow the processes of civic integration (and for Hauser assimilation) that Jewish and Catholic immigrants experienced. They held that the Civil Rights Movement heralded a steady march toward "inclusion," that analyses of power were a "minority viewpoint," and that calls for power might increase discrimination.[94]

The strand of racial thought with which consensus frameworks were in tension treated conflict as foundational. Beginning in the mid-1960s, a loosely linked set of theories featured notions like institutional racism (meaning something much broader than it did in Lohman and Reitzes's work in the late 1940s), power, and internal colonialism. Blurring lines between systemic and relational theorizing, 1960s conflict-based theories of American racism built on concepts of social system associated with the interwar Chicago School and the Caste and Class School, as well as notions of discrimination as a system of the 1940s.[95] These analyses also drew on a long tradition of African-American anticolonial and internationalist thought. They often emerged from scholars with ties to Black Power activism, frequently circulating in African-American-led academic journals such as the *Journal of Afro-American Issues, Review of Black Political Economy, The Black Scholar,* and *Freedomways.* At the same time, conflict approaches claimed a central place in *The Negro American,* with thinkers like Kenneth Clark and St. Clair Drake bringing theories of power, institutional racism, and the colonial analogy into more mainstream social scientific settings as well.[96] Theories of internal colonialism challenged

Parsons, "Introduction," xx, xxv, xxvii; Hauser, "Demographic Factors in the Integration," 71, 95–96, 99–100; and Parsons, "Full Citizenship for the Negro American?" 712. On the tensions leading to the publication of *The Negro American,* see Geary, "Racial Liberalism, the Moynihan Report."

On consensus versus conflict frameworks, see Winant, "Dark Side of the Force."

Singh, *Black Is a Country*; Von Eschen, *Race against Empire*; and Kelley, "But a Local Phase of a World Problem." For an analysis of the literature on "internal colonialism," including debates over the concept of exploitation and its relationship to discrimination, see Katz, *Undeserving Poor,* chap. 2, especially 71–84.

both methodological and liberal individualism when explaining racialized poverty, contesting, as Michael Katz argued, "liberal discourse, whether expressed as the culture of poverty, the residue of discrimination, or the lack of human capital."[97]

This scholarship maintained that interlocking social, political, and economic mechanisms produced white supremacy in the era of formal equality much as they had in colonial contexts or under de jure segregation. In contrast to analyses of systemic discrimination of the 1930s and 1940s, however, because the formal legal systems that had stood at the heart of Jim Crow were no longer the linchpin of post-1960s white supremacy, post-1964 analysts faced more difficulty clarifying, delineating, and, especially, quantifying the causal mechanisms generating the new racial system and its inequalities. Clark, for example, emphasized that America's racial ghettos represented "social, political, educational, and – above all – economic colonies," and both he and St. Clair Drake described "a system of social relations" that deprived its victims of the material goods they helped produce.[98] Despite their emphasis on the cohesiveness of white supremacist systems, theorists of institutional racism conceded that discrimination's consequences could be easier to discern than its mechanisms. Stokely Carmichael (later Kwame Ture) and Charles Hamilton's *Black Power* (1967), at once a radical manifesto and a document whose core terminology moved into the social scientific mainstream, distinguished between "individual racism" and "institutional racism," calling the latter "less overt" and "far more subtle" because it was "less identifiable in terms of specific individuals committing the acts." As Carmichael and Hamilton wrote, when a bigot killed five children bombing a black church, "that is an act of individual racism, widely deplored by most segments of the society." In contrast, when "... five hundred black babies die each year because of the lack of proper food, shelter and medical facilities ... that is a function of institutional racism."[99] The remedy for these more hidden but pervasive forms of racism was a redistribution of not only resources – Clark and Drake suggested that guaranteed income and preferential hiring of racial minorities might be necessary – but also power.

While prioritizing changes to political and economic systems, this literature also registered active debates about the utility of African-American capitalism, collectivism, and self-help, and whether separatist politics or efforts to mobilize

---

[97] Katz, *Undeserving Poor*, 73–74; and Singh, *Black is a Country*, 174–211.
[98] Clark, *Dark Ghetto*, 11; Clark, "Introduction," xi–xii, xvii–xviii; and Drake, "Social and Economic Status of the Negro," 4.
[99] Carmichael and Hamilton, *Black Power*, 4.

African-American power within electoral systems were preferable.[100] Though the concepts of institutional racism and systemic discrimination had more staying power in American social science than the more elaborate theories of internal colonialism, much of this body of systemic criticism faced some marginalization – partly because it was deemed overly political but not sufficiently scientific – from the academic mainstream. By the late 1970s, one historian notes, internal colonialism, and much of the radical critique of institutional racism that went with it, "fell out of favor ... from a combination of its radical sponsorship" and "location outside the mainstream of American social science..."[101] Of course these paradigms, as we will see, would persist in black studies and ethnic studies programs; they would also see a revival during and after the 1990s in critical race theory, anticolonial and antiracist sociological traditions, and histories of race and racism.

A second strand of research, published in mainstream sociology and economics journals and with little connection to African-American radicalism, focused on intergenerational social mobility and racial disparities in labor markets. Like its radical counterpart, this literature pointed more clearly to the consequences than the precise causes of racial disparity. Some of this work focused on the relationship between discrimination and human capital in shaping racially disparate patterns of inter- and intragenerational social mobility. A wave of sociological literature on racial dissimilarity in socioeconomic status built on data collected in the US Census Current Population Survey (1962) and Peter Blau and Otis Dudley Duncan's *The American Occupational Structure* (1967). These data inspired a generation of quantitative sociologists to explore occupational mobility, while others focused on education's capacities for equalizing both educational and social opportunities.[102] Economists also measured social mobility across the life course and between generations, asking about the relative importance of human capital, skill mismatch, and racial discrimination in generating racial disparities in hiring, promotion, and wages.[103]

---

[100] Clark, "Introduction," xi–xviii, xi–xii, xvii–xviii; Drake, "Social and Economic Status of the Negro," 4; Carmichael and Hamilton, *Black Power*; Singh, *Black Is a Country*, chap. 5; and Sugrue, *Sweet Land of Liberty*, chaps. 10 and 12.

[101] Katz, *Undeserving Poor*, 81–82, citing Kelley, *Freedom Dreams*, 95. For a few examples of these sizable literatures, see Crenshaw, *Critical Race Theory*; Lipsitz, *Possessive Investment in Whiteness*; Winant, "The Dark Side of the Force," 567; and Fields and Fields, *Racecraft*.

[102] Blau and Duncan, *American Occupational Structure*; US Bureau of the Census, "Lifetime Occupational Mobility of Adult Males"; Coleman et al., *Equality of Educational Opportunity*; and Jencks et al., *Inequality*.

[103] Simpson and Yinger, *Racial and Cultural Minorities*, 44 and Darity and Mason, "Evidence on Discrimination in Employment," 73–76.

Sociologists and economists interested in the sources of wider patterns of racial disparity in the late 1960s and early 1970s paid particular attention to the relative importance of economic restructuring and labor market discrimination. They found discrimination difficult to measure with available quantitative tools, and patterns of racial inequality easier to precisely delineate than its causes. Health economist Rashi Fein analyzed socioeconomic indicators of racial inequality (in infant mortality, life expectancy, unemployment, income, wealth, and educational attainment) to ask why progress toward equality of opportunity had not proceeded more rapidly. While his methods did not permit the direct measurement of discrimination, Fein reasoned that African-Americans' occupational and income disparities testify to its effects.[104] Others speculated that African-American disadvantages in labor markets were rooted in economic restructuring and would, as a result, persist even with effective antidiscrimination policy. In 1969, surveying existing literature on "Negro disadvantage in the economy," labor economist Charles C. Killingsworth concluded that most analysts overestimated the importance of racial discrimination to patterns of economic disparity; he emphasized, instead, the primary importance of deindustrialization and automation.[105] Still others agreed with radical economist Bennett Harrison that discrimination and economic restructuring worked simultaneously and reinforced one another.[106] And some scholars refused to attribute causality to processes that could not be traced empirically – with discrimination as a prominent case in point. Sociologist Otis Dudley Duncan provided evidence of racial dissimilarity in the relationship between father's occupation, first job, and 1962 occupation among African-American and non-African-American male workers, but did not extrapolate beyond his evidence. All he suggested was that, if the "barriers to Negro mobility (*call them 'discrimination' if you like*)" could be removed, "a rapid convergence of Negro and non-Negro occupational distributions" would result.[107]

Other scholars suggested that deindustrialization and patterns of labor market discrimination intersected in ways that could be quantified – though making causal inferences involved speculation. In their analysis of occupational status among African-American men and racial dissimilarity in patterns of intergenerational social mobility, sociologists Stanley Lieberson and Glenn V. Funguitt distinguished between a traditional notion of discrimination, based in overt racial antipathy, and low status that – though

[104] Fein, "Economic and Social Profile," 106, 121, 129, 130.
[105] Killingsworth, "Jobs and Income for Negroes," 231–32.
[106] Harrison, "Training for Nowhere," B4.
[107] Duncan, "Patterns of Occupational Mobility," 173, 174 (emphasis added), 185.

rooted in histories of racial discrimination – "occurs because the group
occupies an inferior aggregate position on variables which, although racially
neutral, operate to their disadvantage." The pair used statistical modeling
techniques to show that racial and nonracial patterns of social hierarchy
were linked, since discrimination could generate "structural, non-racially
based, social processes," including historical holdovers – even in the absence
of persistent discrimination.[108] In contrast to frameworks like those of Ira
de A. Reid, E. Franklin Frazier, or Robert Weaver, which had depicted labor
or housing market discrimination as an interlocking and organized, if not
deliberately orchestrated, set of systems with roots in public and private policy,
few mid-1960s sociologists and economists depicted the widespread patterns
of discrimination expressed in social immobility as functioning with such
coordination and coherence. Even if the intersecting economic and racial
processes discussed after 1964 had similarly all-encompassing effects – that is,
even if they functioned as a system from the perspective of those discriminated
against – available quantitative methods did not provide clear evidence.

   Faced with similar evidence of racial discrimination's consequences,
scholars working at the intersections of psychology, anthropology, and
sociology made their own speculative analytic leap by drawing attention
to the causal importance of African-American cultural and psychological
pathology to explain social immobility. As historians Alice O'Connor,
Michael Katz, Daniel Geary, and Ellen Herman have carefully chronicled,
by the mid-1960s, a flourishing literature relied on psychological notions
of pathology (including concepts like frustration and ego disruption), as
well as sociological/anthropological notions of social disorganization and
"the culture of poverty," to explain African-American poverty.[109] Though
culturally poverty theorists tended to be political liberals supportive of civil
rights measures, compensatory educational programs, job training, and, for
a time, even job creation, their frameworks generated a deprivation-oriented
research agenda in which, as O'Connor has argued, "the object of research
was poor people and the question was what distinguished them – money
or culture – from everyone else."[110] Daniel Patrick Moynihan's contribution
to *The Negro American* argued that, despite the "moral grandeur of the
Negro revolution," which made it "more than normally difficult to speak

---

[108] Lieberson and Fuguitt, "Negro-White Occupational Differences," 199, 205–206.
[109] Herman, *Romance of American Psychology*, 186–207; O'Connor, *Poverty Knowledge*;
     Katz, *Undeserving Poor*; and Geary, *Beyond Civil Rights*.
[110] O'Connor, *Poverty Knowledge*, 197 and Ryan, *Blaming the Victim*, cited in O'Connor,
     Poverty Knowledge, 209.

of these matters," statistics on African-American unemployment and "family breakdown" told of a crisis. While a small group of middle-class African-Americans had experienced improved economic circumstances, most African-American workers did not see any improvement in economic opportunities. These economic dislocations, Moynihan maintained, developed alongside "a serious weakening of the Negro social structure, specifically the Negro family" – though the causal relationships, which were the crux of the issue, were difficult to tease out.[111]

As reflected in *The American Negro* collection, scholars agreed that racial disparity across housing, occupational status, employment, education, and criminal justice stood at the heart of the post–Civil Rights Act race issue. They also shared the view that something had changed in the processes of discrimination with the arrival of formal equality. But a number of fault lines were evident too. Some were empirical. How could the racial discrimination that blocked African-American mobility be quantified? How did legalized patterns of discrimination in the past generate racial inequalities after these systems had been dismantled? And by what mechanisms did nonracial economic structures and racial discrimination intersect? Others were normative. Was racial integration an ideal worth pursuing? Were employment programs that featured racial preferences or guaranteed annual incomes desirable? And what types of inequality were in fact a social problem?

The available data described much better than explained the mechanisms generating racial inequality in the decade and a half following the Civil Rights Act. One set of causal theories drew implicitly on the Cold War era psychology of prejudice and economics of discrimination to suggest that many discriminatory agents acting in aggregate blocked minority opportunities – but these approaches lacked clear methods for quantifying this large-scale aggregation of discrimination. Other theories – those generally criticized for victim-blaming – treated minority psychology and culture as the mechanism linking past discrimination and present inequality. The major exceptions were theories of power, internal colonialism, and institutional racism, which brought assumptions about systems – especially the notions of political-economic system of anticolonialism, at least by analogy – back to the center of social scientific research on the race issue. But this approach met with skepticism in some of the mainstream academy for being associated with radicalism, insufficiently quantitative, or causally imprecise. Nonetheless, through much of the 1960s and 1970s, the solution to the problem at hand,

[111] Moynihan, "Employment, Income, and the Ordeal," 136–37.

at least as articulated by the liberals publishing in multidisciplinary volumes, was social intervention, especially compensatory education, job training, job creation, and, for some, racial preferences. Where *The Negro American*'s politically diverse, cross-disciplinary range of authors could agree was that effective antidiscrimination measures and job creation were essential.

5.5 Multidisciplinarity, Causal Ambiguity, and Colorblindness, 1975–2000

In the last quarter of the twentieth century, social scientific research on racial injustice and inequality continued to reflect the theoretical and disciplinary multiplicity of the preceding eras. Individualized explanatory frameworks persisted; psychological research on prejudice continued; economists interested in rational actors became leading voices on the topic; and, beginning in the 1970s, paired testing studies sought to measure the sources of racial inequality in housing or labor markets. By the 1990s, conservative "colorblindness" discourse re-emphasized the importance of individual dispositions, while also suggesting the definitional importance of law, by treating any racial categorization as a form of discrimination and popularizing notions of "reverse racism."

Systemic and relational theories circulated as well, most clearly in the movement of "institutional racism" into the social scientific mainstream, but also in debates among economists and quantitative sociologists about how the racial and economic sources of radical disparity interacted.[112] And yet, critics of explanations that prioritized discriminating individuals continued to struggle with how to depict the interlocking sociological, cultural, economic, and political sources of racial inequality in years when discrimination was no longer formalized in law and state policy – and when available research methods were still better at quantifying individual perpetrators and victims of racial injustice than systems. A number of economists experimented with new methodological approaches in the hopes of teasing out the causal importance of discrimination and the presumably "nonracial" (though always, O'Connor reminds us, racialized) sources of racial disparity.[113] Legal theorists focusing on "disparate impact" accepted the causal ambiguity that ran through these quantitative analyses and defined discrimination

---

[112] Pettigrew, *Racial Discrimination in the United States*, x and Simpson and Yinger, *Racial and Cultural Minorities*, x, 3.

[113] Darity and Mason, "Evidence on Discrimination in Employment"; Arrow, "What Has Economics to Say about Racial Discrimination?"; O'Connor, *Poverty Knowledge*, chap. 10; and Katz, *Underclass Debate*.

in terms of its consequences, with important implications for policy and legal remedy. There were notable exceptions to causal ambiguity. Douglass Massey and Nancy Denton's *American Apartheid* (1993) returned attention to the centrality of segregation in generating urban concentrated poverty, while also emphasizing that the roots of segregation lay in law and state policy.[114] A generation of urban historians and sociologists would follow suit in chronicling the ways that state policy and action, from redlining to urban renewal, segregated the metropolitan landscape. For others, however, especially those in fields that required scholarship to be conducted at a large scale to count as rigorous, the task of theorizing – and especially quantifying – systemic sources of racial inequality remained complex.

The shifting political, economic, and ideological context of the last third of the twentieth century – one marked by rising wealth and income inequality, the rollback of Great Society social protections, the declining power of unions, the halting of school desegregation (and resegregation), intensifying residential segregation, and disinvestment in the nation's urban cores – encouraged social scientists to continue examining the mechanisms that reinforced racial and socioeconomic inequality.[115] Economic downturns in the aftermath of the 1973 oil crisis were followed by sharp increases in socioeconomic inequality. As the Nixon and Reagan administrations, and the courts they shaped, attacked labor, welfare, healthcare, and school desegregation policies, encouraged declining union membership, and allowed "the real value of the minimum wage, welfare benefits, and other social protections to erode," the United States gained the auspicious designation of surpassing other Western democracies in incarceration and childhood poverty rates.[116] The ideological context in which late twentieth-century research on race and inequality was developed had changed as well. Beginning in the mid-1970s and accelerating throughout the 1980s and 1990s, a newly emboldened conservative movement, fueled by think tanks and research institutions, took aim at an expanded welfare state and color-conscious policy

---

[114] Massey and Denton, *American Apartheid*. On urban history, politics, and sociology, see Sugrue, *Origins of the Urban Crisis*; Sugrue, *Sweet Land of Liberty*; Erickson, *Making the Unequal Metropolis*; Lipsitz, *How Racism Takes Place*; and Reed, *Stirrings in the Jug*. For a few examples of these critical paradigms, see Crenshaw, *Critical Race Theory*; Fields and Fields, *Racecraft*; Kelley, *Freedom Dreams*; and Lipsitz, *Possessive Investment in Whiteness*.

[115] Kantor and Brenzel, "Urban Education and the 'Truly Disadvantaged'"; Sugrue, *Origins of the Urban Crisis*; and Sugrue, *Sweet Land of Liberty*, chap. 14.

[116] Katz, *Undeserving Poor*, 156; Orfield and Eaton, *Dismantling Desegregation*; and Sugrue, *Sweet Land of Liberty*, chap. 13.

mechanisms.[117] Throughout the 1980s and 1990s, amid conservative attacks on "dependence," the "devolution" of public authority, and an embrace of market models across a range of public policy sectors, liberal social knowledge saw "a broader ideological realignment" that – on questions of poverty and, in some ways, on race – moved "analysts to the 'neutral' center in a spectrum that had shifted dramatically to the right."[118]

In this political and ideological context, mainstream liberal research on race both reflected the interdisciplinary sensibilities of the 1920s, 1930s, and 1940s and incorporated broadly systemic, including power-attuned, theories that had previously been associated with radicalism. At the same time, some raised questions about a kind of causal ambiguity embedded in these newly popular explanations of racism. Both Harvard social psychologist Thomas Pettigrew's *Racial Discrimination in the United States* (1975) and George Eaton Simpson and J. Milton Yinger's reissued *Racial and Cultural Minorities* (1985) assumed that personality-based approaches to discrimination were insufficient without a wider multidisciplinary, systemic, and relational framing.[119] Simpson and Yinger presented discrimination as "manifestations of the struggle for 'power, prestige, and income' between and within societies," and argued that "civil rights, 'internal colonialism,' desegregation, integration, discrimination, pluralism, genocide, apartheid" were the essential concepts any "student of contemporary life must learn to use."[120] Pettigrew's edited volume also distinguished between (1) "the concepts of prejudice and individual racism," which were "phenomena of individuals" and (2) "discrimination and institutional racism," which were best viewed at the "societal level."[121]

Pettigrew also exposed the ambiguity on causality that occasionally surfaced in what he termed the "societal" level, which included both systemic and relational theories. He presented institutional racism as "that complex of institutional arrangements that restrict the life choices of black Americans in comparison to those of white Americans," but admitted that "such a definition can rightfully be challenged as too all-encompassing," since it covers "virtually all of the nation's institutions and their operations." Suggesting that this was not a consequence of the concept itself but

---

[117] Rodgers, *Age of Fracture*, 114; Crenshaw, "Color Blindness, History, and the Law," 283; and Guinier, "From Racial Liberalism to Racial Literacy," 93.

[118] O'Connor, *Poverty Knowledge*, 243–44, 284; Katz, *Undeserving Poor*, 156; and Katz, *Price of Citizenship*.

[119] Simpson and Yinger, *Racial and Cultural Minorities*, 20–25 and McKee, *Sociology and the Race Problem*, 297.

[120] Simpson and Yinger, *Racial and Cultural Minorities*, x, 3.

[121] Pettigrew, *Racial Discrimination in the United States*, x.

instead represented "a reasonably accurate picture of American society," Pettigrew maintained that (1) institutional racism supported individual racism; (2) "racist institutions need not be operated by racists nor designed with racist intentions to limit black choice"; and (3) both discrimination and institutional racism were hard to fight because they involved a "vast, interlocking system that spans all of the various institutions of American society."[122] Pettigrew was one of the few scholars to precisely name these questions about the trickiness of pinning down causal mechanisms in systemic theories. When such theories were divorced from colonial analogies and directed toward the era of formal equality (rather than the era of enslavement or de jure segregation), this causal ambiguity posed challenges for policymakers as well as social scientists.

 While also concerned with the "societal level" sources of the race issue, another group of social scientists – quantitative sociologists and economists – devised a different set of theories that served as an alternative to Cold War individualism. Building on work from the mid-1960s, this literature on African-American unemployment focused on the sources of racial inequality – most notably whether and how racial and economic patterns acted independently or intersected when explaining racial disparity. While less concerned with the collusive nature of real estate interests or the ways discrimination was institutionalized in law and state policy than thinkers of the 1930s and 1940s, these theories might still be termed systemic since (like interwar social ecology) they focused on the evolution of broad economic and social systems, emphasizing the causal power of processes like deindustrialization, automation, and demographic shifts, while also treating widespread patterns of racial discrimination. Like Pettigrew, they exhibited a kind of causal ambiguity by largely eliding questions about the precise ways that intersecting institutions, systems, or structures caused the disparities that their methods effectively measured but had more trouble explaining.

 Some research on the sources of late twentieth-century racial inequality, which expanded amid public debate over the "urban crisis" and the "underclass," focused on the economic systems responsible for racial disparity, but assumed these could be understood in isolation from systematized patterns of racial injustice. For example, economists associated with the University of Wisconsin Institute for Research on Poverty incorporated 1970s economic stagnation, rising income inequality, the collapse of middle- and working-class wages, and the "steady decline in work opportunities" in their

---

[122] Pettigrew, *Racial Discrimination in the United States*, x–xii.

conclusion that "slow growth and high unemployment" were responsible for rising poverty rates among African-American urban residents. In this view, economic growth would inevitably aid the poorest. A different group of left-leaning institutionalist economists, including Barry Bluestone, Bennett Harrison, Robert Kuttner, and David Gordon, put more emphasis on the political sources of economic restructuring and deindustrialization, rather than treating it as a natural or inevitable process.[123]

Scholars of "split labor markets" and "spatial mismatch" also emphasized the economic, and downplayed the racial, sources of inequality. Work on "split labor markets" emphasized that many "racial and cultural minorities" remained "caught" in the labor market's bottom rungs, as the economy increasingly produced fewer of the stable, unionized jobs that could secure a middle-class life with only a high school education.[124] While John Kain's work on "spatial mismatch" in the 1960s had recognized the policies that generated residential segregation, the literature that later took up his thesis emphasized a presumably race-neutral spatial distance, not (as O'Connor has observed) "a set of interlocking, racialized institutional barriers to employment opportunities for blacks." A range of economists and sociologists obscured, then, the functioning of racial systems, by describing processes that generated racially segmented labor markets – including white flight and the suburbanization of manufacturing jobs – as "a straightforward response to naturalized market forces rather than to industry practices and government policies that were themselves influenced by race."[125]

The debate over the interrelation of systemic racial discrimination and economic restructuring reached a high point in discussions of William Julius Wilson's *The Declining Significance of Race* (1978) and *The Truly Disadvantaged* (1987), and of Douglas Massey and Nancy Denton's *American Apartheid* (1993).[126] In an effort to reclaim discussions of urban social pathology from conservatives, Wilson stressed socioeconomic shifts like deindustrialization, "skill and spatial mismatch," and the movement of middle-class African-Americans to the suburbs. By elevating class over race as the factor that most boldly shaped "life chances for blacks," the 1978 volume implied that the state-sanctioned processes generating residential segregation – the racial systems Robert Weaver, St. Clair Drake, and Horace Cayton had described – had

---

[123] O'Connor, *Poverty Knowledge*, 259, 261–62.
[124] Simpson and Yinger, *Racial and Cultural Minorities*, 63–65 and O'Connor, *Poverty Knowledge*, 223–24.
[125] O'Connor, *Poverty Knowledge*, 260–61, 262–64.
[126] O'Connor, *Poverty Knowledge*, 265; Wilson, *Declining Significance of Race*; Wilson, *The Truly Disadvantaged*; and Massey and Denton, *American Apartheid*.

declined in importance, while "race-neutral" economic restructuring was instead to blame (see Chapter 6: The Black Ghetto).[127]

In contrast, Douglass Massey and Nancy Denton's *American Apartheid* (1993) represented the return of sociological attention to systematic and state-sanctioned racial discrimination – most notably, attention to the causal power of segregation, the interlocking institutional forces that generated it, and the concentrations of poverty that it created. To Massey and Denton, segregation was far from a historical "holdover" that was "fading progressively over time." They argued that few realized the extent of residential segregation, especially for African-Americans, or "the degree to which it is maintained by ongoing institutional arrangements and contemporary individual actions." Emphasizing the importance of Myrdal's work on the causal importance of segregation, and dedicating the volume to Kenneth Clark, Massey and Denton argued that the "present myopia regarding segregation is all the more startling because it once figured prominently in theories of racial inequality."[128]

While economists were centrally involved in discussions of the relative importance of the racial and nonracial (both social and economic) sources of racialized inequality, beginning in the 1970s they also brought new methods and theoretical approaches to the study of racial discrimination, as a topic some defined separately from racial inequality. Many of these new economic approaches to discrimination defied easy categorization as individualistic or systemic.[129] By this time, economists were paying attention to, and beginning to question, Becker's "taste for discrimination" framework, and they also experimented with a range of new measurement techniques to tease out discrimination's relationship to other factors generating inequality. The notion of "statistical discrimination" – in which discriminating employers made false assumptions about characteristics like education level that were presumably, but not necessarily, linked to race – provided one possible "market-based explanation" that avoided employing Becker's concept of "taste."[130] The literature assessing the relative importance of a "human capital gap," on the one hand, or "a discrimination gap," on the other, suggested that discrimination was a residual – whatever remainder was left over after human capital differences had been accounted for. Other economists employed the

---

[127] O'Connor, *Poverty Knowledge*, 269–74 and Rodgers, *Age of Fracture*, 123.
[128] Massey and Denton, *American Apartheid*, 1–3.
[129] Arrow, "What Has Economics to Say about Racial Discrimination?" 93–94.
[130] Arrow, "What Has Economics to Say about Racial Discrimination?" 94, 96–97 and Darity and Mason, "Evidence on Discrimination in Employment," 68.

"Blinder–Oaxaca decomposition procedure" to distinguish discrimination from other group attributes – a statistical approach that "involves estimation of separate earnings or occupational status regressions for a reference group – for example, all males or all white males – and all other groups whose labor market outcomes are being compared against them."[131]

A broader range of policymakers and researchers also measured the extent of discrimination, whether in employment, loans, or housing, through multivariate analyses in which discrimination was treated as the residual variable.[132] While studies of discrimination as residual could posit that "some unknown share, possibly all, of the residual is suspected of being due to discrimination," this approach made it difficult to delineate the severity and extent of discrimination, to be sure about the size of the residual, and to precisely identify (and thus report) discriminatory events.[133]

Another strand of economic research on racial (and gender) discrimination that developed in the 1970s and expanded in subsequent decades – one that returned attention to individual discriminating actors to avoid the limits of the residual approach – involved "auditing" or "paired testing." While concerned with the system-wide effects of discrimination in labor or housing markets, this method leaned toward the individualistic, since it relied on an implicit causal model in which the aggregate actions of many discriminatory individuals or firms generated the inequalities in question.[134] With origins in the world of policy, think tanks, and social reform, as well as in social science, the approach involved two testers/auditors, paired for shared characteristics (experience, education, income, etc.) except for the factor (often race, gender, or ethnicity) "presumed to lead to discrimination." Both applied for a job, rental, or mortgage and patterned outcomes were carefully measured. Paired testing researchers proved useful in the legal arena, since their research measured the sources and mechanisms of discrimination, not only its consequences – while also providing fair employment or housing advocates with evidence of their progress.[135]

In its emphasis on the causal importance of many individuals acting in aggregate, paired testing was an exception to the broad shift away from

[131] Darity and Mason, "Evidence on Discrimination in Employment," 67–68.
[132] Fix, Galster, and Struyk, *Clear and Convincing Evidence*, 7–8 and Price and Mills, "Race and Residence in Earnings Determination," 1, 17.
[133] Fix, Galster, and Struyk, *Clear and Convincing Evidence*, 7–8.
[134] Fix, Galster, and Struyk, *Clear and Convincing Evidence*, 11, 12.
[135] Wienk et al., *Measuring Race Discrimination in American Housing Markets*, ii, 3–5; Fix, Galster, and Struyk, *Clear and Convincing Evidence*, 1, 3–5, 11; and Oh and Yinger, "What Have We Learned from Paired Testing in Housing Markets?" 21.

dispositional, intent-based frameworks. Employment discrimination litigation was one especially visible arena that registered this turn from the intent of the discriminator to the "disparate impact" of patterns of discrimination. In *Griggs* v. *Duke Power Company* (1971), the Supreme Court endorsed the notion that apparently race-neutral tests could, in fact, be discriminatory, regardless of employers' intentions, if they had a "disparate impact" by excluding some groups of applicants.[136] Affirmative action programs in government contracts, employment, and higher education admissions also focused on results, rather than intentions, when providing evidence of discrimination and proposing remedies, often expanding minority representation in these sectors significantly. Still, almost as soon as affirmative action policies began they were challenged. The rejection, in *University of California* v. *Bakke* (1978), of racial quotas and logics of compensatory justice, alongside the case's embrace of the "diversity rationale" for racial preferences, ushered in an era where, as sociologist John D. Skrentny puts it, "affirmative action has become separated from *discrimination*."[137] Federal programs that set aside contracts for minority-owned businesses also faced attack, in *Richmond* v. *J.A. Croson* (1989), "based in part on the argument … that claims of historic discrimination were 'inherently immeasurable'" – that only "measurable current and ongoing discriminatory acts" could generate legal remedy.[138]

Affirmative action provided one touchstone – welfare reform the other – for a final, though influential, development in social scientific approaches to racial discrimination in the late twentieth century: the rise of conservative colorblindness. The ascent of colorblind racial logics in law, social science, and conservative social policy was one part of a fracturing of social scientific thought on race in response to the Civil Rights Movement's partial successes undermining discrimination, segregation, and blocked opportunity structures.[139] Colorblind racial logics gained new influence, drawing on older intellectual tendencies: individualistic frameworks that equated racial harm with individual prejudice and intentionality; structural-functionalist frameworks in which racial conflict would die out in a teleological drive toward consensus; tendencies to biologize the dispossessed; black conservative traditions, including those that prioritized

---

136 Dobbin, *Inventing Equal Opportunity*, 110, 112, 129.
137 Skrentny, "Introduction," 11; Sugrue, *Sweet Land of Liberty*, 505–8; and Dobbin, *Inventing Equal Opportunity*, chap. 6, especially 134.
138 Sugrue, *Sweet Land of Liberty*, 509–10.
139 Winant, "Dark Side of the Force," 568, 566.

self-help; and free market economics.[140] Beginning in the 1970s, and accelerating for the remainder of the century, colorblindness gained strength from a conservative ideological sector seeking to reenvision civil rights with race neutrality as its defining ideal.[141]

What was most important about the colorblind turn, and associated notions of "reverse racism," from the perspective of the social science of racial discrimination, was its equation of all racial categorization – and the use of race in any law or public policy – with discrimination. As conservative intellectual Charles Murray put it in 1984, "My proposal for dealing with the racial issue in social welfare is to repeal every bit of legislation and reverse every court decision that in any way requires, recommends, or awards differential treatment according to race.... Race is not a morally admissible reason for treating one person differently from another. Period."[142] The race-blind notion would move to the center of conservative efforts to rollback school desegregation, as well as affirmative action in education and employment, shifting the meaning of seminal court cases like *Brown* v. *Board* from "a clarion call to an excuse not to act."[143] A dismissal of both systemic and relational thinking on the race issue, such an approach denied not only legacies of past oppression but also its ongoing, systematic manifestations. In an ironic twist, however, this framework returned attention to the causal power – and categorizing work – of legal systems, not simply individuals. Yet colorblind conservatives did so in order to promote policies that Reid, Weaver, and Myrdal would certainly have opposed, since they treated discrimination as a historical memory, not an ongoing process, and suggested that civil rights legislation, in and of itself, had solved the race problem.[144]

In the last quarter of the twentieth century, the fields that had been associated with postwar "social relations" frameworks – psychology, sociology, and anthropology – continued to provide leading voices in scholarship on race, though economists would take on a greater role than they had previously. Many sociologists and economists treated the problem to be explained as racial inequality and debated the relative causal importance of changes in the structure of the economy and evolving racial systems. Economists applied new statistical and investigative techniques to the measurement of not only racial inequality but also discrimination, in

[140] Winant, "Dark Side of the Force," 567–69.
[141] Winant, "Dark Side of the Force," 568 and Rodgers, *Age of Fracture*, 127–28.
[142] Murray, *Losing Ground*, 223, cited in Winant, "Dark Side of the Force," 566.
[143] Guinier, "From Racial Liberalism to Racial Literacy," 93 and Crenshaw, "Color Blindness, History, and the Law," 285.
[144] Rodgers, *Age of Fracture*, 130.

some cases paying attention to the social context of discrimination, while in others treating discrimination as the decontextualized aggregate of many individual actions. Social scientific concerns with the consequences, rather than causes, of racial injustice had important parallels in the legal and policy realm, as disparate impact and affirmative action litigation made clear. Despite their concern with the causal power of legal categorization, colorblind frameworks recentered moral and political individualism by disembedding discrimination from context – that is, from the concerns with power, social structure, political economic system, and historical setting that systemic and relational theories of the race issue had long prioritized.[145] At the same time, traditions that built on those interwar and Black Power–era tendencies – from the African-American academy and from grassroots antiracist movements – moved to the center of many academic fields in the mid-1990s, especially history, sociology, anthropology, legal studies (in critical race theory), black studies, ethnic studies, and urban studies.

5.6 Conclusion

Racial discrimination was not only "the problem of the twentieth century," but was also one of the major social problems that occupied the century's social scientists.[146] In the long post–World War II era, however, just how *social* this problem actually was concerned scholars across the disciplines. Many assumed that this multifaceted issue demanded multidisciplinary analysis. A classic example of social science shaped by, and often produced in the hopes of advancing, social and political transformation, scholarship on the race issue stood in a complex relationship to the monumental, though incomplete, egalitarian politics of the long civil rights era.[147] Indeed, in the half-century following World War II, as the struggle against legal discrimination and segregation gained momentum and reached key legislative milestones, scholars of the race issue faced basic questions about discrimination: Who or what can discriminate? How can discrimination be measured? And is racial inequality in the absence of intentional or provable discrimination evidence of a persisting race problem? In the era of formal equality, answering these questions became especially vexing.

From the late 1940s through the 1990s, the relative influence of disciplinary perspectives on questions of discrimination changed, paralleling the rising

---

[145] Rodgers, *Age of Fracture*, 130, 132.
[146] Du Bois, *Souls of Black Folk*, 10.
[147] Hall, "Long Civil Rights Movement."

authority of individualistically oriented psychological and economic frameworks in the post–World War II study of social problems. Interwar and wartime analyses of the race issue had drawn on sociology, anthropology, psychology, economics, and political science to theorize prejudice as intertwined with race relations, but social scientists centered intersecting systems (social, cultural, legal, and political-economic) when explaining discrimination's mechanisms. Beginning in the early Cold War era, however, individually oriented – critics called them "atomistic" – theories gained ground, especially in psychology, economics, and across the behavioral sciences. The legacies of this turn to the individual persisted throughout the late twentieth century in paired testing techniques; in psychologists' efforts to probe prejudiced personalities and, by the 1990s, "implicit biases"; in economic work that finally took up Becker's call for analyzing the costs of discrimination; and, in complex ways, in colorblind paradigms.[148]

And yet, the story of shifting disciplinary jurisdiction in the social science of racial discrimination is more complex than a simple rise of individualistic approaches in and from psychology and economics. Between the passage of the Civil Rights Act and the 1990s, the reality of formal equality moved racial inequality – as opposed to racial discrimination and often questions about the relationship between the two – to the center of scholarship. The era of formal equality raised questions that were at once scientific and political: How could a scholar quantify the causes and mechanisms of racial discrimination, without resorting to race as a variable or embracing a dispositional approach?[149] At what point and by what processes did many individual acts of discrimination – still widespread, most acknowledged, even in a landscape where "whites only" signage no longer announced the processes at work – become a racial system? More broadly, to what systems, structures, and institutions should social scientists look when investigating the systemic and institutional character of racial injustice in the post–Civil Rights Act era? In the absence of legal segregation and discrimination, was racial inequality a problem for American liberalism?

The task of delineating the "vast interlocking system" that Pettigrew described in 1975 as the heart of the race issue occupied scholars for the remainder of the century.[150] The political importance of this task increased

---

[148] For an example of current literature on implicit bias, see Staats et al., *State of the Science*. On paired testing, see Fix, Galster, and Struyk, *Clear and Convincing Evidence*; Arrow, "What Has Economics to Say about Racial Discrimination?"; and Posner, "Gary Becker's Contributions to Law and Economics."

[149] Zuberi, *Thicker Than Blood* and Zuberi, "Deracializing Social Statistics."

[150] Pettigrew, *Racial Discrimination in the United States*, xi–xii and Winant, "Dark Side of the Force," 571.

in the Reagan and Clinton years, an era of rising socioeconomic inequality and steady rightward drift in the political spectrum.[151] From the 1990s through the early twenty-first century, a broad range of scholars – critical race theorists; sociologists and historians of white privilege; sociologists, economists, and anthropologists concerned with urban segregation; and scholars focused on policing and criminal justice systems – returned to the systemic and relational theories that had dominated the 1930s and 1940s. These scholars provided sophisticated answers to questions about how racism functioned "without racists."[152] While the need for historical analogy to explain the causes and mechanisms of racial inequality in the era of formal equality – *American Apartheid* and *The New Jim Crow* provide clear examples – suggests the complexity of the task at hand, the long-term impact of new analyses of racial systems in centers of social scientific and political power remains to be seen.[153]

Bibliography

Adorno, Theodor, Else Frenkel-Brunswik, Daniel Levinson, and R. Nevitt Sanford. *The Authoritarian Personality*. New York: Harper & Row, 1950.

Alexander, Michelle. *The New Jim Crow: Mass Incarceration in the Age of Colorblindness*. New York: New Press, 2010.

Allport, Gordon. *The Nature of Prejudice*. Reading: Addison-Wesley, 1954.

Alpers, Benjamin. *Dictators, Democracy, and American Public Culture: Envisioning the Totalitarian Enemy, 1920s–1950s*. Chapel Hill: University of North Carolina Press, 2003.

Aptheker, Herbert. "The Negro People in America: A Critique of Gunnar Myrdal's 'An American Dilemma'." In *Herbert Aptheker on Race and Democracy: A Reader*, edited by Eric Foner and Manning Marable, 184–97. Urbana: University of Illinois Press, 2006.

Arrow, Kenneth. "Models of Job Discrimination." In *Racial Discrimination in Economic Life*, edited by A. H. Pascal, 83–102. Lexington: D. C. Heath, 1972.

Arrow, Kenneth. "What Has Economics to Say about Racial Discrimination?" *Journal of Economic Perspectives* 12, no. 2 (1998): 91–100.

Backhouse, Roger E. "The Transformation of U.S. Economics, 1920–1960, Viewed Through a Survey of Journal Articles." In *From Interwar Pluralism to Postwar Neoclassicism*, edited by Mary S. Morgan and Malcolm Rutherford, 85–107. Durham: Duke University Press, 1998.

[151] Katz, *Price of Citizenship*; O'Connor, *Poverty Knowledge*, chaps. 10–11; and Crenshaw, "Colorblindness, History, and the Law."

[152] Bonilla-Silva, *Racism without Racists*; Crenshaw, *Critical Race Theory*; and Lipsitz, *Possessive Investment in Whiteness*.

[153] Massey and Denton, *American Apartheid* and Alexander, *New Jim Crow*.

Backhouse, Roger E. "Economics." In *The History of the Social Sciences since 1945*, edited by Roger E. Backhouse and Philippe Fontaine, 38–70. Cambridge: Cambridge University Press, 2010.

Baker, Lee D. *From Savage to Negro: Anthropology and the Construction of Race, 1896–1954*. Berkeley: University of California Press, 1998.

Becker, Gary. *The Economics of Discrimination*. Chicago: University of Chicago Press, 1957.

Bernstein, Michael A. *A Perilous Progress: Economists and Public Purpose in Twentieth-Century America*. Princeton: Princeton University Press, 2001.

Bettelheim, Bruno, and Morris Janowitz. *Dynamics of Prejudice*. New York: Harper, 1950.

Blau, Peter M., and Otis Dudley Duncan. *The American Occupational Structure*. New York: John Wiley & Sons, 1967.

Bogardus, Emory S. "Measuring Social Distance." *Journal of Applied Sociology* 9 (1925): 299–308.

Bonilla-Silva, Eduardo. *Racism without Racists: Color-Blind Racism and the Persistence of Racial Inequality in the United States*. Lanham: Rowman & Littlefield, 2010.

Bradbury, William C., Jr. "Racial Discrimination in Federal Employment." Unpublished manuscript for PhD diss., Department of Sociology, Columbia University, n.d.

Brick, Howard. *Transcending Capitalism: Visions of a New Society in Modern American Thought*. Ithaca: Cornell University Press, 2006.

Bulmer, Martin. *The Chicago School of Sociology: Institutionalization, Diversity, and the Rise of Sociological Research*. Chicago: University of Chicago Press, 1984.

Chen, Anthony S. *The Fifth Freedom: Jobs, Politics, and Civil Rights in the United States, 1941–1972*. Princeton: Princeton University Press, 2009.

Chicago Commission on Race Relations. *The Negro in Chicago: A Study of Race Relations and a Race Riot*. Chicago: University of Chicago Press, 1922.

Ciepley, David. *Liberalism in the Shadow of Totalitarianism*. Cambridge: Harvard University Press, 2006.

Clark, Kenneth. *Prejudice and Your Child*. Boston: Beacon Press, 1955.

Clark, Kenneth. *Dark Ghetto: Dilemmas of Social Power*. New York: Harper & Row, 1965.

Clark, Kenneth. "Introduction: The Dilemma of Power." In *The Negro American*, edited by Talcott Parsons and Kenneth B. Clark, xi–xviii. Boston: Beacon Press, 1966.

Cohen-Cole, Jamie. "Thinking about Thinking in Cold War America." PhD diss., Princeton University, 2003.

Cohen-Cole, Jamie. "Instituting the Science of Mind: Intellectual Economies and Disciplinary Exchange at Harvard's Center for Cognitive Studies." *British Journal for the History of Science* 40, no. 4 (2007): 567–97.

Coleman, James S., Ernest Q. Campbell, Carol J. Hobson, et al. *Equality of Educational Opportunity*. Washington, DC: US Department of Health, Education, and Welfare, 1966.

"Conference on Research in Human Relations." Harriman, NY, 28 February–1 March 1953, folder 100, box 11, series 910, Record Group 3.1, RF, Rockefeller Foundation Archives, Rockefeller Archive Center.

Converse, Jean M. *Survey Research in the United States: Roots and Emergence, 1890–1960*. Berkeley: University of California Press, 1987.

Cox, Oliver Cromwell. "An American Dilemma: A Mystical Approach to the Study of Race Relations." *Journal of Negro Education* 14, no. 2 (1945): 132–48.

Cox, Oliver Cromwell. *Caste, Class, and Race*. New York: Monthly Review Press, 1971. First published 1948 by Doubleday (New York).

Crenshaw, Kimberlé Williams. *Critical Race Theory: The Key Writings That Formed the Movement*. New York: New Press, 1995.

Crenshaw, Kimberlé Williams. "Color Blindness, History, and the Law." In *The House That Race Built: Black Americans, U.S. Terrain*, edited by Wahneema H. Lubiano, 280–88. New York: Pantheon Books, 1997.

Darity, William A., Jr., and Patrick L. Mason. "Evidence on Discrimination in Employment: Codes of Color, Codes of Gender." *Journal of Economic Perspectives* 12, no. 2 (1998): 63–90.

Dobbin, Frank. *Inventing Equal Opportunity*. Princeton: Princeton University Press, 2009.

Drake, St. Clair. "The Social and Economic Status of the Negro in the United States." In *The Negro American*, edited by Talcott Parsons and Kenneth B. Clark, 3–46. Boston: Beacon Press, 1966.

Drake, St. Clair, and Horace Cayton. *Black Metropolis: A Study of Negro Life in a Northern City*. New York: Harper & Row, 1962. First published 1945 by Harcourt Brace (New York).

Du Bois, W. E. B. *The Souls of Black Folk*. New York: Bantam Books, 1989. First published 1903 by A. C. McClurg & Co. (Chicago).

Dudziak, Mary. *Cold War Civil Rights: Race and the Image of American Democracy*. Princeton: Princeton University Press, 2000.

Duncan, Otis Dudley. "Patterns of Occupational Mobility Among Negro Men." In *Racial Discrimination in the United States*, edited by Thomas F. Pettigrew, 167–86. New York: Harper & Row, 1975.

Erickson, Ansley T. *Making the Unequal Metropolis: School Desegregation and Its Limits*. Chicago: University of Chicago Press, 2016.

Fein, Rashi. "An Economic and Social Profile of the Negro American." In *The Negro American*, edited by Talcott Parsons and Kenneth B. Clark, 102–33. Boston: Beacon Press, 1966.

Fields, Barbara J., and Karen Fields. *Racecraft: The Soul of Inequality in American Life*. London: Verso, 2012.

Fix, Michael, George Galster, and Raymond Struyk, *Clear and Convincing Evidence: Measurement of Discrimination in America*. Washington, DC: The Urban Institute, 1993.

Gaither, H. Rowan, Jr. *Report of the Study for the Ford Foundation on Policy and Program*. Detroit: The Ford Foundation, 1949.

Geary, Daniel. "Racial Liberalism, the Moynihan Report & the *Dædalus* Project on 'The Negro American'." *Daedalus* 141, no. 1 (Winter 2011): 53–66.

Geary, Daniel. *Beyond Civil Rights: The Moynihan Report and Its Legacy*. Philadelphia: University of Pennsylvania Press, 2015.

Gerstle, Gary. "The Protean Character of American Liberalism." *American Historical Review* 99, no. 4 (1994): 1043–73.

Gilman, Nils. *Mandarins of the Future: Modernization Theory in Cold War America*. Baltimore: Johns Hopkins University Press, 2003.

Gilmore, Glenda. *Defying Dixie: The Radical Roots of Civil Rights, 1900–1950*. New York: W. W. Norton and Co., 2008.

Gordon, Leah N. *From Power to Prejudice: The Rise of Racial Individualism in Midcentury America*. Chicago: University of Chicago Press, 2015.

Greenwood, John D. *The Disappearance of the Social in American Social Psychology.* Cambridge: Cambridge University Press, 2004.

Guinier, Lani. "From Racial Liberalism to Racial Literacy: *Brown v. Board of Education* and the Interest-Divergence Dilemma." *Journal of American History* 91, no. 1 (2004): 92–118.

Hall, Jacquelyn Dowd. "The Long Civil Rights Movement and the Political Uses of the Past." *Journal of American History* 91, no. 4 (2005): 1233–63.

Harrison, Bennett. "Training for Nowhere." *The Washington Post*, November 19, 1972.

Hauser, Philip M. "Demographic Factors in the Integration of the Negro." In *The Negro American*, edited by Talcott Parsons and Kenneth B. Clark, 71–101. Boston: Beacon Press, 1966.

Herman, Ellen. *The Romance of American Psychology: Political Culture in the Age of Experts.* Berkeley: University of California Press, 1995.

Hinton, Elizabeth. "Creating Crime: The Rise and Impact of National Juvenile Delinquency Programs in Black Urban Neighborhoods." *Journal of Urban History* 41, no. 5 (2015): 808–24.

Hinton, Elizabeth. "'A War within Our Own Boundaries': Lyndon Johnson's Great Society and the Rise of the Carceral State." *Journal of American History* 102, no. 1 (2015): 100–12.

Holloway, Jonathan Scott. *Confronting the Veil: Abram Harris Jr., E. Franklin Frazier, and Ralph Bunche, 1919–1941.* Chapel Hill: University of North Carolina Press, 2002.

Holloway, Jonathan Scott, and Benjamin Keppel, eds. *Black Scholars on the Line: Race, Social Science, and American Thought in the Twentieth Century.* Notre Dame: University of Notre Dame Press, 2007.

Horowitz, Eugene L. "'Race' Attitudes." In *Characteristics of the American Negro*, edited by Otto Klineberg, 139–247. New York: Harper & Row, 1944.

Horowitz, Eugene L., and Ruth Horowitz. "Development of Social Attitudes in Children." *Sociometry* 1 (1938): 301–38.

Igo, Sarah E. *The Averaged America: Surveys, Citizens, and the Making of a Mass Public.* Cambridge: Harvard University Press, 2007.

Isaac, Joel. "The Human Sciences in Cold War America." *Historical Journal* 50, no. 3 (2007): 725–46.

Jackson, John P., Jr. *Social Scientists for Social Justice: Making the Case against Segregation.* New York: New York University Press, 2001.

Jackson, Thomas F. *From Civil Rights to Human Rights: Martin Luther King Jr. and the Struggle for Economic Justice.* Philadelphia: University of Pennsylvania Press, 2007.

Jackson, Walter A. *Gunnar Myrdal and America's Conscience: Social Engineering and Racial Liberalism, 1938–1987.* Chapel Hill: University of North Carolina Press, 1990.

Jencks, Christopher, Marshall Smith, Henry Acland, et al. *Inequality: A Reassessment of the Effect of Family and Schooling in America.* New York: Harper & Row, 1972.

Jencks, Christopher, Marshall Smith, Henry Acland, et al. *Who Gets Ahead? The Determinants of Economic Success in America.* New York: Basic Books, 1977.

Jewett, Andrew. *Science, Democracy, and the American University: From the Civil War to the Cold War.* Cambridge: Cambridge University Press, 2012.

Johnson, Charles S. *The Negro in American Civilization: A Study of Negro Life and Race Relations in the Light of Social Research.* New York: Henry Holt & Co., 1930.

Johnson, Charles S. "Race Relations and Social Change." In *Race Relations and the Race Problem: A Definition and an Analysis*, edited by Edgar T. Thompson, 271–305. Durham: Duke University Press, 1939.

Kantor, Harvey, and Barbara Brenzel. "Urban Education and the 'Truly Disadvantaged': The Historical Roots of the Contemporary Crisis, 1945-1990." In *The Underclass Debate: Views from History*, edited by Michael B. Katz, 365-402. Princeton: Princeton University Press, 1993.

Katz, Irwin, and Patricia Gurin, eds. *Race and the Social Sciences*. New York: Basic Books, 1969.

Katz, Michael B., ed. *The Underclass Debate: Views from History*. Princeton: Princeton University Press, 1993.

Katz, Michael B. *The Price of Citizenship: Redefining the American Welfare State*. New York: Metropolitan Books, 2001.

Katz, Michael B. *The Undeserving Poor: America's Enduring Confrontation with Poverty*. 2nd ed. New York: Oxford University Press, 2013.

Katznelson, Ira. "Was the Great Society a Lost Opportunity?" In *The Rise and Fall of the New Deal Order, 1930-1980*, edited by Steve Fraser and Gary Gerstle, 185-211. Princeton: Princeton University Press, 1989.

Kelley, Robin D. G. *Hammer and Hoe: Alabama Communists during the Great Depression*. Chapel Hill: University of North Carolina Press, 1990.

Kelley, Robin D. G. "But a Local Phase of a World Problem: Black History's Global Vision." *Journal of American History* 86, no. 3 (1999): 1045-77.

Kelley, Robin D. G. *Freedom Dreams: The Black Radical Imagination*. Boston: Beacon Press, 2002.

Killingsworth, Charles C. "Jobs and Income for Negroes." In *Race and the Social Sciences*, edited by Irwin Katz and Patricia Gurin, 194-273. New York: Basic Books, 1969.

Klarman, Michael. *From Jim Crow to Civil Rights: The Supreme Court and the Struggle for Racial Equality*. New York: Oxford University Press, 2004.

Konvitz, Milton R. "Discrimination and the Law." In *Discrimination and National Welfare: A Series of Addresses and Discussions*, edited by Robert M. MacIver, 49-64. New York: Harper and Brothers, 1949.

Lagemann, Ellen Condliffe. *The Politics of Knowledge: The Carnegie Corporation, Philanthropy, and Public Policy*. Chicago: University of Chicago Press, 1989.

Lieberson, Stanley. *A Piece of the Pie: Blacks and White Immigrants since 1880*. Berkeley: University of California Press, 1980.

Lieberson, Stanley, and Glenn V. Fuguitt. "Negro-White Occupational Differences in the Absence of Discrimination." In *Racial Discrimination in the United States*, edited by Thomas F. Pettigrew, 187-205. New York: Harper & Row, 1975.

Lipsitz, George. *The Possessive Investment in Whiteness: How White People Profit from Identity Politics*. Philadelphia: Temple University Press, 1998.

Lipsitz, George. *How Racism Takes Place*. Philadelphia: Temple University Press, 2011.

Lohman, Joseph D., and Dietrich C. Reitzes. "Notes on Race Relations in Mass Society." *American Journal of Sociology* 58, no. 3 (1952): 240-46.

MacIver, Robert. *The More Perfect Union: A Program for the Control of Inter-group Discrimination in the United States*. New York: Macmillan, 1948.

MacIver, Robert, ed. *Discrimination and the National Welfare: A Series of Addresses and Discussions*. New York: Harper & Bros., 1949.

Massey, Douglas, and Nancy Denton. *American Apartheid: Segregation and the Making of the Underclass*. Cambridge: Harvard University Press, 1993.

Masuoka, Jitsuichi, and Preston Valien, eds. *Race Relations: Problems and Theory, Essays in Honor of Robert E. Park*. Chapel Hill: University of North Carolina Press, 1961.

Matthews, Fred H. *Quest for an American Sociology: Robert E. Park and the Chicago School.* Montreal: McGill-Queen's University Press, 1977.

Mayor's Commission on Conditions in Harlem. *The Complete Report of Mayor LaGuardia's Commission on the Harlem Riot of March 19, 1935.* New York: Arno Press, 1969.

McAuley, Christopher A. *The Mind of Oliver C. Cox.* Notre Dame: University of Notre Dame Press, 2004.

McKee, James B. *Sociology and the Race Problem: The Failure of a Perspective.* Urbana: University of Illinois Press, 1993.

Medema, Steven G. "Wandering the Road from Pluralism to Posner: The Transformation of Law and Economics in the Twentieth Century." In *From Interwar Pluralism to Postwar Neoclassicism*, edited by Mary S. Morgan and Malcolm Rutherford, 202–24. Durham: Duke University Press, 1998.

Merton, Robert K. "Discrimination and the American Creed." In *Discrimination and the National Welfare: A Series of Addresses and Discussions*, edited by Robert MacIver, 99–126. New York: Harper & Bros., 1949.

Minow, Martha. *In Brown's Wake: Legacies of America's Educational Landmark.* Oxford: Oxford University Press, 2010.

Moynihan, Daniel Patrick. *The Negro Family: The Case for National Action.* Washington, DC: Office of Policy Planning and Research, March 1965. Reprinted in *The Moynihan Report and the Politics of Controversy*, edited by Lee Rainwater and William L. Yancey. Cambridge: Massachusetts Institute of Technology Press, 1967.

Moynihan, Daniel Patrick. "Employment, Income, and the Ordeal of the Negro Family." In *The Negro American*, edited by Talcott Parsons and Kenneth B. Clark, 134–59. Boston: Beacon Press, 1966.

Murphy, Kevin M. "How Gary Becker Saw the Scourge of Discrimination." *Chicago Booth Review*, June 15, 2015. http://review.chicagobooth.edu/magazine/winter-2014/how-gary-becker-saw-the-scourge-of-discrimination

Murray, Charles. *Losing Ground: American Social Policy 1950–1980.* New York: Basic Books, 1984.

Myrdal, Gunnar. *An American Dilemma: The Negro Problem and Modern Democracy.* New York: Harper & Bros., 1944.

Nicholson, Ian. *Inventing Personality: Gordon Allport and the Science of Selfhood.* Washington, DC: American Psychological Association, 2003.

O'Connor, Alice. *Poverty Knowledge: Social Science, Social Policy, and the Poor in Twentieth-Century U.S. History.* Princeton: Princeton University Press, 2001.

O'Connor, Alice. *Social Science for What? Philanthropy and the Social Question in a World Turned Rightside Up.* New York: Russell Sage Foundation, 2007.

Oh, Sun Jung, and John Yinger. "What Have We Learned from Paired Testing in Housing Markets?" *Cityscape* 17, no. 3 (2015): 15–60.

Orfield, Gary, Susan Eaton, and the Harvard Project on School Desegregation. *Dismantling Desegregation: The Quiet Reversal of Brown v. Board of Education.* New York: New Press, 1996.

Park, Robert E. "Our Racial Frontier on the Pacific." *Survey Graphic* 9 (May 1926): 192–96. Reprinted in *Race and Culture: Essays in the Sociology of Contemporary Man*, edited by Robert E. Park, 138–51. Glencoe: Free Press, 1950.

Parsons, Talcott. "Introduction: Why 'Freedom Now,' Not Yesterday?" In *The Negro American*, edited by Talcott Parsons and Kenneth B. Clark, xix–xxiii. Boston: Beacon Press, 1966.

Parsons, Talcott. "Full Citizenship for the Negro American? A Sociological Problem." In *The Negro American*, edited by Talcott Parsons and Kenneth B. Clark, 709–54. Boston: Houghton, Mifflin, 1966.

Parsons, Talcott, and Kenneth B. Clark, eds. *The Negro American*. Boston: Beacon Press, 1966.

Patterson, James T. *Freedom Is Not Enough: The Moynihan Report and America's Struggle over Black Family Life – From LBJ to Obama*. New York: Basic Books, 2010.

Pettigrew, Thomas. "Complexity and Change in American Racial Patterns: A Social Psychological View." In *The Negro American*, edited by Talcott Parsons and Kenneth B. Clark, 352–62. Boston: Beacon Press, 1966.

Pettigrew, Thomas, ed. *Racial Discrimination in the United States*. New York: Harper & Row, 1975.

Pettigrew, Thomas, ed. *The Sociology of Race Relations: Reflection and Reform*. New York: Free Press, 1980.

Phelps, Edmund S. "The Statistical Theory of Racism and Sexism." *American Economic Review* 62, no. 4 (1972): 659–61.

Platt, Jennifer. *A History of Sociological Research Methods in America, 1920–1960*. Cambridge: Cambridge University Press, 1996.

Polenberg, Richard. *War and Society: The United States 1941–1945*. New York: Lippincott, 1972.

Pooley, Jefferson, and Mark Solovey. "Marginal to the Revolution: The Curious Relationship between Economics and the Behavioral Sciences Movement in Mid-Twentieth-Century America." In *The Unsocial Social Science? Economics and Neighboring Disciplines since 1945*, edited by Roger E. Backhouse and Philippe Fontaine, 199–233. Durham: Duke University Press, 2010.

Posner, Richard A. "Gary Becker's Contributions to Law and Economics." *Journal of Legal Studies* 22, no. 2 (1993): 211–15.

Price, Richard, and Edwin Mills. "Race and Residence in Earnings Determination." *Journal of Urban Economics* 17, no. 1 (1985): 1–18.

Pritchett, Wendell E. *Robert Clifton Weaver and the American City: The Life and Times of an Urban Reformer*. Chicago: University of Chicago Press, 2008.

Reardon, Sean F. "The Widening Academic Achievement Gap between the Rich and the Poor: New Evidence and Possible Explanations." In *Whither Opportunity: Rising Inequality, Schools, and Children's Life Chances*, edited by Greg Duncan and Richard Murnane, 91–116. New York: Russell Sage Foundation, 2011.

Reed, Adolph L., Jr. *Stirrings in the Jug: Black Politics in the Post-Segregation Era*. Minneapolis: University of Minnesota Press, 1999.

Reid, Ira de A. "What Segregated Areas Mean." In *Discrimination and the National Welfare: A Series of Addresses and Discussions*, edited by Robert MacIver, 7–14. New York: Harper & Bros., 1949.

Reitzes, Dietrich C. "Collective Factors in Race Relations." PhD diss., University of Chicago, 1950.

Rodgers, Daniel T. *Age of Fracture*. Cambridge: Belknap Press of Harvard University Press, 2011.

Rose, Arnold M. *Studies in the Reduction of Prejudice: A Memorandum Summarizing Research on Modification of Attitudes*. Chicago: American Council on Race Relations, 1947.

Ross, Dorothy. *The Origins of American Social Science*. Cambridge: Cambridge University Press, 1991.

Ryan, William. *Blaming the Victim*. New York: Random House, 1971.

Savage, Barbara D. *Broadcasting Freedom: Radio, War, and the Politics of Race, 1939–1948*. Chapel Hill: University of North Carolina Press, 1999.

Schrecker, Ellen W. *No Ivory Tower: McCarthyism and the Universities*. New York: Oxford University Press, 1986.

Scott, Daryl Michael. *Contempt and Pity: Social Policy and the Image of the Damaged Black Psyche, 1880–1996*. Chapel Hill: University of North Carolina Press, 1997.

Scott, Daryl Michael. "Postwar Pluralism, *Brown v. Board of Education*, and the Origins of Multicultural Education." *Journal of American History* 91, no. 1 (2004): 69–82.

Selig, Diana. *Americans All: The Cultural Gifts Movement*. Cambridge: Harvard University Press, 2008.

Sheatsley, Paul B. "White Attitudes Toward the Negro." In *The Negro American*, edited by Talcott Parsons and Kenneth B. Clark, 303–24. Boston: Beacon Press, 1966.

Simpson, George E., and J. Milton Yinger. *Racial and Cultural Minorities: An Analysis of Prejudice and Discrimination*. New York: Plenum Press, 1985. First published 1959 by Harper & Bros. (New York).

Singh, Nikhil Pal. *Black Is a Country: Race and the Unfinished Struggle for Democracy*. Cambridge: Harvard University Press, 2004.

Skrentny, John D. *The Ironies of Affirmative Action: Politics, Culture, and Justice in America*. Chicago: University of Chicago Press, 1996.

Skrentny, John D. "Introduction." In *Color Lines: Affirmative Action, Immigration, and Civil Rights Options for America*, edited by John D., Skrentny, 1–28. Chicago: University of Chicago Press, 2001.

Solovey, Mark. "Riding Natural Scientists' Coattails onto the Endless Frontier: The SSRC and the Quest for Scientific Legitimacy." *Journal of the History of the Behavioral Sciences* 40, no. 4 (2004): 393–422.

Solovey, Mark. *Shaky Foundations: The Politics-Patronage-Social Science Nexus in Cold War America*. New Brunswick: Rutgers University Press, 2013.

Southern, David. *Gunnar Myrdal and Black-White Relations: The Use and Abuse of An American Dilemma, 1944–1969*. Baton Rouge: Louisiana State University Press, 1987.

Staats, Cheryl, Kelly Capatosto, Robin A. Wright, and Victoria W. Jackson. *State of the Science: Implicit Bias Review*. Columbus: Kirwan Institute for the Study of Race and Society, 2016. http://kirwaninstitute.osu.edu/my-product/2016-state-of-the-science-implicit-bias-review

Stanfield, John H. *Philanthropy and Jim Crow in American Social Science*. Westport: Greenwood Press, 1985.

Steinberg, Stephen. *Race Relations: A Critique*. Stanford: Stanford University Press, 2007.

Stouffer, Samuel, et al. *The American Soldier*. 2 vols. Princeton: Princeton University Press, 1949.

Sugrue, Thomas J. *Origins of the Urban Crisis: Race and Inequality in Postwar Detroit*. Princeton: Princeton University Press, 1996.

Sugrue, Thomas J. *Sweet Land of Liberty: The Forgotten Struggle for Civil Rights in the North*. New York: Random House, 2008.

Thompson, Edgar T., ed. "Introduction." In *Race Relations and the Race Problem: A Definition and an Analysis*, 3–45. Durham: Duke University Press, 1939.

Tilly, Charles. *Durable Inequality*. Berkeley: University of California Press, 1998.

Tilly, Charles. *Identities, Boundaries, and Social Ties*. Boulder: Paradigm Publishers, 2005.

Carmichael, Stokely, and Charles V. Hamilton. *Black Power: The Politics of Liberation in America*. New York: Vintage Books, 1967.

US Bureau of the Census. "Lifetime Occupational Mobility of Adult Males, March, 1962." Current Population Reports, ser. P-23, no. 11 (May 1964).

US National Advisory Commission on Civil Disorders. *Report of the National Advisory Commission on Civil Disorders*. New York: Bantam Books, 1968.

Van DeBurg, William. *A New Day in Babylon: The Black Power Movement and American Culture, 1965–1975*. Chicago: University of Chicago Press, 1992.

Von Eschen, Penny. *Race Against Empire: Black Americans and Anticolonialism, 1937–1957*. Ithaca: Cornell University Press, 1997.

Weaver, Robert. "A Needed Program of Research in Race Relations and Associated Problems." *Journal of Negro Education* 16, no. 2 (1947): 130–35.

Weaver, Robert. *The Negro Ghetto*. New York: Harcourt, Brace, and Co., 1948.

Weaver, Robert. "Effect on Housing." In *Discrimination and the National Welfare: A Series of Addresses and Discussions*, ed. Robert MacIver, 25–35. New York: Harper & Bros., 1949.

Weaver, Robert. *Negro Labor: A National Problem*. New York: Harcourt, Brace, 1946.

Wienk, Ronald E., Clifford E. Reid, John C. Simonson, and Frederick J. Eggers. *Measuring Racial Discrimination in American Housing Markets: The Housing Market Practices Survey*. Washington, DC: Department of Housing and Urban Development, Division of Evaluation, 1979.

Williams, Robin M., Jr. "Review and Assessment of Research on Race and Culture Conflict," Paper V, Conference on Research in Human Relations, February 1953, box 11, folder 99, box 11, series 910, RG 3.1, Rockefeller Foundation Archives, 3.

Williams, Robin M., Jr. *Strangers Next Door: Ethnic Relations in American Communities*. Englewood Cliffs: Prentice-Hall, 1964.

Williams, Robin M., Jr. *The Reduction of Intergroup Tensions: A Survey of Research on Problems of Ethnic, Racial, and Religious Group Relations*. New York: Social Science Research Council, 1947.

Wilson, William Julius. *The Declining Significance of Race: Blacks and Changing American Institutions*. Chicago: University of Chicago Press, 1978.

Wilson, William Julius. *The Truly Disadvantaged: The Inner City, the Underclass, and Public Policy*. Chicago: University of Chicago Press, 1987.

Winant, Howard. "The Dark Side of the Force: One Hundred Years of the Sociology of Race." In *Sociology in America: A History*, edited by Craig Calhoun, 535–71. Chicago: University of Chicago Press, 2007.

Yu, Henry. *Thinking Orientals: Migration, Contact, and Exoticism in Modern America*. Oxford: Oxford University Press, 2001.

Zuberi, Tukufu. *Thicker Than Blood: How Racial Statistics Lie*. Minneapolis: University of Minnesota Press, 2001.

Zuberi, Tukufu. "Deracializing Social Statistics: Problems in the Quantification of Race." In *White Logic, White Methods: Racism and Methodology*, edited by Tukufu Zuberi and Eduardo Bonilla-Silva, 127–36. Lanham: Rowman & Littlefield, 2008.

6

The Black Ghetto

George C. Galster

This chapter provides a brief history of how social scientists over the last half of the twentieth century have conceptualized and diagnosed the phenomenon whereby disproportionate concentrations of lower-income black households reside in particular urban neighborhoods that are deprived in multiple domains.[1] For expositional simplicity, I will call this phenomenon "the ghetto," fully recognizing that this terminology has evolved in its meaning and usage, and has been the subject of much analytical and political contention.[2] Indeed, the central theme of this chapter is that what scholars and policymakers thought the ghetto was, why it existed, and what (if anything) should be done about it has shifted dramatically during the period under investigation. Indeed, though there was a growing recognition that the ghetto represented a serious social problem immediately after World War II, a clear public consensus did not emerge until the late 1960s due to a coincidence of progressive politics, multiple social movements, sensational television coverage, and scholarly attention.

In overview, diagnoses of the ghetto can be categorized by their relative emphasis on class, race, and/or space, and whether the framing is individual, social, or systemic.[3] In other words, diagnoses differ in how they answer two questions: Is the ghetto problem primarily one of

---

[1] Though focusing on blacks, I acknowledge that other low-income minorities (especially Latinos) are sometimes concentrated in disadvantaged urban neighborhoods, though in lower numbers. Jargowsky, *Poverty and Place*. Nevertheless, over the last century, it is the black demographic aspect of this phenomenon that has been the consistent, predominant focus of scholarship and public discourse.

[2] The term "ghetto" has evolved substantially in its meaning since its introduction over 500 years ago (see Haynes and Hutchinson, "The *Ghetto*" and Duneier, *Ghetto*) and some have argued that it should no longer be used. See Small, "Four Reasons to Abandon."

[3] Here, I adopt the same terminology as Gordon, *From Power to Prejudice*, 9–10.

poverty, discrimination, or segregation? Does the root cause rest with shortcomings of the individual, the societal forces and structures in which the individual is embedded, or the nature of oppression inherent in the capitalist system?[4]

In this chapter, I will advance three arguments related to the evolution of diagnosing the ghetto. First, since the 1970s, the dominant explanation increasingly has emphasized class and de-emphasized race, though the significance of the spatial dimension remains highly contested to this day. Second, after World War II, the individualistic framing has become increasingly dominant in class, race, and space dimensions, while the systematic view has correspondingly withered since the 1970s and the social view remains contested. Third, sociologists have been the primary advocates for an analysis employing both spatial and social perspectives, whereas neoclassical economists and political scientists played key roles in promoting an individualistic, class-oriented framing.

I will also consider how federal policy prescriptions have been influenced by, and influenced in some cases, these evolving scholarly perspectives on the ghetto. I will argue that federal policy explicitly directed at ameliorating problems associated with the ghetto through either desegregation or development programs has proven distinctly cyclical since its inception in the 1960s. Initiatives have tended to be more comprehensive and better funded during Democratic administrations, attempting to both economically develop the ghetto and to reduce barriers to exit for those who wished to do so. By contrast, Republican administrations have tended to respond punitively, if at all, to issues associated with the ghetto and eschew desegregation initiatives; any efforts to develop the ghetto were market-oriented and underfunded. It is sometimes possible to draw compelling links between contemporary scholarship and resultant federal policies related to the ghetto. However, the dominant role of ideology in conferring power on research – in particular, whether the research was consistent with political presuppositions – is most clear. Democratic administrations have found the social/spatial diagnoses more resonant with their priors, whereas Republican ones have found the individualistic/ class diagnoses so.

---

[4] The analysis of the nature, causes, and consequences of poverty and racial discrimination is much broader, of course. Since these are the subjects of chapters by Alice O'Connor (Chapter 4: Poverty) and Leah N. Gordon (Chapter 5: Discrimination), however, I focus here only on aspects that have an explicitly urban or spatial component relevant to framing the discourse on the ghetto.

6.1 The Emerging Ghetto

Europe provided the primary source of labor during the long period of American industrialization prior to World War I.[5] This changed dramatically with the disruptions induced first by the war and then by postwar immigration restrictions. Instead, Northern industry would be fueled by the first "great migration" of rural Southern blacks: 1.5 million by 1940.[6] As sociologists and economists have retrospectively documented, the ghetto was largely created during this interwar period by this massive interregional migration by blacks confronting an interlocking set of discriminatory barriers erected by private and public actors in Northern metropolitan areas.[7]

Most contemporary mainstream sociologists, however, did not see the emerging ghetto as a social problem, but as an unremarkable, generic manifestation of a general process of segregation characterizing all modern metropolises. This perspective can be traced to the dominance of Robert Park, head of the Department of Sociology at the University of Chicago. Park's "ecological" view of urbanization gave primacy to the intergroup dynamics of competition, invasion, succession, and consolidation, which "naturally" yielded clustering of different racial, ethnic, and socioeconomic status groups.[8] This view minimized the importance of race: Black segregation was fundamentally no different than the segregation of the myriad ethnic groups who had earlier immigrated to Northern cities.[9] Like previous immigrants, blacks would become less segregated over time as they became acculturated to the urban environment.[10] Spatial arrangements did not impose serious impediments for ghetto residents, in this view. Instead, any adverse conditions associated with ghettos (such as poverty or lawlessness) could be traced to personal or cultural shortcomings of the residents. Even the prominent black PhD sociologist E. Franklin Frazier took a corresponding position in *The Negro Family in Chicago* (1931). His work emphasized differentiation of status and behaviors *within* the black

---

[5] Sugrue, "Structures of Urban Poverty," 85–117.

[6] Jones, "Southern Diaspora," 46.

[7] Massey and Denton, *American Apartheid* and Cutler, Glaeser, and Vigdor, "Rise and Decline of the American Ghetto."

[8] Park and Burgess, *The City*.

[9] Wirth was the first to introduce the term "ghetto" into the sociological literature in his 1928 book by the same name, but he focused upon Jewish enclaves while asserting that his analysis was applicable to "black belts" and other areas of ethnic concentration. Wirth, *The Ghetto*.

[10] Burgess, "Residential Segregation in American Cities."

community, and his diagnosis of social problems there hinged on the preexisting economic and cultural characteristics of recent black migrants from the rural South.

Unsurprisingly, this period witnessed no efforts by the federal government to intervene in ghettos with an aim to improve their quality of life or the opportunities of their residents.[11] Though the political barriers to do so were undoubtedly impenetrable at all levels of government during this era, mainstream sociology's diagnosis of the ghetto implicitly supported this conservative, laissez-faire position. Why intervene in a "natural" residential sorting process that was essentially benign and would not permanently disfavor blacks?

To be sure, some dissenting scholarship emerged during the interwar period arguing that the ghetto was special in its origins and its spatial reification: Blacks faced unusual constraints in both attempting to settle in nonblack areas of the city and exerting power over their own neighborhoods, compared with other groups.[12] Indeed, in a foreshadowing of what would periodically occur over the next century, major ghetto civil disturbances in Chicago in 1919 and Harlem in 1935 spawned diagnostic studies that identified police repression and widespread discriminatory practices in housing and labor markets as prime means of restricting Northern blacks' socioeconomic opportunities.[13] Moreover, Clifford Shaw, a prominent Chicago School criminologist, argued that particular neighborhoods encouraged truant, delinquent, or criminal acts.[14] This social framing – that social-interactive characteristics of urban spaces could have powerful, independent effects on individual behavior and social outcomes – set the stage for Kenneth Clark's research after World War II and a resurgent "neighborhood effects" literature spawned by William Julius Wilson in the 1980s.

---

[11] On the contrary, beginning in the late 1930s, the federal government enacted many segregationist policies, especially as they related to public housing and federally backed home mortgages. Jackson, *Crabgrass Frontier* and Massey and Denton, *American Apartheid*. State governments in the South had their own set of comprehensive segregationist laws, of course. Local governments across the North also enacted a variety of formal and informal policies aimed at holding the color line. Freund, *Colored Property*.

[12] Of course, this point had been made decades earlier by Du Bois' formulation of the "color line" in *The Philadelphia Negro*.

[13] Johnson, *Negro in Chicago* and Greenstein, *Or Does It Explode?*

[14] Shaw, *Delinquency Areas*. Shaw's 1929 work reprises commentary from the nineteenth century that "slums" bred a variety of antisocial behaviors that spilled over to the wider society. Katz, "Urban 'Underclass' as Metaphor," 8–9.

6.2 Reformulating the Ghetto

With the end of the Great Depression and the concomitant industrial expansion triggered by the onset of World War II, the second "great migration" began; it would eventually add five million blacks to Northern cities from 1940 to 1970.[15] The influx of war workers of all races into the major industrial cities of the North generated intense competition for scarce private and public space. Increasingly, this competition turned violent, most notably in the murderous Detroit race riot of 1943. The crushing housing shortages of the war years badly degraded the physical, psychological, and sanitary conditions of the ghetto, as blacks were crammed into squalid, overcrowded habitations. These new realities called for a reformulation of the ghetto concept.

In the mid-1940s, hegemony of Chicago School sociologists' formulation of the ghetto fractured. A new generation of black sociologists, institutional economists, and social psychologists reformulated the term "ghetto" in ways that emphasized its distinctive causes, its spatiality, and its role in perpetuating racial inequality (see Chapter 5: Discrimination). Most notably, sociologists St. Clair Drake and Horace Cayton argued in *Black Metropolis* (1945) that the Jewish ghetto recently imposed by the Nazis across Europe had analogous features with enforced racial segregation in Northern US cities. Racially restrictive covenants attached to property deeds, steering and exclusion by real estate agents, and redlining by mortgage lenders took the place of barbed wire and armed guards, but the end results were as damaging, they claimed. Despite the constraints, the black ghetto developed a flourishing culture and a vibrant middle-class enclave, which Drake and Cayton called "Bronzeville." Whether the simile about Jewish and black ghettoes was perfect or not was beyond the point. In their view, the ghetto was not a generic, benign, "natural" phenomenon as the Chicago School asserted. Rather, it was distinctive: an intended consequence of concerted individual, institutional, and governmental actions aimed to subjugate. Once established, it manifested a set of (mostly) inferior living conditions and institutional structures in the ghetto that were self-perpetuating because they adversely affected the life-chances of residents.

Appearing almost simultaneously was another monumental treatise that echoed many of the themes of Drake and Cayton: Gunnar Myrdal's *An American Dilemma* (1944). This was the first major work on racial inequality written by an economist (in this case, one from Sweden taking an institutionalist

---

[15] Jones, "Southern Diaspora," 46.

perspective), though, in fairness, it was a broadly interdisciplinary, collective effort involving many famous sociologists of the day.[16] In a foreshadowing of events a half-century later, Myrdal's research was funded by one of the largest grants ever provided by a charitable foundation, the Carnegie Corporation, and became the dominant scholarly work on the topic for over two decades. Myrdal's work focused on race relations in the United States in general and the South in particular, where the vast majority of blacks lived. Nevertheless, when he did diagnose the Northern urban ghetto, Myrdal broke definitively with the Chicago School, emphasizing the primary roles played by whites' actions and beliefs in enforcing segregation, not blacks' inherent inferiority. Though Myrdal admitted there were problematic aspects of ghetto life, these could be traced to white prejudice and the discriminatory actions that it motivated. Myrdal's formulation of the ghetto paid heed to the race, class, and space dimensions alike; his diagnostic framing was predominantly individualistic, though cognizant of institutionalized manifestations of individual whites' prejudice (see Chapter 5: Discrimination).[17]

Myrdal provided two seminal conceptualizations that would be resurrected and modified in the 1960s and again in the 1990s. The first he called the "theory of the vicious circle." Whites' racial prejudices led them to commit individual discriminatory acts and encourage their companies, institutions, and governments to do the same. This comprehensive web of barriers – segregation chief among them – frustrated and impoverished blacks, thereby perpetuating their inferior socioeconomic status and physical living conditions. These numerous inferiorities, in turn, reinforced the veracity of whites' prejudices, thus completing the mutually reinforcing dynamic. Myrdal also advanced the closely related "principle of cumulation": The panoply of domains in which the conditions of ghettos could be described – employment, family stability, crime, health, education – were closely interrelated.[18]

The third towering work of scholarship during this period was institutional economist Robert Weaver's *The Negro Ghetto* (1948). It focused on the plight of Northern ghetto residents as it related to overcrowded and unsanitary housing conditions spawned by the rapid growth of the

---

[16] In particular, sociologists like Horace Cayton and St. Clair Drake, and social psychologists like Kenneth Clark, contributed background research papers upon which Myrdal drew. Myrdal hired thirty-seven scholars for his project; remarkably, twelve were black. Duneier, *Ghetto*.

[17] Gordon, *From Power to Prejudice*.

[18] Though Drake and Cayton did not employ Myrdal's terminology, they wrote about analogous concepts and relationships.

ghetto during World War II. Besides tackling the usual topics of restrictive covenants and steering as ghetto-builders, it took an unsparing view of the segregationist role played by the early Federal Housing Administration and public housing programs. As such, it began to sketch in the housing market mechanisms that had been overlooked by the Chicago School when analyzing residential sorting, and by Myrdal in his focus on the rural South.

The fourth intellectual pillar of this era is the work of social psychologists Kenneth and Mamie Clark.[19] They conducted a series of innovative, well-publicized human experiments that they claimed revealed the psychological damage that segregation wrought on the psyches of black children in the form of internalized inferiority. Publications describing their early findings did not focus on ghettoization or public policy specifically; these aspects of their work would come to the fore during the 1960s, as I will show below.

These sets of scholars shared a common value, quite different from their predecessors, that social science should not only understand the world, but also assist in changing it for the better. Explicit in their work was the normative position that the ghetto represented a social problem demanding a collective response because it harmed the black community. Despite the unambiguously progressive implications of this scholarship, there was precious little in the way of similarly progressive federal policy that followed during the 1940s.[20] Two notable exceptions (both in 1948) were the Supreme Court case *Shelley* v. *Kraemer* (1948), which forbade local governments from enforcing racially restrictive real estate covenants, and President Harry Truman's Executive Order 9981, which abolished racial discrimination and segregation in the military.

The immediate postwar period witnessed the near-merger between what the interwar social problems literature often termed the "urban problem" and the "race problem." A spate of highly publicized race riots, most notably in Detroit in 1943, and the aforementioned scholarly works, had captured the public's attention.[21] The use of the term "ghetto" spiked in scholarly and popular books published after 1945, though faded quickly in subsequent years.[22] One can only speculate about why the nascent notion of ghetto as social problem and the interventionist rhetoric of social science at the time had such

---

[19] See especially Clark and Clark, "Development of Consciousness of Self"; Clark and Clark, "Racial Identification and Preference"; and Clark and Clark, "Negro Child." This and subsequent work is presented in Clark, *Prejudice and Your Child*.

[20] To be fair, the majority decision in the *Brown* v. *Topeka Board of Education* case of 1954 ended by quoting from *An America Dilemma* (Myrdal), though I consider this in the next section.

[21] Galster, *Driving Detroit*.

[22] Duneier, *Ghetto*.

little impact on public opinion or policy. The general (white) public appeared unconvinced that the ghetto constituted a social problem; they could either preserve the racial status quo in the city or render the issue mute by moving to the suburbs. Indeed, reactionary politicians in the North often fanned whites' fears of racial desegregation as a means of thwarting progressive proposals.[23] Perhaps exhaustion with New Deal, class-based domestic policies gave way to a new focus on fighting international communism.

6.3 The Disappearing Ghetto

During the first two decades following World War II, metropolitan America and its ghettos were rapidly transforming. The black migration from the South, though unstinting, morphed from an unskilled, rural exodus into a more educated, urban one.[24] Urban renewal policies bulldozed vast swaths of old ghettos and displaced their residents into newly forming ones. Segregation was the rule in the burgeoning public housing program.[25] The rapidly growing income of whites, elimination and deconcentration of manufacturing jobs, and federal homeownership and highway transportation policies spawned rapid suburbanization of whites.[26] Suburban municipalities strived to hold the color line through both legal exclusionary zoning regulations and a variety of illegal ones.[27] In concert, these forces led to more racial tipping of neighborhood housing markets, concomitant expansion of the ghettos' boundaries and class differentiation within them, and a steady rise in residential segregation.

Yet, as rapidly as the ghetto was evolving, alongside the term's rise to prominence in the immediate postwar period, the ghetto virtually disappeared as a topic of large-scale social scientific investigation during the 1950s.[28] The few sociological books on the subject published between 1950 and 1965 were essentially backward-looking, comparative treatises on residential segregation. Though continuing Chicago School framing, they

---

[23] Sugrue, *Origins of the Urban Crisis* and Galster, *Driving Detroit.*
[24] Lemann, *Promised Land.*
[25] Hirsch, *Making the Second Ghetto.*
[26] Jackson, *Crabgrass Frontier* and Sugrue, "Structures of Urban Poverty."
[27] Freund, *Colored Property.*
[28] In commenting upon the dearth of research during the period, sociologist Mitchell Duneier writes, "By 1965 ... it had been two decades since any important, book-length work of social science on the U.S. ghetto had appeared." Duneier, *Ghetto,* 113. Gary Becker published his path-breaking neoclassical economics treatise *The Economics of Discrimination* in 1957, but it did not consider racial segregation or ghettoization.

did introduce to the field quantitative measures of segregation subjected to multiple regression statistical analysis.[29]

It was through interdisciplinary efforts during the 1950s that some advances were made in understanding how the housing market created and responded to segregation, building on the work of Robert Weaver. The philanthropically funded Commission on Race and Housing sponsored a large, multidisciplinary investigation of the housing conditions facing minorities in the United States, though it did not focus solely on blacks or on ghettos. The multiyear research program, directed by social work professor Davis McEntire, reported its findings as *Residence and Race*, published in 1960.[30] This initiative also spun off two other relevant books, appearing the same year. Economist Luigi Laurenti's *Property Values and Race* and urban planners Chester Rapkin and William Grigsby's *The Demand for Housing in Racially Mixed Areas* explored how neighborhood housing markets responded to racial transition and whether prices of equivalent dwellings were higher or lower in segregated white and black neighborhoods.[31]

What proved to be the most politically influential scholarly works during the 1950s were, as it turns out, published the prior decade. The majority opinion in *Brown v. Topeka Board of Education*, the landmark 1954 Supreme Court case outlawing school segregation, heavily cited work by both the economist Myrdal and the social psychologists Clark and Clark. This is one of the clearest illustrations of social science affecting a public body's decision, with far-reaching policy impacts. The federal civil rights initiatives during the decade aimed at enforcing the *Brown* imperative in the South. Civil rights organizations' efforts took on the same geographic focus. Restoring individual rights by dismantling Southern de jure segregation was an indisputable moral imperative. Northern urban ghettoization was clearly a lower priority for scholars, the public, and policymakers alike during the 1950s and early 1960s.

6.4 The Front-Page Ghetto and a Nascent Federal Response

Any inattention to the ghetto or its ambiguous status as a social problem evaporated during the mid-1960s. A remarkable confluence of mass social movements (aimed particularly at rectifying racist housing, employment,

---

[29] Duncan and Duncan, *Negro Population of Chicago* and Taeuber and Taeuber, *Negroes in Cities.*

[30] McEntire, *Residence and Race.*

[31] Laurenti, *Property Values and Race* and Rapkin and Grigsby, *Demand for Housing in Racially Mixed Areas.* These analyses built on the seminal work in racial tipping by urban planner Wolf, "Invasion-Succession Sequence as a Self-Fulfilling Prophecy."

and police practices) and widespread civil disturbances in Northern cities were brought home vividly by television, radio, magazines, and newspapers. A corresponding upsurge in scholarship and blue-ribbon commissions aimed at deciphering the "urban crisis" conjoined to bring the ghetto to the forefront of American consciousness.[32] The general public came to view the ghetto as a social problem that posed a serious threat to their well-being, spawning a number of federal government initiatives.

From the social science perspective, the mid-1960s marked a mushrooming of research springing from multiple disciplines, each scrambling for supremacy in the halls of academe and the corridors of power. Some research resurrected decades-old ideas and others advanced entirely new ones about the nature and causes of the ghetto. Scholarly debates raged about whether the phenomenon should be seen primarily in race, class, or spatial terms, and whether the framing should be individualistic, social, or systemic. This eclectic body of work typically offered clear, if dramatically different, policy prescriptions.

Much of this new research was individualistic in its framing, though it differed dramatically in methods employed and the degree to which race, class, or space were emphasized in the analysis. This is illustrated by four famous diagnoses of the ghetto emerging from new disciplinary sources: neoclassical economics, anthropology, public policy, and political science.[33] John Kain was one of the first neoclassical economists to delve into urban racial issues, stimulating what would become a major new subfield.[34] His path-breaking thesis, backed up by cutting-edge, regression-based statistical analysis, emphasized race and space: A substantial part of black unemployment in the ghetto could be traced to a "spatial mismatch" between where discriminatory barriers forced ghetto residents to live and burgeoning employment prospects in the suburbs.[35] The growing residence–

---

[32] Katz, *Undeserving Poor*, chap. 3.

[33] The neoclassical paradigm is based on the notion of the autonomous, rational, well-informed individual who attempts to maximize utility (or, in the case of entrepreneurs, profits), subject to various financial and other constraints. Myrdal was a Swedish institutional economist not wed to the neoclassical paradigm that was ascending during the post–World War II period to its current dominance in America; his work was largely a synthesis and extension of sociological research.

[34] The seminal 1964 book by William Alonso, *Location and Land Use*, investigated spatial patterns of urban residence and modeled the origins of segregation by income groups, but did not consider the issue of race.

[35] Kain, "Housing Segregation, Negro Employment." Remarkably, debate over the theory and evidence related to this "spatial mismatch hypothesis" has continued for half a century; see Lens, "Employment Accessibility."

workplace gap meant that blacks would be less likely to find out about employment opportunities and, even if they were to, would be less able to commute to them because of the design of metropolitan transit systems.

A contrasting methodological approach involving personal observation and interviews conducted in poor neighborhoods was used by anthropologist Oscar Lewis. His work (most famously, *La Vida*, 1966) focused on what he termed "the culture of poverty": a set of adaptations to a deprived, hopeless existence. Key features of this culture, on Lewis' account, were inability to defer gratification, casual sexual relationships and family structures, and isolation from mainstream institutions and values. In Lewis' view, the culture of poverty was passed between generations and, once acquired, represented an indelible trait of the individual. The culture of poverty was not, however, a unique feature of the ghetto (or a consequence of racial segregation), but rather for Lewis a condition of all poverty-stricken communities (see Chapter 4: Poverty).

A third methodological approach to diagnosing the ghetto involved nontechnical syntheses of prior scholars' claims, coupled with descriptive summaries of secondary data. Public policy analyst Daniel Patrick Moynihan's *The Negro Family* (1965) drew on the work of Frazier, Clark, and the Chicago School, but emphasized racial differences in family structure.[36] He famously argued that the legacy of slavery, Reconstruction, and the Great Migration had taken a severe toll on the black family by reducing black males' efficacy and employment prospects – and thereby their status claims as breadwinning potential heads of households. The female-headed, welfare-dependent families that resulted were, in his view, ill-suited to raise productive, socially adjusted children (males in particular), especially in the modern urban milieu. Political scientist Edward Banfield's *The Unheavenly City* (1968) synthesized ideas from Moynihan, Lewis, and others in his diagnosis.[37] Banfield saw the core issue as the "present orientation" of "lower-class" individuals (who, he asserted, comprised the bulk of the ghetto population): an inability to conceive of and plan for the future. This psychological defect, in his view, was at the root of all the socially problematic behaviors associated with the ghetto, and was inculcated

---

[36] Moynihan's educational background is difficult to categorize, with his undergraduate degrees in naval science and history, a stint at the London School of Economics, and a PhD in international relations. Today he would probably be listed as an interdisciplinary public policy analyst. In this role, he produced *The Negro Family* as an internal document for the Johnson administration, but it was leaked to the press and eventually published by the Department of Labor.

[37] Banfield, *Unheavenly City*.

in children by their parents. The only effective potential policy – raising children from lower-class families in state-run institutions – violated human rights; so, best to not waste resources on other antipoverty efforts. It is difficult to overstate the scholarly and political controversies and, ultimately, the policy impact, that the works of Moynihan, Lewis, and Banfield engendered.[38] I leave the details of these points to the chapter by Alice O'Connor (see Chapter 4: Poverty). Suffice it to summarize here that they all emphasized an individualistic perspective and class-based framing of the ghetto. Individuals and their families were ultimately responsible for their disadvantaged plight; contemporary social forces and institutional structures generating racial discrimination and segregation played only a minor role. Little wonder that this perspective generated widespread condemnations from progressives as racist, sexist, and "blaming the victim." It is similarly easy to understand why the emphasis on dysfunctional families and subcultures drew conservative admirers.

These aforementioned analyses all neglected Myrdal's admonition to formulate racial issues in America in terms of cumulative causation in multiple domains; instead, they saw unidirectional causation, with typically a single (though different) causal agent. The exception to this generalization was the continuing work of Kenneth Clark, based on his ethnography of living and running a social service agency in Harlem. In *Youth in the Ghetto* (1964) and *The Dark Ghetto* (1965), Clark made it clear that the issues confronting blacks in the rural South and the urban North were different, though the wounds of segregation arose whether it was de jure or de facto.[39] He introduced the idea of an interlocking "tangle of pathologies" arising out of the sensed powerlessness of ghetto residents, primarily caused by its economic isolation and "colonization" by white-controlled institutions. In his clearly systemic analysis of the gamut of race, class, and space domains, Clark argued that the ghetto would only improve if blacks could control the major institutional influences upon it.

Anthropologists conducting fieldwork in the ghetto also offered pointed rejoinders to Moynihan, Lewis, and Banfield with social diagnoses involving patterns of mutual causation, though they may not have identified them as such. Elliot Liebow, in his 1967 *Tally's Corner*, argued that idleness in the ghetto was more a product of disability than present orientation, and that intergenerational patterns were produced by similar, longstanding structural constraints on individual opportunity, not by a culture of

---

[38] Katz, *Undeserving Poor*, chap. 3.
[39] Clark, *Youth in the Ghetto* and Clark, *The Dark Ghetto*.

poverty.[40] Ulf Hannerz, in *Soulside* (1969), and Lee Rainwater, in *Behind Ghetto Walls* (1970), while forthrightly describing many shocking behaviors of "lower class Negroes," emphasized that they were adaptations to a set of equally shocking constraints in the larger social structures.[41] In her 1974 *All Our Kin*, Carol Stack demonstrated the strength, organizational resilience, and resourcefulness of the matriarchal family structure and its extended networks.[42] Though critical of welfare rules that discouraged marriage and wealth accumulation, she nevertheless saw welfare as a crucial financial lifeline for many black families.

The final noteworthy piece of 1960s social science was not primary research, but rather an evidence-based report mandated by the Johnson administration: *The Report of the National Advisory Commission on Civil Disorders*.[43] The summers from 1964 to 1967 were convulsed by mass civil disturbances in ghettos in dozens of American cities. President Lyndon Johnson commissioned a blue-ribbon panel of political, civic, and business leaders to weigh in on why the ghettos were burning and what should be done. What diagnosis of the ghetto – and its associated policy prescription – would they choose from the potpourri of scholarship available to them? Given its progressive predilections, it is not surprising that the Kerner Commission (as it was known) advanced the full panoply of scholarly diagnoses emphasizing race and space (i.e., an amalgam of the Myrdal, Clark, and Kain arguments) that would logically lead to a comprehensive, activist federal desegregation effort.[44] The report offered a powerful critique of the racist nature of previous government housing, education, policing, and social service policies. Its comprehensive set of recommendations aimed at desegregating the ghetto, primarily through strengthened civil

[40] Liebow, *Tally's Corner*.
[41] Ulf Hannerz, *Soulside* and Rainwater, *Behind Ghetto Walls*.
[42] Stack, *All Our Kin*.
[43] National Advisory Commission on Civil Disorders, *Report of the National Advisory Commission on Civil Disorders*.
[44] As in all such cases, the commission relied heavily on their staff's synthesis of existing research and the editorial choices of its executive director, David Ginsburg. In this case, the staff was led by Anthony Downs, a neoclassical urban economist and public choice theorist with a background in real estate consulting. Ginsburg, the executive director, was a lawyer and long-time policy advisor with roots in New Deal liberalism. Ginsburg wrote many of the report's memorable phrases: "[The United States was] moving toward two societies – one black, one white, separate and unequal," and "white society is deeply implicated in the ghetto...White institutions created it, white institutions maintain it and white society condones it." Ironically, President Johnson distanced himself from the report, reputedly upset that it gave insufficient praise to his civil rights legislative achievements.

rights initiatives to thwart discrimination in housing, mortgage, and labor markets, and the replacement of concentrated, high-rise public housing projects with small-scale, scattered-site developments across the suburbs.[45] Elements of this prescription would be pursued by every Democratic administration since.

The prerequisites for such a desegregation effort seemed in place by the middle of 1968.[46] The Civil Rights Act of 1964 and the Voting Rights Act of 1965 had been joined within two months of the Kerner Commission's report by the Fair Housing Act of 1968. Dorothy Gautreaux had filed her landmark civil rights suit against the recently created Department of Housing and Urban Development (HUD), led by none other than Robert Weaver, and the Chicago Housing Authority, challenging segregated public housing.[47] A desegregation policy agenda similar to that advanced in the Kerner Commission's report seemed a foregone conclusion for the next Democratic president to be elected in November 1968.

Another, lower-profile policy approach, community development, was also coalescing at the same time, out of two distinct Great Society legislative threads. The Economic Opportunity Act of 1964 aimed to improve the well-being of low-income (not necessarily ghetto) communities through federally funded Community Action Programs designed and implemented by Community Action Agencies that were substantially governed by low-income residents themselves. One feature of this program encouraged the formation of Community Development Corporations (CDCs), nonprofit organizations for ghetto development that could seek corporate, philanthropic, and governmental grants to support their activities.[48] The Model Cities program, begun in 1966, funneled federal aid to cities for rebuilding and rehabilitating blighted areas.[49] To reduce the negative consequences of the prior urban renewal program, Model Cities also mandated citizen participation. Though neither of these programs was exclusively aimed at ghettos, they proved de facto means for improving the quality of life and economic opportunities of ghetto residents,

---

[45] Gillon, *Separate and Unequal.*

[46] A contemporary synthesis of the liberal, integrationist consensus about diagnosis and prescription for ghetto problems is summarized in Grier and Grier, *Equality and Beyond.*

[47] Polikoff, *Waiting for Gautreaux.*

[48] The first CDC, Bedford-Stuyvesant Restoration Corporation, began in 1967 in New York City with the support of Democratic Senator Robert Kennedy, Republic Senator Jacob Javits, and Republican Mayor John Lindsay.

[49] Frieden and Kaplan, *Politics of Neglect.*

while leaving segregation intact.[50] In addition, they all gave low-income residents a nontrivial voice in the formulation of programs affecting their neighborhoods, though they undoubtedly did not go as far as Kenneth Clark would have wished in the direction of local control.[51] Interestingly, the community development effort was launched with little foundational evidence for its efficacy beyond Clark's exhortations.[52] Some of this support would be supplied after-the-fact in the 1970s, a clear instance of policy leading scholarship.[53]

Perhaps a more fundamental consequence of the antipoverty and urban development policies of Johnson's Great Society initiative was the creation of new social scientific infrastructure during the late 1960s. Federal seed money and, later, research contracts, were instrumental in establishing several nonpartisan, multidisciplinary "think tanks" focused on evaluating and devising social welfare programs, most notably the Urban Institute, the Institute for Research on Poverty, and the Manpower Development Research Corporation (later, MDRC). An independent effort spearheaded by urban land-grant universities created the Council of University Institutes for Urban Affairs (later renamed the Urban Affairs Association), a scholarly organization aiming to promote and legitimize interdisciplinary urban research. Though all these organizations remain important sources of scholarship to this day, none has been primarily focused on the ghetto phenomenon.

Thus, by the end of 1968, it was plain that an unusually robust (if often mutually opposing) body of social scientific research, emanating from a wide variety of disciplines and intellectual framings, was competing for political attention in a social problem realm that the public now deemed of utmost salience. This research offered a diverse menu of fundamentally conflicting diagnoses of the ghetto, as well as prescriptions for public policy. Three dominant siloes of strategy – dispersal, development, and disengagement – had emerged and would frame the terms of the debate for the next fifty years.[54] Which would prove temporarily dominant was determined primarily by the political ideology of those in power in Washington, not definitive new scholarship, since each political position could selectively cite research supporting their predetermined policy perspective.

---

[50] Fine, *Violence in the Model City.*
[51] Lemann, *Promised Land.*
[52] For deeper background discussion, see Katz, *Undeserving Poor.*
[53] See the review in Harrison, "Ghetto Economic Development."
[54] For excellent contemporary statements of these alternative positions, see Downs, "Alternative Futures for the American Ghetto"; Kain and Persky, "Alternatives to Gilded Ghetto"; and Edel, "Development versus Dispersal."

6.5 Disputation, Deracialization, and Benign Neglect

Of course, Democrat Hubert Humphrey lost the 1968 presidential election to Republican Richard Nixon. Though the bulk of the prior administration's Great Society initiatives continued, most of the new desegregation programs advocated in the Kerner Commission report were ignored. Moynihan, Lewis, and Banfield had argued for single-factor causes of the ghetto. Though each highlighted a different aspect, they agreed that the dysfunctional culture of the ghetto would not be altered appreciably through public intervention.[55] These views provided an intellectual foundation for Nixon's political predilection to ignore the ghetto, in what became known as a policy of "benign neglect."[56] Things changed little under the post-Watergate replacement president, Gerald Ford, and his centrist Democratic successor, Jimmy Carter.[57] As quickly as the ghetto had obtained front-page visibility from 1965 to 1968, it dissolved into the background noise of a nation struggling with the decade-long economic malaise triggered by the Arab oil embargo of 1973 while simultaneously riven by strident protests against the Vietnam war, environmental degradation, and sexism. The public salience of the ghetto as a social problem clearly waned.

It was, perhaps, inevitable following the iconoclastic 1960s that most academic disciplines were rent by epistemological and ideological divisions that became glaringly apparent during the 1970s.[58] While an individualistic framing of racial inequality and the ghetto had become increasingly dominant across the social sciences during the postwar period, a new set of scholars employing the systemic, Marxian paradigm rose to prominence.[59] To some extent, all took as their touchstone Kenneth Clark's increasingly radical views about how white-controlled governments, businesses, and institutions kept the ghetto in a subordinate, exploited, "colonial" position economically,

---

[55] O'Connor, *Poverty Knowledge*, chap. 3.
[56] The phrase was coined by Moynihan, then a White House advisor, in 1970. In some cases, Nixon's policies regarding race could be better described as reactionary than as benign. In 1970, Nixon fired his Secretary of HUD, George Romney, for aggressively pursuing legal action against Warren, Michigan, a suburb of Detroit, which had received federal grants while excluding black residents. Nixon called a moratorium on the construction of any further public housing in 1972. His "Southern strategy" was clearly designed to win white support for the Republican party by de-emphasizing previous desegregation policies and emphasizing "law and order" instead. See Chapter 7: Crime.
[57] President Carter's only notable urban initiative, Urban Development Action Grants, was neither large in scale nor targeted on the basis of race, and thus had no perceptible impact on the quality of life in ghettos.
[58] Gouldner, *Coming Crisis of Western Sociology*.
[59] Gordon, *From Power to Prejudice*.

socially, and politically. Prominent works of the early 1970s using the Marxian political economy perspective to understand the structures of oppression in capitalism included economists Michael Vietorisz and Bennet Harrison's *Economic Development of Harlem*, William Tabb's *Political Economy of the Black Ghetto*, and Daniel Fusfeld's *The Basic Economics of the Urban Racial Crisis*, sociologist Robert Blauner's *Racial Oppression in America*, and geographer David Harvey's *Social Justice and the City*.[60] This body of work not only challenged the dominant individualistic framing of mainstream social scientists but implied that their mathematically and statistically sophisticated, positivist orientation had reached the point of diminishing returns in understanding and influencing issues of social justice.[61]

The mainstream's common reaction to this leftist challenge was to either dismiss its scholarship as "subjective," "ideologically driven," and "methodologically naïve," or to ignore it entirely. Neoclassical economics continued its individualist framing, while pushing the boundaries of what was known about race, segregation, discrimination, and housing markets through the use of cutting-edge research methods.[62] John Kain and John Quigley's *Housing Markets and Racial Discrimination* (1975) showed with multiple regression modeling how discriminatory barriers forced blacks to pay higher prices for comparable dwellings and reduced their chances to become homeowners.[63] Thomas Schelling's *Micromotives and Macrobehavior* (1978) used game theory to explain why a great extent of residential segregation across neighborhoods could occur even if that was not the preferred outcome of either most whites or blacks.[64] Finally, a team of economists at HUD documented incontrovertibly the rampant incidence of housing discrimination in forty metropolitan areas using the new research method of "paired testing," in which carefully matched black and white investigator teammates separately responded to real estate advertisements and recorded how they were treated.[65]

---

[60] Vietorisz and Harrison, *Economic Development of Harlem*; Tabb, *Political Economy of the Black Ghetto*; Fusfeld, *Basic Economics of the Urban Racial Crisis*; Blauner, *Racial Oppression in America*; and Harvey, *Social Justice and the City*.
[61] Often explicitly, such as Harvey, *Social Justice and the City*.
[62] In fairness, some economists took a social perspective when examining institutionalized racism, such as Downs, *Opening Up the Suburbs*.
[63] Kain and Quigley, *Housing Markets and Racial Discrimination*.
[64] Schelling's *Micromotives and Macrobehavior* expanded upon and generalized seminal articles published earlier.
[65] Wienk et al., *Measuring Racial Discrimination in American Housing Markets*. This was the first installment of what would become a roughly once-every-decade replication. Turner et al., *Housing Discrimination against Racial and Ethnic Minorities*, is the latest.

At the same time, a transformative perspective on ghettoization arose out of mainstream sociology that elevated the factor of class. William Julius Wilson's *The Declining Significance of Race* argued that the success of the emerging black middle class – both in terms of achieved status and suburban residence – indicated that lack of education in the face of a deindustrializing economy, not labor market discrimination, was now the prime obstacle to black socioeconomic advancement.[66] Wilson argued, moreover, that the black community itself, less bound by common racial identity, was increasingly split along class lines. *The Declining Significance's* 1978 publication was an eerie, "back to the future" moment in sociology. Fifty years after its heyday, the Chicago School's view had returned: The ghetto could be defined without reference to structural racism and external forces of control focused most intensely on black people. Though generating great dissent, this view came to dominate much of the academic and policy discussion over the ensuing forty years.[67] The previous decades of perspective that emphasized the intersection of space and race had now shifted to one emphasizing class.

All this foment in academia must be juxtaposed against the retreat from ghetto desegregation or development on the federal level. The closest thing to a federal intervention in the ghetto was the Minority Enterprise Small Business Investment Company program, enacted in 1972, which aimed to facilitate equity-capital investing in small firms located in the ghetto. Its implicit (and hopeful) notion was that if government can't fix the situation, maybe aspiring black capitalists can. Meanwhile, the Nixon administration ushered in an era of increasingly punitive federal responses to urban unrest in the form of tougher anticrime, antidrug legislation that would have disproportionate impacts on the ghetto's underground economy (see Chapter 7: Crime).

Despite underwhelming efforts from the White House, the 1970s witnessed some legislative and judicial achievements in the realm of civil rights. Congressional passage of the Equal Credit Opportunity Act of 1974, the Home Mortgage Disclosure Act of 1975, and the Community Reinvestment Act of 1977 demonstrated that discrimination by mortgage lenders against minority individuals or their neighborhoods would no longer be tolerated. A federal court decided in favor of the plaintiff in the Gautreaux case in 1974, imposing a desegregation remedy that offered

[66] Wilson, *Declining Significance of Race.*
[67] This included Kenneth Clark and the Association of Black Sociologists. Duneier, *Ghetto.*

former black tenants of segregated public housing scattered-site public housing or rental vouchers for use in racially diverse neighborhoods in Chicago and its suburbs.[68] Numerous local school segregation suits were also resolved during this period, with intradistrict mandatory busing of students the typical remedy. On a more regressive note, a lower-court decision mandating that Detroit suburban school districts participate in busing, on the grounds that they were partially responsible for residential segregation through their exclusionary zoning, was struck down by the Supreme Court in *Milliken* v. *Bradley* (1974).

6.6 The Emergence of the Underclass and Concentrated Poverty in a "Post–Civil Rights" Era

By the end of the 1970s, the ghetto had become a very different place than the one that had been set on fire during the 1960s. On the plus side, there were more transfers flowing into the ghetto economy due to enhancements in Social Security, unemployment insurance, and Aid to Families with Dependent Children, plus the addition of new Great Society programs such as Medicare, Medicaid, and food stamps. More black mayors had been elected, conferring a modicum of political power on the ghetto. On the negative side, the ghetto remained a geographically isolated place; though black–white segregation had peaked in most metropolitan areas in 1970, it remained extreme during ensuing decades.[69] Many middle-class blacks had moved out (increasingly to suburbs) and conflicts over who would control the emerging crack cocaine trade made the ghetto an increasingly violent place.[70] The deindustrialization of central cities that began after World War II was now an inescapable reality after the lackluster economic performance of the 1970s.[71]

These changes in the ghetto context dovetailed nicely with the conservative socio-racial agenda that rose to prominence after the election of Ronald Reagan in 1980. His administration framed the modest political, economic, and geographic gains of a few middle-class blacks as proof that racism had largely ceased, thanks to civil rights laws and the increasing racial tolerance of whites as revealed in opinion polls. Indeed, this view suggested that America had become a "post–civil rights" society where any remaining poverty could not be attributed to social or systemic barriers

---

[68] Polikoff, *Waiting for Gautreaux.*
[69] Cutler, Glaeser, and Vigdor, "Rise and Decline of the American Ghetto."
[70] Lake, *New Suburbanites.*
[71] Sugrue, "Structures of Urban Poverty."

but, instead, to personal failures. It was a framing that elevated class, while diminishing the roles of race and space. It was to resonate with, and spawn, much scholarship during the period. The exception was Marxian and other systemic diagnoses, which were effectively marginalized in public and political discourse, and remain so today.

This new framing corresponded with the emergence of a new term: "underclass." The underclass was roughly defined as perpetually poor, often antagonistic, ghettoized blacks who relied on illegal activities and welfare as alternatives to low-wage work. Social work professor Douglas Glasgow, in *The Black Underclass* (1980), and journalist Ken Auletta, in *The Underclass* (1982), helped popularize and sensationalize the term.[72] Political scientist Charles Murray supplied a comprehensive framework for diagnosing the underclass in his 1984 *Losing Ground*. In the book, well funded by the conservative Manhattan Institute, Murray argued that Great Society programs had unwittingly encouraged the dysfunctional norms and behaviors of the underclass, by stripping away self-reliance and the pride that comes with working. To avoid losing more ground in the fight against poverty, Murray called for the abolishment of the entire social safety net.[73]

Though "underclass" clearly had racial connotations in colloquial discourse, a new book by William Julius Wilson, *The Truly Disadvantaged* (1987), would deracialize the discourse, subtly transforming the conception of the ghetto into one where class and space were in the foreground: "concentrated poverty" became the key frame.[74] The MacArthur Foundation had funded Wilson to write *The Truly Disadvantaged*, which picked up where *The Declining Significance of Race* left off, focusing the class analysis in the geographic terms of the Northern ghettos. In the new book, Wilson revealed how race intersected with class in a new way. In the past, a subordinate caste was all that mattered for every black. Now, the class system expressed itself spatially, with middle-class blacks increasingly segregated from lower-class ones and increasingly living with white and other nonblack neighbors. The lower-class

[72] Glasgow, *Black Underclass*; and Auletta, *The Underclass*. Wilson, in *The Declining Significance of Race*, had used the ill-defined term "underclass" (asserting that it comprised one-third of the black population), but had not investigated its spatial aspects. By 1990, he started advocating against using the term because it reinforced the notion of "undeserving poor" and promoted blaming the victim. Katz, "Urban 'Underclass' as Metaphor," 21. For additional discussion, see Katz, "Urban 'Underclass' as Metaphor."

[73] Murray, *Losing Ground*. Murray's argument built on the work of several economists from the mid-1970s who argued that redistributive policies were ineffective in improving aggregate social welfare because of interdependent utility functions and offsetting private transfers. Fontaine, "Beyond Altruism?"

[74] Wilson, *Truly Disadvantaged*.

blacks left behind in the ghetto increasingly suffered from this separation through a variety of "concentration effects" that made their poverty more desperate and durable, not necessarily from discrimination per se.[75]

Channeling Kain while rejecting Murray, Wilson claimed that increasing joblessness in the ghetto (especially for young males) proceeded from a mismatch of skills and space. Deindustrialization (and concomitant growth of professional jobs) in the inner city meant that there were few jobs nearby for which many young blacks were appropriately skilled. Low-skilled jobs were not only increasingly distant, but also unknown since ghetto residents could only tap into socially isolated networks that provided little information about job prospects. This fundamental structural force of deindustrialization was abetted by black middle-class relocation that followed from the recent fair housing and lending laws. This increasing class segregation within the black community meant that the underclass lost role models, collective efficacy, and much of their neighborhood institutional infrastructure.

Wilson acknowledged that there were legitimate issues regarding the values and behaviors of the underclass residing in concentrated poverty neighborhoods, as Moynihan, Banfield, Lewis, and Murray had all argued. But Wilson saw these, fundamentally, as adaptive responses to lack of opportunities, not root causes. For example, for Wilson, it was not welfare that led black women to have children without being married, but rather the lack of "marriageable males" due to evaporation of their employment prospects (and, often, their incarceration). Wilson's formulation strongly opposed the "culture of poverty" notion that poverty was self-perpetuating; adolescents could break out, if only given the opportunity. Wilson broke with not only conservative/individualistic, but also Marxian/systemic, perspectives, seeing instead of an exploited colony a residual ecological niche isolated from mainstream society. His proposed federal prescription: a class-based policy of guaranteed jobs that, though race-neutral on its face, would provide disproportionate benefits to poor blacks.

The Truly Disadvantaged proved influential (and controversial) along many dimensions.[76] Perhaps the book's most enduring legacy, however, is

---

[75] In worrying over the contagious effects of a concentrated, deprived population, Wilson echoed the work of several nineteenth-century scholars. Katz, "Urban 'Underclass' as Metaphor."

[76] Massey and Denton, *American Apartheid*; Jencks, *Rethinking Social Policy*; and Wacquant, "Three Pernicious Premises in the Study." These authors were leading sociologists who decried the deracialization of the ghetto and its replacement by the concept of concentrated poverty. For a review of the sociological reaction to Wilson, see Small and Newman, "Urban Poverty after *The Truly Disadvantaged*."

that it brought to the fore the notion of "neighborhood effects." Susan Mayer and Christopher Jencks were some of the first to question the empirical basis of whether neighborhoods generated independent effects, suggesting that what was being observed by Wilson may be due to households with certain characteristics selecting into particular neighborhoods.[77] Nevertheless, in another article, they described a variety of mechanisms that could indeed make the neighborhood an independent causal agent in individual outcomes.[78] Quantifying neighborhood effects accurately has since become a burgeoning subfield within economics, sociology, and geography.

Ironically, while Wilson was in the midst of de-racializing the concept of the ghetto, mainstream economics and geography were engaged in a furious battle over what role(s) race played in creating residential segregation.[79] For example, geographer William Clark prominently argued that segregation was primarily due to households acting freely on the basis of their homophily preferences concerning the racial composition of neighborhoods – subject only to the constraints imposed by their income and wealth.[80] This economist retorted that preferences were contingent and shaped by the legacy of institutionalized, government-sanctioned exclusion, blockbusting, and redlining, and that contemporary evidence on the persistence of discrimination provided by paired-testing studies were compelling reasons to reject the notion of segregation as the "natural" product of the housing market.[81]

Desegregation efforts pursued by the Republican Presidents Ronald Reagan and George H. W. Bush during the 1980s generally continued the minimalist trajectory established in the prior decade, but with two deviations, one left and one right. On the left, Congress enacted the Fair Housing Initiative Program in 1987 and the Fair Housing Amendment Act in 1988. The former provided federal financial assistance to local, nonprofit civil rights organizations to investigate fair housing complaints, and the latter expanded civil rights protections to families with children, established a more efficient system for adjudicating complaints, and toughened

---

[77] Mayer and Jencks, "Growing Up in Poor Neighborhoods."
[78] Jencks and Mayer, "Social Consequences of Growing Up."
[79] Radical political economists offered their last holistic effort to frame the ghetto in Fusfeld and Bates, *Political Economy of the Ghetto*. Thereafter, their influence in most US academic circles waned.
[80] Clark, "Residential Segregation in American Cities."
[81] Galster, "Residential Segregation in American Cities." For a review of this and subsequent debates over the origins of segregation, see Dawkins, "Recent Evidence on the Continuing Causes."

penalties for violations. Arguably, both efforts gained traction from the aforementioned 1977 national study documenting rampant housing market discrimination, despite the passage of the Fair Housing Act in 1968.[82]

In a rightward shift, the Department of Justice (DOJ) argued that the use of race in any decision-making (such as affirmative action) was neither warranted nor legal.[83] The most dramatic illustration of this position in the field of housing was the DOJ's 1984 suit against a large New York City housing development that was employing occupancy quotas to maintain a racially diverse clientele.[84]

Like residential desegregation, ghetto economic development was a fraught policy realm during the 1980s. The idea of "enterprise zones," tax-free sectors created to spur innercity job creation, rose to prominence in the United States as "supply-side economics" gained influence. Despite some powerful advocates, it never became federal policy.

6.7 Scholarly and Policy Sclerosis

Though, by design, this history focuses on the 1940s to the 1980s, it is important to note that the major themes and debates that dominated the discourse on the ghetto by the close of the 1980s remain unresolved today. Social scientific scholarship and federal policy in this realm over the last three decades can be described as sclerotic: advancing along the increasingly hardened lines established earlier in the postwar era. The Banfield–Murray individualist framing of the ghetto as essentially a collection of lower-class people embedded in a dysfunctional culture who, for whatever reason, are so damaged that they are beyond help remains a dominant line of thought.[85] Not only do these individuals not deserve public assistance, but such assistance will actually make their plight worse through its perverse disincentives for work and marriage. This view reached its policy apotheosis with the passage of two acts in the mid-1990s that set the course of federal responses to the ghetto to this day. The Violent Crime Control and Law Enforcement Act of 1994 led to billions in federal expenditures for prison construction and more police officers, increasing incarceration rates for

---

[82] Wienk et al., *Measuring Racial Discrimination in American Housing Markets*.
[83] These shifting political winds clearly influenced Wilson's view that only deracialized, class-based policy proposals had any political credibility.
[84] The Supreme Court eventually ruled in favor of the DOJ in *U.S. v. Starrett City and Associates* (1988).
[85] Gans, *War against the Poor*.

young black males.[86] The Personal Responsibility and Work Adjustment Act of 1996 set lifetime limits on receipt of cash welfare (Temporary Assistance to Needy Families) and mandated that recipients work or participate in approved educational programs. These policies sapped economic vitality from the ghetto, exacerbated the incarceration of its young men, and intensified the dysfunctional dynamic of police–community relations that we have recently seen manifested as an epidemic of police violence directed toward black citizens.

The Myrdal–Weaver–Kerner Commission notion that the ghetto is primarily a spatial product of historical and contemporary acts of racial discrimination in housing and mortgage markets also persists alongside the contrary, Chicago School view that segregation is a natural phenomenon primarily due to voluntary choices undertaken within the context of an unfettered market context. Social scientists from several disciplines have convincingly documented over the last thirty years both the persistence of housing discrimination and the vital role played by white homeseekers in avoiding predominantly black or racially mixed neighborhoods for a variety of reasons, but still cannot agree on which factor predominates.[87] Federal fair housing and desegregation policy have continued to vacillate depending on presidential administration. The Bill Clinton era was marked by aggressive antidiscrimination and desegregation efforts using paired testing and public housing court cases, respectively, while the Barack Obama administration developed regulations to incentivize local jurisdictions to dismantle barriers to affordable housing. By contrast, the George W. Bush and Donald Trump administrations evinced indifference if not hostility to these initiatives.

[86] Though the "war on drugs" had been begun during the Nixon administration, this Act considerably ramped up the adverse impacts on the ghetto.
[87] On the persistence of housing discrimination, see Massey and Denton, *American Apartheid*; Yinger, *Closed Doors, Opportunities Lost*; Immergluck, *Credit to the Community*; Immergluck, *Foreclosed*; Ihlanfeldt and Mayock, "Price Discrimination in the Housing Market"; and the review of paired-testing studies of discrimination in Oh and Yinger, "What Have We Learned from Paired Testing in Housing Markets?" On white homeseekers' avoidance, see Ellen, *Sharing America's Neighborhoods*; Charles, *Won't You Be My Neighbor?* and Krysan et al., "Does Race Matter in Neighborhood Preferences?" On the disagreement about prevailing factors, see, for example, economists Cutler, Glaeser, and Vigdor, "Rise and Decline of the American Ghetto" and Bayer, McMillan, and Rubin, "What Drives Racial Segregation?" For sociology examples, see South, Crowder, and Pais, "Metropolitan Structure and Neighborhood Attainment"; and Spivak and Monnat, "Influence of Race, Class, and Metropolitan Area Characteristics." And for planners, see Kucheva and Sander, "Structural versus Ethnic Dimensions." See also Dawkins' review, "Recent Evidence on the Continuing Causes."

Wilson's social/class/spatial conception of the ghetto as socially isolated, concentrated disadvantage set in motion a multidisciplinary effort focused on measuring neighborhood effects that continues to expand at this writing.[88] Technical methodological controversies dominated this effort, with economists leading the effort to debunk the first-generation sociological work that followed Wilson by arguing that their approaches could not identify causal relationships unambiguously.[89] Instead, they placed their trust in the largest random control trial in social science history – the Moving to Opportunity (MTO) demonstration – funded by HUD and a consortium of foundations, and launched in 1994.[90] Families (primarily black) in ghettoized public housing projects were randomly assigned to (1) receive a housing rental voucher with a requirement that it be used in a census tract with 10 percent poverty or less for at least a year, plus mobility counseling to assist recipients making this move; (2) receive a generic housing rental voucher; or (3) serve as controls.[91] Extensive interviews at baseline, five years, and ten years after assignment were used to assess outcomes for adults and children in multiple domains. A multidisciplinary MTO team headed by prominent economists concluded that neighborhood effects were limited in scope and modestly sized.[92] Subsequently, numerous studies tried to overcome the challenges to causal inference by using natural experiments to get quasi-random assignments of households to neighborhoods or by employing a variety of advanced econometric techniques. The vast majority of these third-generation studies have identified sizable neighborhood effects in many outcome domains, though impacts were often heterogeneous by ethnicity, age, and gender.[93] Most notable in impact, because they were highly respected economists, Raj Chetty, Nathaniel Hendren, and Lawrence Katz recently reanalyzed MTO data and found sizable effects from moving to low-poverty neighborhoods for poor, minority children if they completed the move before age 12.[94] Apparently, children can be rescued from the adverse influences of the

[88] See reviews in Brooks-Gunn, Duncan, and Aber, *Neighborhood Poverty* and Sampson, Morenoff, and Gannon-Rowley, "Assessing 'Neighborhood Effects'." The first effort to econometrically model concentrated poverty was undertaken by Jargowsky, *Poverty and Place.*
[89] Manski, *Identification Problems in the Social Sciences.*
[90] Polikoff, *Waiting for Gautreaux* and Briggs, Popkin and Goering, *Moving to Opportunity.*
[91] The MTO design proved not to be the definitive test of neighborhood effects, however, for several reasons. Sampson, "Moving to Inequality."
[92] Sanbonmatsu et al., *Impacts of the Moving to Opportunity.*
[93] See the review in Galster and Sharkey, "Spatial Foundations of Inequality."
[94] Chetty, Hendren, and Katz, "Effects of Exposure to Better Neighborhoods on Children."

ghetto if they are given the chance early in life, as Kenneth Clark had hypothesized.

One new effort attempted to conceptualize the ghetto in a way that synthesized class, race, and space dimensions of the phenomenon as well as individualistic and social frames. Expanding upon Myrdal's notion of cumulative causation and incorporating other sociologists' examples of vicious circles, this author attempted to integrate all these seemingly conflicting arguments into a holistic conceptual framework for understanding the ghetto as the intersection of race, space, and poverty, coining the term "metropolitan opportunity structure."[95] This model contended that multiple dimensions of spatial context (social-interactive, environmental, institutional, etc.) – at multiple geographic scales of neighborhood, jurisdiction, and metropolitan area – altered individual residents' values and behaviors by shaping what they perceived as feasible and most desirable. These perceptions, which were also contingent on race, gender, and class, affected choices that influenced their achieved socioeconomic status. When aggregated over space, these values and behaviors led endogenously to alterations in the metropolitan opportunity structure – especially regarding segregation – that abetted race–class inequalities.[96]

With economists' longstanding methodological skepticism and early MTO analyses creating considerable uncertainty about the putative harms of concentrated poverty or neighborhood effects in general, conservatives were able to maintain their individualistic, nonsocial, a-spatial framing with little amendment. If only law and order were restored, debilitating social safety net programs dismantled, and the free market allowed to reign, ghetto poverty would be cured.[97] Progressives, on the other hand, remained fragmented both in conceptualizing the ghetto and prescribing what interventions to take.[98] Both the Clinton and Obama administrations took

---

[95] Galster and Killen, "Geography of Metropolitan Opportunity." Robert Merton used the term "opportunity structure" but it was different on many grounds, primarily in that it did not have spatial or cumulative causation components. Merton, *Opportunity Structure*.

[96] This model has been refined and updated in Galster and Sharkey, "Spatial Foundations of Inequality."

[97] Porter, "Competitive Advantage of the Inner City."

[98] For fair housing/dispersal rationale, see sociologist Squires, *Fight for Fair Housing* and lawyer and policy analyst Orfield et al., "High Costs and Segregation." For the ghetto development rationale, see urban planners Imbroscio, "Beyond Mobility" and Goetz, *One-Way Street of Integration*. Recent efforts to find common ground between the desegregation and development policy camps were made by planners Turner, "Beyond People versus Place" and Dawkins, "Toward Common Ground."

some initiatives to develop the ghetto economically (e.g., Empowerment Zones, HOPE VI, Choice Neighborhoods), and advanced others to encourage its residents to move elsewhere with better opportunities (e.g., counseling and small-area subsidy adjustments for rental voucher holders). These efforts by Democratic administrations can best be viewed as token gestures, not comprehensive programs. This undoubtedly reflects the prevailing American public opinion that the ghetto's significance as a social problem has steadily waned since the late 1960s.

6.8 Conclusion

The dominant conceptualizations by social scientists of the nature and origins of the urban black ghetto in the mid–twentieth century have evolved significantly. The sociologists' individualistic view of the ghetto in the 1920s as a natural, generic process experienced by all lower-class urban immigrants gave way in the mid-1940s to the economist Myrdal's social view that blacks suffered from a unique racism creating a process of cumulative causation. During the 1960s, a welter of competing theories of the black ghetto emerged from a variety of disciplinary homes that differentially emphasized class, race, and space dimensions of the phenomenon while employing the full gamut of individualistic, social, and systemic framings. In the ensuing decade, sociologists, economists, and political scientists alike tended to drift toward individualistic, class-based formulations that de-emphasized race and space. By the late 1980s, sociologist Wilson had swung the ghetto discussion toward a social class space, one of economic dislocation that produced economic segregation and the resultant evils of concentrated poverty through neighborhood effects. Nevertheless, a steady stream of analyses produced by sociologists, economists, and planners from the 1960s through the end of the century endeavored to maintain the notion that the ghetto had a peculiarly racial dimension at its heart, though the framing of this dimension was often individualistic. Over the last three decades, neoclassical economists staked out the heights of methodological superiority when it came to quantifying the neighborhood effects that were implicit in the rationale for desegregation or ghetto redevelopment policies. Their initial skepticism has evolved into a tentative acknowledgment of the contingent power of context, based on a new generation of research coming primarily from quantitative sociology and economics.

A scan of this evolution of thought leads to three conclusions. First, since the 1970s, the dominant explanation of the ghetto has increasingly emphasized class and de-emphasized race, though the significance of the spatial dimension remains highly contested to this day. Second, after World War II, the individualistic framing has become increasingly dominant in class, race, and space dimensions, while the systematic view has correspondingly withered since the 1970s and the social view remains contested. Third, sociologists have been the primary advocates for an analysis employing both spatial and social perspectives, whereas neoclassical economists and political scientists have played key roles in promoting an individualistic, class-oriented framing.

The public's perception of the ghetto as a critical social problem emerged in the late 1960s as the televised imagery of "race riots destroying our cities" proved irresistible. Public pressure from multiple quarters prompted the first comprehensive package of federal responses. Since then, federal prescriptions for the ghetto have been politically cyclical, juxtaposed on a downward trend in the public salience of the issue. The individualist, class-based framings of some sociologists and political scientists, especially Moynihan, Banfield, and Murray, provided the underpinnings for the conservative strategy of laissez-faire, punctuated by punitive anticrime and antiwelfare initiatives, consistently pursued by Republican administrations. By contrast, progressives have had to negotiate often-shifting conceptual ground when approaching ghetto policy formulation. Even when agreeing on diagnoses, liberal scholars and Democratic administrations alike have been unable to coalesce around a core strategy, instead endlessly debating whether desegregation or development was preferable and putting forward minimalistic prototypes of both approaches that were virtually preordained to never reach scale. This cyclical pattern of ghetto policy is clearly attributable to ideological differences, not to the varied power of contemporaneous social scientific analyses.

Bibliography

Alonso, William. *Location and Land Use*. Cambridge: Harvard University Press, 1964.
Auletta, Ken. *The Underclass*. New York: Random House, 1982.
Banfield, Edward C. *The Unheavenly City: The Nature and Future of Our Urban Crisis*. Boston: Little, Brown, 1968.
Bayer, Patrick, Robert McMillan, and Kim S. Rubin. "What Drives Racial Segregation? New Evidence Using Census Microdata." *Journal of Urban Economics* 56 (2004): 514–35.
Becker, Gary S. *The Economics of Discrimination*. Chicago: University of Chicago Press, 1957.
Blauner, Robert. *Racial Oppression in America*. New York: Harper & Row, 1972.
Briggs, Xavier de Souza, Susan J. Popkin, and John Goering. *Moving to Opportunity: The Story of an Experiment to Fight Ghetto Poverty*. New York: Oxford University Press, 2010.

Brooks-Gunn, Jeanne, Gregory J. Duncan, and J. Lawrence Aber, eds. *Neighborhood Poverty*. 2 vols. New York: Russell Sage Foundation, 1997.

Burgess, Ernest W. "Residential Segregation in American Cities." *Annals of the American Academy of Political and Social Sciences* 140 (1928): 105–15.

Charles, Camille Z. *Won't You Be My Neighbor? Race, Class and Residence in Los Angeles*. New York: Russell Sage Foundation, 2006.

Chetty, Raj, Nathaniel Hendren, and Lawrence Katz. "The Effects of Exposure to Better Neighborhoods on Children: New Evidence from the Moving to Opportunity Experiment." Working Paper no. 21156. Cambridge: National Bureau of Economic Research, 2015.

Clark, Kenneth B. *Youth in the Ghetto: A Study of the Consequences of Powerlessness and a Blueprint for Change*. New York: Harlem Youth Opportunities Unlimited, 1964.

Clark, Kenneth B. *The Dark Ghetto: Dilemmas of Social Power*. New York: Harper & Row, 1965.

Clark, Kenneth B. *Prejudice and Your Child*. Middletown: Wesleyan University Press, 1988. First published 1963 by Beacon Press (Boston).

Clark, Kenneth B., and Mamie P. Clark. "The Development of Consciousness of Self and the Emergence of Racial Identification in Negro Preschool Children." *Journal of Social Psychology* 10 (1939): 591–99.

Clark, Kenneth B., and Mamie P. Clark. "Racial Identification and Preference among Negro Children." In *Readings in Social Psychology*, edited by E. L. Hartley, 169–78. New York: Holt, Rinehart, and Winston, 1947.

Clark, Kenneth B., and Mamie P. Clark. "The Negro Child in the American Social Order." *The Journal of Negro Education* 19 (1950): 341–50.

Clark, William A. V. "Residential Segregation in American Cities: A Review and Interpretation." *Population Research and Policy Review* 5 (1986): 95–27.

Cutler, David M., Edward L. Glaeser, and Jacob L. Vigdor. "The Rise and Decline of The American Ghetto." *Journal of Political Economy* 107 (1999): 455–506.

Dawkins, Casey. "Recent Evidence on the Continuing Causes of Black–White Residential Segregation." *Journal of Urban Affairs* 26 (2004): 379–400.

Dawkins, Casey. "Toward Common Ground in the U.S. Fair Housing Debate." *Journal of Urban Affairs* 40 (2018): 475–93.

Downs, Anthony. "Alternative Futures for the American Ghetto." *Daedalus* 97 (1968): 1331–38.

Downs, Anthony. *Opening Up the Suburbs*. New Haven: Yale University Press, 1973.

Drake, St. Clair, and Horace R. Cayton. *Black Metropolis: A Study of Negro Life in a Northern City*. Chicago: University of Chicago Press, 1993. First published 1945 by Harcourt Brace (New York).

Du Bois, W. E. B. *The Philadelphia Negro*. Philadelphia: University of Pennsylvania Press, 1899.

Duncan, Otis, and Beverly Duncan. *The Negro Population of Chicago: A Study of Residential Succession*. Chicago: University of Chicago Press, 1957.

Duneier, Mitchell. *Ghetto: The Invention of a Place, the History of an Idea*. New York: Farrar, Strauss and Giroux, 2016.

Edel, Matthew. "Development versus Dispersal." In *Readings in Urban Economics*, edited by Matthew Edel and Jerome Rothenberg, 307–24. New York: Macmillan, 1972.

Ellen, Ingrid Gould. *Sharing America's Neighborhoods: The Prospects for Stable Racial Integration.* Cambridge: Harvard University Press, 2000.

Fine, Sidney. *Violence in the Model City: The Cavanaugh Administration, Race Relations, and the Detroit Riot of 1967.* Ann Arbor: University of Michigan Press, 1989.

Fontaine, Philippe. "Beyond Altruism? Economics and the Minimization of Unselfish Behavior, 1975–93." *History of Political Economy* 44 (2012): 195–233.

Frazier, E. Franklin. *The Negro Family in Chicago.* Chicago: University of Chicago Press, 1931.

Freund, David M. P. *Colored Property: State Policy and White Racial Politics in Suburban America.* Chicago: University of Chicago Press, 2007.

Frieden, Bernard J., and Marshall Kaplan, eds. *The Politics of Neglect: Urban Aid from Model Cities to Revenue Sharing.* Cambridge: Massachusetts Institute of Technology Press, 1975.

Fusfeld, Daniel R. *The Basic Economics of the Urban and Racial Crisis.* New York: Holt, Rinehart, and Winston, 1973.

Fusfeld, Daniel R., and Timothy Bates. *The Political Economy of the Ghetto.* Carbondale: Southern Illinois University Press, 1984.

Galster, George C. "Residential Segregation in American Cities: A Contrary Review." *Population Research and Policy Review* 7 (1988): 93–112.

Galster, George C. *Driving Detroit: The Quest for Respect in the Motor City.* Chicago: University of Chicago Press, 2012.

Galster, George C., and Sean Killen. "The Geography of Metropolitan Opportunity: A Reconnaissance and Conceptual Framework." *Housing Policy Debate* 6 (1995): 7–44.

Galster, George C., and Patrick Sharkey. "Spatial Foundations of Inequality: An Empirical Overview and Conceptual Model." *RSF: The Russell Sage Journal of the Social Sciences* 3 (2017): 1–34.

Gans, Herbert J. *The War against the Poor: The Underclass and Antipoverty Policy.* New York: Basic Books, 1995.

Gillon, Steven M. *Separate and Unequal: The Kerner Commission and the Unraveling of American Liberalism.* New York: Basic Books, 2018.

Glasgow, Douglas G. *The Black Underclass: Poverty, Unemployment and Entrapment of Ghetto Youth.* San Francisco: Jossey-Bass, 1980.

Goetz, Edward. *The One-Way Street of Integration: Fair Housing and the Pursuit of Racial Justice in American Cities.* Ithaca: Cornell University Press, 2018.

Gordon, Leah. *From Power to Prejudice: The Rise of Racial Individualism in Midcentury America.* Chicago: University of Chicago Press, 2015.

Gouldner, Alvin W. *The Coming Crisis of Western Sociology.* New York: Basic Books, 1970.

Greenstein, Cheryl. *Or Does It Explode? Black Harlem in the Great Depression.* Oxford: Oxford University Press, 1991.

Grier, George, and Eunice Grier. *Equality and Beyond: Housing Segregation and the Goals of the Great Society.* Chicago: Quadrangle Books, 1966.

Hannerz, Ulf. *Soulside: Inquiries into Ghetto Culture and Community.* New York: Columbia University Press, 1969.

Harrison, Bennett. "Ghetto Economic Development." *Journal of Economic Literature* 12 (1974): 1–37.

Harvey, David. *Social Justice and the City.* Baltimore: Johns Hopkins University Press, 1973.

Haynes, Bruce and Ray Hutchinson. "The *Ghetto*: Origins, History, Discourse." *City & Community* 7 (2008): 347–52.

Hirsch, Arnold R. *Making the Second Ghetto: Race and Housing in Chicago, 1940–1960.* Cambridge: Cambridge University Press, 1983.

Ihlanfeldt, Keith R., and T. Mayock. "Price Discrimination in the Housing Market." *Journal of Urban Economics* 66 (2009): 125–40.

Imbroscio, David. "Beyond Mobility: The Limits of Liberal Urban Policy." *Journal of Urban Affairs* 34 (2012): 1–20.

Immergluck, Dan. *Credit to the Community: Community Reinvestment and Fair Lending Policy in the United States.* New York: M. E. Sharpe, 2004.

Immergluck, Dan. *Foreclosed: High-Risk Lending, Deregulation, and the Undermining of America's Mortgage Market.* Ithaca: Cornell University Press, 2011.

Jackson, Kenneth. *Crabgrass Frontier: The Suburbanization of America.* Oxford: Oxford University Press, 1985.

Jargowsky, Paul A. *Poverty and Place: Ghettos, Barrios, and the American City.* New York: Russell Sage Foundation, 1997.

Jencks, Christopher. *Rethinking Social Policy: Race, Poverty, and the Underclass.* Cambridge: Harvard University Press, 1992.

Jencks, Christopher, and Susan E. Mayer. "The Social Consequences of Growing Up in a Poor Neighborhood." In *Inner-city Poverty in the United States,* edited by Lawrence Lynn and Michael McGeary, 111–86. Washington, DC: National Academy Press, 1990.

Johnson, Charles S. *The Negro in Chicago: A Study of Race Relations and a Race Riot.* Chicago: University of Chicago Press, 1922.

Jones, Jacqueline. "Southern Diaspora: Origins of the Northern 'Underclass'." In *The "Underclass" Debate: Views from History,* edited by Michael Katz, 27–54. Princeton: Princeton University Press, 1993.

Kain, John F. "Housing Segregation, Negro Employment, and Metropolitan Decentralization." *Quarterly Journal of Economics* 82 (1968): 175–97.

Kain, John F., and Joseph Persky. "Alternatives to the Gilded Ghetto." *The Public Interest* 14 (1969): 74–87.

Kain, John F., and John M. Quigley. *Housing Markets and Racial Discrimination.* New York: National Bureau of Economic Research, 1975.

Katz, Michael B. "The Urban 'Underclass' as Metaphor for Social Transformation." In *The "Underclass" Debate: Views from History,* edited by Michael Katz, 3–23. Princeton: Princeton University Press, 1993.

Katz, Michael B. *The Undeserving Poor: America's Enduring Confrontation with Poverty.* 2nd ed. Oxford: Oxford University Press, 2013.

Krysan, Maria, Mick P. Couper, Reynolds Farley, and Tyrone A. Forman. "Does Race Matter in Neighborhood Preferences? Results from a Video Experiment 1." *American Journal of Sociology* 115 (2009): 527–59.

Kucheva, Yana, and Richard Sander. "Structural versus Ethnic Dimensions of Housing Segregation." *Journal of Urban Affairs* 40 (2017): 329–48.

Lake, Robert. *The New Suburbanites.* New Brunswick: Center for Urban Policy Research, Rutgers University, 1981.

Laurenti, Luigi. *Property Values and Race.* Berkeley: University of California Press, 1960.

Lemann, Nicholas. *The Promised Land: The Great Black Migration and How It Changed America*. New York: Vintage Books, 1992.

Lens, Michael. "Employment Accessibility among Housing Subsidy Recipients." *Housing Policy Debate* 24 (2014): 671–91.

Lewis, Oscar. *La Vida: A Puerto Rican Family in the Culture of Poverty, San Juan and New York*. New York: Random House, 1966.

Liebow, Elliot. *Tally's Corner: A Study of Negro Streetcorner Men*. Boston: Little, Brown, 1967.

Manski, Charles. *Identification Problems in the Social Sciences*. Cambridge: Harvard University Press, 1995.

Massey, Douglas S., and Nancy A. Denton. *American Apartheid: Segregation and the Making of the Underclass*. Cambridge: Harvard University Press, 1993.

Mayer, Susan E., and Christopher Jencks. "Growing Up in Poor Neighborhoods: How Much Does It Matter?" *Science* 243 (1989): 1441–45.

McEntire, Davis. *Residence and Race: Final and Comprehensive Report to the Commission on Race and Housing*. Berkeley: University of California Press, 1960.

Merton, Robert K. *Opportunity Structure: The Emergence, Diffusion, and Differentiation of a Sociological Concept, 1930s–1950s*. New York: F. Adler & W. S. Laufer, 1995.

Moynihan, Daniel P. *The Negro Family: The Case for National Action*. Washington, DC: United States Department of Labor, Office of Planning and Research, 1965. www.dol.gov/dol/aboutdol/history/webid-moynihan.htm.

Murray, Charles. *Losing Ground: American Social Policy 1950–1980*. New York: Basic Books, 1984.

Myrdal, Gunnar. *An American Dilemma: The Negro Problem and Modern Democracy*. New York: Harper & Row, 1944.

National Advisory Commission on Civil Disorders. *Report of the National Advisory Commission on Civil Disorders*. New York: Bantam Books, 1968.

O'Connor, Alice. *Poverty Knowledge: Social Science, Social Policy, and the Poor in Twentieth-Century U.S. History*. Princeton: Princeton University Press, 2001.

Oh, Sun Jung, and John Yinger. "What Have We Learned from Paired Testing in Housing Markets?" *Cityscape* 17 (2015): 15–59.

Orfield, Myron, Will Stancil, Thomas Luce, and Eric Myott. "High Costs and Segregation in Subsidized Housing Policy." *Housing Policy Debate* 25 (2015): 574–607.

Park, Robert E. "The Urban Community as a Spatial and Moral Order." In *The Urban Community*, edited by Ernest W. Burgess, 3–21. Chicago: University of Chicago Press, 1926.

Park, Robert E., and Ernest W. Burgess. *The City*. Chicago: University of Chicago Press, 1925.

Polikoff, Alexander. *Waiting for Gautreaux: A Story of Segregation, Housing, and the Black Ghetto*. Evanston: Northwestern University Press, 2007.

Porter, Michael. "The Competitive Advantage of the Inner City." *Harvard Business Review* 73 (1995): 55–71.

Rainwater, Lee. *Behind Ghetto Walls: Black Families in a Federal Slum*. Chicago: Aldine, 1970.

Rapkin, Chester, and William C. Grigsby. *The Demand for Housing in Racially Mixed Areas*. Berkeley: University of California Press, 1960.

Sampson, Robert J. "Moving to Inequality: Neighborhood Effects and Experiments Meet Social Structure." *American Journal of Sociology* 114 (2008): 189–231.

Sampson, Robert J., Jeffrey D. Morenoff, and Thomas Gannon-Rowley. "Assessing 'Neighborhood Effects': Social Processes and New Directions in Research." *Annual Review of Sociology* 28 (2002): 443–78.

Sanbonmatsu, Lisa, Jens Ludwig, Lawrence F. Katz, Lisa A. Gennetian, Greg J. Duncan, Ronald C. Kessler, Emma Adam, Thomas W. McDade, and Stacy Tessler Lindau. *Impacts of the Moving to Opportunity for Fair Housing Demonstration Program after 10 to 15 Years.* Washington, DC: U.S. Department of Housing and Urban Development, Office of Policy Development and Research, 2011.

Schelling, Thomas C. *Micromotives and Macrobehavior.* New York: W. W. Norton, 1978.

Shaw, Clifford R. *Delinquency Areas: A Study of the Geographic Distribution of School Truants, Juvenile Delinquents, and Adult Offenders in Chicago.* Chicago: University of Chicago Press, 1929.

Small, Mario L. "Four Reasons to Abandon the Idea of 'The Ghetto'." *City & Community* 7 (2008): 389–98.

Small, Mario L., and Katherine Newman. "Urban Poverty after *The Truly Disadvantaged*: The Rediscovery of the Family, the Neighborhood, and Culture." *Annual Review of Sociology* 27 (2001): 23–45.

South, Scott J., Kyle Crowder, and Jeremy Pais. "Metropolitan Structure and Neighborhood Attainment: Exploring Intermetropolitan Variation in Racial Residential Segregation." *Demography* 48 (2011): 1263–92.

Spivak, Andrew L., and Shannon M. Monnat. "The Influence of Race, Class, and Metropolitan Area Characteristics on African-American Residential Segregation." *Social Science Quarterly* 94 (2013): 1414–37.

Squires, Gregory D. *The Fight for Fair Housing: Causes, Consequences, and Future Implications of the 1968 Federal Fair Housing Act.* New York: Routledge, 2017.

Stack, Carol. *All Our Kin: Strategies for Survival in a Black Community.* New York: Harper & Row, 1974.

Sugrue, Thomas J. "The Structures of Urban Poverty: The Reorganization of Space and Work in Three Periods of American History." In *The "Underclass" Debate: Views from History*, edited by Michael Katz, 85–117. Princeton: Princeton University Press, 1993.

Sugrue, Thomas J. *The Origins of the Urban Crisis: Race and Inequality in Postwar Detroit.* Princeton: Princeton University Press, 1996.

Tabb, William. *Political Economy of the Black Ghetto.* New York: W. W. Norton, 1970.

Taeuber, Karl E., and Anna F. Taeuber. *Negroes in Cities.* Chicago: Aldine, 1965.

Thompson, Wilbur. *A Preface to Urban Economics.* Baltimore: Johns Hopkins University Press, 1965.

Turner, Margery Austin. "Beyond People versus Place: A Place-Conscious Framework for Investing in Housing and Neighborhoods." *Housing Policy Debate* 27 (2017): 306–14.

Turner, Margery Austin, Rob Santos, Diane Levy, Doug Wissoker, Claudia Aranda, and Rob Pitingolo. *Housing Discrimination against Racial and Ethnic Minorities 2012.* Washington, DC: U.S. Department of Housing and Urban Development, Office of Policy Development and Research, 2013.

Vietorisz, Michael, and Bennet Harrison. *Economic Development of Harlem.* New York: Praeger, 1970.

Wacquant, Loïc. "Three Pernicious Premises in the Study of the American Ghetto." *International Journal of Urban and Regional Research* 21 (1997): 341–53.

Weaver, Robert C. *The Negro Ghetto*. New York: Russell and Russell, 1948.

Wienk, Ronald, Clifford Reid, John Simonson, and Fred Eggers. *Measuring Racial Discrimination in American Housing Markets: The Housing Market Practices Survey*. Washington, DC: U.S. Department of Housing of Urban Development, Office of Policy Development and Research, 1979.

Wilson, William Julius. *The Declining Significance of Race*. Chicago: University of Chicago Press, 1978.

Wilson, William Julius. *The Truly Disadvantaged: The Inner City, the Underclass, and Public Policy*. Chicago: University of Chicago Press, 1987.

Wirth, Louis. *The Ghetto*. Chicago: University of Chicago Press, 1928.

Wolf, Eleanor P. "The Invasion-Succession Sequence as a Self-Fulfilling Prophecy." *Journal of Social Issues* 13 (1957): 7–20.

Yinger, John M. *Closed Doors, Opportunities Lost*. New York: Russell Sage Foundation, 1995.

7

Crime

Jean-Baptiste Fleury

In 1968, brushing aside almost fifty years of social scientific research, Gary Becker wrote that "a useful theory of criminal behavior can dispense with special theories of anomie, psychological inadequacies, or inheritance of special traits and simply extend the economist's analysis of choice."[1] The remark illustrates the confidence displayed at the time by an increasing number of economists investigating problems traditionally considered outside their domain of expertise. But Becker also hinted at a major intellectual change: As crime became untethered from other social issues (including poverty and race) in the public discourse and policy interventions, its study gradually turned away from the socioeconomic causes of criminals' behavior so dear to sociologists and social psychologists. Social scientists were now focusing on crime's efficient *management,* welcoming the contributions of economists, political scientists, and operations researchers, which seemed better suited to the pressing need to rationalize public policies.

In the preceding decades, sociologists and social psychologists had helped establish a social scientific consensus, one that relegated once-prevalent biological explanations to quackish obscurity. Although these postwar social scientists failed to develop a fully integrated approach, they successfully positioned crime and delinquency as enfolded within the broader dynamics of deviance, urbanization, family life, and subculture formation. They located the causes of criminal behavior, for the most part, in the social environment. By the early 1960s, their environmental approach grounded a number of initiatives that, with the support of federal agencies and philanthropic foundations, sought to integrate "delinquents" into their communities by fostering empowerment and legitimate opportunities, culminating in Lyndon Johnson's Wars on Poverty and Crime.

---

[1] Becker, "Crime and Punishment," 170.

Yet these theories would soon be called into question, as public attention shifted to "law and order" in the decade's second half, in the wake of a crime-rate surge and social unrest in the country's urban cores. The uptick in crime, together with the racialized visibility of the riots, was seized by conservative politicians to drive a wedge in the electorate and to discredit Great Society welfare policies. The new political attention on crime as a standalone problem led, indirectly, to the creation of cross-disciplinary programs bringing together economists, operations researchers, legal scholars, psychologists, sociologists, and political scientists under the "criminal justice" label. These programs forged a distinctive approach to crime as an isolated problem primed for rational management. The new schools and departments of "criminal justice," in other words, incubated a social scientific outlook that prioritized cost-effectiveness, rational behavior, and deterrence – "systems of crime control and the broader political economy."[2] The public policy landscape, in turn, largely shifted to street-crime prevention, leading to a revival – mere decades after their decisive repudiation – of biological modes of explanation.

7.1 Carving Out a Place for Social Scientists

In the interwar era, sociologists, psychologists, and legal scholars successfully established the primacy of environmental factors over biological determinants in the explanation for criminal behavior. The belief that specific morphological, physiological, and mental traits engendered criminal behavior had indeed grounded the analyses of European "criminal anthropologists" during the second half of the nineteenth century.[3] This movement was epitomized by the so-called Positive School and its notorious members Cesare Lombroso and Raffaele Garofalo (who coined the term "criminology"). Originally influenced by evolutionary theory, they traced the "criminal type" to lags in evolution.[4] By the mid-1910s, however, a number of landmark studies by physicians and psychiatrists had expanded the range of causal factors to family dynamics and economic or social conditions.[5] In Great Britain, Charles Goring's large-scale 1913 statistical study of British

[2] Laub, "Life Course of Criminology in the United States," 1.
[3] Davie, "Impact of Anthropological Criminology."
[4] Garofalo, *La criminologie.*
[5] Garofalo considered education and economic factors but discarded their importance in motivating criminal behavior. It appears that Lombroso's school was portrayed as the founder of modern criminology by early twentieth-century criminologists. Yet, the Positive School's influence during the early twentieth century may have obscured previous works, for instance those of Adolphe Quételet or André-Michel Guerry, which already emphasized environmental factors. See Lindesmith and Levin, "Lombrosian Myth in Criminology."

inmates authoritatively rejected the Positive School's notion of a "criminal type."[6] In the United States around the same time, William Healy warned against any monocausal theory. A physician and a psychologist trained in psychoanalysis, Healy stressed that delinquents had to be considered in their complexity, with environmental and psychological factors, such as weak parental control, poverty, mental conflict and repression, and/or "abnormal" sexuality, taken into account.[7]

Healy's work was widely acclaimed and paved the way for the development of an approach that sought to identify the multiple factors that contribute to crime, and estimate their relative weight or predictive powers. Among the prominent adopters of this approach were Sheldon and Eleanor Glueck, Harvard legal scholars deeply influenced by Healy's work.[8] Beginning with the widely praised *Five Hundred Criminal Careers* in 1930, the Gluecks regularly published detailed longitudinal studies of criminals or delinquents that won massive influence within criminology. They underlined how social forces – such as economic or class conditions – were intertwined with individual-level factors, like a broken home, age, intelligence, psychological dysfunction, school misconduct, parental supervision, or working habits. Two decades after their first book, criminologists were still debating which factors were decisive, with the Gluecks somewhere in between the two extreme positions: one that emphasized biological causes (e.g., the anthropologist Earnest Hooton) and the other that stressed environmental factors (as with Chicago School sociologists).

Ernest Burgess, a leading Chicago School figure alongside Robert Park, was also influenced by Healy's use of case studies, inductive techniques, and psychoanalysis, but argued that his analysis left little room for the study of social forces and the diagnosis of the social pathology of crime.[9] Although Burgess' own attempt to build predictors of "expectancy rates" of parole violations – which became a fast classic in the field – relied quite significantly

---

[6] Goring, *English Convict*, 15–18. Skepticism about the "positive school" approach had been mounting at the end of the nineteenth century, especially in Great Britain. For an account of the context of late nineteenth-century British criminology, see Davie, "Impact of Anthropological Criminology."

[7] Healy, *Individual Delinquent*, 30–31, 24–29.

[8] Sampson and Laub, *Crime in the Making*, 33–34.

[9] Burgess, "Study of the Delinquent as a Person." On the influence of Healy on Burgess, see Gitre, "Importing Freud" and Chapoulie, "Ernest W. Burgess et les débuts d'une approche sociologique." Gitre also addresses the dissemination of Freud's ideas in the social sciences (especially at Chicago) through the work of social scientists such as Hermann Adler (who replaced Healy at the Institute of Juvenile Research), Healy, Burgess, and others.

on individual-level factors, the influential work of his protégés pointed to broad social forces, instead, as the major causes of delinquency.[10] Clifford Shaw's and Henry McKay's work, from the late 1920s on, linked crime rates to social factors like residential instability, ethnic heterogeneity, and poverty, while treating "under the roof" variables like broken families as insignificant.[11] This first ecology of delinquency, in effect, applied Park and Burgess' portrayal of the city as a natural organism, in which social and cultural equilibria within specific urban areas were constantly disturbed by forces like migration, influencing in turn the geographic distribution of delinquency.

These developments had certainly benefited from late nineteenth-century changes in the US judicial system, which introduced a distinction between adult criminals and young offenders, labeled "delinquents," who were processed through juvenile courts and separately confined in youth clinics. Healy headed the first of these clinics, the Juvenile Psychopathic Institute of Chicago, where Burgess created a sociological research section in 1926, naming Shaw as the director and McKay as a research assistant.[12] In Massachusetts, meanwhile, the Gluecks maintained ties with the Judge Baker Foundation, another youth clinic that Healy codirected with Augusta Bronner shortly after his departure from Chicago in 1917.[13] These institutions, host to multidisciplinary research on psychoanalysis, the biology of learning, and physical growth, provided social scientists with a reservoir of subjects on which to build empirical analyses.[14]

Rising public anxiety about crime in the 1920s, linked to fears over immigration, resistance to Prohibition laws, and the increasing visibility of urban gangs, spurred the work of social scientists, as many cities, states, and eventually the federal government began to focus on crime reduction. Burgess' work on parole prediction was quickly tested and adopted in the early 1930s in Illinois, where judges relied heavily on parole boards to individualize sentencing.[15] Cities and states also summoned social scientists to help them build criminal surveys in the 1920s (e.g., the Gluecks in Boston), at a time when

[10] Burgess, "Is Prediction Feasible in Social Work?" See also Bulmer, *Chicago School of Sociology*, 124 and Harcourt, *Against Prediction*.
[11] Shaw and McKay, "Social Factors in Juvenile Delinquency."
[12] Grisso, "Forensic Evaluation in Delinquency Cases," 316 and Bulmer, *Chicago School of Sociology*, 124.
[13] Glueck and Glueck, *One Thousand Juvenile Delinquents*, i–xxii.
[14] These social scientists were interested in illegal or deviant activities broadly conceived. As he focused on antisocial behavior, Healy explicitly neglected the distinction between "delinquency" and "crime." Healy, *Individual Delinquent*, 3.
[15] Harcourt, *Against Prediction*, 48, 58–59.

crime statistics were useless or nonexistent. By the end of the decade, many still believed that a nation-wide crime report was sorely needed. This argument was taken up by the social scientists working for President Herbert Hoover's Wickersham Commission, established in 1929 to explore law enforcement and lawlessness. In the Commission's reports, they argued forcefully for a system of statistics that would not only measure crime, but also help identify its causes and evaluate the judicial and penal systems.[16] Eventually, though, Congress chose the Federal Bureau of Investigation's (FBI) Uniform Crime Index, a method that fell short of the Commission's ambitious vision and that, over subsequent decades, would be criticized time and again.[17] The Wickersham report, nevertheless, granted public visibility to the multicausal approach of Shaw and McKay, Healy, and the Gluecks. The report notably concluded that environmental factors were far more important than race and immigration, and dismissed explanations for crime rooted in biology.[18]

The report's scientific rigor was, however, soon questioned. In their 1933 *Crime, Law, and Social Science*, Jerome Michael and Mortimer Adler formulated sharp criticisms that were taken seriously by the community of criminologists. In particular, they pointed to the lack of abstract and rigorous causal theory, which prevented empirical research to yield any solid generalizations and useful policy recommendations. During the second half of the 1930s, two major contributions would move the debates to a higher level of abstraction. The first one, by the Chicago-trained sociologist Edwin Sutherland, was directly related to Michael and Adler's critique. Arguably the leading criminologist in the 1930s and 1940s, Sutherland was dissatisfied with the prevailing multicausal approach. Dismissing the Gluecks' studies as mere data collecting, Sutherland believed that a proper theory required a single causal explanation, one capable of explaining any type of criminal behavior. During the second half of the 1930s, he developed a monocausal theory, "differential association," which conceptualized criminality as learned behavior through interaction with members of specific groups.[19] These interactions determined how individuals interpreted their own condition, and how positive or negative attitudes toward the violation of law were transmitted to them. In 1938, a second important contribution also put the study of crime on higher theoretical ground, with the work of Robert

---

[16] US National Commission on Law Observance and Enforcement, *Report on Criminal Statistics*, 4.

[17] Gage, "Counting Crime."

[18] US National Commission on Law Observance and Enforcement, *Report on the Causes of Crime*, 16–17.

[19] Sutherland, *Principles of Criminology*.

Merton – then a graduate student at Harvard – who analyzed deviance within a functionalist framework, focusing on the interplay between a set of culturally defined goals and "acceptable modes of achieving these goals." Crime and delinquency, Merton argued, were the adaptive behavior of what he termed the "innovative" type, a subset of whom pursued their goals by "relinquishing the institutional [legitimate] means." This made crime and delinquency "culturally oriented if not approved" responses to social circumstances.[20]

By the 1940s, then, social scientists had developed strong theoretical arguments to discredit the role of biological factors for crime. Sutherland's work went a bit further: His rejection of multiple causation extended to multidisciplinary analysis, and successfully made crime the privileged turf of sociology.[21] Criminology's higher level of abstraction also led sociologists to reflect on criminology's appropriate subject matter, beyond the narrowly legal definition of crime: Merton studied deviance; University of Pennsylvania's rising criminologist, Thorsten Sellin, considered the determination and violations of "conduct norms"; and Sutherland's analysis of "white collar" criminality questioned social scientists' exclusive focus on reported street crime and delinquency.[22] With Merton gaining increasing stature within sociology, and Sutherland building a hub of American criminology at the University of Indiana (training future influential scholars such as Albert Cohen, Donald Cressey, and Lloyd Ohlin), their distinctive contributions had laid the foundations for the field's postwar mainstream.

7.2 Delinquent Subcultures

In the postwar period, social scientists gradually refined Merton and Sutherland's approaches with the aim to improve criminology's scientific status. Eventually, a dominant view emerged from research on the cultural dimensions of juvenile delinquency, which appeared to social scientists as well as private philanthropic foundations as a promising framework to integrate cross-disciplinary research on the links between relative deprivation and crime.

This consensus approach only emerged during the second half of the 1950s, though. Postwar debates in criminology, mostly led by sociologists,

---

[20] Merton, "Social Structure and Anomie," 673, 672.
[21] On Sutherland's opposition to the Gluecks and scientific positivism, see Laub and Sampson, "Sutherland–Glueck Debate."
[22] Sutherland, "White-Collar Criminality."

were primarily concerned with questions of method, a reflection of the preceding decade's advances.[23] Sutherland's devastating critique of multifactor analysis had notably pressured those criminal "actuaries" interested in predictive studies to question their empirical methods. Consequently, calls for methodological refinement – fewer variables, for example, or attention to statistical significance – overshadowed the older debates over the primacy of "personal" or "situational" factors in criminal or delinquent behavior.[24] Sutherland's work on white-collar crime also stirred intense debate over the field's proper subject matter, as he recommended investigation of a wider range of criminals, including white collars, and of crimes, than those defined within the narrow confines of the "traditional criminal code."[25] In keeping with Burgess, the debates pitted those who supported a legal definition of crime as law-breaking against the norm-violating definitions advanced by Sutherland and Merton.[26] And, indeed, white-collar crime successfully developed into its own subfield in the late 1940s, with contributions from many prominent sociologists. Yet its integration within criminology remained intensely debated, with most criminologists agreeing with Donald Newman, that white-collar law-breaking was "a legitimate area of criminological research, although ... customarily set apart as a special type or 'behavior system' of crime."[27]

These debates reveal that by the mid-1950s, criminology was still struggling to obtain the legitimacy won by sociology's postwar mainstream, with its joint embrace of survey analysis and structural-functionalism "symbolized by the pairing of [Samuel] Stouffer and [Talcott] Parsons at Harvard and [Paul] Lazarsfeld and Merton at Columbia."[28] Merton was not publishing extensively on delinquency at the time and many details of Sutherland's differential association theory, easily equated with a Chicago

---

[23] Mannheim, "American Criminology," 293. Advanced studies and research on criminology were conducted primarily within sociology departments, with the notable exception of Harvard and Berkeley. At Berkeley, August Vollmer had created the Bureau of Criminology within Berkeley's political science department in 1939. Yet, the training was mostly oriented toward the needs of policemen. A professional association, the American Society of Criminology, was created in 1941 with most of its members only remotely related to sociology. The first sociologist to serve as the president of the society was Walter Reckless in 1964. See Morris, "American Society of Criminology."
[24] Schuessler, "Parole Prediction," 428.
[25] Newman, "White-Collar Crime," 737.
[26] For an overview of these debates, see Tappan, "Who Is the Criminal?" and Aubert, "White-Collar Crime and Social Structure."
[27] Newman, "White-Collar Crime," 735–36.
[28] Abbott and Sparrow, "Hot War, Cold War," 285.

tradition that was losing its shine, had scarcely been "subjected to the test of empirical research."[29] In contrast to the wider sociology discipline, many remained dissatisfied with criminology's lack of a "systematic theory" underpinning most of its empirical findings and predictive techniques.[30]

During the second half of the 1950s, refinements of the two leading frameworks – differential association and Merton's anomie theory – were intended to raise criminology's scientific status. Differential association was revised with a view to answering critics (e.g., the Gluecks) who argued that the theory poorly explained why some individuals became delinquents while their neighbors did not.[31] Using social psychological concepts drawn from symbolic interactionism and role theory, some of its advocates insisted that individuals behaved in accordance with the way they expect to be perceived by others.[32] Meanwhile, they sought to operationalize Sutherland's theory and test it empirically.[33] Following Gresham Sykes and David Matza, criminologists developed a social psychological theory whereby delinquents shared most of the mainstream law-abiding values, but escaped self-blame by rationalizing their criminal acts with "techniques of neutralization" such as denial of the victim or condemnation of the condemners.[34] These refinements of differential association theory, however, did not spread beyond social psychology. Not only were cross-disciplinary exchanges scarce, but proponents of differential association also engaged in boundary work, feeding the sense among a number of social scientists that Sutherland's framework stood as an instance of sociological imperialism.[35]

Theories of delinquent subcultures formed another important strand of thought, one that merged differential association with Merton's functionalism. Starting with Albert Cohen's 1955 *Delinquent Boys* and

---

[29] Cressey, "Application and Verification," 43 and Abbot and Sparrow, "Hot War, Cold War," 296.
[30] The lukewarm reception of the Gluecks' 1950 longitudinal study among sociologists illustrates these criticisms, which applied to most research on prediction in the 1950s. See, for instance, Reiss, "Unraveling Juvenile Delinquency."
[31] Glaser, "Sociological Approach to Crime and Corrections."
[32] Matsueda, "Current State of Differential Association Theory."
[33] For example, Short, "Differential Association and Delinquency."
[34] Sykes and Matza, "Techniques of Neutralization."
[35] Glaser, "Sociological Approach to Crime and Corrections," 686. A compelling illustration of boundary work is provided in Cressey, "Differential Association Theory and Compulsive Crimes," which rejects psychiatric explanations even in the case of compulsive crime. On the links between differential association and psychiatry, see also Hartung, "Critique of the Sociological Approach to Crime and Correction," 733–34.

followed by the works of, among others, Harvard anthropologist Walter Miller, Richard Cloward (a student of Merton's), and Lloyd Ohlin (a student of Sutherland's), this approach argued that delinquent subcultures were a collective response to the difficulties that individuals faced. Following Cohen, social scientists built typologies of subcultures and theoretical explanations for their formation, contributing to what arguably became the most influential strand in criminology until the second half of the 1960s. There were disagreements about whether the values of these subcultures were different from those of the poor and working class, or whether they emerged within specific family contexts (e.g., single-mother households), but, by the early 1960s, Cloward and Ohlin's *Delinquency and Opportunity* laid out what was arguably the most influential view. They argued that most delinquents strove to attain the economic status of the middle class, in the face of no real legitimate means to do so. In what was labeled the "opportunity theory," differences in access to various illegitimate means to achieve economic success explained the different forms of delinquency.

Criminology's fusion of differential association and Mertonian functionalism during the second half of the 1950s existed alongside a number of projects aimed at combining psychological, social-psychological, and psychoanalytic insights to form a comprehensive and integrated approach. One index of this new interest was a 1955 conference organized by the Division of the Juvenile Delinquency of the Children's Bureau, which brought Merton and psychoanalyst Erik Erikson together. Another marker was a 1958 special issue on juvenile delinquency in the *Journal of Social Issues*, published by the American Psychological Association, which gathered Cohen and Miller, together with psychologists and social psychologists such as Albert Bandura, Richard Walters, and William and Joan McCord. With the prospect of a "synthesizing approach to American social problems," efforts were undertaken that nonetheless took note of Merton and Erikson's words of caution about the extent to which the sociologists' and psychologists' differences in perspective could be reconciled.[36] Most followed Merton's views that a division of labor between sociologists and psychologists should prevail, with the former specializing in subculture formation and the latter locating delinquency either in pathological family dynamics or the process of ego formation.[37] Although

---

[36] McCord, "Introduction," 3 and Merton, "Concluding Comments and an Example," 79.
[37] Merton, "Concluding Comments and an Example," 79. For psychological analyses, see McCord and McCord, "Effects of Parental Role Model on Criminality" and Erikson, "Ego Identity and the Psychosocial Moratorium."

not the robust form of interdisciplinarity that some wished for, the new settlement was a step beyond the polarized debate that prevailed through to the early 1950s, which had set environmental explanations against personal factors. Because "no single field can offer a complete answer," most agreed that psychological, social-psychological, and sociological insights complemented, rather than supplanted, each other.[38]

By the early 1960s, social scientists reached a rough agreement about the causes of delinquency. As illustrated by subculture studies, sociologists shifted away from the interwar concern about the destabilizing effects of immigration and urbanization. Social scientists were now emphasizing the link between delinquency and the values and socioeconomic problems of lower-income communities. Although delinquency and gang crime were increasingly associated with racial minorities, social scientists maintained the prewar stance that crime was predominantly related to the social environment, not race per se: The dominant view was that higher rates of delinquency among African-Americans and in segregated neighborhoods were the product of poverty, cultural deprivation, and discrimination.[39]

Interestingly, this emerging mainstream had arisen from studies of juvenile delinquents. To some extent, delinquency was a topic that allowed the social scientist to escape the definitional conundrum raised by the white-collar debates, because of its rather loose legal definition; delinquent behavior ranged from truancy, misdemeanors, and simple antisocial behavior, to more severe property offenses, violent acts, and sexual offenses. Scientists could, to some extent, cherry-pick their favored definition of crime, making delinquency a rallying point for different methodological viewpoints.[40] But studying the causes of delinquency also provided answers to a growing public concern that peaked during the second half of the 1950s.[41] Delinquency rates were on the rise, and – while criminal statistics might not have been reliable – newspaper articles painted an alarming picture of youth criminality, which resonated with fears of communism and social disintegration. Meanwhile, the Senate began an almost decade-long series of hearings on the topic, and a number of local antidelinquency committees and organizations sprouted at the time.[42]

[38] McCord, "Introduction," 3.
[39] Flamm, *Law and Order*, 17.
[40] See Tappan, "Who Is the Criminal?" 99. The Gluecks, for instance, narrowed down the types of offenses in their definition of delinquency. See Glueck and Glueck, *Unraveling Juvenile Delinquency*, 13.
[41] For a thorough historical account of the problems of juvenile delinquency in postwar America, see Gilbert, *Cycle of Outrage*.
[42] Gilbert, *Cycle of Outrage*, 76, 63–64.

Since the late 1940s, philanthropic foundations had played no small role in supporting various antidelinquency programs, including social scientific studies.[43] But the most influential program emerged from the Ford Foundation's attempts to fight relative deprivation, in particular by improving schooling, from the mid-1950s on. In this endeavor, officials of the foundation found in Cloward and Ohlin's work the theoretical underpinnings they needed. Ford funded their research at Columbia School of Social Work and developed the Mobilization for Youth community action program (CAP), initiated by the board of directors of the Henry Street Settlement House in New York City to fight rising delinquency in the area, and cosponsored with the National Institute of Mental Health. The philosophy behind the project was similar to another significant Ford-sponsored urban renewal program, "Gray Areas," which emphasized the need to integrate people within mainstream community and its values.[44] The program promoted employment and educational support for young people, but also called for deeper reforms to broaden access to legitimate opportunities by improving job prospects and schooling. These demonstration programs sought to revise urban policies by combining the foundation's monies with the financial and institutional contributions of cities and the federal government.[45] In early 1961, Ford's programs inspired the creation of the President's Committee on Juvenile Delinquency and Youth Crime. Ohlin served as the liaison with the Department of Health, Education, and Welfare (HEW), which, after the Juvenile Delinquency and Youth Offenses Control Act of 1961, distributed $30 million over three years to support pilot projects in crime control in the form of local community action-empowering programs.

In addition to support for these early attacks on poverty, HEW's funds sponsored a number of multidisciplinary research projects. One of them was held under the auspices of the social sciences division at the University of Chicago. Its head, the sociologist Morris Janowitz, sought to study

[43] For instance, Ohlin's, Miller's, and the Gluecks' research was funded by, respectively, the Russell Sage Foundation, the National Institutes of Health, and the Ford Foundation. By 1957, Ford had made juvenile delinquency an important aspect of its Youth Development program. A radical study of Russell Sage's funding activity found that Ohlin was, at the time, the largest recipient of Russell Sage's money (about a million dollars in cumulated grants in the 1950s and 1960s). Schulman, Brown, and Kahn, "Report on the Russell Sage Foundation."
[44] See Marris and Rein, *Dilemmas of Social Reform* and O'Connor, "Ford Foundation and Philanthropic Activism."
[45] See O'Connor, "Ford Foundation and Philanthropic Activism."

"community organization" "as the basis of a preventive attack on juvenile delinquency." Reminiscent of Ford's goal to revamp urban policies, the project sought to integrate new social scientific knowledge with the practices of social workers and school teachers, and to improve the coordination of government, social welfare agencies, and local communities.[46] What makes the Chicago project particularly interesting was Janowitz's hiring of the economist Belton Fleisher to estimate the empirical relationship between employment and delinquency. Recommended by the Chicago labor economist H. Gregg Lewis, Fleisher was arguably one of the first postwar economists to work on crime and delinquency.[47] Janowitz had hired Fleisher because studies by sociologists had "not been adequate in scope to deal with the complexity of the problem," as their research lacked an adequate policy orientation.[48] Eventually, in spite of Janowitz's plea to integrate the analysis of economic conditions within a framework emphasizing subcultures, the rigor and immediate policy implications of Fleisher's analysis impressed HEW officials.[49] This hinted at an interesting development that would create many tensions during Johnson's second mandate, namely, his conflation of the wars on crime and poverty.

7.3 The Politicization of Street Crime and Law and Order in the 1960s

Paradoxically, the consensus idea that crime and delinquency were symptoms of broader social issues was sharply challenged during the 1960s, as street crime and civil unrest rose to the forefront of public debate. One result of the changed political climate was to call into question what was labeled the "rehabilitative ideal."[50]

The increasing involvement of the federal government in matters of crime under Kennedy – a sea change in the history of US politics – played an

---

[46] Janowitz, "Proposal for Curriculum Development in Juvenile Delinquency and Crime Control," n.d., box 27, folder 3, Morris Janowitz Collection, Special Collections Research Center, University of Chicago Library.
[47] Lewis was a key player in the neoclassical turn of labor economics. He supervised many innovative PhD dissertations at Chicago, among which was Becker's 1955, *The Economics of Racial Discrimination*.
[48] Fleisher, *Economics of Delinquency*, 7 and Janowitz, "Final Progress Report," n.d., box 29, folder 2, Morris Janowitz Collection, Special Collections Research Center, University of Chicago Library.
[49] Jack Otis to Morris Janowitz, August 6, 1963, box 28, folder 14, Morris Janowitz Collection, Special Collections Research Center, University of Chicago Library.
[50] Garland, *Culture of Control*.

important role in these developments, if only because its new prominence made the federal government more accountable for public safety.[51] After Kennedy's small-scale attacks on delinquency, Johnson launched a full-fledged War on Poverty – an ambitious series of social welfare policies grounded on the belief that crime and delinquency were intertwined with other poverty-related problems such as discrimination and segregation of minorities, urban problems, and inequalities in access to many legitimate opportunities (see Chapter 4: Poverty). In line with the prevailing consensus, the Community Action Program (CAP), modeled after Ford's Mobilization for Youth, distributed funds on a decentralized basis to empower local communities. Yet it would only take Johnson a few months to make street crime a social (and federal) problem on its own, when he reframed the War on Poverty as a War on Crime.[52] In 1965, the Law Enforcement Assistance Act complemented the CAP with a small-scale crime control program that supported experimental law enforcement methods.[53] The surge in reported crime, together with the wave of race riots beginning in Harlem in 1964 and culminating in the "long summer" of 1967, convinced Johnson to consider the problem of street crime itself.[54] Student protests would only add to this climate of unrest. With Republicans conflating street crime and civil disorders in a political rhetoric focused on "law and order" (see later), crime quickly became an especially charged issue in political discourse and public opinion.[55] Johnson would become the first US president to regularly submit "to Congress messages or speeches specifically on crime."[56]

Indeed, Johnson established two important crime-related commissions, both of which gathered leading social scientists to reflect on causes and furnish policy recommendations: the first on crime, in 1965, chaired by the Attorney General Nicholas Katzenbach, and the second on civil disorders, in 1967, chaired by Illinois Governor Otto Kerner. The two commission reports supported Johnson's liberal creed that policy should target the socioeconomic root causes of crime and unrest. Likewise, they

[51] Crime policies were predominantly a prerogative of the states.
[52] See, for instance, Flamm, *Law and Order* and Weaver, "Frontlash."
[53] See, for instance, Beckett, *Making Crime Pay*, 91 and Hinton, *From the War on Poverty to the War on Crime.*
[54] Flamm asserts that the rate of property crime rose "73 percent from 1960 to 1967. The rate of violent crime (murder, robbery, forcible rape, and aggravated assault) rose 57 percent – and doubled by 1969. Between 1965 and 1969 the overall crime rate increased by double digits every year." Flamm, *Law and Order*, 125.
[55] Flamm, *Law and Order*, 2. See also Beckett, *Making Crime Pay*. Republicans' focus on law and order began during Barry Goldwater's presidential campaign against Johnson in 1964.
[56] Marion, *History of Federal Crime Control Initiatives*, 38.

promoted community empowerment, community integration of young people (in particular through the creation of "Youth Service Bureaus"), and the development of community relations programs within police departments.[57] Finally, they recommended increased spending on welfare programs directed at schooling, housing, training, and employment. Although economic analysis was conspicuously absent from both reports, most recommendations were compatible with the Council of Economic Advisers' endorsement of the War on Poverty at a time when the economics profession and various international institutions (such as the OECD) grew increasingly interested in the economics of education and human capital ideas (see Chapter 3: Education).[58]

The commission reports identified the typical criminal or rioter as coming from a dysfunctional family background, and they also supported welfare policies that would keep families together. In the second half of the 1960s, however, linking family disorganization to poverty and crime inescapably raised the issue of race (see Chapter 6: The Black Ghetto). Daniel Patrick Moynihan's controversial 1965 *The Negro Family* argued that a "tangle of pathology" within African-American families, highly dependent on welfare and lacking father figures, had worsened socioeconomic disparities and generated delinquency. Like Moynihan's, the Kerner report argued that innercity segregation had fostered family and social disorganization, with poverty and unemployment, notably, preventing black males from their socially designated roles as fathers and breadwinners.[59] Rioting was "the behavioral response of men who were attempting to assert some form of power and control," according to some of the Kerner Commission experts. Reflecting the postwar consensus on prejudice marked by the characteristic themes of "social pathology, wounded masculinity, matriarchal families, and problematic self-esteem," these views would remain highly influential in both public policy circles and the social scientific literature until at least the late 1980s (see Chapter 5: Discrimination).[60]

The racial aspects of crime and unrest moved to center stage during Johnson's second term. Riots broke out in segregated neighborhoods, and

---

[57] These conclusions were not sociologists' only. Psychologists were also supporting these views, on the grounds that welfare policies were not a monetary or socioeconomic remedy to poor conditions, but a way to bolster self-esteem. See Herman, *Romance of American Psychology*, 223–25.

[58] See Teixeira, "Portrait of the Economics of Education."

[59] See Herman, *Romance of American Psychology*, chap. 8, for a thorough description of psychologists' work for the Kerner Commission.

[60] Herman, *Romance of American Psychology*, 222, 220, 201. See Hinton, *From the War on Poverty to the War on Crime*, for an analysis of the influence of these views.

reported crime figures showed that African-Americans were overrepresented as offenders, notably in violent crimes.[61] Yet public opinion polls at the time showed increasing polarization along racial lines regarding the causes of crime and civil disorders.[62] For many African-Americans, past and present racism, as well as police brutality, were major causes of unrest. Minority leaders and radicals presented social unrest as political upheaval.[63] Influenced by the Black Panther Party and other minority movements, many activists rejected the idea – epitomized by the Moynihan report – that black innercity family life was a pathological shadow of white middle-class culture. Racial progress "could no longer automatically be equated with 'integration.'"[64] While many liberal social scientists – including Moynihan and those on the Kerner Commission – also blamed racism and discrimination, their integrationist posture was increasingly rejected by activists and protesters, leading a number of social scientists and policy officials to question community empowerment policies as potential contributors to unrest.[65]

These developments made structural-functionalism look "ill equipped" to address deep-seated conflict between groups.[66] In this changing social and intellectual landscape, criminologists were highly supportive of a number of approaches that studied the formation and consequences of "status assignment" by a group on another. Howard Becker's 1963 *Outsiders* stood as a landmark statement of the emerging field of "labeling" theories that, grounded in symbolic interactionism, studied how individuals' self-image and behavior are affected by the very act of labeling certain acts as deviant. Taking the problem from a slightly different angle, conflict theory – which reemerged after a 1966 article by sociologist Austin Turk – focused on the role that culture and group conflicts played in the production of legal and informal definitions of what counts as a deviant or criminal act.[67] Because status ascription was imposed by the dominant, Turk's hypothesis that disadvantaged populations would be far more likely to be found delinquent paved the way for the subsequent emergence of radical criminology (see later).

---

[61] President's Commission on Law Enforcement and Administration of Justice, *Challenge of Crime in a Free Society*, 44.

[62] Flamm, *Law and Order*, 83–84.

[63] See Flamm, *Law and Order* and Hinton, *From the War on Poverty to the War on Crime*, for a depiction of how these events were qualified as upheaval or riots.

[64] Jackson, *Social Scientists for Social Justice*, 3.

[65] See, for instance, Fogelson, "Review Symposium" and Moynihan, *Maximum Feasible Misunderstanding*. Moynihan wrote that "empowerment" was promoted to the point that communities believed they could bypass or override "the city, the state, the world."

[66] Winant, "Dark Side of the Force," 565.

[67] Turk, "Conflict and Criminality."

During the second half of the 1960s, many whites took crime figures at face value and increasingly feared the surge in unrest and street crime – race-tinged anxiety that Republican political campaigns at the state and federal level increasingly fanned. In the wake of Barry Goldwater's 1964 presidential campaign, Republicans successfully seized "law and order" as a rallying cry to capture white working-class and middle-class discontent, conservative voters, and those who had opposed desegregation in the South a decade earlier. Illustrated by Ronald Reagan's successful 1966 gubernatorial campaign in California, as well as Richard Nixon's 1968 presidential campaign, conservative discourse demonized civil rights activism and linked civil disorder with street and violent crimes, implicitly targeting African-Americans.[68] By setting aside discrimination, racism, and poverty as root causes, to focus instead on individual choice, morality, and family disintegration, many conservatives made the Great Society state itself responsible for welfare dependency, frustration, and violence among low-income and minority communities.[69] Though most social scientists shied away from describing race as a determinant of crime, Republicans successfully appealed to sectors of the US electorate by drawing selectively on Moynihan's report or Marvin Wolfgang and Franco Ferracuti's 1967 analysis of African-Americans' violence-prone subculture.[70]

These attacks on liberal policies were strengthened by pointed criticisms of empirical research that, according to critics, failed to support the consensus tenets of mainstream criminology. The Harvard political scientist James Q. Wilson, among others, attacked the Crime Commission's recommendations precisely because the dearth of systematic evidence could not support "its generalizations and recommendations."[71] Wilson's remarks hinted at the stream of countervailing evidence that questioned the conclusion, supported by the subculture approach, that delinquency was concentrated in urban low-income communities.[72] Research, moreover, that had attempted to operationalize Sutherland's differential association theory had not held up under systematic testing. Even prominent sociologist Donald Cressey conceded the empirical limits of differential association in 1960, an admission

---

[68] See Weaver, "Frontlash."
[69] Beckett, *Making Crime Pay*, 34.
[70] Wolfgang and Ferracuti, *Subculture of Violence*. By 1987, the book was still mentioned as a landmark analysis of violent subcultures. See Sampson, "Urban Black Violence."
[71] Wilson, "Reader's Guide to the Crime Commission's Report"; Douglas, "Review of *The Challenge of Crime in a Free Society*," 665; and Savitz, "Review of *The Challenge of Crime in a Free Society*," 300.
[72] Gibbs and Erickson, "Major Developments in the Sociological Study," 27–28.

bolstered by the attacks of Travis Hirschi and Hannan Selvin, among others, on the principle of single causation. At a time when theoretical innovations appeared scant, many found that the bulk of theoretical analysis in criminology had never really met the standards of proper empirical analysis.[73] For these reasons, scholars such as Moynihan were skeptical of community empowerment policies, and warned against the dangers that a group of social scientists, supported by a few foundations' impressive pocketbooks, would impose their values on society, bypassing the sovereignty of citizens.[74] Moreover, a number of comments pointing to the dearth of social scientific knowledge on law enforcement, its deterrent effect, and on the functioning of the criminal justice system, nurtured conservatives' insistence on shifting the emphasis away from offenders' rehabilitation toward public safety, deterrence, and punitive measures.[75] Because they were associated with rehabilitation and socioeconomic explanations of crime, sociologists were often portrayed as soft-hearted and ideologically driven scholars.[76] By the end of Johnson's term, increasing doubts were cast on the possibility of solving the crime problem through welfare policies alone.

In the meantime, new ways of thinking about crime emerged in the aftermath of attempts by officials in Washington, who had been skeptical of the CAP since its beginning, to restore a more centralized approach to policymaking. Around the same time, the government extended the Department of Defense's Program Planning and Budgeting System (PPBS) to all federal agencies in 1965, hoping that cost–benefit and systems analyses would bring value-free criteria into public decision-making.[77] This strong concern for cost-effectiveness provided a fertile ground for the development of alternative approaches to crime. Because "rational" policymaking depended heavily on the quality of empirical data, the Johnson administration gathered forty-one social scientists to produce a complementary "social report" that would account for social progress in the country.[78] The endeavor was one

---

[73] Cressey, "Epidemiology and Individual Conduct"; Hirschi and Selvin, "False Criteria of Causality"; Hirschi and Selvin, *Delinquency Research*; and Gibbs and Erickson, "Major Developments in the Sociological Study."
[74] See Moynihan, *Maximum Feasible Misunderstanding*.
[75] See Wilson, "Reader's Guide to the Crime Commission's Report," 2.
[76] James Kilpatrick's comment "that the [Crime] Commission's staff talked with too many sociologists, and not with nearly enough cops" provides a typical illustration. Quoted in Flamm, *Law and Order*, 56.
[77] See, for instance, Jardini, *Thinking through the Cold War*, 310 and Amadae, *Rationalizing Capitalist Democracy*, 68.
[78] US Department of Health, Education, and Welfare, *Toward a Social Report*. See also Fleury, "Drawing New Lines."

instance of a broader movement led by social scientists determined to help transform the policymaking process by constructing "social indicators" that would accurately inform responses to social ills.[79] Leading HEW's initiative, the sociologist Daniel Bell and economist Mancur Olson hoped to construct indicators with similar aggregative and interpretative characteristics as those already established for the economy. In the case of crime, Bell and Olson explored ways to overcome the limitations of the FBI report by weighting offenses by their relative seriousness (an approach initially developed by Marvin Wolfgang), as well as by computing the net monetary loss due to crime, including foregone earnings.[80] Many social scientists warned against such "economic philistinism," some doubting the very possibility of building social indicators for policy purposes.[81] Yet, from the late 1960s, systems analysis and economic conceptualization emerged as promising frameworks for integrating social scientific research into policymaking, paving the way for the study of deterrence and law enforcement.[82]

By 1968, crime had emerged as a standalone social problem, distinct from poverty, and a decisive one for the presidential election's outcome. Even before the end of Johnson's presidency, liberals' defeat was illustrated by the passing of the 1968 Omnibus Crime Control and Safe Streets Act. Increasingly skeptical of philanthropic foundations' support of political activism – in particular of local empowerment initiatives taking the form of registration campaigns – Congress also passed a law in 1969 that prohibited foundations from using their funds for political lobbying and elections. At the beginning of Nixon's term, then, the intellectual and political tide regarding the causes, prevention, and control of crime and delinquency had turned.

7.4 The Emergence of "Crime Control"

The 1968 Omnibus Crime Control and Safe Streets Act marked a significant shift toward crime *control*, in both policymaking and criminological research. In the wake of the 1967 Crime Commission, the Act relied on the concept of a "criminal justice" system to centralize and rationalize activities related to

---

[79] Springer, "Social Indicators, Reports, and Accounts," 2.
[80] Bell, "Idea of a Social Report" and US Department of Health, Education, and Welfare, *Toward a Social Report.*
[81] Gross and Springer, "New Goals for Social Information," 218 and Reiss, "Putting Sociology into Policy."
[82] Savitz welcomed systems analysis as "the wave of the future." Savitz, "Review of *The Challenge of Crime in a Free Society,*" 301.

the control of street crime and civil unrest.[83] The Act led to the creation of the Law Enforcement Assistance Administration (LEAA), a federal agency providing financial support to the states through block grants, under the condition that "statewide comprehensive law enforcement plans" were established.[84] Consequently, significant support went to police operations and, to a lesser extent, social scientific research aimed at improving law enforcement and efficiency of correctional procedures. LEAA's influence on social scientific research grew stronger in time, as its grants became increasingly tied to "agency-defined research projects."[85] Overall, the annual stream of LEAA funds kept rising throughout the 1970s, totaling $10 billion by 1981.[86] In the meantime, these grants progressively replaced other sources of federal money that once came from agencies that addressed the "social conditions of crime – such as urban development, housing, and health."[87]

With the aim to upgrade educational requirements within enforcement agencies, the LEAA also fostered the massive development of "criminal justice" departments during the 1970s (they had more than tripled by 1976), through, for instance, the "consortium grants" given in 1973 to seven universities to develop specific doctoral degree programs.[88] With a strong vocational aspect, these cross-disciplinary curricula gathered law enforcement professionals, legal scholars, economists, social psychologists, sociologists, psychologists, operations researchers, statisticians, and sometimes chemists and computer scientists, to study the organized response to crime by the various subsets of the criminal justice system, in particular correctional institutions, law courts, and the police.[89] It is thus fair to say that although sociology remained the leading discipline within these departments in the 1970s, its leadership weakened. As criminology progressively moved away from sociology departments, the curricular prominence of sociological theory and methods receded too, in favor of more policy-oriented knowledge and techniques related to crime control,

[83] Orleans, "Criminal Justice, the Sociology of."
[84] Harman, "Bloc Grant," 142.
[85] Savelsberg, Cleveland, and King, "Institutional Environments and Scholarly Work," 1278.
[86] Beckett, *Making Crime Pay*, 38, 91 and Hinton, *From the War on Poverty to the War on Crime*, 2.
[87] Short and Hughes, "Crime, Criminologists, and the Sociological Enterprise," 637.
[88] Leijins, *International Conference on Doctoral-Level Education*, 5. The consortium universities were Arizona State, Eastern Kentucky, Michigan State, Northeastern, Portland State, the University of Nebraska at Omaha, and the University of Maryland, College Park.
[89] Leijins, *International Conference on Doctoral-Level Education*, 5.

which emphasized statistics – the Federal Criminal Justice Statistics Program standing, by 1977, as "the fourth largest federal statistical program in the entire government" – and applications to the criminal justice and correctional systems.[90] Interestingly, specialized outlets in criminology proved much more attractive for crime control and policy-related papers than traditional sociology outlets, the latter publishing, albeit on a modest scale, a higher share of "traditional" works about strain or learning theory.[91]

Following funding and institutional change in the 1970s, social scientific research progressively broke away from its main concern with criminal behavior and the social psychological forces driving it, to focus on crime control, the criminal justice system, and "the larger system of political economy."[92] This opened the way for a new type of cross-disciplinary relationship that placed operations research (OR) at the core of a nexus linking economists, statisticians, legal scholars, political scientists, and sociologists. Best illustrated by Alfred Blumstein's landmark works, OR gathered many discipline-specific concepts and empirical results within a model of the criminal justice system designed as an "input/output process involving institutions and individuals using diverse resources to achieve social goals or output."[93] Deeply related to program budgeting policies at the national and local level – after all, evaluation programs were being implemented by the RAND Corporation within a number of police departments at the time – this approach spurred a flourishing cross-disciplinary literature addressing problems related to the allocation of resources within law enforcement agencies and to the measurement of the cost of crime.[94] These endeavors also incorporated the recent developments in statistics designed to overcome the limitations (and underestimation) of FBI crime figures, in particular the victimization surveys by sociologists.[95]

The increased attention paid to the performance of the criminal justice system supported economists' managerial view that – because both crime and its prevention were costly – there existed an optimal balance

---

[90] Leijins, *International Conference on Doctoral-Level Education*, 2. See also Bruns and O'Hearn, *Criminal Justice Doctoral Education*.
[91] Savelsberg, Cleveland, and King, "Institutional Environments and Scholarly Work."
[92] Laub, "Life Course of Criminology in the United States," 6.
[93] "The Cost of Crime and of Social Defense against Crime," 196.
[94] Sullivan, "Economics of Crime." On the implementation of OR within police departments, see Bottoms, "Operations Research and Computers in Law Enforcement" and Jardini, *Thinking through the Cold War*, 315.
[95] The first National Crime Victimization Survey was published in 1973, and the emergence of these studies was massively supported by LEAA funds. See Skogan, "Review of *Surveying Crime*."

Jean-Baptiste Fleury

of enforcement and crime in a given society. The point was forcefully stated in Gary Becker's widely influential article of 1968.[96] The two central notions on which it was built, rational choice and deterrence, were rapidly assimilated within the other social sciences as well. OR is an obvious example, as it was customarily conflated with economic analysis. But rational choice and cost-effectiveness made their way into political science through Wilson's work, in particular his massively influential *Thinking about Crime*, which welcomed OR and economics as means to "to test the efficacy of alternative crime control strategies."[97] In sociology, both Travis Hirschi's social control theory, which sought to analyze why individuals did not break the law, and Lawrence Cohen and Marcus Felson's late 1970s "routine activity" theory, which stressed the role that situational incentives play in the occurrence of crime, relied on some form of rational behavior.[98] Moreover, sociologists' traditional skepticism toward deterrence started to wane with the works of Jack Gibbs and Charles Tittle, which contributed to the debate – largely dominated by economists – on the effect of severity and probability of punishment on crime.[99] One should note that economics' increasing influence on the social scientific discourse did not imply that noneconomists wholeheartedly embraced its assumptions.[100] Overall, most of them remained aware of rational choice's limitation and – judging from the debates on the deterrent effect of capital punishment, reinvigorated by Isaac Ehrlich's econometric studies in the mid-1970s – noneconomists appeared more cautious than economic students of crime on the conclusiveness and applicability of research on deterrence.[101]

Even so, the emerging mainstream trend in criminology systematized what had become, since the late 1960s, a consensus view among policymakers and officials, namely, that welfare policies aiming at the root causes of crime were ineffective at curbing crime.[102] This appraisal was notably shared by

[96] Becker, "Crime and Punishment."
[97] Wilson, *Thinking about Crime*, xxii.
[98] Cohen and Felson, "Social Change and Crime Rate Trends."
[99] See, for instance, Tittle, "Punishment and Deterrence of Deviance" and Gibbs, *Crime, Punishment, and Deterrence*.
[100] The cross-disciplinary conference organized by the American Enterprise Institute in 1972 shows that the dialogue between economists and sociologists on matters of crime control remained difficult even when they shared common beliefs about deterrence. See Rottenberg, *Economics of Crime and Punishment*.
[101] See, for instance, the report of the Panel on Research on Deterrence and Incapacitative Effects, which, among other things, evaluated Ehrlich's results. Note that Ehrlich was a student of Becker's in the mid-1960s.
[102] Hinton, *From the War on Poverty to the War on Crime*, 181–82.

a number of Nixon's advisers, notably Moynihan, Wilson, and political scientist Edward Banfield, and by a number of other social scientists later labeled "neoconservatives." To them, Johnson's welfare policies were biased misuses of social scientific research that only reflected the almost utopian values of a new class of experts. The critics wished to promote, instead, a more pragmatic use of social science, combined with a sharp reduction in the scope of government's intervention – ideas that they successfully publicized in Irving Kristol and Daniel Bell's *The Public Interest*, first published in 1965.

Yet the shift in scholarly and institutional focus to criminal justice and crime control was heavily criticized by many scholars within the academic community.[103] Social scientists feared, first, that the vocational aspect of these curricula would lead to a "smothering of social science knowledge."[104] A decade after their creation, such a tension was registered within LEAA-sponsored programs in criminal justice, between the "professional" and the "social scientific" aspects, or whether particular doctoral students should be awarded a PhD or a DCrim.[105] But the criticisms extended to the policy-oriented research that Ehrlich's or Wilson's works exemplified too, revealing how debates over the scientific character of crime control–related research were enmeshed with policy and political considerations. To some, such as Cressey, "doing something about crime," especially when it was equated with a racially or class-biased pursuit of criminals, had nothing to do with the pursuit of truth.[106] Opposing Wilson's comments about the uselessness of sociology, Cressey forcefully retorted that only empirical generalizations about the root causes of criminal behavior could ground a scientifically sound fight against crime.

Another strand of attack on criminology during the 1970s came from a radical "new criminology," grounded in a series of foundational critiques of sociological and psychological criminologies, and of Becker's economics of crime.[107] A burgeoning subfield – thanks to the leading role of Berkeley's Department of Criminology and a new journal, *Crime and Social Justice* – radical criminology focused on the relationship between crime and political or institutional structures, where conflict over power

---

[103] Webb and Hoffman, "Criminal Justice as an Academic Discipline," 348.
[104] See, for instance, Cressey, "Criminological Theory, Social Science," 173.
[105] Bruns and O'Hearn, *Criminal Justice Doctoral Education*.
[106] Cressey, "Criminological Theory, Social Science."
[107] On the first type of critique, see Taylor, Walton, and Young, *New Criminology*. For a critique of Becker's economics of crime, see Gordon, "Capitalism, Class, and Crime."

stood as a central process behind law-making and status ascription.[108] To radicals, the criminologist helped the state rationalize penal practices and law enforcement – reflected, in other words, the "values of the State," and helped reinforce the criminalization of working classes' or minorities' behavior by the power elite.[109] Increasingly linked to Marxian thought and drawing together the insights of political economy, philosophy, the sociology of deviance, and political science, radicals sought to redefine the "true" crimes of capitalist societies, in particular alienation, racism, imperialism, exploitation, and political oppression of dissenters. Yet, after a promising start, the movement quickly lost momentum, as many scholars eventually rejected radicals' dogmatism. By the 1980s, the field had mostly "excommunicated radical criminology from the American scene."[110]

While radicals' ambitious program failed to convince social scientists, economists' endeavors to redefine criminal law within a framework inspired by the works of Ronald Coase, Harold Demsetz, Becker, and, perhaps most importantly, Richard Posner, proved quite successful. This view analyzed law as a tool for public policy aiming at maximizing society's wealth and limiting government's intervention, thanks notably to its deterrent effect. Although a number of legal scholars interested in the economic approach argued for a redistributive role for law, and questioned economists' focus on deterrence, the scholarship that addressed criminal law in particular was heavily indebted to Becker's early definition of crime as uncompensated harm and his focus on fines as optimal punishment. Research on the topic would eventually take off in the mid-1980s with Posner's reformulation of crime as "market bypassing," written, like most of his work, for an audience of legal scholars.[111] Closely tied to the University of Chicago and neoliberal circles such as the Mont Pèlerin Society, the movement did not suffer the fate of radicals, and kept expanding in the 1980s. One reason might be that, in contrast to the radicals, the economic analysis of legal rules was never orthogonal (but quite complementary) to the topical problems related to the rational management of crime through law enforcement and deterrence.

By the early 1980s, indeed, the cost-efficiency of the criminal justice system was becoming a pressing issue that concerned not only economists

---

[108] Greenberg, *Crime and Capitalism*, 3.
[109] Platt, "The Prospects for Radical Criminology," 2.
[110] Koheler, "Development and Fracture of a Discipline," 536.
[111] Posner, "Economic Theory of Criminal Law." See also Posner, *Economic Analysis of Law*. For an overview of the debates between economists and legal scholars on the use of economic analysis to study law, see Hackney, *Under Cover of Science* and Marciano and Medema, "Disciplinary Collisions."

but also other social scientists and policymakers, as the first consequences of the "get tough on crime" policies, promoted ever since Nixon, were being felt. With the hope that deterrence would prevent future crime, anticrime policies during the 1970s had promoted harsher punishments, the militarization of police forces, and the development of surveillance techniques.[112] Policymakers' focus on street crime had made African-Americans the primary target of crime control policies, a trend worsened by the war on drugs initially declared under Nixon, but strongly revived under Reagan. By the time of Reagan's election, the movement of mass incarceration had dramatically changed the racial composition of prisons, while the cost of incarceration put huge strains on public finance. This pressing issue strengthened the development of predictive analysis in the 1980s, a subfield that had been rejuvenated by the 1972 longitudinal study by Marvin Wolfgang, Robert Figlio, and Thorsten Sellin.[113] Because its main result showed that a small fraction of delinquents contributed to most delinquency, Wolfgang's study recommended allocating crime control resources to targeted criminals, thus setting the stage for research on "career criminals" and selective incapacitation in the 1980s, with drugs becoming an important causal factor of crime in the social scientific and public discourses.[114] Predictive analyses that could be used, for instance, to estimate the probabilities of parole violation, or to "distinguish the high-rate offenders from the more numerous ordinary offenders," would be at the heart of decision guidelines that were used on a voluntary basis by parole boards.[115] Finally, the development of predictive research on sentencing in the 1980s certainly benefited from the implementation, in a number of states and cities, of mandatory sentences, in particular for drug-related felonies, unlawful gun possession, or recidivism.

The focus on the prevention of future crime also helped encourage the revival of biological explanations. The British psychiatrist Hans Eysenck assumed a leading role in the revival, as he focused on the role of inherited traits of the cortical and autonomic nervous systems, to which difficulties in both learning and inhibiting antisocial behavior were related.[116] Although his early works stretched back to the mid-1960s, Eysenck's work became increasingly influential in the 1970s and spurred a stream of studies that

[112] See Hinton, *From the War on Poverty to the War on Crime.*
[113] Wolfgang, Figlio, and Sellin, *Delinquency in a Birth Cohort.*
[114] Hinton, *From the War on Poverty to the War on Crime.*
[115] Blumstein et al., *Criminal Careers and "Career Criminals,"* vi. On guidelines, see Goldkamp, "Prediction in Criminal Justice Development."
[116] Hollin, *Psychology and Crime,* 55–58.

illustrated the change in predictive methods away from clinical to statistical prediction in the psychiatry of crime of the early 1980s.[117] Moreover, the mid-1980s revival of studies emphasizing heredity while exploring the links between criminality and personality traits – IQ in particular – opened the way for the merging of political science and psychology, thanks to the collaboration between Wilson and the psychologist Richard Herrnstein.[118] In 1994, *The Bell Curve*, coauthored by Herrnstein and conservative political scientist Charles Murray, framed the former's findings on IQ and crime within a broader picture of America's social (and racial) inequalities, with conclusions that left little room for social welfare policies. Although Eysenck and Herrnstein held different positions on rational choice and the potential for the rehabilitation of criminals, they both made biological explanations of criminal behavior highly influential again.

7.5 Conclusion

On the eve of the late-1990s historic drop in crime rates, Bill Clinton's 1994 Violent Crime Control and Law Enforcement Act, the largest federal crime control bill at the time, toughened punishment and expanded federal oversight, illustrating that the "tough on crime" stance had crossed the political divide. Meanwhile, the links between research on crime control and policymaking kept tightening. Wilson and George Kelling's 1982 "broken windows" theory, which argued that police should systematically address misdemeanors in order to prevent the development of a seriously criminogenic environment, reached high levels of respectability, as its implementation through New York City's mid-1990s "quality of life policing" seemed to offer strong empirical validation.[119]

Yet the dominance of crime control research programs should not conceal the increasing fragmentation of social scientific knowledge: Not only did this orientation not replace other research programs on crime but its most important theoretical developments remained discipline-specific. Although research was already splintered as early as the interwar period, when biological, psychological, and sociological explanations of crime coexisted, social scientists were less committed to building an integrated interdisciplinary approach after the 1980s, with criminal justice programs as a case in point.

---

[117] Eysenck and Gudjonsson, *The Causes and Cures of Criminality*, ix.
[118] See Wilson and Herrnstein, *Crime and Nature* and Herrnstein and Murray, *The Bell Curve*.
[119] Harcourt, "Reflecting on the Subject."

Over time, the shifts in methodological mainstreams and leading cross-disciplinary relations were always related to the interaction between debates about the relevant criteria for proper scientific research, on the one hand, and public policy concerns for delinquency or crime control, on the other. A byproduct of the criminal justice turn in the 1970s, criminology's separation from sociology mirrored the dissociation of crime from poverty in the public and policy discourses. By the 1980s, sociology had lost its dominant position. Biological explanations resurfaced after years of rejection, and economics and political science established themselves as promising challengers. OR and psychological or psychiatric research on personal traits provided cross-disciplinary frameworks capable of integrating social scientific and biological knowledge into policy-relevant material.

One distinctive aspect of the changes that occurred in the late 1960s, and that divided scholars both within and outside criminology, concerned the relationship between research and public policy.[120] From scholarship driven by social reform built on social scientific knowledge independent of government's oversight, a significant chunk of criminological research seemed to have become tethered to crime-control policy. While this dependence pressured a number of criminologists to constantly reevaluate their achievements through the prism of policy-relevance, the broad shift to criminal justice – to making the penal system "work" – proved alarming to the growing ranks of political scientists, historians, and criminologists who warned that crime, and its management, had become the foundation of a new, less democratic, and racially polarized American civil and political order.[121]

Bibliography

Abbott, Andrew, and James Sparrow. "Hot War, Cold War: The Structures of Sociological Action, 1940–1955." In *Sociology in America: A History*, edited by Craig Calhoun, 281–313. Chicago: Chicago University Press, 2007.

Amadae, Sonja. *Rationalizing Capitalist Democracy: The Cold War Origins of Rational Choice Liberalism*. Chicago: University of Chicago Press, 2003.

Aubert, Vilhelm. "White-Collar Crime and Social Structure." *American Journal of Sociology* 58, no. 3 (1952): 263–71.

Becker, Gary S. "Crime and Punishment: An Economic Approach." *Journal of Political Economy* 76, no. 2 (1968): 169–217.

Becker, Howard S. *Outsiders: Studies in the Sociology of Deviance*. New York: Free Press, 1963.

[120] See Petersilia, "Policy Relevance and the Future of Criminology," 397.
[121] Simon, *Governing through Crime*, 6.

Beckett, Katherine. *Making Crime Pay: Law and Order in Contemporary American Politics*. Oxford: Oxford University Press, 1997.

Bell, Daniel. "The Idea of a Social Report." *The Public Interest* 15 (Spring 1969): 72–105.

Bell, Daniel. *The End of Ideology*. Cambridge: Harvard University Press, 2000.

Blumstein, Alfred, Jacqueline Cohen, and Daniel Nagin, eds. *Deterrence and Incapacitation: Estimating the Effects of Criminal Sanctions on Crime Rates. Panel on Research on Deterrent and Incapacitative Effects*. Washington, DC: National Academy of Sciences, 1978.

Blumstein, Alfred, Jacqueline Cohen, Jeffrey A. Roth, and Christy A. Visher, eds. *Criminal Careers and "Career Criminals"*. Washington, DC: National Academy Press, 1986.

Bottoms, Albert M. "Operations Research and Computers in Law Enforcement: Some Cases Studies of American Police Experience." *Computers & Operations Research* 1, no. 1 (1974): 149–65.

Bruns, Gilbert H., and Carolyn O'Hearn. *Criminal Justice Doctoral Education: Issues and Perspectives*. Washington, DC: National Criminal Justice Educational Consortium Reports 4, 1976.

Buchanan, James. "Student Revolts, Academic Liberalism, and Constitutional Attitudes." *Social Research* 35 (1968): 666–80.

Bulmer, Martin. *The Chicago School of Sociology*. Chicago: University of Chicago Press, 1984.

Burgess, Ernest. "The Study of the Delinquent as a Person." *American Journal of Sociology* 27, no. 6 (1923): 657–80.

Burgess, Ernest. "Is Prediction Feasible in Social Work? An Inquiry Based upon a Sociological Study of Parole Records." *Social Forces* 7, no. 4 (1929): 533–45.

Chapoulie, Jean-Michel. "Ernest W. Burgess et les débuts d'une approche sociologique de la délinquance aux Etats-Unis." *Déviance et Société* 27 (2003): 103–10.

Clinard, Marshall B. "Sociologists and American Criminology." *Journal of Criminal Law and Criminology* 41, no. 5 (1951): 549–77.

Cloward, Richard A, and Lloyd E. Ohlin. *Delinquency and Opportunity: A Theory of Delinquent Gangs*. Glencoe: Free Press, 1960.

Cohen, Albert K. *Delinquent Boys: The Culture of the Gang*. Glencoe: Free Press, 1955.

Cohen, Lawrence, and Marcus Felson. "Social Change and Crime Rate Trends." *American Sociological Review* 44, no. 4 (1979): 588–608.

"The Cost of Crime and of Social Defense Against Crime: Summary of the Second International Symposium in Comparative Criminology." *Acta Criminologica* 4 (1971): 193–208.

Cressey, Donald. "Application and Verification of the Differential Association Theory." *Journal of Criminal Law and Criminology* 43, no. 1 (1952): 43–52.

Cressey, Donald. "The Differential Association Theory and Compulsive Crimes." *Journal of Criminal Law, Criminology, and Police Science* 45, no. 1 (1954): 29–40.

Cressey, Donald. "Epidemiology and Individual Conduct: A Case from Criminology." *Pacific Sociological Review* 3, no. 2 (1960): 47–58.

Cressey, Donald. "Criminological Theory, Social Science and the Repression of Crime." *Criminology* 16, no. 2 (1978): 171–91.

Davie, Neil. "The Impact of Anthropological Criminology in Britain (1880–1918)." *Histoire de la criminologie 4, l'Anthropologie criminelle en Europe*, 2005.

Douglas, Jack. "Review of *The Challenge of Crime in a Free Society: A Report by the President's Commission on Law Enforcement and Administration of Justice*." *American Sociological Review* 32, no. 4 (1967): 664–66.

Erikson, Erik. "Ego Identity and the Psychosocial Moratorium." In *New Perspectives for Research on Juvenile Delinquency*, edited by Ellen Witmer and Ruth Kotinsky, 1–23. Washington, DC: US Department of Health, Education, and Welfare, 1956.

Eysenck, Hans, and Gisli Gudjonsson. *The Causes and Cures of Criminality*. New York: Springer, 1989.

Flamm, Michael. *Law and Order: Street Crime, Civil Unrest and the Crisis of Liberalism*. New York: Columbia University Press, 2005.

Fleisher, Belton M. *The Economics of Delinquency*. Chicago: Quadrangle Books, 1966.

Fleury, Jean-Baptiste. "Drawing New Lines: Economists and Other Social Scientists on Society in the 1960s." In *The Unsocial Social Science? Economics and Neighboring Disciplines since 1945*, edited by Roger E. Backhouse and Philippe Fontaine, 315–42. Durham: Duke University Press, 2010.

Fogelson, Robert. "Review Symposium." *American Political Science Review* 63, no. 4 (1969): 1269–75.

Gage, Beverly. "Counting Crime: J. Edgar Hoover, the Wickersham Commission, and the Problem of Criminal Statistics." *Marquette Law Review* 93, no. 4 (2013): 1109–18.

Garland, David. *The Culture of Control: Crime and Social Order in Contemporary Society*. Chicago: University of Chicago Press, 2001.

Garofalo, Raffaele. *La criminologie*. Paris: Félix Alcan, 1888.

Gibbs, Jack P. *Crime, Punishment, and Deterrence*. New York: Elsevier, 1975.

Gibbs, Jack P., and Maynard Erickson. "Major Developments in the Sociological Study of Deviance." *Annual Review of Sociology* 1 (1975): 21–42.

Gilbert, James. *A Cycle of Outrage: America's Reaction to the Juvenile Delinquent in the 1950s*. Oxford: Oxford University Press, 1986.

Gitre, Edward. "Importing Freud: First-Wave Psychoanalysis, Interwar Social Sciences, and the Interdisciplinary Foundations of an American Social Theory." *Journal of the History of the Behavioral Sciences* 46, no. 3 (2010): 239–62.

Glaser, Daniel. "The Sociological Approach to Crime and Corrections." *Law and Contemporary Problems* 23, no. 4 (1958): 683–702.

Glueck, Sheldon, and Eleanor Glueck. *One Thousand Juvenile Delinquents*. Cambridge: Harvard University Press, 1934.

Glueck, Sheldon, and Eleanor Glueck. *Unraveling Juvenile Delinquency*. New York: The Commonwealth Fund, 1950.

Goldkamp, John S. "Prediction in Criminal Justice Policy Development." *Crime and Justice* 9 (1987): 103–50.

Gordon, David. "Capitalism, Class, and Crime in America." *Crime and Delinquency* 19, no. 2 (1973): 163–86.

Goring, Charles. *The English Convict: A Statistical Study*. London: H. M. Stationery Office, 1913.

Greenberg, David. *Crime and Capitalism*. Philadelphia: Temple University Press, 1993.

Grisso, Thomas. "Forensic Evaluation in Delinquency Cases." In *Handbook of Psychology: Forensic Psychology*, vol. 11, edited by Alan M. Goldstein, 315–34. Hoboken: John Wiley & Sons, 2003.

Gross, Bertram, and Michael Springer. "New Goals for Social Information." *Annals of the American Academy of Political and Social Science* 388, no. 1 (1967): 208–18.

Hackney, James R. *Under Cover of Science.* Durham: Duke University Press, 2007.

Harcourt, Bernard E. "Reflecting on the Subject: A Critique of the Social Influence Conception of Deterrence, the Broken Windows Theory, and Order-Maintenance Policing New York Style." *Michigan Law Review* 97, no. 2 (1998): 291–389.

Harcourt, Bernard E. *Against Prediction: Profiling, Policing and Punishing in an Actuarial Age.* Chicago: University of Chicago Press, 2007.

Harman, Douglas. "The Bloc Grant: Readings from a First Experiment." *Public Administration Review* 30, no. 2 (1970): 141–53.

Hartung, Frank E. "A Critique of the Sociological Approach to Crime and Correction." *Law and Contemporary Problems* 23, no. 4 (1958): 703–34.

Healy, William. *The Individual Delinquent.* London: Little, Brown, 1915.

Herman, Ellen. *The Romance of American Psychology: Political Culture in the Age of Experts.* Berkeley: University of California Press, 1995.

Herrnstein, Richard J., and Charles Murray. *The Bell Curve: Intelligence and Class Structure in American Life.* New York: Free Press, 1994.

Hinton, Elizabeth. *From the War on Poverty to the War on Crime: The Making of Mass Incarceration in America.* Cambridge: Harvard University Press, 2016.

Hirschi, Travis, and Hanan Selvin. "False Criteria of Causality in Delinquency Research." *Social Problems* 13, no. 3 (1966): 254–68.

Hirschi, Travis, and Hanan Selvin. *Delinquency Research: An Appraisal of Analytic Method.* London: Transaction Publishers, 1967.

Hollin, Clive. *Psychology and Crime: An Introduction to Criminal Psychology.* London: Routledge, 1989.

Hollin, Clive. "Criminal Psychology." In *Oxford Handbook of Criminology*, edited by Mike McGuire, Rod Morgan, and Robert Reiner, 43–77. Oxford: Oxford University Press, 2012.

Jackson, John P., Jr. *Social Scientists for Social Justice: Making the Case against Segregation.* New York: New York University Press, 2001.

Morris Janowitz Collection. Special Collections Research Center, University of Chicago Library.

Jardini, David. *Thinking through the Cold War: RAND, National Security and Domestic Policy, 1945–1975.* Meadows Land: David Jardini.

Koheler, Johann. "Development and Fracture of a Discipline: Legacies of the School of Criminology at Berkeley." *Criminology* 53, no. 4 (2005): 513–44.

Laub, John H. "The Life Course of Criminology in the United States: The American Society of Criminology 2003 Presidential Address." *Criminology* 42, no. 1 (2004): 1–26.

Laub, John H., and Robert J. Sampson. "The Sutherland–Glueck Debate: On the Sociology of Criminological Knowledge." *American Journal of Sociology* 96, no. 6 (1991): 1402–40.

Leijins, Peter P. *International Conference on Doctoral-Level Education in Criminal Justice and Criminology.* College Park: Institute of Criminal Justice and Criminology, University of Maryland, 1977.

Lindesmith, Alfred, and Yale Levin. "The Lombrosian Myth in Criminology." *American Journal of Sociology* 42, no. 5 (1937): 653–71.

Mannheim, Hermann. "American Criminology: Impressions of an European Criminologist." *British Journal of Sociology* 5, no. 4 (1954): 293–308.

Marciano, Alain, and Steven G. Medema. "Disciplinary Collisions: Blum, Kalven, and the Economic Analysis of Accident Law at Chicago in the 1960s." In *Law and Economics as Interdisciplinary Practice*, edited by Magdalena Malecka and Peter Cserne, 53–75. New York: Routledge, 2020.

Marion, Nancy E. *A History of Federal Crime Control Initiatives, 1960–1993.* Westport: Praeger Publishers, 1994.

Marris, Peter, and Martin Rein. *Dilemmas of Social Reform: Poverty and Community Action in the United States.* Chicago: Aldine, 1973.

Matsueda, Ross. "The Current State of Differential Association Theory." *Crime and Delinquency* 34 (1988): 277–306.

Mccord, Joan, and William Mccord. "The Effects of Parental Role Model on Criminality." *Journal of Social Issues* 14, no. 3 (1958): 66–75.

Mccord, William. "Introduction." *Journal of Social Issues* 14, no. 3 (1958): 3–4.

Merton, Robert K. "Social Structure and Anomie." *American Sociological Review* 3, no. 5 (1938): 672–82.

Merton, Robert K. "Concluding Comments and an Example of Research." In *New Perspectives for Research on Juvenile Delinquency*, edited by Ellen Witmer and Ruth Kotinsky, 75–92. Washington, DC: US Department of Health, Education, and Welfare, 1956.

Michael, Jerome, and Mortimer, J. Adler. *Crime, Law, and Social Science.* New York: Harcourt, Brace & Co, 1933.

Miller, Walter B. "Lower Class Culture as Generating a Milieu of Gang Delinquency." *Journal of Social Issues* 14, no. 3 (1958): 5–19.

Morris, Albert. "The American Society of Criminology: A History, 1941–1974." *Criminology* 13, no. 2 (1975): 123–67.

Moynihan, Daniel Patrick. *The Negro Family: The Case for National Action.* Washington, DC: US Government Printing Office, 1965.

Moynihan, Daniel Patrick. *Maximum Feasible Misunderstanding.* New York: Free Press, 1969.

Newman, Donald J. "White-Collar Crime." *Law and Contemporary Problems* 23, no. 4 (1958): 735–53.

O'Connor, Alice. "The Ford Foundation and Philanthropic Activism in the 1960s." In *Philanthropic Foundations: New Scholarship, New Possibilities*, edited by Ellen Condliffe Lagemann, 169–94. Bloomington: Indiana University Press.

Orleans, Myron. "Criminal Justice, Sociology of." In *International Encyclopedia of the Social and Behavioral Sciences*, edited by James D. Wright, 214–18. New York: Elsevier, 2015.

Petersilia, Joan. "Policy Relevance and the Future of Criminology." In *Contemporary Masters in Criminology*, edited by Joan McCord and John H. Laub, 389–408. New York: Plenum Press, 1995.

Platt, Tony. "Prospects for a Radical Criminology in the United States." *Crime and Social Justice* 1 (1974): 2–10.

Posner, Richard A. *Economic Analysis of Law.* Boston: Little, Brown, 1973.

Posner, Richard A. "An Economic Theory of the Criminal Law." *Columbia Law Review* 85, no. 6 (1985): 1193–1231.

President's Commission on Law Enforcement and Administration of Justice. *The Challenge of Crime in a Free Society*. Washington, DC: US Government Printing Office, 1967.

Reiss, Albert. "Unraveling Juvenile Delinquency. II. An Appraisal of the Research Methods." *American Journal of Sociology* 57, no. 2 (1951): 115–20.

Reiss, Albert. "Putting Sociology into Policy." *Social Problems* 17, no. 3 (1970): 289–94.

Rottenberg, Simon. *The Economics of Crime and Punishment*. Washington, DC: American Enterprise Institute, 1973.

Sampson, Robert J. "Urban Black Violence: The Effect of Male Joblessness and Family Disruption." *American Journal of Sociology* 93, no. 2 (1987): 348–83.

Sampson, Robert J., and John H. Laub. *Crime in the Making*. Cambridge: Harvard University Press, 1995.

Savelsberg, Joachim, Lara Cleveland, and Ryan King. "Institutional Environments and Scholarly Work: American Criminology, 1951–1993." *Social Forces* 82, no. 4 (2004): 1275–1302.

Savitz, Leonard. "Review of *The Challenge of Crime in a Free Society*." *Social Force* 46, no. 2 (1967): 300–1.

Schuessler, Karl F. "Parole Prediction: Its History and Status." *The Journal of Criminal Law, Criminology, and Police Science* 45, no. 4 (1954): 425–31.

Schulman, Jay, Carol Brown, and Roger Kahn. "Report on the Russell Sage Foundation." *Critical Sociology* 2, no. 4 (1972): 2–34.

Shaw, Clifford, and Henry McKay. "Social Factors in Juvenile Delinquency: A Study of the Community, the Family, and the Gang in Relation to Delinquent Behavior." In *Report of the National Commission on Law Observance and Enforcement, Causes of Crime*. Vol. 2. Washington, DC: US Government Printing Office, 1929.

Short, James F. "Differential Association and Delinquency." *Social Problems* 4, no. 3 (1957): 233–39.

Short, James F., and Lorine A. Hughes. "Criminology, Criminologists, and the Sociological Enterprise." In *Sociology in America: A History*, edited by Craig Calhoun, 605–38. Chicago: University of Chicago Press, 2007.

Simon, Jonathan. *Governing Through Crime*. Oxford: Oxford University Press, 2007.

Skogan, Wesley G. "Review of *Surveying Crime*, by the National Research Council." *The Journal of Criminal Law and Criminology* 69, no. 1 (1978): 139–40.

Springer, Michael. "Social Indicators, Reports, and Accounts: Toward the Management of Society." *Annals of the American Academy of Political and Social Science* 388, no. 1 (1970): 1–13.

Steinmetz, George. "American Sociology before and after World War II: The (Temporary) Setting of a Disciplinary Field." In *Sociology in America: A History*, edited by Craig Calhoun, 314–66. Chicago: University of Chicago Press, 2007.

Sullivan, Richard F. "The Economics of Crime: Introduction to the Literature." *Crime and Delinquency* 19, no. 2 (1973): 138–49.

Sutherland, Edwin H. *Principles of Criminology*. New York: J. B. Lippincott Company, 1939.

Sutherland, Edwin H. "White-Collar Criminality." *American Sociological Review* 5, no. 1 (1940): 1–12.

Sykes, Gresham M., and David Matza. "Techniques of Neutralization." *American Sociological Review* 22, no. 6 (1957): 664–70.

Tappan, Paul. "Who Is the Criminal?" *American Sociological Review* 12, no. 1 (1947): 96–102.

Taylor, Ian, Paul Walton, and Jock Young, *The New Criminology: For a Social Study of Deviance*. London: Routledge & Kegan Paul, 1973.

Teixeira, Pedro. "A Portrait of the Economics of Education, 1960–1997." In *Toward a History of Applied Economics*, edited by Roger E. Backhouse and Jeff Biddle, 257–88. Durham: Duke University Press, 2000.

Tittle, Charles. "Punishment and Deterrence of Deviance." In *The Economics of Crime and Punishment*, edited by Simon Rottenberg, 85–102. Washington, DC: American Enterprise Institute.

Turk, Austin T. "Conflict and Criminality." *American Sociological Review* 31, no. 3 (1966): 338–52.

US Department of Health, Education, and Welfare. *Toward a Social Report*. Washington, DC: US Government Printing Office, 1969.

US National Commission on Law Observance and Enforcement. *Report on Criminal Statistics*. Washington, DC: US Government Printing Office, 1929.

US National Commission on Law Observance and Enforcement. *Report on the Causes of Crime*. Vol. 1. Washington, DC: US Government Printing Office, 1929.

Weaver, Vesla M. "Frontlash: Race and the Development of Punitive Crime Policy." *Studies in American Political Development* 21 (2007): 230–65.

Webb, Vincent J., and Dennis E. Hoffman. "Criminal Justice as an Academic Discipline: Costs and Benefits." *Journal of Criminal Justice* 6 (1978): 347–55.

Wilson, James Q. "A Reader's Guide to the Crime Commission's Report." *The Public Interest*, no. 9 (Fall 1967): 64–82.

Wilson, James Q. *Thinking about Crime*. Rev. ed. New York: Basic Books, 2013.

Wilson, James Q., and Richard, J. Herrnstein. *Crime and Human Nature: The Definitive Study of the Causes of Crime*. New York: Simon & Schuster, 1985.

Winant, Howard. "The Dark Side of the Force: One Hundred Years of the Sociology of Race." In *Sociology in America: A History*, edited by Craig Calhoun, 535–71. Chicago: University of Chicago Press, 2007.

Wolfgang, Marvin, and Franco Ferracuti. *The Subculture of Violence*. London: Routledge & Kegan Paul, 1967.

Wolfgang, Marvin, Robert Figlio, and Thorsten Sellin. *Delinquency in a Birth Cohort*. Chicago: University of Chicago Press, 1972.

8

Addiction

Nancy D. Campbell

American appetites for morphine were so fully established during the nineteenth century that historian David F. Musto termed such use the "American disease."[1] Although the term "addiction" was not used in the United States until the turn of the twentieth century,[2] nonmedical traffic in opium, coca, and morphine was soon outlawed by the Harrison Act (1914), with heroin following in 1924. Legal distinctions inscribed by law and policy were rarely clear in practice. Legitimate medical use was policed; law enforcement effectively criminalized those prescribing or using "narcotics."[3] Prosecutions that tested the constitutionality of the Harrison Act had the "immediate effect [of driving] tens of thousands of addicts to underworld connections."[4] Denizens of urban vice districts were among the first to sniff heroin; injection was not central to the "opium problem" (as it was called in the 1920s) until after World War II.[5] Stigmatizing terms such as "addicts," "dope fiends," or "junkies" applied to users of illicit narcotics; by the late 1920s, more than one-third of federal prisoners were incarcerated on drug charges.[6] In 1929, the US Congress embarked on a "New Deal for the Drug Addict," creating two large Narcotic Farms designed to rehabilitate

---

[1] Musto, *American Disease*.
[2] Courtwright, *Dark Paradise*, x–xi. Etymologically speaking, the term "addiction" is an "auto-antonym" that encompasses both positive desires and negative connotations and consequences. See Rosenthal and Faris, "Etymology and Early History."
[3] Enforcement was uneven; some physicians quietly continued maintaining patients on morphine until legal questions were settled; see Herzberg, "Entitled to Addiction?"
[4] Maurer and Vogel, *Narcotics and Narcotic Addiction*, 7.
[5] Terry and Pellens, *Opium Problem*; see also Keire, "Dope Fiends and Degenerates."
[6] Lindesmith, "Dope Fiend Mythology." Although the sociologist Alfred R. Lindesmith dismantled the mythic status of the "dope fiend," the term was later rehabilitated as a social identity; see Waldorf, *Careers in Dope*.

addicts through fresh air and hard work, vocational training, and science.[7] Congress expressed great faith that scientists from the US Public Health Service would find a cure for addiction. Their narrowly defined science left little room for a social science of "addiction" to take root.

Mandated to search for a cure, the small laboratory that opened in 1935 at the Lexington, Kentucky, Narcotic Farm became part of the National Institute of Mental Health (NIMH) in 1948 and was formally named the Addiction Research Center (ARC). Social science entered the study of addiction via NIMH, which took a "scattershot" approach to funding natural as well as social and psychological sciences for the next two decades (see Chapter 9: Mental Illness). However, the ARC's experimental studies dominated the field until the late 1960s, when the federal research apparatus was reorganized in keeping with the Nixon administration's consolidation into separate agencies for research, treatment, and services in mental health, alcohol abuse and alcoholism, and drug abuse. In 1975, the ARC became the intramural research branch of the National Institute on Drug Abuse (NIDA), the federal agency that funds large-scale social surveys and research ranging from behavioral to epidemiological to historical to neurophysiological to ethnographic. A shifting succession of diverse disciplines has comprised addiction research, each competing to define addiction on their terms. This chapter tells the story of the succession of social sciences concerned with addiction, as historically and culturally specific moments of "becoming."

Since the 1990s, NIDA's portfolio has narrowed to neuroscience, genetics, and translational clinical applications, with proportionate disinvestment in social science. However, economics in the form of services evaluation and research on treatment modalities such as contingency management – a practical outgrowth of behavioral or neuro-economics – expanded the field of addiction treatment research in the late twentieth century. Other social sciences were sidelined, as neuroscience – the least "social" of the many disciplinary claimants to addiction – rose to prominence in the 1990s.

Treated as a crime from 1914 on, the term "addiction" was initially reserved for those considered *most* deviant. Just as "inebriety" applied only to problematic alcohol use, "addiction" was reserved for those determined by the social norms of their period to be using narcotics in problematic ways (including committing crimes to service drug habits). The term was typically applied to those using illegal opiates (e.g., opium, morphine, and heroin). "Addiction" has fallen in and out of fashion, passing through a dizzying array of synonyms: the "opium problem" in the 1920s; "narcotics

[7] Campbell, "A New Deal for the Drug Addict" and Campbell, Olsen, and Walden, *Narcotic Farm.*

addiction" from the 1930s through the 1950s; "drug dependence" from the mid-1960s to the 1970s; "drug abuse" from the 1970s on; as well as "chemical dependence," "substance use disorder," and "behavioral addictions."[8]

Each new term brought these jurisdictional disputes to new expert communities, cultures of consumption, and attempts to supplant stigma with science.[9] New substances came to the forefront in each moment of "becoming." Not until the late twentieth century was there consensus that cocaine was addictive; nor was the term "addiction" applied to nonsubstance-related behaviors such as eating, exercise, or gambling until recently.[10] This chapter charts interactions between a succession of contending natural and social sciences, each constructing an always tenuous but overlapping cultural authority over this social problem. New bids to redefine "addiction" make new claims of problem ownership. Sometimes new contenders displaced former contenders almost completely, as when neuropharmacology or biological psychiatry displaced psychoanalysis, or when behavioral approaches displaced those based in older experimental modes. More often a congeries of disunified social, natural, and psychological sciences coexisted in fractious multiplicity. Each subsection takes up these moments.

As new entrants came to the social sciences of "addiction" – sociology, social psychology, experimental and clinical psychology, psychopathology, neurophysiology, behavioral pharmacology, epidemiology, ethnography, and, ultimately, economics and neuroscience – addiction became a different kind of social problem. This was a contentious and interactive process, during which drugs and their users became meaningful objects and subjects of knowledge in both material and symbolic ways. For those studying postwar social problems, addiction provides a microcosm for studying social change in science, policy, and politics. Once constituted as a social problem, struggles for cultural authority over addiction ensued between qualitative and quantitative sociologists; cultural anthropologists; social psychologists, psychiatrists, social workers, and other clinicians; and law, legal studies,

---

[8] As a historian of science and medicine who specializes in addiction research and treatment, I typically adopt the terms used within the epistemic communities I study. Thus, my own terms change with the times.

[9] This dynamic remains evident in attempts to dislodge drug use from categorically pejorative moral judgments through neuroscientific and metabolic constructions of addiction as a "chronic relapsing brain disorder." See Campbell, *Discovering Addiction*.

[10] The high-water mark for the possibility of a research emphasis on controlled use came in 1977, when the National Research Council convened an extremely multidisciplinary group, including one economist, Thomas Schelling, which was made to craft research agendas. See National Research Council, *Common Processes in Habitual Substance Use*.

"police science," and law enforcement. Each of these disunified sciences has contributed knowledge about addiction, following the contours of public policy responsive to shifts in drug-using populations and patterns. Yet, the least social among these sciences – neuroscience – ultimately won out.

8.1 Becoming Social Learners: From Early Twentieth Century "Dope Fiends" to the Psychopathology of the 1930s

The early twentieth-century idea that addiction was rooted in individual failings predominated when psychiatrist Lawrence C. Kolb developed the first diagnostic criteria. Kolb's criteria, with their focus on psychopathology, were intended to delink addiction from crime.[11] The first chief medical officer of the Lexington Narcotics Farm, Kolb operated this 1,500-bed hybrid clinical-penal facility from 1935 up to World War II. The modal opiate addict admitted to the facility prior to the war was a white, male, aged over forty-five, unemployed "dope fiend." Studying such individuals was difficult; few social scientists found ways to access and explore the topic. Only two social science dissertations on opiate addiction were produced in the 1930s, both emerging from the University of Chicago Department of Sociology. Criminologist Edwin Sutherland directed Bingham Dai's 1933 dissertation, published in Shanghai under the title *Opiate Addiction in Chicago* (1937).[12] Fellow doctoral student Alfred R. Lindesmith obtained permission to interview inmates of the Lexington Narcotics Farm and Fort Leavenworth Prison (then the country's largest). Lindesmith's permission was revoked "on the grounds that what [he] proposed to do was already being done by their personnel."[13] Both investigators interviewed and observed local opiate addicts navigating social contexts in Chicago, where notions of psychopathology or mental hygiene did not seem salient as prevailing causes of addiction.

---

[11] Kolb, "Drug Addiction in Its Relation"; Kolb, "Types and Characteristics of Drug Addicts" and Kolb, "Pleasure and Deterioration from Narcotic Addiction." See also Acker, *Creating the American Junkie* and Acker, "Addiction and the Laboratory."

[12] Dai, *Opium Addiction in Chicago*. Dai veered toward studying personality rather than sociology, spending his later career teaching at Duke medical school. His papers are archived at the Belk Library at Appalachian State University: www.collections.library.appstate.edu/findingaids/rb8007

[13] See Lindesmith, *Addiction and Opiates*, a revised edition of *Opiate Addiction*, which was in turn based on his 1937 dissertation, "The Nature of Opiate Addiction." Quotations concerning the revocation of permission come from the *Addiction and Opiates* volume, 6.

Lindesmith, in particular, presented a social scientific account of how opiate users came to understand themselves as getting "high" or "hooked," arguing that addiction involved social learning.[14] Like Kolb, he opposed reducing addiction to crime; unlike Kolb and the evolving federal addiction research apparatus, he did not find explanatory power in the concept of psychopathology. Lindesmith became an ardent critic of US drug policy during the criminalization of the 1950s, when mandatory minimum sentences were first imposed by the Boggs Act in 1951.[15] Lindesmith himself was subjected to career-long repression at the hands of Harry J. Anslinger's Federal Bureau of Narcotics (FBN).[16] Documenting the *presence*, rather than absence, of social norms among opiate addicts, Lindesmith and other Chicago-trained sociologists used their city as a social laboratory – and as a platform from which to criticize contemporary drug policy reform. They excoriated older concepts such as Durkheim's *anomie*, the idea that society must regulate insatiable appetites or risk unleashing a state of normlessness. Durkheim had portrayed the driving force of human insatiability in terms akin to the structure of addiction: "The more one has, the more one wants, since satisfactions received only stimulate instead of filling needs."[17] Indebted to Durkheim's concept, Robert K. Merton's 1938 articulation of social strain theory, "Social Structure and Anomie," has been lauded as "the most influential single formulation in the sociology of deviance."[18] Merton argued that modern society exerted control over basic drives rooted in biology. "Nonconformity" was a retreat from modernity but also an adaptation to structural limitations. Merton classified addicts as "retreatist," arguing that social structures pressured them to reject commonly accepted cultural goals and institutionalized means for obtaining them. He grouped addicts along with a motley crew of "true 'aliens'": "psychotics, psychoneurotics, chronic autists, pariahs, outcasts, vagrants, vagabonds, tramps, chronic drunkards, and drug addicts."[19] Strain theory infused mid–twentieth-century social science, accompanied

---

[14] This idea was key to a line of sociological investigation continued later by Howard S. Becker's dissertation and article "Becoming a Marihuana User," which formed the core of his 1963 book *Outsiders*.
[15] Sentences increased in 1956 after the Senate's Illicit Narcotics Traffic hearings (known as the Daniel Hearings), which were televised from seven US cities in 1955–1956.
[16] Keys and Galliher, *Confronting the Drug Control Establishment*; McWilliams, *The Protectors*; and Valentine, *Strength of the Wolf*.
[17] Durkheim, *Suicide*, 248.
[18] Quoted in Short, "Criminology, Criminologists, and the Sociological Enterprise," 615.
[19] Merton, "Social Structure and Anomie," 677.

by the more psychiatric register of maladaptation and maladjustment – the two dominant lexicons for discussing drug addiction as a social problem. Writing against Merton's influential thesis that drug addicts, chronic drunkards, and mentally disabled persons rejected social conventions, Lindesmith argued that these persons had their own social norms. Chicago sociologists following Lindesmith – notably Howard S. Becker after World War II – sought to suspend moral judgment in extending notions of commitment to the "moral careers" and actual activities of their addict-subjects.[20] Drawing on conceptual and practical insights drawn from sociology of work and the professions to the social science of addiction, they criticized the medicalization of addiction and the term "addict," substituting "drug user" instead.[21] The sociological documentation of social norms among opiate addicts was essential to destigmatize language and recognize the work of belief, commitment, and interpretation occurring within the context of drug-using social worlds. This "second," postwar Chicago School (as described later) conflicted sharply with postwar ARC researchers such as Abraham Wikler and Harris Isbell, who studied pharmacological effects in "postaddicts," creating scales, instruments, and methods by which to make "subjective" effects discernible in "objective" terms.[22] Much acrimony from these conflicts was directed toward Lindesmith, before and after the war.[23] Dominated by neurophysiologists and pharmacologists hostile to social science, the ARC joined forces with the FBN, which in turn supplied scientists with seized and confiscated drugs for laboratory experiments. Both official entities played authoritative roles in global and domestic drug control; the ARC supplied clinical data for the World Health Organization/ United Nations expert committees involved in global drug control prior to the 1970s.[24] Both bodies were far more influential than one academic sociology professor – yet FBN agents visited Lindesmith's University of Indiana office and threatened his employment and reputation.[25]

[20] Lindesmith, *Opiate Addiction*, 5; quoted in Becker, *Tricks of the Trade*, 197. See also Becker, "Notes on the Concept of Commitment," which imports the notion of "side bets" from economist Schelling, "Essay on Bargaining," addressed later in the chapter.
[21] On the importance of work to Chicago-style sociology, see Denzin, *Symbolic Interactionism and Cultural Studies*, 8; Hughes, *Men and Their Work*; and Frazier, *Black Bourgeoisie*.
[22] Fine, *A Second Chicago School?*
[23] Keys and Galliher, *Confronting the Drug Control Establishment*, 21.
[24] Musto and Korsmeyer, *Quest for Drug Control*.
[25] Key and Galliher. As a self-declared partisan, Lindesmith had difficulty getting federal funding, although others were funded to test if his theories could be "applied." See McAuliffe and Gordon, "Test of Lindesmith's Theory of Addiction."

Without mention of his unit's revocation of Lindesmith's access, ARC Research Director Harris Isbell dismissed Lindesmith's 1947 *Opiate Addiction*:

> This book is based on information which the author obtained by interviewing 60 to 70 morphine addicts in the course of a sociologic study of drug addiction which was carried out fifteen years ago. The writer has been publishing articles on drug addiction based on this same material since that time. A perusal of this book forces one to the conclusion that the author has, in large part, accepted the views of the confirmed addicts who formed his case material as being the correct ones concerning addiction.[26]

Mischaracterizing Lindesmith as downplaying the "seriousness of the narcotic situation," casting treatment as "hopeless," and relying on subjects from the "fringes of the underworld," Isbell took special aim at Lindesmith's inductive techniques. Interviews of active users came in for abuse not least because Lindesmith had paid his informants by "buying them a meal in a cheap restaurant or bar, or by giving them fifty cents or a dollar after an interview."[27] To Isbell, modern addiction research could *only* be accomplished in the laboratory.

8.2 Becoming "Juvenile Delinquents": The post–World War II Spike in Heroin Use

In 1948, the federal mental health research and services apparatus was consolidated as the NIMH. In these years – the late 1940s through the mid-1950s – young men were recruited into heroin use in growing numbers, as heroin and the technological means to inject it became widely available in urban drug markets. Recruited to narcotics addiction in their teens or early twenties, these "juvenile delinquents" engaged in activities such as smoking, drinking, reading comic books, and premarital sex. Expert communities formed in law, medicine, social work, and the social and natural sciences in order to respond. Most social studies of narcotic addiction from this period involved subjects who were court-mandated to institutionalized treatment, mutual aid, or professional expertise. New drugs, populations, and modes of expertise arose in the addiction arena. The changing thought styles – and the material and social practices and figures with which they were associated – passed through rhetorical registers ranging from early psychoanalytic, psychiatric, physiological, and pharmacological concepts to what might be viewed as the sociological "overturning" of such explanations.[28]

---

[26] Isbell, "Review of *Opiate Addiction*," 1342.
[27] Lindesmith, *Addiction and Opiates*, 6.
[28] Becker, *Outsiders*, 76–78 and Courtwright, *Dark Paradise*.

Postwar addiction social science was caught in a polarized debate over whether addiction's etiology lay in psychopathology and personality maladjustment, or in sociological causes such as social strain, anomie, deprivation, and interactions between "objective environment," family formation, and individual or personal characteristics. Sociologist John A. Clausen, chief of the NIMH Laboratory of Socio-environmental Studies, captured the dueling views:[29] "Narcotics addiction is both a psychophysiological state and a social category," he wrote in a 1957 paper. "It is the product of a behavior learned in a social context and cannot be adequately understood apart from that context."[30] Social scientists found in addiction a problematic concept and lexicon tailor-made for contention over what forms of knowledge production would prevail as authoritative – and what kinds of expertise were thus needed to address the national crisis. The construction of narcotics addiction as juvenile delinquency attracted researchers interested in how larger social and demographic processes of change, legal definitions, and "stereotypes of the addict" shaped post–World War II heroin addiction. Researchers understood the need for interdisciplinary approaches; sociologists, psychologists, social workers, and social psychologists jockeyed for problem ownership. The "troubled individual" was seen as vulnerable to heroin addiction in the mid–twentieth century. Unfit for democratic citizenship, heroin addicts were cast as "enemies within," threatening the postwar nation with abnormal appetites and anomie.

Juvenile delinquency was positioned as both cause and consequence of narcotic addiction, lending credence to those who saw addiction as a crime and thus as a matter of policing and law enforcement. This view sharpened and became dominant during the 1950s through a series of congressional hearings on the "Illicit Drug Traffic"; however, it was also contested by a cadre of professionals who saw addiction as a disease that needed to be treated as a public health problem. The latter group made their views known through the American Bar and American Medical Associations.[31] Thus, drug addiction became intensely politicized on the national stage during a decade when policy inclined toward criminalization

---

[29] At inception, NIMH had only two working laboratories: the Addiction Research Center in Lexington, Kentucky, and the Laboratory of Socio-Environmental Studies headed by Clausen. Trained as a sociologist at the University of Chicago, Clausen published *Sociology and the Field of Mental Health* in 1956 and thus contributed to the growing field of psychiatric epidemiology.

[30] Clausen, "Social and Psychological Factors," 34.

[31] American Bar Association/American Medical Association, *Drug Addiction: Crime or Disease?* The episode is recounted in Campbell, *Using Women*.

more than ever before. Law enforcement's failure to contain addiction through the mandatory sentencing minimums of the 1950s created openings for the demographically inclined social scientific effort that soon emerged at the ARC. Still the world's sole laboratory dedicated to studying addiction, the ARC had drifted away from locating addiction's etiology in psychopathology, and toward underlying neurophysiological aspects of drug effects. Not until 1962 did the ARC hire *any* social scientists.

A small Social Sciences Division opened under the leadership of John O'Donnell, who became a linchpin of the more mainstream sociological and demographic studies of narcotic addiction and treatment evaluation – at far remove from Lindesmith's critical approach.[32] This in-house sociology produced knowledge for the sake of governing drug users, controlling drug traffic, and administering drug treatment efficiently and effectively. ARC social scientists supplied information necessary for governance, not only of the institution within which they were housed, but also with follow-up studies useful to those administering and regulating carceral institutions. Social science was tolerated, but only in a subordinate role within an ecological niche dominated by neurophysiology and behavioral science. ARC researcher Abraham Wikler was a case in point – an experimental researcher who studied how social signals or environmental cues could "trigger" physiologically "strong urges to use" when subjects who had not used narcotics for at least six months returned to neighborhoods where their habits had once flourished.[33] Despite his recognition of the importance of social cues in precipitating relapse, Wikler disdained the methods, analyses, and conclusions of Lindesmith-style sociology, turning instead to behavioral theories of classical and operant conditioning for explanations of this phenomenon.

For their part, the few outside social scientists studying addiction rarely cited the scientific findings of ARC investigators, "for fear that the opinions expressed would introduce an initial and perhaps decisive bias into the investigation."[34] Anthropologists and sociologists conducting observational and ethnographic studies via interviews and careful follow-ups with active users yielded conclusions markedly different from the neurophysiological, behavioral, and experimental orthodoxy produced at the ARC. Premised on Lindesmith's idea that interactive and symbolic processes of social

---

[32] Absorbed into the intramural research program of the National Institute on Drug Abuse (NIDA) in the late 1970s, the ARC moved to the medical campus of the Johns Hopkins University in Baltimore, Maryland.
[33] Wikler, "Conditioning Factors in Opiate Addiction."
[34] Lindesmith, *Addiction and Opiates*, 7.

learning were involved in producing addiction, he and his allies entered into "historically specific academic and political conflicts that pitted qualitative sociologists against quantitative sociologists, the fledgling discipline of sociology against medicine, psychiatry, and psychology, and advocates of therapy for addicts against those who would simply punish them."[35] Mutual antagonisms were territorial struggles for jurisdiction, resources, and, above all, cultural authority over who would become privileged interpreters of the phenomenology of visceral experiences of drug effects. Neurophysiologists of addiction characterized subjective effects such as euphoria, tolerance, dysphoria, and withdrawal in unassailably scientific terms, attempting to solve perennial puzzles: Why do some individuals exposed to drug use become addicted and others do not? Why are drug effects subject to such a wide range of individual variation?[36] Was juvenile delinquency only for the "abnormal" or "psychopathological" individual, the "troubled teen"? ARC scientists believed that the degree of drug exposure better predicted dependence than did psychological abnormality or sociological deprivation, shearing off both from "physical" or "neurophysiological" dependence. By the mid-1960s, they had redefined "drug dependence" as a matter of drugs – rather than psyche or society. They bitterly defended their claims, disputing what they perceived, improbably, as the dominance of sociological approaches.

Addiction was a cognitive, rational, and interpretive process, according to Lindesmith, whose social learning framework remained a prominent sociological theory of addiction, much to the chagrin of the neurophysiologists.[37] To Lindesmith, the social process commenced with initial drug exposure, during which individuals might use opiates but not interpret themselves as addicts. But an interpretive process ensued when they stopped using opiates, suffered flu-like symptoms, and were either told by others or consciously recognized withdrawal distress as such. Only after that process of becoming – of internalized social recognition – did individuals act or identify as addicts, on Lindesmith's view.

With evident dissatisfaction, the nation's recently retired leading authority of narcotic addiction, Lawrence Kolb, summarized Lindesmith's position: "the main theme of his story is that an addict is not an addict unless he knows it."[38] As Kolb detected, sociological theories posed a challenge to

[35] Weinberg, "Lindesmith on Addiction," 156.
[36] Today's explanations for this long-observed phenomenon include epigenetic vulnerability and pharmacogenetics, rather than older explanations such as "addictive personality," "proneness," or "susceptibility."
[37] Lindesmith, *Opiate Addiction*, 5; quoted in Becker, *Tricks of the Trade*, 197.
[38] Correspondence to Victor Vogel, quoted in Acker, *Creating the American Junkie*, 257n54.

the body of work on psychiatric, psychological, and physiological aspects of addiction. Antipathy between the competing models was cast in explicitly political terms during the 1950s, but was, at base, a disagreement over what counted as knowledge and who counted as knowledge producers.

ARC researchers scorned Lindesmith's theory that addiction was attributable to the "individual reaction[s] to the withdrawal symptoms which occur when the drug effects are beginning to wear off."[39] They suggested he become better acquainted with the Lexington facility, apparently forgetting their prior denial of access.[40] Wikler characterized addiction as the result of an "interdependency of subjective and physiologic processes in the human organism."[41] Interestingly for a scientist also a trained analyst, Wikler rarely mentioned psychoanalysis in his published works.[42] However, he did cite Sandor Rado and chided Lindesmith for his failure to appreciate psychodynamics, his naïveté about Kolb's classification system, and for his "post hoc reasoning."[43] But Wikler particularly disdained Lindesmith's account of the linguistic aspects of the social learning process, by which people came to "label" themselves addicts – aspects central to what later became known as labeling theory and, in a wider frame, symbolic interactionism. Wikler treated sociological reasoning as an incursion onto the terrain of psychoanalysis, psychodynamics, and, above all, neurophysiology.

8.3 Becoming a Marijuana User: The Sociology of Deviance in the 1950s and 1960s

What about nonopiates? In the early 1950s, Howard S. Becker, with Lindesmith in mind, took up the study of an apparently nonaddictive substance, marijuana. Becker was a Chicago sociology graduate student who had worked as a jazz musician as he came of age in Chicago during the war. He knew, first- and second-hand, the familiar experience of smoking marijuana without getting high – an experience that shaped his 1951 dissertation and subsequent article, "Becoming a Marihuana User," and,

---

[39] Lindesmith, *Opiate Addiction*, 87.
[40] Wikler, "Review of *Opiate Addiction*."
[41] Wikler, "Review of *Opiate Addiction*," 74.
[42] Long forgotten psychoanalytic theories of addiction were hotly debated in the early twentieth century; see Campbell, "Conceptual Migration from 'Intoxication of Desire' to 'Disease of Democracy.'"
[43] There was some basis for this; Lindesmith, according to Keys and Galliher, "collected much of his data without a firm idea of his method." Keys and Galliher, *Confronting the Drug Control Establishment*, 53.

eventually, his 1963 book *Outsiders: Studies in the Sociology of Deviance.*[44] Becker's insight was that drug users engaged in a line of activity amounting to a "career," albeit a "deviant" one – an insight that remained fruitful for decades. Like Lindesmith, Becker became a public intellectual, speaking about drug use on the campus lecture circuit in the 1960s; attending the Kennedy administration's 1962 White House conference on drug abuse; and publishing papers on marijuana and LSD. Becker described himself as studying "how people learn to interpret [ambiguous] inner sensations."[45] He interacted with other sociologists to build up commitments to certain "lines of activity" or "lines of behavior" that were later named "labeling theory" and "symbolic interactionism."[46]

Becker was impressed, in methodological terms, with Lindesmith's use of "analytic induction," because the approach centered perspectives held by research subjects rather than by researchers.[47] Paired with ethnographic techniques and labeling theory, analytic induction enabled, in Becker's later description, "real knowledge of the process of addiction or the world of addicts."[48] Becker, in his own work, invoked the concepts of the "moral entrepreneur" and the "career," a sequence of movements between social positions, contingencies, and the "commitments" that bind interests to behaviors.[49] Conventional people, in Becker's account, become committed to conventional norms and institutions; deviants have little stake in such conventional codes of conduct.[50] When people used narcotics or marijuana, "illegitimate routines" and deviant identifications became their "controlling" or "master" social status. Reversals of status, on this view, were rare once career trajectories had moved toward deviance.

Shifting away from explanations of addiction rooted in psychopathology and neurophysiology, symbolic interactionists – as the broad approach

[44] Becker, "Becoming a Marihuana User." As I was writing this chapter, Becker generously shared his draft introduction and conclusion for a new edition of *Outsiders*. In "Why I Deserve No Credit" (for marijuana policy reform), Becker considers the broader social contexts in which these changes have taken place. It is to him that I dedicate this chapter, and to whom I owe the inspiration to divide the chapter into separate sections on the trajectory of "becoming" represented by each of the social sciences of addiction.
[45] Author's interview with Howard Becker, January 4, 2005.
[46] Becker, *Outsiders*, 27.
[47] Acker, *Creating the American Junkie* and Becker, *Tricks of the Trade*, 197, 204. The methodology can be traced to the five volumes of W. I. Thomas and Florian Znaniecki in *The Polish Peasant in Europe and America*. On Lindesmith's formative contribution to symbolic interactionism, see Keys and Galliher, *Confronting the Drug Control Establishment*, 50.
[48] Becker, *Tricks of the Trade*, 200.
[49] Becker, "Becoming a Marihuana User" and Becker, *Outsiders*, 24, 27.
[50] Becker, *Outsiders*, 17, 20.

would come to be known by the late 1960s – were critical of the notion
of juvenile delinquency and sought to produce "social" rather than
"individual" explanations. Chicago-trained sociologist Harold Finestone's
1957 study "Cats, Kicks, and Color" was one of a handful of ethnographic
treatments of 1950s heroin use and dealing in an interactionist key. "Cats,"
Finestone wrote, were "young colored drug users" who could not conform
to prevailing opportunity structures and instead engaged in a "form of
fantasy" that was "an extreme form of the adolescent 'youth culture.'"[51]
Membership of drug-using subcultures, on Finestone's view, was driven
by desire to reduce frustration caused by isolation. Embracing a "dead-end
type adjustment," the cat's commitments imparted social status, identity,
style, and an ethical code in subdominant social worlds.

Chicago sociologists were among the few who charted such social worlds.
Marshal B. Ray wrote a 1958 master's thesis on "Cure and Relapse among
Heroin Addicts": "The social world of addiction," he wrote, "contains a loose
system of organizational and cultural elements, including a special language
or argot, certain artifacts, a commodity market and pricing system, a system
of stratification, and ethical codes. The addict's commitment to these values
gives him a status and an identity."[52] Abstinence was a barrier to both status
and identity, because, in Ray's terms, "addict[s] attempt to enact a new
social reality."[53] By closing the gap between self-perception and external
definition, the addict enacted a symbolic process of "becoming," worked
out through language, interpretation, and enactment. This process enabled
the person to differentiate between the symbolic meanings and activities
of the social world of the "addict," and those occurring in the social world
of nonaddicts (referred to as "square" or "straight" in the parlance of the
time). Symbolic interactionist sociology, and labeling theory in particular,
were tailor-made for studying drug-using social worlds, working out
theories of social learning, methods of analytic induction, and shoring up
the conceptual framework of symbolic interaction as a form of sociological
analysis.[54] Beyond Chicago and the narcotic farms in Lexington and Fort
Worth, Texas, another important laboratory for social scientists had
emerged: New York City.

---

[51] Finestone, "Cats, Kicks, and Color," 3, 10, 12.
[52] Quoted in Becker, *Outsiders*, 164.
[53] Quoted in Becker, *Outsiders*, 175–76.
[54] See Clarke, "Controversy and the Development"; Fujimura, "On Methods, Ontologies,
and Representation in the Sociology of Science"; Star, "Sociology of the Invisible"; Star,
"Listening for Connections"; and Strauss, "Discovering New Theory."

8.4 Becoming Social-Psychological: *The Road to H* in 1950s New York

Long the epicenter of the illicit drug trade in the United States, New York was viewed by anthropologists, sociologists, and social psychologists as an urban laboratory for studying deviant subcultures. From 1949 to 1954, NIMH funded a neighborhood-level social-psychological study of heroin addiction in the city's five boroughs, headquartered at New York University.[55] When social psychologist Isidor Chein – director of NYU's Research Center on Human Relations and coauthor of the famous US Supreme Court *amicus curiae* brief in *Brown v. Board of Education* – undertook to study narcotic addiction, he recognized that he knew little about the subject. The NYU team turned to experimental psychologist and psychometrician Conan Kornetsky, who had recently relocated from living onsite at the Lexington Narcotics Farm while completing a doctorate at the University of Kentucky. Published as *The Road to H* (1964), the resulting study relied on psychometrics and a proto-epidemiological mapping of the incidence of heroin use at the neighborhood, household, and individual levels in the three boroughs in which it was concentrated. In addition, *The Road to H* provided career-long accounts of heroin users, beginning with family configuration, parenting style, and psychosexual development; characterizing their initiation into heroin use primarily by peers; and tracing the treatment experiences and in-hospital behaviors of heroin users recruited to the habit in the postwar period.

The NYU team avoided using the term "addict," because they found that occasional users were often included in the juvenile drug treatment program from which they recruited subjects. Defining addiction "in the Lindesmith sense," Chein noted that "a person does not become an addict in the true sense of the word until he has experienced withdrawal symptoms, or at least anticipates withdrawal; it is only then that his style of life becomes adjusted to the fact of his dependence."[56] The NYU researchers emphasized that social and psychological context, attitudes and beliefs, and cultural variations together shaped drug-using "style[s] of life" in ways that required a more "social" psychology rather than a narrowly "scientific" one. "It is not merely the scientific layman who fails to make the necessary distinctions," Chein wrote. "The scientific researchers have also not made them, not exclusively because of a lack of sophistication, but also because

---

[55] Chein et al., *The Road to H*.
[56] Chein, "Status of Sociological and Social Psychological Knowledge," 148.

of the practical exigencies of the circumstances under which they must do their research."[57]

Social researchers, Chein's team included, cited the drug user's social world to explain how mistrust, "hopelessness and futility," denial of dignity, and social dislocation led to rejection of conventional social norms for "tragically real" reasons.[58] Social psychologists like Chein adopted epidemiological approaches to map pathways into heroin use; to foreground structural determinants such as family configurations where fathers were absent and mothers dominant; to draw attention to degrees of neighborhood-level social organization, socioeconomic status, and status deprivation; and to locate personality factors indicating maladjustment to modernity. Caught up in the national furor over juvenile delinquency, social psychologists furnished explanations such as barriers to economic opportunity, differential opportunity structures,[59] delinquent subcultures,[60] and "malignant familial environments."[61]

Psychologist Charles Winick, for example, conducted studies of physicians addicted to narcotics, who were not, given their status, considered "deviant." Yet, addiction presented an occupational hazard to them, as for jazz musicians, who Winick also studied.[62] His works were regularly cited in sociological, anthropological, and psychiatric circles, most notably his suggestion that, as addicted persons became older, they "matured out" of the drug-using life.[63]

8.5 Becoming Epidemiological in the 1970s

Heroin use was so widespread by the 1970s that emphasis on individual pathology and personality maladjustment was considered impractical in policy circles.[64] As drug use widened beyond the racial-ethnic formations and class base of the 1950s, social scientists were called upon to testify in policy arenas such as White House conferences and Congressional hearings. In these contexts, epidemiological and statistical reasoning became a shared currency, resting on the analogy between addiction and contagious disease.

---

[57] Chein, "Status of Sociological and Social Psychological Knowledge," 151.
[58] Chein, "Status of Sociological and Social Psychological Knowledge," 158.
[59] Cloward and Ohlin, *Delinquency and Opportunity*.
[60] Cohen, *Delinquent Boys*.
[61] Chein et al., *The Road to H*.
[62] Winick, "Use of Drugs by Jazz Musicians."
[63] Winick, "Maturing Out of Narcotic Addiction."
[64] Hughes et al., "Natural History of a Heroin Epidemic," 1000.

As the 1960s revealed new drug use patterns, the basic terms of epidemiology began to be applied to the study of addiction, renamed "drug abuse" in this era. The 1966 Narcotic Addict Rehabilitation Act (NARA) required treatment to be provided in all communities from which addicted persons came. As this decentralization of drug treatment occurred, the ARC Social Science Section conducted demographic studies of admissions to both federal narcotic farms, along with longitudinal follow-ups on patients residing in Kentucky,[65] Puerto Rico,[66] and New York City.[67] ARC researchers John Ball and Carl D. Chambers, in their 1970 book *The Epidemiology of Opiate Addiction in the United States*, made the case for community-based aftercare.

"Civil commitment" was the policy motor of a newly decentralized addiction treatment system underwritten by federal contracts with treatment providers, such as the Salvation Army, faith-based organizations, and private clinics. The NARA legislation effectively meant that drug treatment had to be provided in every small city or town from which a drug addict hailed. Civil commitment and methadone maintenance hit New York City at more or less the same time. The standalone outpatient methadone clinic system (a product of regulatory compromise between federal agencies later in the 1970s) was built upon the post-NARA decentralized infrastructure of the late 1960s. Responsibility for drug treatment became a matter of state oversight, even as the federal government maintained primary responsibility for research. States' needs to establish treatment effectiveness required, however, enlisting social scientists to evaluate new treatment modalities, including the experimental methadone maintenance programs springing up in US cities.

In the new "epidemic" climate, social scientists studied the postwar spike in heroin use, reframing that surge as an explicitly epidemiological problem. In their 1972 study "Natural History of a Heroin Epidemic," Patrick Hughes and coauthors showed that the incidence and prevalence of heroin addiction "followed the course of contagious diseases, fluctuating from periods of epidemic spread on the one hand to relatively quiescent periods on the other."[68] Their study emerged from a multimodality treatment program directed by physician and neuropharmacologist Jerome H. Jaffe, who was appointed head of the Nixon White House's Special Action Office for Drug Abuse Prevention (SAODAP) in 1971. The vestiges of that office became the NIDA.

[65] O'Donnell, *Narcotic Addicts in Kentucky.*
[66] Zahn and Ball, "Factors Related to Cure of Opiate Addict."
[67] Vaillant, "Twelve-Year Follow-up of New York Narcotic Addicts," I–IV.
[68] Hughes et al., "Natural History of a Heroin Epidemic."

Epidemiological understandings of addiction abounded in this period. In 1973, Robert DuPont, a Washington-based methadone treatment provider and NIDA's founding director, argued that the post–World War II heroin epidemic of the late 1940s and early 1950s had formed the endemic background against which recent birth cohorts initiated heroin use.[69] Hand-drawn data illustrated his point in an address to the Center for Metropolitan Studies. In the talk, DuPont noted that "endemic addicts started using heroin almost as a matter of course" because the drug was constantly present in their communities.[70] During epidemics, more "normal," "middle class," white people got swept into heroin use, but later exited and left behind the poor, black, and Spanish-speaking people living in the centers of America's cities.[71] For DuPont, the "lifestyle of the street addict, which included crime and participation in the underworld heroin supply system," had become more acceptable to this generation than those preceding it.[72] This "generation," in other words, had little to lose by entering the illicit economy; members discounted the costs of becoming a "street heroin addict" or a "welfare mother" (similar categories in DuPont's analysis). In DuPont's early 1970s appraisal, heroin and welfare appeared as racial and political problems of modern urban life. These were the economic problems that the early NIDA sought social scientists – and, this time, economists – to interpret and understand.

Although periodic alarms sounded concerning white middle-class recruitment into heroin use – and whites remained numerically the majority of persons with addiction[73] – the geography of endemic postwar heroin use was understood as black, urban, and Latino.[74] Such racialized associations were themselves endemic by the time 1970s political elites looked to their postwar antecedents. Meanwhile, media coverage of Congressional allegations that drug use was rampant among US soldiers in Vietnam propelled the search for expertise on drug abuse. Applying insights gained in Abraham Wikler's conditioning studies at Lexington, which found that relapse hinged on social cues, the Nixon administration's Jerome Jaffe enacted a Vietnam-based drug-testing program. He also hired

---

[69] DuPont included an appendix with hand-drawn graphs for every birth cohort from 1921 to 1954, showing a clear rise in the late 1940s.
[70] DuPont, "Perspective on an Epidemic," 4; quoting Dorland, *Dorland's Illustrated Medical Dictionary.*
[71] DuPont, "Perspective on an Epidemic," 23–24.
[72] DuPont, "Perspective on an Epidemic," 24.
[73] Mills, "We Are Animals in a World."
[74] Moore, *Going Down to the Barrio.*

the sociologist of mental health Lee N. Robins, who worked to refine the tools of psychiatric epidemiology to study the drug-using habits of returning veterans.[75] Robins' Vietnam Drug User Study followed two groups of 500 enlisted men who returned stateside in 1971, one a general sample and the other men who had tested positive for narcotics use in Vietnam. The veterans were interviewed within a year of their release from service, and again in 1974. Challenging assumptions about the inevitability of relapse among opiate users reinforced by ARC research, Robins' study concluded that few regular users of opiates in Vietnam became addicted to heroin upon return.[76] These unanticipated findings challenged narrowly biological definition of addiction. The Robins study also represented growing federal investment in epidemiological social science.

8.6 Becoming Ethnographic from the 1950s to the 1980s

Addiction social science presented a challenging mosaic of conceptual and methodological approaches, definitions, and enactments that shifted rapidly in the late 1960s, as a veritable knowledge explosion rocked the research monopoly carefully constructed and stably maintained by the ARC across the previous three decades. Drug ethnography arose as a science of conduct designed to investigate the moral universe within which illicit drug use took place. Most ethnographic research networks were situated in major cities like New York City, Chicago, and San Francisco, where field-based, qualitative research could cluster. The main challenge for the addiction ethnographer – at once conceptual, methodological, and political – was to describe the "typical" drug user with the immersive participant-observation and documentary style of ethnographic realism.[77]

In contrast to the West Coast, Chicago-tinged sociology of figures like Alan Sutter and Dan Waldorf,[78] ethnographers working in New York

[75] Robins had studied social patterns of mental health and illness, and later directed the NIMH Epidemiologic Catchment Area Study, the largest study of its kind, for the Carter administration. See Campbell, "Spirit of St Louis"; Robins, *Follow-up of Vietnam Drug Users*; Robins, *Vietnam Drug User Returns*; Robins, Davis, and Nurco, "How Permanent Was Vietnam Drug Addiction?"; Robins, Davis, and Goodwin, "Drug Use by U.S. Army Enlisted Men in Vietnam"; and Robins, Helzer, and Davis, "Narcotic Use in Southeast Asia and Afterward."
[76] Vietnam veterans experienced higher rates of alcoholism, suicidality, and early mortality than did the matched nonveteran sample.
[77] Ethnographers have been generally reflexive about such matters since the 1980s. See Bourgois and Schonberg, *Righteous Dopefiend.*
[78] See Sutter, "World of the Righteous Dope Fiend."

City were more influenced by cultural anthropology and Columbia-style sociology than the Chicago example. In 1969, anthropologists Edward Preble and John Casey published a classic account of heroin-using subcultures in Manhattan.[79] Noting how much *work* it was to hustle and maintain an active heroin habit, Preble and Casey documented in naturalistic detail how structural constraints affected subcultural bonds between heroin users and sellers. "Taking Care of Business" tracked changes in drug markets, such as pricing and purity, and social demographics such as age, education, skills, and labor-market participation. Connecting drug policy, economies of scarcity during heroin droughts or "panics," and patterns of connection within social networks, Preble and Casey documented what heroin users and sellers actually said and did (rather than what social or psychological theory predicted they would say and do). Critical of "escape theory" – the notion that heroin users sought to escape "from their psychological problems and from their responsibilities in social and personal relationships" – Preble and Casey argued that "taking care of business," the fast-paced, daily quest to satisfy a heroin habit, *was* the "quest for a meaningful life, not an escape from life. And the meaning does not lie, primarily, in the effects of the drugs on their minds and bodies; it lies in the gratification of accomplishing a series of challenging, exciting tasks, every day of the week."[80]

Observation-based social science, Preble and Casey's work included, was both empirical and interpretive. Funded by state and municipal agencies in cities grappling with drug abuse, anthropologists and other ethnographers approached fieldwork very differently than those working in laboratories producing experimental and behavioral research. Just as the federal research monopoly exercised by the ARC from the 1930s to the 1960s gave way, drug-using subcultures began to proliferate. Ethnographers documented these changes. After a brief tenure at the Lexington Narcotics Farm in its waning days, Michael Agar wrote *Ripping and Running* (1973), a linguistic anthropology that characterized the behaviors and language of heroin users as adaptive within an "addict subculture" constituted in opposition to mainstream actions and intentions.[81] Studies of drug users in so-called natural settings were confined almost entirely to male subjects until the path-breaking 1981 publication of Marsha Rosenbaum's *Women on Heroin*, which argued that heroin-using women were oppressed as *women*, and responded in ways that narrowed their life options, commitments, and

[79] Preble and Casey, "Taking Care of Business."
[80] Preble and Casey, "Taking Care of Business," 3.
[81] Agar, *Ripping and Running*.

careers.[82] Treatment, according to Rosenbaum's informants, exerted a form of social control over their habits and their lives.[83]

Ethnographers served as privileged reporters of social change. Preble joined Columbia-trained sociologist Bruce D. Johnson at the National Development and Research Institutes (NDRI), a New York City research foundation that specialized in ethnography. Their team produced a major study, also called *Taking Care of Business*.[84] From 1978 to 1983, their "storefront research" project involved 211 subjects and built upon Preble and Casey's methodology in East and Central Harlem. Ex-addicts administered detailed surveys documenting all activities that either generated economic benefit or enabled individuals to avoid expenditures.

Taking Care of Business provided realistic estimates of the economic consequences of heroin addiction based on actual interactions within heroin markets, and documented the influx of cocaine into these markets immediately prior to the appearance of crack-cocaine. Tying together the economic consequences of the "multiproblem" lifestyles of most heroin users, the research team found that most heroin users were "economically productive"[85] as "discount salesmen" in an underground, stolen-goods economy from which other residents of inner-city neighborhoods benefited.[86] Comparing this economy to government tax breaks extended to luxury housing developers, Johnson and colleagues predicted that "thousands of heroin users ... will continue to be very active in taking care of business."[87] Their ethnographic approach to documenting real economic transactions in an illicit economy differed from the investigations by actual economists, which gathered some steam over this same period.

8.7 Becoming Economic from the 1960s

Centering on markets and consumers acting within them, economists began in the late 1960s to cast drugs as commodities produced, distributed, bought, and sold. Their early ventures into analyzing the heroin trade cast users in simple terms, as consumers seeking to maximize "euphoric utilities." With characteristic bravado, economist Gary S. Becker announced, in an

---

[82] Rosenbaum, *Women on Heroin*, 105.
[83] Rosenbaum, *Women on Heroin*, 121.
[84] Johnson et al., *Taking Care of Business*. This was a posthumous publication for Preble, who died in 1982.
[85] Johnson et al., *Taking Care of Business*, 183.
[86] Preble and Casey, "Taking Care of Business" and Johnson et al., *Taking Care of Business*.
[87] Johnson et al., *Taking Care of Business*, 185, 194.

important 1968 paper, that he would set aside "special theories of anomie, psychological inadequacies, or inheritance of special traits" in his approach to criminal behavior.[88] He would, instead, extend the "economist's usual analysis of choice" to the optimal allocation of resources for deterring crime.[89] Along a similar track, fellow economist Simon Rottenberg arrayed the social costs of drug law enforcement on a continuum stretching from "energetic enforcement" to "police inaction."[90] Asking how resource allocation was structured in clandestine markets and what policing strategies were optimal in a "cartellized" trade where police made far less money than criminals, he divided clandestine marketers into "amateurs" and "organized professionals."[91] Energetic law enforcement could, he argued, reinforce professional incumbents' monopoly, or disrupt and thereby open the drug trade to competition by easing up on new entrants.[92]

To a striking degree, economists often turned to biological addiction research rather than the ethnographic and observational studies discussed above. Without considering how divided addiction researchers were over definition, etiology, and methodology, most economists tended to choose one of the contending theories and cite one or two decontextualized studies in their search for models, explanations, and predictions. Whereas other social scientists sought etiological explanations for the widening prevalence of drug use in the late 1960s – and as natural scientists moved further into characterizing its neurophysiological dimensions as resulting from opioid receptors in the brain – Becker's approach to crime in general was to focus on policy to optimize the resources allocated to enforcement or punishment.

Economists saw addiction as a domain for refining theory, and particularly for testing the limits of rational choice theory with seemingly "irrational" behaviors. In the 1977 paper "De Gustibus Non Est Disputandum," George

[88] Becker, "Crime and Punishment," 170.
[89] Becker, "Crime and Punishment," 208–9.
[90] Rottenberg, "Clandestine Distribution of Heroin."
[91] Rottenberg, "Clandestine Distribution of Heroin," 81.
[92] There was, internal to the discipline, some dissent. Cuban political economist Raul A. Fernandez, whose dissertation was on the "Costs and Benefits of Rehabilitation of Heroin Addicts," castigated Rottenberg for treating heroin addiction as if it was the same as "addiction to science-fiction novels, cigarettes, candy, and marshmallows." Defining addiction as a metabolic dependence or "cellular, biological need for heroin [that was] similar to the biological need for water," Fernandez insisted that addictive commodities were unlike the typical kind, and that, therefore, drug markets operate differently from other markets. See Fernandez, "Costs and Benefits of Rehabilitation of Heroin Addicts"; Fernandez, "Clandestine Distribution of Heroin, Its Discovery and Suppression," 487; and Fernandez, "Problem of Heroin Addiction."

Stigler, together with Becker, assured economists that addictions could simply be treated as stable "tastes." The manifesto-like paper furthered the case for applying the tools of microeconomics to marriage, crime, and other "markets" formerly deemed beyond its scope. Stigler and Becker cast music appreciation, for example, as a beneficial addiction, an investment in "consumption capital" that "accumulated with exposure and age." Undesirable addiction they treated differently: "where H is a harmfully addictive commodity," consumption capital diminished with exposure and did not accumulate.[93]

Even "euphoria" was, in their treatment, a commodity, one accompanied by a form of "euphoric capital." They posited that the "effect of exposure to euphoria on the cost of producing future euphoria reduces the consumption of euphoria as exposure continues" – and predicted, as a result, that heroin use would grow with exposure even when the "amount of euphoria fell."[94] Addiction resulted, they claimed, from inelastic demand; thus, measures of elasticity could be used to derive the relative benefits and harms of the addictions. Harmful addictions occurred with low elasticity; beneficial addictions were correlated with high elasticity. Policies such as excise taxes affected "addicts," by reducing consumption among those addicted to beneficial goods, but not for inelastic-demand, harmful goods.[95]

Other economists modeled addiction as dynamic, conflictual, and downright ambivalent. Arguing that Stigler and Becker had dismissed the role of compulsion in stabilizing preferences, Gordon C. Winston asserted that addictive commodities differed from the ordinary sort: "anti-markets," he observed, form for "addiction control devices" (or "tricks people play on themselves, or pay others to play"). Some people, in other words, want to quit so badly that they are willing to pay for abstinence, treatment, an "economic paradox of markets in which people buy the ability *not* to consume." Instances where controlling, regulating, or stopping consumption was difficult, more broadly involved personal conflict and inconsistent behavior across time. Sometimes persons behaved as if they wanted to quit; at other times, they did not. "Consumer behavior" was difficult to read, according to Winston, into microeconomic models of consumer behavior.[96]

Becker and Kevin Murphy insisted, nevertheless, that addictive behavior was "usually rational," involving "forward-looking rationalization with

[93] Stigler and Becker, "De Gustibus Non Est Disputandum," 80.
[94] Stigler and Becker, "De Gustibus Non Est Disputandum," 80–81.
[95] Stigler and Becker, "De Gustibus Non Est Disputandum," 81.
[96] Winston, "Addiction and Backsliding," 299.

stable preferences."[97] To render addiction tractable to microeconomic theory, Becker and Murphy drew on behavioral notions of intermittent reinforcement. Behavioral pharmacologists had demonstrated that intermittent reinforcement was most likely to "produce reliable and distinctive patterns of behavior."[98] Unstable "steady states" of this kind were, of course, important for "rational 'pathological' addictions" in Becker and Murphy's terms.[99] They had, in effect, rationalized out contradiction; the rational addict abruptly ceased the addiction, on their construal, when the long-term benefits of quitting outweighed its short-term costs.[100] Theirs was a model in which it really was possible to "just say no," to go "cold turkey." It was no accident that economists seeking to explain addiction attributed to Becker and Murphy's model the status of a "dominant force."[101]

Becker-style economic theories of addiction, in turn, intrigued behavioral pharmacologists, who evolved experimental methods for testing choice or "drug discrimination," "delay discounting," and a treatment modality called "contingency management" that is modeled on token economies.[102] Economic theories found their way into addiction treatment; behavioral pharmacologists empirically tested economic theories that addressed impulse control and learning.[103] Therapies based on contingency contracting and management put economic approaches to work in clinical research settings.[104] Yet, formal traffic between economists and substance abuse researchers remained so sluggish that William D. Lerner and James M. Raczynski located fewer than a dozen economic studies of substance abuse by the late 1980s.[105] Indeed, many failed to recognize the relevance of economics to addiction. British health economist Christine Godfrey recalled that when she began her career, "The strength and depth of economic research in addiction had been quite limited," as few economists "seemed to want to

[97] Becker and Murphy, "Theory of Rational Addiction," 675.
[98] Leslie, "History of Reinforcement."
[99] Becker and Murphy, "Theory of Rational Addiction," 676.
[100] Becker and Murphy, "Theory of Rational Addiction," 693.
[101] Vuchinich and Heather, *Choice, Behavioral Economics and Addiction*, 24; aspects of Rational Addiction Theory (RAT) have since been demonstrated invalid.
[102] Balster, Walsh, and Bigelow, "Reflections on the Past 40 Years"; Bickel and Marsch, "Toward a Behavioral Economic Understanding of Drug Dependence"; and Stitzer, Bigelow, and Liebson, "Behavior Therapy in Drug Abuse Treatment."
[103] See Ainslie, "Specious Reward."
[104] Behavioral pharmacologists put token economies to work in treatment settings; see Kirby, Petry, and Bickel, "Heroin Addicts Have Higher Discount Rates"; Crowley, "Contingency Contracting Treatment of Drug-Abusing Physicians"; Bigelow, Stitzer, and Liebson, "Role of Behavioral Contingency Management."
[105] Lerner and Raczynski, "Economic Shaping of Substance Abuse."

interact with other addiction researchers and policymakers."[106] Economists, tellingly, turned to study legal drugs because they could get accurate and timely data via legitimate and legal routes. Becker and Murphy, for example, obtained data on cigarette consumption in most US states from 1955 to 1985 in order to conduct an empirical test of their model.[107] They found that cigarettes were addictive – an underwhelming finding in the world of most researchers studying addiction, regardless of perspective.

8.8 Becoming Neuroscience: Shifting Priorities in the 1980s and 1990s

Dissatisfied with the NIMH approach to addiction research and seeking to address the problem of street crime or "mugging," the Nixon administration wrested drug abuse research, education, and prevention from the NIMH in the early 1970s, and created a new entity called the NIDA. The Reagan administration continued to redirect NIMH priorities away from "social problem" research, including drug abuse and alcohol problems.[108] NIDA priorities helped to marginalize some existing strands of addiction research, though "natural history" and ethnography of "hidden populations" continued alongside epidemiological assessments of incidence, prevalence, correlates, and social determinants for different classes of psychoactive drugs. The resulting mix of supported research, according to the authors of a major study from the period, "implied different and to some extent contradictory considerations in the research design."[109]

There was a crucial development afoot, as funding priorities shifted. NIDA specialized in basic, medicinal chemistry, behavioral studies of drug effects, and ongoing longitudinal surveys such as "Monitoring the Future." Beginning in the 1990s, the agency added neuroscience to its funding register. Those studying real-world drug-using subcultures struggled to find a place amid the onslaught of behavioral and neuroscientific research funded by NIDA. Ethnography, for example, continued to win funding, but mainly for the purposes of governance and surveillance. Characterized as

---

[106] *Addiction*, "Conversation with Christine Godfrey," 261.
[107] Becker, Grossman, and Murphy, "Empirical Analysis of Cigarette Addiction."
[108] Kolb, Frazier, and Sirovatka, "National Institute of Mental Health."
[109] O'Donnell et al., *Young Men and Drugs*. One of NIDA's first sociological monographs, *Young Men and Drugs* showed how a range of social science approaches explained "periods of risk" that made young men more likely to initiate drug use. The study showed spikes in three classes of illicit drug use in 1969 – marijuana, psychedelics, and stimulants – *before* the rising opiate (heroin) use of the early 1970s.

a "creative, but unruly stepchild" in an evidence-based world, ethnography found its way into "rapid-ethnographic assessment."[110] So-called state ethnographies were funded in the mid- to late-1980s out of recognition that more quantitative data collections methods missed rapidly changing or emergent practices in drug subcultures and noninstitutionalized or nontreatment-seeking populations. As a result, drug ethnography assumed a surveillant cast during the public health crisis of HIV/AIDS, a time when ethnographers and public health outreach workers were often one and the same. Studying the actual practices of intravenous drug users (then referred to as IVDUs), NIDA regarded qualitative research as "useful for studying emergent and little-understood phenomena and for learning more about hidden populations: 'the homeless and transient, chronically mentally ill, high school dropouts, criminal offenders, prostitutes, juvenile delinquents, gang members, runaways, and other 'street people.'"[111] In this mode, ethnographers moved beyond the "stereotyped and manipulative responses that drug users often develop for professional ears," in order to achieve rapport with informants.[112] Ethnography was presumed useful for penetrating hidden regions of social life and "special populations" that behaved differently from "not-so-special" populations.

Ethnographic constructions of crack-cocaine use produced in the late 1980s and early 1990s revealed a nightmare world that confirmed alarm about the decline and degradation of the quality of life in low-income urban environments.[113] Ethnographies of crack-cocaine-using women of color located them in a highly gender- and race-specific scene of sexual and reproductive degradation. Set in "high-risk locations" that signaled social disorganization, such studies subjected drug-using women to higher levels of scrutiny and surveillance, linked to women's responsibility for social reproduction. Studies recommended interventions into social norms and inequalities that governed relationships within these settings.

These ethnographies emphasized the new moral dilemmas indigenous to the context of street drug use. Some of the studies revealed ethical reflections among drug users that were, indeed, not dissimilar from those of nondrug users. Continuing in the tradition of Lindesmith and Howard S. Becker, the moral economies of the 1990s revealed that drug users differentiated between "bad addicts" and "good abusers" (who regarded limits, did not harm others,

---

[110] Messac et al., "Good-Enough Science-and-Politics of Anthropological Collaboration."
[111] Lambert and Weibel, *Collection and Interpretation of Data*, 1.
[112] Ratner, *Crack Pipe as Pimp*, 4.
[113] Sterk, *Fast Lives*; Williams, *Cocaine Kids*; and Williams, *Crackhouse*.

and followed standards of conduct designed to reduce drug-related harm, such as breaking off the tips of used needles). Women faced perplexing moral dilemmas in these places – for instance, how to seek treatment without losing custody of children. The NIDA-funded "Careers in Crack" study at the National Development and Research Institutes (NDRI) in New York City continued the lineage of Preble and his protégé, Bruce D. Johnson. They foregrounded how informants reproduced and resisted stigmatizing stereotypes – following in the footsteps of Lindesmith and Becker. Anthropologist Philippe Bourgois and photographer Jeff Schonberg, in a notable example, published a photo-ethnography situating drug-using communities as undergoing social suffering.[114] Reflecting on the "socially constructed and experientially subjective" character of the truths they documented in their book, they acknowledged that addiction was "a slippery and problematic concept" that was both embraced and resisted by "destitute addicts embroiled in everyday violence."[115]

Still, the aims of drug control sat in uncomfortable relation to the more critical goals of social science. While ethnographers supplied countervailing representations, attempting to reorient drug policy, public health, and law enforcement away from further stigmatization and surveillance, they also moved outside treatment programs and institutions to produce knowledge essential for governing well – essential for public health, harm reduction, and ethical treatment of vulnerable populations pioneered in studies of HIV/AIDS. When NIDA was absorbed into the National Institutes of Health in the early 1990s, the agency set out to raise the profile of substance abuse research by investing heavily in neuroscientific ways of knowing addiction.[116] Imperatives to "translate" basic research into clinical practice were repeatedly invoked; through it all, addiction has been understood as an individual, behavioral problem propelled by genes, alleles, trauma, or epigenetics, and "bad choices" driven by these influences. Given the emphasis on the individual implied by neuroscience, the least "social" science won out.

Bibliography

Acker, Caroline J. "Addiction and the Laboratory: The Work of the National Research Council's Committee on Drug Addiction, 1928–1939." *Isis* 86, no. 2 (1995): 167–93.
Acker, Caroline J. *Creating the American Junkie: Addiction Research in the Classic Era of Narcotic Control.* Baltimore: Johns Hopkins University Press, 2002.

---

[114] Bourgois and Schonberg, *Righteous Dopefiend.*
[115] Bourgois and Schonberg, *Righteous Dopefiend,* 5.
[116] National Academy of Science Committee to Identify Strategies to Raise the Profile of Substance Abuse and Alcoholism Research, *Dispelling the Myths about Addiction.*

Addiction. "A Conversation with Christine Godfrey." *Addiction* 108, no. 2 (2013): 257–64.

Agar, Michael. *Ripping and Running: A Formal Ethnography of Heroin Addicts.* New York: Seminar Press, 1973.

Ainslie, George. "Specious Reward: A Behavioral Theory of Impulsiveness and Impulse Control." *Psychology Bulletin* 82, no. 4 (1975): 463–96.

American Bar Association/American Medical Association. *Drug Addiction: Crime or Disease? Interim and Final Reports of the Joint Committee of the American Bar Association and the American Medical Association on Narcotic Drugs.* Bloomington: Indiana University Press, 1961.

Ball, John C., and Carl D. Chambers, eds. *The Epidemiology of Opiate Addiction in the United States.* Springfield: Charles C. Thomas, 1970.

Balster, Robert L., Sharon L. Walsh, and George E. Bigelow. "Reflections on the Past 40 Years of Behavioral Pharmacology Research on Problems of Drug Abuse." *Journal of Drug Issues* 39, no. 1 (2009): 133–52.

Becker, Gary S. "Crime and Punishment: An Economic Approach." *Journal of Political Economy* 76, no. 2 (1968): 169–217.

Becker, Gary S., Michael Grossman, and Kevin M. Murphy. "Rational Addiction and the Effect of Price on Consumption." *American Economic Review* 81, no. 2 (1991): 237–41.

Becker, Gary S., Michael Grossman, and Kevin M. Murphy. "An Empirical Analysis of Cigarette Addiction." *American Economic Review* 84, no. 3 (1994): 396–418.

Becker, Gary S., and Kevin M. Murphy. "A Theory of Rational Addiction." *Journal of Political Economy* 96, no. 4 (1988): 675–700.

Becker, Howard S. "Becoming a Marihuana User." *American Journal of Sociology* 59, no. 3 (1953): 235–42.

Becker, Howard S. "Notes on the Concept of Commitment." *American Journal of Sociology* 66, no. 1 (1960): 32–40.

Becker, Howard S. *Outsiders: Studies in the Sociology of Deviance.* New York: The Free Press, 1963.

Becker, Howard S. *Tricks of the Trade: How to Think about Your Research While You're Doing It.* Chicago: University of Chicago Press, 1998.

Bickel, Warren K., and L. A. Marsch. "Toward a Behavioral Economic Understanding of Drug Dependence: Delay Discounting Processes." *Addiction* 96, no. 1 (2001): 73–86.

Bigelow, George E., Maxine L. Stitzer, and Ira A. Liebson. "The Role of Behavioral. Contingency Management in Drug Abuse Treatment." In *Behavioral Intervention Techniques in Drug Abuse Treatment,* edited by John Grabowski, Maxine L. Stitzer, and Jack E. Henningfield, 36–52. NIDA Research Monograph 46. Washington, DC: US Government Printing Office, 1986.

Bourgois, Philippe. "Anthropology and Epidemiology on Drugs: The Challenges of Cross-Methodological and Theoretical Dialogue." *International Journal of Drug Policy* 13, no. 4 (2002): 259–69.

Bourgois, Philippe, and Jeff Schonberg. *Righteous Dopefiend.* Berkeley: University of California Press, 2009.

Campbell, Nancy D. *Using Women: Gender, Drug Policy and Social Justice.* New York: Routledge, 2000.

Campbell, Nancy D. "'A New Deal for the Drug Addict': The Addiction Research Center (ARC), Lexington, Kentucky." *Journal of the History of the Behavioral Sciences* 42, no. 2 (2006): 135–57.

Addition 317

Campbell, Nancy D. *Discovering Addiction: The Science and Politics of Substance Abuse Research*. Ann Arbor: University of Michigan Press, 2007.

Campbell, Nancy D. "'The Spirit of St Louis': The Contributions of Lee N. Robins to North American Psychiatric Epidemiology." *International Journal of Epidemiology* 43, no. S1 (2014): i19–28. https://doi.org/10.1093/ije/dyt223

Campbell, Nancy D. "The Conceptual Migration from 'Intoxication of Desire' to 'Disease of Democracy': Addiction, 'Narcotic Bondage,' and North American Modernity." In *The Pharmakon*, edited by Hermann Herlinghaus, 93–124. Heidelberg: Winter Verlag, 2018.

Campbell, Nancy D., J. P. Olsen, and Luke Walden. *The Narcotic Farm: The Rise and Fall of America's First Prison for Drug Addicts*. New York: Harry N. Abrams, 2008.

Chein, Isidor. "The Status of Sociological and Social Psychological Knowledge Concerning Narcotics." In *Narcotic Drug Addiction Problems*, edited by Robert B. Livingston, 146–58. Bethesda: National Institute of Mental Health, 1958.

Chein, Isidor, Donald Gerard, Robert Lee, and Eva Rosenfeld. *The Road to H: Narcotics, Delinquency, and Social Policy*. Boston: Basic Books, 1964.

Clarke, Adele E. "Controversy and the Development of Reproductive Sciences." *Social Problems* 37, no. 1 (1990): 18–37.

Clausen, John A. *Sociology and the Field of Mental Health*. New York: Russell Sage Foundation, 1956.

Clausen, John A. "Social and Psychological Factors in Narcotics Addiction." *Law and Contemporary Problems* 22, no. 1 (1957): 34–51.

Cloward, Richard A., and Lloyd E. Ohlin. *Delinquency and Opportunity: A Theory of Delinquent Gangs*. Glencoe: The Free Press, 1960.

Cohen, Albert K. *Delinquent Boys: The Culture of the Gang*. Glencoe: The Free Press, 1955.

Courtwright, David C. *Dark Paradise: A History of Opiate Addiction in America*. Enlarged ed. Cambridge: Harvard University Press, 2001.

Crowley, Thomas J. "Contingency Contracting Treatment of Drug-Abusing Physicians, Nurses, and Dentists." In *Behavioral Intervention Techniques in Drug Abuse Treatment*, edited by John Grabowski, Maxine L. Stitzer, and Jack E. Henningfield, 68–83. NIDA Research Monograph 46. Washington, DC: US Government Printing Office, 1986.

Dai, Bingham. *Opium Addiction in Chicago: A Dissertation*. Shanghai: Commercial Press, 1937.

Denzin, Norman. *Symbolic Interactionism and Cultural Studies: The Politics of Interpretation*. New York: Wiley-Blackwell, 1992.

Dorland, W. A. Newman. *Dorland's Illustrated Medical Dictionary*. Philadelphia: W. B. Saunders Co., 1957.

Dunlap, Eloise, Bruce D. Johnson, H. Sanabria, E. Holliday, V. Lipsey, M. Barnett, W. Hopkins, I. Sobel, D. Randolph, and Ko-lin Chin. "Studying Crack Users and Their Criminal Careers: Scientific and Artistic Aspects of Locating Hard-to-Reach Subjects and Interviewing Them about Sensitive Topics." *Contemporary Drug Problems* 17, no. 1 (1990): 121–44.

DuPont, Robert L. "Perspective on an Epidemic." Unpublished manuscript. Washington Center for Metropolitan Studies. October 29, 1973.

Durkheim, Emile. *Suicide: A Study in Sociology*. Translated by John Spaulding and George Simpson. Glencoe: The Free Press, 1951.

Felix, Robert H. "The Technique of Mass Approach to the Problems of Mental Health." *Neuropsychiatry* 2, no. 1 (1952): 48–62.

Fernandez, Raul A. "The Clandestine Distribution of Heroin, Its Discovery and Suppression: A Comment." *Journal of Political Economy* 77, no. 4 (1969): 487–88.

Fernandez, Raul A. "Costs and Benefits of Rehabilitation of Heroin Addicts." PhD diss., Claremont Graduate School, 1973.

Fernandez, Raul A. "The Problem of Heroin Addiction and Radical Political Economy." *American Economic Review* 63, no. 2 (1973): 257–62.

Fine, Gary Alan, ed. *A Second Chicago School? The Development of Postwar American Sociology*. Chicago: University of Chicago Press, 1995.

Finestone, Harold. "Cats, Kicks, and Color." *Social Problems* 5, no. 7 (1957): 3–13.

Frazier, E. Franklin. *Black Bourgeoisie*. Glencoe: The Free Press, 1957.

Fujimura, Joan. "On Methods, Ontologies, and Representation in the Sociology of Science: Where Do We Stand?" In *Social Organization and Social Process: Essays in Honor of Anselm Strauss*, edited by David Maines, 207–48. Hawthorne: Aldine de Gruyter, 1991.

Geer, Blanche, Everett C. Hughes, Anselm Strauss, and Howard S. Becker. *Boys in White: Student Culture in Medical School*. Piscataway: Transaction Publishers, 1961.

Grob, Gerald N., and Howard H. Goldman. *The Dilemma of Federal Mental Health Policy: Radical Reform or Incremental Change?* New Brunswick: Rutgers University Press, 2006.

Herzberg, David. "Entitled to Addiction? Pharmaceuticals, Race, and America's First Drug War." *Bulletin of the History of Medicine* 91, no. 3 (2017): 586–623.

Hughes, Everett C. *Men and Their Work*. Glencoe: The Free Press, 1958.

Hughes, Patrick H., Noel W. Barker, Gail A. Crawford, and Jerome H. Jaffe. "The Natural History of a Heroin Epidemic." *American Journal of Public Health* 62, no. 7 (1972): 995–1001.

Huizinga, Johan. *Homo Ludens: A Study of the Play Element in Culture*. Boston: Beacon Press, 1955.

Isbell, Harris. "Review of *Opiate Addiction*, by Alfred R. Lindesmith." *Journal of the American Medical Association* 137 (1948): 1342.

Johnson, Bruce D., Paul J. Goldstein, Edward Preble, James Schmeidler, Douglas S. Lipton, Barry Spunt, and Thomas Miller. *Taking Care of Business: The Economics of Crime by Heroin Abusers*. Lanham: Lexington Books, 1985.

Keire, Mara L. "Dope Fiends and Degenerates: The Gendering of Addiction in the Early Twentieth Century." *Journal of Social History* 31, no. 4 (1998): 809–22.

Keys, David Patrick, and John F. Galliher. *Confronting the Drug Control Establishment: Alfred Lindesmith as a Public Intellectual*. Albany: State University of New York Press, 2000.

Kirby, Kris N., Nancy M. Petry, and Warren K. Bickel. "Heroin Addicts Have Higher Discount Rates for Delayed Rewards than Non-Drug-Using Controls." *Journal of Experimental Psychology* 128, no. 1 (1999): 78–87.

Kolb, Lawrence C. "Pleasure and Deterioration from Narcotic Addiction." *Mental Hygiene* 9 (1925): 699–724.

Kolb, Lawrence C. "Drug Addiction in Its Relation to Crime." *Mental Hygiene* 9 (1925): 74–89.

Kolb, Lawrence C. "Types and Characteristics of Drug Addicts." *Mental Hygiene* 9 (1925): 300–13.

Kolb, Lawrence C., Shervert H. Frazier, and Palul Sirovatka. "The National Institute of Mental Health: Its Influence on Psychiatry and the Nation's Mental Health." In

American Psychiatry after the War, edited by R. C. Menninger and J. C. Nemiah, 207–31. Washington, DC: American Psychiatric Press, 2000.

Lambert, Elizabeth, and W. Wayne Weibel. *The Collection and Interpretation of Data from Hidden Populations*. NIDA Research Monograph 98. Rockville: National Institute on Drug Abuse, 1990.

Lerner, William D., and James M. Raczynski. "The Economic Shaping of Substance Abuse." In *Learning Factors in Substance Abuse*, edited by Barbara A. Ray, 62–73. NIDA Research Monograph 84. Washington, DC: US Government Printing Office, 1988.

Leslie, Julian C. "A History of Reinforcement: The Role of Reinforcement Schedules in Behavior Pharmacology." *The Behavior Analyst Today* 4, no. 1 (2003): 98–108.

Lindesmith, Alfred R. "Dope Fiend Mythology." *Journal of Criminal Law and Criminology* 31, no. 2 (1940): 199–208.

Lindesmith, Alfred R. *Opiate Addiction*. Bloomington: Principia Press, 1947.

Lindesmith, Alfred R. *Addiction and Opiates*. Chicago: Aldine, 1968.

Lindesmith, Alfred R., and Anselm L. Strauss. *Social Psychology*. New York: Dryden Press, 1949.

Maurer, David W., and Victor H. Vogel. *Narcotics and Narcotic Addiction*. Springfield: Charles C. Thomas, 1954.

McAuliffe, William E., and Robert A. Gordon. "A Test of Lindesmith's Theory of Addiction: The Frequency of Euphoria among Long-Term Addicts." *American Journal of Sociology* 79, no. 4 (1974): 795–840.

McWilliams, John D. *The Protectors: Harry J. Anslinger and the Federal Bureau of Narcotics, 1930–1962*. Cranbury: Associated University Presses, 1990.

Merton, Robert K. "Social Structure and Anomie." *American Sociological Review* 3, no. 5 (1938): 672–82.

Messac, Luke, Daniel Ciccarone, Jeff Draine, and Philippe Bourgois. "The Good-Enough Science-and-Politics of Anthropological Collaboration with Evidence-Based Clinical Research: Four Ethnographic Case Studies." *Social Science & Medicine* 99 (2013): 176–86.

Mills, James. "We Are Animals in a World No One Knows." *LIFE Magazine* 58, no. 8 (February 26, 1965): 66–81.

Moore, Joan W. *Going Down to the Barrio: Homeboys and Homegirls in Change*. Philadelphia: Temple University Press, 1991.

Musto, David F. *The American Disease*. Oxford: Oxford University Press, 1999.

Musto, David F., and Pamela Korsmeyer. *The Quest for Drug Control: Politics and Federal Policy in a Period of Increasing Substance Abuse, 1963–1981*. New Haven: Yale University Press, 2002.

National Academy of Science Committee to Identify Strategies to Raise the Profile of Substance Abuse and Alcoholism Research. *Dispelling the Myths about Addiction*. Washington, DC: National Academy of Science Press, 1997.

National Research Council. *Common Processes in Habitual Substance Use: A Research Agenda*. Washington, DC: The National Academies Press, 1977.

O'Donnell, John A. "Narcotic Addiction and Crime." *Social Problems* 13, no. 4 (1966): 374–85.

O'Donnell, John A. *Narcotic Addicts in Kentucky*. Chevy Chase: National Institute of Mental Health, 1969.

O'Donnell, John A., Harwin L. Voss, Robert R. Clayton, Gerald T. Slatin, and Robin G. Room. *Young Men and Drugs: A Nationwide Survey*. Rockville: NIDA Research Monograph 5, 1976.

Preble, Edward, and John D. Casey. "Taking Care of Business: A Heroin User's Life on the Street." *International Journal of the Addictions* 4 (1969): 1–24.

Ratner, Mitchell S. *Crack Pipe as Pimp: An Ethnographic Investigation of Sex-for-Crack Exchanges.* New York: Lexington Books, 1993.

Robins, Lee N. *Follow-up of Vietnam Drug Users.* Special Action Office Monograph, Series A, no. 1. Washington, DC: Executive Office of the President, 1973.

Robins, Lee N. *The Vietnam Drug User Returns.* Special Action Office Monograph, Series A, no. 2. Washington, DC: US Government Printing Office, 1974.

Robins, Lee N., Darlene H. Davis, and Donald W. Goodwin. "Drug Use by U.S. Army Enlisted Men in Vietnam: A Follow-up on Their Return Home." *American Journal of Epidemiology* 99, no. 4 (1974): 235–49.

Robins, Lee N., Darlene H. Davis, and David N. Nurco. "How Permanent Was Vietnam Drug Addiction?" *American Journal of Public Health* 64 (1974): 38–43.

Robins, Lee N., John E. Helzer, and Darlene H. Davis. "Narcotic Use in Southeast Asia and Afterward: An Interview Study of 898 Vietnam Returnees." *Archives of General Psychiatry* 32, no. 8 (1975): 955–61.

Rosenbaum, Marsha. *Women on Heroin.* New Brunswick: Rutgers University Press, 1981.

Rosenthal, Richard J., and Suzanne Faris. "The Etymology and Early History of 'Addiction.'" *Addiction Research and Theory* 27, no. 5 (2019): 437–49. https://doi.org /10.1080/16066359.2018.1543412

Rottenberg, Simon. "The Clandestine Distribution of Heroin, Its Discovery and Suppression." *Journal of Political Economy* 76, no. 1 (1968): 78–90.

Ryder, Harl E., and Geoffrey M. Heal. "Optimal Growth with Intertemporally Dependent Preferences." *Review of Economic Studies* 40, no. 1 (1973): 1–31.

Schelling, Thomas C. "An Essay on Bargaining." *American Economic Review* 46, no. 3 (1956): 281–306.

Schelling, Thomas C. *Micromotives and Macrobehavior.* New York: W. W. Norton & Company, 1978.

Schelling, Thomas C. *Strategies of Commitment and Other Essays.* Cambridge: Harvard University Press, 2006.

Short, James F., Jr., with Lorine A. Hughes. "Criminology, Criminologists, and the Sociological Enterprise." In *Sociology in America: A History,* edited by Craig Calhoun, 605–38. Chicago: University of Chicago Press, 2007.

Star, Susan Leigh. "The Sociology of the Invisible: The Primacy of Work in the Writings of Anselm Strauss." In *Social Organization and Social Process: Essays in Honor of Anselm Strauss,* edited by David Maines, 265–83. Hawthorne: Aldine de Gruyter, 1991.

Star, Susan Leigh. "'Listening for Connections': Introduction to Symposium on the Work of Anselm Strauss." *Mind, Culture and Activity* 2, no. 1 (1995): 12–17.

Sterk, Claire E. *Fast Lives: Women Who Use Crack-Cocaine.* Philadelphia: Temple University Press, 1999.

Stigler, George J., and Gary S. Becker. "De Gustibus Non Est Disputandum." *American Economic Review* 67, no. 2 (1977): 76–90.

Stitzer, Maxine I., George E. Bigelow, and Ira Liebson. "Behavior Therapy in Drug Abuse Treatment: Review and Evaluation." *NIDA Research Monograph* 58 (1985): 31–50.

Strauss, Anselm. "Discovering New Theory from Previous Theory." In *Human Nature and Collective Behavior: Papers in Honor of Herbert Blumer,* edited by Tomatsu Shibutani, 46–53. Englewood Cliffs: Prentice-Hall, 1970.

Sutter, Alan G. "The World of the Righteous Dope Fiend." *Issues in Criminology* 2, no. 2 (1966): 177–222.

Terry, Charles E., and Mildred Pellens. *The Opium Problem*. Montclair: Patterson Smith, 1928.

Thomas, W. I. "The Problem of Personality in the Urban Environment." In *The Urban Community*, edited by Ernest W. Burgess, 38–47. Chicago: University of Chicago Press, 1926.

Thomas, W. I., and Florian Znaniecki. *The Polish Peasant in Europe and America*. Boston: Gorham Press, 1919.

Vaillant, George E. "A Twelve-Year Follow-up of New York Narcotic Addicts. I. The Relation of Treatment to Outcome." *American Journal of Psychiatry* 122 (1966): 727–37.

Vaillant, George E. "A Twelve-Year Follow-up of New York Narcotic Addicts. II. The Natural History of a Chronic Disease." *New England Journal of Medicine* 275 (1966): 1282–88.

Vaillant, George E. "A Twelve-Year Follow-up of New York Narcotic Addicts. III. Some Social and Psychiatric Characteristics." *Archives of General Psychiatry* 15 (1966): 599–609.

Vaillant, George E. "A Twelve-Year Follow-up of New York Narcotic Addicts. IV. Some Characteristics and Determinants of Abstinence." *American Journal of Psychiatry* 123 (1983): 573–84.

Valentine, Douglas. *The Strength of the Wolf: The Secret History of America's War on Drugs*. Brooklyn: Verso Books, 2004.

Vuchinich, Rudy E., and Nick Heather, eds. *Choice, Behavioral Economics and Addiction*. Amsterdam: Pergamon Press, 2003.

Waldorf, Dan. *Careers in Dope*. Englewood Cliffs: Prentice-Hall, 1973.

Weinberg, Darin. "Lindesmith on Addiction: A Critical History of a Classic Theory." *Sociological Theory* 15, no. 2 (1997): 150–61.

Wikler, Abraham. "Review of *Opiate Addiction*, by Alfred R. Lindesmith." *American Journal of Psychiatry* 105 (1948): 74–75.

Wikler, Abraham. "Conditioning Factors in Opiate Addiction and Relapse." In *Narcotics*, edited by Daniel M. Wilner and Gene G. Kassebaum, 85–100. New York: McGraw-Hill, 1965.

Williams, Terry. *The Cocaine Kids: The Inside Story of a Teenage Drug Ring*. Boston: De Capo Press, 1990.

Williams, Terry. *Crackhouse: Notes from the End of the Line*. New York: Penguin Books, 1993.

Winick, Charles. "Narcotics Addiction and Its Treatment." *Law and Contemporary Problems* 22, no. 1 (1957): 9–33.

Winick, Charles. "The Use of Drugs by Jazz Musicians." *Social Problems* 7, no. 3 (1959–1960): 240–53.

Winick, Charles. "Physician Narcotic Addicts." *Social Problems* 9, no. 2 (1961): 174–86.

Winick, Charles. "Maturing Out of Narcotic Addiction." *Bulletin on Narcotics* 14, no. 1 (1962): 1–7.

Winston, George. "Addiction and Backsliding: A Theory of Compulsive Consumption." *Journal of Economic Behavior and Organization* 1, no. 4 (1980): 295–324.

Zahn, Margaret A., and John C. Ball. "Factors Related to Cure of Opiate Addiction among Puerto Rican Addicts." *International Journal of the Addictions* 7, no. (1972): 237–45.

9

Mental Illness

Andrew Scull

Mental illness, as the eminent historian of psychiatry Michael MacDonald once aptly remarked, is "the most solitary of afflictions to the people who experience it; but it is the most social of maladies to those who observe its effects."[1] Serious forms of mental disturbance represent an intractable intellectual puzzle while imposing immense costs – both material and nonmaterial – on both individual sufferers, their immediate social circle, and society at large. One might expect the subject, therefore, to be of great interest to social scientists of all sorts. On its face, economists ought surely to be interested in the financial costs, both direct and indirect, that mental illness imposes, or in estimating the respective efficacy of differing approaches to the treatment and management of mental illness. To the extent that mental illness is accompanied by – indeed defined by – disturbances of mental function, psychology would seem to have a natural interest in exploring abnormal mental states, and perhaps in developing ways of responding to and treating disturbances of emotion, reason, and cognition. As for sociology, a host of topics suggest themselves: the social location of mental illness; the possible role of social factors in the genesis of mental disturbance and in its resolution; the role and impact of the family and the immediate interactional circle of the patient in identifying, responding to, and coping with insanity; and the nature of organized responses to the problems mental illness poses, just to mention a few. Most anthropologists during the first half of the twentieth century focused their attention on non-Western societies, but for the past three-quarters of a century, they too have increasingly turned to the study of developed societies, the United States prominently among them, and here too one might expect to find a distinctive disciplinary lens being trained upon the problem of mental illness.

[1] MacDonald, *Mystical Bedlam*, 1.

Mental illness was recognized as a serious social problem requiring innovative social and political responses in the very early national period, very soon after the United States achieved political independence. Serious mental disturbance almost immediately renders many sufferers incapable of work, and incapable of caring for themselves. Unless they possess a great deal of independent wealth, even moderately prosperous and economically well-off individuals swiftly find themselves impoverished. The fear and uncertainty associated with their emotional and/or cognitive problems likewise quickly create serious problems for their families and society more broadly. All across Europe and North America, as work and home became increasingly separated, and geographical mobility increased, the traditional approach of relying on families to care informally for their deranged members proved increasingly unworkable. Before the middle of the century, every country in Europe and the United States had concluded that these issues compelled state intervention on a massive scale. The preferred solution, which was adopted everywhere, was the construction of networks of increasingly vast asylums, built and maintained at public expense. Save for the problems posed by crime, mental illness was the first social problem to secure sustained and massive shifts in social policy, and the state asylum systems, in the United States and abroad, soon became the largest single item in many if not most states' budgets. The expenditure of massive amounts of tax money to construct and maintain what historians refer to as asylumdom is the more remarkable, given the general hostility in this period to this sort of expansion of the state into daily life (a move that in other sectors would often be deferred until the advent of the proto-welfare state), and is concrete testimony (if the awful pun can be forgiven) to the pressing nature of the social problem mental illness represented in an increasingly mobile industrial and urban society. The logic of the market was suspended remarkably early when it came to the case of the mentally ill.[2]

Asylum systems were established in an era of utopian optimism about the possibility of curing mental patients. The institutions and their routines were promoted as curative. Though these expectations were disappointed within a matter of decades, the symbolic and practical challenges posed by mental illness ensured their survival, though increasingly they were justified as means of keeping dangerous and biologically defective souls under lock and key, preventing disturbed people who were labeled as degenerate from adding to what seemed to be an ever-larger population of mentally defective people.

[2] Scull, *Psychiatry and Its Discontents*, 38–53.

Between 1900 and 1940, the numbers of mental patients confined in American mental hospitals quadrupled, increasing at a rate of more than double the general population growth. That pattern persisted after World War II, reaching a peak in 1955, when, on an average day, America's state and county mental hospitals contained 558,000 patients. A series of experimental treatments adopted by psychiatrists during the 1920s and 1930s – fever treatments, deep sleep and insulin comas, shock therapies, and lobotomies, to name but some – proved powerless to stem the remorseless rise in patient populations, and the strain on government budgets grew steadily more pressing. New York State, for example, spent nearly a third of its annual budget (excluding debt service) on its state hospital system. The pressing nature of the problem provoked regular concern among the nation's governors (and would shortly lead to some abrupt shifts in social policy). Mental illness was perhaps the nation's largest and most intractable social problem, and one that had already begun to attract the attention of social scientists who sought to apply their expertise to major issues of public policy.

9.1 Early Social Science and the Problem of Mental Illness

The kinds and degrees of involvement of the major social sciences with the problems posed by mental illness have, however, been very different, and have followed quite separate intellectual trajectories. More than a century ago, the various social sciences began to establish themselves in the American university system, and to organize themselves into increasingly self-conscious and organized academic disciplines, each with their own distinctive approach to some aspects of the social world, and, increasingly, with distinctive methodologies and cultures. From the very outset, American sociology placed great emphasis on the examination of various forms of social pathology.[3] Indeed, the study of "nuts, sluts, and perverts" was one of the key defining features of the distinctive vision of sociology that was the Chicago School. The study of the social and cultural dimensions of mental illness was in certain respects a foundational feature of the discipline, and it would retain a prominent place in sociology until the last quarter of the twentieth century.

Given that psychological disturbances are a constitutive feature of most forms of mental illness, one might have expected that the problems of abnormal psychology would have been central to the new discipline as it began to distinguish itself from philosophy in the late nineteenth-century, but in fact that was not the case. Psychology moved rapidly to ground itself

[3] Mills, "Professional Ideology of the Social Pathologists."

in the laboratory, as an experimental science taking its cue from the natural sciences rather than the social sciences. At the University of Chicago, for instance, where President Robert Maynard Hutchins instituted a division of academic disciplines into the now-taken-for-granted divisions of the biological sciences, the humanities, the social sciences, and the physical sciences, his original plan to place psychology in the social science division was fiercely resisted by the department, which successfully fought to be part of the biological sciences, insisting that this placement would "offer better scientific foundations for psychological training."[4]

Those ties to biology had, it is true, begun to weaken in the late 1930s, though no clear intellectual direction developed to replace it in the war years, in part because of the recruitment of several key faculty to the war effort and in part because of the absence of clear departmental leadership. But postwar, the Chicago department recruited James Grier Miller, a former Harvard Junior Fellow, and the head of the Veterans Administration Clinical Psychology Section, as its new chair. In doing so, the department brought in someone who had already established a pioneer program for training clinical psychologists at the university, and who expressed the then-impolitic notion that "[psychological] research in the clinic could be more significant than in the laboratory." Miller's arrival marked that department's increasing distance from its earlier affiliations, and, more importantly, set it on a trajectory that other academic departments of psychology would soon emulate.[5]

For the first four decades of the twentieth century, clinical psychology had occupied a vestigial place in the discipline, and was mostly devoted to the development of diagnostic tests of various sorts, most notably measures of intelligence and aptitude. The hegemony of the medical specialties of psychiatry and neurology was left unchallenged. Psychoanalysis, rejected or ignored by mainstream American psychiatry in the years before World War II, did, of course, advance an increasingly elaborate theory of the psychological origins of mental disorder and develop a distinctive therapeutic intervention of a psychological sort. But American devotees insisted that only licensed physicians could train and practice as psychoanalysts. They trained new practitioners at Freudian institutes organized outside the world of the university. And their psychological theories enjoyed essentially no purchase or influence within the experimentally oriented academic departments of American universities.

[4] Fontaine, "Walking the Tightrope," 353.
[5] Fontaine, "Walking the Tightrope," 351.

The social science where psychoanalysis *did* come to exercise considerable intellectual influence was anthropology. Freud's speculative *Totem and Taboo* and his claims about the universality of the Oedipus complex certainly contributed to this early attention.[6] Notwithstanding an early critical review by the Berkeley anthropologist A. L. Kroeber, and Franz Boas's objections to the evolutionist anthropology Freud endorsed, the emphasis on culture and personality that quickly became the leading strand in American anthropology readily absorbed an interest in psychoanalysis.[7] Among Franz Boas' early students, figures like Ruth Benedict, Edward Sapir, and Margaret Mead all produced work which bore clear evidence of psychoanalytic preoccupations. And under the guise of psychological anthropology, the interest in marrying anthropology and psychoanalysis persisted well into the 1980s.[8] With the partial exception of the Hungarian-French anthropologist Georges Devereux,[9] who trained in anthropology at Berkeley, and later practiced a psychoanalytically influenced ethno-psychiatry at the Menninger Clinic in Topeka, Kansas, and more briefly in Houston, Philadelphia, and New York before returning to Paris in 1963, this strand within American anthropology exhibited only passing concern with mental illness (let alone the problems of mental illness in an American context), and most anthropological work on the subject came later, once many in the profession had transferred their intellectual attention to the ethnography of modern industrial societies.[10]

Most of the emerging social science disciplines thus gave some attention to the problems posed by mental illness, but among the major social sciences, it was undoubtedly sociology that paid the closest and most sustained attention to them. The Ivy League universities, with the exception of Columbia, tended to shun the discipline (rather as Oxford and Cambridge did in Britain). Harvard didn't start its sociology department until 1930, and Princeton waited until 1960 to launch an independent department. It was the University of Chicago under Robert Park and Ernest Burgess that played the most prominent role in establishing the discipline in the United States, and in important ways, the sociologists they trained were the heirs to the social survey tradition that had emerged in late nineteenth-century

[6] Freud, *Totem and Taboo*.
[7] Kroeber, "*Totem and Taboo*."
[8] See Levy, *Tahitians*; Gehrie, "Psychoanalytic Anthropology"; Spiro, *Oedipus in the Trobriands*; and Spiro, *Culture and Human Nature*.
[9] Devereux, *Reality and Dream*.
[10] See, for example, Kleinman, *Social Origins of Stress and Disease*; Lakoff, *Pharmaceutical Reason*; Luhrmann, *Of Two Minds*; and Martin, *Bipolar Expeditions*.

Britain (see Chapter 4: Poverty). Chicago sociologists treated the city as their laboratory, and set forth to document its structures and its pathologies, including its mental pathologies.[11]

Like their British predecessors, Chicago sociologists employed a mixture of methods. Statistical techniques were employed alongside ethnographic observation. Efforts to map the statistical distribution of social problems across different regions of the city were matched by detailed ethnographic descriptions of particular neighborhoods. Psychoses were only one of a number of what were termed "social pathologies" that formed the subject matter of much of their sociology, alongside homelessness, alcoholism, suicide, homicide, prostitution, juvenile delinquency, and crime. Characteristically, these researchers sought to link the psychological disorientation that characterizes mental illness (and other forms of deviant behavior) to the social disorganization they saw as characterizing particular neighborhoods. Across a variety of studies, they sought to connect the prevalence of anonymous and transitory social relationships to the weakness of social ties and the breakdown of both neighborhoods and individuals.[12]

One of the leading European psychoanalysts, Franz Alexander, had been invited by the University of Chicago's Hutchins in 1930 to come and lecture on Freud's theories. The lectures were not a success with its primary audience. Indeed, his claims were greeted with disdain, hostility, or indifference by the medical faculty.[13] He did manage to secure a more sympathetic hearing with a handful of philosophers and social scientists, however, and Edward Gitre has shown that sociologists like William Ogburn, John Dollard, and Ernest Burgess expressed some sympathy with psychoanalysis, and in indirect ways its doctrines had some influence on the ways they approached mental illness and social pathology more broadly.[14]

The culmination of the Chicago School's perspective on the sociological study of mental illness came with the publication of Robert E. Faris and Henry Warren Durham's 1939 monograph *Mental Disorders in Urban Areas*.[15] It was a book, characteristically, that – title notwithstanding – focused primarily on Chicago, though C. W. Schroeder later attempted to extend its findings to other cities.[16] In a broader sense, the fascination with deviance that runs through most of prewar Chicago sociology resurfaces in much of post–World

[11] Park, Burgess, and McKenzie, *The City*.
[12] See Faris, *Chicago Sociology* and Bulmer, *Chicago School of Sociology*.
[13] Scull, "Creating a New Psychiatry."
[14] Gitre, "Importing Freud."
[15] Faris and Dunham, *Mental Disorders in Urban Areas*.
[16] Schroeder, "Mental Disorders in Cities."

War II sociology. And the preoccupation of many of its leading lights with ethnographic approaches to the study of social life likewise reemerges from the mid-1940s onwards, as the era of total war morphs into the Cold War that followed almost immediately after the ending of open hostilities. These enduring traditions underlay many of the classic studies from the 1950s and 1960s that were devoted to the sociology of mental illness.

9.2 The Impact of War

The war years transformed American society in myriad ways. Not the least of those transformations was the increased power of the federal government, a development that had profound effects on the future of the American university and on the sciences, both social and natural. Fighting Hitler and Hirohito required the unprecedented mobilization of American society. Previous barriers to the expansion of the powers of the federal government, both ideological and legal, simply vanished in the face of the need to wage total war. The consequence was a vast and permanent increase in the size and reach of Washington, and once earlier barriers had been breached, the expansion of federal authority and reach only accelerated in the following decades. In war's shadow, and then in the face of the outbreak of the Cold War in the late 1940s, obstacles to the expanded scope of federal authority simply melted away.

Before the war, federal involvement with medical and scientific research, let alone research in the social sciences, had been vanishingly small. In the second half of the 1940s, its involvement started down the path of exponential growth that has continued ever since. With federal funding, the process of knowledge-creation, the very shape of academic disciplines, and the major characteristics of the academy were irrevocably altered. These dramatic changes were felt with great force in the social as well as the natural and biological sciences. And among certain social sciences, federal largesse had particularly obvious effects, nowhere more so than in the relationship between them and the problems associated with mental illness.

Even before America's entrance into World War II in December 1941, American psychiatrists had raised the problems that mental illness would likely pose for the military. The shell-shock epidemic that had been so notable a feature of World War I was a forcible reminder that psychiatric casualties in combat units could pose massive costs and dangers to troop morale and fighting effectiveness. Leading psychiatrists proposed, and Washington accepted, that screening techniques should be developed to exclude those likely to break down under the stresses of combat. When the program was implemented, 1.7 million potential draftees were rejected on psychiatric grounds. The expectation was that this would sharply limit psychiatric problems among the troops.

The attempt to short circuit the problem was a massive failure. As we periodically need to be reminded, it is not just that modern industrialized warfare generates mass casualties, but that many of those casualties are not just physical, but mental. The shell-shock of the trenches would be replaced in the 1940s by combat exhaustion or combat neurosis (which in their turn would later be relabeled as post-traumatic stress disorder), but the pattern was always the same: Massive numbers of psychiatric casualties were spawned by the horrors of combat. The rate of psychiatric breakdowns among the American armed forces was more than twice as high as in World War I.[17] Many of these casualties were permanently scarred and harmed. The military command thus faced the immediate emergency of dealing with soldiers who had broken down, with potentially devastating effects on fighting efficiency and morale; and the postwar problems posed by disabled veterans with grave and ongoing psychiatric problems.

Both during and immediately after the war, therefore, the problems associated with mental illness were newly salient, and in a context that temporarily reduced some of the stigma that so readily attaches itself to those suffering from mental disorders. The exigencies of breakdowns under combat conditions demanded responses from the military command, and on a huge scale. By the end of the war, the armed forces were employing as many medics to treat psychiatric emergencies as the total number of psychiatrists that had existed in 1940. That perforce meant the employment of rapidly and inadequately trained manpower. Psychiatrists claimed that prompt treatment close to the front was spectacularly successful. Their gullible military superiors accepted many of these largely spurious claims. The myth was thus born that psychiatrists possessed effective outpatient treatments and, postwar, the center of gravity in the profession moved rapidly from institutional psychiatry to outpatient and office treatment. Moreover, since the origins of psychiatric breakdown among the troops was seen as the product of stress and social-psychological pressures, and their treatment, such as it was, predominantly consisted of brief psychotherapeutic interventions, the war contributed much, albeit indirectly and unintentionally, to the rise of psychodynamic psychiatry, and to the general acceptance of the view that many forms of mental disorder had psychological roots and could be treated by psychological therapies.[18]

[17] Shephard, *War of Nerves*, 327.
[18] Scull, *Psychiatry and Its Discontents*, 197–201.

That intellectual shift in psychiatry's center of gravity helped to alter the public's sense of the causes and appropriate treatment of mental illness. Over time, it also broadened the public's view of mental illness and therapy far beyond the sorts of severely disturbed individuals who were then confined in mental hospitals. In an increasingly affluent postwar America, these shifts underpinned the rapid growth of an office-based psychiatry, and fostered the notion (reinforced in neo-Freudian child-raising manuals like Dr. Spock's, in self-help books, and in the general culture, especially the portrayals of psychiatry in the movies) that milder forms of mental illness were rooted in psychological travails and could be effectively treated using psychotherapy. It was a set of changes that underpinned the extraordinary expansion of the market for psychiatric services, and something that unintentionally helped to create a novel space for psychology to colonize and set up in competition with medics.

The problems posed by psychiatrically disabled veterans were profound, and did not vanish with the end of hostilities. On the contrary, tens of thousands of soldiers required ongoing hospitalization, and hundreds of thousands of others were in receipt of pensions and in need of attention for lesser forms of psychiatric disorder. The Veterans Administration thus was in the forefront of federal involvement in the problems created by mental illness. And from 1949 onwards, spurred by the creation of the National Institute of Mental Health (NIMH), the federal government entered the mental health sector in an ever-increasing way, providing massive flows of dollars to fund the training of new professionals, and to underwrite a broad array of research on mental illness, much of which flowed to the social sciences. From the early nineteenth century onwards, mental illness (unlike physical illness) had been recognized as a problem that in the last analysis depended upon subventions from the public purse. Indeed, the vast majority of the half million and more patients who crowded America's mental hospitals in the years after the war were there at public expense. But the treatment of the mentally ill had always fallen on the shoulders of the states, not the federal government. The uniquely American ideologically rooted opposition to public healthcare helps to explain why, even after the war, federal involvement in the mental health sector remained largely confined to research and training, rather than the direct provision of services. (Veterans, as they had been since the Civil War, were and remain an exception to this pattern of rejection of "socialized medicine.")[19]

---

[19] Skocpol, *Protecting Soldiers and Mothers*.

9.3 The Advent of Clinical Psychology

During the war, the mismatch between the number of trained psychiatrists and the demand for treatment of psychiatric casualties among the troops had prompted the recruitment of some psychologists to treatment teams – a move made easier by the fact that the treatments on offer were essentially supportive and psychotherapeutic in nature, and by the existence of military hierarchies that enabled medics to remain in overall charge. As many as 1,700 psychologists could now claim such experience. In the aftermath, the lengthy training for new psychiatrists ensured that shortages of trained manpower remained great, and to ease the strain, and to allow certification of psychologists who had found that they enjoyed the challenges of clinical work, some of the federal training dollars were diverted into newly created programs to train psychologists as therapists. A 1946 survey of every psychologist and psychologist-in-training who had served in the military showed how powerful the demand was for such training. "Hundreds of [these psychologists] had practiced psychotherapy for the first time and many intended to return to school for further training in this field."[20] PhD-granting departments were essentially bribed with federal dollars to set up such programs and to admit eager students to the new specialty.

There was fierce resistance in some departments of psychology to these initiatives. "Applied" work in university settings has traditionally been regarded with suspicion, and "theoretical" work routinely carries the highest prestige.[21] Wedded to this view, and to the laboratory-based, natural science–aping, research-oriented model of their discipline, some high-status departments like Harvard, Princeton, and the University of Pennsylvania rejected the very idea of establishing such programs.[22] Others, however, were more easily swayed. In 1940, there was not a single psychology department offering a PhD program in clinical psychology.[23] In short order, that now began to change, and as that happened, so the center of gravity of psychology as a social science began to shift, and to shift irrevocably.

Chafing at their subordinate position in the social division of labor, clinical psychologists sought to bolster the legitimacy of their new profession and to obtain a greater degree of professional autonomy. Leaders of the movement realized that their legitimacy depended upon close ties to university departments, and a curriculum that combined clinical training and

[20] Herman, *Romance of American Psychology*, 84, 92, 94.
[21] Abbott, *System of Professions*.
[22] Seligman, *Hope Circuit*, 179.
[23] Farreras, "Before Boulder," 19.

demonstrated competence in research methodology. At a 1949 conference held in Boulder, Colorado, and funded by the US Public Health Service's Division of Mental Hygiene, the nuts and bolts of just such a program were hammered out. What became known as the "scientist-practitioner model" was the core of the new approach, which appropriated the mantle of science and combined it with supervised clinical training, emphasizing "the necessity of an academic background in general and experimental psychology as the foundation for training in clinical psychology… ."[24]

Politically, this was an extraordinarily astute program.[25] By requiring two years of basic training in psychological science, it encouraged the model's acceptance by existing academic departments. The influx of large numbers of federally funded clinical psychologists brought tremendous amounts of new funding to the discipline, and the prospect of adding substantial numbers of new research faculty. The "scientist-practitioner" model ritually bowed to the superior knowledge and standing of the researchers, provided a "scientific" basis for the new professionals' practice, and created a means of distinguishing the properly trained from the quack. Confining ourselves only to the top ten departments in the discipline, the number of members of the American Psychological Association (APA) employed in these universities rose from 309 in 1945 to 1,163 in 1965, as federal dollars allowed the hiring of ever-increasing quantities of research staff, and the establishment of a multitude of centers, laboratories, institutes, and bureaus.[26]

As early as 1947, the Veterans Administration was underwriting the training of 200 clinical psychologists. From 1949 onwards, the newly established NIMH advanced much larger sums to underwrite graduate and professional training, and while the bulk of the Institute's funding was committed to the training of psychiatrists, a substantial volume of federal funding was diverted to clinical psychology, subsidizing the hiring of additional faculty in psychology departments, and providing stipends to would-be practitioners.[27] The upshot was a dramatic expansion of the field. In 1945, the APA had 4,173 members. By 1960, there were more than 18,000 – a reflection of the fact that five times as many doctorates in psychology had been awarded in the 1950s as in the preceding decade. By the turn of the century, membership exceeded 80,000, and those numbers continued to rise, reaching a peak of more than 92,000 in 2008. National Science

---

[24] Farreras, "Historical Context," 169.
[25] Baker and Benjamin, "Creating a Profession."
[26] Rice, *Economic Costs*, 64–66.
[27] Rice, *Economic Costs*, 64–66; see also Grob, *From Asylum to Community*, 65.

Foundation data suggested that by 1964, more than two-thirds of American psychologists with a doctorate were working in the mental health field, and the number of clinicians had continued to grow at a remarkable rate.

Unquestionably, then, the demographic profile of American psychology has been decisively altered by the discipline's developing connections to the mental health sector. For some decades, however, the professional association continued to be dominated by laboratory-based, academically oriented psychologists, who continued to monopolize the highest offices in the profession's councils, a reflection of the greater prestige that still accrued to those committed to basic research rather than applied psychology. It was an intellectual and institutional dominance aided by the willingness of the NIMH bureaucracy, and especially of its first director, Robert Felix, to interpret his mandate to underwrite federal funding of research in extraordinarily broad and wide-ranging terms. Though NIMH from the outset developed some intramural research capacity, the overwhelming bulk of its support for research was directed externally, to fund peer-reviewed research on matters related in some fashion to mental illness. Those boundaries might have been narrowly or broadly drawn. In the event, they were difficult to discern, since a huge range of topics were regarded as legitimate subjects for research support. Emphasizing the enormous direct and indirect costs of mental illness, Felix and his staff successfully lobbied Congress for escalating levels of federal support. An initial budget of $9 million in 1949 grew to $14 million in 1955, $50 million by 1959, and $189 million by 1964.[28]

Remarkably, more than half of these funds went to psychology, and only a small fraction to psychiatry. In 1964, for example, 60 percent of NIMH research funding went to psychologists, and a mere 15 percent to psychiatrists.[29] Academic psychiatry in the postwar years had moved in a heavily psychoanalytic direction, with virtually all major university departments headed by psychoanalytically trained psychiatrists or sympathizers. Relying primarily on the clinical case history, and oriented for the most part toward practice, not large-scale research, such scholars were neither equipped nor inclined to compete for the research dollars NIMH now proffered.[30] Little more than 2 percent of the NIMH research grants paid out between 1948 and 1963 went to psychoanalysts or psychoanalytic institutes, and even when one looks solely at grants for research on psychotherapy, the picture is little different, with analysts

[28] Grob, *From Asylum to Community*, 68.
[29] Brand and Sapir, "Historical Perspective," 66–67.
[30] Paris, *Fall of an Icon*.

garnering a mere 7 percent of this money.[31] By contrast, the experimental, laboratory-based, and statistical character of academic psychology, and its conformance with the hypothesis-testing empiricism that was seen as the hallmark of "science," made it far more capable of developing research programs that satisfied the requirements of peer review. Guided by their academic colleagues, clinically oriented psychologists were soon equally adept at modeling their grant proposals along these lines. And, crucially, this led clinical psychology to develop therapeutic interventions that targeted particular symptom-complexes for modification, and that could claim some degree of empirical, "scientific" validation.

Where psychoanalysts spoke in grandiose terms about reconstructing entire personalities (a reconstruction that did not lend itself to measurement or proof, and that seemed to take an eternity to realize), clinical psychologists could offer tested, time-limited interventions that promised measurable improvement in symptoms. Cognitive-behavioral therapies that presented themselves as possessing statistical validation would prove an important comparative advantage when psychotherapists sought insurance reimbursement, and helped clinical psychologists to legitimize their profession to a larger public. Once psychiatry elected to abandon psychoanalysis and re-embrace its identity as a biologically oriented specialism – a shift that derived in part from the psychopharmacological revolution and rapidly gathered pace from 1980 onwards, with the publication of the third edition of the American Psychiatric Association's *Diagnostic and Statistical Manual* (DSM) – the pathway was open for clinical psychology to cement its jurisdictional sway over much of the psychotherapeutic enterprise.

The absence of any clear understanding of the etiology of mental illness in the mid–twentieth century had encouraged Felix to adopt an eclectic-scattershot approach to the question of what types of research to fund. Even research with only the most tangential relationship to NIMH's ostensible mission was supported – at least that was so until the advent of the Reagan presidency in 1980, when the socially activist agenda of some of the projects brought an abrupt halt to the more peripheral projects, and a move to focus on "neutral," biomedical research. Any continuing unease among academic psychologists about the growing presence of "applied" psychology was thus largely assuaged by the flow of support for basic research on cognition, perception, personality, and social psychology, and even for such esoteric fields as comparative psychology, or research on the psychology of the

[31] Hale, *Rise and Crisis of Psychoanalysis*, 252.

animal kingdom.[32] Central or tangential to providing solutions to the problems posed by mental illness, it scarcely seemed to matter to Felix and his minions. And for an extended period, the clinical and applied portions of psychology seemed content to be led by the ever-smaller fraction of the profession that claimed the mantle of pure psychological science.

But not indefinitely. Numerically, clinical psychologists had become the dominant fraction of psychology less than a decade after World War II, and they were not unaware that they were regarded with barely concealed contempt by their purely academically inclined colleagues.[33] In the late 1970s, a group that defiantly called themselves the "dirty dozen" (there were actually fourteen of them) began to organize, plotting a takeover of the APA, and organizing their fellow clinical psychologists to form a voting block that, by 1980, had succeeded in replacing the profession's leadership with an essentially unbroken parade of practitioners. Simultaneously, many of the conspirators (their self-description) were active in a movement to establish free-standing proprietary schools of clinical psychology. The old "scientist-practitioner" model was dismissed as a redundant captive of the ivory-tower academic psychologists.[34] Having done a deal with the devil that many of them saw applied psychologists as being, psychology's mandarins now were forced to retreat to the more comfortable surroundings of an alternative professional association, the American Psychological Society (later renamed the Association for Psychological Science to emphasize its self-identity), and to a handful of congenial divisions of the now-vast APA.

From a public policy point of view, the availability of a large population of professional psychologists trained in psychotherapy would prove to have powerful effects on how mental illness was conceptualized, approached, and treated. As will be analyzed in more detail below, the passage of a revised diagnostic manual by the American Psychiatric Association in 1980 prompted a swing back to biology on the part of psychiatrists, encouraged by the growing symbiotic relationship between psychiatry and the pharmaceutical industry, which did much to "educate" the public about biology and mental illness. The changing psychiatric landscape also coincided with a major shift in the delivery of all forms of medicine toward managed care. These two developments squeezed psychoanalytic psychiatry and brought about its rapid decline.

---

[32] Rice, "Research Grants Program."
[33] Seligman, *Hope Circuit*, 179–82.
[34] Seligman, *Hope Circuit*, chap. 18 and Wright and Cummings, *The Practice of Psychology*.

Insurance companies baulked at paying for unproven psychotherapy that cost large sums and lasted for months and years. They greatly preferred the laboratory-tested and far briefer symptomatic treatments that had developed under the rubric of cognitive-behavioral therapy, and found that, when offering lower reimbursement rates for this form of psychotherapy, they could still attract clinical psychologists to practice. Medics, by contrast, were disinclined to accept this sharp decrease in their incomes. The upshot has been a dramatic shift in how mental illness, broadly defined, is being defined and dealt with as a social problem. Psychiatrists, exploiting their monopoly over prescription drugs, have emphasized the notion that mental illness is brain disease and distanced themselves from the provision of psychotherapy.[35] Clinical psychologists have moved into the space the physicians have vacated, and along with psychiatric social workers, have become the primary providers of psychotherapy.

9.4 Sociology and Mental Illness in the Postwar Era

If the encounter with mental illness has thus had an enormous impact on the discipline of psychology and in turn has helped to reshape the treatment of mental ills, its impact on sociology has been far more muted. Perhaps mercifully for those outside the guild, sociology never attracted the levels of mental health funding that transformed its sister social science, and society has been spared a horde of applied sociologists ministering to society's mental health. It has perforce remained a comparatively small, largely academic discipline. The social dimensions of mental illness are hard to miss, however, and as we have seen, members of the Chicago School and other prewar American sociologists were interested from the discipline's very earliest years in the sociological study of mental health issues. Nor was the NIMH shy about extending its largesse in this direction, and if it never acquired the riches showered upon psychology, sociology did manage to acquire a respectable amount of funding from federal sources, funding that largely ceased with the advent of the Reagan years.

Wartime experience had altered psychiatry's approach to mental illness, as we have seen, but it had also had profound effects on public perceptions of mental illness, as well as inducing politicians to pay greater attention to the issue. The prewar focus on psychosis had been associated with a binary perception of the differences between the mad and the sane, and

[35] Mojtabai and Olfson, "National Trends in Psychotherapy" and Harris, "Talk Doesn't Pay so Psychiatry."

a related attitude toward the social problems presented by the mentally ill, one that emphasized the biological inferiority of those confined in the mental hospital, and the necessity of separating them from the larger society. Psychiatric breakdowns during the war among populations prescreened for alleged susceptibility to mental illness, and among soldiers who were seen as heroically performing their patriotic duty, were widely interpreted to mean that, under sufficient stress, everyone was prone to mental breakdown. The whole approach to combat neurosis emphasized the social and psychological dimensions of mental illness as a social problem, and the leadership of the newly formed NIMH had absorbed this lesson. Hence their willingness, even eagerness, to fund work in the social sciences that might contribute to the understanding of the social dimensions of mental disturbance and to resolving the social problems associated with it. It was a vision that would continue to animate federal policy in this arena through the Carter years. Only with the arrival of Reagan and the neoliberal outlook that he brought with him, was the stress on the social and psychological dimensions of mental illness abandoned, to be replaced by a renewed emphasis on biology. It is a stance that has come to dominate federal policy in the decades since.

Substantively, much of the work in the 1950s built upon the intellectual foundations provided by the Chicago School, with its dual emphasis on quantitative and ethnographic techniques. Large-scale studies of social class and mental illness, mental illness and the family, and popular conceptions of mental illness were undertaken, and in some cases stretched over several decades. Simultaneously, the centrality of the mental hospital in the provision of mental health services in these years, and the relevance of sociological perspectives for studying these complex organizations meant that the asylum and its pathologies became a focus of a good deal of funded research.

In the early 1950s, much of the social science research that was undertaken was collaborative in nature. It linked psychiatrists and other mental health professionals with sociologists, in a pooling of academic resources. At Yale, for example, the chair of the sociology department, August B. Hollingshead, joined with the chair of the psychiatry department, Fritz Redlich, to supervise a long-running examination of the links between social class and mental illness.[36] Some of their associates, and separate

---

[36] Hollingshead and Redlich, *Social Class and Mental Illness* and, for a critique, Scull, "Mental Health Sector and the Social Sciences in Post-World War II USA, Part II."

groups working within the Biometry Branch at NIMH, looked instead at mental illness and family dynamics.[37]

But these early interdisciplinary collaborations did not last. To an increasing extent, the sociological literature on mental illness adopted a more critical stance toward psychiatry and toward psychiatric institutions. The shifting intellectual climate was evident as early as 1956, when Ivan Belknap published an ethnographic study of a Texas mental hospital. Belknap's central conclusion is that "mental hospitals are probably themselves obstacles in the development of an effective plan of treatment for the mentally ill." "In the long run," he continued, "the abandonment of the state hospital might be one of the greatest humanitarian reforms and the greatest financial economy ever achieved."[38] Such disparaging attitudes are equally evident in later works such as Dunham and Weinberg's 1960 *The Culture of the State Mental Hospital* and Perrucci's *Circle of Madness*, published in 1974.[39] But they undoubtedly reached their apogee in Erving Goffman's devastating 1961 portrait of mental hospitals as "total institutions," which became one of the most famous and enduring works of mid–twentieth century sociology.[40]

If Goffman's *Asylums* presented a searing critique of American mental hospitals as engines of degradation and destruction that falsely put on a medical gloss – a book that helped to make Goffman one of the most prominent sociologists of his generation – it did not, as is often thought, constitute his last word on the subject. Goffman's first wife endured an ongoing struggle with mental illness, and eventually committed suicide in 1974. Perhaps this direct acquaintance with the realities of psychosis had a sobering effect. In any event, less than a decade after his book appeared, Goffman returned to the subject of mental illness. This time he stressed "the social significance of the confusion [the mental patient] creates," and argued that the disturbances to the social order that followed "may be as profound and basic as social existence can get." Where in his earlier work, he had spoken of "contingencies" and of the "betrayal" of mental patients into the mental hospital, now in a more chastened mood he acknowledged that

[37] Myers and Roberts, *Family and Class Dynamics in Mental Illness*; Greenblatt, Levinson, and Williams, *Patient and the Mental Hospital*; Leighton, Clausen, and Wilson, *Explorations in Social Psychiatry*; Rennie and Srole, "Social Class Prevalence and Distribution"; and Yarrow et al., "Psychological Meaning of Mental Illness."
[38] Belknap, *Human Problems of a State Mental Hospital*, xi, 212.
[39] Dunham and Weinberg, *Culture of the State Mental Hospital* and Perrucci, *Circle of Madness*.
[40] Goffman, *Asylums*.

"mental symptoms are not, by and large, incidentally a social infraction. By and large, they are specifically and pointedly offensive ... It follows that if the patient persists in his symptomatic behavior, then he must create organizational havoc and havoc in the minds of members of society."[41]

Such statements implied that Goffman had moved away from the central argument of *Asylums*, that the crucial factor in forming a mental patient was the impact of the institution, not his illness. Yet, he remained as savagely critical as he had ever been about psychiatry as a "tinkering trade." The havoc that mental illness gave rise to is, he asserted, something "that psychiatrists have dismally failed to examine." As for the "curative" institutions they presided over, "patients recover more often than not ... in spite of the mental hospital, not because of it." Psychiatry's therapeutic claims verged on the fraudulent, and asylums had proved to be "hopeless storage dumps trimmed in psychiatric paper." And while it was true that they "served to remove the patient from the scene of his symptomatic behavior" (something Goffman concedes "can be constructive"), "the price the patient has had to pay for this service has been considerable: dislocation from civil life, alienation from loved ones who arranged the commitment, mortification due to hospital regimentation and surveillance, and permanent posthospital stigmatization. This has been not merely a bad deal; it has been a grotesque one."[42]

During the 1960s, the intellectual gulf between sociology and psychiatry grew wider still. Within five years of the appearance of *Asylums*, the California sociologist Thomas Scheff had authored a still more radical assault on psychiatry, dismissed the "medical model" of mental illness as a failed ideological construct, and attempted to replace it with what he called a "societal reaction model." Mental patients, on the account he presents in *Being Mentally Ill*, were victims of socially exclusionary practices – victims, most obviously, of psychiatrists and their institutional power to define them as pathological, to confine them, and to damage their future life chances.[43] In a line of criticism that echoed the contemporary arguments of the renegade psychiatrist Thomas Szasz,[44] Scheff contends that psychiatrists had spent centuries trying to legitimize their authority and particular perspective on mental disturbance, and yet "there is no rigorous knowledge of the cause, cure, or even the symptoms of functional mental disorders." Instead of continuing to pursue this will o' the wisp, sociology offers a more

[41] Goffman, "Insanity of Place," 387, 368, 357.
[42] Goffman, "Insanity of Place," 357, 369.
[43] Scheff, *Being Mentally Ill*.
[44] Szasz, *Myth of Mental Illness*.

compelling perspective: "a theory of mental disorder in which psychiatric symptoms are considered to be labeled violations of social norms, and stable 'mental illness' to be a social role." As for the etiology of insanity, "societal reaction [not internal pathology] is usually the most important determinant of entry into that role."[45]

Among sociologists specializing in the study of deviance, societal reaction theory enjoyed a broad popularity and acceptance in the 1960s and 1970s (see Chapter 8: Addiction).[46] Scheff's work stood as one of the principal works in that tradition, and the popularity of its claims drew derision and hostility from the ranks of psychiatrists, who bristled at its denigration of their professional competence, and derided its failure to acknowledge the reality of psychosis.[47] Internally, too, Scheff's thesis came under increasing attack. The British sociologist David Morgan subjected it to scathing theoretical criticism,[48] while American critics sought to demolish its claims on empirical grounds.[49] In the face of devastating objections to his original theory, Scheff was eventually forced to retreat from his more extreme claims, though the publication of new editions of his book testified to a continuing attachment among some sociologists to his work. By the third edition of *Being Mentally Ill*, however, little remained of the initial argument, its bolder claims having been quietly abandoned.[50] To be sure, labeling and the stigmatization of the mentally ill have remained objects of sociological research, but few would now argue that these phenomena, real though they may be, have the etiological significance once attributed to them.[51]

9.5 Transformations of American Psychiatry

Sociologists and historians who have sought to understand the place of mental illness in American society have had to come to terms with four major interrelated changes that have characterized the psychiatric sector in the past half-century or so. The first has been the progressive abandonment of the prior commitment to segregative responses to serious mental illness.

---

[45] Scheff, *Being Mentally Ill*, 7, 25, 28.
[46] Scull, "Competing Perspectives on Deviance."
[47] Roth, "Psychiatry and Its Critics."
[48] Morgan, "Explaining Mental Illness."
[49] Gove, "Societal Reaction as an Explanation for Mental Illness" and Gove and Howell, "Individual Resources and Mental Hospitalization."
[50] Scheff, *Being Mentally Ill*, 3rd ed.
[51] Link, "Mental Patient Status, Work, and Income"; Link et al., "Social Rejection of Former Mental Patients"; and Thoits, "Self-Labeling Processes in Mental Illness."

The mental hospital, which had been the first-line response to cases of serious mental illness from the 1840s onwards, has all but vanished from the scene. Second, psychoanalysis, which dominated American psychiatry from the end of World War II into the 1970s, has seen its hegemony collapse with quite remarkable speed. Since that period, psychoanalysis has not attracted the most talented younger psychiatrists, and has grave difficulty sustaining its training institutes. All the major academic departments of psychiatry, which were almost universally led by psychoanalysts or those sympathetic to psychoanalysis, are now dominated by biological psychiatrists and neuroscientists. Third, in place of talk therapy, psychiatric practice is now heavily dependent on dispensing drugs, and deeply in thrall to the multinational pharmaceutical houses. The psychopharmacological revolution that began in the early 1950s has transformed both popular and professional ideas about the origins and appropriate treatment of mental disorders. Fourth (and closely connected to these other revolutionary changes), American psychiatry has embraced the neo-Kraepelinian revolution. Beginning with the publication of the third edition of the American Psychiatric Association's *Diagnostic and Statistical Manual of Mental Disorders* (DSM) in 1980, the field has adopted a tick-the-boxes approach to treating mental illness. Because insurance reimbursements are tied to the use of DSM diagnoses, even the competing profession of clinical psychology has been forced to adopt this approach, and its links to the prescription drugs that now form the lynchpin of psychiatric practice have spread the influence of the DSM worldwide.

Sociologists have played a crucial role in analyzing the sources and impact of most of these changes, and their research has been highly influential among others attempting to make sense of these profoundly important developments. Deinstitutionalization, for example, was originally presented as a grand reform, ironically just as the mental hospital first had been.[52] From the mid-1970s, however, a more skeptical set of perspectives emerged. Psychiatrists had assumed that the new generation of antipsychotic drugs had been the primary drivers of the change. A series of studies demonstrated the fallacy of this claim.[53]

Though mental hospital populations, after increasing steadily for more than a century, had begun to decline from a peak of 558,000 in 1955, the

---

[52] Rothman, *Discovery of the Asylum*; Scull, *Museums of Madness*; and Scull, *Most Solitary of Afflictions*.

[53] Scull, "Decarceration of the Mentally Ill"; Scull, *Decarceration*; Lerman, *Deinstitutionalization and the Welfare State*; and Gronfein, "Psychotropic Drugs."

decrease in patient numbers was quite slow at first, and only began to accelerate by the mid-1960s. The fast decline largely coincided with the passage of the Community Mental Health Centers Act in 1963, in the months before John F. Kennedy's assassination. Did the new federally supported community programs help to usher in the change in policy, and what had prompted the new legislation?

Kennedy's sister Rosemary, who was possibly mildly mentally retarded, at the instigation of her father had been lobotomized in the early 1940s, with catastrophic results. Perhaps as a consequence, the Kennedy family had taken an unusual degree of interest in mental health matters. Kennedy's sister Eunice Shriver had played an active role in the creation of the Special Olympics, and the family foundation had been active in supporting research into mental retardation at Harvard.[54] Kennedy's interest in mental health issues was an extension of this family concern.[55]

In December 1961, Kennedy formed an Interagency Task Force on Mental Health, bringing together high-level officials from a variety of government departments (including Rashi Fein from the Council of Economic Advisers, one of the few economists with an academic interest in mental health issues). Crucially, both the director of NIMH, Robert Felix, and his deputy, Stanley Yolles, were members of the task force and, perhaps not surprisingly, NIMH came to play the major role in drafting the recommendations that formed the basis of the new legislation that passed in 1963. Till then, as we have seen, the provision of mental health services (with the important exception of the Veterans Administration) had been entirely in the hands of the states, which remained committed to the traditional state hospital system. NIMH insiders viewed the mental hospitals with suspicion, if not outright hostility, and seized the opportunity to expand the agency's bureaucratic empire, seeing community-based treatment as an alternative vehicle that would permit NIMH's involvement for the first time in the direct provision of mental health services. As Gerald Grob puts it, under this approach, "The role of the NIMH would ... undergo a major expansion. Its mission to provide advice and oversee the creation of these new centers required a corresponding increase in the size of its regional staffs."[56]

To legitimize the proposed new centers, Felix and his cohorts invoked the language of the prevention of mental illness and the maintenance of mental health, giving the new clinics the task of implementing programs

---

[54] Berkowitz, "Politics of Mental Retardation."
[55] Shorter, *Kennedy Family and the Story of Mental Retardation.*
[56] Grob, *From Asylum to Community,* 222.

to realize these goals. That meant that community mental health services from the outset had an extraordinarily wide mandate, not least because it was not obvious, then as it is now, how to reach such ambitious goals. The rhetoric of the superiority of community care sat alongside the complete absence "of any evaluation of the claims that comprehensive centers could obviate mental hospital care within a generation."[57]

In practice, implementation of the new policy was completely haphazard. The federal subsidies designed to encourage states to build the centers proved insufficient, and attempts under Kennedy's successor, Lyndon Baines Johnson, to provide funding for professional staff were largely stymied by the claim that they represented the thin end of the wedge of socialized medicine. There had been no attempt to provide any systematic linkage between the community programs and the existing state hospital system and, in any event, those running the new centers wanted nothing to do with such a difficult and unattractive patient population. From the outset, as Ronald Rieder shows, they sought an entirely different clientele: "'good patients' [rather] than chronic schizophrenics, alcoholics, or senile psychotics" – i.e., those with mild forms of mental disorder, or with more diffuse needs for support.[58]

This deliberate policy of discrimination against ex–state hospital patients and refusal to meet their needs meant that these places played essentially no role in the accelerating decline of the mental hospital census that marked the late 1960s and 1970s.[59] Within less than a decade of their creation, as temporary federal support began to vanish, "the relationship between the speciality of psychiatry and centers became problematical ... Centers were largely staffed by clinical psychologists, social workers, or non-professional staff – groups that had neither interest in nor experience with the severely mentally ill."[60] Rapidly spiraling into irrelevance, the community mental health legislation likewise provides no explanation for the growing abandonment by the states of the traditional mental hospital.

As they looked for alternative explanations of the shift in social policy, amid a growing recognition of the defects of so-called community care (in reality, community neglect), some scholars have argued that sociologists' systematic deconstruction of the claim that the mental hospital provided a

[57] Grob, *From Asylum to Community*, 224.
[58] Rieder, "Hospitals, Patients, and Politics," 11.
[59] Chu and Trotter, *Madness Establishment*; Kirk and Thierren, "Community Mental Health Myths"; Windle and Scully, "Community Mental Health Centers"; Rose, "Deciphering Deinstitutionalization"; and Gronfein, "Incentives and Intentions in Mental Health Policy."
[60] Grob, *From Asylum to Community*, 256.

therapeutic function, or even valuable sheltered care, was of considerable importance in undermining the legitimacy of these institutions and in reorienting social policy. Critical sociologists, on this view, smoothed the way toward the abandonment of segregative modes of controlling madness. But empirical work undertaken from a variety of perspectives has demonstrated that neither these shifts in sentiment nor the psychopharmacological revolution that began with the introduction of phenothiazine under the trade names Thorazine (in the United States) and Largactil (in Europe) were the primary factors behind the emptying out of the Victorian bins. The drugs revolution, and the fact that the overwhelming majority of psychiatrists no longer practiced in mental hospitals, meant that psychiatry made little effort to defend the mental hospital. And it is true that the sociological critiques of total institutions helped to distract attention from the lack of alternative provision for deinstitutionalized patients, and to give a humanitarian gloss to a policy of malign neglect. But both of these factors were not the primary force behind the emptying of institutions. What drove things instead was a conscious shift in social policy, much of it provoked by fiscal concerns.[61]

Soon after the publication of DSM III, the re-biologization of psychiatry and the revised importance of psychiatric classification drew increased scholarly attention. Sociologists took the lead in critically examining the processes through which successive editions of the manual had been produced. (There were revisions published in 1987, 1994, 2000, and 2013.) Close attention was paid to both the intended and unintended implications of the manual's widespread use and to the controversial issue of the steady accretion of new psychiatric diagnoses. And criticism was directed at the DSM's emphasis on interrelater reliability in the diagnostic process at the expense of any sustained attention to questions about the validity of the categories that were created.[62] The related phenomenon of the psychopharmacological revolution likewise drew increased interest for its effects on the intellectual orientation of the psychiatric profession and in the form of critical examinations of the role of the pharmaceutic industry.[63]

---

[61] Kirk and Thierren, "Community Mental Health Myths"; Aviram, Syme, and Cohen, "Effects of Policies and Programs"; Windle and Scully, "Community Mental Health Centers"; Scull, *Decarceration*; Rose, "Deciphering Deinstitutionalization"; Gronfein, "Incentives and Intentions in Mental Health Policy"; and Grob, *From Asylum to Community*, chaps. 9, 10.

[62] Kirk and Kutchins, *Selling of DSM*; Kutchins and Kirk, *Making Us Crazy*; Horwitz and Wakefield, *Loss of Sadness*; Horwitz and Wakefield, *All We Have to Fear*; and Greenberg, *Book of Woe*.

[63] Healy, *Antidepressant Era*; Healey, *Creation of Psychopharmacology*; and Hertzberg, *Happy Pills in America*.

All of this work was undertaken in a context where much of the federal money that had once underwritten sociological work on mental illness had been sharply curtailed. In the 1960s and 1970s, NIMH continued the policy it had adopted in its earliest years, defining its mandate broadly and funding an extensive array of psychological and sociological research. In the years of the Great Society, the agency was subjected to political pressures to direct funding toward the solution of a broad array of social problems. NIMH underwrote work on crime, drug and alcohol addiction, suicide, and even rape – all topics that could be construed to bear on mental health issues. During the 1980s, however, this pattern of research funding abruptly altered, and not in ways that favored sociology, or other social sciences come to that.

The Republican administration elected in 1980 promptly ordered NIMH to redirect its funding priorities away from social problem–oriented research toward work more directly pertinent to the understanding of mental disorders.[64] This shift in the political winds occurred just as psychiatry itself was largely abandoning its concern with the social, and embracing a biologically reductionist view of mental illness. Social factors went from being directly relevant in the eyes of most psychiatrists, to being marginal at best to their central concerns. Political pressures to avoid controversial and sensitive work on the sociological dimensions of mental disorder were thus reinforced by the demands of psychiatry for an increased focus on neuroscientific and psychopharmacological research. In the words of Steven Sharfstein, in a presidential address to the American Psychiatric Association, the profession had decisively moved from "the biopsychosocial model [of mental illness] to...the bio-bio-bio model."[65]

9.6 Economics and Mental Illness

This analysis of the connections of the social sciences to the mental health sector has proceeded over a large territory and nearly three-quarters of a century without once mentioning the social science that regards itself as the most highly developed and important of the social sciences: economics. That neglect on my part largely parallels that discipline's own neglect of the problems associated with mental illness. Through the end of the 1950s, there were remarkably few exceptions to this disciplinary silence. To be sure, some of the epidemiologists working in the Biometry Branch of the NIMH had training in economics, and its series of statistical notes on occasion

---

[64] Kolb, Frazier, and Sirovatka, "National Institute of Mental Health."
[65] Sharfstein, "Big Pharma and American Psychiatry."

attempted to quantify the direct and indirect costs of mental illness, but this sort of applied work did not appeal to mainstream economists, or make any mark in their professional journals. There was one large monographic study of the economics of mental illness published by a major economist. Rashi Fein, a health economist then at the University of North Carolina, produced the volume in 1958, but it was the exception that proves the rule.[66]

The book's appearance was no accident. Nor did it reflect Fein's independent decision to focus his analytic lens on the particular topic. Rather, Congress had established a Joint Commission on Mental Illness and Health in 1955, and that body had commissioned Fein to tackle these issues, just as it commissioned reports from other social scientists to inform its deliberations: work on popular conceptions of mental health; on the sources and shortages of trained professional manpower; on schools and mental health; on religion and mental health; and so forth. Both Fein and those employing him acknowledged that prior work in this area was scarce, and the data needed for a systematic analysis were sparse. Fein was able to assemble some reasonably reliable information on the direct costs of coping with mental illness. State budgets, for example, provided some data on this front. But the more important task of assessing the indirect costs to society that mental illness brought in its train proved largely beyond him. The territory was, of course, by its very nature, ambiguous and subject to conflicting interpretations. But Fein's estimates on the burdens placed on individuals, families, and society at large, while the best available, were unreliable and in many respects obviously only a little better than guesswork.

Five years later, Kenneth Arrow (already in receipt of the John Bates Clark medal that marked him as one of the leading economists of his generation, and who would later win a Nobel Prize in Economics in 1972) published a classic paper on the welfare economics of healthcare.[67] But neither this seminal paper nor the extraordinary economic impact of healthcare expenditures in general, and mental health care costs in particular, sufficed to attract mainstream economists to undertake research and to publish in this area. Health economics, to be sure, began to attract a modicum of attention, as economists sought to understand the dynamics of private healthcare markets, and the relationship between healthcare expenditures and morbidity and mortality. But a stigmatized and impoverished

---

[66] Fein, *Economics of Mental Illness.*
[67] Arrow, "Uncertainty and the Welfare Economics."

population of mental patients, largely provided for through the public sector, seemed to have little attraction to the field.

A discipline founded on the notion of "rational man" perhaps also found what by definition required a focus on the irrational to be a particularly unappetizing subject for its investigations. Some may object to this characterization of the field, pointing out that the Nobel Prize–winning economist Gary Becker pioneered the extension of economic reasoning to a whole variety of behaviors that had previously been seen as outside the domain of economic reasoning. These included even such seemingly irrational behaviors as crime and addiction, and extended to realms also traditionally not seen as relevant to practitioners of the dismal science, such as marriage and family life. Though initially treated as something of a pariah, Becker eventually became one of the most highly respected economists of his generation, and his work has attracted many followers.

Fundamentally, however, Becker's approach still depended on the classic economic idea of rational choice. Criminals, for example, on his account, embrace a life of crime having calculated its payoff, based on their assessment of the opportunities, risks, and rewards confronting them.[68] Becker then concluded, in neo-Benthamite fashion, that deterring crime was best done by increasing its cost (see Chapter 7: Crime). Addiction, another apparent embrace of irrational behavior, was likewise "explained" for him as a behavior embarked upon "to maximize utility over time ... we claim that addictions, even strong ones, are usually rational in the sense of involving forward-looking rational maximization with stable preferences" and that this theory "permits new insights into rational behavior" (see Chapter 8: Addiction).[69]

I am concerned here with the question of whether or not economists seek to analyze social problems, not with the usefulness or validity of the theories they offer. Consequently, I shall offer no commentary on the merits of Becker's scholarship, beyond noting that most social scientists in other disciplines have found these arguments crude and unpersuasive. Instead, I simply observe that these attempts to extend rational economic analysis to include apparently irrational behaviors have not extended, so far as I am aware, to the case of mental illness. That is a significant omission, since for many, the defining characteristic of madness is irrationality. Indeed, it is the break the psychotic makes with the reality the rest of us think we share, and their nonresponsiveness to common sense, everyday attempts to modify their behavior in the ways we

[68] Becker, "Crime and Punishment."
[69] Becker and Murphy, "Theory of Rational Addiction," 675.

usually employ to rein in deviance, that is the very essence of their condition. It is always possible that economists will redefine rationality in a way that allows them to see psychosis as a kind of "forward-looking rational maximization," but I fear that such attempts are likely to be met by those with direct experience of serious forms of mental illness as intellectual constructs worthy only of Jonathan Swift's Grand Academy of Lagado.[70]

Becker notwithstanding, economic theory is overwhelmingly concerned with what Robert Solow has called "'greed, rationality, and equilibrium' through mathematical model-building," none of which are prominent features of most mental illness.[71] It matters, too, I think, that economics has constructed the sharpest disciplinary boundaries of any of the social sciences, and that its professional elites enjoy a tight degree of control over the ranking of individual academic economists and university departments unmatched by their "sister" disciplines. As David Hollinger has noted, the "discipline's relative isolation remains beyond dispute."[72] That isolation is largely voluntary and self-imposed, but it does mean that the focus on the mental health sector that can be seen elsewhere in the social sciences is more readily ignored by economists, and that the opportunities for interdisciplinary work involving, say, psychologists or sociologists are scarce, here as elsewhere. Nancy Campbell (Chapter 8: Addiction) has noted a similar disinclination among applied economists focusing on addiction to engage with other social scientists, and a failure to incorporate other scholars' empirical findings into their model-building, a phenomenon confirmed by the British economist Christine Godfrey.[73]

On the margin, the advent of the Reagan administration brought some increased intellectual attention to the ways in which the tools of economics might be brought to bear on mental health issues. The preceding Carter administration had set up a commission on mental health services which reported in the shadow of Carter's electoral defeat. Its proposals were anathema to the incoming Republicans and were quickly jettisoned. Research on the social dimensions of mental illness that had been a mainstay of the commission's deliberations were now regarded with suspicion if not outright hostility. On the other hand, a senior member of the NIMH staff, Carl Taube, had long been arguing for a more extensive employment of economic ideas and techniques to the problems of the mental health sector. Taube's advocacy

[70] Swift, *Gulliver's Travels*, part III, chap. 5.
[71] Quoted in Hollinger, "Disciplines and the Identity Debates," 345.
[72] Quoted in Hollinger, "Disciplines and the Identity Debates," 345.
[73] *Addiction*, "Conversation with Christine Godfrey."

until then had produced little in the way of concrete results. Before the 1980s, as Thomas McGuire has shown, "there was no work at all on the economics of mental health ... [and] no academically-based economist was working on any variety of economics and mental health."[74]

Beginning in 1980, however, NIMH commenced funding what became a series of biennial conferences on the economics of mental health, in a transparent attempt to stimulate interest in the field. To a degree, this did succeed in creating a community of researchers working on such issues as how the nature of incentives built into different insurance regimes affected consumer behavior and the demand for mental health services;[75] how state regulation might have effects on the provision and shape of mental health insurance;[76] how to model and estimate the costs of competing treatment alternatives;[77] and broader questions of cost.[78]

Over time, work in this field became steadily more technical, and following broader trends in the discipline, emphasized statistical modeling.[79] It attracted a small coterie of dedicated researchers, and can reasonably claim to be an established subfield of applied economics. But while similar federal stimulus had an enormous impact in reshaping the discipline of psychology, and a smaller but very noticeable impact on sociology, it would be grossly mistaken to suggest that anything comparable can be observed in the discipline of economics.

On the contrary, mental health economics remains a small, isolated part of the economic enterprise, its prestige almost nonexistent and its practitioners marginalized. One measure of its lowly status is the venues in which its devotees are forced to publish: in edited volumes, government-supported monographs, and specialized, low-impact journals whose major readership lies outside the ranks of trained economists. Major mainstream economics journals display zero interest in publishing research on this stigmatized subject matter, and it is simply not possible to build a serious academic career in economics without access to these venues.

[74] McGuire, "Research on Economics and Mental Health," 1.
[75] McGuire and Weisbrod, *Economics and Mental Health*; Frank and Lave, "Effect of Benefit Design on the Length"; Keeler, Manning, and Wells, "Demand for Episodes of Mental Health Services"; and Christianson, "Capitation of Mental Health Care."
[76] Mitchell, *Psychiatrists' Behavior under Mental Health Insurance Regulation*; Lambert, "Political and Economic Determinants"; and Frank, "Regulatory Policy and Information Deficiencies."
[77] Dickey et al., "Containing Mental Health Treatment Costs."
[78] Rice, *Economic Costs*.
[79] Compare, for example, the impressionistic work of Rashi Fein, *Economics of Mental Illness*, with the papers collected in Frank and Manning, *Economics and Mental Health*.

Applied work, of course, always tends to be less prestigious work in academic circles.[80] But the problems are compounded here by the comparative characteristics of psychology, sociology, and economics as disciplines. Psychology is an enormously disparate field which has great difficulty in enforcing any sort of intellectual or disciplinary orthodoxy. Indeed, as we have seen, the original core of the discipline, as a scientistic, laboratory-based, and experimental enterprise, proved susceptible to the blandishments of external funding for interventionist and practically oriented work. That underwrote a vast expansion of the field, but in the process shifted its political center of gravity in profound ways. One key symptom of the changes that ensued is that what had been the crucial organization at the center of the profession's identity was captured by clinicians. The "scientists" who had previously been the profession's dominant fraction were forced to lick their wounds, and to retire to an alternative organization that defiantly proclaimed it was the home of psychological science.

Though sociology did not experience a similar degree of disciplinary bloat, it has always been a somewhat inchoate and fractious discipline, unable to converge on a single methodological or theoretical paradigm. Instead, it is made up of a congeries of competing factions who seem unable to develop an overarching, coherent vision of how to approach the study of the social. When federal funds were on offer, they were gratefully swallowed, and work on the sociology of mental health flourished. When they shrank and almost vanished, most sociologists moved on, with only the field's original commitment to the study of social problems providing some continuing interest in the subject.

Economics is far more disciplined, in more than one sense. Though in the twenty-first century, behavioral economics has enjoyed steadily increasing status, and has even captured some of the Nobel Prizes on offer, the neoclassical consensus long enjoyed a stranglehold on the field, and continues to dominate most of it. Building ingenious mathematical models has always enjoyed more prestige than engaging directly with the world. It is not without reason that "economists are sometimes accused … of avoiding the complexities of the real world with the determination of Methodists avoiding a local saloon."[81]

Alternative pathways to professional prominence continue to exist in psychology and sociology. By contrast, orthodoxy is far more powerful in economics, and the orthodox powers-that-be have limited interest in the

[80] Abbott, *System of Professions.*
[81] Hollinger, "Disciplines and the Identity Debates," 347–48.

sorts of questions mental health economics perforce focuses upon. Roger Backhouse and Philippe Fontaine have noted the striking contrast "between the protean disciplinary identity of [psychology] and the strong disciplinary identity of [economics]," and one can easily extend that observation to include sociology.[82] An important corollary, which they note, is "the silencing of dissenting voices within [economics]"[83] – a striking contrast with the situation in the other social sciences.

We have seen that World War II had wide-ranging impacts on psychology. The same was emphatically true of economics. Indeed, Paul Samuelson famously dubbed that conflict "the economist's war."[84] Economists saw themselves (and to a significant degree had secured assent to this perception from the political establishment), as having made massive contributions to the conduct of total war. Triumphant and intellectually self-confident, they presented themselves as having played roles comparable in significance to those of the natural sciences. Indeed, economists (Samuelson most notably among them) saw themselves as occupying an intellectual territory that had closer associations with the natural sciences than the social sciences – a stance inseparable from the shedding of prewar interests in Marshallian and institutionalist economics.[85] Theirs was a "rigorous" and mathematical discipline, one that scorned and deprecated nonmathematical reasoning as soft-headed and useless. A sense of intellectual superiority and aloofness pervaded its practitioners, matched by a self-conscious distancing of themselves from interdisciplinary initiatives that did not bow to the superiority of the economists' toolkit.[86] It was, as Jefferson Pooley and Mark Solovey put it, "the self-segregation of the privileged, with economics eager to leave the social or 'behavioral' sciences behind."[87]

That sense of privilege was no delusion. Economics had indeed secured a position in the larger world that other social sciences could only envy. Its centrality to governance was unchallenged. It was greeted with a respect politicians denied to other social sciences, and its insights became crucial to the formation of economic policy and social policy more generally. Its overtly apolitical and technical stance, and its implicit and explicit loyalty to the

---

[82] Backhouse and Fontaine, "Introduction," 10.
[83] Backhouse and Fontaine, "Introduction," 2.
[84] Samuelson, "Unemployment Ahead."
[85] Morgan and Rutherford, *From Interwar Pluralism to Postwar* and Backhouse and Fontaine, "Conclusions."
[86] Pooley and Solovey, "Marginal to the Revolution" and Geary, "Economics and Sociology."
[87] Pooley and Solovey, "Marginal to the Revolution," 201.

superiority of market capitalism only added to its welcome in the halls of the powerful – in sharp contrast to a meliorist discipline like sociology, so easily confused with "socialism." Economists had no need to chase after scraps from the table served up by NIMH. They had far more lucrative and appetizing sources of funding and influence at their disposal. They were, as Daniel Geary puts it, "quite happy to leave messier social issues to sociologists and other social scientists while concentrating on rigorous models of the economy."[88] Mental illness, as one of the messiest of those mercifully marginalized social issues, had, quite understandably when viewed in this perspective, perhaps the least appeal of all to professional economists. By and large, they responded by ignoring it, and all the problems that followed in its wake.

Bibliography

Abbott, Andrew. *The System of Professions*. Chicago: University of Chicago Press, 1988.
Addiction. "A Conversation with Christine Godfrey." *Addiction* 108, no. 2 (2013): 257–64.
Arrow, Kenneth. "Uncertainty and the Welfare Economics of Medical Care." *American Economic Review* 53 (1963): 941–73.
Aviram, Uri, S. Leonard Syme, and Judith B. Cohen. "The Effects of Policies and Programs on the Reduction of Mental Hospitalization." *Social Science and Medicine* 10, no. 11–12 (1976): 571–77.
Backhouse, Roger, and Philippe Fontaine. "Introduction: History of Economics as History of Social Science." In *The Unsocial Social Science? Economics and Neighboring Disciplines since 1945*, edited by Roger E. Backhouse and Philippe Fontaine, 1–21. Durham: Duke University Press, 2010.
Backhouse, Roger, and Philippe Fontaine. "Conclusions: The Identity of Economics – Image and Reality." In *The Unsocial Social Science? Economics and Neighboring Disciplines since 1945*, edited by Roger E. Backhouse and Philippe Fontaine, 343–51. Durham: Duke University Press, 2010.
Baker, David B., and Ludy T. Benjamin, Jr. "The Affirmation of the Scientist-Practitioner: A Look Back at Boulder." *American Psychologist* 55, no. 2 (2000): 241–47.
Baker, David B., and Ludy T. Benjamin, Jr. "Creating a Profession: The National Institute of Mental Health and the Training of Psychologists, 1946–1954." In *Psychology and the National Institute of Mental Health*, edited by Wade E. Pickren and Stanley Schneider, 181–207. Washington, DC: American Psychological Association, 2005.
Becker, Gary S. "Crime and Punishment: An Economic Approach." *Journal of Political Economy* 76 (1968): 169–217.
Becker, Gary S., and Kevin M. Murphy. "A Theory of Rational Addiction." *Journal of Political Economy* 96 (1988): 675–700.
Belknap, Ivan. *Human Problems of a State Mental Hospital*. New York: McGraw-Hill, 1956.
Berkowitz, Edward. "The Politics of Mental Retardation during the Kennedy Administration." *Social Science Quarterly* 61 (1980): 128–43.

[88] Geary, "Economics and Sociology," 299.

Brand, Jeanne L., and Philip Sapir. "An Historical Perspective on the National Institute of Mental Health." Unpublished mimeograph, National Institute of Mental Health, 1964.

Bulmer, Martin. *The Chicago School of Sociology.* Chicago: University of Chicago Press, 1984.

Bush, Vannevar. *Science: The Endless Frontier.* Washington, DC: Government Printing Office, 1945.

Christianson, John Brian. "Capitation of Mental Health Care in Public Programs." In *Advances in Health Economics and Health Services Research*, edited by Richard M. Scheffler and Louis F. Rossiter, 281–311. Greenwich: JAI Press, 1989.

Chu, Franklin, and Sharland Trotter. *The Madness Establishment.* New York: Grossman, 1984.

Devereux, Georges. *Reality and Dream: Psychotherapy of an American Plains Indian.* New York: International Universities Press, 1969.

Dickey, Barbara, Nancy L. Cannon, Thomas G. McGuire, and Jon E. Gudema. "The Quarterway House: A Two-Year Cost Study of an Experimental Residential Program." *Hospital and Community Psychiatry* 37 (1986): 1136–43.

Dickey, Barbara, Paul R. Binner, Stephen Leff, Mark K. Uyeda, Mark J. Schlesinger, and Jon E. Gudeman. "Containing Mental Health Treatment Costs Through Program Design: A Massachusetts Study." *American Journal of Public Health* 79, no. 7 (1989): 863–67.

Dunham, H. Warren, and S. Kirson Weinberg. *The Culture of the State Mental Hospital.* Detroit: Wayne State University Press, 1960.

Faris, Robert. *Chicago Sociology: 1920–1932.* San Francisco: Chandler, 1967.

Faris, Robert, and H. Warren Dunham. *Mental Disorders in Urban Areas: An Ecological Study of Schizophrenia and Other Psychoses.* Chicago: University of Chicago Press, 1939.

Farreras, Ingrid. "Before Boulder: Professionalizing Clinical Psychology, 1896–1949." PhD diss., University of New Hampshire, 2001.

Farreras, Ingrid. "The Historical Context for the National Institute of Mental Health Support of American Psychological Association Training and Accreditation Efforts." In *Psychology and the National Institute of Mental Health*, edited by Wade E. Pickren and Stanley Schneider, 153–79. Washington, DC: American Psychological Association, 2005.

Fein, Rashi. *The Economics of Mental Illness.* New York: Basic Books, 1958.

Fontaine, Philippe. "Walking the Tightrope: The Committee on the Behavioral Sciences and Academic Cultures at the University of Chicago, 1949–1955." *Journal of the History of the Behavioral Sciences* 52, no. 4 (2016): 349–70.

Frank, Richard G. "Regulatory Policy and Information Deficiencies in the Market for Mental Health Services." *Journal of Health Politics, Policy, and Law* 14 (1989): 477–503.

Frank, Richard G., and J. R. Lave. "The Effect of Benefit Design on the Length of Stay of Psychiatric Patients." *Journal of Human Resources* 21 (1986): 321–37.

Frank, Richard G., and W. G. Manning, eds. *Economics and Mental Health.* Baltimore: Johns Hopkins University Press, 1992.

Freud, Sigmund. *Totem und Tabu.* Leipzig: Heller, 1913.

Freud, Sigmund. *Totem and Taboo: Resemblances between the Psychic Lives of Savages and Neurotics.* Translated by A. A. Brill. London: Routledge, 1919.

Geary, Daniel. "Economics and Sociology: From Complementary to Competing Perspectives." In *The Unsocial Social Science? Economics and Neighboring Disciplines since 1945*, edited by Roger E. Backhouse and Philippe Fontaine, 291–314. Durham: Duke University Press, 2010.

Gehrie, Mark J. "Psychoanalytic Anthropology: A Brief Review of the State of the Art." *American Behavioral Scientist* 20 (1977): 721–32.

Gitre, Edward. "Importing Freud: First Wave Psychoanalysis, Interwar Social Sciences, and the Interdisciplinary Foundations of an American Social Theory." *Journal of the History of the Behavioral Sciences* 36 (2010): 239–62.

Goffman, Erving. *Asylums: Essays on the Social Situation of Mental Patients and Other Inmates*. New York: Doubleday, 1961.

Goffman, Erving. "The Insanity of Place." *Psychiatry* 32 (1969): 357–88.

Gove, Walter R. "Societal Reaction as an Explanation for Mental Illness: An Evaluation." *American Sociological Review* 35 (1970): 873–84.

Gove, Walter R., and Patrick Howell. "Individual Resources and Mental Hospitalization: A Comparison of the Societal Reaction and Psychiatric Perspectives." *American Sociological Review* 39, no. 1 (1974): 86–100.

Greenberg, Gary. *The Book of Woe: The DSM and the Unmaking of Psychiatry*. New York: Plume, 2013.

Greenblatt, Milton, D. J. Levinson, and R. H. Williams. *The Patient and the Mental Hospital*. Glencoe: The Free Press, 1957.

Grob, Gerald. *From Asylum to Community: Mental Health Policy in Modern America*. Princeton: Princeton University Press, 1991.

Gronfein, William. "Incentives and Intentions in Mental Health Policy: A Comparison of the Medicaid and Community Mental Health Programs." *Journal of Health and Social Behavior* 26 (1985): 192–206.

Gronfein, William. "Psychotropic Drugs and the Origins of Deinstitutionalization." *Social Problems* 32 (1985): 437–54.

Hale, Nathan. *The Rise and Crisis of Psychoanalysis in the United States*. Oxford: Oxford University Press, 1998.

Harris, Gardiner, "Talk Doesn't Pay so Psychiatry Turns Instead to Drug Therapy." *The New York Times*. March 5, 2011.

Healy, David. *The Antidepressant Era*. Cambridge: Harvard University Press, 1997.

Healy, David. *The Creation of Psychopharmacology*. Cambridge: Harvard University Press, 2002.

Herman, Ellen. *The Romance of American Psychology: Political Culture in the Age of Experts*. Berkeley: University of California Press, 1995.

Hertzberg, David. *Happy Pills in America: From Miltown to Prozac*. Baltimore: Johns Hopkins University Press, 2008.

Hollinger, David. "The Disciplines and the Identity Debates, 1970–1995." *Daedalus* 16 (1997): 333–51.

Hollingshead, August, and Frederick Redlich. *Social Class and Mental Illness*. New York: Wiley, 1958.

Horwitz, Allan, and Jerome Wakefield. *The Loss of Sadness*. New York: Oxford University Press, 2007.

Horwitz, Allan, and Jerome Wakefield. *All We Have to Fear: Psychiatry's Transformation of Natural Anxieties into Mental Disorders*. New York: Oxford University Press, 2012.

Keeler, Emmett B., Willard G. Manning, and Kenneth B. Wells. "The Demand for Episodes of Mental Health Services." *Journal of Health Economics* 7 (1988): 369–92.

Kirk, Stuart, and Herb Kutchins. *The Selling of DSM: The Rhetoric of Science in Psychiatry*. New York: de Gruyter, 1992.

Kirk, Stuart, and Mark Thierren. "Community Mental Health Myths and the Fate of Formerly Hospitalized Patients." *Psychiatry* 38 (1975): 209–17.

Kleinman, Arthur. *Social Origins of Stress and Disease: Depression, Neurasthenia and Pain in Modern China.* New Haven: Yale University Press, 1986.

Kolb, Lawrence C., Shervert H. Frazier, and Paul Sirovatka. "The National Institute of Mental Health: Its Influence on Psychiatry and the Nation's Mental Health." In *American Psychiatry after the War*, edited by Roy W. Menninger and John C. Nemiah, 207–31. Washington: American Psychiatric Press, 2000.

Kroeber, Alfred L. "*Totem and Taboo*: An Ethnologic Psychoanalysis." *American Anthropologist* 22 (1920): 48–55.

Kutchins, Herb, and Stuart Kirk. *Making Us Crazy: DSM: The Psychiatric Bible and the Creation of Mental Disorders.* New York: Free Press, 1997.

Lakoff, Andrew. *Pharmaceutical Reason: Knowledge and Value in Global Psychiatry.* Cambridge: Cambridge University Press, 2005.

Lambert, David A. "Political and Economic Determinants of Mental Health Regulations." PhD diss., Brandeis University, 1985.

Leighton, Alexander H., John A. Clausen, and Robert N. Wilson. *Explorations in Social Psychiatry.* New York: Basic Books, 1957.

Lerman, Paul. *Deinstitutionalization and the Welfare State.* New Brunswick: Rutgers University Press, 1982.

Levy, Robert A. *Tahitians: Mind and Experience in the Society Islands.* Chicago: University of Chicago Press, 1973.

Link, Bruce. "Mental Patient Status, Work, and Income: An Examination of the Effects of a Psychiatric Label." *American Sociological Review* 47 (1982): 202–15.

Link, Bruce, Francis Cullen, Frank James, and John Wozniack. "The Social Rejection of Former Mental Patients: Understanding Why Labels Matter." *American Journal of Sociology* 92 (1987): 1461–500.

Luhrmann, Tanya. *Of Two Minds: The Growing Disorder in American Psychiatry.* New York: Knopf, 2000.

MacDonald, Michael. *Mystical Bedlam: Madness, Anxiety and Healing in Seventeenth-Century England.* Cambridge: Cambridge University Press, 1981.

Martin, Emily. *Bipolar Expeditions: Mania and Depression in American Culture.* Princeton: Princeton University Press, 2007.

McGuire, Thomas G. "Research on Economics and Mental Health: The Past and Future Prospects." In *Economics and Mental Health*, edited by Richard G. Frank and Willard G. Manning, 1–14. Baltimore: Johns Hopkins University Press, 1992.

McGuire, Thomas G., and Burton A. Weisbrod. *Economics and Mental Health.* Washington, DC: US Government Printing Office, 1981.

Mills, C. Wright. "The Professional Ideology of Social Pathologists." *American Journal of Sociology* 49 (1943): 165–80.

Mitchell, J. *Psychiatrists' Behavior under Mental Health Insurance Regulation.* Needham: Health Economics Research, 1984.

Mojtabai, Ramin, and Mark Olfson. "National Trends in Psychotherapy by Office-Based Psychiatrists." *Archives of General Psychiatry* 65 (2008): 962–70.

Morgan, David. "Explaining Mental Illness." *European Journal of Sociology* 16 (1975): 262–80.

Morgan, Mary S., and Malcolm Rutherford. *From Interwar Pluralism to Postwar Neoclassicism.* Durham: Duke University Press, 1998.

Myers, Jerome K., and Bertram H. Roberts. *Family and Class Dynamics in Mental Illness*. New York: Wiley, 1959.

Paris, Joel. *The Fall of an Icon: Psychoanalysis and Academic Psychiatry*. Toronto: University of Toronto Press, 2005.

Park, Robert, Ernest Burgess, and Roderick D. McKenzie. *The City*. Chicago: University of Chicago Press, 1925.

Perrucci, Robert. *Circle of Madness: On Being Insane and Institutionalized in America*. Englewood Cliffs: Prentice-Hall, 1974.

Pooley, Jefferson, and Mark Solovey. "Marginal to the Revolution: The Curious Relationship between Economics and the Behavioral Sciences Movement in Mid-Twentieth Century America." In *The Unsocial Social Science? Economics and Neighboring Disciplines since 1945*, edited by Roger E. Backhouse and Philippe Fontaine, 199–233. Durham: Duke University Press, 2010.

Rennie, Thomas A., and Leo Srole. "Social Class Prevalence and Distribution of Psychosomatic Conditions in an Urban Population." *Psychosomatic Medicine* 18 (1956): 449–56.

Rice, Charles E. "The Research Grants Program of the National Institute of Mental Health and the Golden Age of American Academic Psychology." In *Psychology and the National Institute of Mental Health*, edited by Wade E. Pickren and Stanley Schneider, 61–112. Washington, DC: American Psychological Association, 2005.

Rice, Dorothy. *The Economic Costs of Alcohol and Drug Abuse and Mental Illness*. DHHS Publication Number (ADM) 90-1649. Rockville: US Department of Health and Human Services, 1990.

Rieder, Ronald O. "Hospitals, Patients, and Politics." *Schizophrenia Bulletin* 1 (1974): 9–15.

Rose, Stephen. "Deciphering Deinstitutionalization: Complexities in Policy and Analysis." *Milbank Memorial Fund Quarterly* 57, no. 4 (1979): 429–60.

Roth, Martin. "Psychiatry and Its Critics." *British Journal of Psychiatry* 122 (1973): 373–78.

Rothman, David. *The Discovery of the Asylum: Social Order in the New Republic*. Boston: Little, Brown, 1971.

Samuelson, Paul. "Unemployment Ahead." *The New Republic* 111, no. 11 (1944): 297–99.

Scheff, Thomas. *Being Mentally Ill: A Sociological Theory*. Chicago: Aldine, 1966.

Scheff, Thomas. *Being Mentally Ill: A Sociological Theory*. 3rd ed. New Brunswick: Aldine Transaction, 1999.

Schroeder, C. W. "Mental Disorders in Cities." *American Journal of Sociology* 48, no. 1 (1942): 40–47.

Scull, Andrew. "The Decarceration of the Mentally Ill: A Critical View." *Politics and Society* 6, no. 2 (1976): 173–212.

Scull, Andrew. *Decarceration: Community Treatment and the Deviant: A Radical View*. Englewood Cliffs: Prentice-Hall, 1977.

Scull, Andrew. *Museums of Madness: The Social Organization of Insanity in Nineteenth Century England*. London: Allen Lane, 1979.

Scull, Andrew. "Competing Perspectives on Deviance." *Deviant Behavior* 5 (1984): 275–89.

Scull, Andrew. *The Most Solitary of Afflictions: Madness and Society in Britain, 1700–1900*. New Haven: Yale University Press, 1993.

Scull, Andrew. "The Mental Health Sector and the Social Sciences in Post-World War II USA, Part II: The Impact of Federal Research Funding and the Drugs Revolution." *History of Psychiatry* 22 (2011): 268–84.

Scull, Andrew. "Creating a New Psychiatry: On the Origins of Non-Institutional Psychiatry in the USA, 1900–1950." *History of Psychiatry* 29, no. 4 (2018): 389–408.

Scull, Andrew. *Psychiatry and Its Discontents.* Berkeley: University of California Press, 2019.

Seligman, Martin. *The Hope Circuit.* London: Brealey, 2018.

Sharfstein, Steven S. "Big Pharma and American Psychiatry: The Good, the Bad, and the Ugly." *Psychiatric News* 40 (2005): 3.

Shephard, Ben. *A War of Nerves: Soldiers and Psychiatrists in the Twentieth Century.* Cambridge: Harvard University Press, 2001.

Shorter, Edward. *The Kennedy Family and the Story of Mental Retardation.* Philadelphia: Temple University Press, 2000.

Skocpol, Theda. *Protecting Soldiers and Mothers: The Political Origins of Social Policy in the United States.* Cambridge: Belknap Press, 1992.

Spiro, Melford E. *Oedipus in the Trobriands.* Chicago: University of Chicago Press, 1982.

Spiro, Melford E. *Culture and Human Nature.* Chicago: University of Chicago Press, 1987.

Swift, Jonathan. *Gulliver's Travels.* London: Motte, 1726.

Szasz, Thomas. *The Myth of Mental Illness.* New York: Hoeber-Harper, 1961.

Thoits, Peggy A. "Self-Labeling Processes in Mental Illness: The Role of Emotional Deviance." *American Journal of Sociology* 92, no. 2 (1985): 221–49.

Windle, Charles, and Diana Scully. "Community Mental Health Centers and Decreasing Use of State Hospitals." *Community Mental Health Journal* 12 (1976): 239–43.

Wright, Rogers H., and Nicholas A. Cummings, eds. *The Practice of Psychology: The Battle for Professionalism.* Phoenix: Zeig, Tucker & Thiesen, 2001.

Yarrow, Marian R., Charlotte G. Schwartz, Harriet S. Murphy, and Leila C. Deasy. "The Psychological Meaning of Mental Illness in the Family." *Journal of Social Issues* 11, no. 4 (1955): 12–24.

10

War

Joy Rohde

In 1959, in the midst of escalating tensions with the Soviets over the status of Berlin, political scientist Joseph Schneider asked, "Is war a social problem?" His answer, penned for the *Journal of Conflict Resolution (JCR)*, was a firm "No!"[1] Social problems were challenges that caused so much human suffering or so impeded social progress that they demanded alleviation.[2] War, Schneider argued, "is a necessary condition for the life of the group."[3] It was a natural feature of a state-based international system and a tool for maintaining social cohesion within nations. Far from a social problem, war was a social institution fundamental to the modern political and social order.

Just fifteen years earlier, many social scientists thought quite differently about war. In 1943, members of the Society for the Psychological Study of Social Issues issued a manifesto that insisted, "War can be avoided: war is not born in men; it is built into men." By 1945, over half of the American Psychological Association's membership endorsed the manifesto's claim that war was a pressing social problem requiring "social engineering on a worldwide scale."[4] This was just one expression of a broader social scientific effort to end war that had begun in earnest after World War I. Drawing on social psychology, political science, international law, sociology, and anthropology, scholars had sought since at least the 1920s to create a globally minded citizenry willing to trade national allegiances for international peace.

By the early 1950s, the internationalist project was widely rejected – even by some of its proponents – as an idealistic fool's errand. The causes of this shift were multiple. The failure of democracy in Europe in the 1930s called

---

[1] Schneider, "Is War a Social Problem?" 353.
[2] Bernard, *Social Problems at Midcentury*, 88–112.
[3] Schneider, "Is War a Social Problem?" 354.
[4] Quoted in Herman, *Romance of American Psychology*, 78, 79.

the rationality and reliability of any public – let alone a global one – into serious question. The deepening animosity between the United States and the Soviet Union in the late 1940s and early 1950s made global cooperation and peace seem farfetched. The threat of nuclear war dramatically raised the stakes of foreign affairs and provoked new strategic questions. In this context, many social scientists recast war as a national security challenge. Rather than an aberration to be exorcised, war was a tool of statecraft, one that could be wielded wisely – waged when necessary, threatened when beneficial, and always rationally managed – by social-scientifically informed government officials. Figures in the nation's growing national security agencies invested their resources in these projects, not those geared toward fostering international peace, further eclipsing research that treated war as a social problem.

War was an intellectually generative subject. During the 1950s and 1960s, social scientists pursued a dizzying variety of approaches to armed conflict, including realist international relations theory, game theory, political-military gaming, modernization theory, and quantitative statistical investigations of war's causes. These intellectual traditions sometimes overlapped and sometimes conflicted. While they bore methodological continuities from earlier eras, they represented ideological departures from the interwar period. Each further moved social research away from the values of the social problems tradition and toward managerial approaches to conflict. With an influx of government funding, social scientists shifted their audiences from imagined democratic publics and new international organizations and toward the political and military elites in American national security and foreign policy agencies.

But for some social scientists, scholarly relevance to war would be their undoing. As modernization theory, psychological warfare schemes, and other approaches appeared responsible for at least some of the American failures in the Vietnam War, security-funded social science became synonymous with military hubris and defeat. In the wake of failed battles for hearts, minds, and hamlets, most anthropologists, sociologists, and psychologists withdrew from the study of war. By the middle of the 1970s, war was almost exclusively the domain of political science, and in particular the field of international relations. Under the banner of neorealism, international relations scholars would continue to seek theories, models, and quantitatively proven laws that helped government officials threaten and wield conflict in ways that benefited American national security.

A glimmer of the social problems approached remained in the social sciences even as the security frame gained ground. Interdisciplinary scholars in the field of peace studies toiled away at the margins of the social sciences, seeking the knowledge that would lead to disarmament and peace. Other social scientists continued to attend to the social problems that war could cause or exacerbate, like civilian morale crises, nuclear attack–induced psychological disturbances, or the threats that the military-industrial complex posed to democratic values and institutions. (These subjects are beyond the scope of this chapter.)

The chapter is divided into three parts. The first traces the brief moment in which social scientists viewed war as a social problem demanding international expert reforms. The second explores the period between the end of World War II and the late 1960s, an era in which the social problems approach was replaced by an array of intellectual traditions aimed at wielding war wisely and efficiently. The final section recounts the devastating impact of the Vietnam War on multiple fields, demonstrating that by the late 1970s, war was a security problem, the domain of political scientists intent on maintaining and expanding American dominance in the face of supposedly ruthless enemies.

10.1 War's Brief Career as a Social Problem

In 1942, the world powers were engulfed in their second major war in twenty-five years. University of Chicago political scientist and law professor Quincy Wright ventured a diagnosis: "The lack of consciousness in the minds of individuals that they were related to the world-community" was to blame for World War II.[5] Advances in modern technology, the development of transnational economic relationships, and the spread of modern communications knit the globe together such that "economic, political, and cultural conditions in the most distant countries" affected most people's lives.[6] Political, social, and economic institutions, however, had yet to adapt to these changes. Influenced by the Chicago School theories of social maladjustment and cultural lag, Wright argued that wars were caused by the misfit between the fact of global interdependence, on the one hand, and humanity's outmoded institutional and psychological commitments to national sovereignty, on the other.

Wright's argument implied that war was a social problem that demanded social scientific solutions. Treating war as such might seem unusual, for the social problems frame implied the existence of a cohesive society with shared

[5] Quoted in Selcer, *Postwar Origins of the Global Environment*, 3.
[6] Wright, *Study of War*, 1347.

values and norms. War, by its very nature, implied the existence of separate communities defined by mutual animosity. In fact, Wright argued, the outmoded myth that people lived in separate communities was precisely what made war a social problem. War was caused by the failure of the world's citizens to recognize their mutual social bonds – to embrace the fact that peoples were no longer a collection of autonomous nations, but were themselves a society. By convincing world leaders and the public that war was, in fact, a *social* rather than a legal or political problem, scholars could perhaps eradicate it.

Wright's diagnosis appeared in his mammoth *A Study of War*. The book grew out of a series of meetings convened by Wright and political scientist Charles Merriam in 1926, in which faculty across Chicago's social sciences united to plan an interdisciplinary attack on the intellectual problem of war. The book's two volumes were the product of sixteen years of research by Wright and dozens of collaborators, including Bernard Brodie, Fay Cooper-Cole, Harold Lasswell, and Jacob Viner. Their investigations, sixty-six in total, drew widely from history and political science, law and economics, and psychology and sociology. Funded by the Rockefeller and Carnegie philanthropies, the Social Science Research Council, and the University of Chicago, the project subjected the study of war to the empirical rigors and interdisciplinary commitments of Chicago-style social science.[7] Appropriate for foundation-funded work, *A Study of War* also sought to put social scientific knowledge in service of reform. While Wright dedicated the bulk of his 15,000 pages to scholarly investigation, he concluded by suggesting how social science could help create a "warless world."[8] Peace would follow from the creation of "international and supranational institutions able to adapt individual attitudes, social symbols, public opinions and public policies in every part of the world to modern conditions" of interdependence.[9] Interdisciplinary research into the relationship between psychology and political behavior, public opinion and group formation, and a variety of other subjects would underlay widespread educational efforts to replace "narrow, self-centered" nationalist attitudes with a "widespread sense of world citizenship" shared by everyday citizens and politicians alike.[10]

Wright was far from the only scholar to argue that expert-educated publics were the surest route to ambitious reform. His arguments fit firmly within the Deweyan and Progressive commitments to research, public education,

[7] Griggs, "A Realist before 'Realism.'"
[8] Wright, *Study of War*, 1326.
[9] Wright, *Study of War*, 1332.
[10] Wright, quoted in Throntveit, "A Strange Fate," 365.

and public deliberation as tools that could establish an enlightened world order. For Wright, as for Dewey, appeals to reason could reshape social organization. Wright's arguments also resonated with the optimistic post–World War I pursuit of an international order that commanded attitudinal and cultural affinities as well as legal and political foundations.[11]

If the solution to the problem of war lay in the creation of a psychologically and politically salient world community, the creation of the United Nations at the end of World War II was a step in the right direction – but only a step. Wright warned that peace would elude humanity until nations were willing "to sacrifice a considerable part of their sovereignty."[12] The challenge of cultivating international citizens who were psychically aware of their international ties and tolerant of cultural diversity motivated a number of postwar social research projects. The United Nations Educational, Scientific, and Cultural Organization (UNESCO), for example, spearheaded an international, interdisciplinary study of "Tensions Affecting International Understanding" shortly after the end of World War II. Led by University of Michigan sociologist Robert C. Angell, the "Tensions" project enlisted psychologists, political scientists, anthropologists, and communications experts in an effort to identify the factors that caused widespread conflict and those that fostered international understanding and tolerance. They carried out interdisciplinary empirical studies of "the distinctive character" of national cultures that impeded integration; gauged nationalist and discriminatory attitudes via public opinion surveys; and identified the roles that cultural differences, psychological maladjustment, technological change, and other factors played in generating understanding and aggression.[13] Project participants hoped to design educational programs to reduce tensions, institutionalize "tolerance as a cross-cultural principle," and create the conditions for lasting peace.[14]

While the aspiration to tame war through global social and political reform aligned with the mission of the United Nations, the effort also drew its fair share of scholarly critics. In particular, the project to end war attracted scorn from social scientists skeptical of its Deweyan faith in democratic publics. In the early 1920s, scholars in Europe and the United States questioned whether the public could play any beneficial role in foreign

[11] Bessner, *Democracy in Exile*, 78–79 and Throntveit, *Power without Victory*.
[12] Wright, quoted in Griggs, "A Realist before 'Realism,'" 88.
[13] Quoted in Selcer, "Patterns of Science," 87.
[14] Angell, "Sociology and the World Crisis," 753.

policy.[15] The rise of anti-Semitic and fascist regimes in the 1930s seemed to reinforce their suspicion that the public that liberal internationalists sought to remake as world citizens might actually be profoundly irrational and unreliable. The European crisis of democracy sapped the faith of European thinkers like German sociologist Hans Speier in the potential of participatory democracy. Speier, who emigrated to the United States in 1933, began his career as an advocate of democracy. But the rise of Nazism led him to reject the "Enlightenment conceptions of progress, utopianism, and human perfectibility" implied by a social scientific commitment to democratic participation.[16] Speier's fellow émigré, political scientist Hans Morgenthau, also rejected notions of liberal progress and human perfectibility. Morgenthau's approach to international affairs was rooted in a conviction that humans were motivated above all by the quest for domination. No organization or educational intervention could eradicate the struggle for power from human relationships. The conviction that war was a social problem – one that could be eradicated through mutual understanding – was, for Morgenthau, idealistic sentimentalism.[17]

Events in the five years after World War II seemed to reinforce Morgenthau's and Speier's skepticism of liberal internationalist projects. Deepening enmity between the United States and the Soviet Union dimmed hopes for lasting peace. As it increasingly seemed that US survival might depend not on international cooperation, but on finding a way to maintain the nation's unequal share of world power in the face of a ruthless foe, Morgenthau's star rose. Shortly after the war, he joined the University of Chicago faculty. His hard-nosed rejection of liberal internationalism and human perfectibility – a position referred to as "realist," and opposed in the 1930s and 1940s to the supposed "idealism" of internationalism – earned him a reputation as a leading theorist in the nascent political science subfield of international relations.[18] His methodological approach – qualitative, contextual, often historical analysis – denied the possibility that politics could be known scientifically.

For Morgenthau and other realists, war was not a social problem. It was, instead, a manifestation of the "struggle for power," which Morgenthau declared in his influential *Politics among Nations* (1948) "universal in time and space" and "an undeniable fact of experience."[19] For realists, the international

[15] Rietzler, "International Experts, International Citizens."
[16] Arthur Vidich, quoted in Bessner, *Democracy in Exile*, 74.
[17] Greenberg, *Weimar Century*, chap. 5 and Gunnell, *Descent of Political Theory*, 209.
[18] Greenberg, *Weimar Century*, chap. 5.
[19] Morgenthau, *Politics among Nations*. Quoted in Frei, "Politics among Nations," 64.

system was, and always would be, anarchical. The social scientist's purpose was not to change public perceptions and values through research and education. Instead, social scientists should assist policy elites, providing wise counsel as they pursued the national interest against enemies devoid of moral standards.[20]

Morgenthau's realist theory provided a compelling expression of sentiments and anxieties widely held by American statesmen in the late 1940s and 1950s. George Kennan, whose influential "Long Telegram" helped to establish Cold War containment policy, insisted that policymakers and their advisers "dispense with all sentimentality and day-dreaming; ... our attention will have to be concentrated everywhere on our immediate national objectives" in order to guarantee national survival.[21] Policymakers and diplomats, including Dean Acheson, Paul Nitze, and Henry Kissinger, regularly referenced Morgenthau's ideas to support their policy positions.[22]

In this intellectual and policy climate, social scientific projects to cultivate international cooperation withered. Wright's internationalist message in *A Study of War* was largely forgotten by decade's end.[23] The loss of US nuclear hegemony in 1949 broadened concerns that the United States was a fragile democracy beset by merciless foes. With internationalists increasingly labeled communist sympathizers by the early 1950s, American membership in the United World Federalists, an international organization advocating world government, declined precipitously.[24] In 1951, the University of Chicago Committee to Frame a World Constitution terminated its work in failure. Italian exile G. A. Borgese, one of the committee's founders, explained that "the worlds are two. They can fight it out or they can come to a compromise... . They cannot join in peace."[25] That same year, Angell admitted that the UNESCO "Tensions" project underestimated the moral and cultural divisions among nations. In his presidential address to the American Sociological Society, he conceded that "it seems almost inconceivable that the Soviet Union and the United States could accept a common supranational authority of any kind."[26]

Angell was not willing to give up his faith that social science had important work to do on the international stage. But his agenda for the

[20] On realism, see Bew, *Realpolitik*; Craig, *Glimmer of a New Leviathan*; Guilhot, *Invention of International Relations Theory*; and Freedman, *Future of War*.
[21] Quoted in Price, *Cold War Anthropology*, 4.
[22] Greenberg, *Weimar Century*, chap. 5.
[23] Desch, *Cult of the Irrelevant*, 81.
[24] Baratta, "International History," 382.
[25] Quoted in Baratta, "International Federalist Movement," 346.
[26] Angell, "Sociology and the World Crisis," 751.

sociological study of war was among the Cold War's early intellectual casualties. In his presidential address, he laid out a research agenda for sociologists, calling upon them to apply their expertise in social structures, communications, and attitudes to identify techniques and approaches that would improve allegiance to the United Nations. But his call went almost entirely unheeded. So too did C. Wright Mills' 1958 *The Causes of World War Three*. The impassioned tract called upon sociologists to interrogate the role that the power elite played in creating conflicts, but it quickly went out of print.[27] Between 1945 and 1990, only 4 of 6,500 articles published in major sociology journals addressed nuclear war.[28]

With the deepening of the Cold War, many sociologists turned away from the study of war as a social problem. The few sociologists who continued to focus on war turned to investigating the military as a social organization. Largely funded by the armed services, the small subfield of military sociology coalesced in the 1950s around studies of military occupations, civil–military relations, and the role the military played in development. With international cooperation labeled subversive, the social problems approach to war commanded comparatively little social scientific attention.[29] Less than a decade after Wright's *Study of War*, the social problems approach was waning.

10.2 War as Security Problem

Instead of fostering international understanding, many social scientists took on the urgent project of shoring up American power and strengthening national security. From the end of World War II through the late 1960s, social scientists pursued a variety of intellectual projects aligned with the conviction that the nation was locked in an existential struggle with the Soviets. In the process, they redefined war as a security problem and applied themselves to the maintenance of American national security and international hegemony. This project was, perhaps, less audacious than the pursuit of permanent peace through international understanding. But it was still ambitious. Scholars asked what the next war might be like, if and when it benefited American national interests to wage war, and how statesmen could effectively wield the threat of force against their enemies in order to strengthen American power without triggering violence.

---

[27] Mills, *Causes of World War Three*. See Kurtz, "War and Peace," 76.
[28] Kurtz, "War and Peace," 65.
[29] Kurtz, "War and Peace."

Morgenthau's realist international relations theory, with its emphasis on contextual and qualitative analysis, occupied one influential vein of this scholarship, but other approaches both complementary and competing flourished, including game theory and political-military gaming. As decolonization reshaped geopolitics, social scientists also deployed new categories of conflict, like unconventional warfare, and developed new approaches for the economic and political modernization of new nations. These intellectual trends are the subject of the first half of this section. The section's second half takes up a parallel and complementary pursuit: the development of largely statistical and quantitative studies of war driven by the values of the behavioral revolution, which sought to displace the theorizing of realists like Morgenthau with empirically grounded, predictive tools to manage war.

Each of these intellectual traditions promised to manage wars of all sorts rationally. With this promise, social scientists attracted generous government funding that had the potential to vault them to the forefront of US security policy. In the interwar period, the social scientific study of war had been supported largely by foundation grants. Military and intelligence agencies dramatically expanded their financial support for social science from the 1940s to the 1960s. Intelligence budgets are notoriously difficult to document, but in the early 1960s, the military's social science budget was $15 million – more than its annual budget for R&D in all scientific and engineering fields in the decade prior to World War II.[30] By the late 1960s, at the height of social scientific involvement in the Vietnam War, the Defense Department spent $40 million a year on social science.[31] The period between the end of World War II and the Vietnam War was the heyday of the social science of war – an era of diverse research agendas, full coffers, and institutional expansion.

Yet, this section shows that despite the dominance of national security funds and framings, the social problems–orientation toward war was not fully eclipsed at mid-century. A handful of influential scholars, including Angell and Wright, kept the commitment to peace through social science alive via a new interdisciplinary effort dubbed peace research. That these researchers coexisted and even collaborated with scholars dedicated to war's rational management signals the intellectual eclecticism in the mid-century study of war.

---

[30] Herman, *Romance of American Psychology*, 128–29.
[31] Price, *Cold War Anthropology*, 45–51.

10.2.1 Nuclear Games and Modernizing Nations: Managing War at RAND, MIT, and SORO

The decade after World War II saw unprecedented institutional and intellectual growth in the social science of war. RAND, created by the Army Air Force in 1946 and staffed by civilian researchers, was tasked with providing scientifically grounded recommendations for "preferred methods, techniques, and instrumentalities" for conducting air warfare in the nuclear age.[32] It quickly became known for pioneering novel approaches to war, among them game theory, psychological warfare, and political-military gaming.

RAND's mathematicians were among the first to theorize war as a game. A 1948 report explained that war "is similar to a game of strategy between opposing players." Each seeks to "maximize some function, such as defense," yet neither controls all of the variables.[33] Game theory failed to bear strategic or tactical fruit in its formalist mathematical form. But it was a powerful heuristic device. Bernard Brodie, a RAND strategist who worked on *A Study of War* while a PhD student at the University of Chicago, explained that, when it came to strategy, "What matters is the spirit of the gaming principle, the constant reminder that in war we shall be dealing with an opponent who will react to our moves and to whom we must react."[34] Game theory stressed the mental and communicative, rather than the martial, elements of conflict. As economist and RAND consultant Thomas Schelling explained, war was not merely a "contest of strength," but one of "nerve and risk-taking."[35] It was "always a bargaining process" dominated by "threats and proposals, counterproposals and counterthreats, offers and assurances."[36]

By treating war as an interaction between players, game theory encouraged scholars and policymakers to treat war as a problem of rational, efficient, expert decision-making. Amid a cultural backdrop of books and films like *Red Alert* (1958), *Fail Safe* (1964), and *Dr. Strangelove* (1964), in which unanticipated mistakes and human irrationality threaten nuclear war, strategists offered decision protocols that made choice more bureaucratic, more formal, and thus less dangerous. Schelling argued that game theory could guide both the "rational calculator in full control of his faculties" as well as the "nervous hotheaded frightened desperate decision that might be

[32] Quoted in Desch, *Cult of the Irrelevant*, 125.
[33] Quoted in Leonard, *Von Neumann, Morgenstern, and the Creation of Game Theory*, 309.
[34] Quoted in Ayson, *Thomas Schelling and the Nuclear Age*, 130.
[35] Quoted in Amadae, *Prisoners of Reason*, 87.
[36] Quoted in Kuklick, *Blind Oracles*, 138.

precipitated at the peak of a crisis, that might be the result of an accident or false alarm, that might be engineered by an act of mischief."[37]

During the 1950s and 1960s, American policymakers drew regularly on game theory to justify policies like mutually assured destruction and the American air war in Vietnam. In the hands of game theorists, war was decidedly not a social problem. Rather than an abhorrent cause of human suffering, it was a conceptually bloodless activity, a contest between two faceless choosers whose most relevant characteristics were the national interests they desired to maximize and their ability to follow a set of social-scientifically derived decision protocols. As Schelling wrote, "if we can talk about wars in which tens of millions could be killed thoughtlessly, we ought to be able to talk about wars in which hundreds of thousands might be killed thoughtfully."[38] Far from cooperative, the very production of rational decisions seemed to require the eradication of social instincts like cooperation or empathy.[39]

Game theory's prescriptive embrace of preference maximization bears more than a passing resemblance to contemporary economics. But game-theoretic approaches to war were not imported from economics. Rather, they grew out of interdisciplinary connections between the variety of scholars – mathematicians like John von Neumann, economists like Oskar Morgenstern and Schelling, and political scientists like Brodie – who worried about national survival in the nuclear age. Not until the 1970s and 1980s did game theory make significant inroads into economics.[40] As Robert Leonard has shown, war was too simple of an economic problem to attract sustained interest from the economics community after World War II.[41]

While game theory is perhaps RAND's best-known intellectual product, its social scientists developed a number of other approaches to war. Guided by Weimar émigré and realist thinker Hans Speier, its Social Science Division (SSD) examined "the identification, measurement and control of factors important in (1) the occurrence of war, and (2) the winning of war if it should occur."[42] This mission was managerial in nature, aimed at advising elite military and civilian policymakers who confronted the specter of war. SSD analysts studied psychological warfare, devising programs to

[37] Quoted in Freedman, *The Future of War*, 80.
[38] Quoted in Desch, *Cult of the Irrelevant*, 165.
[39] Amadae, *Prisoners of Reason*.
[40] Amadae, *Rationalizing Capitalist Democracy*; Erickson, *World the Game Theorists Made*; and Weintraub, *Toward a History of Game Theory*.
[41] Leonard, "War as a 'Simple Economic Problem.'"
[42] Quoted in Leonard, *Von Neumann, Morgenstern, and the Creation of Game Theory*, 303. On Speier and the SSD generally, see Bessner, *Democracy in Exile*.

destabilize enemy propaganda. But its political-military game – a simulation of decision-making during crisis – garnered the division more significant policy attention in the 1950s and early 1960s. Concerned that game theory failed to capture the real-world contingencies – individual and group psychology, history, politics, culture, stress, and other qualitative factors – that impacted crisis decision-making, Speier and fellow sociologist Herbert Goldhamer offered the political-military game as a qualitative, experiential technique for producing knowledge about war. The game placed human players in scenarios where they took on the roles and responsibilities of policymakers facing the onset of hypothetical or real-life conflicts. In one 1955 game, Germany (Speier), the United States (Goldhamer), the Soviet Union and France (sociologist Nathan Leites), and Great Britain (historian H. A. Deweerd) played out US security policy toward Western Europe. The Pentagon adopted the technique. In 1964, its Joint War Games Agency brought together high-ranking officials, including McGeorge Bundy, Curtis LeMay, and members of the Joint Chiefs of Staff, to simulate the escalation of the Vietnam War in an effort to assess strategic alternatives. While Speier and Goldhamer had hoped their method would provide scientific knowledge about decision-making, by 1959 they concluded that the technique held little scientific promise. Instead, the simulations were better for assessing specific strategies and training decision-makers.[43]

RAND was only one of a number of new institutes created after World War II to study and manage war. At MIT, a Ford Foundation grant and an infusion of secret CIA funds birthed the Center for International Studies (CIS) in 1952.[44] Its original charter instructed researchers to develop methods, targets, and messages for psychological warfare campaigns against the Soviet Union and its satellites. But the center soon expanded the intellectual terrain of its war-related research. In a secret memo justifying the university's clandestine relationship with the CIA, MIT's provost explained that the "long pull" against communism made it "imperative that we mobilize our resources for research in the broad field of political warfare," just as physical scientists had mobilized to support conventional warfighting.[45] As decolonization yielded new nations, social scientists expanded their purview to nation-building itself. At MIT's CIS, some of the leading social scientists of the postwar generation – including economic historian Walt Rostow, political scientist Gabriel Almond, and sociologist

43 Bessner, "Weimar Social Science in Cold War America."
44 Pooley, "Remobilization of the Propaganda," 25 and Simpson, *Science of Coercion*, 81–82. On the history of CIS, see Gilman, *Mandarins of the Future*, chap. 5.
45 Quoted in Desch, *Cult of the Irrelevant*, 92.

Daniel Lerner – devised theories of political and economic modernization meant to guide new nations through the development process without succumbing to communism. An interdisciplinary school of thought, modernization theory "posited the existence of a common and essential pattern of 'development, defined by progress in technology, military and bureaucratic institutions, and the political and social structure.'"[46] The problems that ostensibly accompanied modernization could, moreover, lead to types of violence over which social scientists claimed expertise in the 1950s and 1960s: guerrilla warfare, insurgency, civil war, and revolution.

The sheer variety of conflict types justified the creation of yet another institution: the Army's Special Operations Research Office (SORO), created in 1956 and housed at American University in Washington, DC. SORO mobilized political scientists, anthropologists, sociologists, social psychologists, and former military officials to build a social science of "unconventional war" – yet another term of art. They marshaled historical and quantitative evidence to identify the political, economic, and psychological variables that correlated with violent revolution; fielded surveys to identify the psychological traits that Latin Americans ostensibly found attractive in their leaders; and sought the organizational factors that facilitated US nation-building efforts overseas.[47]

By claiming to facilitate the alleviation of human suffering, SORO and MIT's CIS appeared to draw on the social problems approach. At a 1962 conference, SORO's associate director, psychologist William Lybrand, explained to an audience of defense officials and social scientists that social knowledge would help the military "create internal conditions and encourage political, social, and economic systems which remove hunger, disease, poverty, oppression, and other sources of discontent" from developing nations.[48] Instead of producing research geared toward public-facing social and educational campaigns to eliminate war, however, modernization theorists and scholars of unconventional war encouraged political and military interventions that were sometimes clandestine and often imposed by elites.[49] At SORO and MIT, as at RAND, the reduction of human suffering and the development of democratic world communities – a centerpiece of the social problems approach – took a backseat to American national security.

[46] Gilman, *Mandarins of the Future*, 3.
[47] Rohde, *Armed with Expertise*.
[48] Quoted in Rohde, *Armed with Expertise*, 34.
[49] Latham, *Right Kind of Revolution*, chap. 5.

10.2.2 Building a Behavioral Science of War

The MIT and SORO researchers who sought scientifically validated knowledge about conflict were influenced by the behavioral revolution which swept through the social sciences in the 1950s.[50] Behavioralism's advocates insisted that social science be "modeled after the methodological assumptions of the natural sciences." Instead of preceding empirical research, theory should follow from the collection of empirical observations – ideally those that could be measured, aggregated, and expressed quantitatively. Only when scholars developed a generalizable body of "tested propositions" that could be applied to social behaviors across time and space could social science earn its rightful status as a science.[51]

Behavioralism shaped a number of intellectual projects related to war in the 1950s and 1960s. The movement reached its apex in a research tradition that went by a variety of names as it emerged in the 1950s and 1960s, including conflict resolution, peace studies, quantitative international politics, or – most simply and aspirationally – international relations. This tradition came to be dominated by international relations experts, but in its early years included political psychologists, sociologists, and a handful of economists, all of whom were united by their devotion to placing the study of war on a behavioral-scientific footing. MIT political scientist Karl Deutsch, a leading figure in the movement, explained that this research had three goals: "to identify generally those conflict situations and states which are likely to lead to war; to evaluate particular conflict situations and the probable lines along which they are likely to develop if left to themselves; and to suggest further possible techniques for controlling or containing such conflict situations so as to prevent them from breaking out into war."[52]

As Deutsch's description implies, the behavioralist study of war promised to manage conflict by developing quantitative indicators and other predictive tools that could alert policymakers to the onset of war and enable them to respond rationally. Military officials were intrigued. In the early 1960s, the Navy contracted with political scientists and political psychologists who sought the signs of emerging conflict in the communications that passed

---

[50] Though "behavioralism" and the "behavioral revolution" were the common labels within political science, the broader movement inclusive of the other social sciences (economics excepted) typically used the sibling "behavioral sciences" phrase. The terms are used interchangeably here.
[51] Quoted in Gunnell, *Descent of Political Theory*, 255, 214.
[52] Quoted in McClelland, "Acute International Crisis," 189.

between nations.[53] The Advanced Research Projects Agency (ARPA) generously bankrolled a variety of efforts to build quantitative measures and models of international affairs beginning in the mid-1960s. It funded Yale's Political Data Program, which published the *World Handbook of Political and Social Indicators*, a volume that included "hard data" on everything from land distribution to riots to voter turnout in 130 countries.[54] And the agency supported University of Hawaii political scientist R. J. Rummel (who sought signs of war in the covariance between adversary nations' population sizes, economic power, geographic proximity, and degrees of press freedom, among other attributes)[55] and University of Michigan political scientist Raymond Tanter (who created a computer infrastructure for preserving and sharing international conflict datasets across institutions).[56] Such research was not confined to defense-supported scholars. At the University of Michigan, J. David Singer launched his Correlates of War (COW) project in 1963, which sought conflict indicators in statistical tests of the "frequency, participants, duration, and battle deaths of all interstate wars" since the Congress of Vienna, the event that international relations scholars agreed established the modern state system.[57]

With its emphasis on prediction, this work embraced the era's managerial orientation toward conflict. Even so, some of its most prominent figures maintained a glimmer of the old social problems frame. Deutsch explained that his systematic quest "to understand war and peace as social processes, with the analytic tools of social science" was directed at "the permanent establishment of peace."[58] That Deutsch's description paralleled some of Quincy Wright's language in *A Study of War* was no accident. Deutsch, Singer, and their intellectual kin traced their ancestry to the University of Chicago scholar. They did not espouse Wright's Deweyan vision of peace through international understanding, however. Rather, they viewed Wright as a founder of the quantitative, empirical study of war. *A Study of War*, after all, had compiled hundreds of pages of quantitative descriptions of conflict. According to Singer, the text proved that "mathematics could help to capture international interactions, statistics could reveal the extent to which certain

[53] Desch, *Cult of the Irrelevant*, 97–98.
[54] Banks, "Review of the *World Handbook*"; Russett et al., *World Handbook of Political and Social Indicators*; and Taylor, Hudson, and Russett, *World Handbook of Political and Social Indicators*.
[55] Young et al., *Utilization of ARPA-Supported Research*, 50–54.
[56] Tanter, *Policy Relevance of Models*.
[57] Morrow et al., "J. David Singer," 591 and Singer and Small, *Wages of War*.
[58] Deutsch, "In Memorium," 107.

conditions and events can and do rise and fall together," allowing scholars to progress "from the anecdotal and impressionistic to the operational and reproducible."[59] Wright's effort to find causal relationships between a people's "warlikeness" and a host of variables – population density, energy production, average annual temperature, social organizational style, number of battlefield honors or casualties, to name just a few – was worthy of emulation.[60]

A handful of influential scholars sought to preserve and extend Wright's normative commitment to peace, and not just his methodological approach. Calling themselves peace researchers, they tended to come from disciplines other than political science. Angell, the sociologist who advocated international understanding as the key to overcoming war, helped create the Center for Research on Conflict Resolution (CRCR) at the University of Michigan in 1959; he directed the center until 1964.[61] CRCR economist Kenneth Boulding, social psychologist Herbert Kelman, and mathematical biologist Anatol Rapoport argued that social science could build peace by attending to the psychological, social, and especially cooperative elements of human affairs. Boulding, a Quaker pacifist, stressed the importance of "love, affection, empathy, and a community of feeling" as critical to understanding war and peace. He lamented that most social science "forgets the ills of society and becomes deaf to the cry of the hungry and blind to the misery of the oppressed."[62] For Boulding, the social scientific study of war should be rooted in moral as well as scientific values. He called on social scientists to build an "intellectual chassis" strong enough to "support the moral engine" which could drive "the abolition of war."[63]

But the CRCR was a broad intellectual tent. It included Singer – who self-identified as a peace studies scholar although he only paid lip-service to eradicating war – among its faculty. Perhaps more revealing of its intellectual and normative breadth, CRCR was the original home of the *JCR*. Founded in 1957 to create a venue for interdisciplinary research that strengthened the study of war "through quantification," the journal's contributors were

---

[59] Singer, "Correlates of War," 450. See also Bueno de Mesquita, "Game Theory, Political Economy, and the Evolving Study."

[60] Wright, *Study of War*. The peace research community also traced its lineage to Lewis Fry Richardson, a British mathematician, meteorologist, and pacifist who spent his free time in the 1920s and 1930s marshaling quantitative evidence – from the rates of arms purchases and the lengths of shared borders to the similarities and differences among nations' cultures and religions – to perform statistical analyses in a search for the causes of war. On Richardson, see Erickson, *World the Game Theorists Made*, 186.

[61] Harty and Modell, "First Conflict Resolution Movement," 734.

[62] Quoted in Fontaine, "Stabilizing American Society," 246, 247.

[63] Quoted in Freedman, *Future of War*, 111.

united in their desire to substitute social science – preferably but not exclusively quantitative – for the unscientific advice of "lawyers, merchants, diplomatists, and military men."[64]

The eclectic scholarship in *JCR*'s pages demonstrates that the peace researchers' social problems frame coexisted with managerial approaches that eschewed any form of moral advocacy. *JCR* also showcased some of the methodological continuities between social problems and managerial approaches to war. The journal's inaugural issue included an article in which Wright advocated for peace via a thoroughgoing program of psychological, social, and political reforms that impressed upon the world's citizens their global kinship and interdependence. Wright called upon international organizations to create a "world intelligence center" that would "enlighten the public by presenting and analyzing factual material indicating the changing atmosphere of world opinion, the changing condition of world politics, and the alternatives available and the probable consequences of adopting each."[65]

Instead of battling over the status of war as a social or managerial problem, the scholars who published in the *JCR* united against their realist interlocutors. Articles by Morgenthau and other realists were unwelcome; advocates of the behavioral science of war scorned realism's pessimistic rejection of science and quantitative empiricism. Singer disparaged realism as mere "speculation and impression."[66] Rapoport objected to its dark conclusions. He wrote that realists "translated the game of strategy (where men may engage in ruthless and cunning to their heart's content *because* it is only a game) into a plan of genocidal orgies, and we call the resulting nightmare 'realism.'"[67] Not surprisingly, realists pushed back, attacking quantitative and empirically minded scholars for their "fetish for measurement" and misguided faith that war could be controlled through science.[68] This so-called second great debate in international relations pitted "historically minded, traditional realists" against "advocates of a sciency approach to politics," including quantitative and formal game-theoretic methods.[69]

Despite this methodological disagreement, realists and behavioralists coexisted in the same institutions, a demonstration of the intellectual

[64] Quoted in Erickson, *World the Game Theorists Made*, 187. On the preference for quantification, see Harty and Modell, "First Conflict Resolution Movement," 731.
[65] Wright, "Project for a World Intelligence Center," 94.
[66] Singer, "Editor's Introduction," 1.
[67] Quoted in Tomás Rangil, "Finding Patrons for Peace Psychology," 105.
[68] Quoted in Ruzicka, "A Fetish for Measurement?" 368. See also Guilhot, *After the Enlightenment*.
[69] Guilhot, *After the Enlightenment*, 153.

flexibility that fueled scholarship in this period. RAND's SSD alone was capacious enough to accommodate the behaviorally minded psychologist John L. Kennedy, who believed in mathematically modeling human behavior, and political scientist Paul Keckskemeti, who vociferously rejected the claim that "rigorously quantitative terms" held the key to understanding human behavior.[70] Similarly, scholars who embraced game theory could also work comfortably with qualitative and realist approaches. Schelling, best known for his game-theoretic understanding of war, directed a political-military game at Camp David in 1958 whose players included high-level Washington policy figures and scholars such as McGeorge Bundy, Alain Enthoven, Carl Kaysen, Henry Kissinger, and Walt Rostow.[71]

The sometimes competing, sometimes overlapping approaches to war at RAND, MIT, and elsewhere reflected a number of shared convictions. For scholars of modernization and unconventional warfare, military-political gamers and game theorists, realists and behavioralists, war was primarily a problem of national security and defense. Funded generously by national security agencies, the study of war was the ambit of scholarly and policy elites rather than the concern of international publics. In the heady period between the end of World War II and the nation's full-scale mobilization in Vietnam, war captivated scholars and government officials. It was just too good to give up. As one social scientist explained in 1970, scholars generally agreed that "war is probably not an a priori evil; wars often accomplish very desirable goals, particularly if they are undertaken to remedy injustice." Instead of eradicating war altogether, the scholarly community was "only interested in reducing wars which emerge from less lofty motives."[72]

An elite minority of scholars – including Wright and Angell – disagreed. Under the guise of peace research, a handful of social scientists from a variety of disciplines continued to insist that war was a social problem that demanded international action guided by social research. But it would be a bloody conflict in Southeast Asia, not the pleas of peace researchers, that would ultimately kill off at least some managerial social scientific approaches to war.

10.3 War as the Territory of International Relations

The Vietnam War was a proving ground for social scientists' managerial approaches to war. In the second half of the 1960s, anthropologist Gerald

[70] Quoted in Bessner, *Democracy in Exile*, 213.
[71] Bessner, *Democracy in Exile*, 224.
[72] Haas, "Three Approaches to the Study of War," 44.

Hickey put the study of unconventional war to the test by advising the US
armed forces how to conduct its military and counterinsurgency programs
for ethnic groups living in the South Vietnamese Highlands. RAND
political scientists interviewed POWs and defectors seeking an answer to
Robert McNamara's query: "Who are the Viet Cong and what makes them
tick?"[73] And Sovietologist Leon Gouré joined Schelling in arguing that
coercive bargaining in the form of escalated bombing campaigns would
quash the insurgency in the South and bring North Vietnam to its knees.[74]

Social scientists' advice failed to deliver a rationally managed war. Gouré's
coercive bargaining produced dead bodies, but not victory.[75] Modernization,
counterinsurgency, and counterrevolutionary projects failed to convert
Vietnamese hearts and minds to the American cause. While some of these
failures seemed to indict the behavioral-scientific approach, realist theorist
Morgenthau blamed Washington, not social science, for US failures. By
escalating the conflict, he argued, policymakers had violated realism's
most fundamental tenet; they traded "sober calculations of power and self-
interest in favor of abstract moral and ideological principles."[76]

Instead of solving the problem of war, social science appeared to have
helped birth a new social problem – the domination of American intellectual,
political, and social life by military values and concerns. Antiwar activists
and even some policymakers attacked the alliance of scholarship and
national security that, they argued, fostered needless American bellicosity.
On Capitol Hill, J. William Fulbright, chair of the Senate Foreign Relations
Committee, argued that the military had used social science as a means to
assume "responsibility for making political judgments," hardly its proper
jurisdiction, "all over the world." Allowing military-funded social science
research to continue, he argued, would only lead "to more Vietnams."[77]
Congress slashed the military's social research budget in 1969.

On campuses across the country, student activists attacked military-
funded social research for its corrosive impact on intellectual and public
life. At American University, home to the Army's SORO, students labeled
the university a "part of the interlocking corporate power elite – the
industrial (exploitation)–military (kill for freedom and/or money)–
education (indoctrination) complex."[78] At MIT, student activists held

---

[73] Elliot, *RAND in Southeast Asia*, 25–28, 53.
[74] Weinberger, *Imagineers of War*, 174–75 and Desch, *Cult of the Irrelevant*, 171–74.
[75] Tomás Rangil, "Rebellions across the (Rice) Fields."
[76] Christoph Frei, quoted in Desch, *Cult of the Irrelevant*, 200.
[77] Quoted in Rohde, *Armed with Expertise*, 110, 115.
[78] Quoted in Rohde, *Armed with Expertise*, 113.

a mock trial of CIS faculty and found them guilty of "crimes against humanity."[79] And at Columbia University, over a thousand protesters called upon the administration to sever the university's ties with Defense Department research institutes. Antiwar intellectuals, including linguist Noam Chomsky and anthropologist Kathleen Gough, referred to scholars who worked on national security problems as "henchmen of the military-industrial complex."[80]

Although activists and policymakers charged security-funded social science with creating a social problem of its own, they did not call upon social scientists to reframe war as a social problem deserving study in its own right. Instead, they demanded institutional and intellectual disinvestment from war altogether. Military officials, burned by the empty promises of their social science advisers, also reduced their support for social research. By the early 1970s, the landscape of the social science of war shifted. American University and the Army cut their ties in 1969, leading to SORO's removal from campus. Modernization theory crumbled under a withering critique of its teleological adherence to unilinear narratives of human progress.[81] RAND analysts continued to work on war-related problems, but the twin pressures of reduced military investment and scholarly skepticism of war-related work drove its leadership to pursue more projects in the domestic sector.[82]

In the wake of these shifts, war-related social science lost much of its disciplinary diversity. Many anthropologists called upon their discipline to abandon the study of war and drop ties to the military to protect their field from the taint of martial values. With the decline of modernization theory and military investments in political and unconventional warfare, sociologists and political psychologists turned away from the study of war too.[83]

The interdisciplinary field of peace research, perhaps counterintuitively, also failed to gain traction. Instead of reviving the study of war as a social problem, the CRCR ran out of funding. By 1970, Boulding, Rapoport, and Kelman had all departed the University of Michigan. The university abolished the center in 1971 and the *JCR* relocated to Yale, home of the behavioralist *World Handbook of Political and Social Indicators*.[84] Over the next decade, the journal's commitment to formal and behavioral methods like game

---

[79] Quoted in Oren, *Our Enemies and Us*, 152.
[80] Quoted in Rohde, *Armed with Expertise*, 120, 99–100.
[81] Gilman, *Mandarins of the Future*.
[82] Rohde, *Armed with Expertise*.
[83] Rohde, *Armed with Expertise*.
[84] See Erickson, *World the Game Theorists Made*; Tomás Rangil, "Finding Patrons for Peace Psychology"; and Harty and Modell, "First Conflict Resolution Movement."

theory and statistical analysis of quantitative empirical data continued. Contributions from sociologists and psychologists declined, and political scientists came to make up the majority of contributions. Game theory's star rose in the 1970s; the study of games rose from 8 percent to 25 percent of *JCR*'s contents within a few years of its transition to Yale.[85] While political scientists dedicated to formal and quantitative studies of war continued to refer to themselves as peace researchers, the pacifist school of peace studies was pushed even further to the margins of social science; its affiliation with peace activism left it chronically underfunded and intellectually suspect among advocates of scientific and formalist approaches.[86]

Political science took center stage in the 1970s in part because the discipline remained sanguine about working on security projects. The American Political Science Association weathered an attempted insurrection in 1968 and 1969 by representatives of the Caucus for a New Political Science, who accused their colleagues of "merely describ[ing] and perpetuat[ing] the social and political status quo."[87] The Caucus fielded Morgenthau – a staunch critic of both the Vietnam War and the scientistic efforts of behavioralist scholars – as their presidential candidate. But he was defeated and the Caucus was quickly relegated to the edges of the profession.[88] Even so, Morgenthau's status in the Caucus indicated the continued salience of realism in international relations, even amidst the behavioralist tide.

Instead of joining the Caucus' political defection, many political scientists argued that the failures of social science in Vietnam demonstrated the need for more – not less – research on the science of war. Political scientist and onetime ARPA program manager Raymond Tanter explained that social scientists had treated the war as a laboratory, but they had done so sloppily. Social scientists and their patrons had identified a variety of social variables to manipulate, from the psychology of Vietnamese peasants to the locations of secure hamlets. But they had no scientific basis to support the hypothesis that their interventions would sway the population toward the South Vietnamese government. The quantitative study of war, Tanter concluded, would provide hard evidence of cause and effect – a "scientific" basis for decision-making.[89]

---

[85] Harty and Modell, "First Conflict Resolution Movement," 738.
[86] Kurtz, "War and Peace."
[87] Quoted in Oren, *Our Enemies and Us*, 162.
[88] Oren, *Our Enemies and Us*, 162–63.
[89] Tanter, *Policy Relevance of Models*, 1.

DARPA (renamed the Defense Advanced Research Projects Agency in the early 1970s) remained optimistic that quantitative studies of war could provide tools to rationally manage conflict. While most federal funding for war-related social science declined precipitously after 1968, DARPA continued to support research that sought validated predictive indicators of conflict through the 1970s.[90] This investment was aided by the conviction, shared among behavioralists since the 1950s, that scholarship's purpose was "not to change the world, but to assist authorities in getting a firmer grip on the existing social order."[91] By the 1970s, scholars who mined quantitative data on war for statistical correlations and laws no longer identified themselves as behavioralists, but they maintained much of behavioralism's ideology. Behavioralism had itself played an important role in moving social science away from the study of social problems. The social problems frame's normative embrace of peace appeared suspect in a climate of anticommunism; but normative commitments to military action, too, were open to critique during and after the Vietnam War. As an ostensibly value-neutral pursuit, the quantitative approach to conflict could offer political safe haven for researchers and their national security patrons in the 1970s.

Unfortunately for researchers and their patrons, however, this work bore little predictive fruit. By the mid-1970s, R. J. Rummel's Dimensionality of Nations had amassed a catalogue of rejected hypotheses. Another seemingly promising DARPA-funded effort, the World Event-Interaction System, fared only slightly better. Created by onetime CRCR affiliate Charles McClelland, it was a computerized catalogue of cooperative and threatening interactions between the world's 160-plus nations, containing over 120,000 event entries by the end of the 1970s. But a multimillion-dollar DARPA project to operationalize the database as a real-time crisis predictor for the US European Command and Ronald Reagan's national security staff in the White House ended in failure in the early 1980s.[92]

Although their quarry eluded them, researchers did not conclude that their efforts were misguided. Instead, they doubled down on their pursuit of statistically validated knowledge about war. For Singer – one of the only CRCR affiliates to remain at Michigan after the Center closed – the painstaking work of amassing datasets and applying statistical tests to conflict became an end in itself. Singer directed the COW project until his retirement in 2002. As he added new datasets and tested new hypotheses

---

[90] Rohde, "Pax Technologica."
[91] Parenti, "Patricians, Professionals, and Political Science," 502.
[92] Rohde, "Pax Technologica."

about war's causes, he trained a generation of international relations experts in quantitative and statistical techniques. COW outlived Singer; his students continue to seek war's definitive correlates.[93]

Even as they fully embraced their policy purpose, however, political scientists worried that their policy relevance was waning. Like other fields shaped by the behavioral revolution of the 1950s and 1960s, the study of war increasingly took the form of arcane discussions of statistical methodology and causal rigor. Between behavioralism and the searing experience of Vietnam, many researchers turned inward, away from policy relevance.[94] The military's eventual disenchantment with the social science of war bore some of the blame for this insularity. The Reagan administration slashed funding for social science broadly in the early 1980s. But by this time, the managerial approach to conflict was firmly entrenched in political science departments and ostensibly multidisciplinary journals like *JCR*, *International Security* (first published 1976), and *Conflict Management and Peace Science* (first published as *Journal of Peace Science* in 1973 and renamed in 1980).

By the 1980s, no single political science approach – game-theoretic, quantitative, or realist – dominated the political scientific study of war. While realists and behavioralists had spilled much ink in the 1950s and 1960s debating whether war could be approached scientifically, the next generation of scholars sought to reconcile the two camps. This new neorealist school of international relations gave pride of place to the role of power in international politics, as Morgenthau had. But it also embraced game-theoretic, quantitative, and other formalist efforts to locate the causes of conflict. Despite the vitriolic debates between realists and advocates of the ostensibly "scientific" study of war embodied in the COW project and formal game theory, international relations offered a broad enough intellectual tent to contain them all.[95]

10.4 Conclusion

In their 1955 textbook *The Sociology of Social Problems*, Paul B. Horton and Gerald R. Leslie reflected on Western nations' hypocrisy when it came to war.

---

[93] "Correlates of War Project," www.correlatesofwar.org. See also Suzuki, Krause, and Singer, "Correlates of War Project."
[94] For example, Azar and Ben-Dak, *Theory and Practice of Events Research* and Singer and Small, *Wages of War*. On the tendency of behavioralism to retreat from policy, see Dryzek, "Revolutions without Enemies," 490 and Gunnell, *Descent of Political Theory*.
[95] Bessner and Guilhot, "How Realism Waltzed Off" and Guilhot, *After the Enlightenment*, chaps. 5–6.

Although Westerners professed to love peace, they "express pride over never having lost a war, build countless statues of military heroes, describe history in terms of battles and wars, and form nonintervention pacts with other nations – strange behaviors for peaceful peoples."[96]

A generation earlier, many social scientists held out hope that they could eradicate Americans' fixation on war. Between World War I and World War II, efforts to rein in human violence and foster international understanding yielded interdisciplinary and internationalist projects. But instead of cementing the perceived need for peace, nuclear proliferation, deepening Cold War tensions, and the growth of a national security state hungry for actionable knowledge, inspired social scientists to create a managerial approach to war. Their project was aided in no small part by the lessons of the European crisis of democracy in the 1930s and 1940s, and the fear that human irrationality and nuclear arsenals posed a cataclysmic risk to humanity.

Perhaps counterintuitively, social scientists viewed human irrationality as more amenable to containment than nuclear weapons. Amid nuclear proliferation and deep enmity between the United States and the Soviet Union, social scientists partnered with government patrons in an effort to maintain and expand American dominance in the face of its enemies. Between the late 1940s and the late 1960s, social scientists worked at new research institutes and devised new methods and theories for managing war efficiently and rationally.

In 1955, Horton and Leslie confronted a "frightening prospect": "war is deeply rooted in the culture of modern nations … only major alterations in that culture offer much hope for its elimination."[97] By the end of the 1970s, the same could be said of international relations. In the wake of the behavioral revolution and the Vietnam War, anthropologists, sociologists, and psychologists retreated from the study of war. This remains true today. Aside from the largely marginalized field of peace studies, war – whether framed as a social or security problem – is no longer a central concern for other social science disciplines. Nor is peace. In academic and policy circles, the suggestion that social science can eliminate war is treated as nothing short of preposterous.

While these shifts may reflect a laudable reduction in the hubris – not to mention hypocrisy – of the social science of war, they also reflect the dramatic hold that national security has over political thought and practice.

---

[96] Horton and Leslie, *Sociology of Social Problems*, 462–63.
[97] Horton and Leslie, *Sociology of Social Problems*, 462–63.

While methodological similarities tie the interwar traditions of Morgenthau, Wright, and others to contemporary neorealism, the ideological goals that motivated the social problems' framing have faded away. Few mainstream international relations scholars or practitioners see permanent peace as a pragmatic pursuit. The study of war continues to be framed in the context of security, statecraft, and the management of conflict in ways that accord with the political status quo. Without a powerful political, financial, and intellectual push in a different direction, the conviction that social science – and political science in particular – is a valuable managerial tool for violence as an instrument of statecraft is here to stay.

Bibliography

Amadae, S. M. *Rationalizing Capitalist Democracy: The Cold War Origins of Rational Choice Liberalism*. Chicago: University of Chicago Press, 2003.

Amadae, S. M. *Prisoners of Reason: Game Theory and Neoliberal Political Economy*. New York: Cambridge University Press, 2015.

Angell, Robert C. "Sociology and the World Crisis." *American Sociological Review* 16, no. 6 (1951): 749–57.

Ayson, Robert. *Thomas Schelling and the Nuclear Age: Strategy as Social Science*. London: Frank Cass, 2004.

Azar, Edward E., and Joseph D. Ben-Dak, eds. *Theory and Practice of Events Research: Studies in Inter-Nation Actions and Interactions*. New York: Gordon & Breach Science Publishers, 1975.

Banks, Arthur S. "Review of the *World Handbook*." *American Political Science Review* 59, no. 1 (1965): 244.

Baratta, Joseph Preston. "The International History of the World Federalist Movement." *Peace and Change* 14, no. 4 (1989): 372–403.

Baratta, Joseph Preston. "The International Federalist Movement: Toward Global Governance." *Peace and Change* 24, no. 3 (1999): 340–72.

Bernard, Jessie. *Social Problems at Midcentury: Role, Status, and Stress in a Context of Abundance*. New York: Dryden Press, 1957.

Bessner, Daniel. "Weimar Social Science in Cold War America: The Case of the Political-Military Game." *GHI Bulletin Supplement* 10 (2014): 91–111.

Bessner, Daniel. *Democracy in Exile: Hans Speier and the Rise of the Defense Intellectual*. Ithaca: Cornell University Press, 2018.

Bessner, Daniel and Nicolas Guilhot. "How Realism Waltzed Off: Liberalism and Decisionmaking in Kenneth Waltz's Neorealism." *International Security* 40, no. 2 (2015): 87–118.

Bew, John. *Realpolitik: A History*. New York: Oxford University Press, 2016.

Bueno de Mesquita, Bruce. "Game Theory, Political Economy, and the Evolving Study of War and Peace." *American Political Science Review* 100, no. 4 (2006): 637–42.

"Correlates of War Project." www.correlatesofwar.org

Craig, Campbell. *Glimmer of a New Leviathan: Total War in the Realism of Niebuhr, Morgenthau, and Waltz*. New York: Columbia University Press, 2003.

Desch, Michael C. *Cult of the Irrelevant: The Waning Influence of Social Science on National Security*. Princeton: Princeton University Press, 2019.

Deutsch, Karl. "In Memorium: Quincy Wright." *Political Science & Politics: PS* 4, no. 1 (1971): 107–9.

Dryzek, John S. "Revolutions without Enemies: Key Transformations in Political Science." *American Political Science Review* 100, no. 4 (2006): 487–92.

Elliot, Mai. *RAND in Southeast Asia: A History of the Vietnam War*. Santa Monica: RAND Corporation, 2010.

Erickson, Paul. *The World the Game Theorists Made*. Chicago: University of Chicago Press, 2015.

Fontaine, Philippe. "Stabilizing American Society: Kenneth Boulding and the Integration of the Social Sciences, 1943–1980." *Science in Context* 23, no. 2 (2010): 221–65.

Freedman, Lawrence. *Future of War: A History*. New York: Public Affairs Press, 2017.

Frei, Christoph. "Politics among Nations: A Book for America." In *Hans J. Morgenthau and the American Experience*, edited by Cornelia Navari, 55–74. Cham: Palgrave Macmillan, 2018.

Gilman, Nils. *Mandarins of the Future: Modernization Theory in Cold War America*. Baltimore: Johns Hopkins University Press, 2003.

Greenberg, Udi. *The Weimar Century: German Émigrés and the Ideological Foundations of the Cold War*. Princeton: Princeton University Press, 2015.

Griggs, Emily. "A Realist before 'Realism': Quincy Wright and the Study of International Politics between Two World Wars." *Journal of Strategic Studies* 24, no. 1 (2001): 71–103.

Guilhot, Nicolas, ed. *The Invention of International Relations Theory: Realism, the Rockefeller Foundation, and the 1954 Conference on Theory*. New York: Columbia University Press, 2011.

Guilhot, Nicolas. *After the Enlightenment: Political Realism and International Relations in the Mid-Twentieth Century*. New York: Cambridge University Press, 2017.

Gunnell, John G. *Descent of Political Theory: The Genealogy of an American Vocation*. Chicago: University of Chicago Press, 1993.

Haas, Michael. "Three Approaches to the Study of War." *International Journal of Comparative Sociology* 11, no. 1 (1970): 34–47.

Harty, Martha, and John Modell. "The First Conflict Resolution Movement, 1956–1971: An Attempt to Institutionalize Applied Interdisciplinary Social Science." *Journal of Conflict Resolution* 35, no. 4 (1991): 720–58.

Herman, Ellen. *Romance of American Psychology: Political Culture in the Age of Experts*. Berkeley: University of California Press, 1995.

Horton, Paul B., and Gerald R. Leslie. *The Sociology of Social Problems*. New York: Appleton-Century-Crofts, 1955.

Kuklick, Bruce. *Blind Oracles: Intellectuals and War from Kennan to Kissinger*. Princeton: Princeton University Press, 2006.

Kurtz, Lester R. "War and Peace on the Sociological Agenda." In *Sociology and Its Publics: The Forms and Fates of Disciplinary Organization*, edited by Terence C. Halliday and Morris Janowitz, 61–98. Chicago: University of Chicago Press, 1992.

Latham, Michael E. *The Right Kind of Revolution: Modernization, Development, and U.S. Foreign Policy from the Cold War to the Present*. Ithaca: Cornell University Press, 2011.

Leonard, Robert J. "War as a 'Simple Economic Problem': The Rise of an Economics of Defense." In *Economics and National Security: A History of Their Interaction*, edited by Crauford D. Goodwin, 261–83. Durham: Duke University Press, 1991.

Leonard, Robert J. *Von Neumann, Morgenstern, and the Creation of Game Theory: From Chess to Social Science, 1900–1960.* Cambridge: Cambridge University Press, 2010.

McClelland, Charles A. "Acute International Crisis." *World Politics* 14, no. 1 (1961): 182–204.

Mills, C. Wright. *The Causes of World War Three.* New York: Simon & Schuster, 1958.

Morgenthau, Hans. *Politics among Nations: The Struggle for Power and Peace.* New York: Alfred A. Knopf, 1948.

Morrow, James D., William Clark, Paul F. Diehl, James Lee Ray, Meredith Reid Sarkees, and Thomas C. Walker. "J. David Singer." *Political Science & Politics: PS* 43, no. 3 (2010): 590–93.

Oren, Ido. *Our Enemies and Us: America's Rivalries and the Making of Political Science.* Ithaca: Cornell University Press, 2002.

Parenti, Michael. "Patricians, Professionals, and Political Science." *American Political Science Review* 100, no. 4 (2006): 499–505.

Pooley, Jefferson. "The Remobilization of the Propaganda and Morale Network, 1947–1953." *MediArXiv*, July 25, 2018. doi:10.33767/osf.io/g9rp4

Price, David H. *Cold War Anthropology: The CIA, the Pentagon, and the Growth of Dual Use Anthropology.* Durham: Duke University Press, 2016.

Rohde, Joy. *Armed with Expertise: The Militarization of American Social Research During the Cold War.* Ithaca: Cornell University Press, 2013.

Rohde, Joy. "Pax Technologica: Computers, International Affairs, and Human Reason in the Cold War." *Isis* 108, no. 4 (2017): 792–813.

Russett, Bruce M., Hawyard R. Alker, Karl W. Deutsch, and Harold D. Lasswell. *World Handbook of Political and Social Indicators.* New Haven: Yale University Press, 1964.

Ruzicka, Jan. "A Fetish for Measurement? Karl Deutsch in the Second Debate." *International Relations* 28, no. 3 (2014): 367–84.

Schneider, Joseph. "Is War a Social Problem?" *Journal of Conflict Resolution* 3, no. 4 (1959): 353–60.

Selcer, Perrin. "Patterns of Science: Developing Knowledge for a World Community at UNESCO." PhD diss., University of Pennsylvania, 2011.

Selcer, Perrin. *The Postwar Origins of the Global Environment: How the United Nations Built Spaceship Earth.* New York: Columbia University Press, 2018.

Simpson, Christopher. *Science of Coercion: Communication Research and Psychological Warfare.* New York: Oxford University Press, 1996.

Singer, J. David. "Editor's Introduction." In *Quantitative International Politics*, edited by J. David Singer, 1–13. New York: Free Press, 1968.

Singer, J. David. "Correlates of War." In *Encyclopedia of Peace, Violence, and Conflict*, 2nd ed., edited by Lester Kurtz, 449–57. London: Elsevier, 2008.

Singer, J. David, and Melvin Small. *The Wages of War, 1816–1965: A Statistical Handbook.* New York: Wiley, 1972.

Suzuki, Susumu, Volker Krause, and J. David Singer. "Correlates of War Project: A Bibliographic History of the Scientific Study of War and Peace, 1964–2000." *Conflict Management and Peace Science* 19, no. 2 (2002): 69–107.

Tanter, Raymond. *The Policy Relevance of Models in World Politics*. International Data Archive Research Report No. 7. Ann Arbor: Department of Political Science, University of Michigan, October 1971.

Taylor, Charles Lewis, Michael C. Hudson, and Bruce M. Russett. *World Handbook of Political and Social Indicators*. New Haven: Yale University Press, 1972.

Throntveit, Trygve. "A Strange Fate: Quincy Wright and the Trans-War Trajectory of Wilsonian Internationalism." *White House Studies* 10, no. 4 (2011): 361–77.

Throntveit, Trygve. *Power without Victory: Woodrow Wilson and the American Internationalist Experiment*. Chicago: University of Chicago Press, 2017.

Tomás Rangil, Teresa. "Rebellions across the (Rice) Fields: Social Scientists and Indochina, 1965–1975." In *The Unsocial Social Science? Economics and Neighboring Disciplines since 1945*, edited by Roger E. Backhouse and Philippe Fontaine, 105–130. Durham: Duke University Press, 2010.

Tomás Rangil, Teresa. "Finding Patrons for Peace Psychology: The Foundations of the Conflict Resolution Movement at the University of Michigan, 1951–1971." *Journal of the History of the Behavioral Sciences* 48, no. 2 (2012): 91–114.

Weinberger, Sharon. *The Imagineers of War: The Untold History of DARPA, the Pentagon Agency That Changed the World*. New York: Alfred A. Knopf, 2017.

Weintraub, E. Roy, ed. *Toward a History of Game Theory*. Durham: Duke University Press, 1992.

Wright, Quincy. *A Study of War*. Chicago: University of Chicago Press, 1942.

Wright, Quincy. "Project for a World Intelligence Center." *Journal of Conflict Resolution* 1, no. 1 (1957): 93–97.

Young, Robert A., James A. Moore, Vivian Moore, et al. *Utilization of ARPA-Supported Research for International Security Planning, Appendices*. Springfield: Consolidated Analysis Centers, Inc., 1972.

Index

Aaron, Henry, 139
Acheson, Dean, 364
Adams, Bert, 94
addiction, 291
 as a disease, 297
 as microcosm for studying social
  change, 292
 biological, 310
 colloquial labels for, 290
 etiology of, 297
 individual failings and, 293
 medicalization of, 295
 politics of representing, 315
 rational choice theory and, 310
 redefinition of, 292
 struggles for cultural authority over, 292
addiction research
 shifting priorities in, 313
Addiction Research Center (ARC), 291,
  295–6, 298, 307
 critique of Lindesmith's approach at, 300
 Social Sciences Section at the, 298, 305
 subordinate role of social science
  at, 298
addicts, 290
 "bad" *versus* "good abusers", 314
 versus drug users, 295
Adler, Mortimer J., 262
Adorno, Theodor W., 75, 190–1
Advanced Research Projects Agency (ARPA),
  372, 378–9
affirmative action, 211
Affluent Society, The (Galbraith, 1958), 144
Agar, Michael, 308
Aid to Dependent Children, 152
Alexander, Franz, 327
All Our Kin (Stack, 1974), 163, 236
Alliance for Progress, 157
Allport, Gordon W., 190–192
Almond, Gabriel A., 127, 369

American Anthropological Association
  (AAA), 24
American Apartheid (Massey and Denton,
  1993), 205, 208–9, 215
American Bar Association (ABA), 297
American Council of Education (ACE), 111
American Dilemma, An (Myrdal, 1944), 74,
  181–3, 187, 228
American Economic Association (AEA),
  145, 154
American Educational Research Association
  (AERA), 110, 127
American Enterprise Institute (AEI), 162, 166
American Historical Association (AHA), 24
American Jewish Committee, 189
American Jewish Congress, 189
American Journal of Sociology (journal), 5,
  86, 94
American Medical Association (AMA), 297
American Occupational Structure, The (Blau
  and Duncan, 1967), 89–91, 98, 200
American Political Science Association
  (APSA), 378
American Psychological Association (APA),
  24, 266, 332, 335, 358
American Psychological Society. *See*
  Association for Psychological Science
American Social Science Association (ASSA), 5
American Sociological Association (ASA), 121,
  see also American Sociological Society
American Sociological Review (journal), 6, 94
American Sociological Society, 5, 9, 28
American Soldier, The (Stouffer, 1949), 188
American Statistical Association, 23
Angell, Robert C., 112, 362, 364, 366, 373, 375
*Annals of the American Academy of Political
  and Social Science* (journal), 117
anomie, 158
 Durkheim's concept of, 294
 Merton's concept of, 265

deterrence
  rational choice and, 278
Detroit race riot (1943), 228, 230
Deutsch, Karl, 371–2
Devereux, Georges, 326
deviance, 151, 301
  functionalist analysis of, 263
  sociology of, 18, 294
Deweerd, H. A., 369
Dewey, John, 109, 113–4, 116, 362
Diagnostic and Statistical Manual of Mental Disorders–III (DSM), 334, 341
differential association theory, 262, 264–5, 273
  operationalization of, 265
  refinements of, 265
  structural-functionalism and, 265–6
disciplinary specialization, 23, 31
disciplines
  boundaries of, 22–4, 31, 34, 52
  boundary work and, 5
  insularity of, 23
discrimination. *See also* racial
    discrimination
  statistical, 209
  systemic, 173
Discrimination and the National Welfare (MacIver, 1949), 173, 181, 185–6
disparate impact, 204, 211
Divorce Revolution, The (Weitzman, 1985), 87
Dollard, John, 179, 327
domestic violence, 155
dope fiends, 290, 293
Downs, Anthony, 35–7
Dr. Strangelove (George, 1964), 367
Drake, St. Clair, 74, 148, 183–4, 198–9, 208, 228
drug addiction
  politicization of, 297
drug ethnography, 314
drug use, 304
  criminalization of, 294
  etiological explanations of, 310
  moral judgments and, 292
  US soldiers in Vietnam and, 306
drug users
  social conventions and, 295
  versus addicts, 295
drugs revolution, 344
drug-using subcultures, 308
Du Bois, W. E. B., 19, 70, 174, 178
Duncan, Otis Dudley, 89–91, 98, 200–1
DuPont, Robert, 306
Durkheim, Émile, 8, 116
Dynamics of Prejudice (Bettelheim and Janowitz, 1950), 191

Easton, David, 33, 38, 127
econometrics, 197
Economic Approach to Human Behavior, The (Becker, 1976), 35, 39, 47
economic development, 154–5
  Third World and, 153–4
Economic Development of Harlem (Vietorisz and Harrison, 1970), 240
economic growth, 26, 80, 84, 150, 153, 155
economic individualism, 176–7, 192–5
Economic Opportunity Act (1964), 237
Economic Theory of Democracy, An (Downs, 1957), 36
economics
  as a style of reasoning, 47, 160
  behavioral, 350
  behavioral sciences and, 35
  development, 154
  disciplinary boundaries in, 348
  discrimination and, 35
  economic history in, 35
  educational research and, 126
  family size and, 81
  farm, 73
  home, 73, 79, 95
  human capital and, 122–5
  hypothetico-deductive modeling in, 33, 36
  institutional, 25, 28–9, 150, 182
  intellectual superiority of, 351
  Keynesian, 155
  neoclassical, 138, 150, 193
  of the family, 95–8
  orthodoxy in, 350
  policy influence of, 26–7, 33, 37, 39, 45–9, 52, 118, 142, 160, 164, 193
  political science and, 36
  postwar consensus of, 45, 143, 193
  poverty and, 38
  quantification of, 30, 193, 197
  rational choice and, 138, 193
  separation from other social sciences, 32
  social analysis and, 22
  social problems and, 2–3, 10, 12, 48, 57
  sociology and, 22
  study of racial discrimination and, 192–5
  welfare, 150
  World War II service of, 32
economics imperialism, 22, 37, 96
Economics of Discrimination, The (Becker, 1957), 193–4
economics of mental health, 349
  minimal impact of federal funding on, 349
  minimal interest of mainstream journals in, 349
economization, 45–8, 57
education
  Americanization and, 109, 117

mass incarceration, 281
Massachusetts Institute of Technology (MIT)
  Center for International Studies at the, 369
Massey, Douglas, 208, 209
Masters of the Universe (Stedman Jones,
  2012), 47
Matza, David, 265
maximum feasible participation, 140, 160,
  see also Community Action Program
  (CAP)
Mayer, Susan, 245
McCarthyism, 34, 189, 190
McClelland, Charles, 379
McClelland, David, 80
McCord, Joan, 266
McCord, William, 266
McEntire, Davis, 232
McGuire, Thomas, 349
McKay, Henry, 261
McKee, James, 190
McLanahan, Sara, 93
McNamara, Robert, 160, 376
Mead, George Herbert, 18
Mead, Margaret, 114, 126, 326
Menninger Clinic, 326
Mental Disorders in Urban Areas (Faris and
  Durham, 1939), 327
mental hospital population, 324
  decline in, 341
mental hospitals
  critique of, 338
mental illness, 339
  as a social problem, 336
  as brain disease, 336
  costs of, 322
  economics and, 36
  economics' neglect of, 345
  language of the prevention of, 342
  military and, 328
  public perceptions of, 336
  social and psychological dimensions of, 337
  social disorganization and, 327
  social policy and, 323
  social sciences and, 322
  sociology and, 336
  sociology of, 326, 328
mental testing, 112, 117
meritocracy, 114
Merriam, Charles E., 24, 30, 361
Merton, Robert K., 1–2, 4, 6, 9, 10, 17, 36, 151,
  158, 186, 263–4, 266, 294
  meeting with Lazarsfeld, 7
Methodenstreit, 22
methodological individualism, 44, 192, 199
methodology, 2, 25, 45, 112, 192, *see also*
  social problems, methodological
  approaches to

Mexico, 154
Michael, Jerome, 262
Micromotives and Macrobehavior (Schelling,
  1978), 240
Middletown (Lynd and Lynd, 1929), 74
Middletown in Transition (Lynd and Lynd,
  1937), 74
Milbank Memorial Fund (MMF), 76
Miller, James Grier, 325
Miller, Walter, 266
Milliken v. Bradley (1974), 242
Mills, C. Wright, 18, 40, 49, 365
Mincer, Jacob, 123–4
Minority Enterprise Small Business
  Investment Company program, 241
Mitchell, Wesley C., 25–6
Mobilization for Youth (MFY), 158, 270
Model Cities program, 237
modern industrial societies, ethnography
  of, 326
Modern Social Imaginaries (Taylor, 2004), 47
modernization theory, 86, 153–4, 370, 377
  family and, 80–2
Mondale, Walter, 38
Mont Pèlerin Society, 280
Montagu, Ashley, 114
Moore, Wilbert, 81
More Perfect Union, The (MacIver, 1948),
  181, 185
Morgan, David, 340
Morgan, James N., 89
Morgenstern, Oskar, 368
Morgenthau, Hans, 363–4, 366, 374, 376,
  378, 380
Moving To Opportunity (MTO), 248
Mowrer, Ernest, 71
Moynihan Report. *See Negro Family, The*
  (Moynihan, 1965)
Moynihan, Daniel Patrick, 88, 122, 140, 155,
  164–5, 168, 202, 234–5, 239, 244, 251,
  271, 274, 279
multidisciplinary team work, 31
Munro, Bennett, 30
Murphy, Kevin, 311, 313
Murray, Charles, 166–7, 212, 243–4, 246,
  251, 282
Myrdal, Gunnar, 74, 148, 181, 187, 209, 212,
  230, 232, 250

Narcotic Addict Rehabilitation Act (NARA,
  1966), 305
narcotics addiction
  as juvenile delinquency, 297
  juvenile delinquency as cause and
    consequence of, 297
  social studies of, 296
Nation at Risk, A (1983), 130

Winston, Gordon C., 311
Wirth, Louis, 189
Wolf, Eleanor, 232
Wolfgang, Marvin, 275, 281
Women on Heroin (Rosenbaum, 1981), 308
Works Progress Administration, 77
*World Handbook of Political and Social
    Indicators* (Russett *et al.*, 1964), 372, 377
World Health Organization (WHO)
    expert committees at, 295
World Revolution and Family Patterns
    (Goode, 1963), 81
World War II, 73, 75, 181

impact on social science, 31
multidisciplinary team work and, 31–3, 37
social scientists' service in, 2, 6, 31–3, 33, 37
Wright, Quincy, 56, 360–1, 366, 372–5, 382

Yale University
    department of psychiatry at, 337
    department of sociology at, 337
Yinger, J. Milton, 206
Yolles, Stanley, 342
Youth in the Ghetto (Clark, 1964), 235

Zorbaugh, Harvey, 147

Printed in the United States
By Bookmasters